Reinhard Stockmann (Hrsg.)
Evaluationsforschung

Sozialwissenschaftliche Evaluationsforschung
Band 1

Reinhard Stockmann (Hrsg.)

Evaluationsforschung

Grundlagen und ausgewählte Forschungsfelder

Leske + Budrich, Opladen 2000

Die Deutsche Bibliothek – CIP-Einheitsaufnahme
Ein Titeldatensatz für diese Publikation ist bei
Der Deutschen Bibliothek erhältlich.

ISBN 3-8100-2656-5

Gedruckt auf säurefreiem und alterungsbeständigem Papier.

© 2000 Leske + Budrich, Opladen

Umschlagbild: Ulrich Thul, Ludwigshafen

Satz: Leske + Budrich
Druck: Druck Partner Rübelmann, Hemsbach
Printed in Germany

Inhaltsverzeichnis

II. Ausgewählte Felder der Evaluationsforschung

Vorwort

Evaluation in Deutschland bietet ein sehr vielfältiges und buntes Bild. In vielen Politikfeldern wird aus den verschiedensten Motiven und Gründen und mit den unterschiedlichsten Ansätzen und Methoden evaluiert. Dennoch wird der Erfolg und die Wirksamkeit der weit überwiegenden Mehrzahl von politischen und sozialen Interventionsprogrammen überhaupt nicht eruiert. Wiederholt hat der Bundesrechnungshof festgestellt, daß in Deutschland nur selten Erfolgskontrollen durchgeführt werden, daß in fast allen Ressorts dafür die Voraussetzungen fehlen und daß in den wenigen durchgeführten Evaluationen oft die vorhandenen methodischen Möglichkeiten zur Ermittlung von Erfolg und Wirksamkeit nicht ausgeschöpft werden.

So bunt wie das Bild der Evaluation ist auch die Gilde derer, die Evaluationen durchführen. Im Unterschied zur USA konnte sich in Deutschland bisher keine sozialwissenschaftliche Evaluationsdisziplin durchsetzen. Die Evaluationsforschung in Deutschland ist fachlich zersplittert, weist nur eine geringe interdisziplinäre Kommunikation und Zusammenarbeit auf und ist noch immer mit dem Makel anwendungsbezogener Auftragsforschung behaftet, deren Wissenschaftlichkeit teilweise bestritten wird.

Allerdings lassen sich erste Professionalisierungserfolge erkennen. Im September 1997 wurde die Deutsche Gesellschaft für Evaluation gegründet, die es sich zur Aufgabe gemacht hat, das Verständnis, die Akzeptanz und die Nutzbarmachung von Evaluation in der Gesellschaft zu fördern, Prinzipien und Qualitätsstandards für Evaluationen zu entwickeln und den interdisziplinären Austausch zu unterstützen. Auch ist eine vermehrte Zahl von Fachpublikationen und ein verstärktes Interesse an Aus- und Weiterbildungsangeboten zu beobachten.

Doch nach wie vor fehlen Lehrstühle, Sonderforschungsbereiche oder wissenschaftliche Institute, die sich mit grundlegenden theoretischen und methodischen Fragen der Evaluationsforschung beschäftigen. Studiengänge, in denen das „Handwerk" des Evaluierens erlernt werden könnte, gibt es nicht. Auch ein außeruniversitärer Aus- und Weiterbildungsmarkt für Evaluatoren ist kaum existent. Bisher gibt es keine deutschsprachige Evaluationszeitschrift und es fehlt an einschlägigen Sammelwerken oder Lehrbüchern zur Evaluationsforschung, die die fachliche Zersplitterung überwinden und das bisher zusammengetragene Wissen bündeln.

Mit dieser im Leske + Budrich Verlag aufgelegten Reihe zur sozialwissenschaftlichen Evaluationsforschung, in der das vorliegende Buch den ersten Band stellt, soll ein Beitrag dazu geleistet werden, diese Lücke etwas zu füllen.

Der Themenband ist so aufgebaut, daß zuerst die Evaluationsentwicklung in Deutschland, in den USA und in Europa charakterisiert wird, bevor grundsätzliche Evaluationsthemen wie die Etablierung gemeinsamer Evaluationsstandards, die Differenz zwischen sozialwissenschaftlicher Grundlagenforschung und anwendungsorientierter Evaluationsforschung sowie Theorie- und Methodenentwicklung in der Evaluationsforschung behandelt werden. Im zweiten Teil des Bandes werden ausgewählte Felder der Evaluationsforschung untersucht.

Als Herausgeber dieses Bandes freut es mich außerordentlich, daß es gelungen ist, auf internationaler, europäischer und nationaler Ebene führende Evaluationsforscher als Autoren und Autorinnen zu gewinnen. Ihnen gilt mein besonderer Dank!

Herzlich zu danken habe ich auch Angelika Nentwig, die sehr freundlich und mit unerschöpflicher Geduld den Kontakt zu den Autoren und Autorinnen gehalten und dafür gesorgt hat, daß alle Beiträge rechtzeitig eingegangen sind.

Ein Dankeschön sage ich auch Nicolà Reade und Anette Becker, die die verschiedenen Texte in eine einheitliche Form brachten.

Bürstadt und Saarbrücken, den 7. Juli 2000   *Reinhard Stockmann*

I. Grundlagen der Evaluationsforschung

Reinhard Stockmann
Evaluation in Deutschland

Ziel des vorliegenden Beitrags ist es, da er zu Anfang dieses Sammelbandes steht, zuerst eine kurze Einführung in die Evaluation zu geben. Dabei sollen auch die Themen abgesteckt werden, die in den einzelnen Beiträgen des Bandes weiter ausgeführt werden. Hauptgegenstand ist dann die Entwicklung der Evaluation in Deutschland, die im Kontext internationaler und europäischer Strömungen sowie im Rahmen nationaler Besonderheiten beschrieben wird. Abschließend werden einige Professionalisierungsdefizite in Deutschland aufgezeigt und Vorschläge zu deren Beseitigung unterbreitet.

1. Evaluation, was ist das?

Auch wenn den meisten Menschen der Begriff „Evaluierung" oder „Evaluation" wenig vertraut sein dürfte[1], ist die Tätigkeit, die damit gemeint ist, so alt wie die Menschheit selbst. Wenn jemand z.b. überprüft, ob gebratenes Fleisch besser schmeckt und bekömmlicher ist als rohes oder wenn jemand ausprobiert, ob bestimmte Pilze oder Pflanzen eßbar sind oder nicht, dann führt er eine Evaluation durch. Evaluationen stellen ein wichtiges Instrument zur Generierung von Erfahrungswissen dar. Sie werden durchgeführt in dem Informationen gesammelt und anschließend bewertet werden, um letztendlich Entscheidungen zu treffen. Die dabei verwendeten Bewertungskriterien können sehr verschieden sein, orientieren sich jedoch sehr oft an dem Nutzen eines Gegenstandes, Sachverhaltes oder Entwicklungsprozesses für bestimmte Personen oder Gruppen. Je nach Kriterienauswahl kann die Nutzenbewertung durch einzelne Personen oder Gruppen dementsprechend sehr unterschiedlich ausfallen.

---

1 Die Begriffe „Evaluierung", „Evaluation" und „Evaluationsforschung" werden hier synonym verwendet. Zu definitorischen Unterschieden vgl. Wottawa & Thierau (1990: 9).

Deshalb kommt es sehr darauf an, wer eine Evaluation in Auftrag gibt, wer sie durchführt, welche Ziele von wem damit verfolgt werden, welche Vorgehensweisen gewählt und welche Methoden angewendet werden. Damit sind schon einige wichtige Fragen umrissen, mit denen sich Evaluationen auseinandersetzen müssen und die in diesem Band behandelt werden.

Wissenschaftliche Evaluationen unterscheiden sich von Alltagsevaluationen lediglich durch die Anwendung empirischer Forschungsmethoden. Diese umfassen dabei die gesamte Bandbreite sozialwissenschaftlicher Forschungsparadigmen. Systematisch sind sie insofern, als die grundlegenden Regeln für die Sammlung valider und relevanter Daten gelten (vgl. Rossi u.a. (1988: 1ff.), Wottawa/Thierau (1990: 9f.), Will u.a. (1987: 12ff.).

Evaluationsforschung kann deshalb als ein Teilgebiet anwendungsbezogener Forschung verstanden werden, die sich von der Grundlagenforschung in einigen Aspekte unterscheidet. *Evert Vedung*, der in diesem Band den Gemeinsamkeiten und Unterschieden von „Evaluation Research and Fundamental Research" nachgeht, hebt hervor: „the basic difference between evaluation research and fundamental research is that the former is intended for use". Während Grundlagenforschung relativ zweckfrei nach Erkenntnissen streben kann, hat Evaluationsforschung einen Auftraggeber, der damit bestimmte Absichten verfolgt. Der Evaluator muß sich deshalb an den Zielbestimmungen seines Auftraggebers orientieren. Ein weiterer wesentlicher Unterschied zur Grundlagenforschung besteht darin, daß Evaluationen immer mit einer Wertung verbunden sind. Während sich Grundlagenforschung weitgehend normativer Urteile enthalten kann, wird bei einer Evaluation immer eine Bewertung verlangt, sie ist Teil des Forschungsauftrags. Dabei kann der Evaluator die Beurteilungskriterien des Auftraggebers bzw. der Zielgruppen, die evaluiert werden übernehmen (z.B. Zielerreichung, Erwartungen der Zielgruppen), oder aber eigene Bewertungskriterien festlegen (z.B. Bedürfnisse der Zielgruppen, Beitrag zum Abbau sozialer oder gesellschaftlicher Ungleichheit).

Keine prinzipiellen Unterschiede sind hingegen zwischen Evaluations- und Grundlagenforschung im Hinblick auf die Auswahl des Untersuchungsgegenstandes sowie die Verwendung von Datenerhebungs- und Analysemethoden zur Identifizierung von Wirkungen und der Bearbeitung der Kausalitätsfrage (Ursache-Wirkungszusammenhänge) zu erkennen.

Gegenstände einer Evaluation können z.B. Personen, Organisationen, Produkte, Reformen, Gesetze, Maßnahmen, Projekte, Programme oder gar Evaluationen selbst sein. Dementsprechend gibt es eine Vielfalt unterschiedlicher Definitionen.

Eine Definition, die sowohl auf die verschiedenen Evaluationsgegenstände paßt, als auch auf die besondere Aufgaben- und Zielbestimmung der Evaluations- im Unterschied zur Grundlagenforschung hinweist, schlägt Donna Mertens vor:

„Evaluation is the systematic investigation of the merit or worth of an object (program) for the purpose of reducing uncertainty in decision making." (Mertens 1998: 219)

Eine ebenfalls weithin akzeptierte Begriffsbestimmung ist die von Peter Rossi/Howard Freeman, die Evaluationsforschung definieren

„als systematische Anwendung sozialwissenschaftlicher Forschungsmethoden zur Beurteilung der Konzeption, Ausgestaltung, Umsetzung und des Nutzens sozialer Interventionsprogramme. Evaluationsforschung bezeichnet den gezielten Einsatz sozialwissenschaftlicher Forschungsmethoden zur Verbesserung der Planung und laufenden Überwachung sowie zur Bestimmung der Effektivität und Effizienz von (...) sozialen Interventionsmaßnahmen." (Rossi u.a. 1988: 3)[2]

Die Evaluationsforschung kann sich mit drei Phasen des politischen Prozesses beschäftigen und dabei drei verschiedene Analyseperspektiven einnehmen (vgl. Schaubild 1):

1. Die Evaluationsforschung kann die Phase der Programmentwicklung behandeln, die die Konzeptualisierung und Ausarbeitung einer geplanten Intervention mit einschließt. Dabei hat die Evaluationsforschung die Aufgabe, „die materiellen, personellen, institutionellen, finanziellen, theoretischen Rahmen- bzw. Eingangsbedingungen eines Programms" zu untersuchen, um zur Erstellung eines Programmdesigns beizutragen (vgl. Brandtstädter 1990b: 217). Dabei sollen möglichst schon frühzeitig negative Effekte eines Programms oder einer Maßnahme abgeschätzt werden (vgl. Hellstern/Wollmann 1980a: 13, 1984: 24; Staudt u.a. 1988: 40f.). Solche Untersuchungen werden „ex-ante evaluations", „input-evaluations" oder „preformative evaluations" (Scriven 1991: 169) genannt.
2. Während der Implementationsphase übernimmt die Evaluationsforschung vor allem Kontroll- und Beratungsfunktionen. Indem Informationen über den Programmverlauf und die Programmergebnisse gesammelt und bewertet werden, sollen Entscheidungshilfen für die Steuerung der Durchführung des Programms gegeben und durch eine frühzeitige Korrekturmöglichkeit Veränderungen des Programmdesigns ermöglicht werden (vgl. Staudt u.a. 1988: 27; Rossi u.a. 1988: 12, 31 u. 63; Wottawa/ Thierau 1990: 54). Solche Evaluationen zur Überwachung der Umsetzung und Ausführung von laufenden Programmen („on-going") werden als „Begleitforschung" (Rossi u.a. 1988: 11) oder als „formative Evaluationen" bezeichnet (vgl. Scriven 1980, 1991). Sie beschäftigen sich mit derselben Phase des politischen Prozesses wie die Implementationsforschung[3] und verfolgen dabei ähnliche Zielsetzungen.
3. Nach Abschluß der Implementation eines Programms kommt der Eva-

---

2   Sinngemäße Definitionen finden sich z.B. bei Wittmann (1985:17); Wottawa/Thierau (1990:9).
3   Zur Implementationsforschung vgl. u.a. Mayntz (1977, 1980, 1983); Windhoff-Héritier (1980, 1983, 1987, 1993); Wollmann (1980, 1994).

luationsforschung die Aufgabe zu, den vollen Umfang der Effekte, die durch ein Programm ausgelöst wurden, zu erfassen und zu bewerten sowie Zusammenhänge aufzudecken (vgl. Wottawa/Thierau 1990: 55; Scriven 1991: 340). Solche Untersuchungen werden als „summative Evaluationen" bezeichnet, und in der Regel ex-post durchgeführt.[4]

Demnach kann das Erkenntnisinteresse in der Evaluationsforschung (1.) mehr darauf gerichtet sein, Programme und den Prozeß ihrer Durchführung und Wirkungsweise zu verbessern, oder (2.) mehr darauf, die Resultate vollzogener policies zu analysieren. Folgende von Jann (1994: 311) für die Politikfeldanalyse getroffene Unterscheidung, läßt sich deshalb auch auf die Evaluationsforschung übertragen:

„Während auf der einen Seite ,*analysis for policy*' im Vordergrund steht, d.h. die Verbesserung zukünftiger *policies* durch die Anwendung wissenschaftlicher Erkenntnisse und Methoden *(science for action)*, ist die zweite Perspektive eher ,*analysis of policy*', mit Erklärung und Verallgemeinerung als vorrangige Zielsetzungen *(science for knowledge)*."[5]

Dementsprechend können Evaluationen mehr *formativ*, d.h. aktiv-gestaltend, prozeßorientiert, konstruktiv und kommunikationsfördernd angelegt sein, oder mehr *summativ*, d.h. zusammenfassend, bilanzierend und ergebnisorientiert. Prinzipiell können beide Evaluations-Perspektiven, bei allen *Phasen des politischen Prozesses* eingenommen werden. Da es in der Planungs- und Designphase eines Programms jedoch kaum Ansatzpunkte für eine summative Evaluation gibt, kann sie in der Durchführung nur formativen Charakter haben. Während der Durchführungsphase sind sowohl formative als auch summative Evaluationen möglich. Ex-post Analysen sind in der Regel summative Evaluationen, da der Gestaltungsaspekt entfällt. Durch entsprechende informationelle Rückkopplungsschleifen für Folgeprojekte können sie jedoch auch formative Bedeutung gewinnen (vgl. Schaubild 1).

Generell können Evaluationen vier Funktionen zugeschrieben werden (vgl. Schaubild 2):

1. Erkenntnisfunktion

Mit Hilfe von Evaluationen werden entscheidungsrelevante Daten gesammelt. Es soll u.a. festgestellt werden, ob die Maßnahmen die Zielgruppe erreichen, welche Bedarfe die Zielgruppe hat, wie es mit der Akzeptanz des Programmes bestellt ist, ob die Träger in der Lage sind, das Programm effektiv und effizient umzusetzen, wie sich die Rahmenbedingungen verändert haben, welche Kausalbeziehungen bestehen etc.. Die durch Evaluationen ge-

---

4   Die terminologische Unterscheidung zwischen formativer und summativer Evaluation geht auf Scriven (1967, 1972a u. b, 1980, 1983, 1991) zurück. Eine aufschlußreiche Gegenüberstellung der Merkmale von formativer und summativer Evaluation geben Wottawa/Thierau (1990: 56). Vgl. auch Rossi u.a. (1988), Will u.a. (1987: 20ff.).

5   Hervorhebungen durch Jann (1994: 311).

sammelten Informationen sollen dann für Steuerungsentscheidungen genutzt werden.

Schaubild 1: Dimensionen der Evaluationsforschung

Phasen des politischen Prozesses	Analyse- perspektive	Erkenntnis- interesse	Evaluations- konzepte
Programm- formulierung/ Planungsphase	ex-ante	„analysis for policy" „science for action"	preformativ/ formativ: aktiv gestaltend, pro- zeßorientiert, kon- struktiv
Implementations- phase	on-going	beides möglich	formativ/summativ: beides möglich
Wirkungsphase	ex-post	„analysis of policy" „science for know- ledge"	summativ: zusammen- fassend, bilanzierend, ergebnisorientiert

2. Kontrollfunktion

Bei der Beobachtung eines Programms und seiner Wirkungen steht zwar in erster Linie das Interesse im Vordergrund, Defizite zu erkennen, um mög- lichst rasch steuernd eingreifen zu können. Gleichzeitig gewinnt man natür- lich aber auch Informationen, die erkennen lassen, ob alle Beteiligten ihre Aufgaben erfüllen, den eingegangenen Verpflichtungen nachkommen etc., so daß direkt oder indirekt auch eine Form von Kontrolle mit Evaluationen ver- bunden ist.

3. Dialogfunktion

Durch Evaluationen werden Informationen bereitgestellt die den Dialog zwi- schen verschiedenen ‚Stakeholdern' (Mittelgeber, Durchführungsorganisati- on, Zielgruppen, sonstige Beteiligte und Betroffene) auf eine solide Grundla- ge stellen. Auf der Basis der ermittelten Ergebnisse kann gemeinsam und für alle transparent bilanziert werden wie erfolgreich die Zusammenarbeit verlief und wo Defizite auftraten, um daraus Konsequenzen für die Gestaltung der weiteren Zusammenarbeit zu ziehen.

4. Legitimitätsfunktion

Die gewonnene Datenbasis bietet die Möglichkeit nachprüfbar nachzuweisen, mit welchem Input, welcher Output und welche Wirkungen über die Zeit hinweg (Prozeßperspektive) erzielt wurden. Bei Ex-post Evaluationen läßt sich zudem die Nachhaltigkeit der Programmwirkungen prüfen. Dadurch können Mittelgeber und Durchführungsorganisationen belegen, wie effizient sie mit Finanzmitteln umgegangen sind und welchen Wirkungsgrad ihre Projekte und Programme erreicht haben.

Sehr oft werden Evaluationen auch *„taktische" Funktionen* zugeschrie- ben. Davon wird dann gesprochen, wenn die Ergebnisse von Evaluationen

nur dazu verwendet werden sollen, um lediglich bestimmte politische Entscheidungen (manchmal sogar nachträglich) zu legitimieren, z.B. weil ein
Programm weitergeführt oder im Gegenteil eingestellt werden soll. Mittlerweile ist es für Politiker auch ‚schick' geworden „to use evaluations as bau-
bles or as bolsters" (Pollitt 1998: 223), als dekorative Symbole für eine moderne Politik, ohne die Ergebnisse von Evaluationen ernsthaft nutzen zu
wollen. Diese Art von ‚taktischer' Funktion läßt sich jedoch kaum mit dem
eigentlichen Zweck von Evaluationen vereinbaren und stellt eher ihre patho-
logische Seite dar. Deshalb wurde sie hier auch nicht in das Aufgabenfeld
von Evaluationen mit aufgenommen (vgl. Schaubild 2).

Schaubild 2: Funktionen von Evaluation

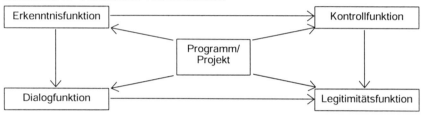

© Stockmann 2000

Da Evaluationen unterschiedliche Analyseperspektiven einnehmen und unterschiedliche Erkenntnisinteressen verfolgen können, werden auch verschiedene theoretische Ansätze, methodologische Paradigmen und Erhebungsmethoden verwendet. Diese unterscheiden sich prinzipiell nicht von den in der
sozialwissenschaftlichen Forschung üblichen Ansätzen und Verfahren. Allerdings gelten *spezielle Anwendungsbedingungen*, da die Evaluationsforschung
in einem Kontext konkreten Handelns agiert und ihrer Intention nach nut-
zungs- und handlungsorientiert ausgerichtet ist (vgl. Weiss 1974: 7 u. 25;
Rossi u.a. 1988: 3; Vedung 1999: 12). Wenn sie darauf abzielt, die Entwicklung von Programminitiativen zu unterstützen, die Planung und Umsetzung
sozialer Interventionen zu beeinflussen und ihre Durchführung zu verbessern,
ist sie „in einem weiten Sinn auch eine politische Tätigkeit" (Rossi u.a. 1988:
183). Indem sie Gestaltungs-, Kontroll-, Steuerungs- und Bewertungsfunk-
tionen innerhalb von Handlungsfeldern der Politik wahrnimmt und ihre Ergebnisse in den Verwaltungs- und Politikprozeß zurückmeldet, wird sie selbst
zu einem Politikum und bewegt „sich notwendig in einem Minenfeld politischer, administrativer und gesellschaftlicher Interessen" (Hellstern/Wollmann
1980b: 61). Evaluationsforscher müssen deshalb die soziale Ökologie ihres
Arbeitsumfeldes berücksichtigen. Verschiedene Interessengruppen sind direkt oder indirekt an den Evaluierungen beteiligt und können die Durchführung behindern oder fördern. Solche ‚Stakeholders' können politische Entscheidungsträger, die Auftraggeber der Evaluation, Durchführungsorganisa-

tionen, Implementationsträger, Programmteilnehmer, Zielgruppen, Projektmitarbeiter, Programmkonkurrenten und andere sein.

Aufgrund dieser *„Dualität"* der *Evaluationsforschung*, die sich darin
ausdrückt, daß sie einerseits Teil der empirischen Sozialforschung ist und
sich ihrer Theorien und Methoden bedient, aber andererseits auch Teil des
politischen Prozesses ist, den sie selbst mit ihren Ergebnissen beeinflußt und
umgekehrt als Instrument zur Entscheidungsfindung für die politische Steuerung wissenschaftsfremden Anforderungen ausgesetzt ist, haben sich im Laufe der Entwicklung der Evaluationsforschung unterschiedliche methodologische Paradigmen herausgebildet. Diese orientieren sich entweder stärker an
wissenschaftlichen Standards oder an den Informationsbedürfnissen der Auftraggeber bzw. der Zielgruppen.

2. Theorien und Methoden der Evaluationsforschung

Da sich die Evaluationsforschung nicht losgelöst von der allgemeinen wis-
senschaflichen Forschung entwickelt, fanden und finden in ihr auch die dort
geführten Debatten mit nicht geringerer Heftigkeit ihre Fortsetzung.

Vor allem in den Anfangsjahren der Evaluationsforschung herrschte ein
positivistisch bestimmter methodologischer Rigorismus vor. Experimentellen
Designs wurde der Vorzug gegeben um „die wahren Zusammenhänge zwischen kausalen Kräften" (Cook/Matt 1990: 20) aufzudecken, damit politische
Entscheidungen über Interventionsprogramme nicht auf falschen Behauptun-
gen hinsichtlich dessen beruhen, was ein Programm leistet und was nicht.
Donald Campbell, der sich die Welt als ein Labor für Sozialexperimente vor-
stellte (vgl. Campbell 1969: 409ff.), mißt deshalb der „internen Validität" die
größte Bedeutung bei Evaluationen zu, d.h. der Sicherheit, daß die Verbindung zwischen zwei Variablen eine kausale Beziehung einer antezedenten Va-
riabeln und ihrer Konsequenz reflektiert (vgl. Cook/Campbell 1979; Scriven
1972, 1980, 1991).

Nicht zuletzt als Reaktion auf diesen methodologischen Rigorismus for-
mierte sich ein Lager von Evaluatoren, das vor allem die instrumentelle
Funktion der Evaluationsforschung für die Entscheidungsfindung im politischen Prozeß in den Vordergrund stellte: Evaluation wird eher als politischer,
denn als wissenschaftlicher Akt gesehen. Aus Gründen der Ethik und wegen
der politischen Nützlichkeit sollten Evaluationen vor allem den Interessen der
Betroffenen dienen. Die Evaluatoren sollen dabei die Rolle von Lehrern
übernehmen und allen beteiligten Parteien bei der Evaluation beratend zur
Seite stehen. Evaluation sollte zu einer Kunst entwickelt werden (vgl. Cronbach u.a. 1981; Cronbach 1982; Wottawa/Thierau 1990: 33).

Das *handlungstheoretische Paradigma* führt diese Gedanken weiter und
postuliert, daß Evaluationen nicht nur die Kontrolle der Qualität von Innova-

tionen beinhalten darf „sondern gleichzeitig die Konstruktion, Optimierung und die Legitimierung der Modellmaßnahmen zu beinhalten habe" (Lange 1983: 256). Daraus ergeben sich folgende, dem konventionellen sozialwissenschaftlichen Forschungsparadigma zuwiderlaufende, methodische Konsequenzen:

–   Nicht die Falsifikation von Theorien oder Hypothesen ist primäres Erkenntnisziel, sondern die Angabe von Handlungsalternativen zur Lösung auftretender Probleme.
–   Die Trennung zwischen Evaluatoren und den Evaluationsobjekten wird aufgehoben. Die Wissenschaftler geben ihre distanzierte Position zum Untersuchungsgegenstand auf und werden zu gleichberechtigten Partnern von den unmittelbar an der Evaluation Beteiligten und den davon Betroffenen (Evaluationsforschung als Aktionsforschung).
–   Nicht die Forschungsfragen des Evaluators stehen im Mittelpunkt des Interesses, sondern die Informationsbedarfe der Zielgruppen.
–   Nicht Wertneutralität in den Aussagen wird angestrebt, sondern im Gegenteil es werden stellungsbeziehende Wertungen verlangt.
–   Gütekriterien der Evaluation sind nicht mehr primär Validität, Reliabilität und Objektivität, sondern Kommunikation, Intervention, Transparenz und Relevanz. (Vgl. Gruschka 1976: 142-151; Weiss 1972: 6f.; Rein 1984: 179; Lachenmann 1987: 320; Staudt 1988: 27f.; Gagel 1990: 45ff.; Schneider-Barthold 1992: 379ff.)

Der positivistisch unterfütterte methodologische Rigorismus wurde zudem vom *konstruktivistischen, interpretativen Paradigma* in Frage gestellt. Das Vorhandensein einer einzigen ‚wahren' Realität wird bestritten. Statt dessen wird angenommen, daß Realität aus verschiedenen Perspektiven sozial konstruiert ist, die in Konflikten zueinanderstehen können. Deshalb verwenden die Anhänger dieses Ansatzes auch andere, mehr qualitativ ausgerichtete Forschungsmethoden, um die Ergebnisse besser in ihrem partikularen Kontext interpretieren zu können. Evaluierungsergebnisse werden deshalb zentral bestimmt durch das spezifische Programm das gerade jetzt (zu einem bestimmten Zeitpunkt), unter spezifischen Umständen und mit ausgewählten Betroffenen (stakeholdern) evaluiert wird. Generalisierungen sind deshalb nur sehr begrenzt möglich. (Vgl. vor allem Guba/Lincoln 1989; Patton 1987; Stake 1983)

Als eine Weiterführung des handlungstheoretischen und des konstruktivistischen Paradigmas kann das *transformative/emanzipatorische Paradigma* betrachtet werden, das die unterschiedliche Machtstellung einzelner Stakeholder-Gruppen hervorhebt, die zur Überbetonung bestimmter Interessen führen kann (vgl. Mertens 1998 und in diesem Band).

Mittlerweile gilt der ‚kalte Krieg' der Paradigmen zwar keineswegs als endgültig beendet. Unterschiedliche Sichtweisen bleiben weiterhin bestehen. Doch es herrscht weitgehend Konsens darüber, daß Evaluationen die Per-

spektiven und Bedürfnisse der Stakeholder zu berücksichtigen haben, und
daß quantitative und qualitative Methoden zu verwenden sind (Multimetho-
denansätze).

Von vielen wird mittlerweile die Auffassung geteilt, „daß eine Untersuchung gleichzeitig strengen wissenschaftlichen Anforderungen genügen und
für den Auftraggeber und andere Interessengruppen von maximalem Nutzen
sein kann" (Rossi u.a. 1988: 10). Sie folgen dabei der kritisch-rationalen For-
schungslogik und halten prinzipiell alle bekannten empirischen Forschungs-
techniken für einsetzbar.

Chelimsky (1995: 6) beschreibt die neuere Entwicklung so:

„We think less today about the absolute merits of one method versus another, and more
about wether and how using them in concert could result in more conclusive findings." Die
eigentlichen Evaluationsfragen rücken dabei mehr in den Vordergrund: „We have learned
that the choice of methods (and measures and instruments and data) depends much more on
the type of question being asked than on the qualities of any particular method." (ebenda)

Über alle theoretischen und methodischen Fragen hinweg besteht zudem Einigkeit darin, daß es vor allem darauf ankommt, daß Evaluationsergebnisse
im politischen Prozeß genutzt werden (vgl. Chelimsky 1995: 8). Damit rückt
das Kriterium der Nützlichkeit von Evaluationsergebnissen für die Auftraggeber und die unterschiedlichen Stakeholder-Gruppen in den Vordergrund.
Seit Mitte der 80er Jahre ist dies ein Schwerpunkt in der Evaluationsdiskussion (vgl. vor allem Patton 1997).

Die Qualität von Evaluationen kann demnach nicht allein an einem Gütekriterium gemessen werden. Neben der Wissenschaftlichkeit der Ergebnisse,
kommt es eben auch darauf an, daß Evaluationen nützlich sind, denn nur
dann werden sie auf politische und soziale Veränderungsprozesse erwirken
können.

Im Zuge der Professionalisierung der Evaluationsforschung haben Ende
der 70er Jahre verschiedene Organisationen in den USA eine Reihe von Kriterien entwickelt mit denen die Qualität von Evaluationen erfaßt werden soll.
Am weitesten verbreitet haben sich die ursprünglich vom „Joint Committee
on Standards for Educational Evaluation" vorgelegten „Standards for Evaluation", die postulieren, daß Evaluationen

–   nützlich sein sollen, d.h. an den Informationsbedürfnissen der Nutzer
    ausgerichtet sind *(Nützlichkeit)*,

–   realistisch, gut durchdacht, diplomatisch und kostenbewußt durchgeführt
    werden sollen *(Durchführbarkeit)*,

–   rechtlich und ethisch korrekt ablaufen und dem Wohlergehen der in die
    Evaluation einbezogenen und von den Ergebnissen betroffenen Personen
    Aufmerksamkeit schenken sollen *(Korrektheit)* und

–   über die Güte und/oder die Verwendbarkeit eines evaluierten Programms
    fachlich angemessene Informationen hervorbringen und vermitteln sollen
    (Genauigkeit).

Mit der *Qualität von Evaluationen* befaßt sich in diesem Band der Beitrag *von Thomas Widmer*, der auch auf die Entstehung, Struktur und den Inhalt der Standards sowie ihre Anwendung in der Evaluationspraxis eingeht.

Die Entwicklung der *Theorien und Methoden* in der Evaluationsforschung, die hier thematisch nur kurz angerissen werden konnte, wird in diesem Band vornehmlich in den Beiträgen von *Barbara Lee* und *Valerie Caracelli* behandelt. Aber auch in dem Beitrag von *Donna Mertens* zur *Institutionalisierung der Evaluation in den USA* finden sich hierzu einige Ausführungen, denn die Geschichte der Evaluationsforschung kann nicht ohne die historische Entwicklung von Paradigmen und den mit ihnen verbundenen Methoden geschrieben werden.

3. Entwicklung der Evaluationsforschung

Im folgenden soll auf die Evaluationsforschung in Deutschland eingegangen werden. Diese wurde vor allem von Entwicklungen in den USA, Europa und in Deutschland selbst geprägt.

3.1 Entwicklung in den USA

Auf systematisch gesammelten Daten basierende Evaluationen sind ein relativ modernes Phänomen. Sie stehen in Zusammenhang mit den Demokratisierungsprozessen dieses Jahrhunderts, und sie wurden ermöglicht durch die Entwicklung sozialwissenschaftlicher Methoden.

In den USA wurden bereits in den *30er und 40er Jahren* Reformprogramme zur Verminderung der Arbeitslosigkeit und der Verbesserung der sozialen Sicherheit im Rahmen des „New Deals" von Evaluationsstudien begleitet (vgl. Deutscher/Ostrander 1985: 17f.).

Als wissenschaftliche Pionierarbeiten der Evaluationsforschung gelten Lewins (1951) Feldstudien, die Arbeit von Lippitt und White über demokratische und autoritäre Führungsstile (Lippitt 1940; White/Lippitt 1953), sowie die Western-Electric-Studie (Hawthorne-Werke) über die psychischen und sozialen Folgen technologischer Innovationen (Roethlisberger/Dickson 1934).

Während des *2. Weltkriegs* versuchte sich die U.S. Army die angewandte Sozialforschung zu Nutze zu machen. In ihrem Auftrag entwickelten Stouffer und seine Mitarbeiter (Stouffer u.a. 1949) Instrumente zur kontinuierlichen Messung der Stimmung in der Truppe und zur Evaluierung bestimmter Maßnahmen im Bereich des Personalwesens und der Propaganda (vgl. Rossi u.a. 1988: 5).

Der eigentliche Boom der Evaluationsforschung setzte in der USA zu Beginn der *60er Jahre* im Gefolge umfangreicher Sozial-, Bildungs-, Gesundheits-, Ernährungs- und Infrastrukturprogramme ein. Von Anfang an waren diese mit dem Auftrag verknüpft, die Wirkungen dieser Programme zu überprüfen. In einem Großteil der Fälle wurden die Evaluationen sogar gesetzlich vorgeschrieben und eigene Haushaltsmittel dafür bereitgestellt.

Am bekanntesten sind die Wohlfahrts- und Reformprogramme der demokratischen Präsidenten John F. Kennedy (1961-1963) und Lyndon B. Johnson (1963-1969). Mit Hilfe des „Feldzugs gegen die Armut" sollte die „Great Society" verwirklicht werden. Die Evaluationsforschung sollte dabei nach Hellstern und Wollmann (1984: 27) Zeuge, Rechtfertigungsinstrument und Stimulator für diese Politik werden.

Mit dem „Economic Opportunity Act" wurde 1964 eine von den Regierungsministerien unabhängige „Behörde für wirtschaftliche Chancengleichheit" (Office of Economic Opportunity) für die Verwaltung und Finanzierung von Programmen gegründet, wie Headstart[6] (Vorschulprogramm für Unterschichtkinder), Jobs Corps (Arbeitsbeschaffungsprogramm für arbeitslose Jugendliche), Manpower Training (Berufsbildung), Gesundheitsdienste und Legal Services (Rechtsberatung). Große Bedeutung errang vor allem das „Community Action Programm", das nicht nur die materiellen Nöte der Bevölkerung abbauen, sondern auch neue Formen der Demokratie und Mitbestimmung auf kommunaler Ebene einführen sollte (vgl. Lachenmann 1977: 31).

Ein ganz wesentlicher Impuls für die Evaluationsforschung ging von der Einrichtung eines Planungs-, Programmgestaltungs- und Haushaltsplanungssystems (Planning, Programming and Budgeting System, PPBS) aus, das im Verteidigungsministerium durch Robert McNamara eingeführt und unter Präsident Johnson 1965 auf den gesamten Regierungsapparat und alle Ministerien ausgedehnt wurde.[7] Unter Präsident Nixon wurde ein Großteil dieses Systems allerdings schon 1971 wieder aufgegeben.

Durch die Reformprogramme entstand ein großer Auftragsmarkt, von dem die Evaluationsforschung stark profitierte. Es wird geschätzt, daß 1976 bereits 600 Mill. $ für die Evaluation von sozialen Dienstleistungsprogram-

---

6   Head Start wurde zu einem der bekanntesten, intensivst evaluierten und umstrittensten sozialpolitischen Programme der USA. An dem zwischen 1965 und 1980 durchgeführten Programm nahmen 7,5 Mill Kinder teil. Es wurden mehr als 50 größere Evaluierungen durchgeführt und etwa 800 Zeitschriftenartikel publiziert. Bis erste Ergebnisse des Head Start Programms vorlagen, war bereits Präsident Richard M. Nixon (1969-1974) im Amt, der die Mittel für die Reformprogramme stark einschränken wollte. Die Evaluierungsergebnisse, die kaum einen Effekt des Vorschulprogramms nachweisen konnten, kamen ihm deshalb gerade recht. Die negativen Testergebnisse lösten eine Welle weiterer Evaluationen und eine umfassende Methodendiskussion aus (vgl. Hellstern/Wollmann 1984: 29 ff.).

7   Deutscher & Ostrander (1985:18) halten die Einführung des PPBS für einen Markstein in der Evaluationsgschichte: „This concept and McNamara's influence are crucial to the history of evaluation research." Dieser Auffassung ist u.a. auch Wittmann (1985: 5).

men aufgewendet wurden (vgl. Wittmann 1985: 9). Das „Evaluationsbusiness" wurde zu einer Wachstumsindustrie.

Als in den *70er* und vor allem *80er Jahren* die Kritik an solchen Programmen wuchs, gingen zwar insgesamt die Mittel für innovative Modellvorhaben zurück, doch die Bedeutung der Evaluationsforschung wurde dadurch nicht geschmälert. Lediglich ihr Schwerpunkt verlagerte sich. Zunehmend rückte das Verhältnis von Kosten und Nutzen, die Effizienz des Managements und die Rechenschaftsberichterstattung in den Mittelpunkt des Interesses. So wurden z.b. sogenannte „Sunset-Gesetze" erlassen, die eine automatische Beendigung der Programme vorsahen, wenn nicht innerhalb einer festgelegten Zeitspanne der Nachweis ihrer Wirksamkeit erbracht werden konnte (vgl. Rossi u.a. 1988: 6). Auch dies stärkte die Rolle der Evaluationsforschung, die mit dem „Government Performance and Result Act" noch einmal deutlich unterstrichen wurde. Dieses 1993 vom US-Kongreß verabschiedete Gesetz, schreibt Mertens in diesem Band: „shifted the focus of federal management and decision making away from preoccupation with the activities that are undertaken under the auspices of federal funding to a focus on the results of those activities". Mittlerweile ist Evaluation in den USA zu einem integrierten Bestandteil von Programmen geworden, um deren Implementation und Wirksamkeit zu überprüfen.[8]

Die *Institutionalisierung der Evaluation in den USA* sowie neuere Entwicklungen, insbesondere auch die Auswirkungen legislativer Einflüsse, werden hier in dem Beitrag von *Donna Mertens* behandelt.

3.2 Entwicklung in Europa

In Europa setzte die „moderne" Evaluationsforschung im Vergleich zur USA mit einer zehnjährigen Verspätung Ende der *60er Jahre* ein. Wie dort gewann sie mit dem Aufkommen umfassender politischer Reformprogramme an Bedeutung und Profil. Schweden, Großbritannien und auch Deutschland werden zu den „frontrunners" (vgl. Leeuw in diesem Beitrag)[9] gezählt. Während diese erste Evaluationswelle getragen wurde von einer neo-keynesianischen Politik, dem Ausbau des Wohlfahrtsstaates und der Verbesserung staatlicher Infrastruktureinrichtungen und dabei noch aus „vollen" Kassen schöpfen konnte, setzten in Folge der Erdölpreiserhöhung von 1973 und der dadurch ausgelösten weltweiten Wirtschaftsrezession staatliche Finanzierungsengpässe ein. Die Diskussion zur Modernisierung von Staat und Verwaltung drehte

---

8 Besonders interessant sind an dieser Stelle die Überlegungen von Derlien (1990: 9f.) über die Auswirkungen unterschiedlicher Verfassungskontexte auf die Bedeutung von Rechnungshöfen und die Funktion von Evaluation.

9 Vgl. zur europäischen Entwicklung auch Derlien (1990); Rist (1990); Wollmann (1997); Pollit (1998); Wollmann (2000).

sich in den westlichen Industrieländern zunehmend um das Problem der Haushaltskonsolidierung. Im Rahmen neo-liberaler und neo-konservativer Strömungen wurde der Rückbau des Sozial- und Wohlfahrtsstaats propagiert.

Bis Mitte der *70er Jahre* wurde die Evaluationsforschung – wie zuvor in den USA – vor allem dazu genutzt, die Effektivität von Programmen nachzuweisen, um die Durchsetzungschancen innovativer Maßnahmen zu verbessern. Evaluationen sollten nicht nur die Wirksamkeit von Programmen belegen, sondern auch zur Korrektur und Steuerung laufender Maßnahmen beitragen. Dabei wurden analytische Interessen und legitimatorische Absichten häufig miteinander vermengt.

Ab Mitte der 70er Jahre gewannen – wie in den USA – Kosten-Nutzen-Erwägungen an Bedeutung und die Administratoren erhofften sich von Evaluationen rationale Entscheidungs- und Argumentationshilfen für die Priorisierung und Selektion von Programmen. In die Evaluierungsforschung wurden große Hoffnungen gesetzt:

„*Öffentlichkeit* und *Parlament* versprachen sich eine verbesserte Kontrolle staatlicher Maßnahmen, die Berücksichtigung von Neben- und Folgewirkungen; der *Verwaltung* eröffnete Evaluierung Eingriffschancen, um eine verbesserte Zielgenauigkeit der Programme, verbesserte Wirtschaftlichkeit der Maßnahmen und Senkung der Kosten zu erreichen; der beteiligten *Wissenschaft* stellte sie nicht nur den Gewinn zusätzlicher Ressourcen, sondern auch die Möglichkeit eines experimentellen Tests ihrer Theorien in Aussicht." (Hellstern/Wollmann 1984: 23)[10]

In den späten *80er und 90er* Jahren bekam Evaluation einen neuen Aufschwung. Die Reform- und Modernisierungsdebatte gewann unter dem Stichwort „New Public Management" neue Konturen, zuerst in Holland, Großbritannien und in den skandinavischen Ländern (vgl. Wollmann 1994: 99). Dabei handelt es sich nicht etwa um ein kohärentes Konzept, sondern eher um ein Bündel von Organisations- und Verfahrensprinzipien mit denen vor allem eine Reduzierung der Staatsaufgaben (insbesondere durch Privatisierung) ein Abbau staatlicher Regelungsdichte (Deregulierung), und die Erhöhung administrativer Effizienz (interne Ökonomisierung, value for money) durch binnenstrukturelle Managementreformen sowie durch die Einführung von Wettbewerb erreicht werden soll. Im Prinzip geht es darum, das an ökonomischer Rationalität orientierte privatwirtschaftliche Unternehmens- und Marktmodell auf den öffentlichen Sektor zu übertragen (vgl. Schröter/Wollmann 1998: 59ff.). Der Evaluation kommt in diesem Kontext vor allem die Rolle zu, die (Kosten-) Effizienz staatlicher Maßnahmen zu überprüfen.

Ein weiterer maßgeblicher Faktor, der auf die Entwicklung der Evaluationsforschung Einfluß nahm, ist in der fortschreitenden europäischen Integration zu sehen, die nicht nur zu einer Ausdehnung eines europäisch bestimmten Verwaltungsregimes führte (vgl. Kohler-Koch 1991: 47ff.) sondern auch zu der Initiierung einer Vielzahl unterschiedlichster Programme. Dies stellt

---

10   Hervorhebungen durch Hellstern und Wollmann.

die Evaluationsforschung, die vor allem national organisiert ist, vor große
Herausforderungen. Zu beobachten ist mittlerweile: „In a variety of sectors –
most notably for the EC Structural Funds – evaluation has been made legally
or conventionally manditory." (Pollitt 1998: 214)

Insgesamt ist sowohl für die EU-Institutionen als auch für die meisten
europäischen Länder im letzten Jahrzehnt eine deutliche Zunahme an Politik-
und Programmevaluationen zu konstatieren, was Christopher Pollitt (1998:
214) zu der Aussage veranlaßt: „These are grand days for European evaluators."

Mit der *Entwicklung der Evaluation in Europa* setzt sich in diesem Band
der Beitrag von *Franz Leeuw* auseinander.

3.3 Entwicklung in Deutschland

Die Entwicklung der Evaluation in Deutschland wurde von den genannten
internationalen und europäischen Strömungen erfaßt und mitgeprägt. Allerdings haben auch eine Reihe *nationaler Rahmenbedingungen* die Evaluationsentwicklung beeinflußt.

Nach einer Phase der „institutionellen Restauration" (Alber 1989: 60)
nahm der Problemdruck in der BRD deutlich zu. Die sogenannte „Bildungs-
katastrophe", ein allgemein konstatierter ‚Reformstau' und die Sorge um die
internationale wirtschaftliche Wettbewerbsfähigkeit führten zu einem breiten
gesellschaftlichen Konsens, daß weitreichende Reformen notwendig seien.
Bereits die große Koalition aus CDU/CSU und SPD (1966-1969) brachte eine Reihe von Vorhaben auf den Weg, die dann in der sozial-liberalen Koalition unter Kanzler Willy Brandt (1969-1974) als Bestandteil einer Politik der
inneren Reform zum Regierungsprogramm erhoben wurde (vgl. Wollmann
2000: 712). Es wurde eine umfassende Staats- und Verwaltungsmodernisierung angestrebt, die auf der Vorstellung beruhte, daß „der Staat als zentrale
gesellschaftliche Steuerungsinstanz fungieren, „aktive Politik" betreiben und
die Gesellschaft langfristig planend gestalten sollte" (Mayntz 1997: 68). Die
Erweiterung der Handlungs- und Gestaltungsfähigkeit des Staates wurde insbesondere von der Einführung neuer Planungsverfahren erwartet, wobei
Evaluation als ein wichtiges analytisches Instrument verwendet wurde. Evaluation erlebte in Deutschland eine erste Blüte. Nicht nur auf der nationalen
Ebene auch die Länder und Gemeinden wurden von Reformeifer erfaßt und
bedienten sich der Evaluation als Steuerungs- und Kontrollinstrument (vgl.
Wollmann 1994, 1998, 1999; Derlien 1976, 1990, 1994). Vor allem in den
Bereichen Bildung und Erziehung, Stadterneuerung und Infrastruktur wurden
umfangreiche und aufwendige Evaluationsstudien durchgeführt.

Dabei griffen die Ministerien weitgehend auf externe Evaluationen zurück, die zumeist öffentlich ausgeschrieben wurden. Vom Aufbau hauseige-
ner Evaluationskapazitäten wurde weitgehend abgesehen. Eine der wenigen

Ausnahmen war das noch junge Bundesministerium für wirtschaftliche Zusammenarbeit, das bereits 1972 ein hausinternes Evaluationsreferat einrichtete (zur *Entwicklung der Evaluation in der staatlichen Entwicklungszusammenarbeit* siehe den Beitrag *von Reinhard Stockmann* in diesem Band).

Das Kanzleramt scheiterte bei dem Versuch: „to use evaluation as its analytical muscle for co-ordinating (and possibly controlling) the ministries „sectoral policies" (Wollmann 1997: 4), so daß es dabei blieb, daß die einzelnen Fachministerien relativ unabhängig voneinander ihre Evaluationen sektorbezogen und speziell an ihren eigenen spezifischen Bedürfnissen und Vorstellungen ausgerichtet durchführten.

Unterstützt wurde der Evaluationsboom durch die Haushaltsreform von 1970. In den Vorläufigen Verwaltungsvorschriften (VV) zu §7 der Bundeshaushaltsordnung (BHO) wurden ausdrücklich Erfolgskontrollen bei ganz oder teilweise abgeschlossenen Maßnahmen vorgeschrieben. Nr. 1.3 der VV-BHO bestimmt:

„1.3 Im Wege der Erfolgskontrolle (Ergebnisprüfung) soll insbesondere untersucht werden

1.3.1 während der Durchführung von mehrjährigen Maßnahmen mindestens jährlich, ob die Zwischenergebnisse im Rahmen der Planung liegen, die Planung anzupassen ist und die Maßnahmen weiterzuführen oder einzustellen sind,

1.3.2 nach der Durchführung von Maßnahmen, ob das erreichte Ergebnis der ursprünglichen oder angepaßten Planung entspricht, die Maßnahmen zu revidieren sind und Erfahrungswerte gesichert werden können." (Bundesrechnungshof 1989: 13 und Anlage 1: 49ff.)

Innerhalb weniger Jahre entstand ein Evaluationsmarkt an dem zwar auch die Universitäten partizipierten, der aber vor allem von einer rasch expandierenden Consultingwirtschaft beherrscht wurde. Hellmut Wollmann kann hierzu nicht nur als Wissenschaftler sondern auch als „Zeitzeuge" zitiert werden: „Commercial research and consultancy firms mushroomed and succeeded to produce the lion's share of the evaluation research funding." (Wollmann 1997: 4)

Doch dem Aufblühen der Evaluation in Deutschland wurde, wie in vielen westeuropäischen Ländern, durch die weltweiten ökonomischen und fiskalischen Auswirkungen der Erdölpreiserhöhung von 1973 ein abruptes Ende bereitet. Mit dem Auslaufen der Modernisierungswelle ging auch die Bedeutung der Evaluation zurück. Das Abklingen der Modernisierungseuphorie ist jedoch nicht nur fiskalischen Zwängen zuzuschreiben, sondern auch der eintretenden Ernüchterung über teilweise bescheidene Reformerfolge. Auch die Evaluation konnte nicht in allen Fällen die in sie gesetzten Erwartungen erfüllen. Oft blieben ihre Ergebnisse widersprüchlich und zu wenig umsetzungsorientiert.

So führten – um nur ein prominentes Beispiel zu nennen – die zwischen Ende der 60er bis Anfang der 80er Jahre mit großem wissenschaftlichen Aufwand betriebenen Evaluationsstudien im Rahmen der Schulversuche mit integrierten Gesamtschulen nicht zu klaren Empfehlungen. Im Gegenteil, die 78 Einzelstudien erwiesen sich hinsichtlich des methodologischen Ansatzes, der Vorgehensweise und der eingesetzten Datenerhebungsmethoden als derart heterogen, daß kein abschließendes Urteil über die Effektivität der neuen Schulform gegenüber dem traditionellen, gegliederten Schulsystem möglich war (vgl. Aurin/Stolz 1990: 269ff.; Fend 1982). Auch wenn dieser „Fehlschlag" des bis dahin aufwendigsten Evaluationsvorhabens als eine Folge übersteigerter Erwartungen gewertet wird, so darf dennoch seine weit über die Grenzen der Bildungsforschung hinausgehende Wirkung auf Entscheidungsträger und Administratoren nicht unterschätzt werden.

Trotz der veränderten internationalen wie nationalen Rahmenbedingungen (fiskale Beschränkungen, Rückbau des Sozialstaats, Aufkommen des Neoliberalismus und Neokonservatismus, Reformernüchterung, Zweifel am Nutzen von Evaluationen, 1974 Führungswechsel in der sozialliberalen Koalition „Wende vor der Wende", 1982 Regierungswechsel: liberal-konservative ‚Wende') konnten Evaluationen eine gewisse Bedeutung beibehalten. Allerdings setzte sich der Ende der 60er Jahre ausgelöste Boom keineswegs fort oder erreichte gar Ausmaße wie in den USA. Von *den Gebieten, in denen Evaluation* (insbesondere im Zusammenhang mit anstehenden Reformen) *Bedeutung gewann,* sind u.a. zu nennen:

- Bildungs-, Erziehungs- und Hochschulpolitik
- Gesundheitspolitik
- Wirtschafts- und Sozialpolitik
- Familienpolitik
- Forschungs- und Technologiepolitik
- Agrarpolitik
- Verkehrspolitik
- Regionale Wirtschafts- und Strukturpolitik
- Städtebau- und Wohnungspolitik
- Arbeitsmarkt- und Beschäftigungspolitik
- Entwicklungspolitik
- Justizvollzug und Kriminologie
- Verwaltungspolitik

(vgl. Lange 1983: 254; Hellstern/Wollmann 1984: 33ff.; Wottawa/Thierau 1990: 56f.; Wollmann 1997: 4f.).

Da in diesem Band nicht alle Bereiche in denen umfangreiche Evaluationen durchgeführt werden und die Evaluationsforschung fest etabliert ist aus Platzgründen berücksichtigt werden konnten, wurden einige beispielhafte Felder ausgewählt:

- *Hellmut Wollmann,* als einer der seit Jahrzehnten ausgewiesenen Evaluationsforscher in Deutschland, setzt sich in seinem Beitrag mit *der Evaluation von Verwaltungspolitik* auseinander. Er untersucht vor allem die Anwendbarkeit konzeptioneller und methodischer Ansätze der Evaluationsforschung auf den Gegenstandsbereich der Verwaltung und Verwaltungmodernisierung. Danach wird der gegenwärtige Stand und das konzeptionelle und methodische Profil der Evaluationsforschung zur Verwaltungsmodernisierung anhand ausgewählter Beispiele dargestellt und ein kurzer Ausblick auf den Diskussions- und Forschungsstand in einigen europäischen Nachbarländern gegeben.

– *Helmut Kromrey*, der sich ebenfalls seit Jahrzehnten mit der Methodik der Evaluation, insbesondere der Implementations- und Wirkungsforschung, in Lehre und Forschung beschäftigt, behandelt in seinem *Beitrag „Qualität und Evaluation im System Hochschule"*. Er unterscheidet drei Paradigmen der Evaluation: Das „Forschungs-" das „Kontroll-" und das „Entwicklungsparadigma" der Evaluation. Anschließend untersucht er, ob eines der drei Paradigmen als besonders geeignet charakterisiert und daher als „Königsweg der Hochschulevaluation" empfohlen werden könnte und welche Alternativen sich anbieten.

– *Xaver Büeler*, Leiter des Forschungsbereichs Schulqualität und Schulentwicklung der Universität Zürich, geht es in seinem Beitrag ebenfalls um ‚Qualität' und wie diese mit Hilfe von *Evaluationen im Schulbereich* gemessen werden kann. Nachdem er die Entwicklung der Qualitätsevaluation in Schulen darstellt und vier Perspektiven der Qualitätsevaluation vorgestellt hat, befaßt er sich mit verschiedenen Evaluationsformen, -methoden und -modellen.

– *Stefan Kuhlmann*, Leiter der Abteilung „Technikbewertung und Innovationsstrategien" im Fraunhofer-Institut für Systemtechnik und Innovationsforschung beschreibt nach einer knappen Darstellung der Entwicklungslinien der staatlichen *Forschungs- und Technologieförderung* die wichtigsten Konzepte, Anwendungsbereiche und Methoden evaluativer Verfahren in diesem Politikfeld. Anschließend geht er auf den strukturellen Wandel in Forschung und Evaluation ein und diskutiert die Konsequenzen für die Verwendung von Evaluationen.

– *Bettina Bangel*, Referentin für Arbeit, Soziales, Gesundheit und Frauen des Landes Brandenburg sowie *Christian Brinkmann* und *Axel Deeke* vom Institut für Arbeitsmarkt- und Berufsforschung untersuchen aus verschiedenen Perspektiven – der Bundesebene, der Landesebene sowie aus europäischer Sicht – die Konzepte, Möglichkeiten, Grenzen und Entwicklungsperspektiven *der Evaluation von Arbeitsmarktprogrammen.*

– *Joseph Huber*, der sich vor allem mit ökologischer Modernisierung und industriegesellschaftlicher Entwicklungstheorie beschäftigt und sein Mitarbeiter *Axel Müller* befassen sich in ihrem Beitrag mit der *Evaluation von Umweltschutzmaßnahmen* in Staat und Unternehmen. Der Schwerpunkt der Beitrages liegt in der Darstellung und Charakterisierung von Evaluationsmethoden zur Erfassung und Bewertung von Umweltschutzmaßnahmen.

– *Reinhard Stockmann* beschäftigt sich mit einem Politikfeld, in dem die Evaluation schon frühzeitig institutionalisiert wurde, der *Entwicklungs-*

politik. Ziel seines Beitrages ist es, die bisherige Evaluationspraxis in der staatlichen Entwicklungszusammenarbeit zu skizzieren, Defizite aufzuzeigen, die derzeitigen Reformbemühungen zu bewerten sowie weiteren Reformbedarf zu benennen.

4. Evaluationsdefizite und Professionalisierungsversuche

Obwohl nach wie vor die meisten Evaluationen von der staatlichen Verwaltung in Auftrag gegeben werden, existieren kaum hausinterne Evaluationsreferate oder auch nur Arbeitshilfen für die Durchführung von Evaluationen.[11] Ein 1989 vom *Bundesrechnungshof (BRH)* angefertigtes Gutachten *zur „Erfolgskontrolle finanzwirksamer Maßnahmen in der öffentlichen Verwaltung"*, kommt zu einem niederschmetternden Ergebnis:

– Nur in drei der untersuchten Ressorts existiert ein „relativ geordnetes Verfahren" (BRH 1989: 35) zur Durchführung von Erfogskontrollen (BMP, BMZ, BMFT).

– In fast allen Ressorts werden schon in der Planungsphase die notwendigen Voraussetzungen für Erfolgskontrollen (Zielformulierung, Festlegung von Ergebnissen, Indikatoren für die Erfolgsmessung) nicht geschaffen (vgl. BRH 1989: 26).

– Versuche durch Evaluationen direkte und indirekte Wirkungen von Programmen oder Maßnahmen zu erbringen sind ausgesprochen selten (vgl. BRH 1989: 29).

– Vorhandene methodische Möglichkeiten zur Ermittlung der Wirksamkeit von Maßnahmen wurden kaum genutzt (ebenda).

– Die Umsetzung von Evaluationsergebnissen ist gering (BRH 1989: 30).

– Bei den für die Erfolgskontrolle zuständigen Mitarbeitern wurde „nur eine relativ gering ausgeprägte Sensibilität für Zweck, Bedeutung und Notwendigkeit dieser Kontrollen festgestellt" (BRH 1989: 38).

Rund zehn Jahre später hat der BRH (1998) eine überarbeitete Neuauflage seiner Studie vorgelegt, in die seine neueren Prüfungserkenntnisse zum Thema Erfolgskontrolle in der öffentlichen Verwaltung eingearbeitet wurden. Die Bilanz fällt keineswegs positiver aus. Erneut wird festgestellt, daß

– nur wenige Erfolgskontrollen durchgeführt werden, und daß deshalb die

---

11 Allerdings gibt es eine Reihe von Ministerien, die Evaluationsaufgaben an nachgeordnete Behörden oder Institutionen übertragen haben, wie z.B. der Bundesanstalt für Straßenwesen, dem Bundesgesundheitsamt, dem Bundesinstitut für Berufsbildungsforschung (BIBB), der Bundesanstalt für Landeskunde und Raumordnung, dem Umweltbundesamt, dem Bundesinstitut für Bevölkerungsforschung, der Bundesanstalt für Arbeitsschutz und Unfallforschung etc.

meisten Ressorts den Erfolg ihrer Maßnahmen nicht hinreichend beurteilen können,

– in fast allen Ressorts die Voraussetzungen für eine systematische Erfolgskontrolle fehlen,
– Wirkungsuntersuchungen, die auch nicht-intendierte Effekte berücksichtigen und die festgestellten Ergebnisse einer Ursache-Wirkungsanalyse
unterziehen nahezu komplett fehlen,
– vorhandene methodische Möglichkeiten zur Ermittlung von Erfolg und
Wirksamkeit nicht ausgeschöpft werden. (Vgl. BRH 1998: 22ff.)

Der *Bundesrechnungshof empfiehlt* deshalb wie schon 1989 die Schaffung
der organisatorischen und methodischen Voraussetzungen für die Durchführung von Erfolgskontrollen, um anschließend die Bewilligung von Haus-
haltsmitteln an die Vorlage von solchen Evaluationen zu binden. Hierfür
empfiehlt der Bundesrechnungshof weiter:

– bei der Erfolgskontrolle die Unterstützung externer Institutionen in An-
spruch zu nehmen,
– Methoden und Verfahren zu entwickeln, die die einzelnen Ressorts in die
Lage versetzen, Erfolgskontrollen durchzuführen und
– Mitarbeiter für die Durchführung von Erfolgskontrollen qualifiziert aus-
und fortzubilden. (Vgl. BRH 1998: 36ff.)

Die Bundesministerien haben die Empfehlungen des Gutachtens von 1998
(wie schon 1989) begrüßt und die Bundesregierung hat sich verpflichtet die
nach §7 der BHO vorgeschriebenen Erfolgskontrollen durchzuführen. Doch
Skepsis ist angebracht. Zwar hat die „rot-grüne" Bundesregierung in ihrer
Koalitionsvereinbarung „Aufbruch und Erneuerung" Reformen zur Modernisierung von Staat und Verwaltung eine hohe Priorität beigemessen und Ende
1999 ein Programm „Moderner Staat – Moderne Verwaltung"[12] verabschie-
det, das die Grundlage für einen umfassenden Modernisierungsprozeß abgeben soll, doch von Evaluation ist dabei kaum die Rede.
Allerdings ist kaum vorstellbar, wie der eigens zur Kontrolle und Steuerung der Programmumsetzung gebildete Staatssekretärsausschuß unter Führung des Innenministeriums, seine Aufgaben ohne Evaluation erfüllen könnte.
Eine Reihe von Anzeichen deuten darauf hin, daß der in Europa zu beobachtende neue *Boom der Evaluation* auch Deutschland erfaßt:

– Mit der nun auch in Deutschland verstärkt geführten Diskussion um
„New Public Management" und neue Steuerungsmodelle „erlebt die
Vorstellung eines umfassenden Steuerungs- und Managementkonzepts
und mit ihr die strategische Akzentuierung und Einbindung der Evaluie-

---

12 Informationen unter www.staat-modern.de

rungsfunktion eine Renaissance" (Wollmann 1994: 99).[13]

– Wie auch in anderen europäischen Ländern sind die Regierungen in Deutschland mit notorischen Budgetproblemen konfrontiert, die eine stärkere Priorisierung und Selektion von Maßnahmen erforderlich machen. Damit steigt prinzipiell auch der Bedarf an Evaluationen, um Daten über die Effektivität und Effizienz von Programmen zu gewinnen, auf deren Basis politisch legitimierte Entscheidungen getroffen werden können. Pollitt (1998: 223) beschreibt die Situation der Regierenden zutreffend: „...they can no longer call on the same reserves of legitimacy and authority which were available to them two or three decades ago. They have to do more with less and do it for a variety of more sceptical and less deferential audiences."

– In Gesetzen oder wichtigen Programmen wurde das Instrument der Evaluation – anders als in den USA – bisher zwar kaum integriert (vgl. Wollmann 1997: 4), doch das Parlament drängt zunehmend auf die Durchführung von Evaluationen. Im Bereich der Entwicklungszusammenarbeit haben z.b. mehrere parlamentarische Initiativen dazu geführt, daß das Bundesministerium für wirtschaftliche Zusammenarbeit und Entwicklung (BMZ) jetzt in größerem Umfang Nachhaltigkeitsuntersuchungen durchführt, um die Frage nach der Wirksamkeit ihrer Projekte und Programme beantworten zu können.

– Der BRH hat sich zu einem der wichtigsten Befürworter von Evaluation entwickelt. Er drängt nicht nur mit eiserner Beharrlichkeit auf die in der BHO verpflichtend vorgeschriebenen Erfolgskontrollen, sondern verlangt auch die Ausweitung der öffentlichen Evaluationsaktivitäten (insb. auf die Überprüfung der Wirksamkeit von Subventionen, die sich jährlich auf rund 36 Mrd. DM belaufen) und führt selbst Wirkungsevaluationen durch.

– In Programmen der EU wird die Durchführung von Evaluationen zunehmend zum Standard (vgl. oben).

– Verstärkt fragen auch Nicht-Regierungsorganisationen, Verbände und Stiftungen Evaluationen, insbesondere Wirkungsevaluationen, ihrer Programme nach.

– Nicht zuletzt könnte auch das Modernisierungsprogramm der Bundesregierung dazu führen, daß Evaluationen als ein wichtiges Instrument für die politische Steuerung eine Aufwertung erfahren.

Die Entwicklung der Evaluation in Deutschland, die trotz Höhen und Tiefen immerhin eine gewisse Kontinuität aufweist (vgl. Wollmann 1997: 5), und

---

13   Die unter dem Stichwort „New Public Management" geführte Reform- und Modernisierungsdebatte begann in Europa vor allem in Holland, den skandinavischen und einigen angelsächsischen Ländern. In Deutschland wurde diese Diskussion lange Zeit weitgehend ignoriert.

die möglicherweise bereits von einem neuen Boom erfaßt ist, steht in eigentümlichen Kontrast zum *Professionalisierungsgrad* dieser Disziplin.

Während die Expansion von Evaluation in den USA nicht nur einen neuen Dienstleistungsmarkt hervorbrachte in dem sich für Sozialwissenschaftler „in einem bisher nicht bekannten Ausmaß Handlungschancen und berufliche Entwicklungsmöglichkeiten bieten" (Wottawa/Thierau 1990: 59), sondern auch zu einem sprunghaften Anstieg der Evaluationsliteratur sowie zur Gründung von Zeitschriften und Berufsverbänden führte und die Ausbildung von Evaluatoren vor allem in postgraduierten Studiengängen an den Universitäten fest verankert ist, ist eine vergleichbare Entwicklung in Deutschland bestenfalls in Ansätzen zu erkennen. Allerdings ist dem Urteil Wittmanns (vgl. 1990: 12) nicht zuzustimmen, daß es in Deutschland keinen Markt für Evaluationsforschung gäbe, da vor allem die gesetzlichen Regelungen, die in verschiedenen Politikfeldern regelmäßige und systematische Evaluationen vorschreiben, fehlen. Die Bundeshaushaltsordnung (§7) bietet sehr wohl gesetzliche Grundlagen und die jahrzehntelangen umfangreichen Evaluationstätigkeiten haben einen Markt geschaffen, auch wenn beides aus der Sicht der Evaluationsforschung keineswegs ausreichend erscheinen mag. Viel erstaunlicher ist jedoch, daß diese Situation zu keiner grundlegenden Professionalisierung in der Evaluation geführt hat.

Es gibt zwar unzählige Studien, Gutachten, Publikationen und sogar einige deutschsprachige Lehrbücher[14], doch fachübergreifende Sammelbände, in denen evaluatorisches Wissen gebündelt und integriert wird, fehlen weitgehend. Eine Evaluationszeitschrift gibt es bisher nicht. In Methodenlehrbüchern und sozialwissenschaftlichen Nachschlagewerken kam das Stichwort „Evaluation" bis vor kurzem noch selten vor.[15] Ein Fachverband – die Deutsche Gesellschaft für Evaluation – wurde im September 1997 gegründet und hat sich – wie vergleichbare Einrichtungen in Europa – zur Aufgabe gemacht, das Verständnis, die Akzeptanz und die Nutzbarmachung von Evaluation in der Gesellschaft zu fördern, Prinzipien bei der Vorgehensweise von Evaluationen zu entwickeln, Qualitätstandards für Evaluationen festzulegen und den interdisziplinären Austausch zu unterstützen. Mit heute rund 200 Mitgliedern

---

14 U.a. Wittmann (1985); Wottawa/Thierau (1990); Bussmann u.a. (1997); Vedung (1999). Das wichtigste Lehrbuch ist nach wie vor eine Übersetzung der englischsprachigen Ausgabe von „Evaluation" von Rossi und Freeman (1999) (dt. 1988). Wichtige Sammelbände: Hellstern/Wollmann (1984); Will/Winteler/Krapp (1987); Mayntz (1980d).

15 Noch in dem bereits in mehreren Auflagen erschienenen Standardwerk zur Methodenausbildung von Schnell/Hill/Esser (1992) kommt das Stichwort Evaluationsforschung nicht vor. In dem empfehlenswerten Lehrbuch zur „Empirischen Sozialforschung" von Andreas Diekmann (1995) werden die Methoden und Probleme der Evaluationsforschung hingegen ausführlich thematisiert. Bortz/Döring (1995) nehmen den Begriff Evaluation in ihrem neuen Lehrbuch „Forschungsmethoden und Evaluation" nicht nur im Titel auf, sondern widmen dem Thema auch ein Kapitel.

weist der Verband bisher jedoch erst eine geringe Intergrationskraft auf. Eine
„evaluation research community" als ein Netzwerk von professionell tätigen
Evaluationsforschern muß sich erst noch herausbilden. Es fehlen Lehrstühle,
Sonderforschungsbereiche und wissenschaftliche Institute, die sich mit
grundlegenden theoretischen und methodischen Fragen der Evaluationsforschung beschäftigen. Studiengänge, in denen die Tätigkeit des Evaluierens
vermittelt werden, gibt es überhaupt keine. Es existiert lediglich eine Reihe
von sozialwissenschaftlichen Studiengängen, in denen Lehrveranstaltungen
zu Evaluation im Rahmen der Methodenausbildung integriert sind. Auch ein
außeruniversitärer Aus- und Weiterbildungsmarkt für Evaluatoren ist kaum
existent.

Die vor über 15 Jahren von Hellstern und Wollmann (1984: 34) getroffene Defizitanalyse trifft deshalb im Kern auch heute noch zu: In der Evaluationsforschung „fehlt vor allem ein sektorale Politikfelder überschreitender
und verschiedene Fachdisziplinen integrierender Fokus, wie er sich in den
USA, aber auch in Kanada und anderen Ländern durch die Gründung eigener
berufsständischer Organisationen auf der regionalen und nationalen Ebene
manifestierte. Auch fehlte in einer immer noch disziplinär und grundlagen-
forschung-bezogenen universitären Forschungslandschaft die Förderung einer anwendungsorientierten Professionalisierung der Evaluationsforschung
durch Stiftungen und staatliche Forschungsorganisationen, wie sie in den
USA für Training, Aus- und Weiterbildung selbstverständlich wurden."

Auch wenn in den letzten Jahren *verstärkte Professionalisierungsbemühungen* festzustellen sind[16], so ist die Evaluationsforschung in Deutschland
dennoch weiterhin fachlich zersplittert, weist nur eine geringe interdisziplinäre Kommunikation und Zusammenarbeit auf und ist noch immer mit dem
Makel anwendungsbezogener Auftragsforschung behaftet, deren Wissenschaftlichkeit teilweise bestritten wird. Diese Mängel haben wesentlich dazu
beigetragen, daß sich bisher – im Unterschied zur USA – *keine eigene sozialwissenschaftliche Evaluationsdisziplin* entwickeln konnte.

Wittmann (1985: 13) hebt hervor, daß die beiden Fächer, die anfangs am
stärksten von der Evaluationsforschung profitierten, die Erziehungswissenschaft und die Psychologie ihre Chancen vor allem professionspolitisch ver-
werteten: „Viele Erziehungswissenschaftler nutzten die Flut der Forschungs-
möglichkeiten mehr, um die Position ihres Wissenschaftsgebiets abzusichern,
denn als Möglichkeit, fächerübergreifende Strategien der Evaluationsforschung zu entwickeln. Vergleichbares gilt auch für die Psychologie." Und
gleichfalls für die Verwaltungswissenschaft, Soziologie und Politische Wissenschaft sowie andere Fächer.[17]

---

16 Gründung der Deutschen Gesellschaft für Evaluation 1997. Seit 1998 eine ad-hoc
    Gruppe Evaluation in der Deutschen Gesellschaft für Soziologie.
17 Überhaupt nicht eingegangen wird hier auf das in der Betriebswirtschaftslehre ent-
    wickelte Konzept des „Controllings" das viele Überschneidungen zu dem Evaluati-

Gudrun Lachenmann (1977: 47) macht vor allem den besonderen Charakter der deutschen Politik, die in viel stärkerem Umfang als in den USA von den Sozialwissenschaften getrennt ist, dafür verantwortlich, daß die Evaluationsforschung in Deutschland keine vergleichbare Entwicklung nahm. Mit dem zunehmenden Übergang von der Ordnungs- zur Planungsverwaltung und der Rezeption „amerikanischer" Planungs- und Evaluationstechniken wandelte sich zwar auch das Politikverständnis. Die Etablierung einer Sozialberichterstattung, Indikatorenkonzepte und eben das gestiegene Interesse an der Evaluationsforschung sind sichtbare Folgen dieser Veränderung. Dennoch gibt es – anders als in den USA – in großen Teilen der Administrationen nach wie vor eine tiefsitzende *Skepsis* gegenüber dem Nutzen von Evaluationen. Nicht selten sind Programmverantwortliche der Auffassung, daß die finanziellen Mittel für das Programm und nicht für „zweifelhafte" Evaluationen ausgegeben werden sollten. Offensichtlich ist es der Evaluationsforschung in Deutschland noch nicht ausreichend gelungen, den Wert von Evaluationen zu vermitteln.

Die *disziplinäre Segmentierung* der Evaluationsforschung und ihre *Sonderstellung* in der Wissenschaft sowie die *institutionelle Zersplitterung* der Evaluation auf administrative Fachressorts, die den Löwenanteil an Auftragsmittel sektor- und ressortbezogen vergeben, haben dazu beigetragen, daß nur wenig übergreifende Fragestellungen entwickelt wurden. Da zudem viele Studien der *Öffentlichkeit nicht zugänglich* gemacht werden, sind sie der wissenschaftlichen Kritik und Diskussion entzogen. Dadurch wird die *Weiterentwicklung* von Theorien und Methoden sowie eine über die Fachgrenzen hinausgehende Wissensakkumulation *erschwert.*

Da *fachliche Standards* (wie die „Program Evaluation Standards" in den USA) bisher in Deutschland nicht etabliert werden konnten, fehlen auch allgemein gültige Qualitätskriterien, nach denen Auftraggeber und –nehmer Evaluationen beurteilen könnten.[18]

Daß der *Evaluationsmarkt* zudem weitgehend von Consulting- und Marktforschungsunternehmen dominiert wird, die nicht in erster Linie an wissenschaftlichen Diskussionen und der Kumulation von Wissen interessiert sind, sondern denen aufgrund ihrer marktwirtschaftlichen Situation vor allem an einer gewinnorientierten Auftragsabwicklung gelegen sein muß, hat sicherlich auch nicht gerade dazu beigetragen, die Evaluation als Disziplin zu pro-

---

onskonzept aufweist (vgl. Horváth 1994; Mayer/Weber 1990; Habersam 1997) sowie auf die Diskussion um lernende Organisationen (vgl. Argyris/Schön 1999; Leeuw u.a. 2000)

18 Wie hoch die Nachfrage nach solchen Standards ist läßt sich auch daran ermessen, daß eine Übersetzung und Erläuterung der Evaluation Standards des Joint Committee on Standards for Educational Evaluation bereits nach kurzer Zeit in einer zweiten Auflage erschienen ist (vgl. Joint Committee 2000). In der Deutschen Gesellschaft für Evaluation gibt es eine Arbeitsgruppe, die sich mit der Etablierung nationaler Standards befaßt.

fessionalisieren. Es fehlen universitäre Einrichtungen oder Forschungsinstitute, die sich mit grundlagenorientierten Fragestellungen und der Theorie- und Methodenentwicklung beschäftigen sowie an der Etablierung fachlichwissenschaftlicher Standards mitwirken.

5. Anforderungen an die Evaluation in Deutschland

Will die Evaluationsforschung den neuen Auftragsboom als Entwicklungschance in Deutschland nutzen, dann müssen nicht nur die benannten Defizite beseitigt werden, sondern dann muß die Evaluationsforschung auch auf die *neuen Herausforderungen* im Rahmen vielschichtiger Globalisierungsprozesse reagieren. Die Einflußmöglichkeiten nationalstaatlicher Politiken sowie die Chance Wandlungsprozesse in den Wirtschafts- und Sozialstrukturen immer noch national definierter Gesellschaften steuernd zu beeinflussen werden sich verändern. Nicht nur die Zahl und Bedeutung supra-staatlicher, national-staatlicher sowie nicht-staatlicher institutioneller Akteure verändern sich, sondern auch die Organisations- und Partizipationsformen, deren Handlungsspielräume, Einflußmöglichkeiten und Steuerpotentiale. Dies wird auch Konsequenzen haben für die Planung, Durchführung und Wirkungsmöglichkeiten sozialer und politischer Programme. Hinzu kommt, daß sich die Ansprüche an die Erfolgsbeurteilung von öffentlichen Maßnahmen in den letzten Jahren stark verändert haben. Während es anfangs noch ausreichte auf den Input (z.B. die eingesetzten Investitionsmittel) zu verweisen und später dazu übergegangen wurde auch den Output zu beziffern (z.B. die Zahl ausgebildeter Fachkräfte) wird heute vor allem nach dem Outcome und dem Impact, also nach den Wirkungen einer Maßnahme gefragt (z.B. ob die ausgebildeten Fachkräfte einen berufsadäquaten Arbeitsplatz gefunden haben oder nicht und ob sie nutzbringend eingesetzt werden können).

D.h. die aufgelegten Programme werden nicht nur komplexer, sondern die Erfolgsmessung wird zunehmend anspruchsvoller und die Wirkungsnachweise sind schwerer zu erbringen. Doch die deutsche Evaluationsforschung ist auf diese Herausforderungen nur ungenügend vorbereitet. Zwar werden in einzelnen Fächern, Sektoren und Ressorts ausgezeichnete Evaluationsstudien durchgeführt, doch aus den genannten Gründen kumulieren diese Erkenntnisse nur unzureichend in einer Weiterentwicklung von Theorie und Methodik der Evaluation.

Wenn die Chancen des derzeitigen Evaluationsbooms nicht erneut für eine *nachhaltige Institutionalisierung von Evaluation als ein wichtiges analytisches Instrument für die Steuerung politischer Entscheidungsprozesse* verspielt werden sollen, sind die bisherigen Professionalisierungsbemühungen in der Evaluationsforschung – denen erste Erfolge nicht abzusprechen sind – deutlich zu verstärken. Hierzu gehört im Einzelnen:

1. Die fachliche Zersplitterung muß einem Fächergrenzen überwindenden Dialog weichen. Hierzu könnte auch die Gründung einer deutschsprachigen Zeitschrift für Evaluation beitragen.
2. Es müssen gemeinsame professionelle Evaluationsstandards entwickelt, akzeptiert, verbreitet und kontrolliert werden. Hierbei könnte die Deutsche Gesellschaft für Evaluation eine zentrale Rolle übernehmen.
3. Es gilt, die Kluft zwischen sozialwissenschaftlicher Grundlagenforschung und anwendungsorientierter Evaluationsforschung zu überwinden. Gezielte Initiativen zur Gründung von Sonderforschungsbereichen und Forschungsschwerpunkten in der DFG könnten zur Weiterentwicklung der wissenschaftlichen Grundlagen der Evaluationsforschung beitragen.
4. Theorie und Methodik der Evaluationsforschung müssen weiterentwickelt und den spezifischen Problemen der politischen Praxis angepaßt und angemessen umgesetzt werden.
5. Es müssen geeignete Organisationsformen zur Dokumentation, Kumulation und Verbreitung des Wissens über Evaluationsforschung gefunden werden.
6. Es müssen universitäre und außeruniversitäre Aus- und Weiterbildungskapazitäten für Evaluatoren, aber auch für Auftraggeber und Nutzer von Evaluationen geschaffen werden.
7. Entsprechend den transnationalen Herausforderungen müssen nationale Grenzen überschritten und die Evaluationsforschung muß konzeptionell und methodisch an die Bedingungen interkulturell vergleichender Untersuchungen angepaßt und weiterentwickelt werden.

Die *Auftraggeber* können diesen Prozeß unterstützen, indem sie

– in einen intensiveren Austausch mit der Wissenschaft treten, um die Einsatzmöglichkeiten von Evaluationen zu verbessern,
– Evaluationsergebnisse nutzen und Evaluationen zu einem wichtigen Steuerungsinstrument ihrer Politik machen,
– mehr Transparenz zulassen und Evaluationsstudien veröffentlichen, so daß sie der wissenschaftlichen Kritik zugänglich sind,
– hohe Qualitätsansprüche an Evaluationen stellen sowie Evaluationsstandards einhalten und dazu bereit sind, die erforderlichen Finanzmittel bereitzustellen,
– Programme nicht nur ex-post evaluieren, sondern bereits im Durchführungsprozeß Monitoring und Evaluationssysteme aufbauen, um steuerungsrelevante Daten zu erhalten.

Eine weitere Professionalisierung der Evaluationsforschung würde dazu beitragen, daß die Disziplin besser als jetzt die anfangs formulierten Aufgaben erfüllen kann, nämlich durch die Sammlung entscheidungsrelevanter Daten Erkenntnisse zu vermitteln und Steuerungspotentiale zu eröffnen, den Dialog zwischen den Stakeholdern zu intensivieren und letztlich die Legitimität von sozialen und politischen Interventionsmaßnahmen und Programmen zu erhöhen.

Literatur

Alber, Jens (1989): Der Sozialstaat in der Bundesrepublik Deutschland 1950-1983. Frankfurt, New York: Campus.

Argyris, Chris u.a. (1999): Die lernende Organisation. Stuttgart: Kett-Kotta.

Aurin, Kurt/Stolz, Gerd E. (1990): Erfahrungen aus der Aufarbeitung von Evaluationsvorhaben am Beispiel der Tätigkeit der Projektgruppe „Gesamtschule" der Bund-Länder-Kommission für Bildungsplanung und Forschungsförderung. In: Zeitschrift für Pädagogische Psychologie. Jg. 4, H. 4, S. 269-282.

Beywl, Wolfgang (1999): Handbuch der Evaluationsstandards. Die Standards des „Joint Committee for Educational Evaluation". In: Klaus Künzel (Hg.): Internationales Jahrbuch der Erwachsenenbildung. Vol. 27, Evaluation der Weiterbildung. Köln, Weimar, Wien: Böhlau. S.: 269-271.

Bortz, Jürgen/Döring, Nicola (1995): Forschungsmethoden und Evaluation. 2. vollständig überarb. und aktualisierte Aufl.. Berlin, Heidelberg, New York: Springer.

Brandtstädter, Jochen (1990b): Evaluationsforschung: Probleme der wissenschaftlichen Bewertung von Interventions- und Reformprojekten. In: Zeitschrift für Pädagogische Psychologie. Jg. 4, H. 4, S. 215-228.

Bundesrechnungshof, Präsident des (1989): Erfolgskontrolle finanzwirksamer Maßnahmen in der öffentlichen Verwaltung. Stuttgart, Berlin, Köln: Kohlhammer.

Bussmann, Werner u.a. (Hg.) (1997): Einführung in die Politikevaluation. Basel, Frankfurt a. Main: Helbing & Lichtenhahn.

Campbell, Donald T. (1969): Reform as Experiments. In: American Psychologist. Jg. 24, H. 4, S. 409-429.

Chen, Huey (1990): Theory-Driven Evaluations. Newbury Park: Sage.

Chen, Huey/Rossi, Peter H. (1983): Evaluating With Sense: The Theory-Driven Approach. In: Evaluation Review. Jg. 7, S. 283-302.

Chen, Huey/Rossi, Peter H. (1980): The Multi-Goal, Theory-driven Approach to Evaluation: A Model Linking Basic and Applied Social Science. In: Social Forces. Jg. 59, S. 106-122.

Chelimsky, Eleanor (1995): New dimensions in evaluation. In: World Bank Operations Evaluations Department (OED): Evaluation and Development: proceedings of the 1994 World Bank Conference Washington D.C.. S. 3-11.

Cook, T. D./Matt, G. E. (1990): Theorien der Programmevaluation. In: Koch, Uwe/Wittman, Werner W.: Evaluationsforschung: Bewertungsgrundlage von Sozial- und Gesundheitsprogrammen. Berlin u.a.: Springer.

Cook, T. D./Campbell, Donald T. (1979): Quasi-Experimentation. Design and Analysis Issues for Field Settings. Chicago: Rand McNally.

Cronbach, Lee J. u.a. (1981): Toward Reform of Program Evaluation. San Franciso u.a.: Jossey-Bass.

Cronbach, Lee J. (1982): Designing Evaluations of Educational and Social Programs. San Francisco u.a.: Jossey-Bass.

Derlien, Hans-Ulrich (1997): Die Entwicklung von Evaluation im internationalen Kontext. In: Bussmann, Werner u.a. (Hg.) (1997): Einführung in die Politikevaluation. Basel; Frankfurt a. Main: Helbing & Lichtenhahn. S. 4-13

Derlien, Hans-Ulrich (1994): Evaluation zwischen Programm und Budget. In: Hofmeister, Albert (Hg.): Möglichkeiten und Grenzen der Programmsteuerung: Controlling und Evaluation. Verwaltungspraxis in Ost und West in Zeiten des Wandels. Schriftenreihe der Schweizerischen Gesellschaft für Verwaltungswissenschaft. Band 21, S. 43-61.

Derlien, Hans-Ulrich (1990b): Genesis and Structure of Evaluation Efforts in Comparative Perspective. In: Rist, Ray C.: Program Evaluation and the Mangement of Government. New Brunswick/London.

Deutscher, Irvin/Ostrander, Susan A. (1985): Sociology and Evaluation Research: Some Past and Future Links. In: History of Sociology. Jg. 6, S. 11-32.

Fend, Helmut (1982): Gesamtschule im Vergleich. Bilanz der Ergebnisse des Gesamtschulversuchs. Weinheim, Basel: Beltz.

Gagel, Dieter (1990): Aktionsforschung – Methoden partizipativer Handwerksförderung. In: Boehm, Ullrich/Kappel, Robert: Kleinbetriebe des informellen Sektors und Ausbildung im sub-saharischen Afrika. Hamburg.

Gruschka, A. (Hg.) (1976): Ein Schulversuch wird überprüft. Das Evaluationsdesign für die Kollegstufe NW als Konzept handlungsorientierter Begleitforschung. Kronberg.

Guba, Egon G./Lincoln, Yvonna S. (1989): Fourth Generation Evaluation. Newbury Park, London, New Delhi: Sage.

Habersam, Michael (1997): Controlling als Evaluation – Potentiale eines Perspektivenwechsels. München und Mering: Rainer Ham.

Hellstern, Gerd-Michael (Hg.) (1984): Handbuch zur Evaluierungsforschung : Band 1. Opladen : Westdeutscher Verlag.

Hellstern, Gerd-Michael/Wollmann, Hellmut (1984): Bilanz – Reformexperimente, wissenschaftliche Begleitung und politische Realität. In: dies.: Handbuch zur Evaluierungsforschung. Bd. 1. Opladen: Westdeutscher Verlag.

Hellstern, Gerd-Michael/Wollmann, Hellmut (1980): Evaluierung in der öffentlichen Verwaltung – Zweck und Anwendungsfelder. In: Verwaltung und Fortbildung. S. 61ff.

Héritier, Adrienne (Hg.) (1993): Policy-Analyse: Kritik und Neuorientierung. Opladen: Westdeutscher Verlag.

Horváth, Péter (1996): Controlling. 6. Aufl. München: Vahlen.

Jann, Werner (1994): Politikfeldanalyse. In: Nohlen, Dieter: Lexikon der Politik. Bd. 2: Politikwissenschaftliche Methoden. (hrsg. von Jürgen Kuz/Dieter Nohlen/Rainer-Olaf Schulze). München: Beck.

Joint Committee on Standards for Educational Evaluation, James R. S. (Hg.) (2000): Handbuch der Evaluationsstandards. Die Standards des „Joint Committee on Standards for Educational Evaluation". Aus dem Amerikanischen übersetzt von Wolfgang Beywl /Thomas Widmer. Deutsche Ausgabe bearbeitet und ergänzt von Wolfgang Beywl/Thomas Widmer/James R. Sanders. 2. Auflage. Opladen: Leske + Budrich.

Koch, Uwe/Wittmann, Werner W. (Hg.) (1990): Evaluationsforschung. Bewertungsgrundlage von Sozial- und Gesundheitsprogrammen. Berlin u.a.: Springer – Verlag.

Kohler-Koch, Beate (1991): Inselillusion und Interdependenz: Nationales Regieren unter den Bedingungen von „International Governance". In: Blanke, Bernhard/W. H. (Hg.): Die Alte Bundesrepublik. Opladen. S. 45-67.

Lachenmann, Gudrun (1987): Soziale Implikationen und Auswirkungen der Basisgesundheitspolitik. In: Schwefel, D.: Soziale Wirkungen von Projekten in der Dritten Welt. Baden-Baden: Nomos.

Lachenmann, Gudrun (1977): Evaluierungsforschung: Historische Hintergründe, sozialpolitische Zusammenhänge und wissenschaftliche Einordnung. In: Kantowsky, Detlef: Evaluierungsforschung und -praxis in der Entwicklungshilfe. Zürich: Verlag der Fachvereine.

Lange, Elmar (1983): Zur Entwicklung und Methodik der Evaluationsforschung in der Bundesrepublik Deutschland. In: Zeitschrift für Soziologie. Jg. 12, H. 3, S. 253-270.

Leeuw, Frans L. u.a. (2000): Can Governments learn? Comparative Perspectives on Evaluation and Organizational learning. New Brunswick: Transaction Publishing.

Lewin, K. (1951): Field Theory in social science. New York: Harper. Deutsch: Feldtheorie in den Sozialwissenschaften. Bern: Huber, 1963.

Lippitt, R. (1940): An Experimental Study of Authoritarian and Democratic Group Atmospheres. Univ. Iowa Stud. Child. Welf., 16, S. 45-195.

Mayer, E. u.a. (Hg.) (1990): Handbuch Controlling. Stuttgart: Poeschel.

Mayntz, Renate (1977): Die Implementation politischer Programme: Theoretische Überlegungen zu einem neuen Forschungsgebiet. In: Die Verwaltung. S. 51ff.

Mayntz, Renate (1980a): Die Entwicklung des analytischen Paradigmas der Implementationsforschung. In: Mayntz, Renate: Implementation politischer Programme. Königsstein: Athenäum.

Mayntz, Renate (1980b): Die Implementation politischer Programme: Theoretische Überlegungen zu einem neuen Forschungsgebiet. In: Mayntz, Renate: Implementation politischer Programme. Königsstein: Athenäum.

Mayntz, Renate (Hg.) (1980c): Implementation politischer Programme. Königsstein: Athenäum.

Mayntz, Renate (1983): Implementation politischer Programme II. Ansätze zur Theoriebildung. Opladen.

Mayntz, Renate (1997): Soziologie in der öffentlichen Verwaltung. Heidelberg: C.F.Müller.

Mertens, Donna M. (1998): Research methods in education and psychology: Integrating diversity with quantitative and qualitative approaches. Thousand Oaks, CA: Sage.

Palumbo, Dennis J./Oliverio, Annamarie (1989): Implementation Theory and the Theory-Driven Approach to Validity. In: Evaluation and Program Planning. Jg. 12, S. 337-344.

Patton, Michael Q. (1997): Utilization – Focused Evaluation: The New Century Text. 3. Aufl. Thousand Oaks, London, New Delhi: Sage.

Patton, M. Q. (1987): Evaluation's Political Inheritency: Practical Implications for Design and Use. In: Palumbo, D. J. (Hg.): The Politics of Program Theory. Thousand Oaks, CA: Sage. S. 100-145.

Pollitt, Christopher (1998): Evaluation in Europe: Boom or Bubble? In: Evaluation. Jg. 4(2), H. 2, S. 214-224.

Rein, M. (1984): Umfassende Programmevaluierungen. In: Hellstern, Gerd-Michael/Wollmann, Helmut: Handbuch zur Evaluierungsforschung. Bd. 1. Opladen: Westdeutscher Verlag.

Roethlisberger, F. J./Dickson, W. J. (1934): Management and the Worker. Cambridge.

Rossi, Peter H./ Freeman, Howard E. (1999): Evaluation. A Systematic Approach. 6 Aufl.. Thousand Oaks u.a.: Sage.

Rossi, Peter H./Freeman, Howard E./Hofmann, Gerhard (1988): Programm Evaluation: Einführung in die Methoden angewandter Sozialforschung. Stuttgart: Enke.

Schneider-Barthold, Wolfgang (1992): Zur Angemessenheit von quantitativen und qualitativen Erhebungsmethoden in der Entwicklungsländerforschung. Vorzüge und Probleme der Aktionsforschung. In: Reichert, Ch./Scheuch, Erwin K./Seibel, H. D.: Empirische Sozialforschung über Entwicklungsländer. Methodenprobleme und Praxisbezug. Saarbrücken: Breitenbach.

Schröter, Eckhard (1998): New Public Management. In: Bandemer, Stephan (Hg.): Handbuch Zur Verwaltungsreform. Opladen. S. 59-69.

Scriven, Michael (1972a): Pros and Cons About Goal-Free Evaluation. In: Evaluation Comment. S. 1-4.

Scriven, Michael (1972b): Die Methodologie der Evaluation. In: Wulf, Christoph: Evaluation. Beschreibung und Bewertung von Unterricht, Curricula und Schulversuchen. München: Piper.

Scriven, Michael (1980): The Logic of Evaluation. California: Edgepress.

Scriven, Michael (1991): Evaluation Thesaurus. Newbury Park u.a.: Sage.

Scriven, Michael (1967): The Methodology of Evaluation. In: Stake, R. E.: AERA Monograph Series on Curriculum Evaluation. Vol. 1 Chicago: Rand McNally.

Scriven, Michael (1983): Evaluation Ideologies. In: Madaus, G. F./Scriven, M./Stufflebeam, D. L.: Evaluation Models: Viewpoints on Educational and Human Services Evaluation. Boston: Kluwe-Nijhoff.

Stake, R. E. (1983): The Case Study Method in Social Inquiry. In: Madaus, G. F. u.a. (Hg.): Evaluation Models. Boston: Kluwer-Nijhoff. S. 279-86

Staudt, Erich/Hefkesbrink, Joachim/Treichel, Heinz-Reiner (1988): Forschungsmanagement durch Evaluation: Das Beispiel Arbeitsschwerpunkt Druckindustrie. Frankfurt a.M.: Campus.

Stouffer, S. A. u.a. (1949): The American Soldier. Vol II: Combat and ist Aftermath. Princeton, NJ: Princeton University Press.

Vedung, Evert (1999): Evaluation im öffentlichen Sektor. Wien, Köln, Graz: Böhlau.

Weiss, Carol H. (1972): Evaluation Research. Englewood Cliffs, NJ: Prentice Hall.

Weiss, Carol H. (1974): Evaluierungsforschung. Opladen: Westdeutscher Verlag.

White, R./Lippitt, R. (1953): Leader Behaviour and Member Reaction in Three „Social Climates". In: Cartwright, D./Zander, A. (Hg.): Group Dynamics, Research and Theory. Evanston, Ill: Row, Peterson and Company, 1953 (1st ed.).

Will, Hermann/Blickhan, Claus (1987): Evaluation als Intervention. In: Will, Hermann/Winteler, Adolf/Krapp, Andreas: Evaluation in der beruflichen Aus- und Weiterbildung. Heidelberg: Sauer.

Will, Hermann/Winteler, Adolf/Krapp, Andreas (Hg.) (1987): Evaluation in der beruflichen Aus- und Weiterbildung. Heidelberg: Sauer.

Will, Hermann/Winteler, Adolf/Krapp, Andreas (1987): Von der Erfolgskontrolle zur Evaluation. In: Will, Hermann/Winteler, Adolf/Krapp, Andreas: Evaluation in der beruflichen Aus- und Weiterbildung. Heidelberg: Sauer.

Windhoff-Héritier, Adrienne (1980): Politikimplementation. Königsstein.

Windhoff-Héritier, Adrienne (1983): Policy-Analyse. Eine Einführung. Frankfurt a.M., New York.

Windhoff-Héritier, Adrienne (1987): Policy-Analyse. Frankfurt a.M., New York.

Wittmann, Werner W. (1990): Aufgaben und Möglichkeiten der Evaluationsforschung in der Bundesrepublik Deutschland. In: Koch, Uwe/Wittmann, Werner W.: Evaluationsforschung: Bewertungsgrundlage von Sozial- und Gesundheitsprogrammen. Berlin u.a.: Springer.

Wittmann, Werner (1985): Evaluationsforschung. Aufgaben, Probleme und Anwendungen. Berlin u.a.: Springer.

Wollmann, Hellmut (1999): Politik- Und Verwaltungsmodernisierung in den Kommunen: Zwischen Managementlehre Und Demokratiegebot. In: Die Verwaltung. (Schwerpunktheft 3).

Wollmann, Hellmut (1998): Evaluation research and politics: Between a science-driven and a pluralist controversy-responsive policy-making model. Potential and limitations. Diskussionspapier. Humboldt-Universität zu Berlin.

Wollmann, Hellmut (1998): Modernisierung der kommunalen Politik- und Verwaltungswelt – Zwischen Demokratie und Managementschub. In: Grunow, Dieter/Wollmann, Hellmut: Lokale Verwaltungsreform in Aktion: Fortschritte und Fallstricke. Basel u.a.: Birkhäuser. S. 400-439.

Wollmann, Hellmut (1998): Kommunale Verwaltungsmodernisierung in Ostdeutschland. Zwischen Worten und Taten. Diskussionspapier. Humboldt-Universität zu Berlin.

Wollmann, Hellmut (1997): Evaluation in Germany. In: European Evaluation Society. Newsletter (3), S. 4-5.

Wollmann, Hellmut (1994): Evaluierungsansätze und -institutionen in Kommunalpolitik und -verwaltung. Stationen der Planungs- und Steuerungsdiskussion. In: Schulze-Böing, Matthias/Johrendt, Norbert: Wirkungen kommunaler Beschäftigungsprogramme. Methoden, Instrumente und Ergebnisse der Evaluation kommunaler Arbeitsmarktpolitik. Basel, Boston, Berlin: Birkhäuser. S. 79-110.

Wollmann, Hellmut (1994): Implementationsforschung/Evaluationsforschung. In: Nohlen, Dieter: Lexikon der Politik. Bd. 2: Politikwissenschaftliche Methoden (hrsg. von Kuz, Jürgen/Nohlen, Dieter/Schulze, Rainer-Olaf). München: Beck.

Wollmann, Hellmut (1980): Implementationsforschung – eine Chance für kritische Verwaltungsforschung? In: Wollmann, Hellmut: Politik im Dickicht der Bürokratie. Beiträge zur Implementationsforschung. (Leviathan Sonderheft 3).

Wottawa, Heinrich T. H. (1998): Lehrbuch Evaluation. 2. Auflage.

Donna M. Mertens

Institutionalizing Evaluation in the United States of America

1. Definitions

Evaluation has many meanings in the United States. One definition that has persisted over time is as follows: Evaluation is the systematic investigation of the merit or worth of an object (program) for the purpose of reducing uncertainty in decision making (Mertens 1998). Alternative definitions tend to emphasize different aspects of the evaluation process. For example, Hadley and Mitchell (1995) define evaluation as "applied research carried out to make or support decisions regarding one or more service programs" (p. 48). Rossi and Freeman (1993) expand the definition of evaluation related to the application of social research procedures as follows: "Evaluation research is the systematic application of social research procedures for assessing the conceptualization, design, implementation, and utility of social intervention programs" (p. 5).

The definition of evaluation includes a statement of purpose for which evaluations are done. This aspect of the definition has been debated in the larger evaluation community. For example, Shadish (1994) calls for an expansion of the definition in terms of the purposes for which evaluations are done. His definition of evaluation included the "use of feasible practices to construct knowledge of the value of the evaluand that can be used to ameliorate the problems to which the evaluand is relevant" (p. 352). (The evaluand is the object of the evaluation, e.g. a social or educational program, a product, a policy, or personnel.) And, Mertens (1999a) suggested extending the definition of evaluation to include the purpose of facilitating positive social change for all relevant stakeholders, including the least advantaged.

Greene (1994) writes about the commonalties that demarcate evaluation contexts and distinguish program evaluation from other forms of social inquiry (such as research). She argues, based on the writings of Patton (1987), Cronbach and associates (1980), and Weiss (1987), that what distinguishes evaluation from other forms of social inquiry is its political inherencey; that is, in evaluation, politics and science are inherently intertwined. Evaluations are conducted on the merit and worth of programs in the public domain, which are themselves responses to prioritized individual and community needs that resulted from political decisions. Thus, program evaluation "is integrally intertwined with political decision making about societal priorities, resource allocation, and power" (p. 531).

In this chapter, I discuss the history of evaluation in the United States in terms of the major approaches that have dominated the evaluation field over the last forty years, factors that have influenced shifts in evaluation approaches, and the institutionalizing of evaluation in terms of professional organizations, standards, guiding principles, and scholarly literature. The historical perspective is followed by a look at current conditions in evaluation in the United States in terms of legislative mandates that are impacting on the field of evaluation and the challenges that are facing evaluators who are operating in this milieu.

2. History

The origins of evaluation in the United States can be traced back to early reform efforts in the 1800s when the government first asked external inspectors to evaluate public programs such as prisons, schools, hospitals, and orphanages (Madaus/Stufflebeam/Scriven 1983). However, most writers peg the beginning of professional evaluation to the early 1960s with the passage of the Great Society legislation that authorized such programs as Head Start to improve poor children's chance for success in school. Evaluation was mandated as a part of that legislative agenda.

Early evaluation efforts in the United States were based on the philosophical assumptions of the positivist and post-positivist paradigms. In education, evaluation emerged from a tradition of testing to assess student outcomes and progressed through an era of specification of objectives and measurement to determine if the objectives had been obtained. Ralph Tyler (cited in Madaus et al. 1983) developed the objectives-based model for evaluation, and Malcom Provus (cited in Madaus et al. 1983) developed the discrepancy evaluation model. In psychology and sociology, evaluation was rooted in the discipline-based social science research methodology. Donald Campbell (see Shadish/Cook/Leviton 1991) and Rossi and Freeman (1993) wrote extensively on the use of quasi-experimental designs as the foundation of evaluation work.

Contemporary evaluators have not abandoned the use of testing, objectives, and quasi-experimental designs, but they have modified and extended these strategies and added new approaches in the ensuing years. Greater sophistication about the complexity of social programs and the political climate in which evaluators work led to the development of more decision-based models of evaluation. As evaluators gained experience with trying to improve social programs, other models of evaluation were developed that tried to address some of the shortcomings of traditional educational assessment or experimental designs. Stufflebeam (1983) was instrumental in pushing the definition of evaluation beyond the achievement of objectives to include the idea that it was a process of providing information for decision making. From his efforts with the Ohio State Evaluation Center and under the auspices of Phi Delta Kappa, Stufflebeam worked with other pioneers in the field of evaluation (including Egon Guba) to develop the CIPP evaluation model. CIPP means:

C = Context
I = Input
P = Process
P = Product

Thus, the CIPP model tries to incorporate many aspects of the program that were not considered under earlier models. The components of the model can be explained by the nature of the evaluation questions asked for each component. For example:

Component	Evaluation Questions
Context	What are the program's goals? Do they reflect the needs of the participants?
Input	What means are required to achieve a given set of goals, in terms of schedules, staffing, budget, and the like?
Process	How were the participants informed of the process? How were the resources allocated? How were the materials adapted?
Product	What is the evidence of outcomes? Should we terminate, continue, or revise this program? Should we decrease or increase funds? Should we merge it with another program?

The context and input phases represent a needs assessment function that evaluation sometimes plays to determine what is needed in terms of goals and resources for a program. Witkin and Altschuld (1995) have written extensively on the process of needs assessment in evaluation. Concerns about the evaluation of the overall context, the input, and the process of a program also led to the emergence of the interpretive/constructivist paradigm with its associated qualitative methods to the world of evaluation.

Stake (1983) combined some of the elements of the CIPP and the discrepancy models in his model of responsive evaluation. He included the idea that evaluation involves the comparison of some observed value with some standard. The standard is to be defined by the expectations and criteria of different people for the program and the observed value are to be based on actually measuring the extent to which those values are manifest in the program. The evaluator's job is to make a comprehensive statement of what the observed program values are with useful references to the satisfaction and dissatisfaction of appropriately selected people. He extended his work in the direction of case study methodology, thus clearing the way for the introduction of qualitative methods in evaluation inquiry.

Stake's work led the way for the introduction of a new paradigm to the evaluation community. Guba and Lincoln (1989) acknowledge the foundation provided by Stake's work in responsive evaluation in their development of what they termed fourth generation evaluation. They conceptualized the four generations this way:

First generation:	Measurement – testing students
Second generation:	Description – objectives and tests (Tyler's work, cited in Madaus et al. 1983)
Third generation:	Judgment – the decision-based models, such as Stake (1983), Scriven (1967); and Stufflebeam (1983)
Fourth generation:	Constructivist, heuristic evaluation

Guba and Lincoln depict the stages of evaluation as generations, with the more recent replacing those that came earlier. It is my perception that the evaluation community does not generally share this depiction, in that many of the methods and models that were developed in evaluation's earlier days continue to have influence on theory and practice.

Theories such as Guba and Lincoln (1989), Patton (1987), Stake (1983), and House (1993) were influential in bringing the interpretive-constructivist paradigm, along with qualitative methods, into evaluation. Greene (1994) notes that qualitative methods were initially contested on both practical and methodological grounds. However, she describe the current situation as a "détente", "signaling the important acceptance of these alternative evaluation methodologies, at least among many evaluation theorists and methodologists" (p. 535). Greene does acknowledge that this acceptance is not universal among all the members of the evaluation community.

Even with the introduction of the interpretive-constructivist paradigm, along with qualitative methods, the evaluation community continued to struggle with the evolution of its theory and practice. House (1993) described the situation this way:

Gradually, evaluators recognized that there were different interests to be served in an evaluation and that some of these interests might conflict with one another. The result was pluralist conceptions of evaluation in which multiple methods, measures, criteria, perspectives, audiences, and interests were recognized. Conceptually, evaluation moved from monolithic to pluralist conceptions, reflecting the pluralism that had emerged in the larger society. How to synthesize, resolve, and adjudicate all these multiple multiples remains a formidable question, as indeed it does for the larger society. Evaluation, which was invented to solve social problems, was ultimately afflicted with many of the problems it was meant to solve. (p. 11)

Factors related to pluralism and a growing awareness of the need to represent multiple perspectives laid the foundation for the emergence of the transformative-emancipatory paradigm in evaluation. While the interpretive-constructivist paradigm evaluators had recognized the importance that values play in the inquiry process, this paradigm did not provide insights into how to justify any particular set of values. House (1993), Sirotnik (1990), Sirotnik & Oakes (1990), Kirkhart (1995) and Mertens (1999a) raise the questions of what social justice and fairness mean in program evaluation. An emerging movement within evaluation is beginning to focus on the meaning of social justice and fairness within evaluation, with the consequent opening of the door to the transformative-emancipatory paradigm of social inquiry for evaluators. As Greene (1994) recognizes, "What importantly distinguishes one evaluation methodology from another is not methods, but rather whose questions are addressed and which values are promoted" (p. 533).

The transformative paradigm is characterized as placing central importance on the lives and experiences of marginalized groups, such as women, ethnic/racial minorities, people with disabilities, and those who are poor. The evaluator who works within this paradigm consciously analyzes asymmetric power relationships, seeks ways to link the results of social inquiry to action and links the results of the inquiry to wider questions of social inequity and social justice (Mertens 1998, 1999a; Mertens/Farley/Madison/ Singleton 1994; Truman/Mertens/Humphries 2000). The transformative paradigm is based on the assumption that diversities of viewpoints exist with regard to many social realities, and that we need to place those viewpoints within a political, cultural, and economic value system to understand the basis for the differences. This leads to the explicit consideration of how to reveal those multiple constructions, as well how to make decisions about privileging one perspective over another.

The introduction of this paradigm into the evaluation community has raised additional challenges that are captured in this remark by M. F. Smith (1994) in which she describes a split within the evaluation community between

...those who wish to use evaluation as a way to promote a favored political agenda and those who wish evaluation to be objective and scientific...These are critical concerns that the field must address, for if we cannot be trusted to be neutral on program topics and objective, to the best of our abilities, then what reason is there for our services? (p. 226)

Mertens (1999a) addressed this seeming conflict between the canons of research that emphasize the search for truth, objectivity, credibility, and validity, and the need to address the concerns of marginalized and less empowered groups. She wrote:

If the heart of objectivity is to avoid bias, then it seems to necessitate inclusion of perspectives of all relevant groups. If we have an awareness of historical conditions in our country and around the world, and understand current social conditions, then we know that certain groups of people have been under- or misrepresented in the world of social inquiry, whether it be evaluation or research. Which is the better role for the evaluator? Dispassionate and distanced, or passionately concerned with ascertaining the truth? And truth is defined as being inclusive of the perspectives of those with the lived experience with the problem whatever it might be – spousal abuse, sexual abuse, poor educational service, or lack of equal access to the justice system.

A good evaluator would want to provide as accurate a picture as possible. When significant voices are missing, the picture is not complete and may actually be a distorted representation of reality. Based on a review of world history, certain groups have been systematically excluded from having meaningful participation in the design, implementation, and use of evaluations that impact them. Can a report be balanced when the voices of important constituencies are missing or inaccurately represented, or lost in the aggregation of data across groups? (p. 6)

Whitmore (1998) explored many of the themes associated with transformational evaluation through the lens of participatory evaluation models that attempt to seek to foster participation in the evaluation for the purpose of increasing understanding of program functions and processes, and to develop skills in systematic inquiry. Transformational participatory evaluation also explicitly recognizes the need for involvement of all legitimate stakeholders, including those with the least power. This is one example where evaluators from the United States have gained insights from approaches that were developed in Latin America, India, and Africa (Brisolera 1998; Mertens 1999b).

The venue for the historical developments in evaluation in the United States has been the professional associations and journals in which the critical issues were discussed. The associations and the documents that they have produced provide another avenue for examining the institutionalization of evaluation in the United States.

3. Associations, Standards, Guiding Principles, and Journals of Evaluation

The American Evaluation Association (AEA) is the primary professional organization whose mission is focused exclusively on evaluation in the United States. AEA was formed in 1986 through the merger of two smaller evaluation associations, Evaluation Network and the Evaluation Research Society. As of the Year 2000, AEA had about 3,000 members with a stated mission to: Improve evaluation practices and methods; increase evaluation use; promote evaluation as a profession, and support the contribution of evaluation to the generation of theory and knowledge about effective human action. The activities of the AEA can be found at their web site: www.eval.org The AEA also manages an active list serve called EvalTalk which has world-wide subscribers.

While AEA is a multi-disciplinary organization, other associations serve evaluators who have specific areas of interest (Cook 1997). For example, economists and political science evaluators tend to belong to the Association for Public Policy Analysis and Management. Their work tends to focus more narrowly on policies than programs and on cash-transfer programs more than other sorts of social service programs. Evaluators who work on programs that examine policies and programs designed to improved physical health tend to belong to the American Public Health Association. The American Educational Research Association has two Special Interest Group of relevancy for evaluators: one that focuses on school-based evaluation issues and the other on research in evaluation.

Codification of a profession's ethics or standards is another hallmark of its institutionalization in society. Evaluation in the United States functions with a set of standards and a set of guiding principles. *The Program Evaluation Standards: How to Assess Evaluations of Educational Programs* was developed by the Joint Committee on Standards for Educational Evaluation (1994). The joint committee was initiated by the efforts of three organizations: the American Educational Research Association, the American Psychological Association, and the National Council on Measurement in Education. Representatives of these organizations were joined by members of 12 other professional organizations (e.g., American Association of School Administrators, Association for Assessment in Counseling, the American Evaluation Association, and the Council of Chief State School Officers). They developed a set of standards that would guide the evaluation of educational and training programs, projects, and materials in a variety of settings. The Standards provide one comprehensive (albeit not all-encompassing) framework for examining the quality of an evaluation.

The Standards are organized according to four main attributes of evaluations:

Utility: These standards are intended to ensure than an evaluation will serve the information needs of intended users.

Feasibility: These standards are intended to ensure than an evaluation will be realistic, prudent, diplomatic, and frugal.

Propriety: These standards are intended to ensure that an evaluation will be conducted legally, ethically, and with due regard for the welfare of those involved in the evaluation, as well as those affected by its results.

Accuracy: These standards are intended to ensure than an evaluation will reveal and convey technically adequate information about the features that determine worth or merit of the program being evaluated.

The Standards are explained through guidelines and illustrative cases. The Standards have been criticized for insufficiently addressing the complexities of conducting intepretive-constructivist evaluations (Lincoln 1995), and for inadequately addressing the concerns about diversity and multiculturalism (Kirkhart 1995; Mertens 1998). Kirkhart (1995) proposed consideration of multicultural diversity in evaluation as an additional attribute for the Standards that would address more specifically concerns about pluralism and diversity in evaluation.

The *Guiding Principles for Evaluators* (Shadish/Newman/Scheirer/Wye 1995) were developed by a task force appointed by the American Evaluation Association's Board of Directors. The process of development is described in a volume of *New Directions for Program Evaluation*, and included lengthy task force deliberations, discussions at Board meetings over a period of a year, direct mailing of a draft to all AEA members seeking feedback, and discussion of the Guiding Principles at symposia at the AEA annual meeting. In 1994, both the AEA Board and the membership voted in favor of adopting the Guiding Principles.

The Guiding Principles are intended to guide professional practice of evaluators, and to inform evaluation clients and the general public about the principles they can expect to be upheld by professional evaluators. The five major categories include:

Systematic Inquiry: Evaluators conduct systematic, data-based inquiries about whatever is being evaluated.

Competence: Evaluators provide competent performance to stakeholders.

Integrity/Honesty: Evaluators ensure the honesty and integrity of the entire evaluation process.

Respect for people: Evaluators respect the security, dignity, and self-worth of the respondents, program participants, clients, and other stakeholders with whom they interact.

Responsibilities for General and Public Welfare: Evaluators articulate and take into account the diversity of interests and values that may be related to the general and public welfare. (American Evaluation Association, Task Force on Guiding Principles for Evaluators 1995: 20)

The *New Directions* volume includes illustrative applications of each of the principles. The AEA expects to examine the principles on a five-year cycle to determine if revisions are needed.

Another important indicator of the institutionalization of a profession is the extent to which a scholarly body of literature is developed. The American Evaluation Association publishes two journals: the *American Journal of Evaluation* and the *New Directions for Program Evaluation* monograph series. There are several other evaluation journals published in the United States, including: *Educational Evaluation and Policy Analysis, Evaluation Review, Evaluation and Program Planning, Evaluation and the Health Professions, Evaluation and Educational Policy,* and *Studies in Educational Evaluation.*

4. Current Influences in Evaluation in the United States

Legislative Influences. In 1993, the Congress of the United States passed legislation that was intended to improve the efficiency and effectiveness of federal programs by establishing a system to set goals for program performance and to measure results. The Government Performance and Results Act of 1993 shifted the focus of federal management and decision making away from a preoccupation with the activities that are undertaken under the auspices of federal funding to a focus on the results of those activities. To this end, the Results Act is intended to improve the efficiency and effectiveness of federal programs by establishing a system to set goals for program performance and to measure results. Specifically, the Act requires executive agencies to prepare multiyear strategic plans, annual performance plans, and annual performance reports. As a starting point, the Act requires virtually every executive agency to develop a strategic plan, covering a period of at least 5 years forward from the fiscal year in which it is submitted. These strategic plans are to include an agency's mission statement, general goals and objectives, and the strategies that the agency will use to achieve those goals and objectives (U.S. General Accounting Agency 1997, Chapter 0: 3)

The requirements of the act have created a systemic presence for evaluation throughout the federal government and all of its programs. Many private foundations have also taken up the practice of requiring performance indicators for projects that they fund. The U.S. General Accounting Office (1997) was asked to report to Congress on the implementation of the Act, including prospects for compliance by federal agencies beyond those who participated in the pilot program under the 1994 phased implementation of the Act. GAO's specific objectives for their report were to (1) assess the status of the Act's implementation efforts; (2) identify significant challenges confronting executive agencies in their efforts to become more results-oriented; and (3) describe ongoing efforts to integrate program, cost, and budget information into a reporting framework that allows for fuller consideration of resource allocations, operational costs, and performance results.

GAO's study reported that the Results Act's implementation to this point has achieved mixed results, which will lead to highly uneven government wide implementation. While agencies are likely to meet the upcoming statutory deadlines for producing initial strategic plans and annual performance plans, GAO found that those documents may not be of a consistently high quality or as useful for congressional and agency decision making as they could be. On a more promising note, OMB selected over 70 performance planning and reporting pilots that were exemplary and that should provide a rich body of experience for agencies to draw on in the future.

GAO's review of efforts to date under the Results Act have shown that to effectively implement the Act, agencies face a variety of significant challenges. One set of challenges arises from the complications of government structure and from program proliferation. Others involve methodological difficulties in identifying performance measures or the lack of data needed to establish goals and assess performance. For example, GAO identified an inadequate ability by the agencies to identify appropriate goals and confidently assess performance. Even when agencies did have data, GAO found that the quality of agencies' performance data was often questionable. Thus, the Results Act has created a milieu in the United States that demonstrates the need for high quality evaluation, however, many challenges face the implementation of the Act.

5. Theoretical Challenges in the Current Environment

Cook (1997) suggests that improved theories of what evaluation means and how it might be carried out are needed in order to approximate more closely the truth about the effects of important social programs. Theory-based evaluation is defined as an approach in which the evaluator constructs a model of how the program works using models based on stakeholders' theories, available social science theory, or both to guide question formation and data gathering (Chen/Rossi 1992). Theory-driven evaluations are seen as a way to mitigate the problems encountered in a more simplistic notion of quasi-experimental design when applied in an evaluation setting. The role of the evaluator is to bring a theoretical framework from existing social science theory to the evaluation setting. This would add insights to the structure of the program and its effectiveness that might not be available to the stakeholders in the setting. Chen and Rossi warn against uncritically accepting the stakeholders' viewpoints as the basis for understanding the effectiveness of a program. They acknowledge that qualitative methods can be used during the program conceptualization and monitoring, but they advocate the use of randomized experiments for assessing program impact. Because theory-based evaluation, as it is conceptualized by Chen and Rossi, is guided by a preference to use structural modeling methods, the kinds of questions formulated for the evaluation are those that fit neatly into causal modeling (Shadish et al. 1991).

Evaluators who struggle to be inclusive and nondiscriminatory in their work have found a number of theoretical perspectives to be helpful in guiding thinking about theory and practice, particularly with regard to dealing with race, gender, disability, and class dimensions in the U.S. and developing countries. An over-arching theoretical framework is provided by the concepts exemplified in the transformative – emancipatory paradigm that was discussed earlier in this chapter (Mertens 1998; Truman/Mertens/Humphries 2000). Feminist theory and critical theory have contributed much to the understanding of this paradigm. While feminists have focused on creating knowledge that improves the position of women in society, transformative theorists have broadened the scope to include an exploration of the experiences of all groups that experience oppression and discrimination on any basis. Thus, evaluation studies within this context is inclusive of the experiences of men and women of any race or ethnicity, with or without disabilities, no matter what their sexual orientation or economic status.

With the move toward the development of performance indicators in evaluation, a new challenge must be faced if the evaluators are to make a contribution to the development and use of indicators that serve to work toward greater social justice and equity. Performance indicators have been criticized for being overly rigid and de-contextualized. Given the weight that feminist and other transformative scholars give to contextual factors in understanding social phenomenon, the development of performance indicators in a decontextualized form is especially problematic.

The elements of a theoretical framework that was developed for the purpose of gaining insight into the challenges researchers and evaluators encounter in this context include: 1) Locating the self in the research/evaluation process in terms of personal, social, and institutional influences on the inquiry process and analysis; 2) Exploring the political/power dimensions of empowerment; 3) Being explicit about the tensions that arise in research and evaluation activities, and relating as much how the tensions remain, rather than how they were resolved; 4) Linking research/evaluation to wider questions of social inequality/social justice; and 5) Balancing theoretical and methodological approaches in discussions and accounts of research and evaluation (Truman et al. 2000). The application of these elements in evaluation are illustrated in *Research and Inequality* with case studies of HIV/AIDS prevention, South Asian women, disabled women in El Salvador; training professionals in economic development, colonial methodologies used in a Norwegian-Tanzanian project, and identifying the needs of street kids in Canada. The framework is used to raise questions about the development and application of performance indicators related to gender, race/ethnicity, disabilities, and social class in these different settings.

Research and Inequality originated from a sub-theme of the International Sociological Association's Fourth International Conference on Social Science Methodology held July 1-5, 1996 at the University of Essex, Colchester, England. Contributors were asked to explicitly identify how their work addressed emancipatory or anti-discriminatory issues both theoretically and methodologically. The issues that formed the framework of this book are represented in over-lapping ways throughout the chapters, with most of the chapters addressing multiple themes.

The relationship between the researcher/evaluator and the participants in the inquiry process, with particular emphasis on the location of self in this process, is illustrated in Carole Truman's chapter, " New social movements and social research", in which she reports her work on a health needs assessment of men who have sex with men in the North Western part of England. She explores the question of her right as a lesbian woman to undertake this needs assessment, as well as the contribution she could make from her formal position in the university system. As a lesbian woman, she felt she brought a knowledge of the broad arena of lesbian and gay politics. At the same time, she recognized the differences between lesbian and gay communities, and thus was conscious of the tensions created by her personal differences in contrast to the client group. She determined that the client (Healthy Gay City/HGC) believed that potential funders of programs related to HIV/AIDS prevention would be responsive to a clear, objective and definable need for safe sex materials, and that engaging Truman as principle investigator, with the weight and status of a professional research organization associated with the university, would off-set the apparent structural inequality of HGC as an organization with relatively low power as compared to the power position occupied by potential funders. Truman also arranged for the project funds to stay in the gay community by recruiting interviewers from the gay community. In this way, she attempted to avoid the exploitative nature of some academic research.

Grindl Dockery explored ways to design research and interact with research participants in order to strengthen the relationship between research process and findings, and social action based on the research. In her chapter, "Participatory research: Whose roles, whose responsibilities?", she reflects on the meaning of participatory research within the context of two cases studies where community groups, consisting of predominantly women, conducted research with the aim of bringing about changes in the delivery of local health services. One case study focuses on the struggle by community groups to keep a local community health center open and the other case study looks at issues related to women's sexuality and sexual health services. Dockery recognizes the danger in seeking participation of people who do not normally have access to influencing service planning in that without a commitment to the political concept of empowerment by those facilitating the process, participation becomes merely a process of manipulation.

Donna M. Mertens, in "Deaf and hard of hearing people in the courts: Using an emancipatory perspective to determine their needs", applied the emancipatory paradigm to the first stage of a training program for judges and other court personnel to improve deaf and hard of hearing people's access to the court system in the United States. The study began with a needs assessment designed to 'listen to the voices' of the deaf and hard of hearing people in order to develop training for judges, other court personnel, and deaf and hard of hearing people and their advocates that validly represented the experiences of those with least power in the court system. The processes used in the study to include diverse voices from the deaf and hard of hearing communities revealed both technical and cultural issues related to improving court access for this population.

Mertens deals with the wider questions of social inequality and social justice within the evaluation of this project. To this end, she designed the study to allow the expression of needs by deaf and hard of hearing people to drive the development of a training program for judges, other court personnel, and deaf and hard of hearing advocates on how to improve access to the courts for this population. Several of the focus group participants were featured in a videotape entitled "Silent Justice" that was used as part of the training. In addition, some were also invited to participate in the training as faculty and on planning teams that developed action plans for improving court access in their state court systems.

Jim Mienczakowski's chapter is entitled "People like us: Ethnography in the form of theatre with emancipatory intentions". In his work, Mienczakowski used the experiences of the health consumer community representing schizophrenic psychosis and institutionalized detoxification processes as a way of communicating to groups of health and student communities. He terms the medium ethnographically derived theatre because the meanings and explanations of the performances are negotiated with audiences in forum discussion at the close of each performance. Thus, the potential is created to share insights and negotiate explanations with an eye to provoking change amongst those who play an active part in the construction of health services.

Joan B. Cohen-Mitchell entitled her chapter "Disabled women in El Salvador reframing themselves: A case study of an economic development program for women". The women in the study had been framed by society, i.e., they had been assigned a fixed identity and with that identity their possibilities in the world were determined. Society had defined them as "not able". However, Cohen-Mitchell constructed her research in a way that facilitated the women in changing their self-perceptions. Her case study examines the way that poor disabled women in El Salvador could participate in a collaborative process that would alter and/or create development programs in their immediate environment in ways that would potentially impact their lives. Cohen-Mitchell draws on the tenets of participatory and feminist research in order to design research that can be tied to the emancipation of people from oppressive structures.

In Ann Ryen's "Colonial methodology", she explores methodological challenges in cross-cultural research in a Tanzanian-Norwegian collaboration in which structured interviews were used in short term projects. If the cross-cultural dimension is underestimated, the population may become a victim of methodological discrimination. Differences in understanding may be related to gender-role expectations, conceptions of time, and criteria for determining status. Different uses of language and norms of politeness can lead to misunderstandings. Use of structured interviewing without observation and participatory research could be viewed as colonial methodology that objectifies the Africans if the interpretation is made through the researcher's cultural eyes.

In "Defining without discriminating; Ethnicity and social problems", Jacques Rheaume and Shirley Roy report the challenges they faced in a study to define the ever-changing population of street youth in major urban centers in Canada. In their study, street youth referred to homeless, twelve-to-eighteen year old children of both genders from a variety of cultural back grounds: French-Canadians, English-Canadians, and various cultural minorities. The major concern of the first year was the social construction of the research categories and the methodological implications of the various options considered.

6. Questions remaining

Through examining the historical and current status of evaluation in the United States (and other countries), we can come to understand how to begin addressing some pressing questions, such as: How can we use theoretical foundations to shape a framework that will allow us to engage in evaluation practice that is useful to program managers and funders, as well as anti-discriminatory and transformative? What does evaluation practice need to embrace when it has at its heart the potential to empower and to contribute to ending the exclusion of relatively powerless groups of people? How can evaluators be responsive to issues of unequal access to project participation or benefits, or unsubstantiated generalization of benefits across groups when specific sub-groups may not be benefiting equally based on sex, race/ethnicity, disability, or other characteristics? These are complex issues that are difficult to capture in a single number that indicates a program's success or failure. Our sensitivity to those theoretical elements and contextual issues is essential to developing theory-based approaches and defining performance indicators that are capable of demonstrating the results of programs and contributing to the transformation of the lives of those who have traditionally been excluded from power.

References

American Evaluation Association, Task Force on Guiding Principles (1995): Guiding Principles for Evaluators. In: Shadish, W. R./Newman, D./Scheirer, M. A./Wye, C. (Eds.): The American Evaluation Association's Guiding Principles. San Francisco: Jossey-Bass. pp. 19-26.
Brisolera, S. (1998): Participatory Evaluation History. In: Whitmore, B. (Ed.): Understanding and practicing participatory evaluation. (New Directions in Evaluation, Vol. 80). San Francisco: Jossey-Bass.
Chen, H. T./Rossie, P. H. (1992): Using theory to improve program and policy evaluation. Westport, CT: Greenwood.

Cohen-Mitchell, J. A. (2000): Disabled women in El Salvador reframing themselves: A case study of an economic development program for women. In: Truman, C./Mertens, D. M./Humphries, B. (Eds.): Research and Inequality. London: Taylor & Francis.

Cook, T. D. (1997): Lessons learned in evaluation over the past 25 years. In: Chelimsky, E./Shadish, W.R. (Eds.): Evaluation for the 21st Century. Thousand Oaks, CA: Sage. pp. 30-52.

Cronbach, L. J./Associates (1980): Toward reform of program evaluation. San Francisco, CA: Jossey-Bass.

Dockery, G. (2000): Participatory research: Whose roles, whose responsibilities? In: Truman, C./Mertens, D. M./Humphries, B. (Eds.): Research and Inequality. London: Taylor & Francis.

Greene, J. C. (1994): Qualitative program evaluation: Practice and promise. In: Denzin, N. K./Lincoln, Y. S. (Eds.): The Handbook of Qualitative Research. Thousand Oaks, CA: Sage. pp. 530-544.

Guba, E. G./Lincoln, Y. S. (1989): Fourth Generation Evaluation. Thousand Oaks, CA: Sage.

Hadley, R. G./Mitchell, L. K. (1995): Counseling research and program evaluation. Pacific Grove, CA: Brooks/Cole.

House, E. (1993): Professional Evaluation: Social Impact and Political Consequences. Thousand Oaks, CA: Sage.

Joint Committee on Standards for Educational Evaluation (1994): The Program Evaluation Standards: How to assess evaluations of educational programs. Thousand Oaks, CA: Sage.

Kirkhart, K. (1995): Seeking multicultural validity: A postcard from the road. Evaluation Practice, 16(1), pp. 1-12.

Lincoln, Y. S. (1995): Standards for qualitative research. Paper presented at the annual meeting of the American Educational Research Association, San Francisco, April 1995.

Madaus, G. F./Stufflebeam, D. L./Scriven, M. S. (1983): Program evaluation: A historical overview. In: Madaus, G. F./Scriven, M./Stufflebeam, D. L. (Eds.): Evaluation Models. Boston: Kluwer-Nijhoff. pp. 3-22.

Mertens, Donna M. (2000): Deaf and hard of hearing people in the courts: Using an emancipatory perspective to determine their needs. In: Truman, C./Mertens, D. M./Humphries, B. (Eds.): Research and Inequality. London: Taylor & Francis.

Mertens, Donna M. (1999a): Inclusive evaluation: Implications of transformative theory for evaluation. American Journal of Evaluation, 20(1), pp. 1-14.

Mertens, D. M. (1999b): Building an international evaluation community. In: Russon, C./ Love, A. (Eds.): Creating a world-wide evaluation community. Kalamazoo, MI: University of Michigan.

Mertens, Donna M. (1998): Research methods in education and psychology: Integrating diversity with quantitative and qualitative approaches. Thousand Oaks, CA: Sage.

Mertens, Donna M./Farley, J./Madison, A./Singleton, P. (1994): Diverse voices in evaluation practice: Feminists, minorities, and persons with disabilities. Evaluation Practice, 1994, 15(2), pp. 123-129.

Mienczakowski, J. (2000): People like us Ethnography in the form of theatre with emancipatory intentions. In: Truman, C./Mertens, D. M./Humphries, B. (Eds.): Research and Inequality. London: Taylor & Francis.

Patton, M. Q. (1987): Evaluation's political inherency: Practical implications for design and use. In: Palumbo, D. J. (Ed.): The politics of program theory. Thousand Oaks, CA: Sage, pp. 100-145.

Rheaume, J./Roy, S. (2000): Defining without discriminating: Ethnicity and social problems. In: Truman, C./Mertens, D. M./Humphries, B. (Eds.): Research and Inequality. London: Taylor & Francis.

Rossi, P. H./Freeman, H. E. (1993): Evaluation: A systematic approach. Thousand Oaks, CA: Sage.

Ryen, A. (2000): Colonial methodology. In: Truman, C./Mertens, D. M./Humphries, B. (Eds.): Research and Inequality. London: Taylor & Francis.

Scriven, M. S. (1967): The methodology of evaluation. AERA Monograph Series in Curriculum Evaluation, 1967, 1, pp. 39-83.

Shadish, W. R. (1994): Need-based evaluation: good evaluation and what you need to know about it. Evaluation Practice, 1994, 15(3), pp. 347-358.

Shadish, W. R./Cook, T. D./Leviton, L. C. (1991): Foundations of program evaluation. Thousand Oaks, CA: Sage.

Shadish, W. R./Newman, D./Scheirer, M. A./Wye, C. (Eds.) (1995): The American Evaluation Association's Guiding Principles. San Francisco: Jossey-Bass.

Sirotnik, K. A. (Ed.) (1990): Evaluation and social justice: Issues in Public Education. New Directions for Program Evaluation, Vol. 45. San Francisco: Jossey-Bass.

Sirotnik, K. A./Oakes, J. (1990): Evaluation as critical inquiry: School improvement as a case in point. In: Sirotnik, K. A. (Ed.) (1990): Evaluation and social justice: Issues in Public Education. New Directions for Program Evaluation, Vol. 45. San Francisco: Jossey-Bass. pp. 37-60.

Smith, M. F. (1994): Evaluation: Review of the past, preview of the future. Evaluation Practice, 1994, 15(3), pp. 215-227.

Stake, R. E. (1983): The case study method in social inquiry. In: Madaus, G. F./ Scriven M./Stufflebeam, D. L. (Eds.): Evaluation Models. Boston: Kluwer-Nijhoff. pp. 279-286.

Stufflebeam, D. L. (1983): The CIPP model for program evaluation. In: Madaus, G. F./ Scriven, M./Stufflebeam, D. L. (Eds.): Evaluation Models. Boston: Kluwer-Nijhoff. pp. 117-142.

Truman, C. (2000): New social movements and social research. In: Truman, C./Mertens, D. M./Humphries, B. (Eds.): Research and Inequality. London: Taylor & Francis.

Truman, C./Mertens, D. M./Humphries, B. (Eds.) (2000): Research and Inequality. London: Taylor & Francis.

United States General Accounting Office. The Government Performance and Results Act (1997): 1997 Government-wide Implementation Will be Uneven. Author: Washington, DC. (Chapter Report, 06/02/97, GAO/GGD-97-109).

Weiss, C. H. (1987): Where politics and evaluation research meet. In: Palumbo, D. J. (Ed.): The politics of program theory. Thousand Oaks, CA: Sage. pp. 47-70.

Witkin, B. R./Altschuld, J. W. (1995): Planning and conducting needs assessment. Thousand Oaks, CA: Sage.

Whitmore, B. (Ed.) (1998): Understanding and practicing participatory evaluation. (New Directions in Evaluation, Vol. 80. San Francisco: Jossey-Bass.

Frans L. Leeuw

Evaluation in Europe

1. Introduction

This chapter discusses some highlights of developments of evaluation in Europe and also describes a number of challenges for the evaluation community for the next years.

First, the question is addressed whether or not evaluation still is an infant industry in Europe.

Secondly, attention is focused on some of the explanatory factors behind the development of evaluation in Europe.

Thirdly, developments within the European Union are described, while finally a number of challenges are put on the agenda.

Evaluation is – as we see it – the application of social science theory and methodology in order to assess both ex-ante and ex-post the implementation, the impact and the side-effects of programs, policies, strategies and other 'tools of governments' (like subsidies, vouchers, levies or communication and information campaigns) on society, including the explanation of those impacts/side-effects. Evaluations are carried out by special research institutions (government/non-government), universities, consultancy firms, audit offices, inspectorates but also by institutions like higher education quality councils, technology assessment institutes etc..

2. Evaluation still an infant industry in Europe?

Evaluation can be an 'infant industry', a 'growth industry' or an 'industry in decline', while perceptions about the type of 'industry' that prevail can differ substantially among stakeholders. During a World Bank Symposium on Evaluation Capacity Building (Picciotto 1998) was referred to programme evaluation as an 'infant industry'. An infant industry is made of numerous firms simultaneously entering into a promising market. A mature market would probably be dominated by a few big international companies, like is the audit industry at present.

To answer this question what the type of 'evaluation industry' we have in Europe, we follow three lines of 'thought'.

The first is to bring together indicators of the level of growth and development of evaluation 'industry' in Europe. We follow the indicators used by Rist, Furubo and Sandahl (2000).

Secondly, we look into the number of professional organizations over Europe as an indicator and describe in particular the European Evaluation Society.

Finally, we use data we earlier gathered (Leeuw et al. 1999) from a survey of evaluation service providers, both private sector consultants and academic research centers.

2.1 Indicators

Rist et al. (2000) use the following indicators in their Atlas-project. This project inventorises where – worldwide – evaluation 'is'. It is a sequel to a study done by Derlien (1989). Its database is produced by the members of the Inteval-Group[1]. However, it should be noted that not all European countries are covered.

Rist et al. use the following indicators (per country)[2]:

1. number of domains in which evaluations take place;
2. supply of evaluators/evaluating organizations;
3. supply of training courses for evaluators;
4. national discourse on evaluation;
5. presence of a profession with its own societies or frequent attendance of international societies in the country;
6. institutional arrangements for conducting evaluations within the public sector/government;
7. institutional arrangements for conducting evaluations within Parliament;
8. evaluation activities are carried out by supreme audit offices (like the National Audit Office in the UK, the Algemene Rekenkamer in Holland or the Court des Comptes in Belgium).

---

1   Inteval is the follow-up group of the IIAS Working Group on Program and Policy Evaluation which started in the mid 1980's with Ray C.Rist (then at the US General Accounting Office) as its chair. In the late 90's the group decided to become more autonomous. Members are evaluation scholars and practitioners of some 20-25 countries (world wide). See the series published by Transaction Publishers, New Brunswick, for more information on the background and productivity of this group. The author of this chapter is a member since its inception.

2   We do not discuss two other criteria they mention: i.e. pluralism within evaluations and the criterion that 'the evaluations done should not only be concentrated on the relations between inputs/outputs or the technical production process' (Rist et al. 2000: 15)

The data produced by the Atlas-group for European countries, including the EU (see section 4) are the following.

Table 1: Indicators of an evaluation culture in Europe

Country	Evaluation activity	Supply of evaluators	Training capacity	National discourse	Organized evaluation meetings	Evaluation infra-structure within the public sector	Evaluation infra-structure within par-liament	Evalua-tions car-ried out by Supreme Audit Offices
Sweden	++	++	+	++	+	++	+	++
Netherlands	++	++	+?	++	+	++	+	++
UK	++	++	+?	+	++	+	?	++
Germany	++	++	+?	+	++	+	++	+
Denmark	++?	++	+	++	+	++?	?	+?
Finland	++	+	+?	+	+?	+	+	+
France	++	+	+	+	++	++	+	+
Switzerland	+	+	+	++	++	0	0	0
Ireland	+	+	0	+	0	+	0	+
Spain	+	0	0	+	++	+	0	0
Italy	0	+	+	+	++	0	0	+
Norway	++	+	+	+	+	++	+	+

Legend: ++ good availability/ coverage
+ moderate availability/coverage
0 no availability.
? insufficient data or interpretation difficulties

From these scores by the Atlas-group some conclusions can be drawn. With regard to the intensity of evaluation activities that take place within the European countries, North and Western Europe are most active. Some of them have already been active for more than two decades (Derlien 1989), an indicator of tenacity. The supply of evaluators also shows relative large differences between the countries, while with regard to training activities the picture is not one of a well-developed 'training/education/transfer culture' within Europe. For example, in many countries there have not been established (university) chairs for evaluation studies. The indicator 'national discourse' shows a similar trend as could be seen with regard to the intensity of evaluation activities. 'Meetings organized' makes clear that if countries are not yet very involved in carrying out evaluations, this does not imply that they are not able to play a role as 'organizer' of debates and meetings. The third congres of the European Evaluation Society for example took place in Rome (1998), the fourth in Lausanne (2000). The 'evaluation infrastructure' within the public sector appears to be more developed than the infrastructure within Parliament, while, finally, the attention paid by national audit offices to evaluation resembles the scores on several other indicators.

In order to make an educated guess about the development of evaluation in Europe we compare these indicators with the analysis Derlien (1989) earlier presented. He referred to countries that participated in the first and the second wave of evaluations since the 1970's. Sweden, Germany and the UK were the countries in Europe detected by Derlien as 'first wave-countries'. This implied that in the 70's and 80's evaluations were going on, that there was (already) some infrastructure, that at least audit offices took an interest in these activities and that there were professional evaluators to be found (to do the job). The US and Canada were also first-wave countries.

The more recent Atlas-data show that Sweden, Germany and the UK are still among the frontrunners. However, a fair amount of other European countries can now be added: Denmark, Netherlands, Norway, France, Finland, Ireland, Italy and Spain. From the Atlas-study (which looks into 15 other countries like the US, Canada, Australia, Israel and China) it also can be deduced that the first wave-European countries as well as the newcomers do perform relatively good (on the basis of the indicators in table 1).

2.2 Evaluation societies

The first evaluation societies being established were those of the UK and the European Evaluation Society. Both had their starting points in the late 1980's. The birth of the EES was stimulated by the Netherlands Court of Audit. This organization also plays (and played) a dominant role in stressing evaluation in the Netherlands in General. The UK Evaluation Society started more within the (research/university) community of evaluation in Great Britain.

Nowadays the following evaluation societies are established or in the process of becoming institutionalized:

- Associazione Italiana de Valuatazione
- Deutsche Gesellschaft fur Evaluation
- European Evaluation Society
- Finnish Evaluation Society
- La Societe Francaise de l'Evaluation
- Swedish Evaluation Network
- Societe Wallonne de l'Evaluation et de la Prospective
- Swiss Evaluation Society
- UK Evaluation Society
- Dutch Chapter of EES

2.3 A survey amongst evaluation providers

Leeuw, Toulemonde and Brouwers (1999) carried out a survey in which one of the questions was the perception of interviewees of the 'market for evaluation in Europe'. Box 1 gives some background information.

Box 1 – A little survey of European evaluators

EES-headquarters in Stockholm did mail 518 questionnaires to persons and organisations in 15 countries (all EU member states minus Luxemburg, plus Switzerland). Ad-
dressees were belonging to one or several of the following lists:
(*) evaluation experts having answered the call for expression of interest recently is-
sued by the European Commission (DG XIX);
(*) consultants within the EES membership;
(*) consultants within the C3E's contact list.
To an unknown extent, the mailing list was biased in favour of evaluators dealing with
socio-economic development policies.
Question #1 concerned the type of organisation the respondent was affiliated with (
private, not for profit, quasi-governmental). Question #2 focused on the total budget of
the organisation, while question #3 dealt with the part of this budget that was directly
related to carrying out evaluations. Question #4 tried to gain an insight into a trend.
We asked: 'compared to the early nineties, has this proportion been stable, increased
or decreased'? Question #5 focused on what the respondents considered their four
biggest markets for evaluations. "Markets" were defined by crossing policy domains
and countries. Question #6 wanted to find out how the evaluation activities in the respondent's organisation were divided given these four markets, while with question #7
we wanted to gain some insight into which share the respondents' organisation has in
these four markets. Finally, we added a question allowing the respondents to add
'qualitative comments' on the situation of the 'evaluation market' in Europe.
The response was very limited. Only 32 of all the questionnaires were returned. This
may be partly explained by outdated addresses in the mailing list. In addition, we had
neither budget nor time for undertaking telephone follow-up. Half of the 32 organisations responding were private (N=16), the other half non-profit (N=8) or quasi-
governmental (N=3). Missing values account for the difference that appear in this paper. For the analysis we brought together the non-profit and quasi-governmental organisations.
Next, we held a workshop during the Third Conference of the Euopean Evaluation Society held in Rome in late 1998 (EES, see below for more information on this society)
in which we also discussed this question. That session is referred to as the 'EES Workshop in Rome'.

Due to the very small number of 32 responses to the EES questionnaire, we
want to limit our conclusions to one statement, i.e. *evaluation appears to be
more a growth market than a market-in-decline*. Most of the organisations
(N=25) report a *growth* in the proportion of their turn-over generated by program and policy evaluations. Only two organisations report a decline, while
the five remaining organisations report that the proportion [compared to the
early 1990's] is stable[3]. This growth is also stressed by one respondent in
these terms: *'evaluation is [becoming a] standard procedure in the policy
process'*. With regard to private sector organisations, five out of 16 have to

---

3   For further analysis we brought together organizations with declining market shares
     and organizations with stable market shares for performing evaluations (labelled
     'stable or decreased').

deal with a decline or a stable percentage of their evaluation activities. This is only true with one (out of 11) non-profit/quasi-governmental organisation.

Table 2 shows that the main 'operating fields' are ranked in the following way: (1) economic development & enterprises[4]; (2) social services & health; (3) development & aid, (4) education, schools & training and (5) technology, innovation & research. Relatively less important are the fields of security, police, justice, agriculture, and the environment.

Table 2 : Means (m) and standard deviations (sd) of approximate percentages of the organizations' evaluation activities by policy domains, divided for private and not private organizations (n = 27)

	PRIVATE (N=16)		NOT PRIVATE (N=11)	
	M	SD	M	SD
ECON	39.4	41.4	29.5	29.5
SOCIAL	12.8	26.1	12.3	16.6
AID	10.3	26.4	.9	3.0
EDUC	9.4	17.3	20.0	31.9
OTHER	4.4	17.5	5.0	7.1
TECH	4.4	17.5	9.0	22.2
AGRIC	2.5	7.7	0	0
INFRA	1.9	7.5	2.7	9.0
ENVIR	1.3	5.0	2.3	4.7
SECUR	1.3	5.0	0	0

ECON: Economic development, Enterprises
EDUC: Education, School, Training
SOCIAL: Social services, Health
AID: Development, Aid and Transition
TECH: Technology, Innovation, Research
INFRA: Basic Infrastructures, Transport
AGRIC: Agriculture, Fisheries, Forestry
ENVIR: Environment
SECUR: Security, Justice, Police

Participants in the workshop organized during the Rome-conference agreed that evaluation demand develops faster at European and national level than at regional and local level. While almost all European policies are now subject to periodic evaluation, a figure of 10% was mentioned about the proportion of regional policies that are subject to periodic evaluations in countries like UK, Denmark, Netherlands and France.

The questionnaire survey cannot inform us about the size of European market(s). It cannot even provide us with an order of magnitude. An interesting figure was given by one of the workshop participants about the overall cost (internal + external) of running a systematic evaluation function. In the

---

4   This first ranking may result from a bias in the mailing list.

case of European Structural Funds in Ireland, this cost amounted to about 1% of the total public expenses involved (CSF Evaluation Unit, 1998) (see also section 4).

Participants in the EES-workshop in Rome acknowledged that many evaluators concentrate on a given policy domain and use evaluation methods and skills that are specific to their field. This is highlighted by one respondent in the following terms: *'Evaluation criteria and methods used in country-wide or sectoral evaluations of aid programmes are still far from having led to commonly accepted definitions and rules, even within the EU. ..Methods have still to be improved but above all an ongoing process of updating and harmonising definitions and methods [is important]'.*

Evaluation activities in Europe seem even more fragmented when we look at national (sub)markets. One can easily understand that foreign evaluators face high barriers when trying to enter into a given national market, especially for reasons of language, knowledge of institutional settings, familiarity with administrative culture. A participant in the workshop stressed that it was even hard to hire an English evaluator in Ireland, although the pool of qualified national consultants is small in the later country.

When it comes to evaluate European-wide policies, this fragmented supply creates a problem. The European Commission hardly finds genuinely European suppliers. Many tenders and contracts involve ad hoc consortia merging national evaluators. We may see the development of a new (quasi)-profession, which consists in gathering a dozen of national evaluators, in making them evaluate a given European policy from various national standpoints, and in working hard to draw a synthetic conclusion for use at European level.

Surprisingly, most of the big audit companies also operate in a fragmented manner, as far as we speak of evaluation which is not part of their core business.

An infant industry also faces problems with unstable standards, like those expressed by several respondents to our questionnaire: *'Evaluations are not yet fully accepted as feedback mechanisms'; 'The evaluation process is becoming routinised and simplified and de-skilled. This is a danger'.* Top-down pressures in favour of evaluation tend to weaken the commitment of civil servants that order evaluations. One participant of the workshop even spoke of cynicism and asked the question whether demand would keep raising or fall if we were no longer obligated to evaluate.

Some present features of the evaluation business were pointed out as typical of the shaky rules that govern an infant industry: over-ambitious terms of reference, evaluators promising much more than they are capable to deliver, ambiguous demand and behaviour with respect to independence.

Moreover, much evaluation activity keeps focusing on resources instead of outcomes, on administrative processes instead of social and economic stakes. There may even be a little drift into what auditors typically do. In the

UK, Mike Power (1994, 1995) referred to the 'Audit Explosion' and the Audit Society. He has put forward the insight that "auditors become second order certifiers of the *form* of systems rather than their *substance*'. He links this development to the knowledge base that underlines the work of auditors and puts forward the hypothesis that "system auditing is attractive because it is easier to audit the system which controls a process than the outputs of that process. A drift from inspection to certification occurs when standards of control replace standards of output" [5]

In the longer run, there is a danger that if we keep calling almost everything an 'evaluation', a *procedural approach* (looking into processes instead of outcomes for example) may be on the horizon that neither is good for evaluation as a profession nor for the ones that are evaluated.

3. Evaluation and the European Union

3.1 A little history

Special attention should be given to evaluation within the EU. Here we use Toulemonde/Summa's overview-study (2000; in press)[6].

"Evaluation of regional economic development programs started in the mid 1980's with a pilot phase covering dozens of programs in the Mediterranean regions. This served as a basis for developing a much wider activity of joint EU-national evaluations. Dating from the early 1980's, the evaluation of RTD (research and technology-development) programs can be considered as one of the forerunners of programmatic evaluation in Europe. This practice had much of the features of the 'first wave' evaluations: heavy reliance upon objectivity and expertise, management and enlightenment perspectives, and an aim to legitimize public interventions (Sand/Toulemonde 1994).

In 1995 a new evaluation scheme was adopted which combines a rolling system of annual monitoring exercises and periodic five-year assessments of all research programs as well as of the framework program. These assessments can be understood as a combination of an ex post evaluation of the previous program, an intermediate evaluation of the current program and an ex ante appraisal of future activities. Compared to the previous scheme of separate intermediate and ex post evaluations the present rolling system is

---

5   This *love for systems* has also been found in the comparative study of the OECD's
    Public Management Group. OECD-PUMA has inventorised developments and con-
    sequences of auditing in some of their member states.
6   This part of the chapter is completely based on the study by Toulemonde et al. (in
    press).

more streamlined and more carefully scheduled to provide information which is timely from the point of view of decision making.

Some of the most influential European policies are of a regulatory nature and involve no or very small public expenditure and no formal programmation. Finalizing and implementing the legislation on the single market, protection of consumers, and environmental regulation are examples of such regulatory policies. Although many evaluations have always occurred in the domain of regulatory policies, EU institutions are not equipped with a formal evaluation system nor even with a database that would record the amount of work undertaken within the various Directorates General. The Council and Parliament pass a small number of "sunset" regulations which include a formal evaluation clause with a given deadline (especially in the field of Competition Policy). Most regulations simply include an obligation to "report" about the results, generally after three years. Usually these reports do not have the name, nor the substance, of evaluations. Systematic ex-post evaluation of European regulations would hardly be feasible since most of them take the form of broad frameworks that must be integrated ("transposed" in European English) into national laws under the responsibility of member states".

3.2 Management Reforms and Evaluation in the 90's

"As a result of developments in the 1980's and in the early 1990's, the autonomous policy making capacity of the EU has increased gradually. The relative size of the European budget (as a percentage of member states' GDP) grew from 0.8% in 1980 to 1.2% in 1993 and the scope of expenditure programs widened in fields such as environment, research, technology, transport, education and culture, as well as in regional redistributional policies and financial assistance to third countries. Simultaneously – and particularly in the aftermath of the difficulties in the ratification process of the Maastricht Treaty – questions concerning democratic accountability and value for money of European level programs began to be raised increasingly in the member states.

To a large extent the concerns for better accountability and value for money in European policy and programs were particularly directed to the Commission as the initiator and executor of Community policies. The European Parliament as well as the Court of Auditors also played an important role in pushing the Commission to account better for what it spends. Against this background the reform wave initiated in the mid-1990's by the Santer Commission is a natural development. Another factor that may have had some influence is the entry of the new Nordic member states, which already had a tradition in accountability and result-oriented public management reform policies. The Santer Commission took two consequent initiatives in reforming the management of EU policy making and spending, one in the field of financial management and control, with particular emphasis on systematic program evaluation, and a later one which focused particularly on internal administrative procedures and staff management. The former is known as 'SEM 2000' – Sound and Efficient Management – and the latter as 'MAP 2000' – Modernization of Administration and Personnel policies".

"The 'Sound and Efficient Management' initiative can be described as an umbrella program covering various reforms in both the Commission's internal financial management and in the Commission's interplay with member states. The 'SEM-2000' process is supervised by a group of personal representatives from member states' ministries of finance. One of the priorities identified for improvements in the Commission's internal financial management was that evaluations of expenditure programs financed from the Community budget should take place on a more systematic, timely and rigorous basis.

In formulating its approach to more systematic program evaluation the Commission could take as its starting point the article of the Treaty establishing the Union (Article 205 of the Maastricht Treaty) stipulating that 'the Commission shall implement the budget... having regard to the principles of sound financial management.' The principle has been further elaborated in the financial regulation covering the establishment and execution of the Community budget, which declares that results of periodic evaluations of Community actions should be taken into account in decisions concerning budgetary allocations, and that all proposals with budgetary consequences should be preceded by evaluations ensuring they yield economic benefits in keeping with the resources deployed. These principles have been translated into procedural requirements, supervised by the Directorate General for Budgets and the Financial Control of the Commission, according to which the operational DGs must describe their evaluation plans and results in the documentation accompanying any proposal with budgetary consequences".

3.3 Towards Systematic Evaluation of All Community Policies

When designing its initiative on more systematic evaluation the Commission acknowledged the existing practices in evaluative work. However, it pointed out that progress had been uneven across policy fields and that large areas of expenditure programs were not covered by any systematic evaluation practices. With support from the representatives of national ministries of finance, and led by the two Nordic commissioners, Liikanen and Gradin, the Commission adopted in May 1996 a memorandum (European Commission 1996) which set out a process of concrete steps to spread best practice in policy and program evaluation across Commission departments. The starting point in the Commission's approach to improving evaluation practices was a decentralized model in which the operational Directorates General are responsible for establishing systematic evaluation procedures for the programs they are executing. The Directorates General for budgets and for financial control were to assist and supervise the spread of best practices, to improve evaluation techniques, and to exercise overall quality control. The following concrete steps were requested by the Commission:

- every operational DG should designate an official or a unit with lead responsibility for evaluation;
- every operational DG should establish annually an evaluation plan identifying programs which will be subject to an evaluation;
- the operational DGs' evaluation plans will be compiled into the Commission's Annual Evaluation Program and presented to the College of Commissioners;
- the DGs for budget and financial control will establishing an Annual Evaluation Review which presents an inventory of evaluation reports finalized during the previous year;
- a network of evaluators will be established to function as an informal forum for constructive peer review and for dissemination of best practice;
- the Directorate General for financial control, in its role of internal auditor, reports to the Commission regularly on the functioning and quality of the systems and organization of evaluation activities that the operational DGs have in place; and
- training, manuals and a 'help desk' function in evaluation matters were to be established by the horizontal financial DGs.

As to the content and type of evaluations, the rule is not one of standardization. On the contrary, the Commission emphasizes that evaluation projects should be tailored to the objectives and delivery mechanisms of the policy or program concerned. However, certain features in the Commission's way of defining and conceptualizing evaluation are of interest. First of all, it takes a fairly broad view on what is included in the concept of evaluation. Not only does it encompass ex post and mid term evaluation, but it also covers ex ante exercises. Ex ante evaluation happens before the policy and program has fully taken shape. Its purpose is to specify the objectives and indicators of success for the program, and to assess the proposed program logic on the basis of criteria such as clarity, evaluability, consistency, feasibility and relevance to the needs. Second, the concept of evaluation is linked to a budgetary perspective: evaluation projects are expected to be framed so that they correspond to identifiable entities in the Community budget and to be timed so that results are available when they are relevant for budgetary decisions.

3.4 Evaluation of European Expenditures: State of Play in 1999

In a stock taking exercise the Santer-Commission, shortly before it resigned, made an assessment on how far the 1996 initiative has achieved its objectives. It concludes that the evaluation systems that are now in place have been fairly successful in providing support for program management and that they contribute to some extent to improved accountability as an increasing number of evaluation reports and an annual evaluation review are published. A third objective set for the evaluation system was to support budgetary decision making and resource allocation – for which the Commission concludes that not fully satisfactory results have been achieved: " The current evaluation system is more likely to produce findings and recommendations that support incremental improvements in programme management and design than judgements that would be of immediate value for addressing problems of resource allocation" (ibid.).

In quantitative terms, the Commission's evaluation activities are significant: during the three years in which a systematic follow-up of evaluation has taken place (1996-98) close to 300 evaluation projects have been initiated by Commission departments. More or less all policy areas are covered by evaluation activities Evaluations on the common agricultural policy have been scarce so far, with only a few minor reports being available. This has been an object of criticism both by academics (Levy 1995; Tangermann/ Buckwell 1999) and by some member states. However, in 1998 an ambitious evaluation program was started for this politically sensitive and controversial area. It can be concluded that, at least in a quantitative and formal sense, the aim to spread out systematic evaluation to all sectors and policy areas has been successful.

Looking at the characteristics of evaluation projects carried out by the Commission reveals something of how far the establishment of an evaluation *culture* has been successful. The annual evaluation reviews (European Commission 1998 and 1999a) show that the typical evaluation project is an intermediate evaluation contracted out to a team of external experts (more than half of the completed projects in 1996-1997 were of this type). About one third of evaluations are of *ex-post* type and about two thirds are carried out at mid-term of the program. Internal evaluations conducted by the Commission departments themselves are exceptional, as are *ex-ante* evaluations as separate projects. The latter is surprising considering the importance this category was given in the Commission's communication on evaluation and the fact that it is included as a general requirement in the financial regulation. A clear increase in the number of *ex-ante* evaluations is shown, however, in the evaluation program for 1999. The quality of evaluation reports was commented upon somewhat critically in the Commission's recent stock taking (European Commission 1999). The Commission has not established any generally applicable quality standards to guide its evaluation activities. In the spirit of the decentralized evaluation system this is considered to be the responsibility of the operational departments. However, guidelines on good practice for managing evaluation were recently established by a working group of Commission's evaluation officials (European Commission 1999b) which recommend that departments should create their own or adopt some existing quality standards for evaluation. At the time of writing, the Directorate General for research and technology policy has started this by establishing a set of quality standards for 5-year assessments and monitoring of the RTD programs (European Commission 1999c).

4. Current developments

4.1 The importance of civil society is increasing

In all of Europe the growing importance of civil society is being recognised. In the States of East and Central Europe, strengthening civil society is a key plank in the transition to democracy. In the European Union the Member States and the Union itself look increasingly to communities, associations, neighbourhoods and other social networks to take on responsibility that existing 'welfare states' seem no longer able to carry. Civic education, new forms of direct democracy, voluntary activities and new ways of involving citizens in decisions are widespread.

Evaluators need to recognise the demands that civil society will make of them. Traditionally evaluators have not seen support for civil society as one of their core concerns. Will it and should it become a core evaluation concern in the future? It is not only a question of who evaluators report to but also of the stance they adopt towards the commissioners of evaluation, to programme beneficiaries and to citizens. Evaluators as advocates, the growth of bottom-up and self-evaluation efforts, citizen juries, the theories of social capital all touch on this aspect of societal evolution. So also do methodological questions: about the validity of qualitative and grass-roots generated data, how to build generalisable evidence from unique case-studies and how to sustain an independent and credible role for evaluators who engage actively in reinforcing civil society.

4.2 Strengthening public management

At different levels – European, national, regional and local – we see continued moves to strengthen public management. Results based management systems, performance indicators, organisational learning, citizens' charters, the growing interest of auditors in 'value for money' studies – all of these impinge on evaluation. Governments are seeking to use these tools and concepts to demonstrate transparency and efficiency. As global markets and competitiveness erode the ability of governments to spend and directly provide services to citizens, improved public management that maximises the benefit of scarce resources is seen as vital.

Public management is not just a matter of the State as traditionally conceived. As followers of the new public management debate will know, government and administration has undergone a revolution over the last ten or fifteen years across the industrialised world. Decentralisation, public/private partnerships, marketisation, privatisation, competitive tendering and new forms of regulation have all become commonplace. Alongside these developments, new forms of accountability – citizens' charters, performance tables, public access to government information – together with new forms of direct democracy (elected burgermeisters and mayors, the use of referenda, internet consultation of citizens), have all come to the fore to make governments more accessible and accountable.

Yet we are not only thinking of the Nation State today in Europe. Arguably the centralised Nation State is being challenged from many directions. With European integration and the single market, the State has to share its powers with European institutions, while growing interdependence requires regional, bilateral and cross-border cooperation. Simultaneously the State is being challenged from within by decentralisation and regionalism.

Where does this all leave the evaluation community in Europe? For commissioners of evaluation and evaluators themselves one of the biggest challenges is how to respond to the all pervasive 'partnership' model within today's public administrations. At European level in the Structural Funds, and at all other levels we see the drive for collaborative government, 'joined-up government', consortia, networks, and compacts. Partnerships that commission evaluation require of evaluators responsiveness to many different stakeholders – while at the same time evaluation is itself a key element in building consensus between different public, private and 'third' sector actors. Performance targets and indicators also pose methodological challenges to evaluators, especially when so often nowadays the 'object' of evaluation is qualitative – the quality of education, social cohesion, innovation potential, and quality of life.

4.3 The ‚Polity‘ and different political traditions

One of the advantages of a European-wide evaluation society is that we are forced to recognise the different national political traditions we have inherited. Evaluation with its concern for 'valuing' – as well as describing, counting and explaining – takes us to the heart of the political process. Politics is after all the means by which choices about values and priorities are supposed to be made in a democratic society. Some would argue that the growth of evaluation as a codified practice is a symptom of the failure of political democracy! This is certainly a big subject – and it is fitting that we should be considering it in a conference in Switzerland, a country where direct democracy and referenda have continued to have such a strong role in political life.

Evaluation within an evolving polity must also address methodological questions of how to make (or help others make) judgements and choices. 'Valuing' poses an inevitable challenge to professionals who have traditionally seen their practice as 'value-free' and 'objective', yet at the same time privileged and taken-for-granted.

4.4 Central topics for evaluation within Europe

These developments, in my opinion, lead to the following ten topics that deserve attention in the next few years.

a) Evaluation as a resource for civil society

The growing importance of civil society in many aspects of contemporary public policy and consequently of evaluation has already been outlined. Evaluators have in the past been more concerned with public agencies and with government than with the demands of community groups, NGOs, the third sector and the like. The relationship between evaluators and the wider society and the kinds of methodological innovations that are now demanded of evaluators by civil society are among those topics that need to be explored in this session. These changes require that evaluators both question and extend their practice, develop new evaluation designs and new ways of handling data that will reinforce the strengthening of community, voluntary and third sector groups.

b) Implications of evaluation for Parliaments

Whilst the main task of Parliaments is to make laws, they have in recent years become increasingly interested in the effects of their decisions. For quite some time and in most countries, there have been measures controlling the regularity of expenses and legality of decisions and other actions. These controls however do not make sure that policies reach their target population and solve the problems they aim at. Many Parliaments have created evaluation bodies to address questions of the effectiveness of policy and of legislation.

What does this imply for the game of coalitions, for the definition of objectives, for the relationship between Parliaments and administrations, for the integration of results from evaluation into the political process, for legislation itself and for the relationship between the Parliaments and other institutions? What is the experience of those countries that locate evaluation mainly within administrations compared with those that give a greater role to evaluation initiated by Parliaments?

c) Partnerships in public policy: implications for evaluation

Many public policies and programmes are currently delivered through partnerships. These partnerships combine public, private and voluntary or third sector bodies. Partnerships may commission evaluations – this is almost the norm in European Structural Funds but is increasingly common in many other national programmes.

Partnerships create new challenges for evaluation. Evaluators need to devise new strategies to cope with multiple stakeholders, each of which has different evaluation agendas. Partnerships are also deservedly themselves becoming the 'objects' of evaluation. For example, one question that evaluators are asking is 'how effective and efficient are partnerships in delivering programmes?' Another question is 'how successful are partnerships in including all interests and building consensus among stakeholders and beneficiaries?'

d) Decentralization & evaluation

Decentralisation introduces new public actors into the evaluation game at regional and local level and this raises the question of building up the capacity of these actors. Decentralisation may also change the rules of the game, i.e. how evaluation itself is conducted. Other questions are: how can evaluations be designed for policies that are delivered in a decentralised fashion by many agencies and across different levels of government? Is it possible to compare performance across different regions? How can we evaluate the impact on civil society of greater decentralisation? How can subsidiarity itself be evaluated? Finally, given that evaluation has in the past often been associated with more centralised forms of government, how are these changes affecting the roles, methods and practices of evaluators?

e) Better performance: who benefits ?

Managers in the public sector are preoccupied nowadays with improving performance and meeting targets. Results-based management emphasises outputs rather than processes – it is argued that too many public sector evaluations in the past have relied on intermediate outcomes. There is also a debate about the extent to which results-based management is already a reality rather than an aspiration. Some argue that though there are many perform-ance and results-focused measurements, the conversion of data and informa-tion into results-based management (including the management of human and social capital) is still far away.

Alongside questions about the validity of indicators and instruments to measure performance are more profound questions about the distorting ef-fects of performance management systems. Social programmes that are diffi-cult to measure may suffer within a performance management culture. Indeed difficulties improving the quality rather than the quantity of public policy are widely acknowledged. Yet new methods to measure the complexity and quality of public policy and delivery are scarce.

f) Evaluation.dot.com?

The role of ICT (information and communication technology) is rapidly in-creasing. Computer-mediated communication, web-based education and the use of Internet as a mechanism of knowledge transfer are central here. We al-ready see innovative approaches to data gathering 'on-line' and the rapid spread of new techniques and methods via websites and electronic conferencing. Some even argue that due to the Internet transaction costs within society can be greatly reduced. ICT and WWW make it possible for citizens to have access to and to findings from evaluations, audits and in-spections more quickly than a decade ago. We are perhaps beginning to see examples of a shift in balance between traditional evaluators and programme beneficiaries and citizens in this regard. Many evaluators have been slow to respond to the opportunities of ICTs. For example is it not parents who are becoming part of the evaluation process when 'school quality maps', that consist of data about the pedagogical quality, learning styles, and perform-ance of schools can be downloaded for free by school, region, type of school and over a number of years? To avoid misunderstanding : this is not the fu-ture but has already been realized by the Netherlands Educational Review Office. This kind of evaluative information plays a role in decision-making processes of parents, grass roots groups and lobby groups but also makes it possible for journalists to comment on the performance of schools.

g) Auditors as Evaluators

Traditionally the primary objective of auditors is to assess whether financial – and/or non financial – information has been presented in financial state-ments and in activity reports in accordance with applicable frameworks. Management has to establish appropriate information systems and ensure that evidence is relevant and competently gathered. Nowadays auditing bodies are also expected to report on value for money, effectiveness and the quality of public programmes. National audit offices are often instructed to inform Parliaments about policy performance or public agencies performance.

Evaluation practice from an audit base often has major (unintended) side effects. Such effects include: the growth of an indicator culture and an increase in the burden of reporting obligations for public sector managers. Among the topics that this session should address are the relationship between auditing and evaluation, the effects that both have on public sector managers and the positive ways in which new roles for auditors can improve the quality of public management.

h) Evaluation for evidence-based policy

Evaluation can be expected to play a central role in the currently fashionable notion of 'evidence-based' policymaking. One may regard this as the latest manifestation of the desire for objectivity and detachment – 'speaking truth to power' – a project which stands in a somewhat tense relationship with the constructivist and/or participative approaches to evaluation. Despite constructivist critiques, the aspiration for rigorous, scientific and independent evaluation is continually renewed, and so is the quest for knowledge about whether, how and why public programmes work or not. In part, this is because even politicians yearn for the special kind of legitimacy that comes from standing above sectional interests and basing policy on 'hard facts' rather than the subjective perspectives of an ever-increasing number of stakeholders and sectional interest groups.

i) Learning from evaluations : who learns and how?

The use and utilization of evaluation are among the evergreen topics in the evaluation community. Under what conditions, through which mechanisms and for whom can evaluation actually become a vehicle for learning and influence decisions, choices and priorities?

The orthodox understanding of how both individuals and institutions learn is rational and linear. However, evidence has been accumulating in the evaluation literature for more than twenty years to indicate that this type of learning is not the only one, and may even be comparatively rare. Instead of a rational cycle of evidence gathering, analysis, judgement and subsequent action, we see a much more variegated pattern. Learning and innovation may be strongly related to crises or political 'hotspots', and presentations of findings may need to be made to 'chime' with current political ideologies and/or institutional territories. Learning may even depend on the messenger as much as the message. For example, the roles of the mass media, lobby groups or grass-root actors have as yet been little researched with respect to evaluation.

j) Evaluation for public managers : resource, duty and/or burden

Public managers must expect to be evaluated and to use the results of evaluation. The effective use of information is a critical component of a public organisation performance management framework. Management has the duty to provide quantitative and qualitative performance information in a cost effective manner. The potential benefits are : (1) to discharge accountability of effective delivery of public policy objectives (2) to assist in the performance measurement of programme delivery and (3) to improve the decision-making process.

But implementation of new performance management systems poses major challenges to organisations. They can be a resource for better management but they can also be seen as a burden. Additionally, even highly developed frameworks are not fully appropriate to meet management needs and requirements.

This topic addresses such questions as: what are the consequence for public sector managers of the growing demands for evaluation and performance data? how can they constructively respond to demands for greater transparency and accountability to citizens, Parliaments and their own Ministers and hierarchies? and what kinds of new frameworks are able to report on performance in ways that avoids creating unnecessary burdens on already overloaded public sector managers?

5. The future

Evaluation in Europe is expanding: more evaluation societies, more studies being commissioned and carried out and slowly but steadily a greater supply of evaluators. There also is a contiunued role for national audit offices, while the attention attached to evaluation by parliament appears to be increasing. Rather slowly one can see developments regarding training and education. Also, we do not see many developments in the field of certification or accreditation of evaluation. As Power (1998) has noted, we more and more live in an accountability society (or, as he calls it: an audit society). This will probably stay on for a number of years. However, it must be noticed that what in principle is true for policy instruments, i.e. that they produce unintended and undesired side-effects, may also be true for the 'policy instrument' of evaluation. This makes it necessary for the evaluation community to be involved in smart and independent monitoring of their own activities.

References

CSF Evaluation Unit (1998): Review of Ongoing Evaluation Function in the Community Support Framework (CSF) for Ireland. Dublin: Department of Finance.

Derlien, Hans-Ulrich (1990): Genesis and structure of evaluation efforts in comparative perspective. In: Rist, R. C. (Ed.): Program evaluation and the management of government, Patterns and prospects ascross eight nations. New Brunswick: Transaction Publishers.

European Commission DG XVI (forthcoming): Evaluation design and management. In MEANS collection: Evaluating Socio-economic Programmes, Volume 1. Luxembourg: OOPEC.

GAO (1998) Program Evaluation; agencies challenged by new demand for information program results. Washington DC.

Leeuw, Frans L. (1996): Performance auditing, new public management and performance improvement: questions and answers. In: Accounting, Auditing and Accountability Journal, 9(2), pp. 92-102.

Leeuw, Frans L. (1999): Evaluation activities in Europe: a quick scann of the market in 1998. In: Evaluation, No.5/99, pp .487-496.

MacKay, Keith (1998): Evaluation in the Australian Government. Paper, Inteval Working Group on Program and Policy Evaluation. Dublin, Annual Meeting, May 21-24.

Paliokas, K./ Rist, Ray C. (1998): The rise and fall (and rise again?) of the evaluation function in the US Government. Paper, Inteval Working Group on Program and Policy Evaluation. Dublin, Annual Meeting, May 21-24.

Picciotto, Robert (1998): Why bother about ECD? In: MacKay, R. L. (Ed.): Public sector performance: the critical role of evaluation. Selected proceedings from a World Bank Seminar. Washington DC. pp. 17-21.

Power, Mike (1995): Audit and the decline of inspection. Paper, Public Finance Foundation. London.

Power, Mike (1994): The Audit Explosion. Demos Publishers.

Power, Mike (1998): The Audit Society. London.

Rist, Ray C./Furubo, J. E./Sandahl, Rolf: The Evaluation Atlas. Transaction Books. Rutgers, in press.

Rossi, P./Wright, J. D. (1984): Evaluation research: an asessesment. In: Annual Review of Sociology, No.10: pp. 331-352.

Summa, Hillka/Toulemonde, Jacques (1998): Evaluation in the European Union. Paper, Inteval Working Group on Program and Policy Evaluation. Dublin, Annual Meeting, May 21-24.

Taylor, M. (1996): Between public and private: accountability in voluntarily organisations. In: Policy and Politics, No.24 (1): pp.57-72.

Thomas Widmer

Qualität der Evaluation – Wenn Wissenschaft zur praktischen Kunst wird

1. Einstieg

Qualität ist ein schillernder Begriff, der sich durch zwei Charakteristiken besonders auszeichnet: Erstens wird er in Wissenschaft und Praxis heutzutage äußerst rege benutzt. Und zweitens ist die Unbeholfenheit gerade jener, die diesen Begriff besonders häufig verwenden, offensichtlich, ihn auch in einer ebenso gehaltvollen wie präzisen *Definition* einzufangen. Ähnliches ließe sich auch zu den aus dem angelsächsischen Raum importierten Wortketten „state of the art" oder „best practice" sagen. Immerhin zeigen diese beiden Termini Ansatzpunkte sprachlicher Art – gemeint sind „Kunst" (vgl. hinsichtlich der Evaluation: Cronbach 1982: 1) und „Praxis" – die zum Begriffsverständnis beitragen könnten. Aber nur schon der Umstand, daß die beiden englischen Formeln gerade im Wissenschaftsbetrieb sehr häufig anzutreffen sind, läßt uns zweifeln. Die Gräben zwischen Wissenschaft einerseits und Kunst sowie Praxis andererseits scheinen ja, wie uns allenthalben glauben gemacht wird, unüberwindbare Hindernisse darzustellen.

Das *Qualitätsmanagement*, so hat sich langsam herumgesprochen, dient nicht der Gewährleistung einer hohen Qualität eines Produktes oder einer Dienstleistung. Vielmehr zielt es darauf ab, die Existenz eines Qualitätssicherungssystems nachzuweisen. Dies vermag vielleicht die Unternehmensleitung zu überzeugen und die Qualitätsberater zu ernähren, Belastung und Begeisterung der Mitarbeitenden halten sich aber im bestem Fall in einem labilen Gleichgewicht und die – in der Ära der Kundenorientierung – so viel Beachtung erhaltende Kundschaft muß feststellen, daß sich ihre Qualitätserwartungen in wenig systematischer Weise erfüllen.

In diesem Artikel wird der Versuch unternommen, die Qualitätsdebatte in anderer Weise und mit dem Ziel zu führen, zu definieren, was Qualität ist. Angesichts dieses hohen Anspruchs erlaube ich mir, die Diskussion auf die *Evaluation* zu beschränken. Dies geschieht nicht nur aus schweizerischer Bescheidenheit, sondern auch, weil ich der festen Überzeugung bin, daß der Ansatz der Evaluation eine eigene Definition von Qualität verdient und gängige Transponierungsversuche „branchenfremder" Konzepte wenig zielführend sind.

Der Beitrag ist wie folgt strukturiert: Im nächsten Kapitel wird auf die Vielfältigkeit der Evaluation eingegangen, um auf eine bedeutende Rahmenbedingung der Debatte zur Evaluationsqualität zu verweisen. Das nachfolgende, dritte Kapitel befaßt sich mit den Erwartungen, die von verschiedener Seite an die Evaluation gerichtet werden. Im vierten Kapitel wird in die Referenzebenen zur Bewertung der Evaluationsqualität eingeführt. Das fünfte Kapitel stellt sodann die Evaluationsstandards vor und im sechsten Kapitel werden mögliche Anwendungen der „Standards" in der Evaluationspraxis aufgezeigt. Das Schlußkapitel enthält eine Zusammenfassung der vorangegangen Überlegungen und verweist auf die Grenzen der „Standards".

2. Vielfältige Evaluation

Der *Ansatz der Evaluation* zeichnet sich durch eine ausgesprochene Reichhaltigkeit auf verschiedenen Ebenen aus. Im folgenden soll kurz diese Vielfalt resümiert werden, da sie eine eminent wichtige Rahmenbedingung der Debatte um die Evaluationsqualität darstellt.

2.1 Gegenstände der Evaluation

Die Unterschiedlichkeit potentieller *Evaluationsgegenstände* – auch Evaluanda genannt – ist enorm. Es läßt sich so gut wie alles in irgendeiner Form evaluieren. Zur Spezifizierung eines bestimmten Evaluationstyps sind vielfältige Begriffe entstanden. An erster Stelle sei hier die prominente Programmevaluation angesprochen, hinzuweisen ist aber auch auf die Produktevaluation, die Personalevaluation, die Projektevaluation, die Reformevaluation, die Gesetzesevaluation, die Maßnahmenevaluation, die Organisationsevaluation, die Politikevaluation oder auch die Evaluation einer Evaluation (sogenannte Meta-Evaluation; vgl. unten, Kapitel 6.2). Ebenso kann auch der Fokus der Evaluation erheblich variieren. So wird etwa unterschieden zwischen der umfassenden Globalevaluation, der spezifischeren Projektevaluation oder einer themenfokussierten Evaluation.

Aber auch bei der zu bewertenden Phase in einer *Wirkungskette*, bestehen maßgebliche Unterschiede. In der Sprache der Politikanalyse kann jede Phase des „policy cycle" einer Evaluation unterzogen worden. So wird etwa die Politikformulierung oder die Politikimplementation (Politikumsetzung; man spricht hier auch von Prozeßevaluationen im Gegensatz zu Wirkungsevaluationen) ebenso evaluiert, wie die drei Stufen der Wirkungsentfaltung, also der „output" (Leistungserbringung), der „outcome" (Wirkungen bei den direkten Adressaten) und der „impact" (gesellschaftliche Auswirkungen).

2.2 Verortung einer Evaluation

Wichtig bei der Spezifikation einer Evaluation ist die Frage nach deren Verortung, wobei die Orte der *Steuerung*, der *Durchführung* und der *Nutzung* zu unterscheiden sind. Mit dem Ort der Steuerung einer Evaluation wird jene Stelle verwiesen, die über die Kompetenzen verfügt, die Funktion(en) einer Evaluation zu definieren und über die Wahl der Evaluationsthematik und - fragestellung zu entscheiden. Nicht zuletzt wird im Rahmen der Evaluationssteuerung auch der Ort der Durchführung und der Nutzung einer Evaluation – also die beiden anderen Verortungen – bestimmt. Mit dem Ort der *Durchführung* wird jene Instanz angesprochen, die sich der operativen Ausführung der Evaluation annimmt, also die relevanten Informationen erhebt, erfaßt und auswertet. Unter dem Ort der *Nutzung* einer Evaluation wird jener Raum verstanden, in dem die Evaluation Ihre Wirkung entfalten soll. Dies kann nicht nur nach Abschluß einer Evaluation mit Vorliegen eines Berichtes der Fall sein, sondern auch während des Evaluationsprozesses oder sogar schon vor Evaluationsbeginn (präventive Wirkungen). Nachfolgende Tabelle zeigt diese drei Dimensionen mit den jeweils idealtypischen Ausprägungen. In der Praxis lassen sich Evaluationsstudien häufig nicht in der durch die Tabelle suggerierten Eindeutigkeit zuordnen; vielmehr sind Mischformen die Regel.

Tabelle 1: Dimensionen der Verortung einer Evaluation

Dimension/ Verortung	Ort der Steuerung einer Evaluation	Ort der Durchführung einer Evaluation	Ort der Nutzung einer Evaluation
Innerhalb der/s Institution/Projektes	Selbstevaluation	Interne Evaluation	Formative Evaluation
Ausserhalb der/s Institution/Projektes	Fremdevaluation	Externe Evaluation	Summative Evaluation

Die Verortung innerhalb respektive außerhalb des Projektes oder der Institution stellt im konkreten Anwendungsfall nicht immer eine trennscharfe Unterscheidung dar. Sie hängt sehr stark von der Definition der Systemgrenzen ab, die Innen von Außen trennen. Dabei ist zu berücksichtigen, daß bei den Beteiligten & Betroffen („stakeholders"[1]) nicht immer Konsens über die Lokalisierung der Systemgrenzen besteht. Die Perspektive hängt auch eng mit der jeweiligen Position des einzelnen Akteurs zusammen.

Die Übersicht in der obenstehenden Tabelle will keineswegs darauf hindeuten, daß nur Kombinationen auf jeweils einer Zeile möglich wären. So ist es durchaus möglich, eine externe Fremdevaluation mit formativer Funktion zu realisieren. Sehr häufig bewegen sich aber konkrete Evaluationsstudien

---

1 Im vorliegenden Text wird die Wortkombinationen Beteiligte & Betroffene in diesem Sinne als terminus technicus verwendet. Um dies zu verdeutlichen, steht zwischen den beiden Begriffen jeweils ein &.

tendenziell eher auf der einen oder anderen Zeile. Weiter kann sich der Charakter einer Evaluation im Zeitverlauf auch verändern. Ursache derartiger Veränderungen sind oft externe Faktoren. Zum Ort der Steuerung und zum Ort der Durchführung ist zu bemerken, daß diese beiden Dimensionen in der Literatur häufig miteinander vermischt werden. So kennt meines Wissens die englische Evaluationsterminologie kein Äquivalent zum deutschen Begriff Fremdevaluation; im Gegensatz zu den anderen drei Typen („self evaluation", „internal" und „external evaluation"). Ich halte es für angemessen, die in der deutschen Sprache mögliche Differenzierung vorzunehmen, da dies zur begrifflichen Präzision beiträgt und eine wesentliche inhaltliche Differenz aufzeigt.

Eine Zusatzbemerkung ist auch zur letzten Spalte der Tabelle nötig, wo die formative und die summative Evaluation aufgeführt sind. Diese beiden, funktional ausgerichteten Begriffe sind unter der Nutzung (oder auch Verwendung) einer Evaluation subsumiert, weil sich die Funktion einer Evaluation sehr stark auf deren Nutzung bezieht. Die formative Evaluation (*Verbesserungsevaluation*) setzt sich zum Ziel, systemintern Lernprozesse auszulösen und Ansatzpunkte zur Verbesserung aufzuzeigen. Die primären Adressaten einer formativen Evaluation sind demzufolge innerhalb des Systems zu finden. Die summative Evaluation (*Bilanzevaluation*) hingegen, ist eher auf Adressaten außerhalb der Systemgrenzen ausgerichtet. Sie soll *Verantwortlichkeit* gegenüber Außenstehenden erzeugen, in dem sie Entscheidungsgrundlagen zur Verfügung stellt oder zur Systemlegitimation beiträgt. Neben den beiden Funktionen der Verbesserung und der Verantwortlichkeit, kann eine Evaluation grundsätzlich zwei weitere Funktionen wahrnehmen. Einmal können Erkenntnisse aus Evaluationen zur *Wissenserweiterung* beitragen. Zum zweiten können Evaluationen auch mit *strategischen* Absichten eingesetzt und so auch instrumentalisiert werden. Die Instrumentalisierung ist jedoch nicht nur hier möglich, sondern auch im Rahmen der anderen drei genannten Funktionen.

2.3 Methodenpluralismus

Die Evaluation zeichnet sich auch hinsichtlich der zum Einsatz gelangenden methodischen Ansätze durch eine große Vielfalt aus. Während sie zwar früher einen eher engen methodischen Zugang verfolgte, ist heute eine recht weitgehende methodische wie erkenntnistheoretische Offenheit festzustellen. Dies gilt sowohl auf der Ebene der epistemologischen Grundannahmen, der Untersuchungsdesigns (Klöti/Widmer 1997) wie auch für die Methodik im engeren Sinne, also die Verfahren der Datenerhebung und der Datenauswertung (Widmer/Binder 1997).

Die unterschiedlichen methodischen Ansätze kennen jeweils ihre spezifischen Vorgehensweisen, Regeln und auch Qualitätskriterien. So folgt ein traditioneller Ansatz, der dem experimentellen Paradigma verbunden ist und eine quantitative Methodik einsetzt, anderen Regeln als ein konstruktivistischer Ansatz, der ein qualitatives Instrumentarium verwendet. Begriffe wie Objektivität, Validität und Reliabilität, geprägt durch ein klassisches Wissenschaftsverständnis, werden in alternativen Ansätzen anders interpretiert. Dadurch wird natürlich die Aufgabe erschwert, über die Ansätze hinweg angemessene Qualitätskriterien zu formulieren.

2.4 Distanz und Umfang einer Evaluation

Die vier Funktionen der Evaluation (Verantwortlichkeit, Verbesserung, Wissenserweiterung und Strategie) haben auch einen Zusammenhang zur Distanz zwischen Evaluation und Evaluandum. Die Evaluation kann, im Falle einer formativen, internen Selbstevaluation, weitgehend Bestandteil des Evaluandums sein. Aber auch wenn es sich um eine Fremdevaluation handelt, sind maßgebliche Differenzen in der Distanz Evaluation – Evaluandum festzustellen. In jenen Fällen, in der die Distanz sehr klein ist, geht die Evaluation fließend in Entwicklung und Beratung über (Organisationsberatung, Programmentwicklung, etc.). Am anderen Ende des Spektrums, also bei Evaluationen, die eine sehr große Distanz zwischen Evaluandum und Evaluation aufweisen, verschwinden die Grenzen zur wissenschaftlichen Forschung oder je nachdem auch zur Kontrolle und Aufsicht. Also auch bezüglich der Distanz einer Evaluation ist ein breites Spektrum an möglichen Ausrichtungen festzustellen. Dies ist in der Diskussion um die Evaluationsqualität angemessen zu berücksichtigen.

Im Zusammenhang mit der Frage nach Qualität einer Evaluation bildet auch ihr Umfang, also die zeitlichen, finanziellen, personellen, materiellen und rechtlichen Ressourcen, welche einer Evaluation zur Verfügung stehen, einen zentralen Diskussionspunkt. Der Umfang von Evaluationen variiert in erheblichem Ausmaß; wobei sich sehr kleine von sehr großen Evaluationen schnell einmal um den Faktor Hundert oder mehr unterscheiden. Unter dieser Voraussetzung überrascht es nicht, daß der Evaluationsumfang oft als ausschlaggebendes Kriterium hinsichtlich der Qualität einer Evaluation dargestellt wird. Meines Erachtens spielt das Kriterium der Größe für die Qualität sicherlich eine Rolle (vgl. dazu die Ausführungen zu Kurzevaluationen in Kapitel 6.2). Ich bin jedoch ebenso überzeugt der Auffassung, daß hierfür auch die bisher genannten Unterschiede zu beachten sind. Weiter spielt für die Bewertung der Qualität einer Evaluation auch eine maßgebliche Rolle, welche Ziele im Rahmen der Evaluation selbst gesetzt (vgl. unten, Kapitel 4) und welche Erwartungen an eine Evaluation gerichtet werden.

3. Erwartungen an eine Evaluation

3.1 Interaktionstheoretisches Modell

Die Evaluation, verstanden als *wissenschaftliche Dienstleistung,* wird mit unterschiedlichen Erwartungen verschiedener Beteiligter & Betroffener konfrontiert. Der Zugang zu diesen Anforderungen soll nachfolgend mittels eines interaktionstheoretischen Modells geleistet werden.

Ausgangspunkt meiner Überlegungen bildet der Umstand, daß die *Evaluation als Prozeß sozialer Interaktion* aufzufassen ist. Die Evaluatorin[2] sieht sich in diesem Prozeß mit einer Vielzahl verschiedener Interaktionen konfrontiert, die ihre Position als äußerst problematisch erscheinen läßt. Sie steht vor der Herausforderung, von verschiedenen Seiten an sie herangetragenen, oft widersprüchlichen Ansprüchen zu genügen. Zur Analyse derartiger Spannungsverhältnisse liegen bereits eine Vielzahl von theoretischen Überlegungen vor, die sich mit dem Verhältnis zwischen Wissenschaft (Theorie) und Politik (Praxis) beschäftigen (vgl. etwa Palumbo/Hallett 1993; Beck/Bonss 1989; Campbell 1984; Habermas/Luhmann 1971; Habermas 1968). Nachstehende Abbildung zeigt das hier vorgeschlagene, nicht an Personen, sondern an funktionalen Rollen orientierte interaktionstheoretische Modell:

Schaubild 1: Interaktionstheoretisches Modell

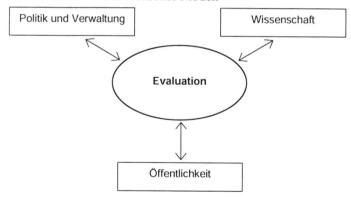

Der Kontext einer Evaluation kann – auf das Wesentliche beschränkt – durch drei verschiedene Akteure beschrieben werden, nämlich (1) Politik und Verwaltung, (2) Wissenschaft und (3) Öffentlichkeit. In diesem Modell werden die

---

2   Ich verwende hier und nachfolgend für die evaluierende Person die weibliche Geschlechtsform, während dem für alle anderen Personen, die männliche Form steht. Selbstverständlich sind in jedem Fall Personen beider Geschlechter gemeint.

für eine demokratisch-verantwortlich (MacDonald 1993) ausgestaltete Evaluation zentralen Interaktionsbeziehungen dargestellt. Diese Beziehungen, die je spezifisch strukturiert sind, sollen nachfolgend kurz charakterisiert werden.

3.2 Interaktion Politik/Verwaltung – Evaluation

Politik und Verwaltung sind zumeist in verschiedenen Rollen am Evaluationsprozeß beteiligt. Sie sind häufig Auftraggeber einer Evaluation, aber oft auch wichtige Informationsquelle und zumeist auch ihr primärer Adressat. Nicht zuletzt sind Politik/Verwaltung auch die intendierten Nutzer einer Evaluation. Im Gegensatz zu anderen hier zu diskutierenden Beziehungen ist das Verhältnis zwischen Politik/Verwaltung und Evaluatorin zumeist vertraglich geregelt. Die Ansprüche, die seitens Politik/Verwaltung an die Evaluation gerichtet werden, lassen sich mit den folgenden Stichworten umschreiben: Nützlichkeit, Zeitgerechtigkeit, politische Opportunität, Anschlußfähigkeit, Sparsamkeit, Praktikabilität und Korrektheit.

Die Evaluatorin andererseits hat ein ausgewiesenes Interesse, die Erwartungen des Auftraggebers auch zu erfüllen. Je nach Organisationsform ist die Evaluatorin finanziell mehr oder weniger stark vom Auftraggeber abhängig. Sie kann zudem, sofern sie den Ansprüchen des Auftraggebers gerecht wird, darauf spekulieren, in Zukunft weitere Aufträge zu erhalten.

Das Verhältnis zwischen Politik/Verwaltung und Evaluation ist somit schwergewichtig ökonomisch und juristisch geprägt.

3.3 Interaktion Wissenschaft – Evaluation

Das Verhältnis von Wissenschaft und Evaluation hat ebenso seine spezifische Struktur. Die Wissenschaft profitiert von der Evaluation vor allem bezüglich zweier Aspekte. Die Evaluation ist in der Lage:

- –Erstens, die gesamtgesellschaftliche Legitimation des Wissenschaftssystems zu unterstützen. Dies geschieht insbesondere dann, wenn sich die Evaluation als praxisrelevant erweist.
- –Zweitens, für wissenschaftliche Erkenntnisse wie Theorien und Methoden empirische Evidenz zu produzieren. Gleichzeitig kann die Evaluation die Fachdisziplinen auch mit zusätzlichem inhaltlichem Wissen alimentieren (vgl. oben, Kapitel 2.2 und 2.4; Funktion der Wissenserweiterung).

Die Evaluation wiederum ist auf die Wissenschaft als Lieferantin wissenschaftlicher Wissensbeständen angewiesen. Die Evaluation kann nur mit Wissenschaft bestehen, da letztere zu ihrer gesellschaftlichen Reputation beiträgt. Ohne die „reine" Wissenschaft würde die Evaluation ihre Daseinsberechtigung als wissenschaftliche Dienstleistung verlieren.

Das Verhältnis zwischen Wissenschaft und Evaluation ist damit hauptsächlich durch den Austausch von Wissen und Reputation geprägt.

3.4 Interaktion Öffentlichkeit – Evaluation

Das Verhältnis zwischen Öffentlichkeit (im Sinne Habermas' als institutionelle Ordnung der Lebenswelt (1981, II: 472)) und Evaluation weist – im Gegensatz zu den oben beschriebenen – eine deutlich andere Qualität auf. Während sich die anderen beiden Interaktionen dadurch auszeichnen, daß eine direkte gegenseitige Abhängigkeit besteht, ist dies hier kaum der Fall. Die Evaluatorin ist damit vordergründig nicht auf eine Interaktion mit der Öffentlichkeit angewiesen. Ihr bietet es sich deshalb geradezu an, auf Interaktionen mit der Öffentlichkeit gänzlich zu verzichten und sich primär in den für sie „lebensnotwendigen" Beziehungen mit Politik und Wissenschaft zu engagieren, was zur Vernachlässigung der Bedürfnisse der Öffentlichkeit führt. Die Evaluation ließe sich so im Dienste von Politik/Verwaltung und/ oder Wissenschaft instrumentalisieren.

Ein demokratisch verantwortungsvoller Evaluationsprozeß erfordert jedoch nicht nur, daß der resultierende Schlußbericht zuhanden der Öffentlichkeit publik gemacht wird. Der Evaluationsprozeß sollte von Beginn weg die Anliegen der Beteiligten & Betroffenen berücksichtigen. Erforderlich ist die Aufnahme eines kommunikativen Diskurses als Antipode zur ‚Entkoppelung von System und Lebenswelt' zur Steigerung der Freiheit des Individuums (in Anlehnung an Habermas 1981, II: 229-293). Dieser Anspruch ist sehr hochgesteckt und in der Praxis wohl kaum jemals vollumfänglich einzulösen. Klaus von Beyme (1991: 269) dazu: „Der Sektor ‚Öffentlichkeit' als Teil der Lebenswelt ist schwerlich je so kommunikativ gewesen, wie im Modell vorgesehen."

Das Verhältnis zwischen Öffentlichkeit und Evaluation ist also primär ethisch-moralisch geprägt und zumindest latent gefährdet.

3.5 Zusammenfassung

Zusammenfassend läßt sich festhalten, daß an die Evaluation vielfältige Erwartungen gerichtet werden, die sich zudem oft gegenseitig konkurrieren. Weiter besteht die Gefahr, daß sich die Evaluation durch spezifische Anforderungen in unausgewogener Weise vereinnahmen läßt. Sich in diesem Spannungsfeld zu bewegen, stellt für alle an der Evaluation Beteiligten hohe Anforderungen. Es läßt sich zudem schließen, daß die Qualität einer Evaluation nicht eindimensional erfaßt werden kann, sondern daß dazu eine Vielzahl unterschiedlicher Aspekte zu berücksichtigen sind und eine eindimensionale Betrachtungsweise zu kurz greifen würde.

4. Referenzebenen der Evaluationsqualität

Die nun dargelegten Ansprüche an die Evaluation lassen sich – inspiriert durch die Vorgehensweise bei der historischen Quellenkritik – nach zwei verschiedenen Bewertungsgrundlagen differenzieren, nämlich nach den inneren und den äußeren Bewertungsgrundlagen. Diese Bewertungsgrundlagen können dazu eingesetzt werden, die Qualität einer Evaluation einzuschätzen. Folgende Tabelle zeigt die jeweiligen Referenzebenen mit den dazugehörigen Bewertungsgrundlagen:

Tabelle 2: Übersicht über die Referenzebenen

Ebene	Gegenstand	Innere Bewertungsgrundlagen	Äussere Bewertungsgrundlagen
Konstruktion erster Ordnung	Programm, Projekt, Massnahme etc.	Ziele des Programms, des Projektes etc.	gesamtgesellschaftliche Bedeutung des Programms
Konstruktion zweiter Ordnung	Evaluation	Ziele der Evaluation	Evaluationstheorie und Evaluationsmethodologie
Konstruktion dritter Ordnung	Meta-Evaluation	Ziele der Meta-Evaluation	....

Die erste Spalte zeigte die Ebene des Gegenstandes, der in der zweiten Spalte aufgeführt ist. Die Evaluatorin kann ein Programm (oder einen anderen Evaluationsgegenstand; Konstruktion erster Ordnung) einerseits auf der Grundlage der Programmziele (innere Bewertungsgrundlage) und andererseits aufgrund der gesamtgesellschaftlichen Bedeutung des Programms (äußere Bewertungsgrundlage) bewerten. Analog läßt sich dies nun auch auf eine Evaluation als Konstruktion zweiter Ordnung beziehen. Die relevanten Bewertungsgrundlagen wären demzufolge erstens die Ziele der Evaluation (innere Bewertungsgrundlage) und zweitens die allgemeine Evaluationstheorie und Evaluationsmethodologie (äußere Bewertungsgrundlage). Wird eine Bewertung (oder Evaluation) einer Evaluation vorgenommen, spricht man auch von einer Meta-Evaluation (vgl. ausführlicher unten, Kapitel 6.2). Selbstverständlich ließe sich dies auf der Ebene der Konstruktion dritter und weiterer Ordnungen weiterführen. Wir folgen hier aber der Auffassung von Michael Scriven, der zu Frage, wer die Meta-Evaluatorin evaluiert, folgendes festhält: „No infinite regress is generated because investigation shows it usually doesn't pay after the first metalevel on most projects and after the second on any" (Scriven 1991: 230).

Hier von Bedeutung ist der Umstand, daß wir, wollen wir die Qualität einer Evaluation untersuchen, grundsätzlich zwei mögliche Bewertungsgrundlagen kennen. Währenddem sich über die Ziele der Evaluation kaum studienübergreifende Aussagen machen lassen, da diese fallspezifisch ausgehandelt werden, konzentrieren wir uns im folgenden auf die äußeren Bewertungsgrundlagen einer Evaluation, also die Evaluationstheorie und Evaluationsmethodologie.

5. Standards der Evaluation

5.1 Entstehung der Standards

Im Zuge der Professionalisierung[3] der Evaluation sind Ende der Siebziger Jahre in den USA verschiedene Initiativen ergriffen worden, um mittels eines Sets von Kriterien die vielfältigen Qualitätsdimensionen von Evaluationen zu erfassen. Diese Kriterien sollten in der Lage sein, die Qualität einer Evaluation hinsichtlich einer allgemeinen Evaluationstheorie und Evaluationsmethodologie – also im Hinblick auf die oben eingeführten äußeren Bewertungsgrundlagen – einzuschätzen. Die mehr oder weniger parallel verlaufenden Bemühungen, ein solches Kriterienset zu formulieren, bezogen sich einerseits auf verschiedene Gegenstandsbereiche der Evaluation und andererseits auf unterschiedliche erkenntnistheoretische Grundprämissen der jeweiligen Urheber. Neben verschiedenen Kriteriensets, die durch eine beschränkte erkenntnistheoretische Ausrichtung geprägt waren, publizierte das 'Joint Committee on Standards for Educational Evaluation' im Jahre 1981 die 'Standards for Evaluation of Educational Programs, Projects and Materials' (Joint Committee 1981), die hinsichtlich ihrer methodologischen Ausrichtung einen vergleichsweise offenen Ansatz verfolgten. In den frühen Achtziger Jahren wurde in der US-amerikanischen Evaluationsgemeinde die Frage, ob auch qualitative Methoden und nicht dem klassischen, (quasi-)experimentell-orientierten Evaluationsverständnis verbundenen Ansätze zulässig seien, heftig und lange Zeit kontrovers diskutiert. Durch ihre erkenntnistheoretische wie methodische Offenheit haben die erwähnten „Standards" des „Joint Committee" die spätere Entwicklung vorweggenommen, die mit sich brachte, daß heute die Daseinsberechtigung alternativer Zugangsweisen nicht (oder kaum) mehr in Frage gestellt wird. Die „Standards" richten sich in erster Linie an Personen, die mit Evaluationen im Bereich von Bildung und Erziehung befaßt waren. Auch die im genannten „Joint Committee" vertretenen Organisationen stammen schwergewichtig aus diesen Bereichen.

Diese „Standards" haben sich in der amerikanischen Evaluationspraxis sehr weit verbreitet, und zwar immer mehr auch in Themenfeldern, die weit über das ursprünglich beabsichtigte Anwendungsfeld der Bildung und Erziehung hinausreichten. Im Jahre 1994 präsentierte das inzwischen auch um nicht nur im Bildungsbereich tätige Organisationen ergänzte „Joint Committee" (Widmer/Beywl 2000: 250) eine überarbeitete Fassung der „Standards", nun unter dem Titel: „The Program Evaluation Standards" (Joint Committee 1994; siehe auch http://www.wmich.edu/evalctr/ic/).

---

3   Zum Professionalisierungsprozeß vgl. das Fünfstufenmodell von Harold Wilensky (1964) sowie – bezogen auf die Evaluation – die Diskussion in Altschuld (1999a: 483-486) sowie die dort angegebene Literatur.

Der Bezug zu Bildung und Erziehung wurde lediglich noch im Untertitel der Publikation erwähnt („How to Assess Evaluations of Educational Programs"). Der Wandel dieser Titelformulierung vollzog (meines Erachtens etwas zögerlich) die in der Anwendung bereits etablierte Praxisänderung, die „Standards" vermehrt auch außerhalb von Bildung und Erziehung einzusetzen.

Im deutschen Sprachraum blieben die „Standards" des „Joint Committee" während langer Zeit wenig beachtet (für eine frühe Ausnahme, vgl. Beywl 1988: 113-23), auch wenn die Evaluation an und für sich, in den Achtziger Jahren bereits einen kleineren Entwicklungsschub erlebte. Aber erst Mitte der Neunziger Jahre begannen sich die „Standards" auch immer mehr im deutschsprachigen Raum zu verbreiten (Widmer 1996a-h; Widmer/Rothmayr/Serdült 1996). Um den Zugang der deutschsprachigen Evaluation zu den „Standards" zu fördern, erschien im Jahre 1999 eine deutsche Übersetzung (Joint Committee 1999). Inzwischen werden die „Standards" auch im deutschsprachigen Raum vermehrt rezipiert (siehe die Hinweise in Kapitel 6), was sich etwa daran zeigt, daß die deutsche Übersetzung der „Standards" bereits nach kurzer Zeit in zweiter Auflage erschienen ist (Joint Committee 2000; siehe auch http://www.uni-koeln.de/ew-fak/WISO/q_kurz.htm).

5.2 Struktur und Inhalt der Standards

Die „Standards" basieren auf der Grundannahme, daß eine Evaluation gleichzeitig nützlich, durchführbar, korrekt und genau sein muß, um die Anforderungen zu erfüllen, die an sie gestellt werden (vgl. oben, Kapitel 3). Eine gute Evaluation soll also die vier Eigenschaften Nützlichkeit, Durchführbarkeit, Korrektheit und Genauigkeit aufweisen. Um diese vier Konzepte faßbarer zu machen, hat das Joint Committee insgesamt dreißig Einzelstandards formuliert, welche den vier Konzepten zugeordnet sind. Im einzelnen lauten die Standards wie folgt (Joint Committee 2000):

N *Nützlichkeit*
Die Nützlichkeitsstandards sollen sicherstellen, daß sich eine Evaluation an den Informationsbedürfnissen der vorgesehenen Evaluationsnutzer ausrichtet.

N1 Ermittlung der Beteiligten & Betroffenen
Die an einer Evaluation beteiligten oder von ihr betroffenen Personen sollten identifiziert werden, damit deren Interessen und Bedürfnisse berücksichtigt werden können.

N2 Glaubwürdigkeit der Evaluatorin
Wer Evaluationen durchführt, sollte sowohl vertrauenswürdig als auch kompetent sein, damit bei den Evaluationsergebnissen ein Höchstmaß an Glaubwürdigkeit und Akzeptanz erreicht wird.

N3 Umfang und Auswahl der Informationen
Die gewonnenen Informationen sollten von einem Umfang und einer Auswahl sein, welche die Behandlung sachdienlicher Fragen zum Programm ermöglichen und gleichzeitig auf die Interessen und Bedürfnisse des Auftraggebers und anderer Beteiligter & Betroffener eingehen.

N4 Feststellung von Werten
Die Perspektiven, Verfahren und Gedankengänge, auf denen die Interpretationen der Ergebnisse beruhen, sollten sorgfältig beschrieben werden, damit die Grundlagen der Werturteile klar ersichtlich sind.

N5 Klarheit des Berichts
Evaluationsberichte sollten das evaluierte Programm einschließlich seines Kontextes ebenso beschreiben wie die Ziele, die Verfahren und Befunde der Evaluation, damit die wesentlichen Informationen zur Verfügung stehen und leicht verstanden werden können.

N6 Rechtzeitigkeit und Verbreitung des Berichts
Wichtige Zwischenergebnisse und Schlußberichte sollten den vorgesehenen Nutzern so zur Kenntnis gebracht werden, daß diese sie rechtzeitig verwenden können.

N7 Wirkung der Evaluation
Evaluationen sollten so geplant, durchgeführt und dargestellt werden, daß die Beteiligten & Betroffenen dazu ermuntert werden, dem Evaluationsprozeß zu folgen, damit die Wahrscheinlichkeit steigt, daß die Evaluation genutzt wird.

D Durchführbarkeit
Die Durchführbarkeitsstandards sollen sicherstellen, daß eine Evaluation realistisch, gut durchdacht, diplomatisch und kostenbewußt ausgeführt wird.

D1 Praktische Verfahren
Die Evaluationsverfahren sollten praktisch sein, so daß Störungen minimiert und die benötigten Informationen beschafft werden können.

D2 Politische Tragfähigkeit
Evaluationen sollten mit Voraussicht auf die unterschiedlichen Positionen der verschiedenen Interessengruppen geplant und durchgeführt werden, um deren Kooperation zu erreichen und um mögliche Versuche irgend einer dieser Gruppen zu vermeiden, die Evaluationsaktivitäten einzuschränken oder die Ergebnisse zu verzerren respektive zu mißbrauchen.

D3 Kostenwirksamkeit
Die Evaluation sollte effizient sein und Informationen mit einem Wert hervorbringen, der die eingesetzten Mittel rechtfertigt.

K Korrektheit

Die Korrektheitsstandards sollen sicherstellen, daß eine Evaluation rechtlich und ethisch korrekt durchgeführt wird und dem Wohlergehen der in die Evaluation einbezogenen und auch der durch die Ergebnisse betroffenen Personen gebührende Aufmerksamkeit widmet.

K1 Unterstützung der Dienstleistungsorientierung
Die Evaluation sollte so geplant werden, daß Organisationen dabei unterstützt werden, die Interessen und Bedürfnisse des ganzen Zielgruppenspektrums zu berücksichtigen und ihre Tätigkeiten danach auszurichten.

K2 Formale Vereinbarungen
Die Pflichten der Vertragsparteien einer Evaluation (was, wie, von wem, wann getan werden soll) sollten schriftlich festgehalten werden, damit die Parteien verpflichtet sind, alle Bedingungen dieser Vereinbarung zu erfüllen oder aber diese erneut zum Gegenstand von formalen Verhandlungen zu machen.

K3 Schutz individueller Menschenrechte
Evaluationen sollten so geplant und durchgeführt werden, daß die Rechte und das Wohlergehen der Menschen respektiert und geschützt sind.

K4 Menschlich gestaltete Interaktion
Evaluatorinnen sollten in ihren Kontakten mit Anderen die Würde und den Wert der Menschen respektieren, damit diese nicht gefährdet oder geschädigt werden.

K5 Vollständige und faire Einschätzung
Evaluationen sollten in der Überprüfung und in der Präsentation der Stärken und Schwächen des evaluierten Programms vollständig und fair sein, so daß die Stärken weiter ausgebaut und die Problemfelder angesprochen werden können.

K6 Offenlegung der Ergebnisse
Die Vertragsparteien einer Evaluation sollten sicherstellen, daß die Evaluationsergebnisse – einschließlich ihrer relevanten Beschränkungen – den durch die Evaluation betroffenen Personen ebenso wie all jenen, die einen ausgewiesenen Anspruch auf die Evaluationsergebnisse haben, zugänglich gemacht werden.

K7 Deklaration von Interessenkonflikten
Interessenkonflikte sollten offen und aufrichtig behandelt werden, damit sie die Evaluationsverfahren und -ergebnisse nicht beeinträchtigen.

K8 Finanzielle Verantwortlichkeit
Die Zuweisung und Ausgabe von Ressourcen durch die Evaluatorin sollte durch eine sorgfältige Rechnungsführung nachgewiesen werden und auch anderweitig klug sowie ethisch verantwortlich erfolgen, damit die Ausgaben verantwortungsbewußt und angemessen sind.

Genauigkeit
Die Genauigkeitsstandards sollen sicherstellen, daß eine Evaluation über die Güte und/oder die Verwendbarkeit des evaluierten Programms fachlich angemessene Informationen hervorbringt und vermittelt.

G1 Programmdokumentation
Das zu evaluierende Programm sollte klar und genau beschrieben und dokumentiert werden, so daß es eindeutig identifiziert werden kann.

G2 Kontextanalyse
Der Kontext, in dem das Programm angesiedelt ist, sollte ausreichend detailliert untersucht werden, damit mögliche Beeinflussungen des Programms identifiziert werden können.

G3 Beschreibung von Zielen und Vorgehen
Die Zwecksetzungen und das Vorgehen der Evaluation sollten ausreichend genau dokumentiert und beschrieben werden, so daß sie identifiziert und eingeschätzt werden können.

G4 Verläßliche Informationsquellen
Die in einer Programmevaluation genutzten Informationsquellen sollten hinreichend genau beschrieben sein, damit die Angemessenheit der Informationen eingeschätzt werden kann.

G5 Valide Informationen
Die Verfahren zur Informationsgewinnung sollten so gewählt oder entwickelt und dann umgesetzt werden, daß die Gültigkeit der gewonnenen Interpretationen für den gegebenen Zweck sichergestellt ist.

G6 Reliable Informationen
Die Verfahren zur Informationsgewinnung sollten so gewählt oder entwickelt und dann umgesetzt werden, daß die Zuverlässigkeit der gewonnen Interpretationen für den gegebenen Zweck sichergestellt ist.

G7 Systematische Informationsüberprüfung
Die in einer Evaluation gesammelten, aufbereiteten und präsentierten Informationen sollten systematisch überprüft und alle gefundenen Fehler sollten korrigiert werden.

G8 Analyse quantitativer Informationen
Quantitative Informationen einer Evaluation sollten angemessen und systematisch analysiert werden, damit die Fragestellungen der Evaluation effektiv beantwortet werden.

G9 Analyse qualitativer Informationen
Qualitative Informationen einer Evaluation sollten angemessen und systematisch analysiert werden, damit die Fragestellungen der Evaluation effektiv beantwortet werden.

G10 Begründete Schlußfolgerungen
Die in einer Evaluation gezogenen Folgerungen sollten ausdrücklich begründet werden, damit die Beteiligten & Betroffenen diese einschätzen können.

G11 Unparteiische Berichterstattung
Die Verfahren der Berichterstattung sollten über Vorkehrungen gegen Verzerrungen durch persönliche Gefühle und Vorlieben irgendeiner Evaluationspartei geschützt werden, so daß Evaluationsberichte die Ergebnisse fair wiedergeben.

G12 Meta-Evaluation
Die Evaluation selbst sollte formativ und summativ in bezug auf die vorliegenden oder andere wichtige Standards evaluiert werden, so daß die Durchführung entsprechend angeleitet werden kann und damit die Beteiligten & Betroffenen bei Abschluß einer Evaluation deren Stärken und Schwächen gründlich überprüfen können.

In der Buchpublikation (Joint Committee 2000) sind diese „Standards" von verschiedenen Ausführungen begleitet, die ihren Einsatz in der Praxis erleichtern. So wird jeder einzelne Standard ergänzt um eine beschreibende Übersicht, um Richtlinien, um Hinweise auf häufig im Zusammenhang mit dem „Standard" begangene Fehler und um ein bis zwei Anschauungsbeispiele, die zuerst dargestellt und dann analysiert werden.

Wie der obigen Darstellung der „Standards" entnommen werden kann, ist die Zahl der Einzelstandards in den vier Gruppen unterschiedlich. Zur Durchführbarkeit werden lediglich drei, zur Genauigkeit insgesamt zwölf Standards aufgeführt. Dies ist jedoch keineswegs in dem Sinne zu verstehen, daß das „Joint Committee" damit eine Gewichtung unter den vier Gruppen beabsichtigt. Vielmehr verzichten die Autoren auf eine Gewichtung der Standardgruppen ebenso wie der Einzelstandards. Der Verzicht wird damit begründet, daß die Bedeutung eines Standards nur im konkreten Einzelfall festgelegt werden kann und deshalb eine generell Gültigkeit beanspruchende Gewichtung nicht angemessen wäre.

Die Frage der Gewichtung ist besonders deshalb von Bedeutung, weil die „Standards" teilweise *konkurrierende Ansprüche* formulieren und so die Evaluatorin in der Praxis recht häufig mit der Frage konfrontiert ist, welche Standards gegenüber anderen Vorrang genießen sollten. Beispielsweise kann im konkreten Fall ein Widerspruch der durch die Standards K3 ,Schutz individueller Menschenrechte' und K6 ,Offenlegung der Ergebnisse' formulierten Ansprüche entstehen, nämlich etwa dann, wenn die Publikation der Evaluationsresultate die Respektierung individueller Rechte gefährden kann. Die fehlende innere Konsistenz der „Standards" ist aber keineswegs als Schwäche einzuschätzen, wird dadurch doch gerade das oben (Kapitel 3) beschriebene Spannungsfeld abgebildet, in dem sich die Evaluation zu bewegen hat.

Die „Standards" formulieren *Maximalansprüche*. Sie sind keine Minimalstandards, die festlegen, was absolute Pflicht ist, sondern formulieren, was eine gute Evaluation anstreben sollte. In der Praxis wird es auch kaum je möglich sein, alle dreißig Einzelstandards in vollem Umfang zu erfüllen. Trotzdem sollten alle Beteiligten – nicht nur die Evaluatorin – anstreben, die „Standards" so weit wie möglich zu berücksichtigen.

Der Evaluation steht mit den „Standards" ein Instrument zur Verfügung, das die Evaluationsqualität in präziser Form umschreibt und der Vielfalt der Evaluation gebührend Rechnung trägt.

6. Anwendung der Standards in der Evaluationspraxis

6.1 Vorbemerkungen

Die Anwendungsmöglichkeiten der „Standards" in der Evaluationspraxis sind vielfältig. Im folgenden soll der Versuch unternommen werden, Einblick in die verschiedene Anwendungsformen zu geben und diese anhand von Beispiele zu konkretisieren.

Zuvor ist aber die Frage der generellen Anwendbarkeit der „Standards" zu klären, präziser gefaßt also auf die Frage einzugehen, ob die aus den USA stammenden und für die Bereiche Bildung und Erziehung entwickelten „Standards" in anderen Themenfeldern und im deutschsprachigen Umfeld einsetzbar sind. Da diese Frage schon an anderer Stelle behandelt wurde (Widmer/Beywl 2000), kann ich mich hier auf eine knappe Darstellung beschränken. Aufgrund einer ausführlichen Argumentation wird dort im Grundsatz folgendes festgestellt: „Zusammenfassend empfehlen wir aufgrund der bisherigen Erfahrungen die Anwendung der „Standards" auf Evaluationen in Deutschland, Österreich und der Schweiz, und zwar auch dann, wenn Evaluationen außerhalb des Bereiches Bildung und Erziehung durchgeführt werden" (Widmer/Beywl 2000: 257). Die Diskussion zeigt aber auch deutlich, daß die „Standards" nicht unreflektiert übernommen werden sollten, sondern daß es angezeigt ist, die Angemessenheit der „Standards" zu überprüfen und je nach Ergebnis gewisse Anpassungen vorzunehmen. Diese Anpassungsleistung bewegt sich jedoch gemäß dem bisherigen Erfahrungsstand in einem eng beschränkten Rahmen. Grundlegende Änderungen sind kaum zu erwarten.

6.2 Meta-Evaluation

Der Begriff der Meta-Evaluation, der bereits oben kurz angesprochen wurde (siehe Kapitel 4; vgl. dazu auch den Standard G12 'Meta-Evaluation'), bedarf einer etwas eingehenderen Erläuterung. Insbesondere ist auf die Differenzen zu anderen Ansätzen zu verweisen, die ebenfalls auf bereits bestehende Evaluationsstudien rekurrieren.

Neben der *Meta-Evaluation* sind dies einerseits die *Evaluationssynthese* und andererseits die *Meta-Analyse* (vgl. dazu und zum folgenden Tabelle 3). Diese beiden Instrumente sind auf die inhaltlichen Ergebnisse der zugrundeliegenden Evaluationsstudien ausgerichtet. Dies unterscheidet sie grundlegend von der Meta-Evaluation, die eine Bewertung einer oder mehrerer Evaluationen vornimmt. Für die beiden substantiell-orientierten Ansätze werden als Untersuchungsbasis Evaluationsstudien benötigt, die zur der inhaltlich interessierenden Thematik Aussagen machen. Dabei ist der Fokus der Meta-Analyse, die quantitativ ausgerichtet ist, typischerweise deutlich enger als bei der Evaluationssynthese. Die Meta-Analyse benötigt zwingend eine ausreichende Zahl bestehender Evaluationsstudien, die zu einer spezifischen Fragestellung quantitative Aussagen machen. Auch beim qualitativen Ansatz der Evaluationssynthese ist eine thematische Bündelung der Ausgangsstudien erforderlich, wobei diese aber nicht so eng gefaßt sein muß.

Tabelle 3: Übersicht über Evaluationsinstrumente dritter Ordnung

Instrument	Umschreibung
Evaluationssynthese	Inhaltliche Synthese verschiedener Evaluationsstudien (zumeist qualitativ) (Globalevaluation/Querschnittsanalyse)
Meta-Analyse	Quantitative Integration der Ergebnisse verschiedener Evaluationsstudien ('research synthesis')
Meta-Evaluation	Evaluation von Evaluation(en): Systematische Bewertung der Qualität einer oder mehrerer Evaluationsstudien

Die Meta-Evaluation hingegen hat eine deutlich andere Zielsetzung. Sie verfolgt die Absicht, in einer systematischen Weise den Wert und die Güte einer Evaluation zu bestimmen, oder mit anderen Worten, die Qualität einer Evaluation einzuschätzen. Um eine solche Bewertung vornehmen zu können, werden Bewertungskriterien benötigt. Wie in Kapitel 4 ausgeführt, sind dafür einerseits die Evaluationsziele zu berücksichtigen (innere Bewertungsgrundlagen) und andererseits die Evaluationstheorie und Evaluationsmethodologie (äußere Bewertungsgrundlagen). Zur präziseren Fassung der äußeren Bewertungsgrundlagen lassen sich die Evaluationsstandards einsetzen.

Meta-Evaluationen lassen sich, wie eine Evaluation, in ganz unterschiedlicher Weise ausgestalten. Meta-Evaluationen können Selbst- oder Fremdevaluationen sein, sie können intern oder extern durchgeführt und formative oder summative Funktionen erfüllen.

Ein Beispiel für eine externe „Fremd-Meta-Evaluation" mit summativem Charakter bildet eine Studie, die im Auftrag des Schweizerischen Nationalfonds (SNF) in der ersten Hälfte der 90er-Jahre erarbeitet wurde (Widmer 1996a-h). Darin werden zehn schweizerische Evaluationsstudien in detaillierten qualitativen Fallstudien ex-post einer Bewertung unterzogen. Die Studie diente unter anderem dazu, die Qualität der schweizerischen Evaluationspraxis zu erfassen. Sie kommt zum Schluß, daß die untersuchten Evaluationen hinsichtlich Nützlichkeit, Durchführbarkeit und Korrektheit allgemein betrachtet eine hohe Qualität erreichen, daß hingegen bei der Genauigkeit noch Verbesserungsmöglichkeiten bestehen.

Eine weitere, ebenfalls vom SNF finanzierte, Studie ging mit einer analogen Vorgehensweise der Frage nach, ob Evaluationen mit geringem Umfang und kurzer Untersuchungsdauer (sogenannte Kurzevaluationen) gute Evaluationen sein können (Widmer/Rothmayr/Serdült 1996). Dabei wurden 15 Evaluationsstudien unterschiedlichen Umfangs im Hinblick auf ihre Qualität miteinander verglichen. Die Meta-Evaluation zeigt unter anderem, daß Kurzevaluationen unter bestimmten Bedingungen durchaus auch gute Evaluationen sein können, wobei die Risiken, daß sie in irgendeiner Form mißlingen, deutlich höher ausfallen, als dies bei umfangreicheren Evaluationsstudien der Fall ist.

6.3 Ratgeber für die Evaluationspraxis

Die „Standards" dienen jedoch nicht nur der Bewertung einer Evaluation, sondern sind primär darauf ausgerichtet, die Evaluatorin bei der Planung und Umsetzung eines Evaluationsprojektes zu unterstützen. In diesem beratenden und nicht regulativen Sinne können die „Standards" auch als Leitlinie in der Evaluationspraxis dienen. Damit sind sie in der Lage, einen Gestaltungsbeitrag an die Evaluationspraxis zu leisten. Dies gilt speziell für die jedem Einzelstandard beigefügten Richtlinien (Joint Committee 2000).

Seitens der Evaluationspraktiker (Evaluatorin, wie Auftraggeber und Adressaten) wird an den „Standards" häufig bemängelt, daß es schwierig sei, sich in den „Standards" zurechtzufinden. Dies wird zumeist mit der hohen Zahl an Einzelstandards in Verbindung gebracht. Mittels des in der Buchfassung enthaltenen funktionalen Inhaltsverzeichnisses läßt sich diese Schwierigkeit jedoch leicht überwinden. Die funktionale Übersicht ordnet nämlich jeweils den hauptsächlichen evaluativen Tätigkeiten ein bestimmtes Set von Einzelstandards zu, die für die spezifische Tätigkeit von besonders hoher Relevanz sind. Die funktionale Übersicht stellt das, die praktische Anwendung der „Standards" erleichternde, Orientierungswissen bereit. Nachstehende Tabelle stellt diese Angaben in der Form einer Funktion-Standard-Matrix zusammen.

Tabelle 4: Funktionale Übersicht (in Anlehnung an Joint Committee 2000: 13-6)

Standard / Funktion	N 1	N 2	N 3	N 4	N 5	N 6	N 7	D 1	D 2	D 3	K 1	K 2	K 3	K 4	K 5	K 6	K 7	K 8	G 1	G 2	G 3	G 4	G 5	G 6	G 7	G 8	G 9	G 10	G 11	G 12
Entscheid zur Evaluation																														
Definition des Problems																														
Evaluationsdesign																														
Informationssammlung																														
Informationsauswertung																														
Berichterstattung																														
Budget der Evaluation																														
Vertragliche Vereinbarung																														
Evaluationsmanagement																														
Evaluationspersonal																														

Diese Matrix erlaubt es, die jeweils besonders relevanten Einzelstandards zu eruieren und daraus Checklisten zu generieren, die dem Bedürfnis nach Übersichtlichkeit ausreichend Rechnung tragen. Dieser vereinfachende Checklisten-Ansatz hat sich auch in äußerst kleinen, von Laien durchgeführten Selbstevaluationsprojekten als ein äußerst praktisches und nützliches Hilfsinstrument erwiesen. Die Checklisten erlauben es den Evaluierenden, die Selbstreflexion zur eigenen Tätigkeit gezielt zu systematisieren.

Der Checklisten-Ansatz hat aber auch einen bedeutenden Nachteil, der an dieser Stelle nicht unerwähnt bleiben sollte. In den „Standards" wird ausdrücklich davor gewarnt, sich strikte auf die jeweils als relevant deklarierten Standards zu beschränken (Joint Committee 2000: 13). Man läuft nämlich so Gefahr, daß im konkreten Einzelfall fälschlicherweise durchaus relevante Einzelstandards unbeachtet bleiben. In Anbetracht der Vorteile ist der Checklisten-Ansatz aber trotzdem zu empfehlen. Um die genannte Gefahr zu minimieren, empfiehlt sich eine regelmäßige Überprüfung der Angemessenheit der eingesetzten Checklisten.

6.4 Qualitätssicherung

In der täglichen Evaluationspraxis zeigen sich immer wieder Qualitätsprobleme. Beteiligte & Betroffene vertreten nicht selten die Auffassung, daß eine bestimmte Evaluationsstudie qualitativ unbefriedigend ausgefallen sei. Auch wenn hinter derartigen Vermutungen oft ganz andere Motive stecken, ist es nicht von der Hand zu weisen, daß Evaluationen nicht immer den Anforderungen genügen. Ursachen für auffällige Qualitätsmängel im Evaluationsbereich sind unter anderem folgende:

–   Der Markt der Evaluation hat im deutschsprachigen Raum deutlich expandiert. Die Nachfrage nach dieser wissenschaftlichen Dienstleistung ist äußerst stark gestiegen. Das Angebot ist dieser Entwicklung zwar gefolgt, wobei aber nicht selten Evaluationsanbieter am Markt auftreten, denen die nötigen Grundlagen und Erfahrungen fehlen.

–   Im Gegensatz zu anderen, bereits ex-ante präzis zu umschreibenden Leistungen, sind durch soziale Interaktionen geprägte Dienstleistungen – wie Bildung, soziale Arbeit, Beratung und auch Evaluation – nicht leicht zu fassen. Dies erschwert es dem Auftraggeber, sich im Markt zu orientieren.

Die „Standards" erlauben es dem Auftraggeber[4], die Evaluation fachlich fundiert zu bewerten. Die Sicherung eines hohen Qualitätsstandards ist beson-

---

4   Ob die Evaluation intern oder extern ausgeführt, spielt hier keine Rolle. Auch bei internen Evaluationen existiert üblicherweise ein Auftraggeber, auch wenn die Evaluatorin in diesem Fall nicht in einem rechtlichen Auftragsverhältnis, sondern in einem Angestelltenverhältnis steht.

ders dort von großem Interesse, wo häufig Evaluationen in Auftrag gegeben werden oder eigentliche Evaluationsprogramme im Einsatz sind.

Die „Standards" können aber auch dazu verwendet werden, einen Konflikt zwischen Auftraggeber und Evaluatorin zu bewältigen. Der Autor des vorliegenden Beitrages hatte beispielsweise vor einiger Zeit eine Anfrage einer Organisation erhalten, ob er eine Evaluationsstudie im Hinblick auf ihre Qualität begutachten könne. Die Organisation war mit der Evaluation äußerst unzufrieden und erwog, der Evaluatorin das vereinbarte Honorar wegen Nicht-Erfüllens des Vertrages vorzuenthalten. Mittels der „Standards" begutachtete ich die Evaluation. Das resultierende Gutachten wies auf verschiedene, zum Teil schwerwiegende Mängel der Evaluation hin. Da sich die „Standards" aber nicht auf die Leistung der Evaluatorin beschränken, sondern die Evaluation als Ganzes betrachten, enthielt das Gutachten auch verschiedene Hinweise auf Versäumnisse des Auftraggebers bei der Auftragsvergabe und der Projektbegleitung. Unter diesen Umständen hat sich die Organisation nach Vorliegen des Gutachtens dazu entschlossen, das Honorar an die Evaluatorin auszuzahlen.

Die Motive zur Begutachtung einer Evaluationsstudie können aber auch ganz anders gelagert sein. So läßt etwa das schweizerisches Bundesamt für Gesundheit regelmäßig Evaluationsofferten sowie Zwischen- und Schlußberichte zu externen Evaluationen durch einen unabhängigen Sachverständigen begutachten. Dies erfolgt mit dem Ziel, eine möglichst fundierte Offertauswahl treffen respektive Qualitätsmängel in den Berichten erkennen zu können. Weiter wird natürlich damit auch die Absicht verfolgt, präventive Wirkungen zu erzielen. Auch in diesem Kontext haben sich die „Standards", die der Autor bei derartigen Begutachtungen regelmäßig einsetzt, als äußerst hilfreich erwiesen.

Die Eidgenössische Finanzkontrolle (EFK), traditionell im Revisionsbereich tätig, führt vermehrt sogenannte Wirtschaftlichkeitsprüfung durch. Um in diesem Bereich die Qualität der Abklärungen zu sichern und Hinweise auf Weiterbildungsbedürfnisse der Mitarbeitenden zu erhalten, prüft ein internes Gremium die durchgeführten Wirtschaftlichkeitsprüfungen. Dieses Gremium setzt dazu ein Set von Kriterien ein, die sich stark auf die „Standards" des Joint Committee beziehen.

Ein letztes Beispiel für den Einsatz der „Standards" zur Qualitätssicherungen bildet eine Meta-Evaluation zu drei externen Evaluationen von Reformprojekten im Rahmen der Verwaltungsreform wif! (Wirkungsorientierte Führung der Verwaltung des Kantons Zürich), die sich an den Prinzipien des „New Public Management" orientieren. Im Hinblick auf weitere, in Zukunft durchzuführende externe Evaluationen im selben Kontext wurde ich damit beauftragt, drei bereits durchgeführte respektive laufende Projektevaluationen anhand der „Standards" zu bewerten. Daraus wurden Empfehlungen für die zukünftige Durchführung von Evaluationen im Rahmen der Verwaltungsreform abgeleitet.

6.5 Didaktisches Hilfsmittel in Aus- und Weiterbildung

Im Rahmen von universitären Lehrveranstaltungen im Evaluationsbereich lassen sich die Evaluationsstandards als didaktisches Instrument einsetzen. Die „Standards" eignen sich dazu in idealer Weise. Als wertvoll erwiesen sich in diesem Zusammenhang die in der Buchfassung (Joint Committee 2000) enthaltenen, ergänzenden Materialien, besonders auch die zu jedem Standard vorliegenden Anschauungsbeispiele. Eine andere Möglichkeit, die „Standards" im Unterricht zu verwenden, besteht in Fallstudien, bei denen die Studierenden die Aufgabe erhalten, eine bestehende Evaluationsstudie im Lichte der „Standards" kritisch zu hinterfragen. Auch bereits bestehende Meta-Evaluationen (siehe Kapitel 6.2), in deren Rahmen die „Standards" eingesetzt wurden, eignen sich hervorragend als Anschauungsmaterial für die Lehre. Im projektorientierten Studium, dienen die „Standards" den Studierenden – ähnlich, wie dies oben (Kapitel 6.3) für die Evaluationspraxis geschildert wurde – als Ratgeber für die Projektarbeit. Die Studierenden erhalten in diesem Rahmen jeweils projektphasenspezifische Aufträge zur Bewertung der eigenen Projektarbeit anhand der „Standards".

Aber auch in der Weiterbildung haben sich die „Standards" als äußerst hilfreich erwiesen. Teilnehmende, die eine sozialwissenschaftliche Grundausbildung absolviert haben, jedoch über kein evaluationsspezifisches „know how" verfügen, sind anhand der „Standards" in der Lage, die Spezifika der Evaluation in Relation zu den Sozialwissenschaften zu erkennen. Aber auch für Personen, die über keine einschlägigen Vorkenntnisse verfügen, aber Selbstevaluationen durchführen werden, erweisen sich die „Standards" als hilfreich. In diesem Kontext ist vor allem der oben geschilderte Checklisten-Ansatz auf großes Interesse gestoßen (siehe Kapitel 6.3).

6.6 Adaption durch Fachgesellschaften

Die „American Evaluation Association" (AEA), weltweit die größte Evaluationsvereinigung, setzt die „Program Evaluation Standards" als Ergänzung zu den von der Gesellschaft selbst erarbeiteten „Guiding Principles for Evaluators" ein (AEA 1995). Auch die „Australasian Evaluation Society" (AES) und weitere Fachgesellschaften verwenden die „Standards" des „Joint Committee". (vgl. dazu Beywl/Widmer 2000).

Im Rahmen ihrer Bemühungen um eine Professionalisierung der Evaluation in der Schweiz, hat die Schweizerische Evaluationsgesellschaft (SE-VAL), eine Vereinigung von privaten und universitären Evaluatorinnen sowie von Evaluationsverantwortlichen der öffentlichen Hand, eine Arbeitsgruppe mit dem Auftrag betraut, Evaluationsstandards für die Schweiz zu entwickeln. Nachdem sich die Arbeitsgruppe vorerst intensiv mit verschiedensten, bereits bestehenden Dokumenten (vgl. dazu auch die Hinweise in

Beywl/Widmer 2000) auseinandergesetzt hatte, beschloß sie, ausgehend von den „Standards" des „Joint Committee", schweizerische Evaluationsstandards zu entwickeln. Dabei folgte die Arbeitsgruppe der Grundstruktur der Standards und nahm an den einzelnen Standards gewisse Änderungen vor. Das resultierende Papier (Widmer/Landert/Bachmann 1999) umfaßt noch 27 Einzelstandards und wurde im Frühling 1999 durch die Mitgliederversammlung der SEVAL mit großem Interesse zur Kenntnis genommen. Es befindet sich zur Zeit in der Diskussion bei den interessierten Kreisen. Gemäß Planung sollen die Mitglieder der SEVAL im Herbst 2000 anläßlich der nächsten Jahresversammlung über die Evaluationsstandards befinden.

6.7 Standards in Rechtstexten und Handbüchern

Im Zuge der zunehmenden Verbreitung von Evaluationsstandards erscheinen diese auch immer häufiger in Texten mit rechtlicher Verbindlichkeit. Dabei stehen entsprechende Festlegungen in Ausschreibungen und Evaluationskontrakten im Vordergrund. Allmählich werden die Bezugnahmen auf Evaluationsstandards fester Vertragsbestandteil, was sich etwa darin zeigt, daß regelmäßige Auftraggeber externer Evaluationen entsprechende Klauseln in ihre Mustertexte für Evaluationsverträge aufnehmen. Damit entwickeln sich die Evaluationsstandards – im Gegensatz zur Situation in den Achtziger und der ersten Hälfte der Neunziger Jahre, als die Evaluationsstandards in der deutschsprachigen Evaluationspraxis nur selten überhaupt bekannt waren – sukzessive zu einem allgemein perzipierten und auch akzeptierten Referenzpunkt der Evaluationspraxis.

Dies zeigt sich auch darin, daß zunehmend in Handbüchern und Manualen diverser Projekte, Programme und Organisationen auf Evaluationsstandards Bezug genommen wird. Diese Dokumente haben zwar im Regelfall keinen Rechtscharakter, leisten aber einen bedeutenden Beitrag zur Verbreitung von Evaluationsstandards, besonders auch bei den entsprechenden Projektverantwortlichen, die häufig im Evaluationsbereich Auftraggeberfunktionen wahrnehmen. Ein Beispiel dieser Art bildet das Handbuch zur bereits oben angesprochenen Verwaltungsreform wif! im Kanton Zürich (wif!-Stab 2000, Kapitel 3: 10-20)

Sukzessive scheint sich diese Entwicklung auch in verbindlichen, rechtlichen Erlassen niederzuschlagen. Im Moment ist es zwar noch zu früh, dies als allgemeine Tendenz darzustellen. Aber es gibt Beispiele, die in dieser Richtung deuten. So wird an der Universität Zürich zur Zeit ein Reglement über eine Evaluationsstelle erarbeitet, das auf die durch die SEVAL empfohlenen Evaluationsstandards (Widmer/Landert/Bachmann 1999) verweist.

7. Schluß

Mit den „Standards" des 'Joint Committee on Standards for Educational Evaluation' steht ein Instrument zur Verfügung, das die Qualitätsbewertung von Evaluationen ermöglicht. Durch ihre konzeptionelle und methodologische Offenheit erlauben sie eine angemessene Qualitätsbewertung von Evaluationen. Besonders adäquat erscheinen die „Standards", weil sie in der Lage sind, das vielfältige Spannungsfeld, in dem sich Evaluation bewegt, praxisnah abzubilden. Durch die Flexibilität der „Standards" eröffnet sich ein weites Feld von Anwendungsmöglichkeiten, sei dies in Meta-Evaluationen, als Ratgeber für die Evaluationspraxis, zur Qualitätssicherung, als didaktisches Hilfsmittel in Aus- und Weiterbildung, aber auch durch die in angepaßter Form erfolgende Weiterverwendung durch Fachgesellschaften, in Rechtstexten oder Handbüchern.

Trotz dieser generell sehr positiven Einschätzung sind an dieser Stelle auch drei eher warnende Hinweise anzuführen, welche die Grenzen der „Standards" aufzeigen sollen:

–   –Die „Standards" formulieren Qualitätsansprüche, die an die Evaluation gestellt werden. Die Angemessenheit in der konkreten Anwendung ist aber sorgfältig zu beobachten, da möglicherweise Änderungen oder Anpassungen erforderlich sind. In jedem Fall repräsentieren die Evaluationsstandards nur die äußeren Bewertungsgrundlagen; die inneren Bewertungsgrundlagen können nur in Kenntnis der spezifischen Evaluationsstudie bestimmt werden.

–   –In letzter Zeit sind in verschiedenen Ländern Debatten über die Zertifizierung und Akkreditierung im Evaluationsbereich geführt worden. Im amerikanischen Bundesstaat Louisiana bestehen Zertifizierungskriterien für Evaluatorinnen im Bildungsbereich (Louisiana State Departement of Education 1996). In der „Canadian Evaluation Society"/"Société canadienne d'évaluation" (CES/SCE[5]) und der „American Evaluation Association" (AEA; Altschuld 1999a & b, Jones/Worthen 1999, Bickman 1999, Smith 1999 und Worthen 1999) laufen zur Zeit Debatten zur Zertifizierung, wobei zum Teil heftige Widerstände angemeldet werden. In der Schweiz arbeitet zur Zeit eine „Groupe de réflexion meta-évaluation" (2000) daran, Standards zur Akkreditierung von Schulen im Bereich der Selbstevaluation zu formulieren. Ohne auf die Diskussion um Akkreditierung und Zertifizierung einzutreten, ist hier zu betonen, daß die „Standards" des „Joint Committee" dafür absolut ungeeignet sind. Erstens handelt es sich um Maximalstandards, die sich nicht dazu eignen, ein obligatorisches Minimum zu definieren. Zweitens ist der Bezugs-

---

5   siehe die entsprechenden Texte auf der Homepage der CES/SCE: http://www. evaluationcanada.ca/devprof.html#certification

punkt der „Standards" nicht die Evaluatorin, wie dies für die Zertifizierung nötig wäre, oder eine Institution, wie für die Akkreditierung erforderlich, sondern die Evaluation.
– Die zukünftige Entwicklung der Evaluation hinsichtlich Theorien, Konzepten, Ansätzen, Methoden und Verfahren ist nicht vorauszusehen.
Deshalb ist darauf zu achten, daß die „Standards" nicht dazu mißbraucht
werden, Weiterentwicklungen des Evaluationsansatzes zu behindern.
Vielmehr sollten die „Standards" einer regelmäßigen Überprüfung unterzogen und bei Bedarf angepaßt werden.

Die Evaluationsstandards des ‚Joint Committee on Standards für Educational
Evaluation' formulieren eine Definition der Evaluationsqualität und können
auch einen Beitrag zur Steigerung der Qualität der Evaluation leisten. Sie
zeigen damit auf, wie Wissenschaft in kunstvoller Weise praxisrelevant werden kann.

Literatur

Altschuld, James W. (1999a): The Certification of Evaluators: Highlights from a Report
Submitted to the Board of Directors of The American Evaluation Association. In: The
American Journal of Evaluation, 20(3), S. 481-493.
Altschuld, James W. (1999b): The Case for a Voluntary System for Credentialing Evalua-
tors. The American Journal of Evaluation, 20(3), S. 507-517.
American Evaluation Association, Task Force on Guiding Principles for Evaluators (1995):
Guiding Principles for Evaluators. New Directions for Program Evaluation 66, S. 19-26.
Beck, Ulrich/Bonss, Wolfgang (1989): „Verwissenschaftlichung ohne Aufklärung. Zum
Strukturwandel von Sozialwissenschaft und Praxis." In: Dies. (Hg.): Weder Sozial-
technologie noch Aufklärung? Frankfurt: Suhrkamp. S. 7-45.
Beyme, Klaus von (1991): Theorie der Politik im 20. Jahrhundert. Frankfurt: Suhrkamp.
Beywl, Wolfgang (1988): Zur Weiterentwicklung der Evaluationsmethodologie. Frankfurt:
Lang.
Beywl, Wolfgang/Widmer, Thomas (2000): „Die „Standards" im Vergleich mit weiteren
Regelwerken zur Qualität fachlicher Leistungserstellung." In: Joint Committee on
Standards for Educational Evaluation (Hg.): Handbuch der Evaluationsstandards.
Opladen: Leske + Budrich. S. 259-295.
Bickman, Leonard (1999): AEA, Bold or Timid? The American Journal of Evaluation,
20(3), S. 519-20.
Campbell, Donald T. (1984): Can We Be Scientific in Applied Social Science? Evaluation
Studies Review Annual, 9, S. 26-48.
Cronbach, Lee J. (1982): Designing Evaluations of Educational and Social Programs. San
Francisco: Jossey-Bass.
Groupe de réflexion meta-évaluation (2000): Mindeststandards für die Selbstevaluation
von Schulen. 3. Entwurf vom 27.1.2000. (unveröff.)
Habermas, Jürgen (1968): Technik und Wissenschaft als Ideologie. Frankfurt: Suhrkamp.
Habermas, Jürgen (1981): Theorie des kommunikativen Handelns. 2 Bde. Frankfurt: Suhr-
kamp.

Habermas, Jürgen/Luhmann, Niklas (1971): Theorie der Gesellschaft oder Sozialtechnologie. Was leistet die Systemforschung? Frankfurt: Suhrkamp.

Joint Committee on Standards for Educational Evaluation (1981): Standards for Evaluations of Educational Programs, Projects, and Materials. New York: McGraw-Hill.

Joint Committee on Standards for Educational Evaluation (1994): The Program Evaluation Standards. Newbury Park: Sage.

Joint Committee on Standards for Educational Evaluation (Hg.) (1999): Handbuch der Evaluationsstandards. Opladen: Leske + Budrich.

Joint Committee on Standards for Educational Evaluation (Hg.) (2000): Handbuch der Evaluationsstandards. 2. Auflage. Opladen: Leske + Budrich.

Jones, Steven C./Worthen, Blaine R. (1999): AEA Members' Opinions Concerning Evaluator Certification. The American Journal of Evaluation, 20(3), S. 495-506.

Klöti, Ulrich/Widmer, Thomas (1997): Untersuchungsdesigns. In: Bussmann, Werner/Klöti, Ulrich/Knoepfel, Peter (Hg.): Einführung in die Politikevaluation. Basel: Helbing & Lichtenhahn. S. 185-213

Louisiana State Department of Education (1996): Certification Criteria for Education Program Evaluators. Baton Rouge: Louisiana State Department of Education.

MacDonald, Barry (1993): „A Political Classification of Evaluation Studies in Education." In: Hammersley, Martyn (Hg.): Social Research. London: Sage. S. 105-8.

Palumbo, Dennis J./Hallett, Michael A. (1993): Conflict Versus Consensus Models in Policy Evaluation and Implementation. Evaluation and Program Planning, 16, S. 11-23.

Scriven, Michael (1991): Evaluation Thesaurus. Fourth Edition. Newbury Park: Sage.

Smith, M. F. (1999): Should AEA Begin a Process for Restricting Membership in the Profession of Evaluation. The American Journal of Evaluation, 20(3), S. 521-31.

Widmer, Thomas (1996a): Meta-Evaluation: Kriterien zur Bewertung von Evaluationen. Bern: Haupt.

Widmer, Thomas (1996b-h): Fallstudien zur Meta-Evaluation. 7 Bände. Reihe „Schlußberichte" des Nationalen Forschungsprogramms „Wirksamkeit staatlicher Maßnahmen" (NFP 27). Bern: Schweizerischer Nationalfonds.

Widmer, Thomas/Beywl, Wolfgang (2000): „Die Übertragbarkeit der Evaluationsstandards auf unterschiedliche Anwendungsfelder." In: Joint Committee on Standards for Educational Evaluation (Hg.): Handbuch der Evaluationsstandards. Opladen: Leske + Budrich. S. 243-257.

Widmer, Thomas/Binder, Hans-Martin (1997): Forschungsmethoden. In: Bussmann, Werner/Klöti, Ulrich/Knoepfel, Peter (Hg.): Einführung in die Politikevaluation. Basel: Helbing & Lichtenhahn. S. 214-255.

Widmer, Thomas/Landert, Charles/Bachmann, Nicole (1999): Von der Schweizerischen Evaluationsgesellschaft (SEVAL) empfohlene Evaluationsstandards. Bern, Genève: SEVAL.

Widmer, Thomas/Rothmayr, Christine/Serdült, Uwe (1996): Kurz und gut? Qualität und Effizienz von Kurzevaluationen. Zürich: Rüegger.

wif!-Stab (Hg.): Wirkungsorientierte Führung der Verwaltung des Kantons Zürich. Projekthandbuch, Aktualisierung 2000. Zürich: wif!-Stab.

Wilensky, Harold L. (1964): The Professionalization of Everyone. The American Journal of Sociology, 70(2), S. 137-158.

Worthen, Blaine R. (1999): Critical Challenges Confronting Certification of Evaluators. The American Journal of Evaluation, 20(3), S. 533-555.

Evert Vedung

Evaluation Research and Fundamental Research

1. The Problem: Differences Between Evaluation and Fundamental Research?

What is the difference between evaluation research and fundamental research? From the outset, however, I will phrase the issue a little bit more specifically: What is the difference between public policy evaluation research and fundamental research on public policy?

Also this second formulation needs some elaboration. I will take public policy to mean reforms, programs, projects, activities, services, products, and similar entities instituted by political and other public sector bodies like parliaments, governments, and government agencies at all levels such as the level of the muncipality, the county, the national state, the European Union, and the global level. I will also include reforms, programs, projects, activities and similar entities launched by non-governmental organizations and enterprises on behalf of some public sector body.

Furthermore, I will make no distinction between evaluation research and evaluation. Both expressions will be taken to mean research or at least research-like enterprises.

At this very general level there is actually a difference between evaluation and basic research, a difference in width. Fundamental research can deal with origins and causes of public policies as well as their implementation and effects. Public policy evaluation, on the other hand, is basically concerned with implementation and effects. Fundamental research on public policy may focus on the front end as well as on the back end of the policy cycle, whereas evaluation research puts its emphasis on the back end. In this sense, fundamental research is broader in its scope than evaluation research.

Actually, a fascinating general feature of evaluation from a sociological and political science point of view is that the output side of government, as opposed to the input side, is stressed. Evaluation puts the influence of government *on* society in the forefront. Evaluation is not concerned with the impact of societal and other contextual factors on government decision-making. The state is not studied as a mere reflection of societal forces, " a committee for the administration of the common affairs of the bourgeoisie," to use Karl Marx' famous phrase (Communist Manifesto: 19). Neither is it examined as a self-contained entity. Evaluation puts the state's, the government's, and the political system's impact on the surrounding society in focus. Through evaluation, the eventual influence of the public sphere is firmly placed as the central concern of social science. Evaluation, in the words of Theda Skocpol (1985), is "bringing the state back in".

While the above mentioned difference between fundamental and evaluation research is a significant one, it does not hit the heart of the matter. So, let us continue our search. For that purpose, we will once again narrow down our problem in the following manner: What is the difference between public policy evaluation research and fundamental research on public policy with the proviso that also the latter is focused on the output side of government interventions?

2. Scheme of Analysis: the Eight Problems Approach to Public Policy Evaluation

Elsewhere, I have phrased the primary problems of evaluation as eight questions (Vedung 1999: 85ff.). I have called this the *Eight Problems Approach to Public Policy Evaluation*. Evaluators may consider some or all of the following eight issues:

Figure 1.1: The Eight Problems Approach to Public Policy Evaluation

---

1. *The purpose problem:*
   For what overall aims is the evaluation launched?
2. *The organization problem:*
   Who should exercise the evaluation and how should it be organized?
3. *The intervention analysis problem:*
   How is the evaluand, that is, the government intervention, normally the policy, the program, the components of policies and programs, or the provision of services and goods, to be characterized and described? Is the evaluand regarded as a means or as a self-contained entity?
4. *The conversion problem:*
   What does execution look like between the formal instigation of the intervention and the final outputs?
5. *The results problem:*
   What are the outputs and the outcomes immediate, intermediate and ultimate of the intervention?
6. *The impact problem:*
   What contingencies (causal factors, operating causal forces) the intervention included explain the results?
7. *The value criterion problem:*
   By what value criteria should the merits of the intervention be assessed? By what standards of performance on the value criteria can success or failure or satisfactory performance be judged? And what are the actual merits of the intervention?
8. *The utilization problem:*
   How is the evaluation to be utilized? How is it actually used?

(Source: Vedung 1999: 86)

I will take the Eight Problems Approach as the point of departure for dissecting the issue of eventual differences between fundamental vs. evaluation research. If we look at the eight questions wherein lie the differences between fundamental and evaluation research?

Problems 3, 4, 5 and 6: No Differences

To begin with, problems 3, 4, 5 and 6 in the list constitute no principal differences between fundamental and evaluation research.

At an early stage, the evaluator must make herself familiar with the *intervention*. She must describe and analyse the intervention (problem 3). How should the intervention be described? What is the nature of the intervention? How should it be depicted? What are the goals of the intervention? If several goals are set, how are they ranked? What range of policy instruments are incorporated in the program? Does the program entail regulatory, economic or communication tools of governance? In case several instruments are involved, how are they combined? If only one type of policy instrument is devised, – for example: regulations – what kinds of regulations are they?

But also the basic social scientist, for instance a political scientist, will raise the same questions. And in answering these questions both types of researchers will use exactly the same data collection methods and data analysis methods. There are no data collection and data analysis methods specific to evaluation. Evaluators will use documentary, interrogatory and observation methods and so will fundamental researchers. Both will analyse text and use statistics, both will employ interviews and questionnaries and both will do site visits and field trips to perform ocular inspection.

Occasionally, of course, the issue of describing the intervention can be lightly dealt with by the evaluator. This is true in self-evaluation conducted by people who already know the program well. This is also true in other evaluations where the potential users of the evaluation are supposed to know the program beforehand. But if intervention description is to be performed there are no discernible differences between fundamental and evaluative research.

Also the conversion problem, problem no. 4, is the same in both types of research. The conversion problem concerns the implementation process between intervention adoption and intervention delivery. What does the implementation process look like? What orders, directives and resources have been given to the central agency? Have the intervention activities reached the eventual intermediaries? Have the intermediaries performed some action? What have the operators at the grass-root level done in preparation of the final output? Evidently, in this stage evaluators follow the program from its birth up to the point immediately preceding the output. But the same implementation processes can be studied by fundamental researchers as well by using the same data collection and data analysis methods.

Problem no. 5, the *results* problem, is also identical to both types of research. In most evaluation analysis, results are characterized in systems terminology. The evaluator may look for the immediate, intermediate and ultimate outcomes, or for outputs like number and size of subsidies granted, number and type of patients treated, or number and sort of information brochures disseminated. Outcomes analysis focuses on intended outcomes as well as perverse results, unintended results outside the target area, or just simply results. Results may thus denote either output and outcomes, outputs only, or outcomes only.

But the same thinking is applied also in basic research. In answering the results question, both the evaluator and the basic researcher may consult several data sources. They might use appropriate statistical records routinely collected by some governmental agency, scrutinize inherited policy documents, do some interviews, send out a questionnaire, make site-visits or resort to participant observation. Data collection triangulation, i.e. a combination of methods, is probably advisable.

Problem 6, can also be raised by both evaluators and basic researchers. Problem 6 concerns the convoluted matter of intervention impact. Has the intervention caused the result? Has it facilitated or counteracted the development? Has it precipitated the outcome, or retarded it, or has it spawned no discernible effect at all?

A good evaluation is concerned with main effects in the target area, perverse or opposite effects (in the target area), side effects (outside the target area), and null effects (in or outside the target area). But the same spectrum of effects can also be investigated by the basic researcher.

The same goes for research designs for the illumination of causal impacts. In principle, the evaluation researcher may chose between randomized experiments, matched experiments, generic controls, reflexive controls, statistical controls and shadow controls as designs for the solution of the causal impact problem. But the same opportunities are available to the basic researcher.

Another research design in causal impact analysis is called process evaluation in evaluation research, process tracing in basic social science. The slight difference in naming notwithstanding, the procedures are the same. Process evaluation and process tracing imply a broad, configurative conception of causative factors. Both seeks to establish a whole pattern of causal interdependencies. They request, among other things, that effects of processes between intervention instigation and intervention results will be probed and clarified. Furthermore, consequences of intervention surroundings are ascertained, factors operative during the formation of the intervention included.

Process analyses concentrate on evaluands in their natural political, administrative, social, and geographic surroundings, may be executed in close interaction with evaluation commissioners and potential users, and will employ hard statistical data, surveys, and questionnaires as well as information produced through qualitative data collection techniques like in-depth interviews, textual analysis, and direct observation through site-visits.

But the point here is that process analysis in evaluation research and process tracing in basic social science do not differ. There are no methodological dissimilarities, basically, between the two.

To sum up, problems 3, 4, 5 and 6 in the Eight Problems Approach to Evaluation constitute no principal differences between fundamental and evaluation research. But what about problem no. 7, the *value criterion* problem?

3. Is There a Difference With Respect to Valuing?

At face value, the value criterion problem seems to differentiate between evaluation and fundamental research. Evaluation must evaluate, i.e. pass judgment on the merit, worth and value of the intervention, its implementation, results, and effects. Evaluation is a normative enterprise. But fundamental research is basically empirical, is it not? Is the passing of judgments really the business of fundamental research? Can and should fundamental social research be normative?

The passing of judgments presupposes the use of value criteria. What value criteria are employed in assessing the worth of an intervention? Evaluators have two options. They may choose descriptive or prescriptive criteria.

In *descriptive valuing*, the evaluator chooses the values of others as criteria. The posture is not that these values are paramount, but that they are perceptions of intervention worth that are grist for the mill of decision-making. In *prescriptive valuing*, the evaluator herself " advocates the primacy of particular values", such as, for instance justice, or equality, regardless of whether these values are adopted by any decision-making body or held by some stakeholding constituency. Prescriptive theories of valuing maintain that some values are superior to others whereas descriptive theories depict values held by others without contesting them or claiming that one value is best or better than some alternative ones.

Figure 1.2 contains a summary of some commonly suggested descriptive and prescriptive criteria for judging intervention merit, worth and value.

The value component of public sector evaluation was long neglected because the answer appeared obvious: the evaluator should avoid setting up criteria of her own; the natural criteria of merit to apply are the initial, stated intervention goals. Since public interventions are inaugurated to achieve some aims, it is natural to assess them in light of these aims.

With time, goal-attainment evaluators discovered practical difficulties. Some government services have very lofty goals which make them worthless as value criteria. Take national defence, for instance. The business of defence is to avoid war. The Swedes have avoided wars since 1813 but is war avoidance really a reasonable benchmark to use in judging defense efforts? It seems far too general to be applied as a criterion to evaluate the effectiveness and efficiency of military defense. Other programs have more specific goals but even these goals are plagued by haziness; particularly difficult to use are goal catalogues with no stated priorities among the goals.

Figure 1.2: Descriptive and Prescriptive Criteria of Merit in Evaluation
Research

Descriptive criteria of merit:
1. Goal-attainment
    a. Goals of global conventions
    b. European Union policy goals
    c. National policy goals
    d. National agency goals
    e. Regional agency goals
    f. Municipal policy goals or goals of municipal commissions
2. Client concerns, expectations, and conceptions of quality
3. Professional conceptions of merit
4. Citizens' expectations and values
5. Merit criteria of diverse stakeholding audiences
Prescriptive criteria of merit:
1. Client needs
2. Equal distribution
3. Public interest

(Source: Vedung 1999: 216)

Responsiveness to client concerns has been suggested as an alternative to public policy and program goals. Is the program or the service acceptable to or highly appreciated by the recipients? The use of client criteria is grounded in political ideologies of the superiority of the market as compared to government provision of services. Since the public sector produces goods or services for certain clients, responsiveness to client tastes is the major value criterion to be met. The client-orientation is also justified by democratic, participatory arguments.

The client model is used particularly in local service provision such as medical service, crime prevention, child care, services to seniors, handicapped, and youth. It is also applied to cultural programs like libraries, museums, zoos, and theaters, recreation programs like national parks, swimming-pools, number and quality of parks, soccer fields, and tennis halls, and other services like trash hauling, street cleaning, snow removal, traffic noise, traffic congestion, and urban transit.

Another set of descriptive criteria are *professional* demands and goals. The pertinent profession is asked to provide yardsticks and judge the quality of the evaluand in peer reviews. Professionals include doctors in medical care, professors in basic research, nurses in services to seniors, and social workers in social service provision. The rationale for this approach is that the value structure in some fields is so complicated that only the expert practitioners themselves can judge the quality of what is performed.

Occasionally, *citizens'* goals are also used as criteria, as when evaluators elicit the opinions of local residents on municipal library services, art exhibitions, sports recreation facilities, or public utilities like electricity, district heating, and garbage collection. This approach is grounded in theories of direct, participatory democracy. All the *stakeholders' goals*, expectations and worries concerning a particular intervention could also be used as criteria. The stakeholder approach is driven by theories of legitimate interest group representation.

Descriptive public sector criteria are mostly plagued by ambiguity. Often, they contradict each other. The evaluator will run into problems, because they are unclear and do not point unambiguously to a distinct outcome. If program goals and other naturally occurring yardsticks such as client concerns are hazy, how can they be the cornerstones in the appraisal? The ensuing result would be fuzzy and vague, to say the least.

Prescriptive strategies have been suggested to avoid the problems of using descriptive criteria. But prescriptive criteria are fraught with other problems.

Figure 1.2 provided some cases of prescriptive criteria. Client needs are one such prescriptive criterion. Needs are very different from goals, express concerns and demands. Goals, concerns, and demands of clients can in principle be described empirically. But needs are not just out there waiting to be described. To argue that somebody needs something is analogous to maintaining that the person will be harmed or detrimentally affected if the thing is not obtained. Many needs theories lean toward a specific theory of justice. But there are several theories of justice. Justice is a central moral concern in evaluation but so are human rights, equality, liberty and utility. Why limit the concern only to justice? Limiting evaluation to needs interpreted as justice is problematic because there are several other candidates. Selecting criteria of merit from needs-based theories of justice may result in evaluations that differ dramatically from the terms used in public policy debates, which will minimize the usefulness of such evaluations. Similar types of reasoning may be directed against other prescriptive criteria such as equal distribution and the public interest.

Evaluation researchers can adopt any of the two types of valuing. Yet, descriptive valuing is easier to handle than prescriptive values because all you have to do is to ask others. In descriptive valuing the evaluator herself does not have to be normative. She is adopting the normative position of others. Prescriptive valuing is intellectually more demanding and requires training in ethics. It means that the evaluator herself must openly advocate some values over others. But certainly, evaluation researchers can adopt prescriptive valuing. However, in that case, she must justify carefully the value criteria chosen.

Admittedly, most basic research as it is conducted in the year 2000, is empirical, not expressly normative. Yet, there is nothing inherently wrong with being abjectly normative even in basic research. A basic researcher, in a similar vein as an evaluation researcher, may chose a set of value criteria, argue in favor of his choices, and apply the criteria as yardsticks in order to value intervention outputs and outcomes. There is nothing in the philosophy of science forbidding basic research to be openly normative. The conclusion is obvious: not even problem no. 7, the criterion problem, singles out evaluation research as something special and different from fundamental research.

But wherein, then, lie the difference or differences? Or maybe there are no differences?

(Shadish/Cook/Leviton 1991: 47ff.). Yes, there is one difference, and a very important one at that. The primary and essential difference between evaluation and basic research concerns *utilization.*

4. Primary and Essential Difference: Evaluation Should Be Useful and Used

An evaluation is supposed to be used in immediate or future debate and decision-making on the problem or intervention at hand. This is not at all the case with fundamental research. Fundamental researchers have no specific application in mind. The basic researcher attempts to live according to the legendary, humorous toast at the Christmas party of the Cambridge economists: "Long live economics and may it never be of any use." In evaluation, use is more or less planned. Basic research may be useful, but its use is accidental and unplanned.

The primary and essential difference, then, between evaluation research and fundamental research is that the former should be useful used. By definition, fundamental research is performed out of pure curiosity without and thoughts about future usefulness. Evaluation research, on the other hand, should not only be useful but also used. The rationale of evaluation research is usefulness and use. This primary difference between evaluation and fundamental research sets the stage for some other major secondary differences between the two research enterprises.

5. What Kinds of Evaluation Uses Are There?

What is meant by use (utilization) in evaluation research? What kind of use should evaluation strive to realize?

There is wild disagreement on the utilization issue among evaluation theorists and practicians. Some argue that evaluation should be scientific and through its results make politics more rational and evidence-based. Some even advocate that evaluation should replace politicking in politics. Politics should be more science-like, if not a science. Others argue that scientification of democratic politics is neither feasible nor desirable. What evaluation may strive to do is to make well-grounded contributions to ongoing policy debates. Evaluators must accept the fact that democratic decision-making is and will be based on many other types of knowledge and insights than evaluation findings, however strongly underpinned. Bascially, I am in favor of the latter position. Yet, for my reasoning here, it is not necessary to take a stand on the kind-of-utilization issue. My deliberation in the sequel will cover all types of utilization, strong as well as weak. For all the diverse and conflicting schools of evaluative thought are united on this particular point: evaluation should be useful and utilized.

It is a fact, then, that use and its synonym utilization carries several meanings. It covers use in the very strong sense of *instrumental use*. Evaluation findings are used instrumentally if adopted by users and employed as means in goal-directed problem solving processes. Evaluation research sets no goals. Goal-determination belongs to the realm of politics. Goal-setting, therefore, is the task of the politicians, or the agencies to which the politicians have delegated their goal-setting powers. The proper role of evaluation is, given politically decided goals and before the reform is inaugurated across the board, to find out through small, but carefully designed field trials the most efficient means to reach the indicated goals. Since the goals have been determined by the politicians, the evaluators can pursue factfinding about means in a purely value neutral and objective fashion. Once the trials are finished, the findings will be communicated back to decision-makers who will adopt them and act accordingly.

A weaker sense of use covers the case when facts and conclusions produced by evaluation are employed to illuminate thinking but does not lead to action. This is called *conceptual use*, or, sometimes, *enlightenment use*. Evaluation results may be incorporated gradually into the users' overall frames of reference. They will gain understanding from the evaluation and become more enlightened. They will receive cognitive and normative insights through the evaluation, but these insights have not been directly instrumental and transformed into action. After due consideration of the findings, program officials and other users conclude that they should do nothing. Yet, the whole procedure contributed to a thorough scrutiny of the premises of the intervention, the illumination of problems, and a deeper apprehension of intervention merits and limitations. In conceptual use, evaluation findings are consulted by the user, even painstakingly studied by him. They make him more informed than before. They may also sway his attitudes. But they do not trigger any action.

In *legitimizing use*, evaluation is seized upon to justify established positions grounded in other considerations, such as for instance political ideology, electoral hopes, coalition expediency or personal idiosyncracies. Evaluation is used to strengthen one's positive or negative stances on either issues or political adversaries and allies. Some evaluation results, deemed suitable to serve political purposes, are appropriated as additional evidence in conflict situations and in political struggles to bolster the case at stake. Other results, believed to be damaging, are either ignored or summarily dismissed. The de facto task of evaluation is to deliver ammunition for political battles, where alliances are already formed and frontlines already exist. Legitimizing use if often referred to as "political ammunition".

The fourth form of evaluation use to be expounded here, *tactical utilization*, asserts that evaluation is employed to gain time or avoid responsibility. The important fact is not the eventual findings, but that an evaluation is appointed and under way. "Look, we cannot say anything or do anything now, because we have an evaluation going. When we have the evaluation we can decide what to do." In tactical utilization, the process of doing evaluation, not the findings of this process, is used. From this case, we may see, incidentally, that evaluation is a process-product concept. It may refer to the process of doing evaluation ("this evaluation took me 15 months to perform"). It may also refer to findings produced by such a process ("this evaluation clearly shows that the intervention has not yet achieved its goals"). Both should be attended to in discussions of evaluation use.

Let us consider a situation where decision-makers want to cover up faulty results and white-wash failures of a specific intervention in order to avoid public debate and deflect criticism. An evaluation is appointed in order to give the impression that the faulty results and failures are taken seriously and that something rational will be done about the problems. The rationale behind the evaluation is to give the handling of the issue an appearance of rationality and placate angry critics. The important thing is that an evaluation is appointed and under way, not that it eventually will produce substantive results. When decision-makers refer to the evaluation as ongoing, they use the evaluation process for tactical purposes.

Finally, we have *discursive use*. Public policy designers are engaged in hobnob search processes with a number of different actors, where evaluators constitute one group only and their knowledge just one set among many. Participants may include administrators, interest group representatives, planners, journalists, clients, political appointees, friends, party members and exercised citizens. The dialogue may serve the purpose of intellectual penetration of a societal problem. However, since disagreements are a commonplace in such "political primeval soups" to borrow a phrase divulged by John W. Kingdon, the exploration procedure will also contain conflict building and conflict resolution. The process from evaluation to future decision in the political system is not linear and unidirectional but unorganized, messy and interactive in a fashion that escapes diagrammatic representation.

Discursive use involves the application of evaluation-informed knowledge in conjunction with further research-based data and other forms of background like common sense, conventional wisdom, intuition, and recipients' own first-hand experiences (Weiss 1979: 206ff.).

In discursive use, public officials endorse "the Open Mouth Principle". They taste, swallow and digest various kinds of information of which evaluation insights on intervention results, intervention costs and intervention structure form only a part. Decision-makers cannot consider outcomes and cost-efficiency only but have to be mindful of legality issues, ethical appropriateness, congruence with due process and democratic values. They must ponder the costs of transforming the intervention, the type of staff needed to implement the change, the stances of client groups and intermediators, and what their fellow party associates believe. They must always calculate the political consequences of their actions, including their chances of reelection. Evaluation findings contribute to the general debate on the issue, may illuminate some users, and may also be used in action but only as one component of a larger body of information.

In sum, there are at least five types of evaluation use:

- 1. instrumental use
- 2. conceptual(enlightenment) use
- 3. legitimizing use
- 4. tactical use, and
- 5. discursive use.

My point here is the following. Whatever kind of use evaluation researchers strive for, they always have some sort of use in mind. It is this emphasis on utilization that distinguishes the business of evaluation research from the business of fundamental research.

6. Importance of the Contract

The general utitilization purpose of evaluation research sets the stage for other differences between evaluation and fundamental research. For instance, evaluators often work for commissioners, who want to use the evaluation for some imminent practical purpose. This makes the issue of the *formal contract* between commissioner and researcher important in evaluation. Lots have been written about what such contracts should contain. It should contain the mutual understandings of the specified expectations and responsibilities of both the commissioner and the evaluator. Such a formal contract clarifies understandings and helps prevent misunderstandings and provide a basis for resolving any future disputes about the evaluation. Without such a contract the evaluation process may be subject to misunderstanding, disputes, efforts to compromise the findings, attack, or withdrawal of cooperation and funds. A contract may prevent the commissioner from burying the report or rewriting it.

The contract issue is much less pressing in fundamental research. Typically, fundamental researchers are tenured and salaried. They don´t need any contracts with outside funding bodies. They toil as their own entrepreneurs with no particular practical purpose in view. In case they have funds from foundations and other research financing bodies, fundamental researchers also have contracts, of course. But these contracts are much less specified because foundations for fundamental research care less about findings.

Because of its orientation toward utilization, evaluation research has *other general purposes* than fundamental research. Evaluation research is performed for either accountability, or intervention improvement whereas fundamental research is performed for basic knowledge advancement.

7. Accountability and Improvement Purposes Are Vital to Evaluation

The key rationale of *accountability* evaluation is to find out whether agents have exercised their delegated powers and discharged their duties properly so that principals can judge their work. Accountability involves two parties, the principal and her agent. The principal issues orders and directives for the agent to follow; the latter is supposed to carry out the will of the former. While the agent is expected to do the accounting, the principal has authority to pass judgements and make decisions on, for instance, continued allocation of funds. However, the accounting can also be performed by some outside body, commissioned by the principal, or by the principal himself. The essence is that accountability evaluation is intended to serve the needs of an external overseeing body.

Accountability is repugnant to both principals and agents. It could be dangerous to both. It belongs to a wider class of phenomena, intimated by dual concepts like

represented – representative,
master – servant,
superior – subordinate,
principal – executive,
mistress – maid,
farmer – farmhand,
employer – employee, and
boss – underling.

Superiors need illuminations of current or past performance of their subordinates to hold them responsible for what they have accomplished. The mistress must check the accomplishments of her maid and call her to account for her actions. The employer must oversee his employee to control that he is doing the right job, and doing it well. Similarly in the public sector, higher-level principals (like agency managers) want to find out whether their lower-level stewards (like agency staff) are performing their tasks properly in order to hold them accountable.

In accountability assessment, information and evaluative judgments are produced to allow decisions on program continuation, expansion, reduction, and termination. Accountability evaluation assembles an information base on which principals may exercise their judgments on resource allocation. Occasionally, the whole rationale and fundamental direction of the intervention may be reviewed and reconsidered. An evaluation can provide evidence on the extent to which intervention objectives remain relevant, whether program activities still address a pertinent societal problem, or if research in the substantive policy area continues to support the kind of policy instruments employed (Hudson/Mayne/Thomlison 1992: 8). On other occasions, only marginal changes are considered. But all in all, the commissioning, performing and utilization of an accountability evaluation is mostly fraught with controversy, disagreements and outright infighting.

In the *improvement* perspective, evaluation aspires to guide intervention amelioration and refinement. The incremental amelioration and revision of intervention operations and intervention direction is basic to the improvement rationale. It is felt that the intervention will continue its operations in the foreseeable future and that it must operate as smoothly and efficiently as possible. The fundamental question is "How can the intervention be made better?". The aim is to make the intervention more stream-lined, effective, efficient, service-oriented, and adapted to client concerns and needs.

The primary customer of improvement evaluation is the personnel responsible for or closely associated with the intervention. It could be front-line program staff, supervisors of front-line personnel, program administrators or even senior managers. Evaluation is seen as a part of the agency's day-to-day management process with learning and corrective actions as a means toward general system improvement as its primary goal. The program improvement perspective conceives of evaluation as an iterative process whereby evaluation findings are fed back into program planning, management, delivery – and fed back fast enough to enable the modification and improvement of currently operating programs. This objective places the priority on speed, flexibility, and relevance in the evaluation rather than on the development of new knowledge according to rigorous methodological standards. In fact, the need for speed and pertinence vis-a-vis a broad range of pressing issues may even obviate the possibility of careful research in the academic sense. On special occasions, for instance, management evaluation may function better if the study is not published.

Accountability evaluation, on the other hand, is not primarily aimed at personnel directly involved with the evaluand but at the superior principals. Evaluation is designed to be a tool for superiors to check their subordinates and keep them and the program responsible for their actions. This is the crucial difference between improvement and accountability evaluation.

Intervention improvement, "intervention modification" or formative evaluation as some authors call this perspective is a worthy and necessary aim for evaluation. It is much less dangerous to the agents than accountability evaluation. Usually, it is therefore much less controversial. Several experts maintain that intervention improvement (and intervention direction reconsideration) must be the major purpose. "Accountability emphasizes looking back in order to assign praise or blame; evaluation is better used to understand events and processes for the sake of guiding future activities," Lee Cronbach wrote in one of his 95 theses on the reformation of evaluation (Cronbach 1980: 4). "In practice," Carol Weiss noted in her textbook (1972a: 17), "evaluation is most often called on to help with decisions about improving programs. Go/no-go, live-or-die decisions are relatively rare ...It is the search for improvements in strategies and techniques that supports much evaluation activity at present."

Accountability and improvement stand out as the most eminent general rationales for doing evaluation. This is not the case at all with fundamental research, which by definition has no such practical purposes. The business of fundamental research is to produce basic knowledge, not knowledge for practical use.

8. Basic Knowledge as a Happy Side-effect in Evaluation

Yet, the production of basic knowledge is sometimes heralded as the task of evaluation research as well. Then, evaluation is seen as fundamental research that seeks to increase the general understanding of reality. It tests broader theories on the ways agencies function, the coping strategies of front-line service deliverers, or the functioning of particular forms of intervention. It augments the collected body of knowledge in some academic field of study. Theory-building and theory-testing are important buzzwords in the basic knowledge perspective. Such research may be devoid of practical implications in the immediate future or even in the longer term. It seeks knowledge for knowledge's sake (Rutman/Mowbray 1983: 27f.).

Several perceptive methodologists accord the basic-knowledge purpose the major role, for example, such proponents of theory-oriented evaluation as Chen (1990), and Fitz-Gibbon et al. (1975). Another group regards basic knowledge as a happy side-effect in relation to improvement and accountability (Chelimsky 1978; Anderson/Ball 1978: 35).

Robert K. Merton, Friedrich A. Hayek, Karl R. Popper and others have taught us to treat unintended side-effects seriously. This is also my attitude toward the basic knowledge outlook on evaluation research. The provision of basic knowledge is not the major task of evaluation; basic knowledge is subordinated under accountability and improvement. Basic knowledge is a side-consideration. Basic knowledge is best regarded as a possible, beneficial side-effect of the primary accountability and improvement purposes.

In sum, evaluation research is done for accountability, improvement and maybe other practical purposes, while fundamental research is done for basic knowledge. While evaluation may contribute to basic knowledge, cases of actual basic knowledge production are best regarded as happy side effects, not as the fundamental rationale.

9. Evaluation as Potemkin villages

To this contrast between evaluation and fundamental research we may add another one: the differing role of *strategic considerations*. Since evaluation always takes place in action settings, it is usually permeated with game-oriented considerations, strategic purposes. This is not at all the case with fundamental research. Or phrased somewhat more carefully, fundamental research is much less permeated by strategic considerations of various kinds than evaluation research. Evaluation may be used by executives to hide shortcomings and failures from their principals, to display attractive images of programs, and in general to provide appearances more flattering than reality. Evaluations are commissioned to gain time, to show up a front of rationality and to disseminate an overly handsome view of the executives' work. These strategic motives for the evaluation are often covert. If disclosed, they would lose their purported beneficial value in the political or administrative power game.

Employed strategically by users, evaluations can be likened to "Potemkin villages" ("Potemkin fronts", "Potemkin scenes"). "Potemkin villages" stands for devices espoused by an agent to camouflage bad conditions to his principal. The expression refers to Empress Catherine II's visit in 1787 to the Crimea where the governor general of the Ukraine, Prince Potemkin, built artificial house fronts along her route to give her a false impression of good conditions. It seems that the prince succceeded with his ruse. During the visit, governor Potemkin, the Empress' former favorite and lover, received the title prince of Tauris (for the expression Potemkin villages, see Vedung 1999: 102).

It seems to me that evaluation research, contrary to fundamental research, becomes part and parcel of political, administrative and personal power games. Assessments are ordered to gain time, to show up a front of rationality or to single-mindedly find traits to defend or destroy the program.

These strategic mostly unacknowledged and hidden rationales mix with the substantive, acknowledged ones in the context of the same evaluation. Evaluations are established to alleviate several problems at the same time.

10. Strategies to Tackle the Utilization Issue in Evaluation

This leads me to my final point about the difference between evaluation research and fundamental research: evaluators are or should be much more concerned with utilization than fundamental researchers. This is obvious from the fact that timing, feedback and use of research is a much more protruding issue in evaluation theory than in the theory of fundamental research. Evaluators must be concerned with utilization for two reasons: to stave off inappropriate utilization and promote appropriate use.

Since evaluation is frequently made to order, it is advisable for the evaluator to consider carefully the first problem in the Eight Problems Approach to Evaluation, the *overall purposes of the commissioner*. True, the evaluator must find out what intervention ingredient the sponsor wants to have investigated. Furthermore, the evaluator should also pay attention to the particular problems that the commissioner wants her to illuminate. In talking about overall evaluation purposes, however, I have something much more far-fetched in mind, namely why the sponsor wants to have these particular things examined. In which decision context will the evaluation be used? Who are the prospective primary users? Is there a hidden agenda behind the evaluation? Is there really a genuine desire with the sponsor to have the intervention and its outputs and outcomes clarified or does he covet a tranquilizer or some legitimizing evidence?

The purpose problem in the overall sense intimated here is something the basic researcher may circumvent. In the academic community, funds for research are allocated on the grounds of basic-knowledge interests alone. Not so in evaluation. A client commissioning an evaluation also has a strategic agenda, in most cases hidden, in mind. Hence, the evaluator must pay attention to the commissioner's deeper purposes in order to be prepared to say no to inappropriate commissions and yes to appropriate ones.

Also the second problem in the Eight Problems Approach to Evaluation can be seen from a utilization angle. How should evaluation work *be organized* in order to promote utilization of results? Who should conduct the evaluation? Should the evaluation be initiated and produced by the affected people themselves or should some external body commission and conduct the assessment?

The organization problem is closely related to problem no. 8 in the Eight Problems Approach to Evaluation. How does evaluation get a hearing in governmental decision-making? The literature is replete with admonitions. The basic-science road would be to publish the best approximation to truth, attend to the resulting scholarly debate, and let the political and administrative process handle the rest. However, I shall discuss situations in which evaluators adopt a consciously active role to use. In this active mode, the broad approaches with subapproaches in figure 1.3 will be briefly covered.

Figure 1.3: Strategies to Enhance Utilization of Evaluation

1. Diffusion-oriented Strategy
   a. Reporting Method
   b. Linkage Method
2. Production-oriented Strategy
3. User-oriented Strategy
4. Metaevaluation (Synthesis Analysis)
   a. Summarizing and synthesizing of several evaluations
   b. Evaluation of the general evaluation function

(Source: Constructed from Vedung 1999: 243)

The diffusion-oriented strategy attempts to improve the dissemination of evaluation results. Production-oriented strategies try to transform the evaluators and their evaluation procedures to increase evaluation use. In user-oriented strategies, finally, the main preoccupation is to render the recipients more evaluation-friendly and susceptible to evaluations. Metaevaluation aspires to improve the evaluation function as a whole.

The *diffusion-oriented strategy* is concerned with making dissemination of evaluation findings as effectual as possible. The idea is, of course, that the recipients must know about the results before they can use them.

Within the diffusion-oriented strategy, I have discerned two sub-approaches: the reporting method and the linkage method. Concentrating on evaluation papers, tracts, and oral briefings, the reporting method attempts to broadcast evaluation output as widely as feasible and make it as recipient-friendly as possible, without compromising on either methodology or facts. The point of the linkage method is the same but here the efforts are institutionalized into formal groups, appointed commissions or some permanent documentation system.

Starting with the *reporting method,* I have collected and organized some possibilities of streamlining and broadcasting evaluation outputs, suggested by Seidel (1983: 52ff.) and other communication experts. The results are shown in figure 1.4.

It is adamant for the success of the reporting method that the evaluator is resolutely committed to utilization, locates the potential users, attempts to avoid unintelligible writing, shuns no effort to fashion her papers and briefings in a user-friendly manner, and assumes the role of an ardent advocate of her results.

Figure 1.4: The Diffusion-oriented Strategy: the Reporting Method

- Reports should display some startling fact that makes people sit up and think;
- Reports ought to be pointed and brief;
- Each written report should be confined to one trenchant issue; if complex, the results should be presented in several brief reports instead of one comprehensive treatise;
- Reports should contain a short and sharp executive summary;
- Potential evaluation clients should be located, preferably in advance;
- Written reports should be fashioned in user language rather than in jargon designed to make simple ideas difficult to grasp;
- Accounts of results should be accompanied by graphics;
- Crucial results should be highlighted stylistically, through the use of clear headings, subheadings, and an appropriate overall organization of the analysis; substantive findings ought to be presented first, methods afterwards; the major substantive results should be stated in unequivocal terminology prior to reservations, not the other way around; it is important that the executive summary starts with the major substantive findings;
- Reasoning on methods should be reduced to an absolute minimum in the bulk of the report; instead methodological considerations ought to be appended as attachments;
- Findings, insights and recommendations ought to be disseminated continually and to many audiences before the final essay is completed;
- Reports should include recommendations for action;
- Reports should be prompt and timely;
- Appropriate managers and other stakeholders should receive copies of written preliminary papers and the final essay;
- Results should be communicated in person;
- Evaluators should become involved in the selling of their findings;
- Evaluators should be around if managers may want to talk;
- Evaluators should talk briefly and often;
- Evaluators should tell stories, performance anecdotes, to illustrate the points;
- Evaluators should engage in public debate.

(Source: Vedung 1999: 244)

The purpose of the second diffusion-oriented subapproach, *the linkage method*, is to promote dissemination by opening up channels into the recipient organization in a sustainable, organized, and systematic fashion. The linkage method involves permanent use of some intermediary agent between evaluators and practitioners.

Advisory commissions are one possible link. Besides the evaluators, such bodies are usually composed of the potential primary recipients of the evaluation, the evaluation sponsors, and producers of other evaluations. The commission members may offer valuable advice concerning how the findings should be diffused within their respective organizations. In addition, they might also function as disseminators themselves.

Another option is to involve opinion leaders. Defined as credible and influential members of their respective communities, opinion leaders operate as gate keepers in particular communication networks, who can obstruct, filter, delay or precipitate flows of information. Dissemination will increase if such gate keepers are appointed members of advisory commissions.

Still another possibility would be to engage an information transfer specialist. Appointed a member of the advisory commission, her task would be to suggest mechanisms for the fostering of communication between evaluators and users.

Also computerized systems designed to make evaluation results better known to conceivable recipients are included in the linkage substrategy. Efforts to incorporate evaluations into new documentation systems and data bases are cases in point.

In sum, the diffusion strategy starts from the assumption that faulty utilization is due to noise and other communication barriers between producers and consumers of evaluation. There might be something to this assumption. It is obvious that before recipients can use any information, they must know about it. It helps, too, if they understand it. Occasionally, evaluation reports are both incomprehensible and little disseminated. Therefore, amelioration of the dissemination function and the prerequisites for communication is important. The diffusion-oriented strategy does not necessitate any changes either in evaluation methodology or in the facts to be reported. Neither does it demand any changes on the recipient side. This seems to explain the popularity of the diffusion strategy. Yet it should be emphasized that utilization of evaluation is not a question of user-friendly reporting and intensified dissemination efforts only. The broadcasting of evaluation results cannot guarantee utilization. There are much more difficult obstacles to utilization than information barriers.

The *production-oriented strategy*, the second major approach to utilization improvement, suggests that evaluation outputs should be made more user-friendly through efforts directed at the evaluation process. The assumption is that evaluations are dismissed or shelved because they are irrelevant, if not faulty. Production strategists do not primarily worry about how to improve communication of substantiated findings or dissemination of oral or written information. The adjustments must probe deeper. The evaluation process as such must be adapted to meet the demands and desires of the conceivable recipients.

One possibility is to adapt evaluation to the stages of program development. To illustrate this important idea, I shall use a four-stage scheme developed by Lee J. Cronbach, as it is summarized in the Shadish, Cook & Leviton volume (1991: 336):

"The *breadboard* stage comes first. The ideas for a program have been provisionally incorporated into field activities on a small scale and are being routinely tinkered with to improve design. The *superrealization* stage is when a suitable design has been constructed and a demonstration study is initiated under conditions that maximize the likelihood of success designers of the model deliver services with no slippage from the plan, expenditures per recipient are high, service recipients are carefully chosen for cooperativeness, and the catchment area is partly cut off from outside perturbations. In the *prototype* stage a program is implemented under conditions that mimic those under which the program would be introduced as policy. Finally, the *operating program* stage is when the program is permanently up and running."

The assumption appears to be that the evaluation must be accommodated to the various stages of program maturity. The four different stages require four different evaluations.

Another feature of the production strategy is responsiveness to user worries. The responsive evaluator should care for the user's questions, not the questions of academic interest only. Various plausible users have diverse information wants in the different stages of intervention maturity. Preferably, the likely recipients e.g. responsible officials at the policy level, program level and local delivery level, program clients, scholars and journalists should frame the questions and then leave them to the evaluator for investigation.

The use of manipulable variables as contingent factors is also recommended. Users are only attentive to contingencies that can be influenced through human action, or more specifically, the user himself. This usually means that suggestions aiming at a complete restructuring of society should be avoided. The underlying notion is that evaluations must be theoretical in order to become practically applicable. Theory in this context stands for explanatory theory. Only when we know what factors condition a beneficial or detrimental outcome, the appropriate conclusions for the future can be drawn. To this end, the responsive evaluator should concentrate on contingencies that humans may change, i.e. manipulable variables.

Still another ingredient in the production-oriented strategy is to adapt evaluation methodology to user needs. On this account, evaluation theorists disagree. Some theorists argue that case studies which attempt to picture the program as a comprehensive whole are best adapted to utilization whereas others maintain that sample surveys and questionnaires are more prone to produce use. Michael Patton asserts that qualitative evaluation methods and designs are more conducive to utilization than the scientific quality of the findings. It is particularly adamant that the utilization-focused evaluator choose softer, process-oriented anthropological methods which ensure close evaluator-user interaction. She ought to apply open-ended interviews and frame the major issues to be investigated in an interactive dialogue with commissioners and users. Then the odds are increased that utilization will happen.

A more far-reaching specimen of the production-oriented approach claims that the recipients, or some sample of them or their trusted representatives, should be consulted by the evaluators throughout all stages of evaluation and utilization. In addition to problem identification, planning for data collection, actual data collection, data processing, and report writing, cooperation should spill over into dissemination and utilization as well. This enhances the probability that the users become committed to the findings, which increase the possibility that they will use the findings or recommend others to do so. It also enables the evaluators to implement their findings. This comes rather close to so-called action research.

The stakeholder-consultation substrategy is strongly endorsed by evaluation theorists, who are frantically preoccupied with utilization. Michael Q. Patton, who has composed treatises on "utilization-focused evaluation", effectively commends this strategy as a vehicle of ensuring that the evaluation will pose questions relevant to potential primary users.

The stakeholder-consultation approach displays several advantages. The crucial rationale is that the chances of providing the right kind of information to recipients will increase. Through active participation, conceivable recipients may ensure that the evaluation will be responsive to issues that real users want to have illuminated.

Another merit is that learning may occur in the evaluation process, i.e. long before the publication of the final tract. By participating in all stages of the evaluation, users will become committed to the results, which will enhance the likelihood that they will use them or recommend others to use them. Often the users will take the results as their own, and claim that they have been thinking along these lines all the time.

Yet there are drawbacks with the stakeholder-consultation substrategy. Researchers risk becoming involved in political processes. The problems that will be addressed may be of minor interest from a research perspective. In choosing between objectivity and usefulness, the second may be preferred. From the point of view of solid research, it is important to separate objectivity and truth from usefulness and use. Invalid knowledge may be used, and valid knowledge may remain unused. Evaluation should not be transformed into something entirely politicized.

The third and final approach to improvement of utilization, the *user-oriented strategy*, engenders making potential evaluation clients more susceptible to utilization. The recipient organization should have an evaluation capacity. There should be active efforts to develop and sustain contacts with external evaluation communities. There are studies that show that to become utilized evaluations need some champion in the recipient organization. Users might also be educated in evaluation. The major approach in this area would be to incorporate evaluation into the management system of the organization. Evaluation should be institutionalized as an ongoing internal affair, like in management by results or management by objectives.

In addition to the three approaches to enhanced utilization hitherto discussed, I shall add a fourth, *metaevaluation*. Metaevaluation usually refers to:

a) a procedure for summarizing and synthesizing the findings of several evaluations of the same program or of an array of similar programs
b) evaluation of the general evaluation function of an organization or a unit

Metaevaluation in the sense that the findings of several evaluations should be summarized and synthesized is often recommended. Frequently, one is struck by the number and diversity of evaluation studies which have been produced in a single public policy sector or on an individual program. Evaluation research is usually designed to solicit practical answers to particular questions. The many evaluation studies have embraced a variety of methodological approaches and data gathering techniques. As a result, when previous studies are viewed in isolation from each other, the lessons learned often appear insignificant, inconclusive, and even contradictory. However, if the findings of past efforts are meticulously synthesized, they may cumulate to a surprising extent. Accordingly, they can be used to build more general explanations of what works and what does not. This could also be done at a cross-national level. A synthesis of results seems to be more useful to decision-makers than a single evaluation effort. In this fashion, metaevaluation or synthesis analysis is an approach to improved utilization of evaluation.

Also metaevaluation in the second sense of auditing of the evaluation function as suggested by Hudson, Mayne och Thomlison (1992: 195ff.) might improve future utilization. Metaevaluation in this sense is often included in a larger evaluation management philosophy suggesting the following. Instead of actually carrying out substantive evaluations, senior management should concentrate on auditing the evaluation function in subordinate bureaus. While lower-level branches are instructed to do self-evaluation of their own performance, higher authorities assumes the task of conducting evaluations of their subordinates' evaluation work. Senior management, for instance, may decide that lower levels ought to perform self-evaluation and summarize the findings in an evaluation essay. The task of senior management would then be to evaluate the evaluation report.

11. Final Word

In conclusion, the basic difference between evaluation research and fundamental research is that the former is intended for use. Evaluation research should be useful and used, but that is not incorporated into the ethos of fundamental research. There are many types of use in evaluation: 1. instrumental use, 2. conceptual use, 3. legitimizing use, 4. tactical use, and 5. discursive use. But whatever kind of use evaluation researchers strive for, they always have some sort of use in mind. It is this emphasis on utilization that distinguishes the business of evaluation research from the business of fundamental research.

The different emphasis of use and usefulness sets the stage for other major differences between evaluation research and fundamental research. The formal contract between the commissioner of an evaluation and the evaluators plays a much more important role in evaluation than in fundamental research. Evaluators pay and must pay attention to the overall general purposes of the actual evaluation, if it is performed for accountability or improvement or if there is some underlying hidden strategic agenda involved. And evaluators pay and should pay attention to various strategies to enhance the utilization of their evaluation results. These strategies are oriented toward diffusion of the results, better evaluation practice, and development of user capacity to receive results. Metaevaluation in the sense of synthesizing of several evaluations and evaluation of the general evaluation function may also enhance use.

References

Anderson, Scarvia B./Ball, Samuel (1978): The Profession and Practice of Program Evaluation. San Francisco: Jossey-Bass.

Bickman, Leonard (Ed.) (1990): Advances in Program Theory. San Francisco: Jossey-Bass.

Braskamp, L. A./Brown, A. D. (Eds.) (1980): Utilization of Evaluative Information. New Directions for Program Evaluation No. 5. San Francisco: Jossey-Bass.

Chelimsky, Eleanor (1978): "Differing Perspectives of Evaluation". New Directions for Program Evaluation, p. 2-18.

Chen, Huey-Tsyh (1990): Theory-Driven Evaluations. Newbury Park, CA: Sage.

Clarke, Alan (1999): Evaluation Research: An Introduction to Principles, Methods, and Practice. Thousand Oaks, CA: Sage Publications [chapter on utilization].

Cronbach, Lee J. & Associates (1980): Toward Reform of Program Evaluation: Aims, Methods, and Institutional Arrangements. San Francisco: Jossey-Bass.

Fitz-Gibbon, Carol Taylor/Lyons Morris, Lynn (1975): "Theory-Based Evaluation." Evaluation Comment, p. 1-14.

Hudson, Joe/Mayne, John/Thomlison, Ray (Eds.) (1992): Action-oriented Evaluation in Organizations: Canadian Practices, Toronto, Ontario: Wall & Emerson.

Karapin, Roger S. (1986): "What's the Use of Social Science? A Review of the Literature". In: Heller, Frank (Ed.): The Use and Abuse of Social Science, p. 236-265. Newbury Park, CA: Sage.

Larsen, Judith K. (1980): "Knowledge Utilization: What Is It?" Knowledge: Creation, Diffusion, Utilization, No.1, p. 421-442.

Leviton, Laura C./ Hughes, Edward F. X. (1981): "Research on the Utilization of Evaluations: A Review and Synthesis," Evaluation Review: A Journal of Applied Social Research, No. 5, p. 525-548.

Lindblom, Charles E./Cohen, David K. (1979): Usable Knowledge: Social Science and Social Problem Solving. New Haven, CN.: Yale University Press

Patton, Michael Quinn (1986): Utilization-Focused Evaluation. Newbury Park. CA: Sage, 2nd ed.

Pawson, Ray/Tilley, Nick (1997): Realistic Evaluation. London: Sage Publications [chapter on evaluation, policy and practice].

Rutman, Leonard/Mowbray, George (1983): Understanding Program Evaluation. Newbury Park, CA: Sage.

Seidel, Andrew D. (1983): "Producing Usable Research: A Selected Review." Policy Studies Review, No. 3, p. 52-56.

Shadish Jr, William R./Cook, Thomas D./Leviton, Laura C. (1991): Foundations of Program Evaluation: Theory and Practice. London: Sage ["knowledge use" treated throughout].

Skocpol, Theda (1985): Bringing the State Back In. Cambridge: Cambridge University Press.

Vedung, Evert (1999): Evaluation im öffentlichen Sektor. Wien, Köln, Weimar, New York: Böhlau Verlag [chapter 14 on utilization].

Weiss, Carol H. (1972): Evaluation Research: Methods of Assessing Program Effectiveness. Englewood Cliffs, NJ: Prentice-Hall. Often used text. Directed to programs.

Weiss, Carol H. (1972b): Evaluating Action Programs: Readings in Social Action and Education. Boston, MA: D C Heath.

Weiss, Carol H. (1977): Using Social Research in Public Policy Making. Lexington, MA: D.C Heath.

Weiss, Carol H. (1979): "The Many Meanings of Research Utilization," Public Administration Review, No. 39, p. 426-431.

Weiss, Carol H. (1981). "Measuring the Use of Evaluation." In: James A. Ciarlo (Ed.): Utilizing Evaluation: Concepts and Measurement Techniques. Newbury Park, CA: Sage. p. 17-33.

Weiss, Carol H./Bucuvalas, Michael J. (1980): Social Science Research and Decision-Making. New York: Columbia University Press.

Barbara Lee
Theories of Evaluation

> I was visiting a research facility recently, which has achieved a modest national reputation in the United States. It receives millions of dollars each year in grants and contracts to do mental health evaluation. Two years ago, several senior faculty decided to develop a program designed to offer graduate students at the University where they were co-located, a certificate program in evaluation.
>
> As I walked through the main lobby, I overheard the chairman of the curriculum committee for the certificate program talking with a visitor. The visitor was wondering out loud what evaluation really was, and what it would mean for someone to be "a certified evaluator", when they completed the certificate program.
>
> The chairman responded to the visitor, smiling. "You can do anything you want with it. No one really knows what evaluation is anyway."

1. Introduction

It is one of the interesting realities of evaluation, that even after over 30 years of discussion and thought about this emerging discipline, most of the people *doing* evaluation still come from training other than as evaluators. Furthermore, the well-known writers in the field of evaluation theory did not receive their formal education in a program designed to produce professional evaluators, although these have been in existence since the late 1970s. Some of this, of course, can be attributed to the relative newness of the profession. Many of the people who shaped the emerging discipline entered it in early or mid-career, mostly from the social sciences, and their interest in evaluation has been long-lived. Their ideas have, for the most part, continued to mature and be elaborated following the energizing debates that have characterized emergence of the field. Yet, it is still curious, that some of the people with well-established careers in evaluation, can comfortably admit that they don't know how to define just what it is.

On the positive side, this has resulted in a wonderful level of creativity and diversity in evaluation methods and thinking. Those educated in sociology, psychology, education, economics, business, and philosophy have brought their particular skills, methods, and professional perspectives to bear on the need to measure and judge value of social programs, where they are tested in the arena of harsh reality. Also, many evaluators have moved to this profession after years of work with the kind of programs within which they are now conducting evaluations. The value of this experiential expertise about what is being evaluated has brought about a general assumption that this is a necessary resource that must be present in any evaluation team. The down side is that relatively few people think inclusively about what evaluation theory is. Even those who are very experienced in doing evaluations easily oversimplify what the field is, apply research methods borrowed from other fields naively, or make evaluation practice (and therefore theory) seem undefined, as the committee chairman did in the example above.

This has been a persistent issue over time. Guba (1969) identified lack of definition of the field and lack of evaluation theory, as two of seven important gaps in the discipline of evaluation. In 1980, House still characterized the state of evaluation practice as marked by vitality and disorder, and Cronbach (1980) also spoke about the need for an evaluation profession that was clear about its role in society and about the nature of its work. Cronbach saw the social importance of evaluation as enormous, but saw its self-understanding as relatively minute. Eleven years later, Shadish (1992) responded to a review of his book on evaluation theory (Shadish/Cook/Leviton 1991), stating that there was even then, not much good theory in evaluation. As late as in 1997, questions were raised about the distinction, if there was one, between research and evaluation. The extended discussion of this topic on EVAL-TALK, an on-line discussion list sponsored by the American Evaluation Association, demonstrated once again that there is not yet full consensus on how to define the discipline of evaluation.

Nevertheless, there has been a great deal of elaboration in the past two decades around the early definitions of evaluation. Also, from Cronbach's (1980) simple definition of evaluation as the process by which a society learns about itself, through many variations by other theorists, several common elements have emerged. These will be considered using Shadish, Cook, & Leviton's (1991) organization of evaluation theory into five components; social programming, knowledge, value, use, and practice. We note that the apparent content of three of these is certainly sufficient in itself to distinguish evaluation from its kissing cousin, research[1], which addresses only construction of knowledge and research practice. However, the definition which is most straightforward, while including the most common and persistent ele-

---

1 There is a saying in self-help organizations that is often referred to as the "KISS" principle – keep it simple, stupid! The allusion here is to the relative simplicity of defining research as systematic inquiry, compared to evaluation, although evaluation professionals need to have a reasonably simple description of what the discipline is, as well.

ments of the discipline of evaluation, is that used by Donna Mertens (1998), who distinguishes evaluation from research in purpose, method, and use.

"Evaluation is the systematic investigation of the merit or worth of an object (program) for the purpose of reducing uncertainty in decision making." (Mertens 1998: 219).

This definition can include specialty areas like product, performance, and personnel evaluation, which are practiced by Michael Scriven and others who are very active in professional evaluation circles internationally. Scriven himself conceptualizes evaluation very broadly as a transdiscipline like statistics, whose methods and theories are used and useful in many contexts and many fields of study (Scriven 1999). In social program evaluation, the demanding nature of problems that must be dealt with to reduce uncertainty in decisions are more complicated than is generally true in applications like product evaluation. I have no dispute with Scrivens characterization of evaluation as a transdiscipline, but for the purpose of discussing evaluation theory, it is convenient to draw the examples primarily from program evaluation, because this tends to cover the largest area of complexity.

The emphasis within any given definition of evaluation, and in the particular evaluation theory or theories based on it, has generally varied depending on the discipline in which the writer was trained, prior to his/her experience in the practice of evaluation. The basic process described in Tyler's objectives-based model for evaluating educational curricula (Tyler 1949; Smith/Tyler 1942), for example, originated in education, which was already measurement oriented. Rossi and Freeman's comprehensive approach to evaluation used examples drawn primarily from sociology. However, the objectives-based evaluation developed first in education came to be widely used by sociologists, and Rossi and Freeman, as well as many other theorists, have had their work widely adapted to several fields besides sociology. Today, in light of models of theory, or meta-theory, such as those found in Shadish, Cook, & Leviton (1991) and in Scriven (1991), later theories are much more likely to be written with conscious attention to possible uses in a broad range of fields and contexts.

2. The activity of evaluation

Even though most people have never discussed the nature of evaluation, virtually all of us know at least what the *activity* of evaluation is. We all do it frequently. It is the action of examining some thing carefully, to determine the value of it – systematic investigation of merit or worth. The two roots of evaluation are information gathered according to some plan which ensures its credibility and objectivity, and a process by which value is assigned. Value determination requires identifying some basis for giving value definition and scale, but value itself is essentially subjective.

We are doing product evaluation when we comparison shop, and choose to skip evaluation if we make an impulse purchase. We are doing evaluation when we try to think through any decision, weighing the pros and cons, and we don't do it when we flip a coin to decide, or ask someone else to tell us what to do, decide that something "feels right", or look for divine inspiration. As an activity, evaluation is an alternative to random or wild guessing, use of insight, adherence to custom, to what we did yesterday, or to what someone instructs us to do, all of which can be valid ways of choosing individual actions. These are alternative ways of making decisions, with different risks and benefits attendant to each one. Society at several levels also uses evaluation to inform decision-making. Evaluation activity is an alternative to using political reasoning, influence by money or other power, following past policy, or taking a vote or referendum, to make informed choices on a course of action when there is more than one alternative.

Historically, there has been a great deal of activity in society designed to measure something about what social programs were doing, that preceded development of evaluation as a discipline. By 1800, statistical reports were in common use by governments, and by 1900, sociologists and other social scientists were conducting many studies around the world, in both industrialized and less industrialized nations. There were also studies of the effectiveness of public education and of specific educational methods. Educators were already evaluating the performance of students, and the step to evaluation of teaching and programs responsible for that performance was a natural one.

One of the earliest examples of a study with an evaluation purpose, was published by Joseph Rice (1897). His study established that time spent in spelling drills did not result in better spelling. At this time governments were also using external inspectors to do evaluations of public programs such as prisons, orphanages, and hospitals, as well as education (Madaus/Stufflebeam/Scriven 1983). Around the same time period, Alfred Binet had created his method for screening out retarded youth, and the concept of the intelligence quotient was introduced. A national committee chaired by Arthur Otis was formed in 1904 in the U.S.A. to study tests for classifying children & determining their progress, and the first group intelligence test was put into use for screening military personnel.

Rossi and Freeman (1982) suggest the driving force for evaluation activity around the beginning of the 20th century was the need for effective and economical means to provide literacy and occupational training, which had become important to maintaining the momentum of the industrial revolution. Evaluation activity at that time was essentially without theory, following a simple, measurement-focused paradigm, which assumed there was one reality that could be known within some probability, that objectivity could be value-free, and that measurement could be quantified. We might even reject much of this activity as "evaluation" today, because the basis for judging merit or value of the programs being studied was rarely thought about. It was widely assumed that if information was objective and available, it would lead naturally to judgements of comparative "goodness", and would be utilized by decision-makers (Scriven 1972, 1973; Shadish et al. 1991; and others).

As the role of government in providing human services expanded rapidly in the aftermath of the Great Depression and World War II, evaluation became institutionalized as integral to governance of social policy, especially in the United States. At the same time that evaluation was being stimulated by government demands for information, business and industry were also utilizing the results of evaluation studies. From these evaluations, our collective understanding of interpersonal interactions and group processes was growing rapidly, led by Kurt Lewin and his students (Patton 1997). Also, the scientific management movement in business and industry gained momentum with its time/motion studies, and this led to application of those methods to educational measurement in the form of the behavioral objectives movement.

Ralph W. Tyler was one of the first to articulate the behavioral objectives approach as a process for assessing educational programs or experiments. The 8-year study for which Tyler was research director, at the Bureau of Educational Research at Ohio State University, was published in 1942, using the measurement of objectives achieved for the outcome evaluation. The study was designed to determine if students from progressive high schools would perform as well in college as those from high schools using conventional, Carnegie-unit curricula (Smith/Tyler 1942). The thoughtfully designed process Tyler used was carefully conceived, and Tyler built on this experience to produce one of the first true theories of evaluation in 1949. The process he described for evaluating educational curricula detailed a process for determining the standards by which a program would be judged, primarily using panels of experts to design objectives for each program, with specific measurements tied to each one. This was the first time both methods of investigation and equally systematic methods of determining value were combined into one theory for judging programs. Guba and Lincoln (1981) described it even thirty years later as "...systematic in nature, elegant, precise, and internally logical" (p. 5). The Joint Committee for Standards in Educational Evaluation (1981) eventually designated Ralph W. Tyler as the "Father of Evaluation".

In the era following the two World Wars, there was an explosion of activity directed at solving social problems. Evaluations in the 1960s and 1970s were concerned with programs of delinquency prevention, family planning and other public health programs, agricultural and community development, pharmacological treatments, rehabilitation programs for felons, and public housing programs, as well as educational programs. No doubt the invention of high-speed computers also encouraged the spread of large scale evaluation activity.

The U.S. government required evaluation as part of many sweeping social programs directed at poverty, crime, illiteracy, and public health, and this requirement, coupled with a growing economy, stimulated the field of evaluation greatly. Through the same period of time, many development projects were funded by the World Bank (Chelimsky/Shadish 1997), which also required evaluation as a condition of funding, thus stimulating evaluation work in many third world countries. Most of these followed the objectives-based model that Tyler had first articulated. The criterion for judgement of value was nearly always how well the program met its objectives.

In the first text on evaluation research, Edward Suchman (1967) quoted Hans Zetterberg, who said that "one of the most appealing ideas of our century is the notion that science can be put to work to provide solutions to social problems." As experience with evaluation of large social programs and education across the world accumulated, people conducting these evaluations began to reflect on their choice of methods and what value seemed to be derived from doing these evaluations. By 1980, it was widely recognized that even the most scientifically sound evaluations were not guiding decisions as evaluators had hoped. The perception of a need for better, more effective methods in evaluation undoubtedly contributed to the formation of organizations where people practicing evaluation could exchange ideas and experience. In the United States in the late 1970's, in addition to subject-specific groups like educational associations, two organizations invited an inter-disciplinary view of evaluation. The academically oriented Evaluation Research Society and the practice oriented Evaluation Network came into existence, later merging into the American Evaluation Association. These organizations, coupled with the veritable explosion of published works on evaluations in the 1960's and 1970's, provided forums in which self-reflective theorizing about evaluation could flourish. The combined stimuli of economics, massive social change in the wake of the industrial revolution and two world wars, and the intellectual stimulation of these organizations and publications dealing with the subject, brought about the emergence of competing theories in evaluation.

3. Evolutionary forces shaping evaluation theory

It is apparent that evaluation activity is an integral part of human enterprise, in spite of the fact that there was little theorizing about it prior to the second half of the 20th century. The activity of evaluation is always initiated when someone perceives the need for information in order to make some kind of decision or choice. Individuals, businesses, organizations and societies all have decisions to make, and evaluation is always intended to provide information, which is expected to be unbiased, about the value of one or more possible choices or decisions. Whether evaluation is of a product (existing or potential), a program, personnel, performance, a major social intervention, or policy, is of little importance, because the basic role or purpose of evaluation is always the same, even though the methods used throughout the process can differ widely. The stimulus for evaluation is the need for information about the value of a program or "evaluand", a term coined by Scriven in 1973 to encompass inclusively a broad array of targets for evaluation such as programs, personnel, or a particular product.

Regardless of what stimulates the desire for information about a social program (the same reasoning applies to other evaluands), evaluation requires an investment of time, money, and attention, before the results are in. Furthermore, spending those resources studying the program can seem to compete with the program's need for resources to actually do the work they are doing, especially if resources are limited or diminishing. There is also bound to be someone or some group of staff or recipients of services, who think the fan (program) is already working well and should be left alone, lest tinkering makes it less effective than it was before the studies. They have to be sold on the idea that the systematically gathered information the evaluator can provide, and its contribution to the decision-making process in and about the program, will have value that exceeds the costs of doing it. Thus the evaluation often competes with what it is evaluating for resources, and is unlikely to win its fair share unless the evaluation does itself prove to be "of value". This is the force, analogous to natural selection for biological evolution, that drives development of evaluation methods and models. Like poorly adapted plants in a desert, evaluation methods in practice which are not so useful or cost-effective will become extinct during times when resources to do evaluation become limited.

The economic tension between evaluation and programs may be the reason that evaluation has been most visible in the United States. It always seems to have enough resources to waste – or to risk wasting – a little, both on programs and on evaluation. Although it is easy, then, to assume that evaluation as a profession and as a discipline will be practiced mostly in countries that are relatively resource rich, this has not proven to be true. If resources are extremely limited, it becomes even more important to know how well, or whether the social programs are succeeding in solving the problems for which they were begun. Where there is at least the possibility that the evaluation will prevent waste of precious resources, or will eventually save more money than it costs, or at least, where some person in power believes that is true, evaluation will be done. Thus, there has also been a lot of development of evaluation practice in the Third World countries, as well as in the industrialized nations. This has been encouraged by agencies such as the World Bank, which funds hundreds of development projects internationally every year, and which requires evaluation as a condition of that funding (Cook 1997). For reasons of both culture and cost, however, the use of experimental methods which has been advocated in the United States, has seen little or no use in the rest of the world.

4. What is "evaluation theory"?

There are two basic uses of the term "theory". According to Webster (1997, 2000), theory is defined as "...systematically organized knowledge applicable in a relatively wide variety of circumstances, especially a system of assumptions, accepted principles and rules of procedure devised to analyze, predict, or otherwise explain the nature or behavior of a specified set of phenomena". A second major definition is that theory is an assumption or guess based on limited knowledge or information. For the sake of realistic humility about the constantly evolving state of evaluation theory, we will keep both definitions in mind.

It does not serve the development of science in any field of study to elevate theory to the level of "truth", or to start treating it as truth. Truth, in fields much older than evaluation, too often turns out to look different and require even radical revision in the light of later discoveries. Nevertheless, it is theories that guide the work that eventually produces new energy sources, agricultural practices that vastly increase the food supply, and produces the kind of information from which significant social change will emerge, as well as better theories. Theory is powerful and important.

In 1972, Alkin (in Weiss 1972: 105-117) proposed that the purpose of evaluation theory is to predict fully the appropriateness of utilizing various evaluation strategies within a system. He said that a theory of evaluation should:

- Offer a conceptual scheme by which evaluation areas or problems are classified
- Define the strategies, including kinds of data, and means of analysis and reporting, appropriate to each of the areas of the conceptual scheme
- Provide systems of generalizations about the use of various evaluation procedures and techniques and their appropriateness to evaluation areas or problems.

Evaluation practice has expanded greatly in the 20th century, and in the last quarter of it a great deal of writing and theorizing was happening about how to do it, why one should do it or not, the ethical dilemmas in doing it, and the philosophical roots of it. One of the early comprehensive evaluation theories was published in 1967. One could argue that except for Daniel Stufflebeam's CIPP model (context, input, process, product), and Tyler's educational model, there was no evaluation theory prior to the 1980s. However, there was publication of several influential books in the 1980s offering competing theories about evaluation and how to do it. In 1980 Cronbach said "evaluation has become the liveliest frontier of American social science" (p. 12).

In addition to the several books published in the early 1980s which met Alkin's criteria for evaluation theory, some writers were moving into meta-theory, i.e., theorizing about evaluation theory itself. Michael Scriven was one of the most visible. Scriven (1991) has characterized evaluation as a trans-discipline whose subject matter is the study and improvement of certain tools for other disciplines, much like mathematics and statistics. In his useful and entertaining book, *Evaluation Thesaurus,* which was in its 4th edition in 1991, Scriven presents an interesting geographical metaphor for evaluation. In his "country of the mind", he conceptualizes the specific evaluation activities within other disciplines, and the complex interconnections between evaluation in specific fields like education or sociology and the core knowledge bases of the discipline of evaluation. Thus, Scriven defines evaluation most broadly, as "...the process of determining the merit, worth and value of things, and evaluations are the products of that process." (Scriven 1991: 1).

Scriven's very general definition is highly inclusive, embracing product and performance evaluation, and evaluation activity like that conducted on popularity of museum exhibits, as well as much evaluation activity without explicit theory or with very simple theories. This inclusion is very practical, because evaluation as a discipline has borrowed its methods and designs from many fields besides sociology and the other social sciences. It continues to do so, as the diversity of practitioners participating in evaluation conferences and on internet discussion groups demonstrates. Scriven's geographic metaphor helps us give appropriate attention to different levels of thinking about evaluation theory, and puts a host of evaluations quite different in subject and methodology into a conceptual pattern that clarifies considerably questions about the nature of evaluation in general.

We should note one other position on evaluation theory. Guba and Lincoln (1989) claimed to dismiss the need for theory on the grounds that all knowledge, including that of how to conduct evaluations, is a socially constructed reality with multiple perspectives on a program, the context, and the methods by which evaluation will be carried out. They claimed that dismissing any belief in an objective reality frees the evaluator to use many different methods, reducing those based on so-called "objective science" to the same status level as case studies and other qualitative methods, and perhaps below them.

Attempting to argue for a "theory-less" characterization of evaluation, however, simply begs the question of what we have learned about the complexities of evaluation practice in the 20th century, and the patterns emerging within theory. Evaluation is a complex process, working within a context that is even more complex, both of which must be understood for evaluation to achieve its purpose. We have multiple purposes for evaluation: to guide decision-making, to enlighten various stakeholder groups, to improve programs, to provide information relative to design of new programs (Shadish/Cook/Leviton 1991). We need theory to help us make some sense out of that complexity. One can believe in both objective and subjective reality, and still choose a wide variety of methods.

Shadish/Cook/Leviton (1991) also took the step into meta-theory. They described five components that they suggest are necessary for a comprehensive evaluation theory, although they caution the reader that there is no necessity for all theories to be comprehensive. The strengths and weaknesses of various theories of evaluation can themselves be evaluated within this framework, which can be applied usefully even to evaluation and theories that fall outside their own definition of social programs. Guba and Lincoln's naturalistic approaches can be examined just as readily within this framework as can other theories of evaluation. Thus we will use this framework to organize the following presentation of major areas of evaluation theory and the current and sometimes enduring debates within each one.

It should be noted that evaluation as a discipline has grown very rapidly, creatively, and in non-linear ways. This is no doubt greatly stimulated by its multi-disciplinary heritage. However, throughout this chapter, the emerging common themes running through different evaluation theories will be emphasized. This does not imply that a meta-theory of evaluation is necessarily evolving. Historically, evaluation theory did not develop along smoothly parallel lines, but in "fits and starts" (Shadish et al. 1991). The framework suggested by Shadish, Cook & Leviton (1991) of knowledge construction, knowledge use, evaluation practice, valuing, and social programming, gathers together ideas that are similar, thus clarifying the most important differences, regardless of the chronology of when the ideas developed.

5. The knowledge component: What counts as acceptable and credible evidence about programs? [2]

Evaluation theory started as a search for truth about effectiveness of solutions to social problems (Shadish et al. 1991: 67). An idea that was recognized early in the emergence of evaluation, was a point made by Suchman (in Weiss 1972: 72). He wrote that " ... to some extent, all programs of planned social change, whether educational, economic, medical, political, or religious, are required to provide "proof" of their legitimacy and effectiveness in order to justify public support." The need for information that would be credible to the public developed as governments got into the business of public solutions to social problems. Early in the history of evaluation, it was generally assumed that "truth" had an objective existence, and was there waiting to be discovered. The question, then, was how to measure it.

---

2   For the sake of brevity, we will use "program evaluation" generically. However, it is assumed that the same concepts and theory can be applied to areas that are not usually thought of as "programs", such as product or activity evaluation.

The method Tyler (1949) used in his theory for making knowledge claims required identifying specific objectives for educational outcomes and how those objectives would be measured. Tyler used content specialists and educational researchers (Guba/Lincoln 1981) to determine the objectives, an approach we would characterize today as a connoisseur model. By using experts to determine the objectives of the program, considerable responsiveness to complexity around cultural values was possible, even though this concern was not explicit. Tyler did not explain how to set the standards against which the value would be judged (i.e., how good is good enough?), nor was there provision for changes in either program or design once a study had begun (what we know as formative evaluation).

Tyler also distinguished between process evaluation (how does the program bring about the change in participants?) and impact evaluation (what kind of change occurred and how much?). Both were considered important to describe and measure. Tyler had great concern for the objectivity, reliability, and validity of the instruments used to test each objective, whether it was a process objective or an outcome. Tyler also discussed design issues related to making cause-effect connections between program and outcome. His model was clearly based on faith in the measurement-oriented scientific paradigm, and Tyler assumed that the results would be useful to the teachers for whom it was primarily designed, many of whom did use it. But because he insisted on *a priori* stipulation of objectives (Guba/Lincoln 1980), the flexibility of the model to change with time and context, adding, deleting, or prioritizing objectives, was very limited. He did, however, build into the process a provision that observed patterns of strength and weaknesses in curriculum would inform a new cycle of evaluation, an example of what would later come to be called continuous quality improvement.

Objectives-based evaluation still persists in the United States in major federal and state programs for supporting remedial educational services and special education for students with handicapping conditions. It is also a common model used in sociology, as well as in public information campaigns and a host of other contexts. This is also the most common form of what we might call " pre-professional" evaluation, asking the basically simple questions of " What did we want to do, and did we do it?"

All of the activities in the early years of evaluation were conceptualized with a strong focus on measurement and objectivity. Computer technology greatly expanded the capacity of these large evaluation studies to do sophisticated data analysis, and critiques of large-scale evaluations led to the promotion of experimental methodology to make evaluation results less open to challenge. Campbell & Stanley (1963) extended the range of designs considered to have scientific credibility with their influential book on quasi-experimental designs. At this point in history the language of evaluation was well under development. The use of science-based models and ideals for measurement in conducting evaluation was strongly reinforced by Donald T.

Campbell (1969) and his influential article on social reforms as experiments. Other writers like Michael Scriven and Lee Cronbach were also strongly committed to the use of science in constructing the knowledge used to support value claims.

Scriven's goal-free approach (1972, 1973) was originally offered as an alternative to the objectives-based approach to evaluation. Goal-free evaluation used both observation and experiment, and was strongly based on the scientific/measurement paradigm, emphasizing the importance of objectivity. At that time Scriven even advocated laboratory experiments in evaluation, although no one ever operationalized just how that would be accomplished, or whether the results would be useful in the more complicated "real" world environment. The goal-free approach put a great deal of power (and therefore risk) in the hands of the evaluators, who would not be told in advance what the people running the program thought was important or "should" be measured. But the difficulty of capturing all program effects made goal-free evaluations all too easy to dismiss or argue against. Michael Scriven and others still place their greatest faith in science, and in the willingness of policy makers and the public to use objectively gathered information as the primary basis for decisions in spite of considerable evidence that this simply does not happen (Patton 1980, 1997; Mertens 1998). One legacy of the goal-free approach, however, is the recognition that there is a need to be alert to the presence of unintended effects of programs, both bad and good, as well as those that are intended.

Other approaches designed specifically to supplement the limitations of Tyler's model were developed. Robert Stake (1967) was one of the early critics who pointed out the limitations of objectives-based evaluation, and who advocated for the concept that evaluation must always include both description and judgement. In his model for Responsive Evaluation, Stake said that the purpose of evaluation was to establish what congruence there was among the intended versus observed outcomes, the antecedents, and the transactions that occurred, linked by logical or empirical contingency. It was one of the first statements characterizing evaluation as a complex, but highly integrated activity, in which the judgement component was as important as science, and the methods of investigation did not rely solely on measurement.

Like Lee Cronbach, Robert Stake's background was in education, but both considered their theories of evaluation to apply across disciplines. Stake recommended case studies using naturalistic methods of observation, and reaction to those observations by program staff, participants, and other stakeholders, as a way to improve the usefulness of evaluation. All approaches to the collection of information, however, were expected to meet standards of objectivity, reliability, and validity. Stake's methods were adapted from those used in anthropology and other disciplines, relying on training, the use of multiple observers, and other techniques to prevent bias. Guba (1969) also strongly criticized the objectives-based model, and later became a leading advocate of naturalistic approaches to gathering information (Guba 1987; Guba/Lincoln 1989), which were designed to get relevant information quickly into the hands of decision-makers. These approaches were particularly successful in smaller, localized, program evaluations, and were especially popular in England, where the goal was to document in an impartial way, the experience of participation (Guba, in Weiss 1972).

In 1971, Stufflebeam et al. (1971) published a book describing the first truly sophisticated theory of evaluation which included all of the components Stake suggested, well elaborated and with methods tied to each one. The CIPP theory structured evaluation as four major components, each of which had specific suggestions on what to assess, how to assess it, and how to link it together with the other components. The four components of the CIPP model were context, input, process, and product, taking its terminology from industrial systems thinking.

The context component included investigating the setting in which a program operated, as well as determination of the program goals, which in turn were derived from the perceived social need the program was intended to fill. The input component included describing the variability among participants as they entered a program, the staff and skills that were necessary to make the program work, and the necessary resources of all kinds that would be required by the program. The process component was the actual activities of the program, complete with the reasons it was believed those activities would be linked to achieving the goals, what we would call the logic model for the program, or program theory today. The final component was product, and this included both desired and unexpected outcomes, thus adding an important element that had been missing in the objectives based approach to evaluation. Stufflebeam described a variety of designs and methods for assessing the products of programs, which again showed strong commitment to measurement and scientific/objective methods for determining value. It was a model that could be used both by evaluators working for the program managers (internal evaluation), and those who came in from the outside under contract to evaluate programs (external evaluation). It clearly favored what was assumed to be the relative objectivity of an evaluator being outside of the program being evaluated. The CIPP model is recognizable today, elaborated as development of the logic model for the program used to design the evaluation, or program theory (Chen 1990).

6. Where the transdisciplines of statistics and evaluation meet

As professional evaluation has become more and more international, cultural diversity of different countries has created another important challenge to measurement-based approaches to evaluation. The scientific, largely quantitative methods used in evaluation had already resulted in considerable emphasis in the profession on skill in the use of statistical analysis. Through the early history of evaluation, statistical analysis emphasized avoiding the mistake of saying the group with the program was different from the control or comparison group (without the program) on measures of success, when it really wasn't (Type I error). The statistics used most commonly were based on comparing groups, which works the best when the amount of variability within each group is not very great compared to the possible effect of a program on the individuals in the group.

However, statistics was developed for use in agriculture, where control of the environment is much simpler and the "individuals" to be measured are far more numerous than in the human world of social problems and programs. Also, unfortunately, measurement of human responses to programs is much more difficult and complicated than the response of corn to different fertilizers. The huge and mostly uniform samples used in agriculture simply did not exist in human society and using differences between program and no-program groups that were statistically significant as the standard for value simply did not work. Too many measurements lacked sensitivity enough to detect the complexity of individual responses to programs. The result was that most evaluations based on measurement did not confirm that there were any differences between people in, and those not in, the programs being evaluated.

Those with insight into statistical logic already knew that if a statistically significant difference was found, one could be very confident there really was an effect of the program, at least on whatever was being measured. But "no difference" usually did not mean that the program was "not working", because there were many other possibilities that would explain finding no differences. Today, even with the new emphasis on using power analysis with statistical findings, the rare occurrence of statistically significant differences between groups with and without the program being evaluated leads to too much belief that "nothing works". This made evaluation not so popular with the people running the programs, most of whom believed very sincerely that the program they were implementing was doing some good.

Another problem in using statistical significance as the value standard is that groups of humans often have variability that causes differences in how different people experience a program. In the decades of large sociological studies of major social experiments, it was generally assumed that if a program worked for the majority of people in a group, that it was valid (true), and would work for other people in general. The resulting concern with "how big a sample do we need", and the importance of "statistically significant differences" is still prevalent. But relevance of these concerns is greatly reduced when it is recognized that both programs and participants are embedded in culture, which is very complex and diverse, even within a single ethnic group, gender, and program. People simply aren't as uniform in their reactions to programs, as plants are to agricultural interventions.

Today there is general recognition of the complexity of measurement in evaluation. As a result, models for measurement now often use strategies like multivariate or structural equation modeling, time series analysis, clustering techniques, hierarchical linear modeling, and network analysis, among many others, to enhance sensitivity to differences. Multiple measures are often used, and measurement designs no longer see "people using program" as a single group. Minimally, gender, age, ethnicity, educational attainment, and economic resources, are consciously used when designing the analysis of results, so that differences in program effectiveness based on those individual characteristics are described and hopefully understood.

The hope of people doing evaluation had been that the standards of scientific measurement, if followed stringently, would produce highly credible evidence about programs. This hope, in practice, proved to be useful primarily in comparing final results of competing programs on simple measures, and provided little useful information about how and why the programs worked or did not work. Now many other methods of investigation are used in evaluation practice, and the information is not frequently not even appropriate for statistical analysis. Narrative analysis and Results Mapping (1999) are examples. However, some new statistical methods have been applied to the task of quantifying complex information. Guttentag (1975) used multi-attribute scaling to combine multiple criteria, and methods such as cluster analysis and Trochim's concept mapping have also used statistical techniques in creative and useful ways.

7. The cold war in evaluation

As theorists advocated different approaches about how to do evaluation, there came to be notable differences between naturalistic and measurement approaches in how roles were defined for the evaluators, in the kinds of activities that characterized an evaluation, and in the reports of results. These differences have been the subject of prolonged and persistent debate, sometimes characterized as the "paradigm wars". A paradigm is a world-view, a general perspective that is inevitably deeply embedded in the socialization of those who use any given one. Paradigms carry with them basic beliefs about the nature of reality, the nature of knowledge about that reality, and how one should approach systematic inquiry into that reality. The strength of a paradigm is that action is guided without needing to be reconstructed in each case. The weakness of paradigms is that the reason for action is hidden in the assumptions of the paradigm (Mertens 1998).

Over the three decades from the late 1960s to the late 1990s, the relative merit and usefulness of measurement and quantitative analysis in the scientific paradigm, versus naturalistic methods and qualitative reporting was debated, often with an adversarial flavor. However, the debate served to bring into consciousness at least for those participating in the fledgling professional organizations for evaluators, the nature of the assumptions hidden within the competing paradigms. Recently, Mertens (1998, 2000) has proposed what she characterizes as an emancipatory/transformative paradigm, although it shares many characteristics with the paradigm that is usually labeled constructivism. Her (1998: 6-21) discussion of the philosophical assumptions of these paradigms is enlightening, and highly recommended. Taken partly from that discussion, in brief, these competing paradigms are:

Positivism/postpositivism – associated with science. It assumes that:

–   Only one reality exists, and is discovered by eliminating alternative explanations
–   Objectivity and neutrality are the only appropriate standard for researchers
–   Methods should be drawn primarily from science and the study of the natural world, and should emphasize detecting cause-effect relationships and generalizability
–   Interpretive/constructivism – looks for meaning only within a particular context. It assumes:
–   Reality is socially constructed from multiple perspectives that may conflict with each other.
–   There is no " objective" reality, and the observer both influences and is influenced by those who are being observed. It is emphasized that the researchers must be conscious of each source of bias, especially their own.
–   Methods are mostly naturalistic, qualitative or narrative, and are directed at explanation of meaning, specific to the particular context, with generalization assumed to be limited

Transformation/emancipation – addresses directly differences in social power by relinquishing control of the evaluation research to the marginalized groups served by the program, assuming that bias is always present, and if any are to be advantaged, it should be those with least power. It assumes that:

–   There are multiple realities *and* these have varied influences on the social, political, and cultural context of both program and evaluation. Differences in program effect and effectiveness linked to diversity in economic status, ethnicity, gender, and disability are specifically addressed.
–   The observer should interact with the observed in a way that empowers the observed, but this does not imply reducing the responsibility of the evaluator(s) for ensuring appropriate standards for the evaluation.
–   Methods are pluralistic and evolving, and should seek to represent diverse voices, rather than to generalize.

The first paradigm is associated generally with science, although this is not strictly necessary. It operates under the assumption that reality is something fixed, and that reality exists apart from the varied biases and interpretations of those who attempt to discover what that reality is. It uses methods that attempt to eliminate the distorting effects of various forms of bias, most commonly by recommending random assignment or other so-called experimental or quasi-experimental methods.

The constructivist paradigm sees reality as constructed by those currently defining it. Therefore, there may be disagreements about what it is in any given evaluation, and that reality must be reconstructed every time a new question is asked. Guba and Lincoln (1989), in *Fourth Generation Evaluation* articulate this position quite thoroughly, stating that truth is: " ... a matter of consensus among informed and sophisticated constructors, not of correspondence with an objective reality." (p. 4). They see "reality" as a description of what is, at any given time, agreed upon as "real", putting the emphasis clearly on context, without necessarily having presumptions about whether the description will generalize to other contexts, even those that are very similar and involve the same program. This assumption about the nature of reality leads to the highest level of particularity, as compared to generalizability. That is, whatever knowledge claims are made by an evaluation, they will apply only to *that* specific program in *that* place, and at *that* time with *those* particular representatives of the stakeholder groups involved.

The transformative/emancipatory paradigm has basic assumptions about the nature of reality and methods of investigation similar to those in the constructivist paradigm. It differs because it explicitly includes the belief that differences in power among various stakeholders within groups, and between stakeholder groups, cause bias inevitably favoring the viewpoints of some groups over others (Mertens 1998, 2000). This paradigm recognizes that even the most so-called "objective" methods of random assignment and other experimental approaches have imbedded within them cultural values that favor the majority, ignore the individual, and tend to invalidate the unique experiences of minority or marginalized individuals. The strategy used is to identify these power relationships, and consciously empower the most disadvantaged groups by letting their questions, choice of methods, and interpretations guide the evaluation arena.

Regardless of individual philosophies about how independent (or not) reality may be from the necessarily flawed perceptions of the individual seeking to define it, in practice most of us experience reality as *relatively* stable. On the other hand, thanks to modern communications, most of us are quite aware of the diversity of viewpoints about virtually any question, and the multiple ways in which almost any finding can be interpreted and used. The common ground of all three paradigms, and variations of them, is the value placed on providing the most credible evidence possible for the knowledge claims made by a program and an evaluation of it. Similarly, we can agree to leave the debate about whether objectivity is truly possible to philosophers like Michael Scriven (1972, 1997), and settle for a practical compromise that respects both objective and subjective reality.

We can also agree that the effects of coercion and fear, as well as of assumed privilege, can lead to important and unpredictable (in direction) bias in our search for truth. Experience with evaluation in many international settings has validated the importance of the issues raised by the transformative paradigm (Mertens 2000). The common ground there is to build into our evaluation designs recognition of, and methods to detect, the pluralism of experience and the biases introduced by differences in power and the perception of how the evaluation results will be used. It implies also that the evaluators must work, as much as possible, directly with the stakeholders that have the least power.

It is certainly a reality, even though it may seem too obvious to mention, that evaluation always involves systematic inquiry and reporting, whether the paradigm is scientific-objective, or relative-subjective. Also, evaluation always involves some form of data collection with methods and instruments that will have credibility specific to the subject matter and the people who are affected in some way by the program and therefore the evaluation, and to the cultural, political, or other context (Patton 1997). It is unlikely that the commitment to using the objective scientific methods whenever that is possible, practical, and credible with those using the evaluation results, will change any time very soon. However, the trend toward methods in evaluation theories other than those thought of as "scientific" for constructing knowledge about programs is very likely to continue. Many writers have pointed out that good evaluation practice generally involves both quantitative and qualitative inquiry (Cook/Reichardt 1979; Cronbach 1980; House 1980; Krathwohl 1980; Patton 1997; Rossi/Freeman 1982; Weiss 1972; and others), and that even science cannot be regarded as being value-free (Nathan 1988; Patton 1997; Mertens 1998). Many different kinds of data, gathered by many different methods, can be relevant to the purpose of evaluation. Even so, all approaches to investigation value certain things. Reliability and accuracy are one of these values. Will the same thing be observed by others at the same time in a similar way, and, and if not, why not? Another general value is for validity – is what we are measuring what we really wanted to measure – which Mertens (1998) usefully breaks down into methodological validity and several others types that bear upon the interpersonal context within which the evaluation will be done.

Regardless of paradigm, the importance of valid comparisons and quantitative data to support claims of value is an accepted need in evaluation practice, as is the expectation that when qualitative methods are used, they must also strive either to be free of individual bias or to make the biases clear. Many of the practical implications for practice of evaluation using the transformative paradigm are yet to be tested, but it has made an invaluable contribution to the discipline of evaluation. Self-awareness of advantage built in by values embedded in culture, and of the consequences when the advantage of some groups is increased over others, can only make the evaluation discipline more valid in the pluralistic, multi-cultural society the world is becoming. Thomas D. Cook (in Chelimsky/Shadish 1997), reflecting on progress in the field of evaluation in the past 20 years, expressed the belief that the "quantitative/qualitative" wars have brought qualitative inquiry into full equality with quantitative methods for all but the diehards. It is fortunate for the discipline if this is true. In the past, the cold war about paradigms was conducted primarily in the academic arena, probably making distinctions that are much less obvious in actual practice of evaluation. In the field, especially outside the national arena, the use of many different kinds of methods is widely recognized as necessary.

It is important to recognize the significance of both subjective and objective experience of all stakeholders, in all its plurality, and valuing both simplicity and complexity can only bring theory and practice closer together, benefiting both. The most recent editions of durable books like those by Rossi and Freeman (1993), Posavac and Carey (1992), and Patton (1997), and other writings like those of Robert Stake (1995), Chen and Rossi (1992), House (1993), and Mertens (1998), reflect this trend. They discuss a wide range of methods and the situations in which they are applicable and credible. Patton and Mertens are particularly even-handed and inclusive about the wide range of qualitative and quantitative data they consider useful, often to meet different evaluative needs, or at different stages of program development, and sometimes as alternatives or cross validation for each other. Worthen et al. 1997, point out that the differences in paradigm have led to a richness of perspective in evaluation, and offer the opinion that the field is still too young to choose a single paradigm. As an alternative, we might simply opt for more clarity about the paradigm or paradigms in use, so that fewer of our assumptions are hidden, especially from ourselves.

8. Value – what kind, how much, to whom, and under what conditions?

In the early years of the profession, many evaluators relied upon such standards as "how well the objectives of the program were met", and it was generally assumed that the measurements used in evaluation were value-free. But programs themselves are designed around specific value decisions about what is important, and the questions asked about programs will differ depending on the particular group and the stake they have in the outcome (Weiss 1972). Both programs and evaluations exist in a profoundly political environment (Weiss 1972; House 1993). Even the scientific, comparative approaches used by Scriven, Campbell, and Rossi, among others, result only in data which must be interpreted, thus bringing in both values and ethics. Shadish et al. (1991) use the Sesame Street evaluation as an example.

Cook et al. (1975) found that children who watch Sesame Street more often do learn some language skills, which is certainly of value to those who designed the program to do exactly that. However, because children from poor families watch it less than those from families with more economic resources, the social effect of the program is to widen the achievement gap between the poor and not poor. By whose standards of value, then, would the program be judged? The answer can only be given when competing values are considered and made clear, and even then it is hard to predict who in what group will choose which value. Evaluation theories differ in how they would treat this kind of issue. Some will advocate for some values over others, such as Scriven, who would choose based on assessment of need. In this case, the need is for higher achievement of children, and the increasing gap between poor and not poor would be considered secondary. Others like Stake and Weiss will describe values and who holds them, without claiming one is superior over the other. This latter approach clearly favors a reality in which plural values compete with each other in the political arena. The former approach is vulnerable to attack by stakeholder groups who perceive or believe their values were not attended to equitably.

Obviously, the data collected in an investigation of a program has no real value until it is interpreted. If "merit" is considered to be as simple as dollars and cents, someone still has to make the decision about whether more is better, or less is better. But even in product evaluation, there are multiple standards that can be applied, and value is ultimately a judgement, not a matter of the relatively stable reality we call "knowledge". Early in the history of evaluation theory, some theorists recognized that the perspective on value would vary depending on the relationship of the people doing the judgement of value with the program or other object of evaluation. Carol Weiss, a sociologist, saw evaluation as a means to enlighten the complex working of institutions (Shadish et al. 1991). She is credited with a career-long recognition of the political and organizational realities within which evaluation takes place, including the origin of the commonly used term "stakeholder".

There are a number of different stakeholder groups whose interest in a program, and therefore basis for judgement of value, will vary. Minimally, this includes: (a) the people funding the program, (b) those funding the evaluation, (c) the staff of the program or those who produce the product, and (d) the intended beneficiaries of the program being evaluated. In the broadest context, because social programs are designed to meet social needs, the larger society within which the program or product is used, the public, is also a significant stakeholder group. Theorists in evaluation have differed in the importance they have given to different stakeholders, and all recognize that no single stakeholder group is made up of people who all hold exactly the same set of values.

Michael Scriven and Peter Rossi, for example, have emphasized the public interest as the most important group of stakeholders. As a natural result, both have emphasized using methods of assessing needs as part of their recommendations. Both seem to believe that it is possible to separate "need" from "want" and "demand", but if the evaluator's perception and interpretation of these is not given primacy, this too becomes a matter of perspective.

There was a recent on-line debate (EVALTALK 1999) about definition of need for people with severe mental illness, which illustrates the differences inherent in the concept of "public good". In that exchange Scriven expressed the belief that there are values external to the recipients or targets of a social program, such as control of symptoms of mental illness, which are primary. This author argued that the same "general public" also places great value on the freedom of individual choice, and on other individual freedoms, and that there are tradeoffs to be made by people taking the medication between symptom control and sexual or creative functioning, for example. People with serious mental illness to live with might see their needs quite differently, and certainly in a more complex way than simply "symptom relief". Even the definition of mental health varies among different stakeholder groups. The kind of programs designed to meet those differing values about what is the true "need", will be quite different. One might target ways to achieve better compliance with medication regimes, while another would emphasize research targeted at finding medications with fewer unwanted side effects. It is obviously a matter of opinion and value choices whether one approach should be valued over another, and in a society that values pluralism, both would be addressed.

Shadish (1991) points out that Scriven discusses the assignment of value with much more detail than most theorists, who agree on the importance of determining the criteria for value, but provide relatively little guidance about how to do that. Scriven's goal-free approach was directly targeted to avoid the bias of focusing evaluation on the outcomes chosen by the program staff or managers. Instead, the evaluator would have to look for all possible outcomes, and is directed to look for the "right things", although the way to determine exactly what those right things are is not clear. In other words, evaluation must evaluate the goals of a program, as well as the attainment of those goals. It is implicit in Scriven's ideas, as well as those who favor quantitative/scientific methodology, that true value is relatively universal, and that the appropriate methods will be able to detect it.

In social policy, a number of different value issues exist, including justice, freedom, human rights, liberty, equality, and utility (Shadish et al. 1991). Cronbach (1980), Weiss (1973, 1992), and Robert Stake (1975) take the broadest perspectives by recommending the evaluator consult with all stakeholders, and when that is impossible, the evaluator should attempt to represent the interests and concerns of the missing stakeholders her/himself. Wholey (Shadish et al. 1991) is concerned mostly with program managers and whether or not goals have been met, and that focus is reasonable considering that his work has primarily been inside the many levels of governmental management. Wholey developed the concept of evaluability assessment, to determine if a program is sufficiently stable and consistent in its operation, to make designing a summative or outcome evaluation relevant, thus emphasizing utility. House emphasizes justice, and Rossi focuses on practicality and utility. Rossi (1993) also places great value on being clear and explicit about whose values are being used, and what those values are, but he implies the existence of values that transcend specific stakeholder groups, as does Scriven. Cronbach (1980) prefers to leave judgement of value up to the decision makers.

Developments in the last decade of evaluation theory have seen a growing interest, especially in the international arena, in combining explicit clarification of the values held by different stakeholder groups and an equally explicit value in equalizing power differences among stakeholder groups. Some approaches like empowerment evaluation (Fetterman 1995) and emancipatory/transformative evaluation (Mertens 1998, 2000), take the position that there is always bias inherent in defining evaluation goals, questions, and methods by those in decision-making positions (usually program management). Stakeholder groups such as those who are homeless, or recipients of welfare, especially those marginalized in the society at large, will have less power to define the standards by which a program will be judged. The empowerment approaches seek these groups out, and use methods explicitly biased to equalize the influence of these less powerful stakeholders with the stronger ones.

A result of the trend toward reversing the usual exercise of power by different stakeholder groups, is that pluralism in value descriptions and democratization tend to be encouraged. The description of whose values under what contingencies, are going to continue to be prominent in the discipline, alongside the recognition of some values about which there is more consensus, such as fairness, absence of bias, accuracy, and credibility of evidence by multiple standards. It is obvious that it is impossible to represent all possible value systems when designing and executing evaluations. The area of value and the appropriate way for evaluators to participate in the determination of value beyond simply collecting information, is less coherent than any other aspect of evaluation theory. Nevertheless, those who practice the discipline of evaluation, recognize that values are built in to every phase of evaluation work. These need to be made clear, or the claims to credibility of evaluation results will suffer greatly.

9. Who cares?! The component of Use

The first evaluation theories emphasized measurement and experimental designs that had the potential to make causal connections, based on an enthusiastic and idealistic belief that reliable, valid data gathered using the methods of social science would be valued and used by policy makers and the public. By the late 1970s, in the practice of evaluation, however, many noticed that evaluations were rarely used. Also, there was a great deal of evaluation activity going on for which the scientific paradigm and experimental or quasi-experimental methods simply did not apply or were impossible to implement. As the limitations of experimental method became more obvious, a variety of tools were being brought in from anthropology, qualitative sociology, and phenomenology (Patton 1997) that it was hoped would yield information of more value to programs, and therefore be more likely to be used. Books like Stake's (1975) work on the responsive evaluation approach and Patton's (1978) book on *Utilization-Focused Evaluation,* became widely used by evaluation practitioners.

Experimental designs are relatively rarely possible, and the more qualitative and more discovery-oriented methods recommended by Stake and Patton were found to be widely useful in the many relatively small, local programs where much evaluation was being done. In case studies and other qualitative approaches, objectivity, or more accurately, bias-avoidance, was achieved primarily by hiring evaluators from outside the program, multiple observers, and by applying tested methods of observation and recording.

Some other perspectives on evaluation were articulated early, that recognized other elements of the context in which evaluation occurred and how that context affected use of evaluation. Carol Weiss was one of these. She emphasized methods for understanding and dealing with the political environment in which evaluation took place (Weiss 1972 and 1973), and dealt with the questions of use of evaluation results in some depth. One result of Weiss's use of decision theory was recognition that there is a general resistance of social programs to change, even when there is good information about what needs to be changed provided by evaluation. This happens not only because those working in the program are invested in its survival, but because the social decision-making process is notoriously slow and dependent on political, rather than rational, processes.

The necessary balance in evaluation theory between scientific rigor and usefulness was seen in several of Cronbach's (1980) theses, such as the 58th, that merit of a program evaluation is not in the form of the inquiry, but in the relevance of the information. That balance is summed up in the 95th thesis: "Scientific quality is not the principal standard; an evaluation should aim to be comprehensible, correct and complete, and credible to partisans on all sides" (Cronbach et al. 1980: 11). Cronbach also recognized that generalization or replication is virtually impossible, expressing a deep respect for the specificity of context effects, which is an idea that should probably be more widely accepted today than it is.

The concern with whether or not evaluation findings will be used continues. Patton's book addresses utilization very directly, and is now in its 3rd edition (1998), continuing to be a useful guide for those wanting to maximize the use of evaluation. This approach is undoubtedly valid especially for internal evaluation, or situations in which decisions are primarily local ones. But the larger the scale of the social problem and program solution, the more difficult it is to see any change at all in response to evaluation findings. This does not necessarily mean the results do not have any effect at all. They may well become part of the evidence that will later have a cumulative effect on policy. Carol Weiss, in particular, advocates for the concept of incremental change in programs, and for the use of methods that will lead to recommendations for improvements of smaller scale. However, she also sees enlightenment to be a major goal of evaluation (Shadish et al. 1991), obviously placing value on social awareness, which may eventually lead to the development of better programs or alternative solutions to the original social need.

At this stage in the development of the discipline of evaluation, all but the diehards Cook (1997) refers to acknowledge that it is legitimate for the evaluator to be concerned about whether and how the results of an evaluation will be used. This overlaps with ethical issues as well as legal ones (Who actually owns the findings? How should an evaluator respond when the results are used inappropriately or suppressed?). At the far end of the range are Patton (1998) and others like Fetterman (1995), whose empowerment evaluation methods are most clearly designed to maximize use. Most will also agree that program improvement is a more important goal than summary judgements about a program's overall worth. Incremental change is accepted, as is the goal of simply informing stakeholders in the evaluation about what a program is doing, how well that seems to be working, and what is responsible for the effects or lack thereof. It is generally agreed that results need to be fed back early, and over time, to those participating in the evaluation, and the formal reports will not necessarily be the most useful way to make findings known. At all stages of the conceptualization, implementation, and completion of evaluation, what the program stakeholders perceive will be of use to them must be attended to. If there are other agendas, these stakeholders will have to be convinced of their usefulness before resources are expended. Especially in evaluations of large social programs, the primary goal is enlightenment, which might later influence policy decisions, and the worth of evaluation is not limited to whether or not results are immediately used in decision-making.

10. Practice: What do we do, under what contingencies, and how do we do it?

There is probably more written about evaluation practice than any other component of evaluation theory. The literature on methods and other aspects of practice is very large, and constantly growing. Evaluators now have a great wealth of methods, models, styles, and reporting formats to draw upon that have been invented, adapted, borrowed, or stolen from many other fields (Chelimsky/Shadish 1997), including economics, personnel assessment, product evaluation and auditing, to name only a few (Scriven 1991). The development of the discipline of evaluation has been anything but linear, with evaluation in industry, social experimentation, education, policy, and other areas, evolving at the same time. In addition, the use of methods first developed in the United States in international settings, as brought about not only creative adaptation of those methods, but the development of new ones (Chelimsky/Shadish 1997). To provide details of practice in all areas where evaluation has been important, far more space would be needed than available here. Nevertheless, certain things are characteristic of evaluation practice in every field, and every setting. These are proposed as the common ground of theory about evaluation practice.

Methods and practice of evaluation are not independent of the setting and context within which it will occur. Because any particular method or model used in practice must be applied to a specific situation or program, intimate knowledge of the evaluand is also needed. Dual expertise is necessary, either in one person, or in an evaluation team, in order to have a sufficiently deep understanding of how any object of evaluation functions, and how it interacts with the context in which it exists and operates. This necessity has resulted in increasing recognition of the synergy created by bringing the skills of those doing the program into partnership with the skills of those designing the evaluation. But in business and industry, as well as other arenas, the decision to evaluate and the methods used are not just a matter of good "scientific" design and credibility. What methods to use is essentially a political decision, over which the evaluator has influence and sometimes veto rights, although a veto of what those contracting for an evaluation wanted to see would undoubtedly result in a search for a more cooperative evaluator.

It is commonly understood by evaluation professionals, that in practice evaluation should be, as much as possible, comprehensive. In Rossi & Freeman (1982), comprehensive evaluation is defined as "analysis covering the conceptualization and design of interventions, the monitoring of program implementation, and the assessment of program utility" (p. 16). They use terms such as "target population, target problem, formative research". These terms require a little adaptation to apply to other kinds of evaluands than "programs", but they do apply. Just as Stufflebeam's CIPP model directed attention at different aspects of the process (context, input, process, product), it is generally accepted now that evaluation should be comprehensive in its thinking, even if there are severe limits on how much of this will be addressed in any particular evaluation. A professional evaluator, whether coming to this role from a formal training program or from one of the social sciences, will always pay attention to what is *not* being done, what is not being evaluated, and whose perspective is being left out. In addition, the evaluator will also consider the possible consequences of those omissions, and make these explicit.

Evaluation practitioners must be aware of the different groups of people whose lives are affected by a program (or other evaluand), and those whose decisions will affect its future (Bryk (Ed.) 1983: 1). At the very minimum, the stakeholder groups include people who deliver a program, those who fund the program (directly and indirectly, as with taxes), and those who are the intended recipients of a program. The stakeholder approach to evaluation can be time-consuming and difficult (Gold, in Bryk 1983). Its purpose is to identify initial expectations of each stakeholder group, both for the program and for the evaluation, to negotiate a workable set of expectations, considering the reality within which the program and its evaluation will operate, and to modify those expectations or the program, as results come in. In practice, much time can be consumed trying to negotiate reasonable compromises to what are often conflicting agendas from different groups.

Although it is generally accepted now that evaluation is, to some degree, accountable to all stakeholder groups, including the general public. However, it is often difficult to resolve competing expectations from different stakeholders, as when a public agency has resources too limited to provide the mental health programs that consumers of those services believe to be essential. As a result, relatively little evaluation practice follows this approach completely. Even so, it would be very difficult to find a professional evaluator who did not acknowledge the importance of being aware of the issues of all stakeholder groups, and the desirability of working or consulting directly with as many as possible.

An important understanding of evaluation practice is that the methods must be appropriate to the questions, meaning financially, culturally, and meaningfully. For example, the 3rd edition of Patton's *Utilization-Focused Evaluation* (1997) provides details of how to establish a working relationship with program staff and other stakeholders, how to assess readiness for evaluation, clarify goals for both the program and the evaluation, describe and monitor the implementation of the program as well as its outcomes, how to focus the evaluation, select methods from both quantitative and qualitative domains, present information, and participate in the judgements about interpretation. Like Rossi and Freeman (1993), Patton's approach is comprehensive, and books by these authors provide a great deal of practical advice about how to approach the complex tasks involved with evaluation.

Other writers such as Posavac&Carey (1997), offer little that is new or innovative in theory of evaluation practice. However, they do provide quite succinct descriptions of most of the practical issues confronted by an evaluator. They discuss different types of evaluations and the situations in which each one is most appropriate. Posavac&Carey discuss the roles of the evaluators, offer some practical advice on how to handle various troublesome attitudes toward evaluation, and help organize the range of evaluation questions that may be asked. They talk about how to set criteria for success, they discuss the ethical issues that will confront an evaluator in the field and how these might be handled, and describe a variety of quantitative and qualitative methods for gathering the information needed in an evaluation. Issues of design and how these affect the credibility of results is covered, as is the development of a reporting plan and reports, and how to encourage utilization.

The CIPP model of Rossi and Freeman (1985, 1993) is still considered a useful way to think about program evaluation, and their writing makes a conscious attempt to include all credible methods into their presentation of how to practice evaluation. They manage to describe trade-offs and priorities (Shadish et al. 1991) for different ways of doing the same evaluation activity, and this is especially clear for impact assessment. They address in some detail how to tailor their model of comprehensive evaluation to a particular situation in which resources are limited, or when the stage of program development varies. This practice maintains the broader perspective of the evaluator much better than the focussing devices recommended by Stake (1975) in responsive evaluation.

Similarly, Patton (1998) provides much "what to do and how to do it" detail about practice, as do Guba and Lincoln (1981), Mertens (1998), Scriven (1982), Cronbach et al. (1980), and other authors who are less well known. In addition, some publishers have specialized in evaluation methods and other writing about evaluation (especially Sage Publications, in the United States), and a review of the titles in their catalogs clearly reveals just how much has happened in the 30 year history of the discipline around methods. Quantitative method books still outnumber qualitative ones, but the gap is clearly narrowing rapidly, and more and more published works take a comprehensive and eclectic position. Furthermore, there is now a trend to more specific methodology in evaluation method books, as experience in practice accumulates in specialty areas. The number of people who come to the profession and practice of evaluation from other fields no doubt contributes a great deal to this creativity and variety of ideas, and there is a great deal of practical experience behind most of the writing.

In the practice arena, it is widely recognized that much greater methodological skill and skill in working with organizations is necessary in evaluation practice today than it was 30 years ago (Posavac & Carey 1997). Programs (or other evaluands) are seen as more complex and dynamic, and often unique to a particular program setting and time in history. Therefore, what works in one place will most likely have to be extensively adapted in order to work in another. Evaluation practice is more sensitive to differences among various stakeholder needs, and Patton (1997), Fetterman (1995) and a few others have provided suggestions about how to accomplish this.

The importance of context for the program and for the evaluation is recognized by virtually all theories about practice. Evaluation practice has become quite sophisticated in methods and perspective, and is much more likely today to be appropriate to a given situation and useful to those who request it. Experience across the globe has added even more insight to the contingencies of evaluation practice, as well as some new methods (Chelimsky/ Shadish 1997; Mertens 2000). Even so, it does not seem likely that the sense of change and excitement on the evaluation frontier noted first more than 20 years ago, is likely to diminish any time very soon. There is ample challenge in the details of evaluation practice, attempting to capture judgments of value for constantly changing social programs and even the needs for which programs are created, for continuing creativity in both theory and practice.

All of this dynamic creativity in evaluation practice suggests that there may be no such creature as a "general practice evaluator". There is simply too much to learn both about the kinds of programs being evaluated and about the methods useful in specific circumstances for anyone to master them all. Practitioners of evaluation *will* be specialists, and a reasonably humble self-image and respect for the collaborative process will no doubt work more consistently than reliance on general skills or research training.

11. Social programming: For whose good? Who benefits, and who is harmed?

The ideas presented by Cronbach and Associates in one of several influential books published in the early 1980s, *Toward Reform of Program Evaluation* (1982*)*, originated in one of the developing forums for evaluation debate, the Stanford Evaluation Consortium, which was established and active from 1973 to 1979. A majority of forum members were educators, but sociology, psychology, statistics, and communication research were also represented. This multidisciplinary composition strongly influenced what emerged from that group, and was a good example of how evaluation theory has been influenced by the challenge of inter-disciplinary discourse. Differences among the varied disciplinary assumptions and approaches revealed early the importance of documenting the social purpose behind both programs and evaluations, as well as how evaluation might affect the social context of the program.

The 95 theses discussed in Cronbach's book (1982), partially a product of the consortium debates, are a mixture of criticism, theory, concepts, ethics, and common sense about the practice of evaluation, access to the information it delivers, and the training and professional development of evaluators. Cronbach, like Weiss, was already conceptualizing evaluation not merely as it was used in education or government, but as a novel political institution, based on the premise that evaluation policies should emerge from the social decision-making process. The 11th thesis, that "A theory of evaluation must be as much a theory of political interaction as it is a theory of how to determine facts", reflected Cronbach's recognition of the importance of this political context, as well as the complexity and subjectivity inherent in it.

Cronbach's (1980) concept of evaluation was frankly biased toward social action and facilitation of a democratic, pluralistic process, stating that the mission of evaluation is to enlighten all participants in a program. It was one of the first works theorizing about evaluation that recognized that even though rigorous, credible methods may be thought to be relatively value-neutral, evaluation as a whole is not. Information can be biased by the choice of questions to ask, and can often be used both to validate, and potentially discredit, any particular program or practice within a program. Cronbach recognized that the most likely effect of comprehensive evaluation would be to encourage pluralism.

Coming from a sociological perspective, Rossi & Freeman (1982, 1993) saw the development of evaluation as powered by growth and refinement of social science research methods. However, they also recognized early the equally important influence of political changes such as the New Deal social programs introduced in the U.S.A. under President Roosevelt's administration in the early 40s, or the programs funded in the 1960s by the War on Poverty in the USA (Patton 1997). The growth of large scale social programs in urban development, technological education, and public health, also brought with it large-scale evaluations in the industrialized countries in Europe, especially France, Belgium, Germany, and England, and in the United States, as well as in Asia, Africa, and Latin America.

What is the effect on society of all this evaluation activity? Rossi and Freeman (1982) note that the types of information evaluations can provide are of use to all policy makers, regardless of political orientation. Information on program efficiency, efficacy, and accountability is useful regardless of the social values and goals of people in politically powerful positions. In democratic political systems, that information is also important to the voters, but the emphasis of some writers in the 1970s and early 1980s that the goal of evaluation was to improve society and make it more democratic, was more bias than necessity. For example, Rossi and Freeman (1982) asserted that evaluation is political and managerial, an input into the complex mosaic from which emerges policy decisions about the planning, design, implementation, and continuance of programs to better the human condition. Clearly that statement would have the same claim to validity if the value was to change the human condition in some way other than to "better" it. The enduring problem in the assignment of value to programs, is that what is desirable to some stakeholders may be undesirable to others. By whose standards, then, is "better" to be measured?

Ernest House (1980) discussed this issue, noting that even the concept of "value" implies some kind of relative "goodness". This further implies judgement of some kind that may be unique to the judge who is making it, as well as to the specific time and context within which it is made. Thus, to understand the unique context of any given evaluation, the implicit values of the stakeholders, the evaluator, and the evaluation itself must be clear, and described with impartiality. This position implies that evaluation in general will encourage political pluralism. House regards the underlying basis of evaluation to be moral values conceived within a pluralist conception of justice. In his view, evaluation is a social decision procedure, with democratic and pluralistic values built in.

As discussed earlier, there is general agreement in evaluation theory, that evaluation is about assigning value, and values are a matter of context and cultural (as well as personal) perspective. Thus, the questions and methods used to answer evaluation questions should be inclusive of values from all stakeholder groups, including the society itself. This means that there will often be competing values. Choices will inevitably result, and thus necessarily introduce some kind of bias. Theories of evaluation need to be clear about the basis for making choices. Theories that that emphasize empowerment and transformation of less-advantaged stakeholders is most clear about how to make those choices.

In the empowerment evaluation model proposed by Fetterman (1995, 1997), the effects of the evaluator and the evaluation upon the program (i.e., interactions within, and with context) were consciously considered. The problem for evaluators is that empowering certain stakeholder groups inevitably encourages the tendency to „take sides" or to become an advocate. In empowerment evaluation, like earlier models, value-pluralism and methods which are, as much as possible, value-neutral, continue to be the ideal. But the choice suggested by empowerment evaluation comes from a recognition that when evaluation is responsive to any particular group, the findings will empower that group. Empowerment evaluation specifically works to increase the power of those affected by the program, and this will be practiced with all stakeholder groups.

Mertens (1998, 2000) carries this concept to a logical, but perhaps controversial conclusion. First, however, she specifically and consciously includes the earlier roles filled by evaluators over three decades as still relevant to all evaluation. In her view, like that of most other theorists, evaluators should investigate programs using a variety of methods appropriate to the values of impartiality and responsive to the varied values of all stakeholder groups. This information should be described with as little (or at least known) bias as possible. Evaluators working within the discipline of evaluation should do their best to measure what is described with awareness of and clarity about the biases imposed by a particular selection of questions and methods, including those coming from the evaluator's own working paradigm. As much as possible, all of what the program and agents of the program and funding agencies, beneficiaries, and victims (those affected negatively by a program) are actually doing to each other is described in a value-neutral way. The consequences, both intended and unintended, of all that „doingness" is also described. The program agents, beneficiaries, and others affected by the program and the evaluation, are helped to clarify the values which they have used in defining the problem the program was intended to address, and from which they have chosen what to measure (if anything).

All stakeholder groups, to the extent possible, are encouraged to an informed judgement of value. At this point, Mertens departs from the paradigms used by other theorists. She states that the conscious goal of evaluation is to offset the natural power differentials that exist among stakeholder groups due to economics, social stigma and marginalization, role in the organization providing the program, and the natural power possessed by those who fund the program and the evaluation. Mertens (1998) view is that evaluation will contribute to power for some stakeholder groups, especially by omitting the perspectives of any one. It should counter this, she suggests, by consciously choosing the most marginalized and disempowered groups around which to design the evaluation, explicitly attempting to transform the balance of power into one that is more democratic and pluralistic. She suggests that the alternative is not neutrality, but potentially harmful reinforcement of the power of the dominant group, and disempowerment of those less privileged.

It is unclear the degree to which this kind of social programming can be applied in practice. Most people in " privileged" groups sincerely believe their privilege is justified and appropriate. Even those with very positive views of human nature can see that this is expecting a great amount of altruistic willingness to put the interests of others and of the whole above themselves and the group of which they are part. In a theoretical situation many of us can probably agree with the worthy goal of equalizing power for the oppressed. But in the world of often-harsh reality, fears about job security and even the appropriate desire to believe one is doing a good job are potent motives to preserve the status quo.

Most theorists would probably agree that " fairness to all stakeholders" is an intended and intentional ethic for evaluators. It is impossible to address a social need without reflecting certain values about social programming, whether we choose to be aware of it or not. Theorists have differed greatly over the years in how much they hold the evaluator responsible for exposing those values and attempting to influence them. The field of evaluation has become more sophisticated over time, and the reality has emerged that it is a highly interactive profession, in which skills in collaboration and working with organizations in a political context are as vital as skill in gathering information and interpreting it appropriately. The most recent theorists in the participatory, empowerment, and transformative models, force the evaluator or evaluation team to consciously " take sides", clearly believing that true neutrality is a practical impossibility. They propose that the choice of which side to take should be based on the belief that power in society should be more equally distributed, and that pluralism in social problem solving in general should be encouraged. Therefore, Mertens (1998) suggests, evaluation should be transformative, aware of and consciously using its own power of influence to enhance democratic pluralism. At the very least, Mertens challenges all evaluators to be aware of how the power of their expertise is affecting those whose lives are affected by programs.

12. Theoretical Common Ground in the Discipline of Evaluation

It has been a running theme throughout this chapter, that over three decades of disciplinary development, there has been considerable convergence among evaluators from many different settings and fields of study about what evaluation should aim to accomplish, and how to accomplish it. This has come about mostly because diversity of evaluation thinking, methods, and motives has been incorporated into impressive methodological and practical pluralism. Because the discipline of evaluation is one in which most practitioners received their primary training in fields other than evaluation, it is particularly important for the common ground of the discipline of evaluation to be recognized. With so many people entering the profession from a whole host of side doors, we risk debating over and over issues that have already gone through much philosophical development in this discipline. The following points are offered to encourage consolidation of experience and argument, and hopefully putting some of the ongoing theoretical differences into perspective. Reviewing these, it seems that there is actually a surprisingly firm foundation of theory about the profession of evaluation, and that each decade has seen significant creativity in thinking about every component of theory. At the very least, it is hoped that this attempt as synthesis will stimulate discussion about what the common ground of the evaluation discipline really is.

Evaluation as a profession and as a discipline, is a complex process of investigating programs, products, processes, performance, or other activities designed in response to a perception of social need, in order to facilitate public (or other defined groups) judgments of their worth or merit.

Evaluation always involves the collection of information about the object of evaluation. This information includes qualitative, quantitative, descriptive, and experiential data, and methods must be adapted to the specific cultural context. For each type of data, the basis for and limits of its claims to credibility is made explicitly clear.

Evaluation always involves making judgements of worth, and makes clear the basis for judgement, who is choosing those values, and the context within which values are chosen and judgements made. Facts and values are inextricably intertwined, and even the most " scientific" methods have built-in bias.

Evaluation is an interactive process, rather than prescription by the evaluator, in which the expertise of all stakeholder groups is (should be) utilized. Evaluation ideally uses methods selected collaboratively by all groups who have a significant stake in the object of evaluation, and the results of the evaluation. These are chosen for their applicability to, and credibility about, the questions of all stakeholders, including the larger society. Methods are chosen in ways that balance cost (human and material) with the potential worth of the evaluation itself, the importance of the social need which the object of evaluation was intended to fill, and the urgency of making decisions of worth.

The object of evaluation is always studied in the context in which it exists or is used. "Value" cannot be separated from the context in which the object of evaluation operates. The evaluation ideally makes clear the nature of that physical, economic, cultural, historical, and political context, and how these elements affect the object of evaluation and the evaluation itself. Because context is essential to judgements of worth, and is never simple, the use of the evaluation itself will be limited when applied to other contexts, and no assumptions of generalizability can be made until there is accumulation of similar evidence, consistently across many different contexts.

Evaluation is self-conscious throughout its process, and monitors the way in which the process of evaluation affects the program being evaluated, the context within which it operates, and the people in different stakeholder groups. It is assumed that there will be complications in most evaluation settings over which the evaluator has no control. However, the evaluator is obligated to be aware and to make clear what these are to those who use the program and the evaluation results.

Evaluative judgements of a program often (maybe always) will be unique to a particular time in history, a particular cultural and political context, and to the particular people who are targeted by the program, product, or other object of evaluation. Both the object of evaluation and its environment are moving targets, changing even as they are observed and described. Conclusions based on an evaluation, therefore, must be appropriately modest.

Evaluation occurs in an ethical context, which includes an absolute commitment to reporting what is "true"[3], including the limits of that truth, and to

---

3   Webster's Dictionary (1982: 1240) defines truth as; (a) conformity to fact or actuality, (b) fidelity to an original or standard, (c) reality's actuality (sounds a little circular!), and (d) a statement proven to be, or accepted as, true. We will avoid the philosophical debate about the nature of reality, and assume that although "truth" may be relative and the understanding of what it is can change over time, what we can agree upon as "truth" is relatively stable over a reasonable period of time. "Facts" will be understood to be snapshots in time, although we hope that the focus will be sharp, the subject of the picture interesting, and the lighting clear. At any given time, any given snapshot will be exactly as if there *was* a truth that was independent of the observer, and, for the moment at least, unchanging. However, if there are multiple observers, it is like looking at a piece of paper with printing on it, but from two different sides. We can then agree on the truth of the matter only by including the content of both sides, or moving to a different level of cognition, i.e., "paper with printing". Subjective, personal interpretations of the printed message and of its meaningfulness may change over time. Thus we understand truth to include both what anyone would see at that ti-

maintain as much impartiality as it is possible to achieve. It is the evaluator's responsibility to maintain this ethical standard.

Evaluation is self-conscious; i.e., it applies its tools of analysis and determination of value to its own theories, activities, patterns, processes, and products. It submits the product of evaluation work to the process of meta-evaluation, determining its strengths and weaknesses, the confidence possible in its conclusions, and the limits to its use in decision-making.

13. Conclusion

At the 1999 conference of the American Evaluation Association in Orlando, FL, there were approximately 1400 people from about 20 different countries who participated. About thirty-five people attended one of the Theories of Evaluation Topical Interest Group meetings. This group included several of the long-time contributors to evaluation theory and writing, but also included people from the new generation of evaluators. In the group was a mix of people who, like the founders of the profession, had come from various fields, mostly from the social sciences or education, but without formal training in evaluation. It did include some people who had been trained in formal academic programs to practice the discipline of evaluation.

The topic for the meeting was the question of whether or not evaluation theory influenced or was helpful in the practice of evaluation. Several people expressed the perspective that when they practice evaluation, theory goes out the window, as they respond to the demands of managing competing agendas from different stakeholder groups, and try to achieve some balance between resources and results, within their particular political context. Others spoke strongly about the influence of evaluation theory on the way they approached an evaluation, negotiated for methods and resources, and thought about the results.

Whether the participants of the discussion believed in the influence of evaluation theory on their practice or not, there were several common themes. They all talked about responding to various groups of stakeholders, and these always included the people who were the targets or recipients of what was being evaluated. They all described using varied methods, both quantitative and qualitative. They all worked in teams, or in teamwork with, the people working in the program being evaluated. They all spoke of the challenge of clarifying the values implicit in their contract for the evaluation, for themselves and for and the staff working in the programs. They all recognized the need for results to be meaningful to all stakeholder groups, including the obligation to be meaningful to the recipients of the program or product. They were all aware of the ethical issues and responsibilities involved in evaluation, including common ethical dilemmas such as who owns (and can therefore edit) the reports, and how to deal with mandated evaluations with inadequate budgets.

---

me and place, and how we each understand what is seen. Both are essential to truth in evaluation.

Shadish's (1992) view was that there is not much good theory, and that the theoretical basis of the evaluation field is in disarray. The theoretical basis of evaluation may not be widely known, even by those practicing in the field, but it seems that as the 21st century begins, there is more common understanding of the major elements of theory in evaluation than might be realized. In the example above, some practitioners denied the effect of theory on their evaluation practice, but the issues they spoke of reflected the same issues prevalent in today's evaluation theories, some of which are listed under " Common Ground" above.

Internationally, in the past 3 decades, evaluation has become institutionalized in such influential organizations as the World Bank and United Nations (Chelimsky/Shadish 1997). The responsibility of the evaluation group for the World Bank, includes oversight of its self-evaluation processes, as well as monitoring and performance evaluation of hundreds of financial and technical assistance projects funded by the World Bank in developing countries (Picciotto 1997). The current trends toward a global economy and increased democracy, will continue to stimulate international demand for evaluation information. In turn, the demand brings with it the challenge of adapting evaluation principles and practices to cross-cultural value systems that impact both methodology and conceptualization of programs and evaluation. It seems that the practice of the discipline of evaluation cannot help but promote diversity of views in a society. And the diversity of values and projects internationally and multi-culturally, cannot help but promote creativity, diversity, and self-reflection in the discipline of evaluation and its theories.

One of the intriguing recent changes is the increasing recognition that definitive evaluation studies will often be quite limited in scope, and that specific evaluation findings are always time-limited in their usefulness, and not likely not to be easily generalized to other settings. As Scriven puts it (1991), " ...yours is not the task of determining truth for the ages, but the best possible advice at the time it is needed." The discipline of evaluation has accumulated an impressive diversity of theories about methods, measurement tools, and practice in an enormous variety of settings. Evaluation theory has come a very long way from the time when measurement was adapted to the task of providing " objective" information to decision-makers. The nature of the discipline ensures that it will continue to study itself, and we can expect continued creativity in evaluation theory.

References

Alkin, Marvin C. (1972): Evaluation Theory Development. In Weiss, C.: Evaluating Action Programs. Boston: Allyn & Bacon.

Aronson, Sidney H./Sherwood, Clarence C. (1973): Researcher versus practitioner: problems in social action research. In: Weiss, C. (1973): Evaluating Action Programs. Boston: Allyn & Bacon.

Bahm, A. J. (1971): Science is not value-free. Policy Sciences, No. 2, pp. 391-396.

Boruch, Robert F. (1974): Bibliograph: Illustrated randomized field experiments for program planning and evaluation. Evaluation, No. 2, pp. 83-87.

Campbell, Donald T. (1969): Reforms as experiments. American Psychologist, No. 24, pp. 409-429.

Chelimsky, Eleanor/Shadish, William R. (Eds.) (1997): Evaluation for the 21st Century: A Handbook. Thousand Oaks, CA: Sage Publications.

Chen, Huey-Tsyh (1990): Theory-Driven Evaluations. Newbury Park, CA: Sage.

Chen, H. T./Rossi, P. H. (1992): Using theory to improve program and policy evaluation. Westport, CT: Greenwood.

Cook, Thomas D./Reichardt, Charles S. (Eds.). (1979): Qualitative and quantitative methods in evaluation research. Beverly Hills, CA: Sage.

Cook, Thomas D./Campbell, Donald T. (1979): Quasi experimentation: Design and analysis issues for field settings. Chicago: Rand McNally.

Cronbach, Lee J. and associates (1980): Toward reform of program evaluation. San Francisco: Jossey-Bass.

Denzin, N. K./Lincoln, Y. S. (Eds.) (1994): Handbook of Qualitative Research. Newbury Park, CA: Sage.

Elliot, J. (1986): Democratic evaluation as social criticism: Or putting the judgement back into evaluation. In: Hammersley, M. (Ed.): Controversies in classroom research. Milton Keynes, England: Open University Press, pp. 28-237.

Fetterman, D. M. (1995): Empowerment Evaluation. Evaluation Practice, No. 15(1), pp. 1-15.

Fetterman, D. M. (1997): Empowerment evaluation and accreditation in higher education. In: Chelimsky/Shadish (1997): Evaluation for the 21st Century: A Handbook, pp. 381-404.

Guba, E. G. (1969): The failure of educational evaluation. In: Educational Technology, No. 9, pp. 29-38.

Guba, Egon G. (1987): Naturalistic evaluation. In Cordray, D. S./Bloom, H. S./Light, R. J. (Eds.): Evaluation practice in review (New directions for program evaluation, No. 34, pp. 23-43). San Francisco: Jossey-Bass.

Guba, Egon G./Lincoln, Y. S. (1981): Effective evaluation. Improving the usefulness of evaluation results through responsive and naturalistic approaches. San Francisco: Jossey-Bass.

Guba, Egon G./Lincoln, Y. S. (1989): Fourth generation evaluation. Newbury Park, California et al.: Sage.

Guttentag, Marcia/Struening, E. L. (Eds.) (1975): Handbook of Evaluation Research, Volumes 1 & 2. Beverly Hills, CA: Sage.

House, Ernest R. (1980): Evaluating with Validity. Beverly Hills, CA: Sage Publications.

House, E. R. (1993): Professional evaluation: social impact and political consequences. Newbury Park, CA: Sage.

Joint Committee on Standards for Educational Evaluation (1981): Standards for the evaluation of educational programs, projects, and materials. NY: McGraw-Hill.

Joint Committee on Standards for Educational Evaluation (1988): The personnel evaluation standards. Newbury Park, CA: Sage.

Krathwohl, David R. (1980): The myth of value-free evaluation. Educational Evaluation and Policy Analysis, No. 2, pp. 37-45.

Lincoln, Yvonna S. (1985): The ERS standards for program evaluation: Guidelines for a fledgling profession. Evaluation and Program Planning, No. 8(3), pp. 251-253.

Lincoln, Yvonna S./Guba, Egon G. (1986): But is it rigorous? Trustworthiness and authenticity in naturalistic evaluation. In: Williams, D. D. (Ed.): Naturalistic evaluation. San Francisco: Jossey-Bass.

Madaus, G. F./Scriven, M. S./Stufflebeam, D. L. (Eds.) (1983): Evaluation models. Boston, MA: Kluwer-Nijhoff.

Mertens, Donna M. (1998): Research Methods in Education and Psychology: Integrating Diversity with Quantitative and Qualitative Approaches. Thousand Oaks, CA: Sage Publications.

Mertens, Donna M. (2000): Transformative theory and evaluation. Theories of Evaluation TIG Newsletter. Theories of Evaluation Topical Interest Group of the American Evaluation Association.

Nathan, Richard P. (1988): Social Science in Government. NY: Basic Books, Inc.

Patton, Michael Q. (1997): Utilization-focused Evaluation (3rd edition). Thousand Oaks, CA: Sage.

Picciotto, Robert (1997): Evaluation in the World Bank. In Chelimsky, E./Shadish, W. R. (Eds.): Evaluation for the 21st Century: A Handbook. Thousand Oaks, CA: Sage.

Posavac, E. J./Carey, R. G. (1992): Program Evaluation: Methods and case studies. Englewood Cliffs, NJ: Prentice Hall.

Results Mapping (1999): http://www.pire.org/resultmapping/FIrst%20page.htm. Chapel Hill, NC: Pacific Institute for Results Mapping Laboratory.

Rice, Joseph Mayer (1897): The futility of the spelling grind. Forum, No. 23, pp. 163-172.

Rossi, Peter H./Freeman, Howard E. (1982): Evaluation: A Systematic Approach. (2nd Edition). Beverly Hills, CA: Sage.

Rossi, Peter H./Freeman, Howard E. (1993): Evaluation: A Systematic Approach. (5th Edition). Newbury Park, CA: Sage.

Schwandt, Thomas A./Halpern, Edward S. (1988): Linking auditing and metaevaluation. Newbury Park, CA: Sage.

Scriven, Michael (1967): The methodology of evaluation (AERA Monograph Series in Curriculum Evaluation, No. 1, pp. 39-83). Chicago: Rand McNally.

Scriven, Michael (1972): Objectivity and subjectivity in educational research. In: Thomas, L. G. (Ed.): Philosophical Redirection of Educational Research. Chicago: University of Chicago Press.

Scriven, Michael (1973): Goal-free evaluation. In: House, E. R. (Ed.): School evaluation: The politics and process. Berkeley, CA: Mc Cutchan, pp. 319-328.

Scriven, Michael (1978): Merit vs. Value. In: Evaluation News, No. 8, pp. 20-29.

Scriven, Michael (1991): Evaluation Thesaurus, 4th Edition. Newbury Park, CA: Sage Publications.

Shadish, William R./Cook, Thomas D./Leviton, Laura C. (1991): Foundations of Program Evaluation: Theories of Practice. Newbury Park, CA: Sage Publications.

Smith, Eugene/Tyler, Ralph W. (1942). Appraising and recording student progress. NY: Harper & Row.

Stake, Robert E. (1967): The countenance of educational evaluation. Teachers College Record, No. 68, pp. 523-540.

Stake, Robert E. (1995): The art of case study research. Thousand Oaks, CA: Sage.

Stake, Robert E. (1975): The countenance of educational evaluation. Teachers College Record, No. 68, pp. 523-540.

Stake, Robert E. (1986): Quieting reform. Urbana: University of Illinois Press.

Stufflebeam, Daniel/Foley, Walter J./Gephart, William J./Guba, Egon G./Hammond, Robert I./Merriman, Howard O./Provus, Malcolm M. (1971): Educational evaluation and decision making. Itasca, IL: Peacock.

Stufflebeam, Daniel (1967): Evaluative Research: Principles and Practice in Public Service and Social Action Programs. NY: Russell Sage.

Suchman, E. (1967): Evaluative Research. New York: Russell Sage.

Tyler, Ralph W. (1949): Basic Principles of Curriculum and Instruction: syllabus for Education 360. Chicago: University of Chicago Press.

Webster's II (1984): New Riverside University Dictionary. Boston, MA: Houghton Mifflin.

Weiss, Carol (1972): Evaluating Action Programs. Boston: Allyn & Bacon.

Weiss, Carol. (1973): Where politics and evaluation research meet. In: Evaluation, No. 1, pp. 37-45.

Weiss, Carol C. (Ed.) (1992): Organizations for Policy Analysis: Helping Government Think. London: Sage.

Williams, David O. (1986): Naturalistic Evaluation (New Directions for program evaluation, No. 3). San Francisco: Jossey-Bass.

Worthen, Blaine R./Sanders, James R. (1973): Educational evaluation: Theory and practice. Worthington, OH: Charles A. Jones.

Worthen, Blaine R./Sanders, J. R./Fitzpatrick, J. S. (1997): Program Evaluation: Alternative approaches and practical guidelines. White Plains, NY: Longman Inc.

Valerie J. Caracelli [1]

Methodology: Building Bridges to Knowledge

Program evaluation draws on a set of social science procedures to systematically collect, analyze, interpret and communicate descriptive and explanatory information about social programs. Until recently evaluation texts tended to detail a tool chest of methods available to the evaluator without concomitant attention to how and when various methods should be used in practice. Initially, evaluators drew on existing methods and theories from the academic disciplines, typically in the social sciences, in which they were trained. However, as a transdiscipline evaluators not only adapted concepts and methods from their disciplines of origin, they also invented or combined methods in a new ways to achieve evaluation purposes. (Scriven 1991; Shadish/Cook/Leviton 1991). Evaluation work is practiced within substantive disciplinary domains, such as, health, education, criminal justice, employment, international aid, and others. Strong linkages between social science theory and theories about the program to be evaluated are necessary (Riggin 1990). Domain-specific evaluator practices are responsive to their contextually unique circumstances.

In 1991, with the publication of Shadish, Cook & Leviton's *Foundations of Program Evaluation,* a knowledge base corresponding to evaluation practice was recognized as one of the five fundamental aspects of program evaluation theory.[2] The authors show how the evaluation theory one chooses can affect the kinds of questions one chooses to answer and the types of methods one uses. Similarly, the framing of questions and method choice may also derive from the theoretical perspectives or values held by the evaluator or his or her paradigmatic allegiances (Bentz/Shapiro 1998; Crotty

---

1 The options expressed in this chapter represent those of the author and should not be construed as the policy or position of the U.S. General Accounting Office.

2 The other four take into account social programming (the nature of social programs an their role in social problem solving), knowledge construction (what counts as acceptable knowledge about the evaluand), values (the role that values and the process of valuing play in evaluation), and knowledge use (how evaluative information can be used in social policy and programming).

1998; Greene 1999; Greene/Caracelli 1997). There are many different bridges evaluators can build to obtain warrant for the assertions they make in connecting the questions addressed to the collection and analysis of data. This chapter addresses three major topics: planning, evaluation strategies, and multiplist approach to inquiry. The chapter begins with planning tasks pertaining to the framing questions, building quality into the study, and the design of an evaluation. Next, the chapter briefly describes evaluation strategies, including several analytic frameworks and various types of evidence. The chapter concludes with a discussion about the use of multiple approaches and methods that assist evaluators in strengthening the credibility and meaningfulness of their work.

1. Planning

1.1 Framing Questions

Design efforts begin with the posing of a question or questions that resonate throughout the evaluation. Reaching agreement with stakeholders involved in an evaluation (sponsors, users, program personnel and others) can be a difficult and challenging task. The formulation of the problem into questions that will be addressed in the evaluation has implications for the kinds of data that will be collected, the data sources, the analyses used, and the conclusions drawn.

Studies may have one key question or may have a cluster of questions depending on the purpose of the evaluation. Three major purposes of evaluation are typically discussed: rendering judgments, facilitating improvements and generating knowledge (Chelimksy 1997; Patton 1997). In this paper the focus will be primarily on evaluation that is undertaken for accountability purposes (rendering judgments).[3] In evaluation done for purposes of accountability there are some typical questions used to assist in program oversight. These questions are listed in table 1.

---

3   More recently this category has been separated into the assessment of merit or worth of the value of a policy or program and oversight and compliance (See Mark, Henry & Julnes, in press). At the U.S. General Accounting Office the former category represents the influence of program evaluation and the later the auditing profession. The agency has combined both frameworks in multi-task accountability assessments.

Table 1: Typical Questions for Program Oversight

Information Category	Example of Typical Question
Description	– Overall, what activities are conducted? By whom? How extensive and costly are the activities, and whom do they reach? – If conditions, activities, and purposes are not uniform throughout the program, in what significant respects do they vary across program components, providers, or subgroups of clients?
Context	– What key aspects of the current and historical context affect program management or program and policy issues? – What stakeholder views are relevant to program and policy issues?
Implementation	– What progress has been made in implementing new provisions? – Have feasibility or management problems become evident? – If activities and products are expected to conform to professional standards or to program specifications, have they done so?
Targeting	– Have program activities or products focused on appropriate issues or problems? – To what extent have they reached the appropriate people or organizations? – Do current targeting practices leave significant needs unmet (problems not addressed, clients not reached)?
Information Quality	– Are information systems adequate for managing the program? Are data reliable? – Are indicators (performance measures) technically sound/valid? – Are analysis procedures appropriate? – Are evaluations conducted on the program technically sound?
Outcome	– What progress has been made toward the objectives and stated goals?
Impact	– What is the impact of the program beyond what would have happened in the absence of the program? – If impact has not been uniform, has it varied across program components, approaches, providers or client subgroups? – Have program activities had important positive or negative side effects, either for program participants or outside the program?
Comparative Advantage	– Is this program's strategy more effective in relation to its costs than others that serve the same purpose?
Prospective	– What are the future needs for a new or changed policy, law, regulation, or program? – What are the possible effects of a new or changed policy? Law? – What are promising practices for future programs?

(Source: Adapted from GAO/PEMD-95-1; GAO/GGD-00-35)

Evaluations done for other purposes may focus on different types of questions. For example, if the focus of the evaluation is organizational learning a series of typical questions appear in Preskill & Torres (1998). Alternative approaches to collaborative evaluation practice are discussed by Cousins & Whitmore (1998).

1.2 Building In Quality

The social program context in which evaluations are carried out is inextricably bound up with politics and social policy decision-making (Patton 1987; Cronbach & Associates 1980; Vedung 1997; Weiss 1987; Greene 2000). Chelimsky (1997) points out that this fact has a number of important implications for evaluation theory and practice. The most critical implication is evaluation credibility. Credibility equates to an evaluation that is both competent and objective, an evaluation that is defensible in the heat of debate. Further, Chelimsky cautions that the appearance of advocacy can have a „dramatically negative and long-term impact on credibility" (p. 59). More recently, Datta (2000) examines the strategies used in evaluation to achieve a non-partisan evaluation. Non-partisan is defined as „an evaluation that is and is regarded by partisans of all persuasions as balanced, fair, and faithful, so that *if methodological quality is high*, debates focus on the implications of the findings for practice or policy, not on the credibility of the findings themselves (p. 3, emphasis in original). Datta provides a set of non-partisan approaches that focus on strategies used in planning, on strategies involving the management of the evaluation, as well as strategies used in the conduct of the evaluation and in reporting and dissemination.

1.2.1 Seven Dimensions of Quality

Accountability studies conducted at the U.S. General Accounting Office (GAO) must ensure that the products are of the highest quality. At GAO seven dimensions of quality are considered essential throughout its assignments and products. These dimensions include Accuracy, Objectivity/Fairness, Context Sophistication, Scope/Completeness, Significance/Value, Timeliness, and Clarity.

- *Accuracy*: Among other attributes, this dimension includes collecting adequate and sufficient evidence; verifying the reliability and validity of data; identifying assumptions used; determining the degree of confidence we can assign to the data; and providing information that is factually correct, complete, and clear.
- *Objectivity and Fairness*: This dimension refers to the unbiased conduct and reporting of GAO´s work.
- *Context Sophistication*: This dimension requires that staff have a thorough understanding of the technical and substantive issues in the assignment, are aware of the political environment, are professionally proficient, and provide useful messages with practical recommendations.
- *Scope and Completeness*: This dimension involves developing well-defined questions, using clear and valid objectives, developing appropriate methodology, making efficient use of time and resources, and acknowledging limitations.

- *Significance and Value*: This dimension places emphasis on doing work with the potential for making important contributions.
- *Timeliness*: This dimension encompasses both planning and reporting.
- *Clarity*: This dimension requires clear and convincing work papers, instruments, and products.

1.2.2 Professional Standards, Guidelines, and Quality Criteria

The Government Auditing Standards (Yellow Book) are important to ensuring the achievement of each quality dimension in performance auditing and evaluation at GAO. The standards applicable to each dimension are also reflected in the Program Evaluation Standards (Caracelli 1999). The dimensions are used prospectively in how a project is planned and designed. For example, as an aid to planning project teams complete a design matrix that serves as a reflexive tool for considering issues pertaining to quality. Technical staff are included as team members to ensure that methodological issues are adequately addressed. The design is reviewed and discussed with key internal staff. Management is involved throughout a project and more formally at specific project milestones, such as job commitment (when the job objectives and design and project plan are reviewed for approval by management) and message agreement (when findings are reviewed). The quality dimensions are also used retrospectively, when fieldwork has been completed, to incorporate quality into the products or outputs of GAO's work.

Consideration of the American Evaluation Association's (AEA) Guiding Principles and the Program Evaluation Standards (1994) represent other ways that quality is built into an evaluation. Certain issues pertaining to quality are guided by the conventions of a discipline that may be predominant, e.g., ethnographic methods. Quality criteria also derive from inquiry frameworks (for an overview of dominant paradigms in evaluation see Greene 1994; Guba 1990). For example, working within a post-positivist framework leads an evaluator to examine criticisms or threats to the validity of a study for their potential effect on a planned or completed study (Cook/Campbell 1979). In constructivist evaluation criteria for establishing the trustworthiness of a study would be considered. (Lincoln/Guba 1985; Erlandson/Harris/Skipper/Allen 1993).

1.3 Maintaining Quality in Creating the Evaluation Design

In any evaluation context there are multiple audiences (stakeholders) with a vested interest in the evaluation. Greene (1994, 2000) describes the complexity of selecting questions and audiences and determining the standards to be used in evaluating programs given the different values and political stances of the various audiences for the study. She makes the case that evaluation methodologies "constitute coordinated frameworks of philosophical assumptions, integrated with ideological views about the role and purpose of social inquiry in social policy and program decision-making, with accompanying value stances" about desired program outcomes, desired ends of the inquiry and method preferences (1994: 531). Greene further characterizes four major genres of evaluation methodologies: postpositivism, pragmatism, interpretivism, and critical, normative science. She uses tables to outline their ideological orientation and key values, audiences, preferred methods and typical evaluation questions. In summary, Greene (1994) observes that what distinguishes one evaluation methodology from another is not methods but whose questions are addressed and which values are promoted.

The design of an evaluation involves several design tasks. Designs are characterized by the manner in which evaluators develop a methodological approach for responding to the defined questions, and formulate a data collection plan and analysis plan for answering the questions with appropriate data. These tasks take into consideration the questions guiding the study, the resource needs and constraints faced by the evaluator or evaluation team, and the information needs of the intended user. Careful design is a critical step toward ensuring the quality of the end product. In the field of evaluation this is a far more complicated scenario than this brief description leads you to expect.

1.4 Design Planning Tool

Notwithstanding the complexity of methodological choices, in the accountability studies done at GAO, a design matrix is a tool used by staff to plan their work and build quality into a project at the outset. Introduced in 1988, the utility of this tool in clarifying the intended design and in preparing the study for review has merited its continued use today (See Hedrick/Bickman/ Rog 1993: 90-91). The matrix addresses key planning issues, such as the problem being addressed, research questions, required information sources, overall design strategy, data collection methods, data analysis methods, limitations, and a statement that anticipates what the analysis could yield. Technical staff are included as team members to ensure that methodological issues are adequately addressed. The design is reviewed and discussed with key internal staff. The study is discussed with the client and terms of agreement are set. Management is involved throughout a project and more formally at specific project milestones, such as job commitment (when the job objectives and design and project plan are reviewed for approval by management) and message agreement (when findings are reviewed).

Research Questions	Information Required	Information Sources	Overall Design Strategy	Data Collection Methods	Data Analysis methods	Limitations	What the analysis will allow you to say
What Does the Sponsor want to know?	**What information is needed to answer the question?**	**Where will the information come from?**	**How will the information be used to answer the question?**	**How will the information be obtained?**	**What will be done analytically with the information?**	**What are the limitations or caveats?**	**What can be reported?**
• Clear and specific	• Types of evidence	• Officials	• Case studies	• Structured Interviews	• Descriptive statistics	• Generalizability	• Not the expected finding
• Fair and Objective	• Physical/	• Program participants	• Computer simulation	• Focus Groups	• Cost/benefit analysis	• Data quality and reliability	• Anecdotal Information
• Politically Neutral	• Observational	• Inventory Records	• Modeling	• Questionnaires	• Inferential statistics (regression analysis)	• Access to records	• Precise statements about sample
• Measurable	• Testimonial	• Data bases	• Nature of available information/gaps	• Visual Inspection	• Qualitative analysis	• staffing/travel constraints	• Extrapolate to larger universe
• Doable	• Documentary	• Laws and regulations	• Rationale for selecting cases, locations, programs	• File Review	• Synthesis		• Cost of various program options
• key terms defined	• Analytical	• Previous Studies	• Relationship between questions				• Impact of program changes
• Scope	• Program Criteria						
• Timeframe	• Agency procedures						
• Population	• Participant rates						
	• Cost Information						
	• Funding levels						

The dimensions of quality are reviewed for each segment of the matrix. To begin, the major issues underlying the project are identified and explained. This helps others understand the political context, identifies potential users, explains stakeholder perspectives, and considers prior research. In the first column the research questions pertaining to the issue or problem are derived. It is through the research questions that methodological issues such as quality, time and cost are raised. If a project is guided by a question that it has neither the time nor resources to answer, the question will need to be renegotiated in order to maintain a high level of quality. The quality dimension of scope and completeness and significance must also be linked to the researchable questions and objectives.

Questions generally undergo a translation process from the policy or practical question that a policy maker or manger has to a researchable question that can be investigated by the project team. For example, a question may broadly ask, How effective are nicotine reduction strategies? The researchable question is more specific, for example, Is nicotine reduction by patch more or less effective than nicotine reduction by nasal spray in smoking cessation programs over a period of six weeks? If the evaluation team has written a question that it cannot answer accurately, fairly, and objectively (so that the question is politically neutral) within the cost and time frame, the question must be revised. Chelimsky (1996) discusses the difficulty of this translation process and with making certain that study questions are the right ones in terms of politics, the values, and the history of issue. Questions generally fall into four types (a) descriptive, (b) normative or comparative, (c) program impact, or (d) prospective.

At GAO normative questions more typically represent audit-emphasis questions; whereas, program impact and prospective questions fall in the domain of evaluation-emphasis questions. Because more than one question may be addressed in a single project, cross-discipline work is often undertaken so that both audit and evaluation frameworks may be used in a single project.

The design matrix is intended to facilitate developing the objectives, scope and methodology of the project and to communicate the design of the project to others. Involving stakeholders early will promote discussion on the major design issues. The matrix is most effective when it is developed through an iterative process that includes all stakeholders. Once the questions have been identified, the information required to answer the questions is detailed in column two. Questions that are evaluative need to stipulate the criteria that will be used to answer the question. For example, compliance with a set of regulations is not the same as meeting a rigorous set of evaluation criteria. Many regulations are too broad to serve as a basis for evaluative conclusions and rigorous evaluation criteria need to be developed.

In column 3 information sources should be detailed so that each data element pertaining to required information has a matching data source. Examples of data sources are previous reports, agency officials, databases, etc.

Column 4 sets forth the overall design strategy including both data collection and analysis techniques. For example, if a case study method is selected a description of how the cases are to be selected would be detailed. Column 5 then provides the specific data collection methods, e.g., structured interview, mail survey, observations, etc. The nature of the universe of cases, or sample selection would be described for mail surveys, for focus groups the basis for selecting participants would be explicit, and so on. In Column 6 the planned analysis methods are laid out, e.g., descriptive statistics, multiple regression, content analysis, as appropriate. The planned analysis can be very specific. Also important for assessing job design is consideration of the limitations, which are detailed in column 7. The limitations pertaining to scope and methodology should explain how potential conclusions and recommendations could be affected. The last column considers other comments, including what the analysis may allow you to say. This column is not used to indicate an expected finding as the research is only being planned at this stage. However, given the choice of data collection methods it may be possible to outline how specific, precise, or how confident we will be in our findings.

2. Evaluation Strategies

There are a variety of ways to depict evaluation strategies, designs, and methods. No single overview chapter can sufficiently condense the range of techniques available. First, this chapter presents several analytic frameworks for conducting evaluation (the frameworks can include different types of data collection methods). Next, types of evidence obtained through different data collection procedures are presented; these sources of evidence may be used in one or more analytic framework. Although written generally from the perspective a particular mode of inquiry, several sourcebooks provide excellent overviews (Berg 2000; Bickman 2000a, 2000b; Bickman/Rog 1998; Denzin 1997; Denzin/Lincoln 2000; Fetterman/Hedrick/Bickman/Rog 1993; Mark/ Henry/Julnes, in press; Maxwell 1996; Mertens 1997; Owen/Rogers 1999; Patton 1990; Patton 1997; Pawson/Tilley 1997; Posavac/Carey 1997; Rossi/ Freeman/Lipsey 1999; Trochim 1999; U.S. GAO 1991; Weiss 1998; Wholey/ Hatry/Newcomer 1994; Posavac/Carey 1997). For simplicity, several evaluation strategies and designs, many used by GAO, are briefly explicated. Surveys and Case Studies are typically used in responding to descriptive and normative questions. Field experiments and the use of available data can be used for explanatory purposes by addressing cause and effect questions. Each of these strategies may call on either qualitative or quantitative information. An analytic framework is the structure within which the existing data or data collected are analyzed. It may serve as the sole basis for a cause and effect inference or may be used in combination with other frameworks to support a cause and effect inference, or in some instances may serve descriptive purposes.

2.1 Analytic Frameworks[4]

Program Theory/Logic models

Beginning in the 1980s a movement toward more theory-oriented evaluation approaches began to take hold. Such evaluations are viewed as emphasizing the conceptual relationship between treatment implementation and outcomes, as well as specifying factors by which a program achieves interim and long-term outcomes. Several terms are used in the literature including program theory, theory-driven/theory-oriented/theory-guided, theory-based evaluations. Common among these terms is that a causal mechanism or causal process is specified with regard to how a program produces its effects (Lipsey 1993). Weiss (1998) elaborates on how theories of change can serve as a guide to evaluation. Logic models are a visual way of depicting the theory, they mirror the theory in that they include (a) program inputs (e.g., resources), (b) program activities (actions taken to implement the program), (c) interim outcomes (the intermediate responses that are expected to lead to desired results, and (d) desired end results. Logic models are commonly used in evaluability assessments; such assessments determine whether the program is ready to be managed for results, helps managers articulate their assumptions about how the program works and examines the logic of the assumptions, and tests the theory with data on program operations and outcomes (Wholey 1994).

One benefit to developing such models is the potential for enhanced communication between evaluator and client. In addition, these models allow for a comparison against the actual data collected for the evaluation so that the viability of the theory can be tested. It is sometimes possible to do this through statistical models and analysis (Chen 1990; Chen/Rossi 1987) or through other types of pattern-matching techniques (Mark 1990; Marquart 1990; Trochim 1985, 1989). The pattern matching approach refers to the specification of a theoretical pattern and its correspondence or match with the acquisition of an observed pattern in the data. The theoretical pattern is derived through a process of conceptualization from extant theories, and ideas or hunches of the investigator or articulated implicit theories of stakeholders. The observed pattern is derived through the task of data organization from observation in the form of impressions, field notes, etc., as well as more formal objective measures. The inferential task of pattern matching attempts to

---

4   Material used in GAO training has been incorporated and supplemented with additional information and references.

relate or link the two patterns and to the extent that correspondence is achieved the theory receives support. To the extent the theory is not supported an opportunity is provided to gain a better understanding of the program and activities that are needed for successful program implementation and achievement of results. (Key concepts in developing and assessing program theory can be found in Patton 1997; Rossi/Freeman/Lipsey 1999; Weiss 1998, for the role of theory in qualitative program evaluation see Greene 1993).

Program Monitoring

Program monitoring is defined as the systematic documentation of key aspects of program performance that are indicative of whether the program is functioning as intended or according to some appropriate standard (Rossi/ Freeman/Lipsey 1999: 6). This evaluation activity builds on program theory and is designed to detail how a program is operating and how well it performs its intended functions. Monitoring is a tool for formative evaluation that assesses program implementation to determine that activities and services are delivered appropriately. Monitoring can help distinguish cases of poor program implementation from ineffective intervention concepts. Common forms of monitoring include process evaluation, management information systems, and performance measurement. Performance measurement distinguishes program outputs, the good and services delivered to participants, from program outcomes, the actual results of the activities the program was designed to achieve, e.g., improved nutrition. Program monitoring provides a means by which managers can assess how well programs are meeting their intended functions and serves as a way of demonstrating accountability to the public and program stakeholders. (Hatry 1999; Newcomer 1997; Rossi/Freeman/Lipsey 1999)

Experimental Designs

Evaluators are interested in assessing the effects of interventions and in attributing outcomes to the intervention when appropriate. Impact evaluation is one form of evaluation that assesses the net effect of a program by comparing program outcomes with an estimate of what would have happened in the absence of the program. Both randomized experiments and quasi-experiments are two types of research designs used to assess treatment intervention effects. They are employed when external factors are known to influence the program´s outcomes. In both cases comparisons are drawn between participants who experience the treatment and those who do not. In this way the designs are intended to isolate the program´s contribution to achieving its objectives. In a randomized experiment, a random process used to assign participants to the treatment is intended to assure that each participant in the study has an equally likely chance of receiving the intervention. This fact makes the design strong against criticisms that something other than the actual intervention caused the effects observed. However it is not always possible to conduct a randomized experiment. Quasi-experiments (before-after designs, interrupted time-series, regression-discontinuity, and nonequivalent group designs) are sometimes used. Each of these designs is vulnerable to certain sources of bias that can decrease the confidence we can place in the results of the study.

The above experimental designs, and others, are reviewed by Reichardt & Mark (1998) and the strengths and limitations of each design type are elaborated. The authors note that a variety of designs are available for estimating the effects of a treatment and no single design is always best. The choice of design can be a „considerable intellectual challenge" both in recognizing the potential threats to validity (criticisms that the conclusion is incorrect) and in elaborating design comparisons so as to minimize uncertainty about the size of the treatment effect (p. 224). The choice of design will depend on the circumstances of the study and how well potential threats to validity and other criticisms can be ruled out. However, some uncertainty will always remain. Evaluators rely on an accumulation of evidence across studies using multiple designs and thus multiple estimates of effects. In rare instances a single project may receive adequate funding for the implementation of multiple designs within a single project. Such projects, when estimates converge across designs, allow for more confidence than if conclusions were based on a single design (Lipsey/Cordray/Berger 1981).

Case Study

A case study is perhaps one of the most diverse analytic strategies and can serve a variety of purposes. It can be used for illustration about a program or policy, as an exploratory technique for generating hypotheses for future study. It can also be used to study program implementation and program effects (usually involving multisite, multimethod assessments or in a cumulative way by bringing many studies together to answer a question). The case study may be „intrinsic," undertaken because of the researchers interest in a particular case (Stake 2000). A case study is also considered a method for learning about a complex instance, based on a comprehensive understanding of that instance obtained by extensive description and analysis of that instance taken as a whole and in its context (GAO 1990). Case studies usually call upon a variety of data sources, e.g., interview, observations or participant observation, documents and other archival materials, physical artifacts. Yin (1998) points out the strengths and weaknesses of each source of evidence and the importance of having the researcher well-versed in a variety of data collection techniques. Analysis may be conducted through triangulation of data sources, the development and use of a logic model, pattern matching, explanation building, and content analysis or thematic reviews. The selection of cases range from selecting a site for convenience to sampling in order to obtain a representative sample. Case studies at multiple sites are also a special topic of study. (For two very different perspectives on case studies see Yin 1998; Stake 1995, 2000.)

Ethnography

An ethnographic approach is one way of conducting qualitative research and comes from the discipline of anthropology. Ethnography is the study of a culture and in evaluation this can translate to the culture of programs or organizations. This framework typically relies on participant observation as part of the field research. The researcher immerses him or herself in the culture and records extensive field notes (and also relies on documents and interviews). Other qualitative traditions to field research include, among others, ethnomethodology, phenomenology, grounded theory, life history, participatory action research, hermeneutics, chaos/complexity theory, clinical research, etc. (See Denzin & Lincoln 2000 for a compendium of approaches; see also Patton 1990; Miles & Huberman 1994 for more general design and analysis issues).

Meta-ethnography synthesizes interpretive ethnographic studies. Emphasis is on interpretation rather than aggregation. The aim through comparison and contrast across studies is to recover the social and theoretical context in which substantive finding emerge (Noblit/Hare 1988). The meta-ethnography is viewed as having synergistic properties that primarily result in enhancing substantive interpretation across studies.

Surveys/Questionnaire

A survey may serve as an analytic framework when it is the sole source of data, e.g., the U.S. Census Survey of Income and Program Participation. Frequently a survey is one method among others that, taken together, are part of a different analytic framework, e.g., a case study. Surveys may be administered to an entire population (people, records, or institutions) or when that is not practical the survey may be administered to a random sample of participants to help ensure generalizability. Surveys may be conducted by mail, telephone, fax, or through the use of the internet (See Dillman 1999 for comprehensive treatment of survey methodology). Typically, the intention of a survey is to determine the incidence, distribution or interrelationship of events or conditions. Groves (1989) discusses the various sources of error than can enter into a study when surveys are used. For example errors associated with the sample frame, missing data, and measurement errors (e.g., bias in the survey question, order of questions, mode of collecting the data, interviewer or respondent characteristics). Typically, reliability is strengthened by pretesting questions so that it is clear that the questions are being interpreted in the same way. It is also important to ensure the construct validity of the survey questions. Pre-testing, expert review, and careful construction of questions are some of the strategies used by researchers. Recently efforts have been made to ground survey construction in cognitive research as a way of improving question construction through a better understanding of how respondents interpret questions (McKay 1995; Schwarz/Sudman 1996; Sudman/Bradburn/Schwarz 1995). (Additional source material on surveys can be found in Fowler 1993; Lavrakas 1993; U.S. GAO 1993).

Research Synthesis

An evaluation synthesis is a systematic procedure for organizing findings from several disparate evaluation studies and summarizing their results. This methodology can be useful for addressing questions that can be answered satisfactorily without conducting primary data collection. A synthesis can answer several different kinds of questions about overall program effectiveness and versions of programs that are working especially well or poorly. It can also identify areas where further empirical information is needed. Cooper & Hedges (1994) provide comprehensive coverage of research syntheses. A short guide for conducting an evaluation synthesis can be found in GAO´s evaluation synthesis transfer paper (GAO/PEMD-10.1.2). The quality of the studies included in the synthesis needs to be considered and any potential bias given the composite of studies that make up the synthesis. The main limitations of an evaluation synthesis pertain to relying on extant data. Policy concerns where there is little or no existing information cannot be investigated through a synthesis. Further, even for those programs where a base of information exists, the synthesis can only respond to questions that existing studies have addressed and is only as current as the studies included in the synthesis.

A *meta-analysis* is a special type of research synthesis in which statistical procedures are used to integrate, synthesize, and make sense of the results from a collection of related empirical studies. By combining the results of several studies a meta-analysis can increase statistical power and the precision of results (Cook/Cooper/Cordray/Hartmann/Hedges/Light/Louis/Mosteller 1992; Lipsey/Wilson, in press, provide useful guidance for conducting a meta-analysis). Lipsey (1997) discusses the linkage between social intervention theory and meta-analysis as an important partnership in learning what evaluation reveals about social programs. For some areas and subject matter a series of meta-analyses may have been conducted. A review of results from a series of meta-analysis can provide an overview of the knowledge base in an area (GAO/PEMD-96-7).

Another type of synthesis is the *Prospective Evaluation Synthesis* (PES). GAO developed the PES as a systematic method for responding to questions about the future, e.g., meeting congressional requests for analyzing proposed legislation, analyzing alternative proposals and projections of various kinds. A prospective synthesis combines (1) a skilled textual analysis of a proposed program (designed to clarify the implied goals of that program and what is assumed to get results); (2) a review/synthesis of evaluation studies from similar programs, and (3) summary judgements of likely success (given a future that is not too different than the past). As in an evaluation synthesis results can vary by changes in the inclusion rules for the synthesis. In addition, different advantages and disadvantages inhere in different models used to weigh criteria when judging quality (GAO/PEMD-10.1.10).

Efficiency Assessment

Public and private funders of programs are concerned about accountability and value of the program given dollars expended. Cost-benefit analysis and Cost-effectiveness analysis are two tools that can be used to address these concerns. Benefit-cost analysis is used to assess the success or failure of a program and to help determine whether the program should be continued or modified, and to assess the probable results of program changes. The analysis (a) determines the benefits of a proposed or existing program and places a dollar value on the benefits; (b) total costs are calculated; (3) costs are compared to benefits. When quantifying benefits is inappropriate, cost-effectiveness analysis can be undertaken. This analysis does not produce a „net benefit" number; however, it can help to compare costs to units of program objectives. Both types of analyses have different purposes and strengths and limitations. Depending on how benefits are valued in dollar terms these two types of analyses may lead to different conclusions about the same program (Key 1999; see also, Key 1994; Levin, 1983; Yates 1996).

Each of the above analytic frameworks is appropriate under different circumstances and each has strengths and some limitations that the evaluator must be aware of. A design or multiplicity of designs is often a piecing together of different elements in order to convey a holistic assessment of the evaluand. Similarly, the data collected within these analytic frameworks must also be artfully crafted to fit within these frameworks. The choices and considerations an evaluator must take into account make evaluation inquiry complex.

2.2 Evidence base

The data collected when using the various analytic frameworks form the evidence base of the study. At GAO researchable questions also frame decisions on four basic types of evidentiary information which serve as the means by which questions will be. The methods chosen for data collection and analysis must provide evidentiary information that conforms to GAO's standards of evidence. Predominantly four types of evidence are used: Documentary, Testimonial, Physical/Observational, and Analytic. Each evidence type requires more elaboration on the various methodological approaches than is provided in this overview. Analysis tasks often involve collating information from various sources (documents, interviews, observations). Several source books provide guidance: Berg 2000; Miles/Huberman 1994; Patton 1990; and Strauss/Corbin 1990.

Documentary Evidence

Documentary evidence includes sources such as, program documents, manuals, minutes of meetings, reports, files and records, regulations, budgets, policy statements, existing statistical or other quantitative data already prepared by an agency, contracts, grants, reports, laws or bills, committee reports, testimonies, published and unpublished studies, newspapers and other broadcast material. For example, documentary evidence frequently involves some sort of record review that may require the development of a data collection instrument. A data collection instrument provides an efficient way to obtain systematic information from records or from direct observation of events. Obtaining documentary evidence involves details about whom to contact for the information, what information should be obtained, how to obtain the information, and a place to record the information. Extracting information from documents is a data reduction task and depending on the nature of the task the reliability of the extraction by more than one coder may have to be assessed. Archival records may either public or private with the latter used in qualitative research for creating case studies or life histories (Berg 2000).

Testimonial Evidence

Testimonial evidence refers to in-person interviews, expert panels (including use of Delphi technique or panel discussions), and focus groups. Gathering testimonial evidence involves a number of techniques associated with qualitative inquiry.

– Personal Interviews. These can range from very structured personal interviews to unstructured, open-ended interviews. Depending on the degree of structure the type of data collected will vary and the analysis techniques will differ. A structured interview may ultimately yield data that may not substantially differ from a quantitative questionnaire. An unstructured interview may require qualitative techniques such as content analysis so that findings can be interpreted. Typically, at GAO a structured or semi-structured interview will be used and a data collection instrument will be developed to gather data by telephone or face-to-face. Staff are expected to ask the same questions, in the same manner, and offer respondents the same set of possible responses or allow for open-ended responses. Error can occur if respondents interpret the questions in different ways or if individuals conducting the interviews are not consistent in their approach. Therefore, questions are pre-tested and reviewed by methods experts and the interviewers are trained to administer the questions in a consistent manner. (See Patton 1990; Seidman 1991; U.S. GAO 1991)

– Expert panels. An expert panel is a formal and systematic method of gathering the opinions of experts in a subject area in a face-to-face discussion setting. Each panelist has an opportunity to address the issues on the agenda (perhaps detailed earlier through a discussion paper). The discussion may be spontaneous or prepared in advance. Panelists are given an opportunity to comment on the presentations of other panelists. Panels are often used to gain insight into a problem or to validate measures created for other research purposes, as well as develop criteria. It is important to obtain the right set of experts for the particular topics. Technical experts may be mixed with policy experts, service users, and program clients to obtain different perspectives on the topic. (See Vedung's (1997) discussion on the pros and cons of peer reviews; see also Worthen/Sanders/Fitzpatrick 1997.)

– Delphi for consensus. The Delphi method is a systematic method of opinion gathering and consensus development. It involves recruiting an appropriate panel, getting each panelist's views before and after getting controlled feedback about the opinions of other panelists. When each subsequent response is requested, the results of the prior data collection effort are given to panelists in summary form. The rounds of data collection continue until a group consensus is established or opinions stabilize. Delphi panels can be problematic if they do not represent the population of interest, in addition care needs to be taken to accurately represent an individual's opinion, especially as opinions change through iterations of data collection. (See Worthen/Sanders/Fitzpatrick 1997)

– Focus groups. Focus groups can be a valuable way to obtain information about issues and in helping staff frame future questions. Typically a group of 8-10 people is led by a moderator to discuss specific issues. Through open-ended questions, participants share their thoughts and experiences. Participants are generally not randomly selected and so generalizability of results is low. Bias can be introduced in a number of ways and care must be taken to accurately summarize the discussion. (Berg 2000; Krueger 1994)

Physical/Observational Evidence

Physical or observational evidence includes observing individuals, property, equipment, buildings and installations, etc. eyewitness information. Observations may be done directly or covertly; they vary in their degree of structure and in the extent to which the observer participates in the setting being observed or retains a spectator role. This type of evidence is frequently used during site visits and is intended to corroborate information provided in documents or personal interviews. Observations or inspections may be used to describe or compare a specific condition with other conditions or against a set of criteria. Observations may be recorded through data collection instruments or in memoranda, photographs, drawings, charts, maps, or physical samples. At GAO observations (which can vary in their degree of structure) may employ instruments that provide categories or rating scales for recording the data. Generally training is required to assure reliability and assessments of inter-rater reliability can also strengthen the credibility of the data. (Webb/ Campbell/Schwartz/Sechrest 1966, 2000. Among other sources, issues in observational fieldwork are detailed in Denzin 1978; Patton 1990).

Analytic Evidence

Analytic evidence includes the analysis of experimental or quasi experimental data, estimates of cost efficiency or dollar savings, case study data, legal analysis, obtaining descriptive statistics or simple comparisons or trends; conducting multivariate or trend analysis. Simulations, sensitivity analysis, quantitative research synthesis, qualitative research synthesis, and content analysis also provide analytic evidence. In addition, reviews of methodologies, checks on the reliability of agency/program datasets or performance monitoring systems, or the development of new strategies for data collection, analysis or evaluation all fall under analytic evidence.

At GAO multiple sources of information are collected and used to provide a comprehensive perspective on a program. The different data sources serve to validate and cross-check findings.

3. A Multiplist Approach to Inquiry: Enhancing Credibility, Meaning, and Utility

Over the past 30 years the field of evaluation has had to grapple with a macro social context that has grown considerably more complex. Evaluation has become increasingly pluralistic; evaluators embrace different perspectives, ideologies, value stances, and methods preferences. Today, bridges to knowledge rely on multiple approaches and methods as a way to assure that evaluative claims are credible and defensible. Although evaluation serves a number of purposes, more recently there has been an emphasis on accountability at all levels of the U.S. government.

At the federal level there has been an increased emphasis on program results. The various reform initiatives such as the Government Performance and

Results Act of 1993 (commonly referred to as GPRA or the Results Act) (P.L. 103-62) have shifted the emphasis from the characteristics of program constituents and the services they receive (process issues) to an increased demand for information on program effectiveness. This shift in perception about what counts as useful information for decisionmaking is also found at state and local levels. Other reform initiatives have been tried in the past and were perceived as failures by policymakers. The Results Act reform initiative begins with the development of an agency's overall strategic plan. Performance monitoring systems are put in place to measure progress toward agency goals and objectives. Typically, however, desired program outcomes (e.g., improved quality of life) are difficult to measure. In practice, performance management systems have not risen to the level of complexity in measurement problems. Further, program measurement systems have been viewed by some as (a) inadequate, potentially distorted, responses to accountability demands (Greene 1999), (b) manipulable and subject to misuse (Perrin 1998), (c) ignoring key elements that need attention by policy-makers and program managers, (d) insufficiently addressing data validity, reliability, and tradeoffs between costs and outcomes achieved, (e) failing to consider the diversity of program environments, and (f) giving inadequate attention to external factors and isolation of net impact of a program .

The problems outlined are ones of theory, methods, measurement, and interpretation. Guidelines drawn from critical multiplism (Cook 1985) and outlined by Dunn (1994) for creating, critically assessing, and communicating policy-relevant knowledge include multiple operationalism, multimethod research, multiple analytic synthesis, multivariate analysis, multiple stakeholder analysis, multiple perspective analysis, and multimedia communications. The logic behind this call for a multiplist approach to inquiry has a long history. It stems from recognition in the social sciences that all methods have inherent biases and limitations. The multi-trait, multi-method matrix was developed as an approach for assessing the construct validity of a set of measures in a study (Campbell/Fiske 1959). This classic article lay the foundation for the importance of establishing both convergent and discriminant validity.

As noted by Sechrest, Davis, Stickle, & McKnight (2000) the idea of method is not very well understood in measurement today. Methods are usually defined in some superficial way and studies may be classified as multimethod simply because two approaches to measurement were used that were not identical and yet they may not at all meet the criteria that they are sufficiently different to justify the study as observing the intent of the multitrait-multimethod matrix (p. 68). Nevertheless, from this classic work the notion of triangulation took hold. The logic of triangulation assumes that the use of only one method to assess a given phenomenon will yield biased or limited results. When two or more methods, with offsetting biases, are used to assess a given phenomenon, and the results converge or corroborate one another, the validity of findings is enhanced (Denzin 1978; Mathison 1988; Webb/Campbell/Schwartz/Sechrest 1966).

Triangulation of data sources can be served by designs that include the use of both qualitative and quantitative methods (mixed methods), providing the methods do not share the same source of bias but rather offset the bias and limitations of the contrasting method type (Shotland/Mark 1987). Greene, Caracelli & Graham (1989) in a review of mixed method studies found that although triangulation was a stated purpose for combining methods, the term was misused and study designs were inappropriate for triangulation purposes.[5] From this review, five purposes for mixing methods were identified: (a) triangulation (the use of mixed-methods for purposes of achieving convergence, corroboration); (b) complementarity (mixed-methods are used to measure overlapping but different facets of a phenomena in order to obtain an enriched, elaborated understanding of the phenomena); (c) development (the sequential use of qualitative and quantitative methods help develop or inform the other method); (d) initiation (the use of mixed-methods by design or during analysis results in fresh perspectives, paradoxes, contradictions, a recasting of the study) and (e) expansion (mixed methods are used for different components of the evaluation and extended the breadth and range of the inquiry).

Drawing on the same set of studies several mixed method analysis strategies were identified (Caracelli/Greene 1993). Current standards provide little guidance on how evidence from multiple perspectives should be put together to provide a coherent assessment. A multidimensional conceptualization of quality in mixed-method studies was developed to set forth some criteria for achieving a quality synthesis of qualitative and quantitative methods (mixed-method collaboration, 1994). Although many criteria generated in this study are typical of those needed to conduct any quality evaluation, a number of criteria were specific to mixed-method studies (e.g., among others, a conceptual framework guided selection of qualitative and quantitative methods; convergent findings are not the result of shared bias between the methods). Several sources provide information on issues related to conducting multiple or mixed-method studies and strategies for designing and analyzing such studies (Brewer/Hunter 1989; Creswell 1994; Greene/Caracelli 1997; Mark/ Shotland 1987; Mertens 1997; Ragin 1989; Reichardt/Rallis 1994; Tashakkori/Teddlie 1998).

Design options for mixed methods that also include elements of different paradigms are discussed in Caracelli & Greene (1999). Two broad classes of designs are identified: Component and Integrated. In a component or coordinated design the different methods are implemented relatively separately and are only brought together at end of the study when drawing inferences and conclusions. Integrated designs result in methods being mixed at multiple

---

5   Triangulation designs require that two or more methods be intentionally used to assess
     the same conceptual phenomenon, be implemented simultaneously, and, to preserve
     their counteracting biases should be implemented independently (Greene et al. 1989).

stages of inquiry resulting in refined interpretations and conclusions. For example, program theory can provide a framework for integrated, holistic evaluations using qualitative and quantitative methods (Chen 1990; Chen 1997). Articulating the program theory, e.g., through the use of a logic model, can serve as a framework for integrating disparate methods, meanings, and understandings (See Cooksy 1999 for an illustration of an evaluation that included multiple sources of data and used a program logic model to guide data collection and reporting). Frameworks such as emergent realism require a mix of methods and perspectives and provide guidance on the selection of methods given the particular purpose served by the evaluation (See Henry/ Julnes/Mark 1998; Mark/Henry/Julnes, in press).

Greene, Benjamin, Goodyear, & Lowe (1999) cite some of the benefits that can accrue from a planned mixed-method study, such as enhanced validity and credibility of inferences, greater comprehensiveness of findings, more insightful understandings, and increased value consciousness and diversity. These attractive benefits are not a simple matter. The practice of evaluation must take into account diverse paradigms, perspectives, value frameworks, methods, and data. This pluralistic enterprise would appear to be best served by a multiplist approach (Cook 1985). Yet such approaches are resource intensive, stakeholders do not always come to some consensual agreement, data from methods do not always converge. We are often faced with what Cook (1985) terms an „empirical puzzle" which raises questions requiring attention to potential problems with our theories and methods. The analytic frameworks and methods outlined here are rarely singly applied in an evaluation. Instead they are arrayed in different configurations depending upon our theories about the program and problems the program is intended to address, the particular questions that guide the evaluation, the skill set and resources of those conducting the study, the user needs for timely information, and other factors. As noted by Datta (1997) a pragmatic approach to design and selection of mixed methods requires systematic consideration of practicality, contextual responsiveness, and consequentiality. This requires a body of knowledge about the practical consequences of our design decisions. As noted at the beginning of this chapter, the study of evaluation practice is a foundational aspect of program evaluation. Such study is necessary if we are to assist in maximizing the potential of policies and programs to ameliorate persistent problems faced by society, assure the accountability of programs, and better serve the needs of the citizenry.

References

Bentz, V. M./Shapiro, J. J. (1998):Mindful Inquiry in Social Research. Thousand Oaks, CA: Sage.

Berg, B. L.(2000): Qualitative Research Methods for the Social Sciences. (4th Ed.). Needham Heights, MA: Allyn & Bacon.

Bickman, L. (Ed.) (2000): Validity & Social Experimentation: Don Campbell's Legacy. (Vol. 1). Thousand Oaks, CA: Sage.

Bickman, L. (Ed.) (2000): Research Design: Don Campbell's Legacy. (Vol. 2). Thousand Oaks, CA: Sage.

Bickman, L./Rog, D. J. (Eds.) (1998): Handbook of Applied Social Research Methods. Thousand Oaks, CA: Sage.

Blalock, H. M. Jr. (1982): Conceptualization and Measurement in the Social Sciences. Newbury Park, CA: Sage.

Brewer, J./Hunter, A. (1989): Multimethod Research: A Synthesis of Styles. Thousand Oaks, CA: Sage.

Campbell, D. T./Fiske, D. W. (1959): Convergent and discriminant validation by the multitrait-multimethod matrix. Psychological Bulletin, 56, 1959, pp. 81-105.

Caracelli, V. (1999): Strengthening Quality at GAO: The Interface of Contemporary Auditing and Evaluation Professions. Paper presented at the annual meeting of the American Evaluation Association, Orlando, Florida. November 4, 1999.

Caracelli, V. J./Greene, J. C. (1993): Data Analysis Strategies for Mixed-Method Evaluation Designs. Educational Evaluation and Policy Analysis, 15 (no. 2), Washington, D.C.: American Educational Research Association, 1993, pp. 195-207.

Caracelli, V. J./Greene, J. C. (1997): Crafting Mixed-Method Evaluation Designs. In: Greene, J. C./Caracelli, V. J. (Eds.): Advances in Mixed-Method Evaluation: The Challenges and Benefits of Integrating Diverse Paradigms. New Directions for Evaluation, No. 74, San Francisco: Jossey-Bass. pp. 19-32.

Chelimsky, E. (1996): From Incrementalism to Ideology and Back: Can Producers of Policy Information Adjust to the Full Spectrum of Political Climates. Distinguished Public Policy Lecture Series, 1996. Center for Urban Affairs and Research, Evanston, Illinois (February 29, 1996).

Chelimsky, E. (1997): The Coming Transformations in Evaluation. In: Chelimsky, E./ Shadish, W. (Eds.): Evaluation for the 21st Century. Thousand Oaks, CA: Sage. pp. 1-26.

Chelimsky, E. (1997): The Political Environment of Evaluation and What it Means for the Development of the Field. In Chelimsky, E./Shadish.W. R.: Evaluation for the 21st Century: A Handbook. Thousand Oaks, CA: Sage. pp. 53-68.

Chen, H.-T. (1990): Theory-driven Evaluations. Thousand Oaks, CA: Sage.

Chen, H.-T./Rossi, P. H. (1987): The theory-driven approach to validity. Evaluation and Program Planning, 10, New York, NY: Pergamon Press, 1987, pp. 95-103.

Cook, T. D./Campbell, D. T. (1979): Quasi-experimentation: Design and Analysis Issues for Field Settings. Chicago: Rand McNally College Publishing Co..

Cook, T. D. (1985): Postpositivist critical multiplism. In: Shotland, R. L./Mark, M. M. (Eds.): Social Science and Social Policy. Beverly Hills, CA: Sage. pp. 21-62.

Cook, T. D./Cooper, H./Cordray, D. S./Hartmann, H./Hedges, L. V./Light, R. J./Louis, T. A./Mosteller, F. (1992): Meta-analysis for Explanation: A casebook. New York, NY: Russell Sage Foundation.

Cooksy, L. J. (1999): The Meta-Evaluand: The Evaluation of Project TEAMS. American Journal of Evaluation. Vol. 20, No. 1, 1999, pp. 123-136.

Cooper, H./Hedges, L. V. (Eds.) (1994): The Handbook of Research Synthesis. New York: Russell Sage Foundation.

Cousins, J. B./Whitmore E. (1998): Framing Participatory Evaluation. In: Whitmore, E. (Ed.): Understanding and Practicing Participatory Evaluation. New Directions for Evaluation. No. 80, 1998, pp. 5-23.

Creswell, J. W. (1994): Research Designs: Qualitative and Quantitative Approaches. Thousand Oaks, CA: Sage.

Crotty, M. (1998): The Foundations of Social Research. Thousand Oaks, CA: Sage.

Cronbach, L. J./Associates. (1980): Toward Reform of Program Evaluation. San Francisco: Jossey-Bass.

Datta. L-e. (1997): A Pragmatic Basis for Mixed-Method Designs. In Greene, J. C./Caracelli, V. J. (Eds.): Advances in Mixed-Method Evaluation: The Challenges and Benefits of Integrating Diverse Paradigms. New Directions for Evaluation, No. 74. San Francisco: Jossey-Bass. pp. 33-45.

Datta, L-e. (2000): Seriously Seeking Fairness: Strategies for Crafting Non-partisan Evaluations in a Partisan World. American Journal of Evaluation, Vol. 21, No. 1, 2000, pp. 1-14.

Denzin, N. K. (1978): The Research Act: An Introduction to Sociological Methods (chap. 10). New York: McGraw-Hill.

Denzin, N. K. (1997): Interpretive Ethnography: Ethnographic practices for the 21st Century. Thousand Oaks, CA: Sage.

Denzin, N. K./Lincoln, Y. S. (Eds.) (2000): Handbook of Qualitative Research (2nd. Ed.). Thousand Oaks, CA: Sage.

Dillman, D. (1999): Mail and Internet Surveys: The Tailored Design Method (2nd Ed.). John Wiley & Sons.

Dunn, W. N. (1994): Public Policy Analysis: An Introduction. (2nd Ed.). Englewood Cliffs, NJ: Prentice Hall.

Erlandson, D. A./Harris, E. L./Skipper, B. L./Allen, S. D. (1993): Doing Naturalistic Inquiry: A Guide to Methods. Newbury Park: Sage.

Fetterman, D. M./Kaftarian, S. J./Wandersman, A. (Eds.) (1996): Empowerment Evaluation: Knowledge and Tools for Self-Assessment & Accountability. Thousand Oaks, CA: Sage.

Fowler, F. J. (1993): Survey Research Methods (2nd Ed). Newbury Park, CA: Sage.

Guba, E. G. (Ed.) (1990): The Paradigm Dialog. Newbury Park, CA: Sage.

Greene, J. C. (1993): The Role of Theory in Qualitative Program Evaluation. In Flinders, D. J./Mills, G. E. (Eds.): Theory and Concepts in Qualitative Research: Perspectives from the Field. New York, NY: Teachers College.

Greene, J. C. (1994): Qualitative Program Evaluation: Practice and Promise. In: Denzin, N. K./Lincoln, Y. S. (Eds.): Handbook of Qualitative Research. Thousand Oaks, CA: Sage. pp. 530-544.

Greene, J. C. (1999): The inequality of performance measurements. Evaluation, 5(2), 1999, pp. 160-172.

Greene, J. C. (1999): Understanding Social Programs Through Evaluation. In: Denzin, N. K./Lincoln, Y. S. (Eds.): Handbook of Qualitative Research (2nd. Ed.). Thousand Oaks, CA: Sage. pp. 981-999.

Greene, J. C./Benjamin, L./Goodyear, L./Lowe, S. (1999): The Merits of Mixing Methods in Applied Social Research (Working Draft), APPAM Conference, Washington, D.C., Nov.6, 1999.

Greene, J. C./Caracelli, V. J. (1997): Advances in Mixed-Method Evaluation: The Challenges and Benefits of Integrating Diverse Paradigms. New Directions for Evaluation, No. 74. San Francisco: Jossey-Bass.

Greene, J./Caracelli, V. J. (1997): Defining and Describing the Paradigm Issue in Mixed-Method Evaluation. In: Greene, J. C./Caracelli, V. J.: Advances in Mixed-Method Evaluation: The Challenges and Benefits of Integrating Diverse Paradigms. New Directions for Evaluation, No. 74. San Francisco, CA: Jossey-Bass.

Greene, J. C./Caracelli, V. J./Graham, W. F. (1989): Toward a Conceptual Framework for Mixed-method Evaluation Designs. Educational Evaluation and Policy Analysis, 11 (no. 3), 1989, pp. 255-274.

Groves, R. M. (1989): Survey Errors and Survey Costs. New York: John Wiley & Sons.

Hatry, H. (1999): Performance Measurement: Getting Results. Washington, D.C.: Urban Institute Press.

Hedrick, T. E./Bickman, L./Rog, D. J. (1993): Applied Research Design: A Practical Guide. Applied Social Research Methods Series, Vol 32. Thousand Oaks, CA: Sage.

Henry, G. T./Julnes, G./Mark, M. M. (Eds.) (1998): Realist Evaluation: An Emerging Theory in Support of Practice. New Directions for Evaluation, No. 78. San Francisco: Jossey-Bass.

Krueger, R. A. (1994): Focus Groups: A Practical Guide for Applied Research (2nd ed.). Thousand Oaks, CA: Sage.

Lavrakas, P. J. (1993): Telephone Survey Methods: Sampling, Selection, and Supervision. (2nd ed.). Applied Social Research Methods Series, v. 7. Newbury Park, CA: Sage.

Lincoln, Y. S./Guba, E. G. (1985): Naturalistic Inquiry. Beverly Hills, CA: Sage.

Lipsey, M. W./Wilson, D. B. (in press, 2000): Practical Meta-Analysis. Sage.

Lipsey, M. W. (1993): Theory as Method: Small Theories of Treatments. In: Sechrest. L. B./Scott, G. G. (Eds.) Understanding Causes and Generalizing About Them. New Directions for Program Evaluation. No. 57, pp. 5-38.

Lipsey, M. W. (1997): What Can You Build With Thousands of Bricks? Musings on the cumulation of knowledge in Program Evaluation. In: Rog, D. J./Fournier D. (Eds.) Progress and Future Directions in Evaluation: Perspectives on Theory, Practice, and Methods, New Directions for Evaluation, No. 76, pp. 7-23.

Mark, M. M. (1990): From Program Theory to Tests of Program Theory In: Bickman, L. (Ed.): Advances in Program Theory. New Directions for Program Evaluation, No. 47. San Francisco, CA: Jossey-Bass. pp.37-51.

Mark, M. M./Henry, G. T./Julnes, G. (in press, 2000): Evaluation: an Integrated Framework for Understanding, Guiding, and Improving Policies and Programs. San Francisco, CA: Jossey-Bass.

Mark, M. M./Shotland, R. L. (Eds.) (1987): Multiple Methods in Program Evaluation. New Directions for Program Evaluation (No. 35). San Francisco, CA: Jossey-Bass.

Marquart, J. M. (1990): A Pattern-Matching Approach to Link Program Theory and Evaluation Data. In: Bickman, L. (Ed.): Advances in Program Theory. New Directions for Program Evaluation, No. 47. San Francisco, CA: Jossey-Bass. pp. 93-107.

Mathison, S. (1988): Why Triangulate? Educational Researcher, 17(2), 13-17, 1988.

Maxwell, J. A. (1996): Qualitative Research Design: An Interactive Approach. Applied Social Research Methods Series, Vol. 41. Newbury Park, CA: Sage.

McKay, R. B. (1996): Cognitive Research in Reducing Nonsampling Errors in the Current Population Survey supplement on Race and Ethnicity. Proceedings of Statistics Canada Symposium 96: Nonsampling Errors. Ottawa, Ontario. pp. 107-117.

Mertens, D. M. (1997): Research Methods in Education and Psychology: Integrating Diversity with Quantitative and Qualitative Approaches. Thousand Oaks, CA: Sage.

Miles, M. B./Huberman, A. M. (1994): Qualitative data analysis: An Expanded Sourcebook (2nd Ed.). Thousand Oaks, CA: Sage.

Mixed-Method Collaboration (1994). Mixed-Method Evaluation: Developing Quality Criteria through Concept Mapping. Evaluation Practice, 15 (no. 2), 1994, pp. 139-152.

Newcomer, K. E. (Ed.) (1997): Using Performance Measurement to Improve Public and Nonprofit Programs. New Directions for Evaluation, no. 75. San Francisco, CA: Jossey-Bass.

Noblit, G. W./Hare, R. D. (1998): Meta-Ethnography: Synthesizing Qualitative Studies, Qualitative Research Methods, No. 11. Thousand Oaks, CA: Sage.

Owen, J. M./Rogers, P. J. (1999): Program Evaluation: Forms and Approaches. Thousand Oaks, CA: Sage.

Patton, M. Q. (1987): Evaluation's Political Inherency: Practical implications for design and use. In: Palumbo, D. J. (Ed.): The Politics of Program Evaluation. Newbury Park, CA: Sage. pp. 100-145.

Patton, M. Q. (1990): Qualitative Evaluation and Research Methods (2nd Ed.). Thousand Oaks, CA: Sage.

Patton, M. Q. (1997): Utilization-Focused Evaluation: The New Century Text (3rd Edition). Thousand Oaks: CA: Sage.

Pawson, R./Tilley, N. (1997): Realistic Evaluation. Thousand Oaks, CA: Sage.

Perrin, B. (1998): Effective Use and Misuse of Performance Measurement. American Journal of Evaluation, 19, No. 3, Greenwich, CT: JAI Press, Inc., pp. 367-379.

Posavac, E. J./Carey, R. G. (1997): Program Evaluation: Methods and Case Studies, Upper Saddle River, N.J.: Prentice-Hall.

Preskill, H./Torres, R. T. (1999): Evaluative Inquiry for Learning in Organizations. Thousand Oaks, CA: Sage.

Ragin, C. C. (1989): The Comparative Method: Moving Beyond Qualitative and Quantitative Strategies. Berkeley, CA: University of California Press.

Reichardt, C. S./Rallis, S. F. (Eds.) (1994): The Qualitative-Quantitative Debate: New Perspectives. New Directions for Program Evaluation, 61. San Francisco, CA: Jossey-Bass.

Riggin, L. J. C. (1990): Linking Program Theory and Social Science Theory. In: Bickman, L. (Ed.): Advances in Program Theory. New Directions for Program Evaluation No. 47. San Francisco, CA: Jossey-Bass.

Rossi, P. H.,/Freeman, H. E./Lipsey, M. W. (1999): Evaluation: A Systematic Approach (6th Edition.). Thousand Oaks, CA: Sage.

Schwarz, N./Sudman, S. (Eds) (1995): Answering Questions: Methodology for Determining Cognitive and Communicative Processes in Survey Research. San Francisco, CA: Jossey-Bass.

Scriven, M. S. (1991): Evaluation Thesaurus (4th Ed.). Newbury Park, CA: Sage.

Sechrest, L./Davis, M. F./Stickle, T. R./McKnight, P. E. (2000): Understanding „method" variance. In: Bickman, L. (Ed.): Research Design: Don Campbell's Legacy, Vol. 2. Thousand Oaks, CA: Sage. pp. 63-87.

Seidman, I. E. (1991): Interviewing as Qualitative Research. New York: Teachers College Press.

Shadish, W. R. Jr./Cook, T. D./Leviton, L. C. (1991): Foundations of Program Evaluation: Theories of Practice. Newbury Park, CA: Sage

Stake, R. E. (1995): The Art of Case Study Research. Thousand Oaks, CA: Sage.

Strauss, A./Corbin, J. (1990): Basics of Qualitative Research: Grounded Theory Procedures and Techniques. Newbury Park, CA: Sage.

Sudman, S./Bradburn, N./Schwarz, N. (1995): Thinking about Answers: The Application of Cognitive Processes to Survey Methodology. San Francisco, CA: Jossey-Bass.

Tashakkori, A./Teddlie, C. (1998): Mixed Methodology: Combining Qualitiative and Quantitative Approaches. Applied Social Research Methods Series, Vol. 46. Thousand Oaks, CA: Sage.

The Joint Committee on Standards for Educational Evaluation (James R. Sanders, Chair) (1994). The Program Evaluation Standards: How to Assess Evaluations of Educational Programs (2nd edition). Thousand Oaks, CA: Sage.

Trochim, W. M. K. (1985): Pattern matching, validity, and conceptualization in program evaluation. Evaluation Review, 9 (5). Beverly Hills, CA: Sage. pp.575-604.

Trochim, W. M. K.(1989): Outcome pattern matching and program theory. Evaluation and Program Planning, 12. New York, NY: Pergamon Press. pp.355-366.

Trochim, W. M. K. (1999): The Research Methods Knowledge Base (2nd Ed.). Ithaca, NY: Cornell University.

U.S. General Accounting Office (1995). Program Evaluation: Improving the Flow of Information to Congress. PEMD-95-1. Washington, D.C.: GAO, January 30, 1995.

U.S. General Accounting Office (2000). Managing for Results: Views on Ensuring the Usefulness of Agency Performance Information to Congress. GAO/GGD-00-35: Washington, D.C.: GAO, January 26, 2000.

U.S. General Accounting Office . Cholesterol Treatment: A review of the Clinical Trials Evidence. GAO/PEMD-96-7. Washington, D.C.: GAO, 1996.

U.S. General Accounting Office (1993). Developing and Using Questionnaires. GAO/PEMD-10.1.7. Washington, D.C.: GAO, 1993.

U.S. General Accounting Office (1992). The Evaluation Synthesis (PEMD-10.1.2). Washington, D.C.: GAO.

U.S. General Accounting Office (1991). Designing Evaluations (PEMD-10.1.4). Washington, D.C.: GAO.

U.S. General Accounting Office (1991). Using Structured Interviewing Techniques (PEMD-10.1.5). Washington, D.C.: GAO.

U.S. General Accounting Office (1990). Prospective Evaluation Methods: The Prospective Evaluation Synthesis (Transfer Paper 10.1.10). Washington, D.C.: GAO.

Vedung, E. (1997): Public Policy and Program Evaluation. New Brunswick, NJ: Transaction Publishers.

Worthen, B. R./Sanders, J. R./Fitzpatrick, J. L. (1997): Program Evaluation: Alternative Approaches and Practical Guidelines (2nd Ed.). White Plains, NY: Longman.

Webb, E. J./Campbell, D. T./Schwartz, R. D./ Sechrest, L. (2000): Unobtrusive Measures (revised edition). Sage Classics 2. Thousand Oaks, CA: Sage.

Webb, E./Campbell, D. T./Schwartz, R. D./Sechrest, L. (1996): Unobtrusive Measures: Nonreactive Research in the Social Sciences. Chicago: Rand McNally.

Weiss, C. H. (1987): Where politics and evaluation research meet. In: Palumbo, D. J. (Ed.): The Politics of Program Evaluation. Thousand Oaks, CA: Sage. pp. 47-70.

Weiss, C. J. (1998): Evaluation (2nd Ed.). Upper Saddle River, NJ: Prentice Hall.

Wholey, J. S./Hatry, H. P./Newcomer, K. E. (Eds.) (1994): Handbook of Practical Program Evaluation. San Francisco, CA: Jossey-Bass.

Wholey, J. S. (1994): Assessing the feasibility and likely usefulness of evaluation. In: Wholey J. S./Hatry, H. P./Newcomer, K. E. (Eds.): Handbook of Practical Program Evaluation. San Francisco: Jossey-Bass. pp. 15-39.

Yin, R. K. (1994): Case Study Research: Designs and Methods: Applied Social Research Methods, vol 5. Thousand Oaks, CA: Sage.

Informations

Web-based guidance:
American Evaluation Association: http://www.eval.org
This site provides a number of links to assist the evaluator in obtaining information that may be helpful in planning and conducting and evaluation. In particular, link to Bill Trochim's Center for Social Research Methods. This site contains an online textbook entitled the Research Methods Knowledge base. This is a comprehensive web-based textbook that addresses subject matter typically covered in undergraduate or graduate courses in social research methods. The text includes such topics as formulating research questions, sampling (probability and non-probability), measurement (surveys, scaling, qualitative, unobtrusive), research design (experimental, quasi-experimental), data analysis and writing the research paper. Theoretical and philosophical underpinnings of research including the idea of validity in research, reliability of measures and ethics are also covered.

The Evaluation Exchange: http://gseweb.harvard.edu/~hfrp
The site provides a forum for sharing information and ideas about evaluation.

Western Michigan University Evaluation Center: http://www.wmich.edu/evalctr/checklists
The site provides information on the logic and methodology of checklists, guidelines for developing checklists and makes available checklists already in use.

The U.S. Centers for Disease Control and Prevention (CDC): www.cdc.gov/eval/index.htm
The CDC Evaluation working group has developed CDC's Framework for Program Evaluation available at the site. The framework guides public health professionals in their use of program evaluation. It lays out steps in program evaluation practice and standards for effective program evaluation. The site also refers practitioners to additional resources that can assist practitioners in conducting an evaluation project.

The U.S. General Accounting Office (GAO): http://www.gao.gov
The U.S. General Accounting Office provides guidance on specific topics, e.g., designing evaluations, case study research, and evaluation synthesis, among others. The General Policies /Procedures and Communications Manual contains guidance for designing evaluations and selecting the appropriate methodology, including describing the major benefits, purposes and limitations of different approaches and specific methods. The Government Auditing Standards (Yellow Book) are important to ensuring the achievement of quality in performance audits and evaluations conducted by GAO. These documents are available under the link to Other Publications at the U.S. General Accounting Office

Other handbooks are also available on the Web:
The Administration on Children, Youth and Families (ACYF), U.S. Department of Human Services has made the Program Managers Guide to Evaluation available on the web at http://www2.acf.dhhs.gov/programs/hsb/CORE/dox/progman.html

The Division of Research, Evaluation and Communication of the National Science Foundation provides a User-friendly Handbook for Project Evaluation and a User-Friendly Handbook for Mixed Method Evaluations at the web site: http://www.ehr.nsf.gov/her/rec/pub/htm. The former publication describes types of evaluations and the evaluation process, including the development of evaluation questions and the collection and analysis of appropriate data to provide answers to these questions. Quantitative techniques are emphasized because many indicators used in projects contributing to knowledge and understanding of mathematics, science, and technology rely on quantitative outcome indicators. The second volume builds on the first but introduces a broader perspective, including the collection and analysis of qualitative data. Experienced evaluators have found that most often the best results are achieved through the use of mixed-method evaluations, which combine quantitative and qualitative techniques.

II. Ausgewählte Felder
   der Evaluationsforschung

Hellmut Wollmann

Evaluierung und Evaluierungsforschung von Verwaltungspolitik und -modernisierung[1] – zwischen Analysepotential und -defizit

1. Problemstellung

Die Politik- und Verwaltungswelt der Bundesrepublik wurde in den vergangenen 40 Jahren von zwei verwaltungspolitischen Modernisierungswellen erfaßt (vgl. Wollmann 2000): in den späten 60er und frühen 70er Jahren von dem um die Stärkung der *politisch-administrativen Planungsfunktion* kreisenden Reformschub und seit den frühen 90er Jahren vom *betriebswirtschaftlichen Managerialismus*, der zunächst in der internationalen, insbesondere angelsächsischen Modernisierungsdiskussion unter dem Stichwort *New Public Management* (NPM) Furore machte und dann auch die Modernisierungsdiskussion in der Bundesrepublik Deutschland als *Neuen Steuerungsmodells* (NSM) ergriff[2].

Bei allen Unterschieden haben die beiden Diskussionsstränge konzeptionell und strategisch vor allem zweierlei gemeinsam (vgl. Wollmann 1994: 103f.; Grimmer/Kneissler 2000: 10):

– War die *Planungsdiskussion* darauf gerichtet, die politisch-administrative Handlungsfähigkeit durch die Stärkung der *Planungs- und Ziel*funktion (*management by objectives*) zu verbessern, wollen *NPM* und *NSM* – an die *Planungs*philosophie unverkennbar anknüpfend und diese unter Rückgriff auf privatwirtschaftliche Managementkonzepte weiterentwickelnd (vgl. Naschold 1995: 94) – die Leistungsfähigkeit (und Wirtschaftlichkeit) öffentlichen Handelns durch eine Steuerung „über Ergebnisse/ Resultate" (*Output*-Steuerung, *management by results*) steigern.

---

1   Der Aufsatz ist Frieder Naschold gewidmet, der am 30. November 1999 im Alter von 59 Jahren unerwartet verstorben ist. Wie kaum ein anderer hat er in den letzten Jahren in der Bundesrepublik die Diskussion um die Modernisierung des Öffentlichen Sektors und deren (international vergleichende) Erforschung und Evaluierung angestoßen und vorangebracht.

2   Aus der inzwischen unübersehbar gewordenen Literatur sei Frieder Nascholds fast schon klassische Schrift (Naschold 1995) genannt. Ansonsten sei auf die einschlägigen Beiträge in dem von Bandemer u.a. herausgegebenen Handbuch (von Bandemer u.a. 1998), etwa Jann (1998); Schröter/Wollmann (1998) mit zahlreichen Referenzen verwiesen.

- Dadurch, daß der *Planungsdiskussion* ebenso wie dem *Managerialismus* die Vorstellung eines in den Phasen: Zielbildung/Planung, Prozeß/Durchführung/Implementation und Wirkung/Kontrolle abrollenden Managementzyklus zugrunde liegt, bildet die (fortlaufende und/oder abschließende) Identifizierung und Rückmeldung *(feedback)* der Ergebnisse und Wirkungen eine integrale Komponente, Phase und Schleife eines (kybernetischen) Steuerungs- und Handlungsmodells (vgl. Naschold 1995: 94)
  - in der *Planungsdiskussion* als *Evaluierungs*funktion (mit überwiegendem *analytischen* und *kybernetischen Akzent)*[3], im *Managerialismus* als *Controlling*funktion (mit stärker *steuerungstheoretischen* Intentionen) (vgl. etwa Richter 1998: 349).

In dem Maße, wie die Politik- und Verwaltungswelt der Bundesrepublik in den vergangenen 30 Jahren zum einen Phasen intensiver verwaltungsreformerischer und modernisierungspolitischer Veränderungsabsichten und -prozesse erlebte und gegenwärtig durchlebt und zum andern hierbei *Evaluierung* bzw. *Controlling* als Funktionen und Verfahren in der Absicht institutionalisiert wurden, die *Transparenz* des Verwaltungshandelns und seiner Wirkungen herzustellen und zu sichern, drängt sich die sozialwissenschaftlich wie verwaltungspolitisch spannende Frage auf, ob, in welchem Umfange und vermöge welcher Verfahren die Verwaltungspolitik selber, insbesondere die von ihr herbeigeführten (organisatorischen, personellen, instrumentellen usw.) Veränderungen und deren Wirkungen, zum Gegenstand von Evaluierung und Evaluierungsforschung gemacht worden sind und gemacht werden.

Diese Frage soll im folgenden in vier Schritten verfolgt werden.

- Zunächst sollen einige begriffliche und konzeptionelle Verständigungen getroffen werden.
- Sodann sollen die konzeptionellen und methodischen Ansätze der Evaluierungsforschung unter dem Blickwinkel ihrer Anwendbarkeit auf den Gegenstandsbereich der Verwaltung und Verwaltungsmodernisierung diskutiert werden.
- Danach sollen der gegenwärtige Stand und das konzeptionelle und methodische Profil der Evaluierungsforschung zur Verwaltungsmodernisierung anhand ausgewählter Beispiele dargestellt werden.
- Schließlich soll ein kurzer Ausblick auf den einschlägigen Diskussions- und Forschungsstand in einigen europäischen Nachbarländern gegeben werden.

---

3   Zur Entstehung und Entwicklung der Evaluierung in der Bundesrepublik vgl. etwa Derlien (1976); Hellstern/Wollmann (1984a, 1984b) für die kommunale Ebene Hellstern/Wollmann (1984c). Vgl. den noch immer sehr instruktiven (frühen) international vergleichenden Überblick bei Levine (1984). Für international vergleichende Überblicke vgl. auch Wagner/Wollmann (1986), Derlien (1990).

2. Begrifflicher und konzeptioneller Rahmen

2.1 Begriffliche Dimensionen der Evaluierung und Evaluierungsforschung[4]

– *Evaluierung/Evaluierungsforschung.* Als *Evaluierung* (im Öffentlichen Sektor) werden verbreitet Analysen verstanden, die darauf gerichtet sind, die Wirkungen politischen und administrativen Handelns, insbesondere von politischen Interventionen, Programmen, Projekten oder Maßnahmen zu erfassen und zu ermitteln, ob die beobachtbaren Veränderungen – intendierte wie nicht-intendierte Wirkungen – auf die politischen Programme, Projekte usw. usw. (oder aber auf andere Faktoren) kausal zurückzuführen seien. Untersuchungen, die sich im wesentlichen darauf beziehen, den Zielerreichungsgrad eines Programms (durch den Vergleich der Ziele, d.h. der intendierten und der tatsächlich erreichten Wirkungen, „Soll-Ist-Vergleich") zu identifizieren, werden vielfach als *Erfolgskontrolle* bezeichnet. Als Evaluierungs*forschung* können Evaluierungsverfahren verstanden werden, die sich zur Aufhellung der relevanten Ziel-Mittel- und Wirkungs-Ursachenzusammenhänge sozialwissenschaftlicher Methoden bedienen. Angesichts dessen, daß Evaluierung in den 60er und 70er Jahren (zumal in den für Politikevaluierung bahnbrechenden USA) vielfach politische Programme (vgl. etwa Hellstern/Wollmann 1984b: 27ff.) zum Gegenstand hatten, wurde in den USA die Bezeichnung *program evaluation* (vgl. Rist 1990) üblich und kam auch in der deutschen Diskussion der Terminus Programmevaluierung und *Programmforschung* in Umlauf[5].

– *Zeitpunkt der Evaluierung.*
- Die *ex-ante* Evaluierung zielt darauf, die Wirkungen und Ursache-Wirkungszusammenhänge eines künftigen Handlungsprogramms/einer Maßnahme vorab abzuschätzen (*pre-assessment).* Sie weist Überschneidungen zur (*ex-ante*) *Kosten-Nutzen-Analyse auf,* mit der die Kosten und Nutzen (von Varianten) einer künftigen Maßnahme vorab ermittelt werden sollen. Demgegenüber ist eine *Evaluierbarkeits-Abschätzung* (*evaluability pre-assessment)* auf die Vorab-Aussage darüber gerichtet, ob sich das interessierende Handlungsprogramm/die Maßnahme für eine Evaluierung eignet.

---

4   Zur Begrifflichkeit der Evaluierung und Evaluierungsforschung vgl. etwa Hellstern/ Wollmann (1984b: 19ff.).

5   Vgl. hierzu insbesondere Derlien (1981a, 1981b), der den Begriff „Programmforschung" seit den späten 70er Jahren propagiert hat; die von ihm mitbegründete *Gesellschaft für Programmforschung* spiegelt in ihrer Bezeichnung diese Begriffswahl programmatisch wider.

- Sodann wird herkömmlich (vgl. Scriven 1972) zwischen *summativer* und *formativer* (oder – in neuerer Diktion – *on-going*) Evaluierung unterschieden. Während jene als abschließende (*ex-post*) Evaluierung erst nach Ablauf des Handlungsprogramms/der Maßnahme durchgeführt wird, ist dieser eigentümlich, möglichst von Anfang an einzusetzen. Sie dient der früh- und rechtzeitigen Rückkopplung von (Zwischen-) Ergebnissen an die relevanten (politischen, administrativen und gesellschaftlichen) Akteure, um etwaige Korrekturen im laufenden Programm-, Projekt- und Maßnahmevollzug zu ermöglichen.
- Der formativen Evaluierung steht das Konzept der Begleitforschung nahe, innerhalb derer wiederum zwischen einer distanzierten, die *analytische* Evaluierungsfunktion betonenden, einer (zusätzlich) *beratenden* und einer sich in den Projektverlauf *aktiv einmischenden* („intervenierenden")[6], Übergänge zur *Aktionsforschung* aufweisenden Variante von Begleitforschung unterschieden wird[7].
- Als Monitoring kann schließlich die deskriptiv-analytische (auf die „Kausalfrage" und -interpretation weitgehend verzichtende) Beobachtung relevanter Ergebnisse (insbesondere mit Hilfe brauchbarer Indikatoren) verstanden werden.
- *Träger von Evaluierung.* Die Evaluierungsfunktion kann entweder von der betreffenden Verwaltungsorganisation selbst als verwaltungsinterne (*interne,* „in house") Evaluierung, und hierbei als *Selbstevaluierung* der operativen Verwaltungseinheit selber wahrgenommen werden. Sie kann aber auch durch *externe* Beratungsorganisationen oder Forschungseinrichtungen durchgeführt werden (*externe-* „*extra muros"-Evaluierung*).
- *Initiierung und Finanzierung von Evaluierung.* Die Evaluierungsuntersuchung kann entweder durch die Beauftragung einer externen Forschungseinrichtung durch die betreffende Verwaltungseinheit und deren Finanzierung aus Mitteln der Verwaltung (z.B. Ressortforschungsmitteln) veranlaßt sein oder aufgrund einer selbständigen Entscheidung einer externen Forschungseinrichtung durchgeführt und aus deren Eigenmitteln und/oder dadurch finanziert werden, daß hierfür Fördermittel (Drittmittel) – in der Regel bei einer „angewandte Grundlagenforschung" fördernden Stiftung (z.B. Hans-Böckler-Stiftung) oder Forschungsfördereinrichtung (z.B. DFG) – eingeworben werden.

---

6 Vgl. kritisch zur „Interventionsforschung" Lutz (1983).
7 Zu der in den 70er Jahren (insbesondere im Kontext der damaligen umfangreichen Schulversuche) geführten lebhaften Diskussion („distanzierte" versus „intervenierende" Begleitforschung) vgl. Hellstern/Wollmann (1983b: 59ff.) mit Nachweisen. Vgl. Lutz (1983) mit einer Kritik der „Interventionsforschung".

2.2 Verwaltungspolitik und verwaltungspolitische Maßnahmen als Gegenstand von Evaluierung

Zunächst ist es zweckmäßig, eine gegenständliche und begriffliche Unterscheidung zwischen *Verwaltungs*[8]- oder *Institutionenpolitik*[9] einerseits und anderen (substanziellen) Politiken (*policies*) andererseits einzuführen und zu verwenden[10].

– Als substanzielle Politiken können die (normalen) sektoralen Politiken verstanden werden, die darauf gerichtet sind, bestimmte sozio-ökonomische, ökologische usw. Veränderungen im Umfeld von Politik und Verwaltung zu beeinflussen und entsprechende Politikziele (als intendierte Wirkungen bzw. Wirkungsketten) zu erreichen. Innerhalb dieser Wirkungen lassen sich wiederum *Outputs* (als unmittelbar angestrebte Veränderungen, z.B. die Ansiedlung bestimmter Betriebe durch regionale Wirtschaftsförderungspolitik) und im weiteren Verlauf der Wirkungskette *Outcomes* (als weitere – verteilungspolitische usw. – Wirkungen, z.B. Senkung der Arbeitslosigkeit, Steigerung der regionalen Wohlfahrt) unterscheiden.

– Demgegenüber ist die Interventionslogik der Verwaltungs- bzw. Institutionenpolitik durch einen Doppel-, wenn nicht Dreierschritt gekennzeichnet. *Zum einen* ist sie zunächst und unmittelbar auf die Veränderung der politisch-administrativen Strukturen und (organisatorischen, personellen, instrumentellen, prozeduralen usw.) Institutionen gerichtet. Insoweit ist sie auf das institutionelle Gehäuse, auf die *polity*[11] gerichtet, in der und durch die „Politik gemacht" („policy making") wird. Insoweit Verwaltungspolitik auf die Gestaltung der institutionellen Logistik der *polity* und Infrastruktur des „Politikmachens" zielt, kann sie als „polity policy" oder „meta-policy-making" (Dror 1968: 7f.)[12] bezeichnet werden. So betrachtet, erweist sich die Einführung und Institutionalisierung der Evaluierungsfunktion selber als ein wesentliches Teilziel und -element der Verwaltungs- und Modernisierungspolitik. *Zum andern* und des weiteren strebt Verwaltungspolitik an, *vermittels* dieser institutionellen Veränderung die Leistungsfä-

---

8   zum Begriff von Verwaltungspolitik vgl. Böhret (1998: 42).

9   Vgl. Knoepfel/Bussmann (1997: 59), die den Begriff „institutionelle Politik" verwenden.

10   Zur Unterscheidung zwischen Institutionen- und „substanzieller" Politik vgl. auch Ritz (1999: 28).

11   Bekanntlich wird in der Policy-Forschung vielfach die Triade „politics, policy und polity" unterschieden, wobei „polity" als das „institutionelle" Arrangement (und Gehäuse) verstanden wird, in dem der politische Auseinandersetzungsprozeß der Akteure („politics") stattfindet und in dem „Politiken" (policies) formuliert und verwirklicht werden.

12   Vgl. hierzu auch Derlien (1981b: 13) unter Verweis auf Y. Dror.

higkeit (Effektivität), Wirtschaftlichkeit (Effizienz) usw. des Verwaltungshandelns *(Performanz, Output)* zu beeinflussen und zu steigern. *Schließlich*
und letztlich sollen die institutionellen und Performanz-Veränderungen
weiterreichende (gesamtwirtschaftliche, verteilungspolitische) Effekte
(Outcomes, z.b. erhöhte Investitionsbereitschaft der privaten Unternehmen, Senkung der Arbeitslosigkeit usw.) bewirken.

2.3 Evaluierung von Verwaltungspolitik: Mehrere Analyseschleifen

Die *normale Politik-/Programmevaluierung* besteht grundsätzlich aus *einer*
Analyseschleife, indem sie darauf gerichtet ist, die Wirksamkeit und Wirkungsweise einer bestimmten Politikintervention (Programm, Maßnahme usw.)
(methodisch gesprochen: als *abhängige Variable)* zu erfassen und zu ermitteln, ob die Politikintervention – oder andere Faktoren – (als *unabhängige
Variablen)* für die beobachteten Veränderungen ursächlich – sind.

Demgegenüber weist die Evaluierung von Verwaltungspolitik von vornherein eine komplexere analytische Architektur dadurch auf, daß bei ihr zumindest *zwei* unterschiedliche Analyseschleifen zu unterscheiden sind.

– Zum einen kann die Verwaltungs- und Institutionenpolitik dadurch selber
   zum Gegenstand der Evaluierung werden, daß sich diese darauf richtet,
   den Verlauf und Stand ("Zielerreichungsgrad") der intendierten institutionellen Veränderungen (methodisch gesprochen: als abhängige Variable) zu erfassen und die diese bestimmenden Faktoren (als unabhängige
   Variablen) zu identifizieren. Hierbei können es sich um eine umfassende,
   das gesamte NSM-Repertoire sowie eher traditionelle Reformbausteine
   umgreifende Veränderungsstrategie oder aber um einzelne Modernisie-
   rungskomponenten (z.B. die Einführung der Dezentralen Ressourcenverantwortung, die Einrichtung von Bürgerämtern oder auch die Institutionalisierung der Evaluationsfunktion, z.B. Controlling, selbst) handeln.
   Die auf die *institutionellen* Veränderungen gerichtete Evaluierung als
   „erste Analyseschleife" soll hier als *Institutionenevaluierung* bezeichnet
   werden. Dadurch, daß sie auf *(inner-administrativ) institutionelle* Veränderungen fokussiert ist, weist sie gegenständliche, konzeptionelle und
   methodische Gemeinsamkeiten mit der sozialwissenschaftlichen Institu-
   tionen- und Verwaltungsforschung zur (politisch-administrativen) Insti-
   tutionenbildung *(institution building)* auf[13].
– Die *zweite* Analyseschleife der Evaluierung gilt der Frage, ob und welche
   Veränderungen im Verwaltungshandeln *(Performanz),* z.B. Beschleuni-

---

13 Als jüngstes Beispiel sind hierfür insbesondere die umfangreichen politikwissen-
    schaftlichen Arbeiten zum Umbruch („Transformation") der politischen und admini-
    strativen Institutionenwelt in Ostdeutschland zu nennen, vgl. etwa die Beiträge in
    Wollmann u.a. (1998), auch Wegrich u.a. (1997).

gung der Entscheidungsverfahren, größere Kosteneffizienz, Qualität der Dienstleistung usw., (methodisch gesprochen: als *abhängige Variable*) auf die Modernisierungspolitik und ihre Maßnahmen (oder aber auf andere Faktoren) (als *unabhängige Variablen*) zurückzuführen sind. Diese Evaluierungsfragestellung wird hier als *Performanzevaluierung* bezeichnet.

– Schließlich kann es in einer *dritten* Analyseschleife darum gehen, im sozio-ökonomischen Umfeld der Verwaltung die beobachtbaren (ökonomischen, ökologischen, verteilungspolitischen usw.) Veränderungen (*Outcomes*) als jene Wirkungen zu identifizieren, auf die auch und gerade die Verwaltungspolitik vielfach „letztlich" zielt.

3. Reichweite des Methodenrepertoires in der Evaluierung von Verwaltungspolitik

Bekanntlich sind beim Design und der Durchführung von Evaluierungsuntersuchungen vor allem zwei konzeptionelle und methodische Probleme zu bewältigen:

– die Konzipierung der Ziele/intendierten Wirkungen (aber auch der nichtintendierten Wirkungen) als der in erster Linie interessierenden *abhängigen* Variablen (*Konzipierungsproblem),*

– die Formulierung eines leistungsfähigen Designs zur Erfassung der relevanten Ursache-Wirkungszusammenhänge (*Kausalitätsproblem).*

3.1 Zielbestimmung und Indikatorenbildung

Die konzeptionellen, methodischen, empirischen und datenökonomischen Probleme, die die Politikevaluierung aufwirft[14], zeigen sich bei der Evaluierung von Verwaltungspolitik aus einer Reihe von Gründen besonders ausgeprägt:

– Zunächst ist an die mögliche „Mehrschleifigkeit" der Evaluierung von Verwaltungspolitik (*Institutionen-, Performanz- und/oder Outcomes-Evaluierung)* zu erinnern, die von vornherein eine die jeweils adressierende Mittel-Ziel- und Ursache-Wirkungs-Schleife sorgfältig und differenziert berücksichtigende Zieldiskussion erheischt.

– Sodann ist zu beachten, daß modernisierungspolitischen Interventionen vielfach eine vieldimensionale Strategie- und Zielstruktur zugrunde liegt,

---

14 Vgl. hierzu ausführlich (am Beispiel des Städtebaus) Hellstern/Wollmann (1983a: 11ff.).

in der gegebenenfalls das gesamte Repertoire der im NPM bzw. im NSM
diskutierten Modernisierungskonzepte und -komponenten, einschließlich
der eher traditionellen (auf die 70er und 80er Jahre zurückgehenden) Reformbausteine, mobilisiert und eingesetzt werden sollen[15]. Es liegt auf der
Hand, daß diese mögliche Konzeptbreite und -heterogenität die Konzipierung der Evaluierung von vornherein vor besondere Probleme stellt,
gleichviel, ob eine *Institutionen-,* eine *Performanz-* oder eine *Outcomes-
Evaluierung* unternommen wird.

Die Voraussetzungen, konzeptionell wie empirisch auf leistungsfähige Indikatoren zurückzugreifen, erscheinen für die Evaluierung von Verwaltungspolitik auf den ersten Blick angesichts dessen als verhältnismäßig günstig,
daß die Bildung und Nutzung aussagekräftiger Indikatoren zur Messung von
Verwaltungshandeln in der Bundesrepublik zum einen in der „Planungsdiskussion" der 60er und 70er Jahre vor allem in der kommunalen Praxis leb-
haft diskutiert worden ist[16] und zum andern der Formulierung und Implementation leistungsfähiger Indikatorensysteme in der gegenwärtigen Modernisierungsdiskussion – im Zusammenhang mit der Definition von *Produkten*
und von *Kennziffern* – besondere Aufmerksamkeit gilt. Allerdings zeigt sich,
daß die Nutzung brauchbarer Daten, einschließlich *Verwaltungsvollzugsdaten,* noch immer in den Anfängen steckt (hierauf soll weiter unten zurückge-
kommen werden).

3.2 „Kausalitätsproblem"

Zunächst sei daran erinnert, daß jedem politischen Handlungsprogramm („Policy") in der Regel – sei es explizit, sei es implizit – eine „Handlungstheorie"
der Akteure, d.h. (hypothetische) Annahmen und Erwartungen darüber zugrunde liegen, daß das angestrebte Handlungsziel als Ergebnis der vom Akteur absichtsvoll in Gang gesetzten Handlungsschritte und Wirkungskette eintreten
werde (zu „impliziten Theorien" in der Politik vgl. Hofmann 1993). Wie man
seit der bahnbrechenden Studie von *Geoffrey Pressman* und *Aaron Wildavsky*
(vgl. Pressman/Wildavsky 1973) weiß, kann das Mißlingen und Verfehlen des
Handlungsziels entweder auf die unzulängliche Implementation einer an sich
richtigen Handlungstheorie („bad implementation") oder aber auf die zugrunde

---

15 Aus der kaum mehr zu übersehenden Literatur zum NSM soll hier auf Jann (1998) mit
    zahlreichen Nachweisen, zum NPM auf Pollitt (1995) (der 8 Komponenten auflistet),
    zur Unterscheidung zwischen NSM-spezifischen und „traditionellen" Modernisie-
    rungselementen auf Wegrich u.a. (1997: 244ff.), Jaedicke u.a. (2000: 21ff.) verwiesen
    werden.

16 Vgl. hierzu die Beiträge in Hellstern/Wollmann (1984c), insbesondere Hellstern/Woll-
    mann (1984d: 29ff.); Wollmann (1994), u.a. mit Hinweisen und Nachweisen der in
    den frühen 80er Jahren im Verband der Deutschen Städtestatistiker geführten (kon-
    zeptionell bemerkenswert fortgeschrittenen) „Indikatorendiskussion".

liegende „falsche" Handlungstheorie („false theory") zurückzuführen sein (vgl. hierzu ausführlicher Wollmann 1999: 12f.).

Sodann sei hervorgehoben, daß die sich der Verwaltungsforschung generell stellenden konzeptionellen und methodischen Probleme für die Evaluierung von Verwaltungspolitik in noch gesteigertem Maße gelten. Wie in der Diskussion der methodischen Potentiale und Grenzen der Verwaltungsforschung verschiedentlich betont worden ist (vgl. etwa Hucke/Wollmann 1980), werden für diese die bei der Gewinnung valider (Ursache-Wirkungs-) Aussagen zu bewältigenden Design- und Methodenprobleme dadurch verschärft, daß im Gegensatz zu anderen Forschungsfeldern (in ausgeprägtem Maße z.B. zur Wahlforschung) die Verwaltungsforschung mit einem Gegenstandsbereich zu tun hat, der – etwa am Beispiel der politisch-administrativen Organisationsstrukturen – in den Makrostrukturen (der Bundes-, Landes-, Kommunalverwaltung, Sonderbehörden usw.) zwar distinkte Grundtypen aufweist, jedoch im Detail – als Ergebnis und in Widerspiegelung der die deutsche Verwaltungsgeschichte kennzeichnenden hochgradigen vertikalen und horizontalen institutionellen Vielgestaltigkeit – eine außerordentlich hohe Variabilität und Varianz zeigt.

Im folgenden seien die in der Evaluierungsforschung (in Anlehnung an die allgemeine sozialwissenschaftliche Methodenlehre) üblicherweise diskutierten methodischen Zugänge mit Blick auf ihre Brauchbarkeit bei der Evaluierung von Verwaltungspolitik, insbesondere bei *Performanz- und Outcomes-Evaluierung*, kurz erörtert[17].

3.2.1 Experimentelle Methode

Die (ursprünglich in der Sozialpsychologie und Kleingruppenforschung entwickelte) experimentelle Methode besteht bekanntlich darin (als „klassische" Methodeneinführung vgl. Campbell/Stanley 1964, 1970), daß zwei Gruppen gebildet werden, die *experimentelle Gruppe* (Zielgruppe), die einem Stimulus („treatment") ausgesetzt wird, und die *Kontrollgruppe*. Indem die Gruppen nach Möglichkeit mit Hilfe von Zufallsverfahren („randomization") gebildet werden, soll erreicht werden, daß sie in möglichst vielen Merkmalen identisch seien („ceteris paribus"), wobei davon ausgegangen wird, daß alle jene Merkmale, in denen die Gruppen identisch sind, als mögliche Einflußfaktoren auf Varianz „neutralisiert" sind. Sodann wird die experimentelle Gruppe der interessierenden Einwirkung, dem „treatment", ausgesetzt, die Kontrollgruppe nicht. Eine sich ergebende Varianz (Wirkung) wird als auf die *Einwirkung* („treatment") kausal zurückführbar interpretiert.

---

17 Für eine ausführliche Methodendiskussion vgl. etwa Hellstern/Wollmann (1977, 1983a: 47ff.) mit „klassischen" Beispielen aus der internationalen Evaluierungsforschung.

Politik- und evaluierungsgeschichtlich geht der *experimentelle* Politik- und Evaluierungsansatz bekanntlich auf die späten 60er und frühen 70er Jahre zurück, wurde zunächst in den USA propagiert (vgl. den klassischen Aufsatz von Campbell 1968) und fand dort in den 70er Jahren in umfangreichen „Sozialexperimenten" (zunächst im bahnbrechenden „Head Start"-Programm, vgl. Hellstern/Wollmann 1977: 430f.; 1984b: 29ff. mit Nachweisen) seinen Ausdruck; auch die Bundesrepublik erlebte in den späten 60er und 70er Jahren in einer Phase groß angelegter „Sozialexperimente" (Gesamtschule versus traditionelle Schule, Einphasen-Juristenausbildung versus traditionelle Zweiphasen-Ausbildung usw., vgl. die Beiträge in Hellstern/Wollmann (1983b) zu den experimentellen Vorhaben) einen Höhepunkt. Inzwischen ist es in der Bundesrepublik um den *experimentellen* Politik- und Evaluierungsansatz still geworden – im Gefolge der allgemeinen Ernüchterung ob der politischen Realisierbarkeit des zugrunde liegenden „Modells rationalen Politikmachens", aber auch als Folge der methodischen und politischen Schwierigkeiten. Angesichts der hohen methodischen (und auch politischen) Anforderungen, die bei der Schaffung der erforderlichen Versuchs- und Untersuchungsanordnung zu erfüllen sind, dürfte sich der experimentelle Politik- und Evaluierungsansatz – jedenfalls in seiner methodisch rigorosen Variante – für die Verwaltungspolitik und -evaluierung nur ausnahmsweise eignen (ähnlich Pollitt 1995: 140).

3.2.2 Quasi-Experimente

Der Versuch, die für das Experiment charakteristischen Vorteile in der Bestimmung von Ursache-Wirkungszusammenhängen zu realisieren, ohne jedoch deren restriktive Bedingungen wie Randomisierung und vollständige Kontrolle aufrecht zu erhalten, führte zu *quasi-experimentellen* Ansätzen, um die Wirkungen innerhalb des tatsächlichen Programm-/Interventionskontextes zu bestimmen. Zum einen wird dadurch die Künstlichkeit der Experimentalsituation vermieden, zum andern werden die Einwände gegen die mangelnde Berücksichtigung der sozialen Realität zumindest abgeschwächt.

Quasi-experimentelle Versuchspläne (vgl. Wollmann/Hellstern 1977: 432ff.) bedienen sich innerhalb ihrer Forschungsdesigns vor allem zweier Kontrollverfahren sowie deren Kombination:

– Untersuchungen im (räumlichen usw.) Querschnitt auf der gleichen Zeitachse (*synchron*) unter Nutzung von Vergleichsgruppen, die mit der Untersuchungsgruppe zwar nicht identisch, jedoch mit ihr in wesentlichen Eigenschaften übereinstimmen (*ceteris paribus*),
– Untersuchungen in der Zeitreihe, d.h. in mehreren zeitlichen Schritten (diachron), indem das Untersuchungsobjekt longitudinal sozusagen in mehrere Untersuchungseinheiten zerlegt wird, um Veränderungen der interessierenden Variablen im Zeitverlauf unter den *ceteris paribus*-Bedingungen, d.h. unter der Annahme zu analysieren, daß der Untersuchungs-

gegenstand in den relevanten Variablenbereichen seine Kontinuität und Identität im Zeitverlauf bewahrt.
– der Verknüpfung von Querschnittsanalysen mit Längsschnittsanalysen durch einen Zeitreihenvergleich.

Der springende Punkt einer *quasi-experimentell* konzipierten Evaluierungsuntersuchung ist mithin die Bildung einer Vergleichsgruppe oder -einheit, die mit der Untersuchungsgruppe/-einheit in möglichst vielen wesentlichen Eigenschaften übereinstimme (*ceteris paribus*). Zwar zeigt sich in der Forschungs- und Evaluierungspraxis, daß ein solches „matching" von Untersuchungs- und Vergleichsgruppe bei heterogenen Gesamtheiten, deren einzelne Einheiten Träger einer Vielzahl von vielfach divergenten Merkmalen sind (beispielsweise Städte und Gemeinden), in einer methodisch anzustrebenden und akzeptablen Weise vielfach nur begrenzt gelingt[18]. Ungeachtet dieser methodischen Schwierigkeiten eröffnet ein *quasi-experimentelles* Vorgehen auch in gerade bei der Evaluierung von verwaltungspolitischen Interventionen, insbesondere im Rahmen einer *Performanzevaluierung*, einen durchaus gangbaren und tragfähigen Evaluierungsansatz. Für die Untersuchungsanordnung ist vor allem darauf zu achten, daß auf der Seite der (nach Möglichkeit mehreren und untereinander homogenen, *ceteris paribus*) Untersuchungseinheiten der interessierende und zu testende Wirkungszusammenhang (etwa zwischen der Einführung dezentraler Ressourcenverantwortung einerseits und Effizienz- sowie Effektivitätsgewinnen andererseits) möglichst präzise gefaßt (operationalisiert) wird und auf der Seite der Vergleichsgruppe (ohne dezentrale Ressourcenverantwortung!) möglichst homogene (*ceteris paribus)* Kommunen ausgewählt werden.

In dem Maße, wie es bei der Evaluierung wesentlich darum geht, im Zeitverlauf eintretende Veränderungen zu erfassen, dürften sich *Längsschnittuntersuchungen* als besonders ergiebig erweisen (vgl. Wollmann/Hellstern 1977: 433; Hucke/Wollmann 1980: 229). Deren einfachste Variante stellt der simple *Vorher-Nachher-Vergleich* (Zustand vor und nach der Intervention) als „Zwei-Zeitpunkte-Reihe" dar, wobei von der Veränderung (Wirkung) auf den „Kausalbeitrag" der Intervention rückgeschlossen wird.

Freilich ist dieser (simple) „praeter-propter"-Schluß den bekannten „Gefährdungen der Validität" (z.B. Einwirkung gleichzeitig laufender Prozesse im Handlungsumfeld, „maturation") ausgesetzt (zu den „threats to validity" vgl. „klassisch" Campbell/Stanley, 1964, 1970). Um dieser methodischen Schwäche abzuhelfen, könnte die reine Zeitreihen-(Vorher-Nachher-) Analyse durch die Hinzunahme einer Kontrollgruppe und deren Zeitreihe (Zeitreihenvergleich) ergänzt werden; freilich sind damit wiederum die Schwierigkeiten mit der Bildung einer methodisch befriedigenden Vergleichsgruppe erkauft.

---

18 Vgl. auch Pollitt (1995: 140): „Yet the promise of standard quasi-experimental design is also distinctly limited".

3.2.3 Pilot-/Modellvorhaben

Sie sind dem *experimentellen* Politik- und Evaluierungsansatz darin ähnlich, daß sie bestimmte institutionelle Regelungen oder Vorgehensweisen fall- und projektweise ausprobieren und Verlauf- und Ergebnis des Pilot-/Modellvorhabens evaluieren sollen. Jedoch unterscheiden sie sich vom Experimentieren im strengen Sinn wesentlich vor allem dadurch, daß auf die bewußte Bildung von Kontroll- oder Vergleichsgruppen in der Regel verzichtet wird und es bei der Evaluierung meist methodisch „lockerer" (etwa auf der Grundlage von Erfahrungsberichten der Projektbeteiligten) zugeht. Innerhalb der damit nur begrenzten Validität, d.h. verallgemeinerungsfähigen Schlüssigkeit ihrer Ergebnisse, sind die Chancen von Pilot- und Modellvorhaben, rasch nutz- und umsetzbare Erfahrungen gezielt zu kumulieren, auch und gerade in der Verwaltungspolitik als hoch zu veranschlagen.

3.2.4 Statistische Verfahren (Korrelationsanalysen usw.)

Die statistische Methode, die mathematische Techniken auf Grundgesamtheiten oder Samples mit einer hinreichend großen Zahl von Merkmalen anwendet, strebt in der Manipulation von Parametern und operationalen Variablen die gleiche Untersuchungslogik an wie die experimentelle Methode. Der Hauptunterschied zwischen der experimentellen und der statistischen Methode ist darin zu sehen, daß jene die *reale Experimentiersituation* zu *manipulieren* sucht, während diese sich einer *gedanklichen (mathematischen) Manipulation* bedient, die versucht, mögliche Ursachen der Variation konstant zu halten oder auszuscheiden. Der Mehrzahl bisher angewandter Verfahren (vgl. Näheres etwa bei Wollmann/Hellstern 1977: 436ff.) liegt meist eine partielle *Korrelationsanalyse* zugrunde. In der politikwissenschaftlichen Forschung sind statistische Verfahren insbesondere in der sog. Output-Forschung angewendet worden, die sich in den USA in Vergleichsuntersuchungen von Einzelstaaten und Gemeinden entwickelte (vgl. Wollmann/Hellstern 1977: 438; FN 87 mit Nachweisen).

Zur Brauchbarkeit von statistischen Verfahren bei der Evaluierung von verwaltungspolitischen Interventionen, insbesondere im Rahmen von *Performanzevaluationen*, ist daran zu erinnern, daß statistische Verfahren vor allem dann (aber auch nur dann) leistungsfähig sind, wenn es sich, wie eine Faustformel besagt, um *viele Fälle und wenige Variablen* (many cases, few variables) (vgl. Lijphart 1971: 685) handelt, wenn, mit anderen Worten, die Untersuchung auf zahlreiche Untersuchungsfälle (typisches Beispiel: Wahlforschung) zurückgreifen kann und die Zahl der Variablen, die als interessierende „operative" (abhängige und/oder unabhängige) Variablen in die Untersuchung einbezogen werden, aufgrund von (theoretischem) Vorwissen, konzeptionellen Vorentscheidungen usw. von vornherein begrenzt werden kann. Angesichts dessen, daß Verwaltungsmodernisierungen inzwischen z.B. in einer großen Zahl von Städten, Gemeinden und Kreisen durchgeführt werden, könnten sich statistische Evaluierungsuntersuchungen in Anlehnung an Ansätze der Output-Forschung als durchaus aussichtsreich erweisen.

3.2.5 Fallstudien, vergleichende (Multi-) Fallstudien

Durch ihren Untersuchungsgegenstand bedingt, steht die Evaluierungsforschung (wie die empirische Verwaltungsforschung insgesamt, vgl. Hucke/Wollmann 1980: 228) vielfach vor einem Dilemma. Auf der einen Seite ist davon auszugehen, daß die auf Implementationsverlauf und -ergebnis des Modernisierungsprojekts einwirkenden Faktoren im natürlichen Handlungsfeld außerordentlich vielfältig und verwickelt und die Anzahl der in Betracht kommenden Untersuchungseinheiten zugleich verhältnismäßig gering sind (Faustformel: „Many variables, small number of cases", Lijphart 1971: 685), was die Anwendbarkeit der die Faustformel „Few variables, many cases" voraussetzenden quantitativ-statistischen Verfahren von vornherein in Frage stellt. Auf der anderen Seite sind Fallstudien auf den Versuch, Erklärungen induktiv, *ad hoc* aus dem gerade untersuchten Fall zu entwickeln, vor allem dann angewiesen, wenn sie in Ermangelung besseren Theoriewissens heuristisch und explorativ vorgehen (zur „explorativen Fallstudie" vgl. Eckstein 1975). Je „fallbezogener" und -spezifischer aber eine Erklärung formuliert wird, um so stärker wird sie dem individuellen Fall auf den Leib geschnitten („explanation tailored to each case", Verba 1967: 113). Zwar besitzen derartige ad hoc-Erklärungen eine hohe *interne Validität* (als Erklärung eben dieses *einen* Falles), entbehren jedoch der *externen Validität*, nämlich einer gesicherten Verallgemeinerungsfähigkeit. Überdies ermangelt die Einzelfalluntersuchung der *Repräsentativität*, nämlich einer Aussage darüber, für wie viele und für welchen Typus aus der Grundgesamtheit er steht.

Um dieser methodischen Schwäche abzuhelfen, sind drei ergänzende Untersuchungsstrategien in Betracht zu ziehen:

a) vergleichender Fallstudien-Ansatz,
b) konzeptionell reflektiert ausgewählte Fallstudien und
c) theoretisch angeleitete Fallstudien.

– Der *vergleichende (mehrere Fälle-) Ansatz* (vgl. Wollmann/Hellstern 1977: 440ff.) hat mit dem quasi-experimentellen Verfahren die Untersuchungslogik gemeinsam, wonach die Überprüfbarkeit des Zusammenhangs zwischen bestimmten Variablen, den *operativen* Variablen, dadurch ermöglicht werden soll, daß andere möglicherweise relevante Variablen kontrolliert, also zu „Parametern" gemacht werden und damit das Zusammenspiel der interessierenden operativen Variablen isoliert untersucht werden kann. Diese Untersuchungslogik findet in der gebräuchlichsten Variante des vergleichenden Vorgehens, dem „Vergleichbare Fälle" -Ansatz (*„comparable cases approach"*) (vgl. Lijphart 1971: 686ff.), darin ihren Aus-

druck, daß für die vergleichende Analyse von vornherein solche Untersuchungsfälle ausgesucht werden, in denen die interessierenden (operativen)
Variablen möglichst große Unterschiede (Varianzen) aufweisen und die
hinsichtlich der übrigen Variablen (Parametern) möglichst gleich (*vergleichbar, ceteris paribus*) seien. So einleuchtend diese Untersuchungslogik *modellhaft* ist, so erheblich sind freilich die Schwierigkeiten ihrer *for-
schungspraktischen* Anwendungen. Die entscheidende Crux liegt auch hier
in den Schwierigkeiten, bei der Auswahl der Untersuchungsfälle das methodische *ceteris paribus*-Gebot einzulösen.

–   Angesichts der methodischen Schwierigkeiten *vergleichender* Fallunter-
suchungen einerseits und wegen des Erfordernisses, bei in aller Regel
sehr knappen Forschungs- und Zeitressourcen die Auswahl auf verhältnismäßig wenige Untersuchungsfälle zu beschränken, kann die *konzeptionell reflektierte Auswahl* („purposeful selection") der Fälle von der
Überlegung angeleitet sein, als entscheidende Auswahlkriterien für die
(in der Regel: wenigen) Fälle solche Merkmale der potentiellen Untersuchungseinheiten zu verwenden, die (aufgrund von theoretischem und
empirischem Vorwissen oder von Plausibilitätsannahmen) als mögliche
Einflußvariablen besonders relevant sind (etwa die Größenklasse von
Kommunen) oder die unter spezifischer Fragestellung der Untersuchung
besondere Aufmerksamkeit verdienen. Ein Beispiel für das letztere Kriterium wäre die Entscheidung zu Beginn einer Evaluierungsuntersuchung
zur kommunalen Verwaltungsmodernisierung, die Auswahl der Kommunen von vornherein auf die *modernisierungsaktiven* zu beschränken und
die modernisierungs*in*aktiven mithin beiseite zu lassen. Eine solche bewußte Zuspitzung (und Verzerrung) der Auswahl hat einerseits den Vorteil, daß Aussagen über fortgeschrittene Modernisierungsfälle und deren
Erfolgsbedingungen zu erwarten sind, birgt andererseits aber den Nachteil, daß Fälle der stockenden oder scheiternden Modernisierung und deren Gründe analytisch und als Lernpotential ausgeblendet blieben.

–   *„Theorie-angeleitete" Fallstudien.* In Anknüpfung an die weiter oben
formulierte Überlegung, daß verwaltungspolitischen Modernisierungs-
strategien und -projekten – wie politischen Programmen und Interventionen insgesamt – explizit oder implizit Handlungs*theorien*, nämlich Annahmen darüber zugrunde liegen, vermöge welcher Handlungsmittel und
-schritte das angestrebte Handlungsziel zu erreichen sei, könnte die Evaluierung von Verwaltungsmodernisierungsprojekten, insbesondere *Per-
formanzevaluierungen,* als Fallstudien begriffen und angelegt werden,
die von der zugrunde liegenden Handlungstheorie angeleitet wird (zum
theorieangeleiteten Konzept einer „realistischen Evaluierung" vgl. jüngst
Pawson/Tilley 1997)[19].

---

19 Das Konzept „theoriegeleiteter" Fallstudien hat Anknüpfungspunkte auch bei Eck-
    stein (1975: 117), der – im Gegensatz zu den noch theoretisch weitgehend blinden

Dem Ziel, den methodischen Schwächen des Fallstudienansatzes abzuhelfen, die insbesondere in der ungesicherten Verallgemeinerungsfähigkeit („externe Validität") und Repräsentativität liegen, können *ergänzende Validierungsstrategien* dienen; zu diesen sind insbesondere den Fallstudien *vorausgehende* oder ihnen *nachfolgende* (*follow-ups*) *Breitenrecherchen* (etwa durch schriftliche Befragung aller oder eines Großteils der in Betracht kommenden Untersuchungseinheiten) zu rechnen, wobei die vorausgehenden dazu dienen können, die Auswahl der Fallstudien informiert anzuleiten und deren Repräsentativität kenntlich zu machen, während die *follow-ups* geeignet sind, die in den Fallstudien gewonnenen Aussagen (Hypothesen) zu überprüfen.

3.2.6 Methodenmix

Wie in der empirischen Verwaltungsforschung insgesamt (vgl. Hucke/Wollmann 1980), zeichnet sich – vor dem Hintergrund der vorstehenden Überlegungen – auch für die Evaluierung von verwaltungspolitischen Maßnahmen ein Methodenprofil und -repertoire ab, in dem die Anwendung quasi-experimenteller und statistischer Verfahren eher die Ausnahme und Fallstudien-Ansätze eher die Regel bilden dürften. Um die spezifischen Stärken der unterschiedlichen Vorgehensweisen zu bündeln und deren jeweilige Schwächen auszugleichen, sollte ein *Methodenmix* (vgl. Wollmann/Hellstern 1977: 448) angestrebt werden, bei dessen konkreter Akzentuierung und Mischung den Besonderheiten des Untersuchungsbereichs, der Fragestellung und – last not least – den verfügbaren Forschungsressourcen (Finanzen, Personal, Zeit) Rechnung zu tragen ist.

4. Evaluierung und Evaluierungsforschung zur Verwaltungsmodernisierung in der deutschen Politik-, Verwaltungs- und Forschungspraxis

Im folgenden Abschnitt soll die gegenwärtige Entwicklung der Evaluierung/ Evaluierungsforschung in der Bundesrepublik vor allem unter der Frage nach ihrem *konzeptionellen und methodischen* Profil diskutiert werden. Aus der Fragestellung und aufgrund der an dieser Stelle gebotenen Kürze ergeben sich hierbei einige wesentliche Einschränkungen:

– Die einschlägigen Evaluierungsansätze und -beispiele werden in erster Linie unter den *konzeptionellen und methodischen* Aspekten erörtert; die *inhaltlichen* Ergebnisse der Evaluierungen müssen an dieser Stelle außer Betracht bleiben.

„explorative case studies" in den „crucial case studies" solche sieht, in denen explizierte Hypothesen einem „Test" („Falsifikationsversuch") ausgesetzt werden.

– Bei der Auswahl instruktiver Evaluierungsbeispiele muß *selektiv* verfahren werden; ein *vollständiger* Überblick über den Forschungsstand, die Forschungseinrichtungen und Forschungsbeteiligten ist hier weder beabsichtigt noch möglich.

Zur Gliederung des Stoffes werden maßgebliche Evaluierungsansätze aufgerufen und vor allem unter konzeptionellen und methodischen Aspekten diskutiert.

4.1 Controlling als verwaltungseigene/-interne Evaluierung (Selbstevaluierung)

Controlling wird im NSM als ein verwaltungsinternes Informationssystem konzipiert und institutionalisiert, das die (laufende) Erfassung relevanter Ergebnisse administrativen Handelns und deren Rückmeldung an die relevanten administrativen und auch politischen Akteure bewerkstelligen soll (vgl. etwa Richter 1998). Hinsichtlich seiner zentralen Aufgabe, handlungsrelevante Informationen mit Hilfe leistungsfähiger Indikatoren zu erfassen und diese „rückzumelden", weist das Konzept des Controlling, wie bereits weiter vorn erwähnt, breite (in der gegenwärtigen NSM-Diskussion allerdings kaum wahrgenommene, geschweige denn genutzte) Gemeinsamkeiten mit den Bemühungen auf, die in den späten 60er und 70er Jahren – vor allem auf der kommunalen Ebene – unternommen wurden, leistungsfähige Systeme der „laufenden Beobachtung" und Evaluierung von Verwaltungshandeln mit Hilfe geeigneter *Indikatoren* zu etablieren (zur kommunalen Ebene vgl. die Beiträge in Hellstern/Wollmann 1984c, für einen Überblicksaufsatz vgl. Hellstern/Wollmann 1984d). Ein wichtiger Unterschied (und Fortschritt) gegenüber dem früheren Verständnis der Evaluierungsfunktion ist freilich darin zu sehen, daß diese im Controlling in eine strategische, durch die Anbindung an die Politik- und Verwaltungsspitze (Machtpromotor) abgesicherte *Steuerungs*funktion eingebettet ist (vgl. Wollmann 1994).

Zwar sind – insbesondere auf der kommunalen Ebene – inzwischen vielfältige Bemühungen zu beobachten, um über die Definition von *Produktkatalogen* und *Kosten-Leistungsrechnungen* verwaltungsinterne Systeme zur Erfassung und Rückmeldung von relevanten Informationen sowohl über die Leistungen („Zielerreichung") als auch über die Wirtschaftlichkeit (Kosten-Ertrags-Relation) von Verwaltungshandeln aufzubauen. Jedoch zeigen sich hierbei, wie die Implementationspraxis augenfällig macht, ernsthafte Schwierigkeiten und Einschränkungen.

– Dies gilt insbesondere für *Produkte* als den konzeptionellen und instrumentellen Dreh- und Angelpunkt des Indikatoren-gestützten Informations-, Evaluierungs- und Rückmeldesystems (vgl. Reichard 1998; Wollmann 1999b). Hierzu an dieser Stelle nur so viel: In der Praxis zeigt sich, daß die Produkt*definition* bislang vielfach kaum mehr leistet, als die bisherigen administrativen *Aufgaben* in eine „modernisierungs*politisch korrekte*" Terminologie umzubenennen; eine brauchbare Präzisierung durch Indikatoren/Kennziffern oder gar Qualitätsmerkmale steht meist noch am Anfang[20]. Hinzu kommt, daß selbst dort, wo brauchbare Indikatoren an sich verfügbar sind, deren empirische Darstellung und „Füllung" hinterherhinkt, zumal die Nutzung der „Verwaltungsvollzugsdaten" hinter ihren Möglichkeiten auffällig zurückbleibt[21].

– Verhältnismäßig fortgeschritten scheint das System der *Kosten-Leistungsrechnung* in der Gegenüberstellung von Kosten und Leistungen. Jedoch sind hierbei vor allem zwei Schwächen zu notieren. Zum einen zeigt sich die (aus der Kosten-Nutzen-Analyse seit langem geläufige) Problematik, daß – zumal unter dem politischen und budgetären Druck, dieses Verfahren für Kosteneinsparungen zu nutzen – in erster Linie solche Kosten und Leistungen erfaßt werden, die sich relativ leicht quantifizieren und „monetarisieren" lassen (z.B. Personalkosten pro Baugenehmigungs- oder Sozialhilfebescheid), während Kosten und Leistungen, die sich einfacher Zählung und „Monetarisierung" entziehen (wie etwa die für den einzelnen Sozialfall aufgewandte Beratungsleistung), unberücksichtigt bleiben.

– Schließlich bleibt hervorzuheben, daß bei der Erfassung der Kosten bislang die erheblichen finanziellen Aufwendungen (*Implementations- und Transaktionskosten*) unberücksichtigt bleiben, die *einmalig* bei der Einrichtung und Unterhaltung der neuen Steuerungselemente (z.B. die – oft sehr hohen – Honorare für die Einführungsberatung durch Consulting-Firmen, verwaltungseigene Personaleinführungskosten, Hardware- und Software-Investitionen, erstmalige Dateninstallation, Schulungskosten usw.) und *laufend* (Personalkosten, Datenfortschreibung usw.) anfallen (vgl. etwa Grunow 1998: 3; Jaedicke u.a. 1999: 257). Realistischerweise sollten auch die *Opportunitätskosten*, also jene „Schattenkosten" veran-

---

20 So zeigte sich in einer Evaluierungsstudie zur (modernisierten) kommunalen Baugenehmigungspraxis (vgl. Jaedicke u.a. 1999; vgl. hierzu unten Fußnote 41), daß die Baugenehmigungspraxis bei der *Produktdefinition* (*Produkt*: Baugenehmigungsverfahren) es bislang verbreitet vorzieht, es bei der qualitativen Umschreibung des Handlungsziels, z.B. „zügige Antragsbearbeitung, Vermeidung von unnötigem Prüfungsaufwand" zu belassen, anstatt in eine quantifizierende Operationalisierung (etwa: durchschnittliche und maximale Bearbeitungszeit je nach Schwierigkeitsgrad) einzusteigen, vgl. Jaedicke u.a. (1999: 126f.) – mit dem Ergebnis: „weniger fortgeschrittener Stand der Indikatorenbildung und damit verbunden die bislang nur in Teilen realisierte Leistungsmessung" (ebda.: 129).

21 Vgl. hierzu Jaedicke u.a. (1999: 251): „... kennzeichnend, daß die Beschleunigung der Baugenehmigungsverfahren zwar zentrales Reformziel ist, quantitative Informationen zur tatsächlichen Dauer der Baugenehmigungsverfahren aber in der Regel nicht erhoben werden bzw. nicht ausgewertet werden, und zwar auch von denjenigen Bauaufsichtsämtern nicht, die in der EDV-Unterstützung der Baugenehmigungsverfahren weit vorangeschritten sind".

schlagt werden, die der Verwaltung dadurch entstehen, daß das mit der Ein- und Durchführung des Modernisierungsprojektes befaßte Personal für andere Aufgaben nicht zur Verfügung steht (vgl. Pollitt 1995: 139).

Ungeachtet dieser Grenzen und Schwierigkeiten stellt das *Controlling* ein aussichtsreiches Instrument der *Performanz- und Outcomes-Evaluierung* dar.

4.2 Interkommunale Vergleichsringe als (inter-kommunale) Selbstevaluierung und Quasi-Wettbewerb

Seit den frühen 90er Jahren hat das Konzept der *interkommunalen Leistungsvergleiche* – als ein strategischer Ansatz, um die Elemente einer *Selbstevaluierung* der Kommunen, ihres interkommunalen Vergleichs („benchmarking"), eines „Quasi-Wettbewerbs" untereinander und eines institutionalisierten interkommunalen Lernprozesses zu verbinden und zu bündeln, zunehmende Verbreitung gefunden[22].

– Den Auftakt gab die *Bertelsmann-Stiftung*, die 1990/1991 das Projekt „Grundlagen einer leistungsfähigen Kommunalverwaltung" begründete. Darauf aufbauend, wurde eine Reihe von Einzelprojekten gestartet, so 1991 das Projekt „Wirkungsvolle Strukturen im Kulturbereich"[23]. 1997 waren bundesweit 150 Städte am kommunalen Leistungsvergleich der Bertelsmann-Stiftung beteiligt, um das Konzept der *regionalen* Vergleichsringe zu verfolgen. Diese sollten aus Gründen der Vergleichbarkeit möglichst aus (mindestens vier bis maximal zehn) Städten ähnlicher Größenordnung bestehen.

– An die Anstöße und Vorarbeiten des Projekts der Bertelsmann-Stiftung anknüpfend, wurde Ende 1996 unter Federführung der KGSt ein IKO-Netzwerk ins Leben gerufen. Das IKO-Netz soll als „internes Informationssystem der Kommunen" fungieren, die sich zu themen- bzw. arbeitsbereichsspezifischen und zum Teil regional organisierten Vergleichsringen zusammenschließen. Ende 1999 arbeiteten insgesamt 400 Kommunen (unter Berücksichtigung von Doppelteilnahme 650) in 64 IKO-Vergleichsringen zusammen. Dabei sind auch hier die Vergleichsringe so angelegt, daß zwischen vier und 25 Kommunen ähnlicher Größenordnung in themenspezifischen Vergleichsringen (Abfall, Bauaufsicht, Bür-

---

22 Der nachstehende Abschnitt zu den Kommunalen Vergleichsringen stützt sich auf eine (ausführliche) Recherche, die Sabine Lorenz gegenwärtig zur Entwicklung und zu den Ergebnissen der Kommunalen Vergleichsringe durchführt.

23 Vgl. das von der Bertelsmann-Stiftung herausgegebene (vierteljährliche) Projektjournal „Podium Leistungsvergleich", zum „Kulturprojekt" eine Vielzahl von (von Marga Pröhl herausgegebenen) Projektberichten. Für eine umfassende Analyse/Evaluierung des Gesamtprojekts „Interkommunaler Vergleich" der Bertelsmann-Stiftung (vgl. Schuster 2000).

gerämter usw., derzeit knapp 30 Fachthemen) zusammenarbeiten (vgl. KGSt, IKO-Netz, Stand Oktober 1999).

Gegenwärtig operieren die beiden Vergleichsring-Netzwerke der Bertelsmann-Stiftung und des IKO-Verbundes noch weitgehend nebeneinander, jedoch ist vorgesehen, die Ersteren in das IKO-Netzwerk zu überführen (vgl. Schuster 2000: 10; Adamaschek 1998).

Den konzeptionellen und instrumentellen Dreh- und Angelpunkt des *interkommunalen Vergleichs* und der *interkommunalen Vergleichsringe* bilden die Vorstellung und das Ziel, (fachverwaltungs-)spezifische Sätze von interkommunal verwendbaren Indikatoren oder, wie in diesem Konzeptzusammenhang vornehmlich gesagt wird, von *Kennziffern* zu konzipieren und empirisch aufzufüllen. In der Entwicklung und Nutzung solcher Indikatoren- bzw. Kennziffern-Sets und ihrer Umsetzung in interkommunalen *Vergleichsringen* sind mehrere für eine (übergreifende) Institutionalisierung der Evaluierungsfunktion in der kommunalen Praxis bedeutsame Funktionen sichtbar:

- Zum einen soll die *vergleichende interkommunale Evaluierung* von Verwaltungsleistungen installiert werden.
- Dadurch, daß angestrebt wird, die für den interkommunalen Vergleich zu entwickelnden Indikatoren-/Kennziffern mit den Produktdefinitionen/Indikatoren abzustimmen, die in den an den Vergleichsringen beteiligten Kommunen beim Aufbau ihrer Controlling-Systeme formuliert werden, kann die *Selbstevaluierung* der einzelnen Kommunen abgestützt werden.
- Zwar sind die in den Vergleichsringen formulierten Kennziffern bislang im wesentlichen darauf gemünzt, bestimmte Verwaltungs*leistungen* (als *Performanz* und *Output*) meßbar zu machen, stellen sich also im wesentlichen als ein *Monitoring* dar. Jedoch sind die interkommunal vergleichenden Diskussionen in den Vergleichsringen geeignet, das Interesse und die Einsichten auf die Auswirkungen unterschiedlicher Organisationsformen, Instrumente usw. auf die (durch die Kennziffern ausgewiesenen) unterschiedlichen Verwaltungsleistungen – im Sinne von *Performanzevaluationen* – zu lenken.
- Mit dem interkommunalen Leistungsvergleich (*benchmarking*) wird ein *Quasi-Wettbewerb* zwischen den Kommunen angeregt.
- Schließlich wird zwischen den Kommunen und ihren Fachleuten ein ständiger *Diskurs- und Lernprozeß* institutionalisiert, den es bislang in dieser Häufigkeit und Verbindlichkeit inter-kommunal nicht gegeben hat.

So überzeugend und tragfähig sich diese konzeptionellen und strategischen Überlegungen und Aussichten *modellhaft* auch darstellen, so schwierig erweist es sich in der kommunalen Praxis, sie zu implementieren und umzusetzen. An dieser Stelle sei nur auf zwei Hindernisse hingewiesen:

- Zum einen zeigen sich bei der bisherigen Arbeit in den Vergleichsringen erhebliche Schwierigkeiten, Indikatoren/Kennziffern zu entwickeln, die

sowohl für den interkommunalen Vergleich taugen als auch auf die sehr
unterschiedlichen organisatorischen, personellen usw. Gegebenheiten der
beteiligten Kommunen passen.

– Ähnlich wie beim Aufbau der Kommune-internen Controlling-Systeme
  und deren Datenbasen, erweisen sich zum andern die hohen Personal-
  und Zeitaufwendungen, die nicht nur die Ersteinrichtung der Kennzif-
  fern-bezogenen Datenbestände, sondern auch und vor allem deren laufende Fortschreibung und Betreuung erfordern, als (zunehmendes)
  Hemmnis. Eine wachsende Zahl von Kommunen scheint sich aus den
  Vergleichsringen wieder zurückzuziehen, da ihnen der Erhebungsauf-
  wand für die fortlaufende Aktualisierung der Kennziffern-Daten unan-
  gemessen hoch im Vergleich zu dem erwartbaren (und vielfach nicht erkennbaren) „Steuerungsgewinn" zu geraten scheint (vgl. Schuster 2000;
  Anke/Grabowski/Wetzel 1999).

4.3 Evaluierung durch öffentliche ausgeschriebene Innovationspreise

In den frühen 90er Jahren wurde eine Veranstaltungsform kreiert, in der die
Evaluierung von Verwaltungstätigkeit auf originelle Weise mit der Initiie-
rung von Wettbewerb zwischen Trägern öffentlicher Verwaltungen bzw.
Kommunen in Gang gesetzt worden ist.

– Im Jahr 1992 wurden auf Initiative von Hermann Hill und Helmut Klages
  die sog. Speyerer Qualitätswettbewerbe initiiert, durch die „Spitzenverwaltungen" identifiziert und prämiiert werden sollen[24]. Hierdurch soll
  insbesondere ein Innovations*wettbewerb* und -*transfer* in der öffentlichen
  Verwaltung angefacht werden[25]. Auch wenn die Wettbewerbe (ungeachtet der von ihren Initiatoren vorsorglich vorgesehenen Widerhaken, vgl.
  Klages 1993) Anlaß zur Vermutung und Kritik geben, daß nicht selten
  PR-erfahrene und -beratene Preiskandidaten sich, ihre Modernisierungspraxis schönredend, in Szene setzen (kritisch Grunow 1998: 14), hat der
  Speyerer Innovationspreis, der seit 1992 etwa im Zwei-Jahres-Takt (1992,
  1994, 1996, 1999, 2000) ausgeschrieben und vergeben wird (vgl. Hill/

---

24 „Kurzprofil" des *Speyerer Qualitätswettbewerbs*. Mehrere Schritte: 1. Öffentliche
    Ausschreibung, 2. Die sich bewerbenden Verwaltungseinheiten (Kommunen, Regie-
    rungspräsidien, staatliche Sonderbehörden) haben einen Fragebogen mit 25 Fragen
    auszufüllen („Selbstbeschreibung als Methode der Informationsbeschaffung", Klages
    1993: 42), 3. Vorauswahl („engere Wahl") durch Wissenschaftler-Praktiker-Jury. Die
    Auswahlkriterien sind u.a.: Ausmaß der Innovationsorientierung, Struktur- und Pro-
    zeßkriterien der Verwaltungsqualität (Wirtschaftlichkeit, Organisationsqualität, Qua-
    lität der Personalarbeit, Produkt- und Serviceorientierung), Effektivität der Quali-
    tätsorientierung (vgl. Klages 1993: 45), 4. Mündliche „Anhörung" der in die „engere
    Wahl" gezogenen „Kandidaten" durch die Jury, 5. Endauswahl durch die Jury.
25 Vgl. Klages (1993: 39f.).

Klages 1993, 1995, 1997, 1999), ohne Zweifel die Diskussion um Verwaltungsmodernisierung und -evaluierung in der Bundesrepublik merklich beflügelt.

–   Auch die Internationale Ausschreibung des Carl Bertelsmann-Preises, den die *Bertelsmann-Stiftung* 1993 dem Thema „Demokratie und Effizienz in der Kommunalverwaltung" widmete (vgl. Bertelsmann-Stiftung 1993), beruhte auf dem Konzept, die international innovativen Kommunen im Wege eines (mehrstufigen) Such- und Auswahlverfahrens zu ermitteln[26]. Abgesehen von der Schockwelle, die das Ergebnis der Preisvergabe (den beiden ausländischen Städten *Phoenix,* Arizona/USA, und *Christchurch,* Neuseeland, wurden die beiden Spitzenplätze zuerkannt, während die Stadt *Duisburg* als Schlußlicht endete) in der deutschen Verwaltungsmodernisierungsszene auslöste und die Diskussion um das *Neue Steuerungsmodell* wesentlich anschob (vgl. Wollmann 2000: 705f.), hat der Bertelsmann-Wettbewerb auch die weitere verwaltungspolitische Forschung und Evaluierung sichtlich beeinflußt[27].

4.4 Verwaltungspolitische „Experimentierklauseln", Pilot- und Modellvorhaben und deren Evaluierung

Geht man von dem weiter oben dargelegten Verständnis des *experimentellen* Politik- und Evaluierungsansatzes aus, wonach dieser die (methodisch kontrollierte) Bildung von *Kontroll-* oder zumindest von *Vergleichs*gruppen voraussetzt, sind die in der jüngsten deutschen Modernisierungspraxis beobachtbaren einschlägigen Projekte nicht als „experimentell" im engeren Sinne zu bezeichnen, sondern dem Typus der *Modell- und Pilotprojekte* zuzurechnen.

---

26   Kurzprofil: Nominierungs- und Auswahlverfahren vollzogen sich in mehreren Schritten: (vgl. Pröhl 1993: 1ff.): a. Formulierung von 7 Kriterien mit Hilfe von Expertengruppe: Leistung unter demokratischer Kontrolle, Bürger- und Kundenorientierung, Kooperation zwischen Politik und Verwaltung, Dezentrale Führung, Potentiale der Mitarbeiter, Innovations- und Evolutionsfähigkeit durch Wettbewerb, b. Nominierung (durch nationale Experten der betreffenden Länder) von je zwei „Kandidaten"– Städten aus 11 Ländern (Finnland, Neuseeland, Großbritannien, Niederlande, Dänemark, Schweden, Norwegen, Japan, Deutschland, USA, Österreich, c. Auswahl einer erstplazierten Stadt je Land durch Expertengruppe der Stiftung, die Bereisung und Untersuchung der erstplazierten Kommunen durch Consulting-Firmen, die Bewertung der nominierten Städte durch eine internationale Expertengruppe der Stiftung auf der Basis von Kurzexpertisen zweier Consulting-Firmen, abschließende Bewertung und Preisvergabe durch die internationale Expertengruppe (vgl. Pröhl 1993: 17ff.; vgl. auch Naschold 1995: 196). Bekanntlich kamen die Städte Phoenix, Arizona (USA) und Christchurch (Neuseeland) auf die Spitzenplätze. Förderung und Projektträger: Bertelsmann Stiftung.

27   Vgl. insbesondere das WZB-Projekt „Neue Städte braucht das Land" (vgl. unten FN 40), für dessen Fallstudien die (ausländischen) Städte der Endrunde der Ausschreibung ausgewählt wurden.

Unter konzeptioneller und methodische Betrachtung verdient die Frage besondere Aufmerksamkeit, welche Vorkehrungen jeweils getroffen wurden, um eine möglichst systematische Auswertung der in den Pilot-/Modellvorhaben gewonnenen Erfahrungen und Einsichten zu sichern.

4.4.1 Brandenburger Modellkommunen, Begleitforschung

Als durchdachtes Handlungs- und Evaluierungskonzept, in dem der Begleitforschung von Anfang an eine Schlüsselrolle zugeschrieben wurde, ist das Förderungsprogramm hervorzuheben, mit dem die Landesregierung des *Landes Brandenburg* die Verwaltungsmodernisierung in 8 Modellkommunen für den Zeitraum von zwei Jahren (September 1995 bis August 1997) in der Absicht förderte, „für die verschiedenartigen Kommunen im Land Brandenburg aus diesen Modellversuchen Erkenntnisse zu gewinnen, um letztendlich in ganz Brandenburg bürgerfreundliche und effiziente moderne Verwaltungen zu schaffen" (zitiert nach Maaß/Reichard 1998: 267). Die Förderung wurde unter den Gemeinden und Kreisen des Landes öffentlich ausgeschrieben, bei der Auswahl der Kommunen „wurden die unterschiedlichen kommunalen Strukturen berücksichtigt" (Maaß/Reichard 1998: 267)[28].

Das Begleitforschungsprojekt[29] war im wesentlichen darauf gerichtet, Verlauf und (Zwischen-) Ergebnis der Verwaltungsmodernisierung in den (8) Modellkommunen zu erfassen und den jeweiligen Verlaufs- und Ergebnisstand – unter Anwendung eines normativen Konzepts von Erfolgsbedingungen – zu bewerten (und zu erklären). Infolge seiner gegenständlichen Fokussierung ist das Projekt in erster Linie als *Institutionenevaluierung*, aufgrund seiner Finanzierungs- und Trägermodalität als von einer (universitätsnahen) Forschungseinrichtung durchgeführte *Auftragsforschung* zu kennzeichnen. Seine Begleitforschungs- und Politikberatungsfunktion kommt vor allem in der Durchführung projektbegleitender Praxis- und Umsetzungsworkshops

---

28 Im Ergebnis wurden zwei Landkreise, eine kreisfreie Stadt, drei kreisangehörige amtsfreie Städte und zwei Ämter gefördert.

29 „Kurzprofil" : Publikationen: Maß/Reichard (1998); Maß (1998), Aufgabenstellung des Projektes: „Die Ergebnissicherung und Evaluierung des Reformprozesses (in den 8 Modellkommunen) sowie der Transfer verallgemeinerbarer Erfahrungen" (Maß & Reichard 1998: 267). Als Maßstäbe „für die Bewertung der Reformdurchführung in den Modellkommunen dient ein aus sieben Kriterien zusammengesetztes idealtypisches Modell...". Folgende Kriterien wurden untersucht und bewertet: Engagement der Führungsspitze; Einbezug der Politik; Einbezug der Mitarbeiter; Reformklima; Prozeßmanagement; Zeitplanung", (ebda.: 268f.). Untersuchungsdesign und Methoden: Fallstudien in den (8) Modellkommunen, Interviews, Dokumentenanalyse, teilnehmende Beobachtung; Untersuchungszeitraum: Herbst 1995/Herbst 1997; Forschungsauftrag des Innenministeriums Brandenburg; Forschungseinrichtung: Kommunalwissenschaftliches Institut der Universität Potsdam.

und in der abschließenden Formulierung eines „Handbuchs" (vgl. Maaß 1998) zum Ausdruck.

4.4.2 Landesgesetzliche „Experimentierklauseln" zur Erprobung neuer Haushaltsverfahren durch die Kommunen

Im Verlauf des Jahres 1994 wurden – nach Vorberatungen einer Arbeitsgruppe der Innenministerkonferenz – in rascher Folge in fast allen Flächenländern durch Novellierung der einschlägigen Landesgesetze, insbesondere der Gemeinde- und Kreisordnungen, sog. Experimentierklauseln eingeführt[30], durch die den Gemeinden die Möglichkeit eröffnet werden sollte, beim zuständigen Landesinnenminister die auf zwei Jahre befristete Freistellung von bestimmten haushaltsrechtlichen Vorschriften[31] zu beantragen. Dabei stand – vor dem Hintergrund der Diskussion um eine Modernisierung der Kommunalverwaltung durch Einführung des *Neuen Steuerungsmodells* – die Absicht Pate, „die rechtlichen Voraussetzungen dafür zu schaffen, neue Steuerungsmodelle auch dort zu erproben, wo organisations- und haushaltsrechtliche Vorschriften des Kommunalverfassungsrechts dem Versuch an sich entgegenstehen" (Innenministerium NRW 1998: 1) und „die Erfahrungen mit der Budgetierung in der Verwaltungspraxis zu erkennen und aus der Praxis kommende Regelungsvorschläge zur Flexibilisierung des Gemeindehaushaltsrechts bei den anstehenden Rechtsänderungen zu berücksichtigen" (Innenministerium Baden-Württemberg 1996: 5). Die der Handhabung der „Experimentierklauseln" zugrunde liegende *Versuchsanordnung* stellte sich – mit Unterschieden zwischen den Ländern – etwa so dar:

– Das kommunale Projekt wurde dadurch eingeleitet, daß die Kommune eine Freistellung von bestimmten rechtlichen Vorschriften beim Innenministerium beantragte (und begründete) und nach der Genehmigung während der zweijährigen „Testphase" entsprechend verfuhr.
– Eine systematische Evaluierung der kommunalen Probeläufe war indessen von keiner Landesregierung – konzeptionell und institutionell – vorgesehen (kritisch Klages 1996: 16). Vielmehr wurde von diesen lediglich vorgeschrieben, daß die Kommunen, die von der „Experimentierklausel" Gebrauch machten, dem zuständigen Innenministerium über ihre Erfahrungen berichten sollten. Nur in einem Teil der Länder wurden die Kommunen über Fragebogen angeleitet und angehalten, ihre Berichterstattung zu vereinheitlichen. Im Falle des Landes *Nordrhein-Westfalen,*

---

30 Für eine Übersicht und Zusammenstellung der landesrechtlichen Regelungen vgl. Rembor (1996: 219ff.) Vorläufer war das Land Schleswig-Holstein mit einer frühen Variante vom 21.9.1993 bzw. 25.10.1993 (vgl. Rembor 1996: 232f.).
31 Insbesondere Abweichung vom Grundsatz der Gesamtdeckung, Ermöglichung von Deckungsfähigkeit zwischen einzelnen Ausgabenansätzen, Ermöglichung der Übertragbarkeit von Ausgabeansätzen in Folgejahren (vgl. Reichard 1998).

wo immerhin fast ein Viertel aller Kommunen von der Experimentierklausel Gebrauch machten und wo diesen für ihre Berichterstattung immerhin ein – die Querauswertung erleichternder – Fragebogen vorgelegt
wurde, erwies sich eine Querauswertung in Bezug auf die Freistellung
von einzelnen Vorschriften indessen dadurch als kaum möglich, daß das
Modernisierungsprofil und -repertoire der berichtenden Kommunen sehr
heterogen war[32]. So gelangte das Innenministerium zu zusammenfassenden Einschätzungen: „Aus den Rückmeldungen ... kein einheitliches
Bild" (IM NRW 1998: 8). Auch im Land *Baden-Württemberg*, in dem
sich knapp 40 Prozent der kreisfreien Städte, Großen Kreisstädte und
Landkreise an den „Experimenten" beteiligten, wurde die Berichterstattung der Kommunen von einem Fragebogen angeleitet, dessen 40 Fragen
insbesondere die praktizierten Budgetierungsregelungen und deren fi-
nanzwirtschaftliche Auswirkungen betrafen (vgl. IM BW 1996: 5).
Demnach berichtete „die Mehrzahl der Kommunen von Einsparungen in
den budgetierten Bereichen, einige stellten keine wesentlichen Veränderungen fest oder konnten keinen Ursachenzusammenhang mit der Budgetierung erkennen" (Strobl 1997: 41).

Vieles deutet darauf hin, daß dieser an sich bemerkenswerte Anlauf und Vor-
stoß, über eine „Experimentierklausel" kommunale Innovationsbereitschaft
anzureizen und die durch die Versuchsvorhaben gewinnbaren Erkenntnisse
zu nutzen, in Ermangelung eines systematischen Evaluierungskonzepts und
-verfahrens weitgehend versandet ist[33].

4.5 Evaluierungsforschung

4.5.1 Evaluierung durch Umfragen

Verlauf und Stand der Verwaltungsmodernisierung auf der kommunalen
Ebene sind zum Gegenstand mehrerer schriftlicher Umfragen des *Deutschen
Städtetages (DSt)*,[34] einer Umfrage der *Kommunalen Gemeinschaftsstelle für*

---

32 „Das Reformspektrum reicht von der Umstrukturierung einzelner Fachbereiche/Be-
    triebe (Pilotprojekte) bis hin zur flächendeckenden Einführung neuer Strukturen, u.a.
    unter Aufgabe der bisherigen Querschnittsämter" (IM NRW 1998: 8).
33 Vgl. Janning (1996: 52): „... nicht erkennbar, wie die vielfältigen Experimente der
    Kommunen durch die Kommunalaufsichtsbehörden empirisch ausgewertet werden".
34 Kurzprofil: DSt-Umfrage 1998 (vgl. Grömig/Gruner 1998: 581f.): *Fragestellung*:
    Verlauf und Stand der Verwaltungsmodernisierung in den Kommunen, Schwerpunkt:
    Institutionenevaluierung; Untersuchungsdesign und -methode: Schriftliche Befragung
    der (266) (west- und ostdeutschen) Mitgliedstädte des Deutschen Städtetages mit Hil-
    fe eines Fragebogens, Rücklauf: 85 Prozent, Untersuchungszeitraum: Frühjahr 1998,
    Forschungsträger: Eigenprojekt des Deutschen Städtetages.

Verwaltungsvereinfachung (KGSt)[35] sowie einer Umfrage des *Deutschen Instituts für Urbanistik*[36] gemacht worden. Die Umfragen richten sich überwiegend darauf, den *Stand* des Modernisierungsprozesses zu ermitteln, sind also in erster Linie als *Institutionenevaluierungen* einzustufen; die Fragen nach der *Performanz* der neuen Strukturen und Verfahren (Wirtschaftlichkeit usw.) bleiben (noch) weitgehend ausgeblendet. Auch wenn die Reliabilität von Umfragen, mit denen die Modernisierungsbereitschaft und Fähigkeit erkundet werden soll, Zweifeln ausgesetzt sein mag (welche Stadt bzw. welcher kommunaler Akteur ist ohne weiteres willens, sich – zumal gegenüber seinem kommunalen Spitzenverband – gegebenenfalls als modernisierungs- „lahm" zu „outen"?), bilden diese ein wichtiges empirisches Auskunftsmittel, insbesondere im Falle der DSt-Surveys, die inzwischen in einer Zeitreihe 1994/1995, 1996 und 1998 vorliegen.

4.5.2 Evaluierungsuntersuchungen als empirische Feldforschung

Der gegenwärtige Stand der der Evaluierungsforschung zuzurechnenden, im wesentlichen auf empirische Feldforschung gestützten Forschungsarbeiten läßt sich etwa so kennzeichnen[37]:

---

35 Kurzprofil: KGSt-Umfrage (vgl. KGSt 1998), Fragestellung: Stand der Verwaltungsmodernisierung; Untersuchungsdesign und Methoden: Schriftliche Befragung der 1430 KGSt-Mitglieder, Rücklauf 43 Prozent, „Chef-Fragebogen" „fragt vor allem nach der Bereitschaft zur Modernisierung und nach der Realisierung von wichtigen Modernisierungselementen; „Expertenfragebogen" fragt nach der konkreten Gestaltung des Modernisierungsprozesses, z.B. durch den Einsatz neuer Instrumente wie der Kosten- und Leistungsrechnung oder des Controlling", (ebda.: 11)), Untersuchungszeitraum: Sommer/Herbst 1997: Forschungsträger: Eigenprojekt der KGSt.

36 Kurzprofil: Difu-Umfrage (vgl. Mäding 1998), Untersuchungsfrage: Stand der Budgetierung, Untersuchungsdesign und Methoden: Schriftliche Befragung aller Städte mit mehr als 50.000 Einwohnern, Rücklauf: 85 Prozent, Untersuchungszeitraum: 1997; Forschungsträger: Eigenprojekt des Difu.

37 Es sei auch an dieser Stelle noch einmal betont, daß in diesem Bericht nur eine *Auswahl* von Forschungsprojekten abgehandelt werden soll und kann, um an *Beispielen*, deren Auswahl nicht frei von subjektiven Präferenzen sein mag, das konzeptionelle und methodische Profil des gegenwärtigen Forschungsstandes zu illustrieren. Für einen umfassenderen Überblick über die sozialwissenschaftlichen Forschungsvorhaben zu „Verwaltungsreformprojekten in Deutschland" siehe die „Transparenzstudie" von Jann/Reichard (1998). Als Ergebnis einer Umfrage bei vermutlich einschlägig arbeitenden Wissenschaftlern wurden insgesamt 72 Projekte identifiziert und u.a. nach mehreren Kriterien (Forschungszielsetzung, Beginn der Projekte, Untersuchungsebene, Forschungsträger, Finanzierung/Auftraggeber) klassifiziert. Allerdings sind die in der „Transparenzstudie" zur Erfassung der Forschungsfragestellung vorgegebenen drei Kategorien: *Analyse/ Theoriebildung; begleitende Beratung; direkte/aktive Beteiligung am Reformprozeß* für die hier von uns verfolgte *Evaluierungs*frage wenig erhellend. Zudem wird in der Transparenzstudie das Ergebnis der Umfrage insoweit

– In ihrer Fragestellung sind die empirischen Untersuchungen überwiegend
mit dem Verlauf und Stand der Verwaltungsmodernisierung befaßt, sind
mithin in erster Linie als *Institutionenevaluierung* einzustufen. Eher
Ausnahmen bilden die Untersuchungen von Naschold[38] und von
Naschold, Oppen & Wegener[39], die ausdrücklich den Anspruch erheben,
die Auswirkungen der institutionellen Veränderungen auf Effizienz der
Verwaltung (in unserem Verständnis: als *Performanzevaluierung)* und
darüber hinaus Demokratie- und Verteilungswirkungen (als *Outcome-
Evaluierung)* zu erfassen. Auch die Studie Jaedicke, Thrun & Wollmann[40] ist über eine *Institutionenevaluierung* hinaus als *Performanzevaluierung* angelegt.

---

als „nicht sonderlich befriedigend" bezeichnet: „Die meisten Antwortenden haben
Mehrfach-Ankreuzungen vorgenommen" (ebda.: 5).

38 Naschold (1995), Untersuchungsfrage: „drei Fragestellungen: die Identifizierung der
strukturellen Entwicklungstrends.... des öffentlichen Sektors" (in 11 OECD-Ländern);
die Abschätzung der Auswirkungen dieser Entwicklung im Sinne ihrer produktiven
Effizienz und ihrer sozialpolitischen Verteilungswirkung; die Analyse der Entwick-
lungskräfte im Modernisierungsprozeß des öffentlichen Sektors", (ebda.: 33), Untersuchung ausdrücklich bezeichnet als „Evaluierungsstudie", (z.B. ebda.: 33, 36); Untersuchungsdesign und Methoden: „Methodenmix" (vgl. ebda.: 38ff.) insbesondere: a.
für 11 – nach Kriterien des „most similar" sowie „most dissimilar approach" (ebda.:
39) ausgewählte – OECD-Länder Sekundäranalyse von OECD-Daten sowie weitere
nationale Dokumente und Interviews, b. Fünf-Länder-Vergleich einer sektoralen Politik und ihrer Steuerungssysteme (am Beispiel der Arbeitsmarktpolitik), c. internationaler Vergleich der Public-Sector-Modernisierung auf kommunaler Ebene unter Einbeziehung von 11 Kommunen aus 10 OECD-Ländern, d.h. der 11 erstplazierten Kommunen des internationalen Wettbewerbs der Bertelsmann-Stiftung (1993) (ebda.:
196ff.), Sekundärauswertung und Eigenerhebungen; Untersuchungszeitraum: 1992/
1994, Forschungsförderung: Hans-Böckler-Stiftung und Eigenförderung; Forschungsträger: Wissenschaftszentrum Berlin.

39 Naschold/Oppen/Wegener (1997), Projekt „Neue Städte braucht das Land", Untersu-
chungsfragen: „Zentrale Forschungsfragen waren drei Dimensionen kommunaler Verwaltungsmodernisierung. Zum einen wurde das Profil der Modernisierung erfaßt, zum
andern die Prozesse des Verwaltungsumbaues („Institutionenevaluierung", d. Verf.)
und schließlich die Wirkungen und Effekte der Verwaltungsmodernisierung auf ein
breites Set von Kriterien, unter anderem Effizienz und Effektivität, Qualität, Demokratie
und Sozialstaatlichkeit sowie Arbeit und Beschäftigung" (Performanz- sowie Ergebnis-
evaluierung, d.Verf.) (Wegener 1998: 337). Forschungsdesign und Methoden: Untersuchung der 10 ausländischen bestplazierten Kommunen des internationalen Wettbewerbs
der Bertelsmann-Stiftung (1993), Interviews, Dokumentenanalyse; Forschungsförderung: Hans-Böckler-Stiftung; Forschungsträger: Wissenschaftszentrum Berlin.

40 Jaedicke/Thrun/Wollmann (1999): Untersuchungsfokus: „Evaluierungsstudie zur Verwaltungsmodernisierung im Bereich Planen, Bauen und Umwelt" (Untertitel), Untersuchungsdesign: a. „Breitenrecherche" in 51 Kommunalverwaltungen (kreisfreien
und kreisangehörigen Städten/Gemeinden sowie Landkreisen); „das Auswahlverfahren... zielte auf die Gewinnung von „Positivfällen, d.h. von modernisierungsaktiven
Kommuen", (ebda.: 42), b. Forschungsdesign: Fallstudien in (10) Kommunen (Her-

– Infolge der Fokussierung auf die verwaltungspolitischen Veränderungs-
  prozesse weist die *Institutionenevaluierung* Schnittmengen mit (angewandter) Verwaltungsforschung und (mit Blick auf den institutionellen
  Umbruch in der ostdeutschen Verwaltung) mit der institutionenbezoge-
  nen Transformationsforschung auf (vgl. etwa Wegrich/Jaedicke/Lorenz/
  Wollmann[41]).

– Die vorliegenden empirischen Untersuchungen sind überwiegend als
  Fallstudien angelegt, sei es, daß sie sich auf diese beschränken (vgl. Kiß-
  ler/Bogumil/Greifenstein/Wiechmann[42], vgl. auch Maaß/Reichard[43], Gerstl-
  berger/Kneissler[44] aber auch Engelniederhammer/Köpp/Reichard, Röber/
  Wollmann[45], sei es, daß ihnen eine umfassendere Analyse des Unter-

---

ten, Wuppertal, Köln, Düsseldorf, Esslingen, Nordhausen, München, Heidelberg, Pas-
sau, Kreis Wesermarsch); Methoden: in „Breitenrecherche": Literaturanalyse, Telefo-
ninterviews, Dokumentenanalyse, in Fallstudien: Interviews, Dokumentenanalyse
(ebda.: 42ff., 62ff.); Projektlaufzeit: 1996/1998; Forschungsförderung: Wüstenrot-
Stiftung; Forschungsträger: IfS Institut für Stadtforschung und Strukturpolitik Berlin.

41 Wegrich/Jaedicke/Lorenz/Wollmann (1997), Fragestellung: Verlauf und Ergebnis der
    institutionellen Transformation und Modernisierung der Politik- und Verwaltungs-
    strukturen in ostdeutschen Kommunen, ansatzweise: Institutionenevaluierung; Unter-
    suchungsdesign und Methoden: a. Sekundäranalyse der DSt-Umfragen (ebda.: 194ff.);
    vertiefende Erhebungen (Telefon- Interviews, Dokumentenanalyse) in 20 „moderni-
    sierungsaktiven" (kreisfreien und kreisangehörigen) Städten (ebda.: 203ff.) sowie in 5
    „modernisierungsaktiven" Landkreisen (ebda.: 213ff.); b. Fallstudien (Interviews, Do-
    kumentenanalyse, teilnehmende Beobachtung) in zwei kreisfreien Städten (Schwerin
    und Neubrandenburg) und zwei Landkreisen (Nordwestmecklenburg und Ludwigs-
    burg) (ebda.: 19ff.); Untersuchungszeitraum: 1995/97; Förderung: Hans-Böckler-Stif-
    tung; Forschungsträger: Humboldt-Universität zu Berlin.

42 Kißler/Bogumil/Greifenstein/Wiechmann (1997): Untersuchungsfokus: „Die Imple-
    mentationsstrategien bei der Einführung eines NSM in den Kommunalverwaltungen",
    (ebda.: 16); Untersuchungsdesign: Fallstudien in (drei) Untersuchungsstädten (Hagen,
    Saarbrücken und Wuppertal, also in „drei im Modernisierungsprozeß eher fortgeschrit-
    tene Stadtverwaltungen" (ebda.: 17; FN 7); Methoden: „Experteninterviews, Gruppen-
    diskussionen, eine Beschäftigtenumfrage... sowie teilnehmende Beobachtung" (in Ha-
    gen) (ebda.: 18) und Dokumentenanalyse sowie Experteninterviews in Saarbrücken und
    Wuppertal (ebda.: 18). Projektlaufzeit: 1992/1996; Forschungsförderung: Hans-Böckler-
    Stiftung; Forschungsträger: Universität Marburg.

43 Vgl. oben FN 39.

44 Vgl. Gerstlberger/Kneissler (2000: 81ff.): *Fragestellung*: Erfassung von „Problemen
    und Schwierigkeiten der Verwaltungsmodernisierungsprozesse" (ebda.: 83), überwie-
    gend *Institutionenevaluierung*; Design und Methode: Fallstudien in 7 Städten (Düs-
    seldorf, Halberstadt, Hamburg, Ludwigshafen, Neustadt, Passau, Saarbrücken) – um
    „Kommunen mit möglichst unterschiedlichen Reformansätzen in das Sample aufzu-
    nehmen"; insbesondere teilstrukturierte Leitfadeninterviews (ebda.: 83); Zeitraum:
    1998, Forschungsförderung. Deutsche Forschungsgemeinschaft; Forschungsträger:
    Forschungsgruppe Verwaltungsautomation/Uni Kassel.

45 Engelniederhammer/Köpp/Reichard/Röber/Wollmann (1999), Untersuchungsfokus:
    Untersuchung der „Realisierung der betriebswirtschaftlich orientierten Verwaltungs-
    reform in Berlin", die auf Senats- und Bezirksebene Berlins im Jahr 1994 in Gang ge-

suchungsfeldes – als Vollerhebung aller in Betracht kommenden Untersuchungseinheiten (so Grunow/Grunow-Lutter[46]) oder als „Breitenanalyse" eines relevanten Ausschnitts von diesen (so Jaedicke u.a.[47] und Wegrich u.a.[48]) vorausging.

– Als Untersuchungs*ebene* beherrschen bislang die *Kommunen* die Agenda der Evaluierungsforschung; als Ausnahme ist auf eine Untersuchung zum Berliner Reformprojekt zu verweisen (vgl. Engelniederhammer et al.[49]).

– International vergleichende Untersuchungen bilden ein wachsendes Forschungsfeld: als Mehrebenen-Analyse (vgl. Naschold 1995)[50], als Städte-Projekt (vgl. Naschold/Oppen/Wegener 1997)[51] und zuletzt als Untersuchung zur zentralen Regierungsebene (vgl. Naschold/Jann/Reichard 1999)[52].

---

setzt worden ist (ebda.: 10); Untersuchungsdesign und Methoden: „Fallstudie" zum Berliner Reformprozeß: Experteninterviews, Dokumentenanalyse, teilnehmende Beobachtung; Projektlaufzeit: 1995/1998; Forschungsförderung: Berlindienliche Forschungsförderung des Berliner Senats; Forschungsträger: Fachhochschule für Verwaltung und Rechtspflege Berlin/Humboldt-Universität zu Berlin.

46   Kurzprofil: Grunow/Grunow-Lutter (2000), Fragestellung: Verwaltungsmodernisierung des Öffentlichen Gesundheitsdienstes auf kommunaler Ebene; Untersuchungsdesign und Methoden: 1. Schritt: teilstandardisierte schriftliche Befragung der Leiter aller Gesundheitsämter (außer Thüringen), Rücklaufquote: 47,8/61,1 Prozent (vgl. ebda.: 56), 2. Schritt: Intensivuntersuchungen zu den Öffentlichen Gesundheitsdiensten in 11 (westdeutschen) Kommunen (4 Städten, 7 Kreisen) sowie einer ostdeutschen Kommune, insbesondere durch Gesprächsleitfaden-gestützte Interviews mit Gesundheitsamts-Personal („Perspektive der Politikfeldvertreter") und kommunalem Leitungspersonal („Perspektive der Modernisierer") sowie schriftliche Befragung von (634) Mitarbeitern der Gesundheitsämter, Rücklaufquote durchschnittlich 60 Prozent; Forschungsförderung: Bundesressortforschungsmittel; Forschungsträger: Akademie für öffentliches Gesundheitswesen, Düsseldorf/Rhein-Ruhr-Institut für Sozialforschung und Politikberatung an der Universität Duisburg.

47   Vgl. oben FN 40.

48   Vgl. oben FN 41.

49   Vgl. oben FN 45.

50   Vgl. oben FN 38.

51   Vgl. oben FN 39.

52   Kurzprofil: Naschold/Jann/Reichard (1999): Modernisierung der zentralstaatlichen Regierungs- und Verwaltungsebene; Fragestellung: Bestandsaufnahme und (ansatzweise) Evaluierung der zentralstaatlichen Verwaltungsreform in sieben Ländern (USA, U.K, Neuseeland, Dänemark, Schweden, Niederlande, Schweiz und Deutschland) insbesondere für vier „Bereiche der Staats- und Verwaltungsreform": neue Steuerungslogik, Finanzmanagement, Personalmanagement und Mehrebenenmanagement (ebda.: 10). Forschungsdesign und Methoden: a. Konzeptformulierung durch das deutsche Autorenteam, b. Abfassung von Berichten durch nationale Experten der ausgewählten Länder, c. Diskussion der „nationalen Berichte" auf internationalem Workshop (März 1999), der „Umsetzungskonferenz" (mit Fachleuten der Bundes-, Landes- und Kommunalverwaltung), ein Querauswertungsbericht durch das deutsche Autorenteam; Untersuchungszeitraum: Mitte 1998/Anfang 2000; Förderung: Hans-

– Aufgrund der in den meisten aufgeführten Studien angewandten Auswahl- und Suchkriterien („modernisierungsaktive" Untersuchungsfälle) (so Kißler u.a.[53]; Jaedicke u.a.[54]; Maaß/Reichard[55]; Naschold[56]; Naschold u.a.[57] 1997) ist der Evaluierungsstand von einem die „modernisierungsaktive" Verwaltung berücksichtigenden und die „modernisierungspassive" Verwaltung vernachlässigenden Bias gekennzeichnet.

– Maßgebliche Anstöße erhielt die Evaluierungsforschung (wie die anwendungsbezogene Verwaltungsforschung insgesamt) durch die Forschungsförderung der *Hans-Böckler-Stiftung*[58], die – unter entscheidender Mitwirkung ihrer Forschungsreferentin Erika Mezger – seit 1990 einen programmatischen Förderungsschwerpunkt „Modernisierung des öffentlichen Sektors" einrichtete. Dabei knüpfte sie an die 1988 von der ÖTV ergriffene Initiative „Zukunft durch öffentliche Dienste" an, die durch die Hans-Böckler-Stiftung begleitet und – insbesondere in Form sog. Gestaltungsprojekte – unterstützt wurde (vgl. Mezger 1998: 29)[59].

5. Internationaler Ausblick

Abschließend sei ein (kaum mehr als summarischer und fragmentarischer) Ausblick auf den Stand der Evaluierung von Verwaltungsmodernisierung im internationalen Vergleich und in anderen europäischen Ländern versucht (vgl. den vorzüglichen Übersichtsaufsatz von Löffler 1998), um die deutsche Entwicklung ansatzweise einzuordnen.

Für *international vergleichende* Untersuchungen ist zunächst auf die eher qualitativ-deskriptiven Länderprofile der OECD (vgl. OECD 1990, 1995) zu verweisen, die wegen ihrer Orientierung auf Verlauf und Stand der länderspezifischen Modernisierungspolitiken als *Institutionenevaluierung* einzustufen sind. Die jüngste international vergleichende Studie von Barzelay 2000 beruht im wesentlichen auf einer (sekundäranalytischen) Auswertung und

---

Böckler-Stiftung, Forschungsträger: Wissenschaftszentrum Berlin/Universität Potsdam.
53 Vgl. oben FN 42.
54 Vgl. oben FN 40.
55 Vgl. oben FN 29.
56 Vgl. oben FN 38.
57 Vgl. oben FN 39.
58 Vgl. hierzu auch die „Transparenzstudie", wonach von den 72 identifizierten Forschungsprojekten knapp 30 Prozent durch die Hans-Böckler-Stiftung gefördert wurden (vgl. Jann/Reichard 1998: 9).
59 Die bekanntesten dieser Gestaltungsprojekte waren der Bürgerladen Hagen (vgl. Kißler/Bogumil/Wiechmann 1994), das Einwohnermeldeamt Kassel (vgl. Abel/Brinkmann/Grimmer 1995) und die Reform des Landkreises Main-Kinzig.

konzeptionell-klassifikatorischen Interpretation verfügbarer nationaler Analysen. Vermöge seines breiten konzeptionellen, methodischen und empirischen Umgriffs hat die bereits erwähnte Studie von Naschold 1995[60] im Konzert der (wenigen) international vergleichenden Abhandlungen einen beachtlichen Platz. Als ein bahnbrechender Fortschritt in der international vergleichenden Evaluierung der Verwaltungsmodernisierung ist das jüngste Werk von Pollitt/ Bouckaert hervorzuheben.

Für die Entwicklung in den anderen europäischen Ländern ist in einem kundigen Überblick festgestellt worden, daß „trotz der global zu verzeichnenden rhetorischen ‚Output-' und ‚Outcome-'Orientierung von Verwaltungsreformern ... Evaluierungen von ‚New Public Management' ein universell defizitärer Bereich" seien (Löffler 1998: 333). Allerdings weisen einzelne Länder ein durchaus lebhafteres Evaluierungsprofil auf, was hier nur anhand von zwei (augenscheinlich verhältnismäßig evaluierungsaktiven) Ländern bzw. Ländergruppen angedeutet werden soll.

– Zum einen sind die skandinavischen Länder zu nennen, die eine (bis in die 30er Jahre zurückreichende) Evaluierungtradition und -kultur besitzen[61]. Eine Reihe der jüngsten Politik- und Verwaltungsreformen, so etwa die Mitte der 80er Jahre eingeführten „freie Kommunen-Experimente" (vgl. Baldersheim 1986: 295 mit Nachweisen) sind denn auch Gegenstand von Evaluierungsuntersuchungen geworden.

– Besonders ausgeprägt scheint in der Schweiz die Evaluierung von New Public Management-Reformen in Gang gekommen zu sein, wie ein Schub neuerer Publikationen unterstreicht (Bussmann 1995, Bussmann u.a. 1997, Hofmeister/Buschor 1999 und insbesondere zuletzt Ritz 1999). Unter den einschlägigen Untersuchungen ist auf Bundesebene vor allem ein Großprojekt zur Evaluierung der FLAG-Ämter (d.h. der Ämter, die „Führung mit LeistungsAuftrag und Globalbudget anwenden) hervorzuheben (vgl. hierzu Ritz 1999: 37ff.).

6. Zusammenfassung

– Zwar hat in Deutschland der Umfang an („„in house") Selbstevaluierungsansätzen (vor allem auf der kommunalen Ebene) und auch das Volumen externer, der Evaluierungsforschung zurechenbarer Forschungen im Verlauf der 90er Jahre deutlich zugenommen. Jedoch muß der Stand

---

60 Vgl. oben FN 38.
61 Vgl. Levine (1984: 121): „Evaluierungen durchziehen das schwedische System schon fast endemisch", vgl. hierzu jüngst Naschold/Jann/Reichard (1999: 30).

der Evaluierungsforschung nach wie vor als durchaus defizitär eingeschätzt werden (so auch z.B. Mezger 1998: 31; Grunow 1998: 1) [62].

– Diese Einschätzung gilt vor allem dann, wenn man in Rechnung stellt, daß es sich bei den bislang verfügbaren Untersuchungen überwiegend um auf Verlauf und Stand der Modernisierungsmaßnahmen gerichtete Studien (*Institutionenevaluierung*) und – sei es konzeptionell oder faktisch – am Rande um *Performanz- oder Outcome-Evaluierungen* handelt. Die bisherige weitgehende Ausblendung der verwaltungsinternen (*Performance*) oder -externen Auswirkungen (*Outcomes*) dürfte nur zum Teil der Tatsache geschuldet sein, daß die modernisierungspolitische Umgestaltung der Organisations-, Personal- usw. -strukturen vielfach noch im Gange und deren Auswirkungen noch kaum zu beobachten sind. Bestimmend für diesen Analyserückstand dürften auf Seiten der Forschung deren Disposition sein, den sehr viel schwierigeren methodischen und empirischen Problemen der Erfassung der Auswirkungen (noch) aus dem Wege zu gehen und sich auf die „einfachere" Institutionenanalyse zu werfen, und auf Seiten der Politik und Verwaltung deren geringe Bereitschaft sein, sich in der prekären Frage von Erfolg oder Mißerfolg der (oft sehr kostspieligen) Modernisierungsmaßnahmen „in die Karten schauen zu lassen".

– Evaluierungsuntersuchungen als Auftragsforschung – also Evaluierungsforschung, die von externen Forschungseinrichtungen im Auftrag und mit finanzieller Förderung der öffentlichen Einrichtungen (Bund, Länder und Kommunen) durchgeführt werden – sind bislang kaum zu notieren. Zum einen steht dies in auffälligem Gegensatz zur Bereitwilligkeit des Bundes, der Länder und der Kommunen, in der Phase der Vorbereitung und bei der internen Durchführung der Modernisierungsprojekte externe Gutachten und Beratungsleistungen (in aller Regel an Unternehmensberatungsfirmen)

---

62 In diesem Zusammenhang ist festzuhalten, daß auch in den 60er und 70er Jahren, als die Policy- und Programmevaluierung auch und gerade in der Bundesrepublik einen geradezu steilen Aufstieg erlebte (vgl. Derlien 1976, Hellstern/Wollmann 1984b), die Evaluierung der Verwaltungsmodernisierung ebenfalls randständig blieb, obgleich umfassende „Regierungs- und Verwaltungsreform" und die Schaffung von Transparenz eine Schlüsselbotschaft jener Politikphase war. Allein zu den kommunalen Gebietsreformen, die zwischen den mittleren 60er und den mittleren 70er Jahren die kommunalen Politik- und Verwaltungsstrukturen in den Bundesländern teilweise radikal umpflügten, wurden umfangreiche (vor allem von der VW-Stiftung geförderte) (Evaluierungs-)Untersuchungen durchgeführt, vgl. Thieme/Prillwitz 1981 sowie die 19 (!) Bände der von v. Oertzen/Thieme herausgegebenen, zwischen 1979 und 1988 erschienenen Schriftenreihe. Allerdings wurde hierzu im Rückblick 1994 (!) festgestellt: „Ob all diese Ziele mit der Umsetzung der Reform erreicht worden sind, ist bis heute nicht abschließend bewertet worden, zumal für die Bemessung der meisten Vor- und Nachteile im Vorher-Nachher-Vergleich klare Indikatoren fehlen" (Hennecke 1994: 556).

in beachtlicher Fülle zu vergeben[63] und hierfür sehr namhafte finanzielle
Mittel aufzuwenden[64]. Zugleich befindet sich der Verzicht auf Evaluierung
in geradezu paradoxem Widerspruch zu dem auf Schaffung von Wirkungs-
und Kosten*transparenz* gerichteten Imperativ der NPM- und NSM-
Philosophie. Politik und Verwaltung sollten – allen der früh- und rechtzeitigen analytischen Durchleuchtung der Modernisierungsprozesse und -
ergebnisse und deren Nutzen und Kosten etwa entgegenstehenden (Macht-
usw.) Interessen zum Trotz – die Erkenntnis- und Handlungschance nutzen, die die Evaluierung der Modernisierungsvorhaben eröffnet.

– Auch wenn die im konzeptionellen und methodischen Fundus der Evaluierungsforschung verfügbaren (im ersten Teil des Aufsatzes angetippten) Po-
litik- und Evaluierungsansätze vermöge der in ihnen vorausgesetzten teilweise recht komplexen Untersuchungsanordnungen erhebliche Anforderungen an die konzeptionelle (und auch politische) Phantasie, die methodische Kompetenz und (last not least) an die verfügbaren Forschungsressourcen stellen (vgl. Pollitt 1995), sollte – um der analytischen Absicherung
des Modernisierungsprojekts willen – eine maximale Nutzung des Metho-
denrepertoires der Evaluierungsforschung unternommen werden. Die Forscher sind gefordert, sich den konzeptionell, methodisch und empirisch bekanntermaßen sehr viel schwierigeren Fragen nach den *Auswirkungen* von
Reformprojekten (*Performanz- und Outcome-Evaluierung*) zuzuwenden,
anstatt den leichteren Weg der *Institutionenevaluierung* zu gehen.

– *Experimentelle* Politik- und Evaluierungsansätze sollten – in der methodischen „weichen" Variante von *Pilot- und Modellvorhaben* – durch die
rechtzeitige Sicherung einer kompetenten Evaluierungsfunktion als in-
stitutionen- und modernisierungspolitische *Lernstrategie* möglichst um-
fangreich genutzt werden.

---

63 Siehe als Beispiel die lange Liste der externen Organisationsuntersuchungen, die die
Landesregierung von Baden-Württemberg seit 1990 (durchweg an Unternehmensberatungsfirmen) vergeben hat, vgl. Innenministerium Baden-Württemberg (1999:
184ff.) Auch in NRW wurde zur Vorbereitung der gegenwärtigen Verwaltungsmodernisierung „die gesamte Landesverwaltung oder zumindest nennenswerte Teile flächendeckend mit Organisationsuntersuchungen überzogen" (Bürsch/Müller 1999: 9).

64 Über die (angesichts der Stundenhonorare der Consulting-Firmen vielfach zweifellos
gewaltigen) finanziellen Beratungsaufwendungen der Öffentlichen Hand wird – ungeachtet der programmatischen „Transparanz"-Forderung der gegenwärtigen Verwaltungsmodernisierung – auffällig wenig bekannt. Die wenigen zufälligen Informationen lassen „die Spitze des Eisbergs" erkennen. So wandte das Land Berlin allein
1994/1995 rund 20 Mio. DM für externe Beratungsleistungen von Consulting-Firmen
auf. Hinzu kamen weitere 5,3 Mio. für Mitarbeiterqualifikation und 3,6 Mio. DM für
IuK-Technik (vgl. Wollmann 1998: 220). Für externe Beratungsleistungen (einschließlich Produkt-Beratung) gab der ostdeutsche Landkreis Ludwigslust jährlich
120.000 DM, der ostdeutsche Landkreis Barnim einmalig 420.000 DM aus, vgl.
Wegrich u.a. (1996: 216). Die Stadt Ludwigshafen entgalt die von ihr beauftragte
Consulting-Firma mit 10.6 Mio. DM, vgl. Grunow 1998.

– Die *(Selbst)Evaluierungskultur,* die in den letzten Jahren (nicht zuletzt durch nationale wie internationale *Qualitätswettbewerbe* und die *interkommunalen Vergleichsringe*) bemerkenswerte Anstöße erfahren hat, sollte als kulturell-kognitive Voraussetzung und Einbettung einer umfassenden Evaluierungs- und Lernfunktion weiter gefestigt werden.

Literatur

Adamaschek, Bernd (1997): Leistungssteigerung durch Wettbewerb in deutschen Kommunen – der interkommunale Vergleich. In: Naschold, Frieder/Oppen, Maria/Wegener, Alexander (Hg.) (1997): Innovative Kommunen. Stuttgart. S. 107ff.

Adamaschek, Bernd (Hg.) (1998): Interkommunaler Leistungsvergleich. 100 spürbare Erfolge. Gütersloh: Verlag Bertelsmann Stiftung. S. 19-125.

Baldersheim, Harald (1996): Nordic Municipalities in Transition: From Free Communes To Free Choice? In: Reichard, Christoph/Wollmann, Hellmut (Hg.): Kommunalverwaltung im Modernisierungsschub? Basel usw.: Birkhäuser. S. 289-307.

Barzelay, Michael (2000): The New Public Management. Improving Research and Policy Dialogue. Berkeley, L.A., Oxford.

Bertelsmann Stiftung (Hg.) (1993): Demokratie und Effizienz in der Kommunalverwaltung, Bd. 1. Gütersloh.

Böhret, Carl (1998): Verwaltungspolitik als Führungsauftrag. In: Bandemer, Stephan von/Blanke, Bernhard/Nullmeier, Frank/Wewer, Göttrik (Hg.): Handbuch zur Verwaltungs-Reform. Opladen: Leske + Budrich. S. 41-46.

Bürsch, Michael/Müller, Brigitte (1999): Verwaltungsreformen in den deutschen Bundesländern. Friedrich-Ebert-Stiftung.

Bussmann, Werner (1995): Wirkungsorientierte Verwaltung, NPM und Evaluationen. In: Hablützel, Peter u.a. (Hg.): Umbruch in Politik und Verwaltung. Bern usw. S. 367-377.

Bussmann, Werner (1997): Evaluation von NPM-Pilotprojekten. In: Gesetzgebung heute. Mitteilungsblatt der Schweizer Gesellschaft für Gesetzgebung. H. 3, S. 137ff.

Bussmann, Werner/Klöti, Ulrich/Knöpfel, Peter (Hg.) (1997): Einführung in die Politikevaluation. Basel/Frankfurt.

Campbell, Daniel (1968): Reforms as Experiments. Wieder abgedruckt in: Caro, F. G. (Hg.) (1971): Readings in Evaluation Research. New York. S. 233ff.

Campbell, Daniel T./Stanley, J. C. (1970): Experimental and Quasi-Experimental Designs for Research on Teaching. In: Ingenkamp, K. H/Parey, E. (Hg.) (1970): Handbuch der Unterrichtsforschung. Teil 1, Weinheim. S. 447ff.

Campbell, Daniel T./Stanley, J. C. (1963): Experimental and quasi-experimental evaluation in social research. Chicago.

Derlien, Hans-Ulrich (1976): Die Erfolgskontrolle staatlicher Planung. Baden-Baden.

Derlien, Hans-Ulrich (Hg.) (1981a): Programmforschung in der öffentlichen Verwaltung. Werkstattbericht 1 der Gesellschaft für Programmforschung. München.

Derlien, Hans-Ulrich (1981b): Stand und Entwicklung der Programmforschung in der öffentlichen Verwaltung. In: Derlien, Hans-Ulrich (Hg.): Programmforschung in der öffentlichen Verwaltung. Werkstattbericht 1 der Gesellschaft für Programmforschung. München. S. 9ff.

Deutscher Städtetag (Hg.) (1998): Verwaltungsmodernisierung: Warum so schwierig, warum so langsam? Eine Zwischenbilanz. DST-Beiträge zur Kommunalpolitik, Reihe A, H. 27. Köln.

Dror, Yehezkel (1968): Public Policymaking Reexamined. Scranton, Pennsylvania.

Eckstein, Harry (1975): Case Study and Theory in Polical Science. In: Greenstein, Fred/ Polsby, Nelson W. (Hg.): Handbook of Political Science, Vol. 7. Reading Mass.

Eichhorn, Peter/Siedentopf, Heinrich (1976): Effizienzeffekte der Verwaltungsreform – Exemplarische Ansätze einer Wirkungsanalyse der territorialen und funktionalen Verwaltungsreform in Rheinland-Pfalz. Baden-Baden.

Engelniederhammer, Stefan/Köpp, Bodo/Reichard, Christoph/Röber, Manfred/Wollmann, Hellmut (1999): Berliner Verwaltung auf Modernisierungskurs. Berlin.

Gerstlberger, Wolfgang/Kneissler, Thomas (2000): Wie Kommunalverwaltungen mit De- zentralisierungstendenzen umgehen: Erkenntnisse aus sieben Fallstudien. In: Kneiss- ler, Thomas (Hg.): Tastende Schritte zu einer neuen Verwaltung. Kassel: Forschungs- gruppe Verwaltungsautomation der Uni Kassel. S. 81-100.

Grimmer, Klaus/Kneissler, Thomas, (2000): Tastende Schritte zu einer neuen Verwaltung. Kassel: Forschungsgruppe Verwaltungsautomation der Uni Kassel. S. 7-19.

Grömig, Erko/Gruner, Kersten, (1998): Reform in den Rathäusern. In: Der Städtetag. (1998), H. 8, S. 581ff.

Grunow, Dieter (1998): Lokale Verwaltungsmodernisierung „in progress"? In: Grunow, Dieter/Wollmann, Hellmut (Hg.): Lokale Verwaltungsreform in Aktion: Fortschritte und Fallstricke. Basel usw.: Birkhäuser. S. 1-25.

Grunow, Dieter/Grunow-Lutter, Vera (2000): Der öffentliche Gesundheitsdienst im Mo- dernisierungsprozeß. Weinheim/München.

Haldemann, Theo (1997): Evaluation von Politik- und Verwaltungsreformen: Institutio- nelle und materielle Auswirkungen von NPM- und WOV-Projekten. In: Gesetzgebung heute. Mitteilungsblatt der Schweizer Gesellschaft für Gesetzgebung, H. 3, S. 63ff.

Haubner, Oliver, (1993): Zur Organisation des 1. Speyerer Qualitätswettbewerbs: von der Idee zum „Ideenmarkt". In: Hill, Hermann/Klages, Helmut (Hg.) (1993): Spitzenver- waltungen im Wettbewerb. Baden-Baden. S. 48-60.

Hellstern, Gerd-Michael/Wollmann, Hellmut (1983a): Evaluierungsforschung. Ansätze und Methoden – dargestellt am Beispiel des Städtebaus. Basel.

Hellstern, Gerd-Michael/Wollmann, Hellmut (Hg.) (1983b): Experimentelle Politik – Re- formstrohfeuer oder Lernstrategie. Bestandsaufnahme und Evaluierung. Opladen.

Hellstern, Gerd-Michael/Wollmann, Hellmut (1983c): Bilanz – Reformexperimente, wis- senschaftliche Begleitung und politische Realität. In: Hellstern, Gerd-Michael/Woll- mann, Hellmut (Hg.) (1983): Experimentelle Politik – Reformstrohfeuer oder Lern- strategie. Bestandsaufnahme und Evaluierung. Opladen. S. 1-75.

Hellstern, Gerd-Michael/Wollmann, Hellmut (Hg.) (1984a): Handbuch zur Evaluierungs- forschung. Bd. 1. Opladen.

Hellstern, Gerd-Michael/Wollmann, Hellmut (1984b): Evaluierung und Evaluierungsfor- schung – ein Entwicklungsbericht. In: Hellstern, Gerd-Michael/Wollmann, Hellmut (Hg.) (1984): Handbuch zur Evaluierungsforschung. Bd. 1. Opladen. S. 17-93.

Hellstern, Gerd-Michael/Wollmann, Hellmut (Hg.) (1984c): Evaluierung und Erfolgskon- trolle in Kommunalpolitik und -verwaltung. Basel usw.

Hellstern, Gerd-Michael/Wollmann, Hellmut (Hg.) (1984d): Evaluierung und Erfolgskon- trolle auf der kommunalen Ebene – ein Überblick. In: Hellstern, Gerd-Michael/ Woll- mann, Hellmut (Hg.) (1984): Evaluierung und Erfolgskontrolle in Kommunalpolitik und -verwaltung. Basel usw. S. 10-59.

Henneke, Hans-Günter (1994): Verwaltungseffizienz und Betroffenenakzeptanz, Leitbild- gerechtigkeit und politische Durchsetzbarkeit. In: Neue Verwaltungswissenschaftliche Zeitschrift, H. 6, S. 555ff.

Hill, Hermann/Klages, Helmut (Hg.) (1993): Spitzenverwaltungen im Wettbewerb. Eine Dokumentation des 1. Speyerer Qualitätswettbewerbs 1992. Baden-Baden.

Hill, Hermann/Klages, Helmut (Hg.) (1995): Lernen von Spitzenverwaltungen (2. Wettbewerb 1994). Baden-Baden.

Hill, Hermann/Klages, Helmut (Hg.) (1996): Jenseits der Experimentierklausel. Stuttgart.

Hill, Hermann/Klages, Helmut (Hg.) (1999): Innovation von Spitzenverwaltungen (4. Wettbewerb 1999). Baden-Baden.

Hofmann, Jeanette (1993): Implizite Theorien in der Politik. Opladen.

Hofmeister, Albert/Buschor, Ernst (Hg.) (1999): Verwaltungsreform in der Schweiz – eine Zwischenbilanz. Bern.

Hucke, Jochen/Wollmann, Hellmut (1980): Methodenprobleme der Implementationsforschung. In: Mayntz, Renate (Hg.): Implementation politischer Programme. Empirische Forschungsberichte. Königstein. S. 212-237.

Innenministerium Baden-Württemberg (1996): Budgetierung bei den Kommunen in Baden-Württemberg, Erfahrungsbericht zur Anwendung von zugelassenen Abweichungen vom geltenden Recht (Experimentierklauseln §49 GemHVO, §41 GemKVO), unveröff. Ms. Stuttgart.

Innenministerium Baden-Württemberg (1999): Zwischenbilanz der Verwaltungsreform. Stuttgart.

Innenministerium Nordrhein-Westfalen (1998): Bericht über die Erfahrungen mit der Anwendung der Experimentierklausel des §126 Gemeindeordnung NW, vervielf. Ms.

Jaedicke, Wolfgang/Thrun, Thomas/Wollmann, Hellmut (1999): Modernisierung der Kommunalverwaltung. Evaluierungsstudie zur Verwaltungsmodernisierung im Bereich Planen, Bauen und Umwelt. Stuttgart.

Jann, Werner (1998): Neues Steuerungsmodell. In: Bandemer, Stephan von/Blanke, Bernhard/ Nullmeier, Frank/Wever, Göttrik (Hg.) (1998): Handbuch zur Verwaltungsreform. Opladen: Leske + Budrich. S. 70-79.

Jann, Werner/Reichard, Christoph (1998): Transparenzstudie: Wissenschaftliche Begleitforschung zu Verwaltungsreformprojekten in Deutschland. Verv. Ms., KWI Universität Potsdam.

Janning, Hermann (1996): Kreis Soest. In: Hill, Hermann/Klages, Helmut (Hg.): Jenseits der Experimentierklausel. Düsseldorf. S. 45ff.

KGSt IKO-Netz (1999): Methodik des IKO-Netzes: Kennzahlen und Vergleichsarbeit. Köln.

KGSt IKO-Netz (2000): Aktuelle Übersicht der IKO-Netz – Vergleichsringe. Stand 20.3. 2000. Köln.

Kißler, Leo/Bogumil, Jörg/Greifenstein, Ralph/Wiechmann, Elke (1997): Moderne Zeiten im Rathaus? Berlin: edition sigma.

Klages, Helmut (1993): Methodenfragen des Verwaltungswettbewerbs. In: Hill, Hermann/ Klages, Helmut (Hg.) (1993): Spitzenverwaltungen im Wettbewerb. Baden-Baden. S. 32-47.

Klages, Helmut (1996): Jenseits der Experimentierklausel – oder zurück ins Diesseits? In: Hill, Hermann/Klages, Helmut (Hg.): Jenseits der Experimentierklausel. Düsseldorf. S. 7ff.

Knöpfel, Peter/Busmann, Werner (1997): Die öffentliche Politik als Evaluationsobjekt. In: Bussmann, Werner/Klöti, Ulrich/Knöpfel, Peter (Hg.): Einführung in die Politikevaluation. Basel/Frankfurt. S. 78ff.

Kommunale Gemeinschaftsstelle für Verwaltungsvereinfachung (KGSt) (1995): Das Neue Steuerungsmodell – Erste Zwischenbilanz. KGSt-Bericht 10/1995. Köln.

Kommunale Gemeinschaftsstelle für Verwaltungsvereinfachung (KGSt) (1998): KGSt-Mitgliederbefragung 1997. Neues Steuerungsmodell und TuI-Einsatz. KGSt-Bericht 10/1998. Köln.

Levine, Robert A. (1984): Programmevaluierung und Politikanalyse in Europa, USA und Kanada – Ein Überblick. In: Hellstern, Gerd-Michael/Wollmann, Hellmut (Hg.): Handbuch zur Evaluierungsforschung. Opladen. S. 94-133.

Lijphart, Arend (1971): Comparative Politics and the Comparative Method. In: American Political Science Review. S. 482ff.

Löffler, Elke (1998): „New Public Management im internationalen" Vergleich. In: Grunow, Dieter/Wollmann, Hellmut (Hg.): Lokale Verwaltungsreform in Aktion: Fortschritte und Fallstricke. Basel usw.: Birkhäuser. S. 323-336.

Lutz, Burkhard (1983): Zur Problematik programmbegleitender Sozialforschung. In: Hellstern, Gerd-Michael/Wollmann, Hellmut (Hg.): Experimentelle Politik. Opladen. S. 256-262.

Maaß, Christian (1998): Brandenburger Kommunen auf dem Weg. Handbuch, Potsdam.

Maaß, Christian/Reichard, Christoph (1998): Von Konzepten zu wirklichen Veränderungen? Erfahrungen mit der Einführung des neuen Steuerungsmodells in Brandenburgs Modellkommunen In: Grunow, Dieter/Wollmann, Hellmut (Hg.): Lokale Verwaltungsreform in Aktion: Fortschritte und Fallstricke. Basel usw.: Birkhäuser. S. 267-285.

Mäding, Heinrich (1998): Empirische Untersuchungen zur Verwaltungsmodernisierung aus dem Deutschen Institut für Urbanistik. In: Deutscher Städtetag, Verwaltungsmodernisierung. Eine Zwischenbilanz. DSt-Beiträge zur Kommunalpolitik. Reihe A, H. 27, S. 9ff., Köln.

Mezger, Erika (1998): Das Netzwerk „Kommunen der Zukunft" und der Beitrag der Hans-Böckler-Stiftung. In: Bogumil, Jörg/Kißler, Leo (Hg.): Stillstand auf der „Baustelle"? Baden-Baden. S. 21ff.

Naschold, Frieder (1995): Ergebnissteuerung, Wettbewerb, Qualitätspolitik. Entwicklungspfade des öffentlichen Sektors in Europa. Modernisierung des öffentlichen Sektors. Sonderband 1. Berlin.

Naschold, Frieder/Reichard, Christoph/Röber, Manfred/Wegener, Alexander (1998): Verwaltungsreform auf der Ministerialebene. Dokumentation. WZB, FS 2, S. 98-205.

Naschold, Frieder/Jann, Werner/Reichard, Christoph (1999): Innovation, Effektivität, Nachhaltigkeit. Internationale Erfahrungen zentralstaatlicher Verwaltungsreform. Berlin.

Naschold, Frieder/Oppen, Maria/Wegener, Alexander (Hg.) (1997): Innovative Kommunen. Internationale Trends und deutsche Erfahrungen. Stuttgart usw. : Kohlhammer.

Nullmeier, Frank (1998): Kennzahlen und Indikatoren. In: Bandemer, Stephan von/Blanke, Bernhard/Nullmeier, Frank/Wever, Göttrik (Hg.) (1998): Handbuch zur Verwaltungsreform. Opladen: Leske + Budrich. S. 339-346.

OECD (1990): Public Management Developments. Survey. Paris.

OECD (1995): Governance in Transition. Public Management Reforms in OECD Countries. Paris.

Pawson, Ray/Tilley, Nick (1997): Realistic Evaluation. London etc.: Sage.

Pressman, J. L./Wildavsky, A. B. (1973): Implementation. Berkeley.

Pollitt, Christopher (1990): Managerialism and the Public Services. The Anglo-American Experience. Oxford.

Pollitt, Christopher (1995): Justification by Works or by Faith? Evaluation the New Public Management. In: Evaluation, vol. 1, no. 2, p. 133-154.

Pollitt, Christopher/Bouckaert, Geert (2000): Public Management Reform. A Comparative Analysis. Oxford.

Pröhl, Marga, (1993): Zielsetzung und Methodik der Preisvergabe. In: Bertelsmann Stiftung (Hg.): Demokratie und Effizienz in der Kommunalverwaltung. Bd. 1. Gütersloh. S. 9ff.

Reichard, Christoph (1998a): Der Produktansatz im „Neuen Steuerungsmodell" – von der Euphorie zur Ernüchterung. In: Grunow, Dieter/Wollmann, Hellmut (Hg.): Lokale Verwaltungsreform in Aktion. Basel usw.: Birkhäuser. S. 85-102.

Reichard, Christoph (1998b): Modernisierungsschub durch Experimentier- und Öffnungsklauseln. Unveröff. Ms.

Rembor, Ralph-Peter (1996): Überblick über vorhandene Experimentierklauseln. In: Hill, Hermann/Klages, Helmut (Hg.) (1996): Jenseits der Experimentierklausel. Düsseldorf. S. 219ff.

Richter, Walter (1998): Controlling im „Konzern" Stadt. In: Bandemer, Stephan von/Blanke, Bernhard/Nullmeier, Frank/Wever, Göttrik (Hg.) (1998): Handbuch zur Verwaltungsreform. Opladen: Leske + Budrich. S. 356-361.

Rist, Ray C. (Hg.) (1990): Program Evaluation and the Management of Government. New Brunswick/London.

Ritz, Adrian (1999): Die Evaluation von NPM. Bern.

Schröter, Eckhard/Wollmann, Hellmut (1998): New Public Management. In: Bandemer, Stephan von/Blanke, Bernhard/Nullmeier, Frank/Wewer, Göttrik (Hg.): Handbuch zur Verwaltungs-Reform. Opladen: Leske + Budrich. S. 59-69.

Scriven, Michael (1972): The Methodology of Evaluation. In: Weiss, C. H. (Hg.): Evaluating Action Programs. Boston. S. 123ff.

Stöbe, Sybille (1998): Output-Steuerung des Verwaltungshandelns. In: Bandemer, Stephan von/Blanke, Bernhard/ Nullmeier, Frank/Wever, Göttrik (Hg.): Handbuch zur Verwaltungsreform. Opladen: Leske + Budrich. S. 323-331.

Strobl, Heinz (1997): Erfahrungen mit der gemeindehaushaltsrechtlichen Experimentierklausel in Baden-Württemberg. In: Kommunalpraxis Baden-Württemberg. Nr. 2/97, S. 39ff.

Thieme, Werner/Prillwitz G. (1981): Durchführung und Ergebnisse der kommunalen Gebietsreform. Baden-Baden.

Thieme, Werner/von Oertzen, H. J. (Hg.) (1979/1987): Die kommunale Gebietsreform. Schriftenreihe (19 Bände). Baden-Baden.

Verba, Sidney (1996): Some Dilemmas of Comparative Research. In: World Politics, p. 111-132.

Wagner, Peter/Wollmann, Hellmut (1986): Fluctuations in the development of evaluation research: do ,regime shifts' matter? In: International Social Science Journal, No.108/1986, S. 205-218.

Wegener, Alexander (1998): Kommunale Verwaltungsrestrukturierung im internationalen Vergleich. In: Grunow, Dieter/Wollmann, Hellmut (Hg.): Lokale Verwaltungsreform in Aktion: Fortschritte und Fallstricke. Basel usw.: Birkhäuser. S. 337-353.

Wegrich, Kai/Jaedicke, Wolfgang/Lorenz, Sabine/Wollmann, Hellmut (1998): Kommunale Verwaltungspolitik in Ostdeutschland. Basel usw.: Birkhäuser.

Wollmann, Hellmut (1994): Evaluierungsansätze und -institutionen in Kommunalpolitik und -verwaltung. Stationen der Planungs- und Steuerungsdiskussion. In: Schulze-Böing, Matthias/Johrendt, Norbert (Hg.): Wirkungen kommunaler Beschäftigungsprogramme. Basel usw.: Birkhäuser. S. 79ff.

Wollmann, Hellmut/Derlien, Hans-Ulrich/König, Klaus/Renzsch, Wolfgang/Seibel, Wolfgang (Hg.) (1997): Transformation der politisch-administrativen Strukturen in Ostdeutschland. Opladen.

Wollmann, Hellmut (1999a): Modernisierung der Kommunalverwaltung in den neuen Bundesländern. Zwischen Worten und Taten. In: Landes- und Kommunalverwaltung, Beilage I/1999, S. 7-13.

Wollmann, Hellmut (1999b): Politik- und Verwaltungsmodernisierung in den Kommunen: Zwischen Managementlehre und Demokratiegebot. In: Die Verwaltung, Bd. 32/1999, H. 3, S. 345-375.

Wollmann, Hellmut (2000): Staat und Verwaltung in den 90er Jahren. Kontinuität oder Veränderungswelle? In: Czada, Roland/Wollmann, Hellmut (Hg.): Von der Bonner zur Berliner Republik. Leviathan Sonderheft 19/1999, S. 694-731.

Wollmann, Hellmut/Hellstern, Gerd-Michael (1977): Sozialwissenschaftliche Untersuchungsregeln und Wirkungsforschung. In: Haungs, Peter (Hg.): Res Publica. München. S. 415-466.

Helmut Kromrey

Qualität und Evaluation im System Hochschule

1. „Evaluation" – Begriff und Funktionen

Was ist Evaluation? Was ist ihr Nutzen? Wie soll man es machen? Fragen dieser Art sind für das System Hochschule nicht nur deshalb schwer zu beantworten, weil die zu evaluierenden „Gegenstände" so vielfältig, die mit Evaluation verfolgten Ziele so widersprüchlich und die für diesen Zweck eingesetzten Methoden und Verfahren nicht unstrittig sind. Schon der Begriff *Evaluation* selbst ist zu einem schillernden Allerweltswort geworden, mit dem je nach Kontext sehr Unterschiedliches verbunden wird. Sieht man einmal von der alltagssprachlichen Verwendung als „wohlklingendes" Fremdwort für jede Form von Bewertung[1] ab, so findet sich die am wenigsten spezifische Verwendung in der politischen Diskussion. Hier bedeutet Evaluation die *Überprüfung und Beurteilung eines Programms oder einer Einrichtung.* Speziell mit dieser Aufgabe betraute Experten formulieren auf der Basis von Informationen, die zu diesem Zwecke gesammelt wurden, ein Evaluationsgutachten. Dieses kann gravierende Konsequenzen für die Zukunft der überprüften Programme oder Einrichtungen haben bis hin zu deren Einstellung oder „Abwicklung".

Von *Evaluation* wird häufig aber auch im Kontext „ganz gewöhnlicher" Umfrageforschung gesprochen. Gemeint ist dann – in Analogie zur Meinungsforschung – die *Erhebung, Aufbereitung und Auswertung bewertender* (also evaluativer) *Aussagen.* In diesem Sinne ist die Fragebogenerhebung der Urteile von Vorlesungsteilnehmerinnen und -teilnehmern über die von ihnen besuchte Veranstaltung eine „Evaluation der Lehre", ist das Sammeln der Auffassungen von Professorinnen und Professoren über das Image verschiedener Universitäten eine „Evaluation der Hochschulen" und ist die Befragung von Personalverantwortlichen in Verwaltung, Wirtschaft und Verbänden über ihre Vorlieben bei der Einstellung akademisch ausgebildeter Mitarbeiter eine „Evaluation der Qualifikation der Absolventen".

In der Methodologie empirischer Sozialforschung schließlich bezeichnet Evaluation das *Design für einen spezifischen Forschungstyp,* durchgeführt im

---

1 „Alltagsevaluationen" können wie folgt charakterisiert werden: Irgendwer bewertet irgend etwas irgendwie unter irgend welchen Gesichtspunkten.

idealtypischen Fall als Feldexperiment mit Kontrollgruppen. Wo die Voraussetzungen dafür nicht in vollem Maße erfüllt sind – und das ist überwiegend der Fall – behilft man sich mit „Ersatzlösungen" für diejenigen Designkomponenten, die nicht idealtypisch realisiert werden können: So tritt etwa das „matching"-Verfahren zur Konstruktion strukturäquivalenter Experimental- und Kontrollgruppen an die Stelle der häufig nicht möglichen Zuordnung durch Randomisierung oder ersetzt die statistische Kontrolle von „Störgrößen" deren nicht realisierbare Abschirmung in der Erhebungssituation. Charakteristisch an solchen quasi-experimentellen Anordnungen ist, daß die generelle Orientierung an der Vorgehens- und Argumentationslogik des Experiments erhalten bleibt. Je nach Erkenntnis- und Verwertungsinteresse kann so verfahrende Evaluation unterschiedliche Schwerpunkte setzen: Sie kann sich als *Begleitforschung* auf den Implementationsprozeß eines Programms beziehen oder als *Wirkungsforschung* auf die späteren Konsequenzen; ihre Ergebnisse können *formativ* direkt in den Prozeß rückgekoppelt werden, oder sie können *summativ* im Nachhinein einen Gesamtüberblick vermitteln. Gemeinsam bleibt bei allen Ausdifferenzierungen des Vorgehens der unmittelbare Bezug zu einem *Programm* (einem Bündel von Maßnahmen zur Erreichung definierter Ziele). Die eigentliche *Evaluation* besteht hier nicht in der Formulierung normativ wertender Urteile, sondern in „technologischen" (Vergleichs-) Aussagen, etwa: Ist das Programm so implementiert worden wie geplant? Hat es die gesetzten Ziele erreicht? Welche Maßnahmen waren besonders effektiv, welche ineffektiv? Welche ungeplanten (erwünschten oder unerwünschten) Nebenwirkungen traten auf?

Die dargestellten Begriffsverwendungen schließen eine zusätzliche und manchmal Verwirrung stiftende Dimension des Begriffs ein: Als Evaluation wird einerseits ein bestimmtes *Tun oder Handeln* bezeichnet: das *Evaluieren*, andererseits aber auch das *Resultat dieses Tuns*: die formulierte bewertende Aussage, das *Evaluationsurteil*. Beides hängt untrennbar zusammen: Damit das *Evaluationsurteil* nicht rein subjektiv bleibt, sondern den Anspruch intersubjektiver Geltung erheben kann, muß das *Evaluieren* nach objektivierbaren Regeln geschehen, muß also einer nachprüfbaren Evaluationsmethodik folgen. So existieren beispielsweise relativ genaue Verfahrensvorschläge für die Gewinnung entscheidungsrelevanter Informationen und für das Erstellen von Evaluationsgutachten durch Sachverständige im Hochschulbereich (vgl. etwa Wissenschaftsrat 1996). Ähnliches gilt für das Evaluieren per Befragung: Zunächst liefert die Methodenlehre empirischer Sozialforschung die Kriterien für die Gestaltung des Prozesses der Datenerhebung; ergänzend formulieren Anhänger dieser Evaluationsstrategie einige Axiome, um von den erhobenen *subjektiven Werturteilen* der je einzelnen Befragten zu *intersubjektiven Evaluationen* zu gelangen.[2]

---

2 Für den Fall studentischer Lehrbewertungen wurden z.B. die folgenden – allerdings bestreitbaren – Axiome formuliert: (1) Urteile (Schätzungen) von Studenten über die

Eine andere Perspektive auf die Evaluation und ihre Methodik eröffnet sich durch die Frage, *zu welchem Zweck* evaluiert werden soll. Nach einem Vorschlag von Eleanor Chelimsky (1997: 100ff.) sind bei grober Einteilung drei *Funktionen von Evaluation* zu unterscheiden, denen methodisch drei „conceptual frameworks" entsprechen:

– Evaluation zur Verbreiterung der Wissensbasis (im folgenden als „Forschungsparadigma" der Evaluation bezeichnet),
– Evaluation zu Kontrollzwecken (im folgenden das „Kontrollparadigma") und
– Evaluation zu Entwicklungszwecken (im folgenden das „Entwicklungsparadigma").

Das „Forschungsparadigma" der Evaluation:

Insbesondere für Universitätswissenschaftler gelten Evaluationsprojekte als Chance, neben dem „eigentlichen" Evaluationszweck grundlagenwissenschaftliche Ziele zu verfolgen. Evaluation gilt in dieser Perspektive als angewandte Forschung, die sich mit der Wirksamkeit von sozialen Interventionen befaßt. Ihr kommt die Rolle eines Bindeglieds zwischen Theorie und Praxis zu (Weiss 1974: 11). Insbesondere staatliche Auftragsforschung eröffnet einen Weg, Zugang zu den internen Strukturen und Prozessen des politisch-administrativen Systems zu erhalten (Wollmann/Hellstern 1977: 456). Alle Anlässe, Aktionsprogramme zur Bewältigung sozialer Probleme zu implementieren, alle Situationskonstellationen, in denen durch neue gesetzliche Regelungen wichtige Randbedingungen geändert werden, alle Bemühungen, technische, organisatorische oder soziale Innovationen zu entwickeln, werfen zugleich sozialwissenschaftlich interessante Fragestellungen auf. Und im Unterschied zu forschungsproduzierten Daten zeichnen sich Untersuchungen unmittelbar im sozialen Feld durch einen ansonsten kaum erreichbaren Grad an externer Validität aus. *Evaluationsforschung* in diesem Sinne wird in erster Linie als Wirkungsforschung, die *Evaluation* selbst als wertneutrale technologische Aussage verstanden, die aus dem Vergleich von beobachteten Veränderungen mit den vom Programm angestrebten Effekten (den Programmzielen) besteht. Evaluatoren, die sich dem Forschungsparadigma ver-

---

Lehre sind verläßlicher als Urteile der Dozenten über die Leistung der Studenten und ebenso verläßlich wie Urteile von Kollegen über die Lehre. (2) Sie legen praktisch dieselben Kriterien für gute Lehre an wie die Dozenten selbst. (3) Sie sind – wenn man etwa 20-30 Studenten urteilen läßt – zuverlässig wie professionelle Testverfahren. (4) Sie sind von anderen Merkmalen der Studenten selbst und der Dozenten wenig beeinflußt (vgl. Schmidt 1980: 51-52). Bisher konnte nur die Geltung des zweiten Axiom belegt werden, wogegen sich die für die Qualität als intersubjektive Urteile entscheidenden Axiome 3 und 4 leider als empirisch falsch erwiesen haben (vgl. Kromrey 1994 und 1995b).

pflichtet fühlen, werden versuchen, wissenschaftlichen Gütekriterien so weit wie möglich Geltung zu verschaffen und Designs zu realisieren, die methodisch unstrittige Zurechnungen von Effekten zu Programm-Elementen durch Kontrolle der relevanten Randbedingungen erlauben.

Das „Kontrollparadigma" der Evaluation:

Im Unterschied zur Wirkungsforschung versteht sich der zweite Typus von Evaluation als Beitrag zur Planungsrationalität durch Erfolgskontrolle des Programmhandelns. Planung, verstanden als Instrument zielgerichteten Handelns, um einen definierten Zweck zu erreichen, muß sich bestimmten Erfolgskriterien (Effektivität, Effizienz, Akzeptanz) unterwerfen. Evaluationen dieser Art werden argumentativ vertreten als eine weitere Kontrollform administrativen Handelns neben Rechtmäßigkeits-Kontrolle (Gerichte), politischer Kontrolle (Parlamente) und Wirtschaftlichkeits-Kontrolle (Rechnungshöfe). Eine schon früh vorgeschlagene, charakteristische Definition lautet: „Der Begriff Erfolgskontrolle impliziert ex-post-Kontrolle von Ausführung und Auswirkung von zu einem früheren Zeitpunkt geplanten Maßnahmen, und Erfolgskontrolle ist immer zugleich Problemanalyse für den nächsten Planungszyklus" (Hübener/Halberstadt 1976: 15). In welcher Weise der Erfolg kontrolliert wird und an welchen Kriterien der Erfolg gemessen wird, ob die Evaluation ihren Schwerpunkt auf output oder outcome des Programms legt oder auf dessen Implementation, hängt ab vom Informationsbedarf der programmdurchführenden und/oder der finanzierenden Instanz.

Das „Entwicklungsparadigma" der Evaluation:

Grundsätzlich anders gelagert sind Problemstellung und Erkenntnisinteresse bei diesem dritten Typus von Evaluationen. Am Beginn steht *nicht* ein bereits realisiertes oder in der Implementationsphase befindliches oder zumindest ausformuliertes Programm; vielmehr geht es darum, Konzepte und Vorstellungen zu entwickeln, die Fähigkeit von Organisationen zur Problemwahrnehmung und -bewältigung zu stärken, beim Strukturieren von Politikfeldern beratend und unterstützend mitzuwirken. So verstandene Evaluation ist im wörtlichen Sinne „formativ", also programmbeeinflussend. Sie ist wesentlicher Bestandteil des Gestaltungsprozesses, in welchem ihr die Funktion der Qualitätsentwicklung und Qualitätssicherung zukommt. Gelegentlich wird diese Konstellation auch als „offene" Evaluation bezeichnet, im Unterschied zu den zuvor geschilderten „geschlossenen" Evaluationen, in denen Problem- und Fragestellungen, methodisches Vorgehen, Bewertungskriterien und die Zielgruppen der Evaluationsberichte von vornherein feststehen.

2. Evaluation im System Hochschule - wie und wozu?

Im Kontext der Qualitätsdiskussion im Bereich Hochschule schwingen – wenn Evaluationen eingefordert werden – fast immer die Erkenntnisinteressen aus allen drei „frameworks" gleichzeitig mit. Natürlich möchte man neues empirisch abgesichertes Wissen darüber gewinnen, wovon erfolgreiches Lehren und Studieren abhängt und wie der Erfolg gefördert (wenn schon nicht garantiert) werden kann – insofern ist das Forschungsparadigma gefragt. Natürlich sollen zugleich Effektivität und Effizienz der Verwendung der in den Hochschulbereich fließenden öffentlichen Mittel kontrolliert werden, sollen die Hochschulen Rechenschaft über ihr Tun ablegen – also ist auch das Kontrollparadigma angesprochen. Und ebenso natürlich soll Evaluation dabei helfen, geeignete Maßnahmen zur Verbesserung der Qualität von Lehre und Studium zu konzipieren, zu implementieren und zu testen – womit schließlich das Entwicklungsparadigma zu seinem Recht kommt.

Trotz solcher unrealistisch hoher Erwartungshaltung wird dann aber nicht selten zugleich in aller Naivität gefordert, Evaluation müsse sich schnell, einfach, mit geringem Kosten- und Arbeitsaufwand realisieren lassen – denn Personalressourcen und Geld sind in den Hochschulen bekanntermaßen außerordentlich knapp. Außerdem darf die Evaluation den laufenden Betrieb nicht „stören" – schließlich ist das eigentliche Ziel der Hochschule die Sicherstellung eines geregelten Angebots für ein ordnungsgemäßes Studium und nicht dessen Evaluation. Übersehen wird bei solchen Rufen nach simplen und belastungsfreien Verfahren in aller Regel die außerordentliche Komplexität des Gegenstands von Evaluationen im System Hochschule: Es existiert weder ein präzise beschreibbares „Programm" mit klar definierten Zielen und ihnen zugeordneten Maßnahmen sowie eindeutig festgelegten Zielerreichungskriterien[3] noch ein konkretes „Produkt", dessen Qualität mit einem Satz von Qualitätsindikatoren durch standardisierte Meßverfahren abgebildet werden kann[4] (dazu später mehr). Zudem muß die Evaluation unmittelbar im aktiven Feld durchgeführt werden und kann – anders als etwa bei politischen

---

3 Ein „Studiengang" zeichnet sich selbst im Falle extrem starker „Verregelung" durch rigide Prüfungs- und Studienordnungen dadurch aus, daß er nur als formaler Rahmen existiert, der in jedem Semester aufs neue empirisch interpretiert und „in die Welt gesetzt" werden muß: durch die jeweiligen Lehrangebote und Prüfungsthemen, durch das jeweilige Lehr-, Beratungs-, Betreuungs- und Prüfungsverhalten des Lehrpersonals, durch die jeweils zum Studieren bereitgestellte Infrastruktur des Instituts oder Fachbereichs und natürlich durch das jeweilige Lern- und Arbeitsverhalten der Studierenden.

4 Ein Produkt „Qualifizierung der Studierenden" ist zwar *allgemein* mit Hilfe von Leerformeln beschreibbar, aber nur *individuell* bei jedem einzelnen Studierenden zu konkretisieren und zudem auch noch in allererster Linie durch die Qualität und die Eigenschaften des „Rohmaterials" determiniert, nämlich durch die individuell eingebrachten Vorkenntnisse und Fertigkeiten sowie das individuelle Studierverhalten.

Pilotprojekten – nicht einen Teilbereich abgrenzen und (zumindest teilweise) von der Umwelt isolieren. Nicht zuletzt ist sie dabei mit zahlreichen Akteuren mit je unterschiedlichen Zielen und Vorstellungen konfrontiert, deren Handeln sämtlich über Erfolg und Mißerfolg des zu evaluierenden Programms wie auch der Evaluation selbst mitentscheidet.

Will Evaluation im System Hochschule dieser Komplexität gerecht werden, ist sie extrem zeit- und ressourcenaufwendig. Soll sie nicht lediglich Selbstzweck sein, sondern Veränderungen (Qualitätsverbesserungen) in Gang setzen, ist sie trotz des mit ihr verbundenen Aufwands bei allen Beteiligten auf *aktive Akzeptanz* – auf Mitwirkungsbereitschaft – angewiesen. Soll diese erwartbar sein, muß sich der Aufwand lohnen: Die Evaluation muß für die Beteiligten einen erkennbaren Nutzen bringen; andernfalls würde jeder von ihr angestossene Prozeß schnell wieder zum Stillstand kommen. Akzeptanz ist darüber hinaus aber auch eine wesentliche Voraussetzung dafür, daß Evaluation überhaupt gültige – und somit verwertbare – Ergebnisse liefern kann. Es ist daher vorab zu klären und für alle Beteiligten erkennbar zu machen, zu welchem Zweck evaluiert werden soll, was mit den zu erhebenden und auszuwertenden Daten geschehen soll. Evaluation darf nicht als „Evaluations-Ritual" erscheinen. Nicht selten geschieht allerdings genau dies: Es wird evaluiert, um eine an die Universität gestellte Forderung nach Evaluation zu erfüllen. Daß in einem solchen Fall möglichst wenig Aufwand getrieben wird und lediglich leicht zugängliche Informationen gesammelt werden, daß zudem vor allem „unproblematische" Daten präsentiert werden (etwa in Lehrberichten, die nicht zum Gegenstand fakultäts-/fachbereichs-interner Diskussion über Lehre und Studium werden), darf nicht verwundern.

Eine geringe Akzeptanz ist auch dann zu erwarten, wenn Evaluation lediglich als *Kontrollinstrument* verwendet werden soll, um – seien die zu Bewertenden nun Lehrpersonen oder ganze Fächer – die „Guten" von den „Schlechten" zu sondern und daran Sanktionen zu knüpfen. Sofern eine solche Evaluation nicht zu umgehen ist, haben die Evaluierten unendlich viele Möglichkeiten, kritische Informationen zu verschleiern und positive Informationen überdimensioniert in den Vordergrund zu rücken. Als Argument für die Verpflichtung zu regelmäßigen Kontrollen wird u.a. vorgetragen, Evaluation sei der Preis, den die Hochschule und ihre Angehörigen für größere Autonomie (etwa in Form von Globalhaushalten) zu zahlen habe. An die Stelle abnehmender staatlicher Kontrolle müsse zunehmende interne Kontrolle und öffentliche Berichterstattung über die effiziente Verwendung der zufließenden Steuermittel treten. Daxner kritisiert diese Tendenz als einen „Weg in die Rechtfertigungsgesellschaft" (1999: 41ff.). Der Wissenschaftsrat erkennt zwar durchaus ein „berechtigtes öffentliches Interesse" an Erhöhung der Transparenz, Rechenschaftslegung und Kontrolle an, sieht aber zugleich einen Zielkonflikt zum (ebenfalls öffentlichen) Interesse an „Qualitätsentwicklung und -sicherung im Lehrbetrieb" sowie der „Verbesserung von Organisationsformen und -strukturen" (Küchler 1996: 6-8); denn ein erfolgversprechendes Verfolgen des letztgenannten Ziels setzt „eine schonungslose Selbstkritik und Selbstanalyse der Fachbereiche" voraus: „Hier kann die öffentliche Dimension der Evaluation eher zu einer Verschleierung als zu einer Behebung bestehender Defizite führen" (a.a.O.: 7).[5]

Weniger strittig als die (öffentliche) Kontrollfunktion der Evaluation ist ihr Einsatz als *hochschulinternes Steuerungsinstrument*, zum Teil verknüpft mit „incentives" z.b. für gute Lehrorganisation und Forschungsleistungen. In manchen Bundesländern wird ein Teil der universitären Sachmittel „nach Leistungs- und Belastungskriterien" vergeben. Zu diesem Zweck ist – soll dies in der Universität routinemäßig und flächendeckend geschehen – ein Raster von möglichst wenigen Indikatoren zu entwickeln, die regelmäßig verfügbar sind und möglichst objektiviert Leistungen und Belastungen eines Fachs oder auch von kleineren Einheiten abbilden: etwa Zahl der Studienanfänger und Betreuungsrelation Studierende/Lehrende (als Belastungsindikatoren), Zahl der Zwischenprüfungen, Examensarbeiten, Studienabschlüsse, Studiendauer der Absolventen, Promotionen, Studienabbrüche etc. (als Leistungsindikatoren). Methodisch sind solche Verfahren nicht unstrittig: Indikatoren können immer nur einen Ausschnitt aus dem gesamten Problemfeld abbilden und auch dies immer nur mit zweifelhafter Gültigkeit. Des weiteren besteht – wenn an die Ausprägung der verwendeten Indikatoren die Verteilung von Mitteln geknüpft wird – die Möglichkeit (und damit die Gefahr), lediglich die durch Indikatoren abgebildeten Bereiche zu „optimieren" und anderes zu vernachlässigen; ganz abgesehen von der Möglichkeit der Umdefinition von Kriterien, um „bessere" Ergebnisse zu erzielen (mehr Studienabschlüsse in kürzerer Zeit kann man auch dadurch erreichen, daß man das Anspruchsniveau senkt). Indikatorensysteme – das ist aus den Erfahrungen der Sozialindikator-Bewegung bekannt – funktionieren nur so lange, wie sie lediglich zu Deskriptions- und Erklärungszwecken (allenfalls auch noch als prognostisches Frühwarnsystem) genutzt werden, so lange also an die Indikatorenwerte keine Sanktionen für diejenigen geknüpft werden, die die Ausprägungen durch ihr Handeln beeinflussen können.

Einen etwas anderen Zungenschlag erfährt die Diskussion um Evaluation als Steuerungsinstrument im Kontext der Forderung nach stärkerer *Wettbewerbsorientierung der Hochschulen*: „Auch ein Hochschulsystem, das staatlich globalgesteuert, aber zunehmend von Wettbewerb und Profilbildung gekennzeichnet ist, muß sich Marktgesetzlichkeiten stärker öffnen. Auch wenn sie

---

5   Konsequenterweise räumt der Wissenschaftsrat in diesem Zielkonflikt der Qualitätsentwicklung Priorität ein und empfiehlt ein Evaluationsverfahren in Eigenverantwortung der Hochschulen mit den Zielsetzungen: „Verbesserung der Transparenz in Studium und Lehre; Förderung der institutionellen Verantwortung der Fachbereiche für die Lehre; Herausbildung von Qualitätssicherungsstrategien in Studium und Lehre ..."; aber auch: „Verstärkung des Wettbewerbs im deutschen Hochschulsystem sowie der Profilbildung an Hochschulen und Fachbereichen nicht nur in der Forschung, sondern auch in der Lehre" (Küchler 1996: 9).

nicht auf Gewinnerzielung hin orientiert sind, müssen Hochschulen sich in
mancher Hinsicht wie Unternehmen verhalten lernen. Das heißt unter anderem,
bei der Planung und Ausgestaltung von Lehrangeboten rascher auf Nachfrageänderungen zu reagieren und auch Studierende als ‚Kunden' ernster zu nehmen" (Landfried 1999: 10). Evaluation schafft in diesem Zusammenhang „ein
Stück Markt-Ersatz, eine Art Quasi-Wettbewerb" (ders.: 11). Mit wem die
Hochschulen über das Medium Evaluation in welcher Form um welche knappen Ressourcen konkurrieren, bleibt allerdings ebenso unbeantwortet wie die
Frage, auf wessen Nachfrageänderungen – und dann in welcher Weise – rascher zu reagieren sei. Auch die „Kundenrolle" von Studierenden bleibt diffus.

An der Schnittstelle von Kontroll- und Wettbewerbsargumentation finden
wir die Vorstellung von *Evaluation als Instrument globaler Qualitäts-„Messung".* Wenn es gelänge, die Qualität der Leistungen der Institution Hochschule und ihrer Gliederungen umfassend, detailliert, gültig und zuverlässig zu
messen, dann stünde damit einerseits ein „objektives" Kontrollinstrument zur
Verfügung; andererseits existierte in Gestalt der Qualitätsmaße auch eine Art
„Währung", die für einen funktionierenden Wettbewerb (etwa um Reputation,
aber auch um öffentliche Finanzmittel, um Forschungsförderung, sogar um besonders leistungswillige Studierende) notwendig scheint. Die wiederholt unternommenen Versuche, „Rankings" von Hochschulen, Hochschulfächern bis hin
zu Lehrveranstaltungen zu erstellen, sind u.a. auch als Bemühung zu verstehen,
Transparenz auf einem solchen Wettbewerbsmarkt zu schaffen.[6]

Beziehen wir das Argument auf den Sektor Lehre und Studium, so gilt
zwar einigermaßen unbestritten als letztliches Kriterium für die Leistungs-
qualität der Hochschule der positive Effekt bei den Adressaten, also der
„Qualifizierungserfolg" bei den Studierenden. Doch ist hier die unerschüt-
terliche Annahme weit verbreitet, daß gute Servicequalität bereits eine weitgehende Gewähr für solchen Erfolg sei. Somit gehört es zu den ersten Aufgaben der Evaluation, die qualitätsrelevanten Dimensionen des Serviceange-
bots zu bestimmen und zu deren Beurteilung Qualitätsindikatoren zu begründen und zu operationalisieren. So wird die Evaluation gleich zu Beginn mit
einem zentralen theoretischen und methodologischen Problem konfrontiert:
der Unbestimmtheit des Begriffs „Qualität". Zwar kann an dieser Stelle nicht

---

6   „Vorreiter" der Hochschulrankings in Deutschland war der SPIEGEL mit einer 1989
     veröffentlichten ersten Rangreihe, der 1993 eine zweite folgte („Welche Uni ist die
     beste?"). „Gerankt" wurde im Hinblick auf „Service-Qualität"; Maßstab für die Qua-
     litätsaussagen waren studentische Urteile (also „Kundenzufriedenheit"). Mittlerweile
     erstellt das Zentrum für Hochschulentwicklung (CHE) gemeinsam mit der Stiftung
     Warentest „Studienführer", die neben den subjektiven Urteilen von Studierenden und
     Hochschullehrern auch „harte" Fakten aufbereiten (für eine Darstellung der SPIE-
     GEL-Rankings s. Hornbostel & Daniel (1995), zum Studienführer s. Hornbostel
     (1999); eine vergleichende Analyse von Hochschulrangreihen liefert Klostermeier
     (1994), kritisch Kreutz u.a. (1992).

im Detail hierauf eingegangen werden[7] – die Sozialwissenschaft befaßt sich im Rahmen der Sozialindikatorenbewegung seit Jahrzehnten damit; für das Gesundheitswesen hat Donabedian ein differenziertes und weit verbreitetes Qualitätskonzept entwickelt (ausführlich Donabedian 1980). Das Fazit jedenfalls ist, daß Qualität angesichts der Vieldimensionalität dieses Konstrukts und seiner unterschiedlichen Bedeutung in unterschiedlichen Kontexten und für unterschiedliche Zielgruppen nicht in einer Weise empirisch abbildbar ist, wie es das wissenschaftliche Konzept „Messen" verlangt.

Dennoch gilt gemeinhin als unbestrittenes Ziel von Evaluation, einen *Beitrag zur Verbesserung von Qualität* zu leisten, hier also: zur Qualität von Studium und Lehre. Kann Qualität schon nicht „gemessen" werden, so kann von der Empirie doch gefordert werden, diejenigen Informationen zur Verfügung zu stellen, die es erlauben, die Güte der zu evaluierenden Sachverhalte aus unterschiedlichen Perspektiven einzuschätzen. Für das Ziel Qualitätsentwicklung und/oder Qualitätssicherung ist allerdings allein mit dem Bereitstellen solcher Informationen durch die Evaluation noch nicht viel gewonnen – denn Qualität entwickelt sich nicht von selbst. Informationen sind allenfalls die notwendige (aber noch nicht hinreichende) Voraussetzung dafür, gezielte Veränderungen dort in Gang zu setzen, wo der evaluierte Sachverhalt verbesserungsbedürftig und verbesserungsfähig erscheint. Selbst wenn alle methodischen und organisatorischen Fragen der Evaluation geklärt sein sollten (s. dazu den folgenden Abschnitt), bleibt daher noch eine wesentliche Entscheidung zu treffen: Wer ist *Träger des Qualitätsentwicklungs-Vorhabens*? Nur in Ausnahmefällen wird dies auch der *Träger des Evaluationsvorhabens* sein (= „interne Evaluation"). Wo Qualitätsentwicklungs-Akteure und Evaluationsinstanz sich unterscheiden (= „externe Evaluation"), ist ein auf gegenseitigem Vertrauen basierendes Verhältnis beider Instanzen die Voraussetzung sowohl für gültige Evaluationsresultate (keine Unterdrückung „problematischer" Informationen, zuverlässige „Schwachstellen"-Analyse) wie für gelingende Umsetzung der Resultate in Maßnahmen zur Qualitätsentwicklung (Formulierung *konstruktiver* und *realisierbarer* Empfehlungen durch die Evaluation, Zusicherung der Vertraulichkeit erlangter interner Kenntnisse, Veröffentlichung nur im gegenseitigen Einvernehmen).[8]

---

7   Der Abschnitt 4 greift das Thema noch einmal auf.
8   Ein Beispiel für die Verknüpfung von Evaluation und Organisationsentwicklung hat kürzlich die Hamburger Hochschule für Wirtschaft und Politik (HWP) vorgestellt (Künzel/Nickel/Zechlin 1999).

3. Welches „Paradigma" der Evaluation ist das beste?

Gegen Schluß des Abschnitts 1 wurden drei „Paradigmen" für die Evaluation skizziert; und es stellt sich nach dem Abriß der Funktionen und Zwecke von Evaluationen im vorigen Abschnitt die Frage, ob eines der drei Paradigmen als besonders geeignet charakterisiert und daher als „Königsweg der Hochschulevaluation" empfohlen werden könnte. Bei diesen Überlegungen ist zu berücksichtigen, daß wir es bei dem zu evaluierenden Leistungsspektrum von Hochschulen nicht mit einem konkret faßbaren „Gegenstand" zu tun haben – anders als im Falle der Güterproduktion, wo sich Effizienz und Effektivität des Produktionsprozesses sowie die Qualität des Produkts (output) relativ leicht beurteilen und in standardisierter Form messen lassen. Hier geht es vielmehr um die Bereitstellung von Dienstleistungen, bzw. noch eingeschränkter: von Humandienstleistungen, die die aktive Mitwirkung der Klienten (hier: der Studierenden) voraussetzen, sollen sie einen „Erfolg" bewirken, also „Qualität" haben, effizient und effektiv sein. Was ist in diesem Fall das „Produkt"? Was ist der „Produktionsprozeß"? Ist es das Vorhalten einer Dienstleistungs-Infrastruktur (geregeltes Lehrangebot und die Informationen darüber in kommentierten Vorlesungsverzeichnissen, Personal für Beratungen und Prüfungen, PC-Räume und Bibliotheken) oder die einzelne Dienstleistung selbst (die Lehrveranstaltung, Prüfung, das Beratungsgespräch)? Oder interessiert nicht eher, was durch die vorgehaltene und realisierte Dienstleistung bewirkt wird (outcome anstelle von output)? Schließlich: Wenn es sich – wie hier – um eine Dienstleistung handelt, die auf die Akzeptanz und das aktive Mitwirken der Adressaten angewiesen ist: Wer oder was ist dann eigentlich zu evaluieren – der Anbieter, der Nachfrager oder beide? Und nicht zuletzt: Wer evaluiert wen?

Das „Entwicklungsparadigma" ist von seiner ganzen Konzeption her auf Innovationsprozesse zugeschnitten. Anzuwenden wäre es also für die Qualitätsentwicklung in einzelnen Lehrveranstaltungen (für Beispiele s. Knäuper/ Kroeger 1999; Peter/Wawrzinek 1995; Kromrey 1996) oder bei der Reform eines Curriculums oder bei Vorhaben der Organisationsentwicklung. Hierfür können offene Evaluationsansätze geeignete Konzepte bereitstellen, etwa das Konzept der responsiven Evaluation (Beywl 1991) oder das einer nutzenfokussierten Evaluation (Patton 1997; Beywl/Joas 2000). Solche Strategien sind jedoch nicht gemeint, wenn die regelmäßige und (in angemessenen Zeitabständen) flächendeckende Evaluation von Lehre und Studium eingefordert wird. Diese Forderung bezieht sich gerade nicht auf wissenschaftlich kontrollierte Innovationsprozesse, sondern auf den Regelbetrieb der Hochschule und ihrer Einrichtungen, u.a. auch um anhand der Ergebnisse einschätzen zu können, ob Reformmaßnahmen und Veränderungen notwendig erscheinen.

Das „Kontrollparadigma" in seiner evaluationsmethodisch ausgearbeiteten Form als Erfolgskontrolle (vgl. etwa Eekhoff/Muthmann/Sievert 1977) setzt klar formulierte und operationalisierbare Ziele und (im allgemeinen out-put-orientierte und quantifizierbare) Zielerreichungskriterien sowie ihre Zu-rechenbarkeit zum Handlungsvollzug der zu evaluierenden Einrichtung vor-aus. Die obigen Ausführungen dürften jedoch gezeigt haben, daß diese Vor-aussetzungen für das Handlungsfeld Humandienstleistungen im System Hochschule nicht gegeben sind. Der von der Politik gewählte Ausweg ist die Ersetzung von Erfolgskontrolle durch ein formalisiertes Berichtswesen: Fast alle Bundesländer verlangen mittlerweile die regelmäßige Erstellung von Lehrberichten in Ergänzung der schon länger üblichen Forschungsberichte.[9] Solche Lehrberichte sind zwar eine Sammlung beschreibender Informatio-nen, die das System Hochschule transparenter und somit auch für Außenste-hende einschätzbarer (also „evaluierbarer") machen, sind aber selbst keine Evaluationen.[10]

Noch anspruchsvoller in den Voraussetzungen für seine Anwendbarkeit ist das „*Forschungsparadigma*", sofern es nach dem Standardmodell der Programmforschung unter Rückgriff auf quasi-experimentelle Designs (s.o., Abschnitt 1) verfahren soll. Dass dieses Modell in der Hochschule flächen-deckend nicht eingesetzt werden kann, ist offensichtlich. Die Universität kann – sowohl aus grundsätzlichen wie aus pragmatischen Gründen – nicht zum Experimentallabor umfunktioniert werden, nur um dadurch evaluierbar zu sein.[11] Aber auch aus weiteren methodologischen Gründen eignet sich die-se Form der Evaluierung nicht.

So könnte beispielsweise das zu bewertende *Programm* des *Diplomstu-diengangs eines Fachs* sein. Als Ziele kämen die an die Studierenden zu vermittelnden Qualifikationen, als Maßnahmen Studienordnung, Studienver-laufspläne, Lehrveranstaltungen, Studieninfrastruktur sowie Betreuung und Beratung durch das Lehrpersonal, außerdem Prüfungsordnung, Prüfungen und andere Leistungskontrollen in Betracht. Für die Messung der Zielerrei-

---

9 Einen Auflistung gesetzlicher Grundlagen zu Evaluation und Lehrberichterstattung fin-det sich bei el Hage (1996: 27ff.). Die Dokumentation gibt auch einen instruktiven Über-blick über staatlich initiierte und/oder geförderte Projekte zur Lehrevaluation seit den 1990er Jahren (S.13ff.), informiert über Methodenfragen und Instrumentenentwicklung und stellt einige der verwendeten Instrumente studentischer Veranstaltungskritik vor.

10 Obwohl durch Landesgesetze vorgeschrieben und ihrem Wesen nach nicht Evaluati-on, sondern Dokumentation, können Lehrberichte dennoch über ihre öffentliche Transparenzschaffungsfunktion hinaus auch hochschulintern von Nutzen sein, als „In-strument des Controlling" und als „Mittel einer von der Hochschule selbst gesteuerten Studienreformarbeit" (Habel 1995: 12); und sie können natürlich auch Evaluationen *enthalten*: Selbstbeurteilungen der Fachbereiche und Institute, Ergebnisse studenti-scher Befragungen. Als „Handreichung für die Praxis" finden sich bei Habel (a.a.O.: 14ff.) Leitfäden für Interviews und Informationserhebungen für Lehrberichte.

11 Allenfalls Lehrexperimente *neben* dem laufenden Lehrbetrieb könnten in dieser Weise evaluiert werden; hier wären z.B. für die Vermittlung des herkömmlichen Stoffs Dop-pelangebote bei Realisierung unterschiedlicher Lernsettings denkbar.

chung böte sich der Zeitpunkt der Beendigung des Studiums (Diplomprüfung oder Studienabbruch) bei den einzelnen Studierenden an.

Ein erstes Bündel von Problemen ergäbe sich hier bereits bei der empirischen Beschreibung der für die Studierenden bis zum Examen relevant gewordenen Maßnahmen. Studienordnung, Studienverlaufspläne und Prüfungsordnung wären für alle im Verlaufe ihres Studiums konstant und somit (im Hinblick auf *Unterschiede* in den erworbenen Qualifikationen) ohne Wirkung. Lehrveranstaltungen dagegen – mit Ausnahme einiger standardisierter Vorlesungen und Übungen insbesondere im Grundstudium – sind auch von ihren Inhalten häufig so stark variierend, daß zusätzlich zu den im Prinzip statistisch kontrollierbaren Unterschieden der studentischen Veranstaltungsauswahl (feststellbar etwa durch Auswertung der Studienbücher) eine zusätzliche Variation in nicht kontrollierbarem Ausmaß hinzukäme. Beratung, Betreuung und Prüfungen schließlich ergeben sich in Interaktionen zwischen einzelnen Studierenden und einzelnen Mitgliedern des Lehrpersonals und wären bei Studienabschluß überhaupt nicht mehr rekonstruierbar.

Als ähnlich problematisch erwiese sich die Erfolgsmessung. Die im Studium zu vermittelnden Qualifikationen sind üblicherweise in den Studiengangsdokumenten (Studien- und Prüfungsordnung) nur sehr vage – falls überhaupt – definiert. Ersatzweise kämen die in Klausuren und Prüfungen erbrachten Leistungen der Absolventen (gemessen in den erzielten Noten) in Betracht. Diese wären allerdings keine direkten Maße der Qualifikationen, sondern lediglich Indikatoren für eine Teilmenge von ihnen. Erfolge/Mißerfolge auf anderen Dimensionen blieben unerkannt. Außerdem wäre zu fragen, wie es um die Gültigkeit dieser Indikatoren bestellt wäre, wenn die Träger des zu evaluierenden Programms die Indikatorausprägungen selbst festlegten (nämlich in Prüfungen und Klausurbenotungen).

Ganz unmöglich schließlich wäre die Zurechnung der Beiträge einzelner Maßnahmen zum festgestellten Studienerfolg der jeweiligen Absolventen. In welcher Weise das Studium verläuft sowie ob und in welchem Ausmaß es erfolgreich abgeschlossen wird, hängt nach allen vorliegenden empirischen Erkenntnissen aus der Bildungsforschung in hohem Maße von Merkmalen in der Individualsphäre der Studierenden ab: wie Lebenssituation, Interesse und Leistungsmotivation, Studienstil und -intensität. Die von den Trägern des Studiengangs beeinflußbaren Gegebenheiten – Studieninfrastruktur, Lehre und Betreuung – können lediglich (wenn sie von schlechter Qualität sind) das Studium erschweren oder (bei guter Qualität) erleichtern; den individuellen Erfolg *bewirken* können sie nicht. Um also den relativen (fördernden oder hemmenden) Beitrag der angebotenen Maßnahmen zum Studienerfolg abschätzen zu können, müßte zunächst der individuelle Eigenbeitrag des jeweiligen Studierenden bekannt sein – eine, wie leicht einsehbar, völlig unrealistische Anforderung, deren Nichterfüllbarkeit in diesem Bereich jede Evaluation im Sinne von Zielerreichungskontrolle prinzipiell unmöglich macht.

4. Der Ausweg: Evaluation durch Umfrageforschung

Wenn Evaluation nach dem Modell der Programmforschung nicht möglich ist, liegt es nahe, das Fällen von Urteilen – also die *Tätigkeit des Evaluierens* – auf dafür geeignet erscheinende Dritte zu verlagern (auf Experten, auf Kunden, auf Betroffene) und die Funktion der Forschung auf das systematische Einholen und Auswerten solcher „Fremd-Evaluationen" zu beschränken. Dies wird in der Tat überall dort so gehandhabt, wo Lehrevaluation betrieben wird.

In besonders systematischer, formalisierter und nachprüfbarer Form geschieht dies in dem *Verfahren der zweistufigen (internen und externen) Evaluation,* wie es im Verbund Norddeutscher Universitäten und von der Zentralen Evaluationsagentur (ZEvA) in Niedersachsen angewendet wird und das auf Empfehlungen der Hochschulrektorenkonferenz (1995) und des Wissenschaftsrates (1996) beruht. Die so durchgeführte Evaluation erfaßt als Gegenstand die Organisation und Durchführung der Lehre und des Studiums innerhalb einer Hochschuleinheit (Fakultät/Fachbereich oder Institut) und hat explizit nicht die Bewertung einzelner Lehrveranstaltungen zum Ziel. Die Hauptelemente des Verfahrens sind (s. HRK 1998a):

– Der Lehrbericht eines Fachbereichs/einer Fakultät als kontinuierliche Sammlung von Basisdaten und Leistungsindikatoren.
– Die interne Evaluation (...), die von einer internen Arbeitsgruppe vorbereitet wird und auf der Analyse der in den Lehrberichten erfaßten Daten und auf Interviews mit Studenten und Personal basiert. Sie führt zu einem kritisch-abwägenden Bericht über die Selbsteinschätzung der erreichten Resultate im Hinblick auf die selbstgesteckten Ziele; sie enthält eine Beschreibung möglicher Hindernisse und Defizite sowie von Maßnahmen zu ihrer Beseitigung, Vorschläge für die Kontrolle und Verbesserung der Qualität der Lehre und die Verteilung von Mitteln für Forschung und Lehre. (...)
– Der Vor-Ort-Besuch der Sachverständigen (Peers), der von der betreffenden Agentur vorbereitet wird, welche die Selbstbewertungsberichte an die Mitglieder der Peer-Group weiterleitet und, falls nötig, den zu evaluierenden Fachbereich um weitere Informationen bittet. Der in der Regel zweitägige Vor-Ort-Besuch schließt Gespräche mit der Universitätsleitung, dem Dekan und den Lehrenden und Studierenden ein, (...).
– Der Evaluations-Bericht der Peers schließt eine kritische Würdigung der internen Evaluation und ihrer tatsächlichen Bedeutung als Mittel der Qualitätssicherung ein, weist auf Probleme hin und gibt Hinweise auf mögliche Lösungen. Vor der Veröffentlichung des Abschlussberichts erhält der evaluierte Fachbereich Gelegenheit, den vorläufigen Bericht zu bearbeiten, um Irrtümer und Mißverständnisse zu korrigieren. Dies findet

im Rahmen einer gemeinsamen Sitzung statt, an der die Mitglieder der Sachverständigengruppe (Peer-Group), Vertreter der evaluierten Einrichtung und der Evaluationsagentur teilnehmen. (...)
– Das „follow up" umfaßt eine Vereinbarung bzw. einen Vertrag zwischen dem Fachbereich und der Universitätsleitung über zu ergreifende Maßnahmen zur Verbesserung von Lehre und Studium, zur Optimierung der Ergebnisse bzw. zur Sicherstellung bestimmter zu erreichender Standards innerhalb eines definierten Zeitraums. (...)" (a.a.O.: 11f.)[12].

Die Evaluierung geschieht in diesem Modell – wie ersichtlich – nicht *durch* die Umfrageforschung, wohl aber (unter anderem) *mit* Umfragen, und wird ergänzt um andere Erhebungen sowie um Daten aus der Hochschulstatistik und um Beobachtung und Diskussion. Für die Evaluation dieses Typs erfüllt die empirische Forschung und deren Methodik nicht die Funktion einer Instanz der Qualitätsentscheidung mittels „objektiver" Daten. Vielmehr finden wir hier ein Beispiel für das Prinzip der „Objektivierung durch Verfahren". Die Sicherung der Intersubjektivität der Ergebnisse wird durch ein darauf zugeschnittenes Verfahrensmodell angestrebt: Die Einbeziehung aller Beteiligten und Betroffenen in den Prozeß soll gewährleisten, daß das für den Zweck der Evaluation relevante Informationsspektrum erfaßt wird. Die Gültigkeit der Ergebnisse, wie sie der Evaluationsbericht dokumentiert, wird durch die Möglichkeit zur Korrektur sowie durch eine gemeinsame Abschlussdiskussion zwischen Evaluatoren und Evaluierten angestrebt (kommunikative Validierung). Damit die Evaluation nicht ins Leere läuft, sondern Anstöße zu Qualitätsverbesserungen gibt, mündet das Verfahren in konkrete Zielvereinbarungen (Festlegung nachprüfbarer Maßnahmen mit expliziten Terminen für die Realisierung). Und um es nicht bei einem einmaligen Anstoß bewenden zu lassen, sondern einen Prozeß kontinuierlicher Qualitätsverbesserung in Gang zu setzen, sind schließlich in regelmäßigen Abständen (von mehreren Jahren) „follow ups" vorgesehen.[13]

---

12 Im selben Heft findet sich auf S. 15f. ein Muster zur Gliederung des Lehrberichts sowie auf S. 17f. ein Vorschlag für eine Gliederung des Evaluationsberichts). „Crucial Points" des Verfahrens diskutiert Bülow-Schramm (1995).

13 Die Realisierung dieses Modells im „Verbund norddeutscher Hochschulen" wird ausführlich dargestellt und diskutiert von Fischer-Bluhm (1995) und Schierholz/Vocke (1997). – Im Auftrag der Bund-Länder-Kommission für Bildungsplanung und Forschungsförderung führt die Hochschulrektorenkonferenz seit 1998 ein „Projekt Qualitätssicherung" durch, das u.a. den Auftrag hat, die Weiterentwicklung von Standards der Evaluation zu unterstützen und auf gemeinsame Standards hinzuwirken, Informationen für Hochschulen bereitzustellen sowie zwischen Hochschulen und Öffentlichkeit zu transportieren. Eines der Instrumente ist die Unterstützung und Durchführung von Tagungen und Workshops an verschiedenen Hochschulstandorten sowie die Veröffentlichung der Tagungsbände in der Reihe „Beiträge zur Hochschulpolitik" (s. Schreier 1998). Auf einem „Nationalen Expertenseminar" wurde am 29.5.1998 ein umfassender Überblick über den Stand der Evaluation in Deutschland gegeben (HRK 1998b).

Es ist leicht nachvollziehbar, daß ein solches Evaluations- und Qualitätssicherungsmodell mit einem hohen Aufwand an Kosten, Zeit und Personal verbunden ist.

Wesentlich weniger anspruchsvoll – sowohl hinsichtlich des Verfahrens als auch hinsichtlich des Bemühens um Objektivierung – ist demgegenüber die weit verbreitete Strategie, die Lehrevaluation allein auf die *Befragung Studierender* zu stützen. Dem liegt offenbar die Gleichsetzung von Betroffen-Sein mit Expertentum zugrunde. Für die Beurteilung der Qualität der Lehre etwa läßt sich die folgende einfache (und auf den ersten Blick auch durchaus plausibel erscheinende) Argumentation rekonstruieren: „Ein aufwendiges Verfahren der Qualitätsbeurteilung durch Evaluations*forschung* ist entbehrlich. Mit den Studierenden verfügt die Hochschule bereits über *die* Experten, die die Lehre aus erster Hand – als tagtäglich von ihr Betroffene – fundiert und zuverlässig beurteilen können. Deren Wahrnehmungen und Bewertungen brauchen nur in standardisierter Form erhoben und pro Lehrveranstaltung in geeigneter Form ausgewertet zu werden, um aussagekräftige Qualitätsindikatoren zu erhalten" (s. oben). Manche Lehrende gehen noch einen Schritt weiter und vertreten unter Verweis auf „jahrzehntelang bewährte Praxis in den USA"[14] die Auffassung, hierzu werde nicht einmal ein detailliertes Instrumentarium benötigt. Vielmehr reichten kurze und damit schnell ausfüllbare Fragebögen aus, in denen von den Studierenden auf wenigen zentralen Dimensionen (typischerweise Didaktik, Angemessenheit von Stoffmenge und Schwierigkeitsgrad, Auftreten der Lehrperson und soziales Klima, Lernerfolgseinschätzung) zusammenfassende Bewertungen erbeten werden. Studierende seien durchaus kompetent, solche Urteile zu fällen, wird – vermeintlich studentenfreundlich – argumentiert. Damit erübrigten sich zugleich auch aufwendige Auswertungsverfahren; Auszählungen und Durchschnittsberechnungen seien hinreichend. Ein Beispiel für diesen Typ von „Einfach-Evaluation" ist das an der Freien Universität Berlin in regelmäßigen Abständen eingesetzte „FU-Studienbarometer", das für die standardisierte Beurteilung eines ganzen Studiengangs mit einer einzigen Fragebogenseite auskommt (s. Kromrey 1999: 62ff.).

In dieser Form eingesetzt, sind mit einer Strategie der Erhebung studentischer Wahrnehmungen und Bewertungen *als* Evaluation von Studium und Lehre allerdings gleich mehrere *Fehlschlüsse* verbunden.

Im Unterschied zur Expertenevaluation anhand vorgegebener Kriterien und auf der Basis systematisch ausgewerteter Informationen mit anschließender kommunikativer Validierung (wie beim Verfahren der peer-Evaluation)

---

14 Übersehen wird dabei, daß mit Studierendenbefragungen in US-Universitäten bewußt Akzeptanzmessung betrieben wird (schließlich sind die Studierenden „Kunden" der Universität, nämlich Abnehmer einer Dienstleistung, die durch zum Teil hohe Studiengebühren die Institution mitfinanzieren). Für die Evaluation der Lehrenden durch die Hochschule ist allerdings die per Befragung ermittelte Akzeptanz nur *ein* Baustein in einem detaillierteren Bewertungsverfahren.

sind die befragten Studierenden „Alltags-Evaluatoren" (vgl. Fußnote 1): Jeder einzelne von ihnen bewertet *irgend etwas* (was er mit dem in der Frage
angesprochenen Sachverhalt ad hoc assoziiert) *irgendwie* („alles in allem"
oder „aus aktueller Erfahrung" oder „mit Blick auf das Wesentliche" oder ...)
unter irgendwelchen Gesichtspunkten (Nutzen für sein Studium oder vermu-
teter Nutzen für den angestrebten Beruf oder aktuelles persönliches Interesse
oder abstrakt-verallgemeinertes Interesse *der* Studierenden oder ...). Die Bedeutung der im standardisierten Erhebungsbogen gegebenen Antworten ist so
nicht mehr rekonstruierbar.

Werden *Globalaussagen* verglichen mit *differenziert erhobenen Beurteilungen* (unter Verwendung von Itemlisten, mit denen vor der Erhebung zu-
sammenfassender Urteile zunächst Detail-Aspekte eingeschätzt werden), so
zeigt sich, daß unter den Studierenden – grob zusammengefaßt – zwei geradezu gegensätzliche Evaluierungsweisen existieren. Nahezu die Hälfte der
Veranstaltungsteilnehmer urteilt so pauschal, daß in der Tat die Verwendung
einfacher und kurzer Erhebungsinstrumente angemessen wäre: Die Tendenz
der Einschätzungen auf *allen* Detail-Items einer Dimension stimmt überein
mit dem zusammenfassenden Gesamturteil, d.h.: Man ist entweder in jeder
Hinsicht zufrieden oder in jeder Hinsicht unzufrieden oder empfindet das
Angebot durchweg als mittelmäßig. Die andere Hälfte der Befragten urteilt in
den Details differenziert (man ist mit dem einen Teilaspekt zufrieden, mit
dem anderen weniger, mit dem dritten unzufrieden) und bildet dann für die
Gesamtbewertung der Dimension einen subjektiven Mittelwert. Bei diesem
Teil der Studierenden gingen bei Verwendung kurzer „Alles-in-allem"-
Fragebögen nicht nur wesentliche Informationen verloren, vielmehr würde
dadurch auch der unzutreffende Eindruck einer einfachen, in sich wider-
spruchslosen Urteilsstruktur erweckt – methodologisch ausgedrückt: Es würde ein *Erhebungsartefakt* produziert.

Ähnlich problematisch ist die Empfehlung „einfacher Auswertungen",
insbesondere in Form isolierter Auszählungen der Antworten auf die einzelnen Fragen und/oder durch Berechnung von Mittelwerten. Auch hier zeigt
die komplexe Analyse differenziert erhobener studentischer Bewertungen die
Unangemessenheit solchen Vorgehens: Zum einen werden von den Befragten
die Einschätzungen hinsichtlich der verschiedenen Dimensionen und Teildi-
mensionen des Evaluationsgegenstands (z.B. Lehrveranstaltung oder Lehrperson) nicht unabhängig voneinander vorgenommen, sondern sie stehen –
selbstverständlich – in einem subjektiv sinnvollen Zusammenhang. Daraus
folgt, daß sich die Einzelurteile jedes Befragten zu einem für seine Wahrnehmung *typischen Urteilsprofil* verbinden und dadurch sozusagen „Gestalt
annehmen". Die isolierte Auszählung einzelner Variablen aber läßt solche
Profile gar nicht erst sichtbar werden. Zum anderen sind sich die Teilnehmer
ein und derselben zu evaluierenden Veranstaltung – eigentlich ebenfalls
selbstverständlich – in ihren Beurteilungen nicht einig. Das liegt nicht nur
daran, daß ihnen für ihre „Alltags-Evaluationen" keine intersubjektiven Ver-

gleichsstandards vorgegeben wurden, sondern insbesondere auch daran, daß es sich bei den Befragten nicht um austauschbare Exemplare *der* Gattung Studierende handelt, sondern um Individuen: mit unterschiedlichen Sozialisationserfahrungen und von daher unterschiedlichen Vorkenntnissen, Interessen und Lernstilen, mit unterschiedlichen Präferenzen und Sympathien/Antipathien für die Lehrperson, mit unterschiedlichen Standorten in ihrem Studiengang, mit unterschiedlicher Einschätzung der Brauchbarkeit ihres Studiums und des zu Lernenden für das Leben außerhalb der Hochschule usw.. Das heißt: Die Gesichtspunkte, unter denen beurteilt wird, sind sehr verschiedenartig; sie *müssen* demgemäß – wenn der Fragebogen ernsthaft und kompetent ausgefüllt wird – zu unterschiedlichen Urteilen führen. Die Berechnung von Mittelwerten, die die studentischen Individualurteile zu Qualitätskennziffern *der* Teilnehmer kondensieren, produziert *Auswertungsartefakte*.

Für Evaluationen durch Befragung führt das zu dem Fazit: Ein komplexer Sachverhalt kann angemessen auch nur durch hinreichend komplexe empirische Erhebungen valide abgebildet werden; und komplexe Interdependenzen im abzubildenden Sachverhalt werden erst durch hinreichend komplexe Analyseverfahren sichtbar. Der Verweis auf die o.g. Gefahren von Fehlschlüssen sollte allerdings nicht als Argument gegen die Verwendung von „Alltagsevaluationen" Betroffener mißverstanden werden. Sie liefern wichtige Informationen darüber, wie das „Dienstleistungsangebot Lehre" bei den Adressaten „ankommt". Um diese aber als gültige Informationen nutzen zu können, ist zuvor im Zuge der Analyse das Kriteriensystem der Evaluierenden zu rekonstruieren. In methodisch angemessener Form kann die Befragung von studentischen Veranstaltungsteilnehmern als wertvolles Informationsinstrument zur Entwicklung von Lehrqualität genutzt werden.

5. Andere Formen des Einsatzes von Befragungen und Erhebungen

Weitere für die Qualitätsentwicklung nutzbare Formen der Umfrageforschung in der Hochschule sind in Lehrveranstaltungen eingesetzte und von Didaktikern schon seit langem empfohlene (kürzere oder längere) Fragebögen als Instrument der *Rückmeldung an die Lehrperson*. Sie dienen nicht der Evaluation, sondern der *Kommunikation* über Lehre und sind vor allem in größeren Veranstaltungen hilfreich, in denen eine direkte Interaktion zwischen Lehrenden und Lernenden nicht mehr ohne weiteres möglich ist. Im Unterschied zu Befragungen *als* Evaluationsverfahren sind der Differenzierungsgrad und die methodische Qualität der Fragebögen ebenso wie die Form der Erhebung zweitrangig. Die Ergebnisse sollen der Lehrperson einen Eindruck von der Sichtweise der Teilnehmer vermitteln, *und* sie sollen der Ausgangspunkt für die Diskussion zwischen Lehrenden und Studierenden über die Lehre sein. Für diesen Zweck sind kurze Fragebögen mit durchaus auch groben Kategorien und zusammenfassend vorzunehmenden Bewertungen sogar von Vorteil: Sie bieten mehr Raum für die Interpretationsphantasie und damit auch mehr Ansatzpunkte für eine engagierte Diskussion.

Gegenstand der Befragung und Bewertung müssen nicht in jedem Fall Lehrveranstaltungen sein. Sinnvolle Fragestellungen können sich richten auf das Curriculum und die übergreifende *Studiensituation* im Fach (Institut, Fakultät/Fachbereich): Wie nehmen die Studierenden die durch Studien- und Prüfungsordnung vorgenommene Definition des Fachs wahr? Wie einleuchtend sind ihnen Struktur und Inhalte des Lehrangebots? Wird der Zusammenhang zwischen Lehre und Prüfungen als hinreichend erkannt? Wie wird die Betreuung empfunden? und vieles mehr. Ebenso sind aktuelle *Kenntnisse über die Studierenden* und ihre Art und Weise des Studierens für die Träger des Curriculums von Bedeutung: Unter welchen persönlichen Bedingungen und wie intensiv wird studiert (etwa Berufstätigkeit neben dem Studium, Anzahl der besuchten Veranstaltungen, zeitlicher Aufwand für das Studium)? Welche inhaltlichen Schwerpunkte setzen die Studierenden dort, wo sie Wahlmöglichkeiten haben? Welche Studierstile sind im Grund-, welche im Hauptstudium anzutreffen? Wie ist das Informationsverhalten der Studierenden? usw. In diesem Zusammenhang kann auch eine Vollerhebung der *Teilnehmerstruktur* in allen Veranstaltungen eines Semesters wichtige Informationen liefern: nicht nur darüber, ob und in welchem Maße eine Veranstaltung ihre definierte Zielgruppe tatsächlich erreicht, sondern auch darüber, ob und in welchem Ausmaß das Fach mit seinen Angeboten Dienstleistungen für andere Fächer liefert (für Nebenfächler, aber auch durch Teilnehmer anderer Fächer, die lediglich spezielle Angebote wahrnehmen und dort erbrachte Leistungen im eigenen Fach anerkennen lassen).

Befragungen müssen sich nicht lediglich an einen Querschnitt der aktuell Studierenden richten. Auch *spezifischere Auswahlen* können nützlich sein: Studienanfänger, Studierende im Grundstudium vor der Zwischenprüfung, Studierende bei Beginn des Hauptstudiums, in der Examensphase. Darüber hinaus werden zunehmend *Absolventenbefragungen* durchgeführt, entweder zur ex-post-Evaluation des Studiums aus der späteren Perspektive von Berufstätigen und/oder als Verbleibstudien ehemaliger Studierender. Schließlich kommen auch „*Abnehmer*"-*Befragungen* vor, insbesondere mit dem Ziel, in potentiellen Berufsfeldern Profile von Anforderungen an das Qualifikationsprofil der Bewerber zu ermitteln. Nicht zuletzt – wenn auch (warum eigentlich?) ganz selten durchgeführt – könnten (und sollten) auch *die Lehrenden* eine Zielgruppe von Erhebungen sein. Eine Konfrontation der Wahrnehmung von Lehre und Lehrpersonen aus der Perspektive der Studierenden mit der Wahrnehmung der Studierenden und ihres Studienengagements durch die Lehrenden dürfte interessante Ergebnisse bringen.

6. Zu guter Letzt: Qualitätsentwicklung ohne Qualitätsbegriff?

Bei aller Unterschiedlichkeit der Argumente der Befürworter von Evaluationen scheint über ein Ziel ihres Einsatzes Einmütigkeit zu herrschen: Sie werden durchgeführt, um die Qualität von Lehre und Studium zu verbessern, um aus den Evaluationsresultaten Hinweise zu gewinnen, *wo* etwas verbesserungsbedürftig ist und *wie* es verbessert werden kann. Wird dieses Ziel akzeptiert, unterstreicht es noch einmal die Notwendigkeit einer *differenzierten* Herangehensweise an das Evaluationsvorhaben: Pauschale Bewertungen und leerformelhafte Aussagen mögen zwar ein geeigneter Ansatzpunkt für das Formulieren von Hypothesen und für das Ingangsetzen von Diskussionen sein; für das Erkennen *konkreten* Veränderungsbedarfs und für die Ableitung *konkreter* Maßnahmen sind sie jedoch keine zuverlässige Basis. Ist man sich auch darüber einig, bleibt aber dennoch eine weitere, ganz zentrale Frage unbeantwortet: Was *ist* eigentlich Qualität von Lehre und Studium?

Zunächst: Eine *Qualität „alles in allem"* existiert nicht. Ein Sachverhalt kann zugleich in einer Hinsicht von ausgezeichneter Qualität, in anderer Hinsicht dagegen fehlerhaft sein. Es sind also verschiedene Aspekte *oder „Dimensionen"* von Qualität – in der Fachdiskussion des Qualitätsmanagements *„Kriterien"* genannt – zu unterscheiden. Zum anderen: Qualitätsaussagen sind Werturteile. Sollen sie intersubjektiv gefällt werden, sind Vergleichsmaßstäbe – Fachausdruck: *„Standards"* – notwendig. Mit der Festlegung, aus wessen Perspektive Kriterien und Standards ausgewählt und formuliert werden, ist dann bereits eine wesentliche Vorentscheidung getroffen. Soll nun die Qualität des Sachverhalts „gemessen" werden – was als Erwartung des öfteren an Evaluationsvorhaben herangetragen wird –, ist das Qualitätskonzept präzise zu definieren und sind die anzulegenden Kriterien und Standards durch geeignete, gültige Indikatoren zu operationalisieren.

Um es an einem einfachen Beispiel zu veranschaulichen: Zu beurteilen sei die Qualität von Autoreifen. Als *Qualitätskriterien* kämen wesentliche Eigenschaften des Objekts selbst in Frage. *Ein* Qualitätskriterium wäre etwa die Haltbarkeit des Produkts, gemessen an der Laufleistung in Kilometern; ein bei der Beurteilung anzulegender *Standard* könnte lauten: mindestens 30.000 km auf glatten Straßen. Andere Kriterien könnten sein: die Bodenhaftung (auf trockener sowie auf nasser Straße), die Sicherheit (bei Überbeanspruchung sowie bei Außeneinwirkung) u.ä. Auch dazu sind meßbare Standards und zuverlässig durchführbare Qualitätstests relativ leicht definierbar.

Nun ist aber – wie oben bereits ausgeführt – die Lehre kein Sachverhalt, dessen Merkmale als Eigenschaften des „Objekts" direkt ablesbar und in diesem Sinne „objektiv" meßbar wären. Vielmehr ist sie eine *Dienstleistung*, deren Produkt sich erst in der Interaktion von Lehrenden und Lernenden herstellt. Bemühungen, die Qualität von Lehre kontextunabhängig verbindlich zu definieren, sind somit von vornherein zum Scheitern verurteilt. Qualität ist

hier keine „*objektive*", dem Gegenstand (dem „*Objekt*") zurechenbare, sondern eine relationale Eigenschaft. Wo dennoch der Versuch unternommen
wird, Merkmale „guter Lehre" aufzulisten, setzt dieser – unabhängig vom
Lehr-Inhalt – an der didaktischen Oberfläche an (Webler 1991: 246)[15]; und
selbst da fällt es schwer, Einigkeit über einen Kriterienkatalog für „gute Didaktik" zu erzielen. Für Einführungsveranstaltungen mit Pflichtcharakter, in
denen ein bei Studierenden eher unbeliebter Stoff vermittelt werden soll,
wird eine andere Didaktik angemessen sein als in Hauptstudienseminaren zu
Spezialthemen mit ausschließlich freiwillig teilnehmenden und interessierten
Studierenden oder als in Trainings zur Vermittlung fachübergreifender
Schlüsselqualifikationen – um nur wenige unterschiedliche Lehr-Lern-Situa-
tionen zu benennen. Und welche Didaktik in diesen Situationen jeweils als
angemessen gelten kann, dürfte von verschiedenen Lehrenden ebenso unterschiedlich eingeschätzt werden wie von Studierenden ohne oder mit Vorkenntnissen, ohne oder mit Leistungsmotivation, mit passiv-konsumierendem
oder mit aktiv-entdeckendem Lernstil. Eine rein formale Definition – als
Qualität der Darbietung – geht jedoch auch *prinzipiell* am Ziel der „Dienstleistung Lehre" vorbei. Lehre soll ja nicht stromlinienförmig nach Rezept-
buch abgespult werden, ihr Ziel ist auch nicht lediglich das Sich-Wohlfühlen
oder die gute oder gar spannende Unterhaltung der Teilnehmer von Lehrveranstaltungen. Sie soll vielmehr Anregungen, Orientierung und – wo nötig –
auch Anstöße zum aktiven Studieren geben. Ihr Ergebnis kann nicht in „Ein-
schaltquoten" oder Zufriedenheits-Kennziffern gemessen werden.

Es bleibt also nur der Ausweg *relativer* Qualitätsdefinitionen, wie dies in
der Diskussion um Qualitätsentwicklung und Qualitätssicherung von Dienstleistungen geschieht. Für Ingenieurwissenschaftler liegt es nahe, auf Qualitätsdefinitionen aus der Industrie zurückzugreifen und sie analog auch für die
Organisation Hochschule anzuwenden (z.B. Weule 1999). So findet sich etwa
in der DIN/ISO-Norm 8402 eine inhalts- und ergebnisbezogene Definition:
„Qualität ist die Beschaffenheit einer Einheit bezüglich ihrer Eignung, fest-
gelegte und vorausgesetzte Erfordernisse zu erfüllen." Für welche Zwecke
die Leistung geeignet sein soll, welche und wessen Erfordernisse festzulegen
und vorauszusetzen sind, müßte demnach zunächst ermittelt werden, bevor
eine Evaluation beginnen kann. Qualität der Lehre – so ist bis jetzt zu resü-
mieren – kann nicht adressatenunabhängig, sondern kann nur zielgruppenori-
entiert bestimmt und realisiert werden. Von Studienanfängern und Fortge-
schrittenen, von gegenwärtig Studierenden und künftigen Absolventen, von
Arbeitgebern und fachwissenschaftlicher community werden unterschiedliche, teils sogar gegensätzliche Erfordernisse geltend gemacht. Die Vorstellung von Lehre als Dienstleistung hat konsequenterweise zur Übernahme des
oben bereits genannten Begriffs der Kundenorientierung in die Qualitätsdis-

---

15   Oder es werden recht abstrakte und damit kaum intersubjektiv prüfbare „erfolgsrele-
     vante Persönlichkeitsmerkmale der Lehrenden" genannt (ders.: 247f.).

kussion geführt – hier allerdings nicht in Analogie zum Wettbewerbsmarkt, sondern als Bezugspunkt für die Definition von Leistungsanforderungen. Soll Lehre ihrem Charakter als Dienstleistung gerecht werden, kann somit ihre Qualität und können Qualitätskriterien nicht extern (von wem auch immer) und auch nicht ein für allemal festgesetzt werden, sondern sie müssen den jeweiligen Gegebenheiten angepaßt und – wo keine direkte Marktabstimmung durch Angebot und Nachfrage wirksam wird – zwischen den Beteiligten „ausgehandelt" werden. Dies findet seinen Niederschlag in einem weiteren, an den DIN/ISO-Normen orientierten Definitionsversuch: „Qualität ist die Erfüllung der gemeinsam (Kunde – Lieferant) vereinbarten Anforderungen – einschließlich der Erwartungen und Wünsche" (Rühl 1998: 22). Die Grundtendenz dieser Definition aus dem Produktionsbereich wird inhaltlich auch auf das Qualitätsmanagement von Dienstleistungen übertragen (DIN/ISO 9001 sowie 9004/2, wo als Anwendungsfall ausdrücklich u.a. auf die Wissenschaft verwiesen wird; ausführlicher dazu Stock 1994).

Es stellt sich die Frage: Ist unter diesen Bedingungen „Qualität der Lehre" in der Universität überhaupt evaluierbar?

Daß für eine flächendeckende Evaluation der Lehre in der Hochschule das methodologische Konzept der Programm- und Wirkungsforschung aus grundsätzlichen wie aus pragmatischen Gründen nicht in Frage kommt, wurde bereits begründet. Es verbleiben damit nur die oben genannten verschiedenen Erhebungsformen vom Typ Befragung, um die für Evaluierungen benötigten empirischen Informationen zu beschaffen. Das Instrumentarium der Umfrageforschung wird daher notgedrungen weit verbreitet zu Lehrevaluationszwecken eingesetzt; es führt aber zugleich – wo dies nicht im Bewußtsein der begrenzten Reichweite von Umfragedaten geschieht – über die oben bereits genannten Schwierigkeiten hinaus zu zahlreichen Problemen der Erhebung und Deutung.

Erhebungs- und Deutungsprobleme, die auf zu geringem Differenzierungsgrad der Frageformulierungen beruhen, wurden bereits hinreichend angesprochen. Hinzu kommen – noch nicht thematisiert – *Probleme der Auswahl* der zu befragenden Informanten. Teilnehmerbefragungen in Lehrveranstaltungen werden üblicherweise in der Mitte des Semesters durchgeführt. Dies hat zur Konsequenz, daß die Ergebnisse in Wahl- und Wahlpflichtveranstaltungen durch den bis dahin wirksam gewordenen Prozeß der Selbstselektion einen positiven Bias aufweisen: Diejenigen anfänglichen Teilnehmer, die die Veranstaltung und/oder die Lehrperson besonders negativ einschätzen, sind nicht mehr anwesend. Pflichtveranstaltungen ohne Wahlmöglichkeit zwischen Alternativangeboten erscheinen dadurch im studentischen Urteil systematisch negativer. Noch ungünstiger wirkt es sich auf die Gültigkeit der Resultate aus, wenn die Fragebögen nicht unmittelbar in der Veranstaltung ausgefüllt und wieder eingesammelt, sondern den Studierenden mit der Bitte um Rückgabe mitgegeben werden. Die Konsequenz dieses Vorgehens ist eine Tendenz zur Polarisierung in den erfaßten Urteilen. Die Ursache ist leicht nachzuvollziehen: Die Befragung verlangt ein aktives Beteiligungsverhalten von den Befragten; dazu sind vor allem diejenigen motiviert, die „etwas mitteilen" wollen – sei es ein besonderes Lob (dieser Fall findet sich besonders in Wahlveranstaltungen), sei es explizite Kritik (vor allem unzufriedene Teilnehmer in Pflichtveranstaltungen). Die Mehrheitsgruppe der „einigermaßen Zufriedenen" ist demgegenüber mangels Motivation zu aktiver Mitwirkung in den Daten deutlich unterrepräsentiert. Eine analoge Verzerrung tritt bei der Erhebung studentischer Aussagen zur Studien-, Betreuungs- und Prüfungssituation in Instituten oder Fakultäten/Fachbereichen auf, wenn sie nicht direkt zu Semesterbeginn, sondern in der Semestermitte anhand einer Stichprobe der im Institut bzw. Fachbereich Anwesenden erfolgt. Diesmal fällt der Bias zugunsten der kontinuierlich Studierenden aus. Wer – aus unterschiedlichen Gründen – die Lehrangebote nur selektiv nutzt (etwa weil er berufstätig ist und sich lediglich zu Semesterbeginn umfassender informiert), wird in diesem Fall gar nicht erfaßt. Damit fallen die Zugehörigen zu einer hinsichtlich des Studierverhaltens gegenwärtig zentralen Gruppe als Informanten vollständig aus.

Ein zweites Problem, das häufig nicht zur Kenntnis genommen wird, hat seine Ursache im (zu Beginn bereits behandelten) ungenauen Sprachgebrauch: Die Erhebung und Auszählung bewertender (also „evaluierender") Aussagen *ist* noch keine Evaluation im wissenschaftlichen oder methodologischen Sinne, sondern ein Verfahren des Sammelns der persönlichen „Alltags-Evaluationen" der Befragten. Die *begriffliche Gleichsetzung des Einsatzes der Umfrageforschung* zum Zwecke von Evaluation und Qualitätsentwicklung in Lehre und Studium *mit Evaluation* verursacht unnötige Verwirrung. Umfrageforschung ist nicht mehr – aber auch nicht weniger – als ein bewährtes Instrument der Informationserhebung; und sie kann als solches ein wichtiger Baustein in einem Konzept von Evaluation und Qualitätsentwicklung sein.

Sinnvollerweise wird man also bei Evaluationsvorhaben innerhalb der Hochschule von einem Konzept ausgehen, das ich zu Beginn als „politischen Evaluationsbegriff" bezeichnet habe: Ein Programm, eine Maßnahme, eine Einrichtung wird auf der Basis zielgerichtet gesammelter und aufbereiteter Informationen von einem Evaluator (z.B. einem ausgewiesenen Evaluationsexperten oder einem Evaluationsgremium) beurteilt, der abschließend ein Evaluationsgutachten mit Empfehlungen erstellt. Für das Gelingen dieses Konzepts ist es wesentlich, zu Beginn Klarheit darüber zu schaffen, welche Ziele verfolgt werden, welcher Informationsbedarf besteht, wer welche Kompetenzen hat. Mindestens die folgenden Fragen sind eindeutig und verbindlich zu beantworten:

Wer ist zuständig für die Koordination und Durchführung des Evaluationsvorhabens? Diese organisatorisch verantwortliche Evaluationsinstanz hat die Aufgabe der unbeeinflußten, methodisch kontrollierten Sammlung und Aufbereitung der für die Urteilsbildung notwendigen Informationen. Sie erhebt Daten, befragt Informanten, sichtet vorhandene Statistiken, macht sich durch eigene Anschauung ein Bild vom Gegenstand der Beurteilung.

Wer evaluiert? Das heißt: Welche Instanz nimmt auf der Basis der zielgerichtet gesammelten Informationen die Bewertungen vor, trifft Qualitätsentscheidungen? Das kann dieselbe Instanz sein, die das Evaluationsvorhaben koordiniert und durchführt. Es kann aber auch z.b. eine vom Fachbereichsrat eingesetzte Kommission aus Vertretern aller universitärer Gruppen sein.

Welche Informationen sind die Basis für die vorzunehmenden Bewertungen (z.B. Befragungsergebnisse *und* Hochschulstatistiken *und* per Beobachtung gewonnene Daten)? Und *wer sind die Informanten* (z.B. Studierende *und* Lehrende *und* die Hochschulverwaltung)?

Was soll evaluiert werden und warum? Ist es die Lehre in Lehrveranstaltungen? Oder die Struktur des Lehrangebots? Sind es die Rahmenbedingungen für das Studieren und für die Lehre? Ist es das Betreuungsverhalten der Lehrenden und/oder das Arbeitsverhalten der Studierenden? Und aus welchen Gründen besteht Interesse an Beurteilungen dieser Gegebenheiten?

Und schließlich: *Zu welchem Zweck soll evaluiert werden?* Was soll mit den Daten geschehen? Evaluation ist kein Selbstzweck (auch wenn es in manchen landesgesetzlichen Regelungen und Erlassen so erscheint). Evaluation ist aufwendig; der Aufwand muß sich lohnen. Durch die Evaluation *allein* wird noch nichts besser. Sie liefert lediglich die notwendigen Informationen als Voraussetzung dafür, Verbesserungsbedarf zu erkennen und erforderliche Veränderungen in Gang zu setzen. Das aber muß *nach* der Evaluation – als „follow up" – auch geschehen, wenn nicht die Motivation der Beteiligten erlahmen soll. Die Evaluation muß münden in konkrete Zielvereinbarungen, oder anders formuliert: in ein Qualitätsentwicklungsprojekt.

Daraus leitet sich die Notwendigkeit einer weiteren Entscheidung ab, die im Abschnitt 2 schon angesprochen wurde: *Wer ist Träger des Qualitätsentwicklungs-Projekts?* Anders formuliert: Wer ist verantwortlich dafür, daß die gelieferten Evaluations-Informationen in konkretes Handeln umgesetzt werden? Dies wird nur in Ausnahmefällen auch der Träger des Evaluationsvorhabens sein.

Wenn Qualität von Dienstleistungen nicht absolut, sondern nur relativ bestimmt und somit auch nur relativ sichergestellt werden kann – nämlich relativ zu den Adressaten (oder „Kunden") der Dienstleistung –, dann hat der Träger des Qualitätsentwicklungs-Projekts zu entscheiden und zu begründen, *für welche Zielgruppe* er die Dienstleistung optimieren will. Das bedeutet immer zugleich eine Entscheidung *gegen* andere potentielle Adressaten. Der Versuch, einem imaginären ‚Durchschnitt' heterogener Zielgruppen mit heterogenen Bedürfnissen und Ansprüchen gerecht zu werden, führt nahezu zwangsläufig zu dem Resultat, daß die Leistung für keine Gruppe von großem Nutzen ist. Die Dienstleistung wird immer auch unter einschränkenden – angesichts knapper werdender Ressourcen im Hochschulbereich: unter zunehmend stärker eingeschränkten – Rahmenbedingungen erbracht. Der Träger des Qualitätsentwicklungs-Projekts wird sich also klarzumachen haben – und wird dies seiner Zielgruppe zu vermitteln haben –, *welche Rahmenbedingungen gestaltbar sind* und welche außerhalb der Möglichkeiten einer Realisierung liegen. Ein Idealkonzept, das Utopie bleiben muß, nützt weniger und schadet mehr als ein Bündel kleiner Schritte in die gewünschte Richtung.

Literatur

Bülow-Schramm, Margret (1995): „Wer hat Angst vor den Evaluatoren?" Der Umgang mit Akzeptanzproblemen von Evaluationsverfahren. In: Handbuch Hochschullehre, D 1.6. Bonn: Raabe.

Chelimsky, Eleanor (1997): Thoughts for a new evaluation society. „Keynote speech" at the UK Evaluation Society conference in London 1996. In: Evaluation, 3(1), S. 97-109.

Daxner, Michael (1999): Evaluation, Indikatoren und Akkreditierung. Auf dem Weg in die Rechtfertigungsgesellschaft. In: Hochschulrektorenkonferenz (Hg.): „Viel Lärm um nichts?" Evaluation von Studium und Lehre und ihre Folgen. Beiträge zur Hochschulpolitik: 4/1999. Bonn: HRK. S. 41-49.

Donabedian, A. (1980): Explorations in quality assessment and monitoring: The definition of quality and approaches to its assessment. Ann Arbor, MI.

Eekhoff, Johann/Muthmann, R./Sievert, O. (1977): Methoden und Möglichkeiten der Erfolgskontrolle städtischer Entwicklungsmaßnahmen. Bonn-Bad Godesberg: Schriftenreihe „Städtebauliche Forschung" , Bd. 03.060.

el Hage, Natalija (1996): Lehrevaluation und studentische Veranstaltungskritik. Projekte, Instrumente und Grundlagen. Bonn: BMBF.

Fischer-Bluhm, Karin (1995): „Gemeinsam geht es besser!" Evaluationsprojekte im Verbund norddeutscher Hochschulen. In: Handbuch Hochschullehre, D 3.3. Bonn: Raabe.

Habel, Edna (1995): „Hochschulen zum Rapport???" Erfahrungen mit internen Lehrberichten und Lehrberichten nach Universitätsgesetz an der Universität Dortmund. In: Handbuch Hochschullehre, D 1.5. Bonn: Raabe.

Hochschulrektorenkonferenz (1995): Zur Evaluation im Hochschulbereich unter besonderer Berücksichtigung der Lehre. Entschließung des 176. HRK-Plenums vom 3.7.1995.

Hochschulrektorenkonferenz (Hg.) (1998a): Evaluation. Sachstandsbericht zur Qualitätsbewertung und Qualitätsentwicklung in deutschen Hochschulen. Dokumente & Informationen 1/1998. Bonn: HRK .

Hochschulrektorenkonferenz (Hg.) (1998b): Evaluation und Qualitätssicherung an den Hochschulen in Deutschland – Stand und Perspektiven. Beiträge zur Hochschulpolitik 6/1998. Bonn: HRK.

Hornbostel, Stefan (1999): Evaluation und Ranking. Führen sie zu mehr Transparenz und Vergleichbarkeit? In: Hochschulrektorenkonferenz (Hg.): „Viel Lärm um nichts?" Evaluation von Studium und Lehre und ihre Folgen. Beiträge zur Hochschulpolitik 4/1999: Bonn: HRK. S. 91-95.

Hornbostel, Stefan/Daniel, H.-D. (1995): Das SPIEGEL-Ranking. In: Mohler, P. (Hg.): Universität und Lehre. Ihre Evaluation als Herausforderung an die Empirische Sozialforschung. Münster: Waxmann. S. 29-44.

Hübener, A./Halberstadt, R. (1976): Erfolgskontrolle politischer Planung – Probleme und Ansätze in der Bundesrepublik Deutschland. Göttingen.

Klostermeier, Johannes (1994): Hochschul-Ranking auf dem Prüfstand. Hochschuldidaktische Arbeitspapiere Nr. 26. Hamburg: IZHD.

Knäuper, Bärbel/Kroeger, Matthias & Studierende (1999): Qualitätssicherung und -verbesserung im Intensivstudium Psychologie: Ein Werkstattbericht zur Lehrevaluation. Berlin: FU Studiengang Psychologie (der Bericht ist auf der Webseite http://userpage.fu-berlin.de/~sciencec/iStudium/ einsehbar).

Kreutz, Henrik/Tarnai, Ch./Wolff, K. E./Zezula, S. (1992): Universitätsrangreihen und die Bewertung der Qualität von Hochschulen, 2 Bde. Erlangen-Nürnberg, Wien: IAS.

Kromrey, Helmut (1994): Wie erkennt man „gute Lehre"? Was studentische Vorlesungsbefragungen (nicht) Aussagen. In: Empirische Pädagogik, Jg. 8, H. 2, S. 153-168.

Kromrey, Helmut (1995a): Evaluation. Empirische Konzepte zur Bewertung von Handlungsprogrammen und die Schwierigkeiten ihrer Realisierung. In: ZSE Zeitschrift für Sozialisationsforschung und Erziehungssoziologie, Jg. 15, H. 4, S. 313-336.

Kromrey, Helmut (1995b): Evaluation der Lehre durch Umfrageforschung? Methodische Fallstricke bei der Messung von Lehrqualität durch Befragung von Vorlesungsteilnehmern. In: Mohler, Peter Ph. (Hg.): Universität und Lehre. Ihre Evaluation als Herausforderung an die Empirische Sozialforschung. Münster, New York, 2. Aufl. S. 105-127.

Kromrey, Helmut (1996): Qualitätsverbesserung in Lehre und Studium statt sogenannter Lehrevaluation. Ein Plädoyer für gute Lehre und gegen schlechte Sozialforschung. In: Zeitschrift für Pädagogische Psychologie, Jg. 10, H. 3/4, S. 153-166.

Kromrey, Helmut (1999): Von den Problemen anwendungsorientierter Sozialforschung und den Gefahren methodischer Halbbildung. In: SuB Sozialwissenschaften und Berufspraxis, Jg. 22, H. 1, S. 58-77.

Küchler, Tilmann (1996): Für eine verbesserte Qualität der Lehre. Empfehlungen des Wissenschaftsrates zur Evaluation der Lehre. In: Handbuch Hochschullehre, D 1.7. Bonn: Raabe.

Künzel, Ellen/Nickel, Sigrun/Zechlin, Lothar (1999): Organisationsentwicklung an Hochschulen. Was geschieht mit den Evaluationsergebnissen? In: Hochschulrektorenkonferenz (Hg.): „Viel Lärm um nichts?" Evaluation von Studium und Lehre und ihre Folgen. Beiträge zur Hochschulpolitik 4/1999, Bonn: HRK. S. 105-119.

Kultusminister- und Hochschulrektorenkonferenz (1994): Umsetzung der Studienstrukturreform. Bonn: HRK.

Landfried, Klaus (1999): Qualitätssicherung als Aufgabe wettbewerblicher Hochschulen. In: HRK (Hg.): Ein Schritt in die Zukunft. Qualitätssicherung im Hochschulbereich. Beiträge zur Hochschulpolitik 3/1999. Bonn: HRK. S. 7-13.

Peter, Lothar/Wawrzinek, Andreas (1995): Dialogische Evaluation. Ein studentisches Evaluationsverfahren. In: Handbuch Hochschullehre, D 3.1. Bonn: Raabe.

Rühl, Werner J. (1998): ISO 9000 – Erfahrungsbericht aus einem technischen Entwicklungszentrum. In: Hochschulrektorenkonferenz: Qualitätsmanagement in der Lehre. TQL 98. Beiträge zur Hochschulpolitik 5/1998. Bonn: HRK. S. 21-46.

Schierholz, Petra/Vocke, Christina (1997): Selbstkritik und Aufbruch. Evaluation im Verbund Norddeutscher Universitäten – Erfahrungen und Konsequenzen. In: Handbuch Hochschullehre, D 3.4. Bonn: Raabe.

Schmidt, Jörn (1980): Evaluation als Diagnose. HDZ-Dozentenkurs. Essen.

Schreier, Gerhard (1998): Das HRK-Projekt Qualitätssicherung – Konzepte und Ziele. In: Hochschulrektorenkonferenz (Hg.): Evaluation und Qualitätssicherung an den Hochschulen in Deutschland. Beiträge zur Hochschulpolitik 6/1998. Bonn: HRK. S. 13-17.

SPIEGEL Spezial (1990): „Welche Uni ist die beste?". Hamburg.

Stock, Wolfgang G. (1994): Wissenschaftsevaluation. Die Bewertung wissenschaftlicher Forschung und Lehre. ifo Diskussionsbeiträge 17. München: ifo Institut für Wirtschaftsforschung.

Webler, Wolff-Dietrich (1991): Kriterien für gute akademische Lehre. In: Das Hochschulwesen, Jg. 39, H. 6, S. 243-249.

Weiss, Carol H. (1974): Evaluierungsforschung. Methoden zur Einschätzung von sozialen Reformprogrammen. Opladen.

Weule, Hartmut (1999): Praktische Probleme der Qualitätssicherung an Hochschulen. In: Hochschulrektorenkonferenz (Hg.): Ein Schritt in die Zukunft. Qualitätssicherung im Hochschulbereich. Beiträge zur Hochschulpolitik 3/1999. Bonn: HRK. S. 45-54.

Wissenschaftsrat (1996): Empfehlungen zur Stärkung der Lehre in den Hochschulen durch Evaluation. In: ders.: Empfehlungen und Stellungnahmen 1996, Band I. Köln.

Wollmann, Hellmut/Hellstern, G.-M. (1977): Sozialwissenschaftliche Untersuchungsregeln und Wirkungsforschung. Zur Chance kritischer Sozialwissenschaft im Rahmen staatlicher Forschungsaufträge. In: Haungs, P. (Hg.): Res Publica. Dolf Sternberger zum 70. Geburtstag. München (1977). S. 415-466.

Xaver Büeler

Qualitätsevaluation und Schulentwicklung

Daß die Gesellschaft sich insgesamt in einem revolutionären Wandel befindet, wird hier vorausgesetzt und nicht weiter thematisiert. Für das Thema dieses Kapitels ist vor allem jener Aspekt dieses Wandels von Interesse, den der Managementguru Peter F. Drucker als Übergang von der Industrie- zur Wissensgesellschaft bezeichnet hat. Gemäß dieser Vision wird Wissen in absehbarer Zeit zum wichtigsten Produktionsfaktor und die sinnvolle Nutzung dieses Wissens zur zentralen Managementaufgabe in den politischen und wirtschaftlichen Organisationen der Zukunft.

Auch der britische Premierminster Tony Blair bezeichnete am Weltwirtschaftsforum im Februar 2000 in Davos folgerichtig „Aus- und Weiterbildung als das Ein und Alles" im Hinblick auf das angebrochene Jahrtausend. Die bisher unternommenen Anstrengungen im Bildungssektor seien sehr ehrgeizig, doch seine einzige Sorge wäre, daß sie nicht ehrgeizig genug seien! Auf diesem Hintergrund ist es nicht erstaunlich, daß 10-15% der gesamten öffentlichen Ausgaben in OECD-Staaten in den Bildungssektor fließen (Bundesamt für Statistik 1999; OECD/CERI 1997). „Das Bildungswesen ist bei uns das größte Unternehmen der öffentlichen Hand, mit den meisten Beschäftigten und den meisten ‚Kunden'. Es gestaltet Millionen von menschlichen Schicksalen mit" (Fend 1998: 357).

Diese offensichtliche Bedeutung des Bildungssektors kontrastiert eigenartig mit dem Umstand, daß im deutschsprachigen Europa bis vor kurzem die Frage, ob diese Mittel auch tatsächlich effektiv und effizient eingesetzt werden, kaum systematisch gestellt wurde. Wohl gab es schon in der pädagogischen Tradition eine geisteswissenschaftliche Reflexion über die Qualität von Schulen. Eine empirische Wende erfuhr die Pädagogik allerdings erst relativ spät (Roth 1962). Bis die empirisch verfahrende Erziehungswissenschaft auch bei uns allgemeine Anerkennung fand, verstrichen nochmals etwa zwei Jahrzehnte. So darf es nicht verwundern, daß erst in den 90er-Jahren methodisch kontrollierte Evaluationen im Schulbereich Einzug gehalten haben. Bevor auf diese Entwicklungen detaillierter eingegangen werden kann, sollen noch einige begriffliche Klärungen vorangestellt werden.

1. Begriffliche Klärung

Der Begriff der *Evaluation* ist ein bedeutungsmässig sehr schillernder. Im Schulbereich konkurriert er mit einer Reihe von weiteren Begriffen, die in teilweise sehr ähnlicher Weise verwendet werden: Schulforschung, Schulqualitätsforschung, Schulentwicklungsforschung, Qualitätsmanagement, Qualitätssicherung usw. Eine scharfe Abgrenzung gegenüber diesen Konzepten ist weder möglich noch sinnvoll, auch wenn dies andernorts versucht wird. Präzisierungen in der Sache werden in der Folge nach und nach eingeführt. Den vielen vorliegenden Definitionsversuchen wird hier kein weiterer angefügt. Stattdessen sollen sechs Kennzeichen von Evaluationsforschung im Bildungsbereich angeführt werden, über die weitgehend Konsens besteht (vgl. Stamm 1998: 21; vgl. Wottawa/Thierau 1998:13f.):

1. Evaluation ist ziel- und zweckorientiert.
2. Evaluation hat eine systematisch gewonnene Datenbasis.
3. Evaluation beinhaltet eine bewertende Stellungnahme.
4. Evaluation bezieht sich auf Bereiche von Bildungsmaßnahmen.
5. Evaluation ist Bestandteil von planvoller Entwicklungsarbeit.
6. Evaluation ist nicht Reform, sondern Mittel zur Reform.

Was aber ist, so kann man weiter fragen, eine *Schule*? Zunächst erwarte ich wenig Widerstand gegen den Vorschlag, Schule als ein System zu betrachten, wobei ich *System* nach dem Begründer der Allgemeinen Systemtheorie von Bertalanffy (1971: 55) folgendermaßen definiere: „A system can be defined as a set of elements standing in interrelations".

Welches sind nun die Charakteristika und die Elemente des Schulsystems? Einem breiten Konsens folgend, wird Schule hier als ein *soziales* System begriffen, dessen Funktion in der „gesellschaftlich kontrollierten und veranstalteten Sozialisation" (Fend 1981: 2) liegt. Alle sozialen Systeme kristallisieren sich um einen bestimmten Typus von Kommunikation aus, im Falle der Schule handelt es sich um erzieherische Kommunikation (vgl. Büeler 1994; Luhmann 1987).

Schulsysteme können durch drei Bestimmungsfaktoren definiert werden: (1) sie sind formal organisiert als Institution, (2) sie sind gekennzeichnet durch die Veranstaltung von absichtlichen und kontrollierten erzieherischen Kommunikationsprozesses, und (3), in ihnen geschieht – latent und/oder manifest – Sozialisation.

Sowohl die Schulqualitäts- wie auch die Schulentwicklungsforschung – um diese zwei Perspektiven der Evaluationsforschung zu unterscheiden – befassen sich mit Schulsystemen. Sie tun dies aber in unterschiedlichen Hinsichten. Ihre Unterscheidung wird verständlicher, wenn man sich vor Augen hält, daß jedes System sich durch eine spezifische raum-zeitliche

Struktur auszeichnet (vgl. untenstehende Definition). Auf die Schule bezogen heißt das:

(Ad a) Das Schulsystems besitzt, wenn man einen *Querschnitt* zur Zeitachse macht, eine bestimmte Raumstruktur. Sie ist gekennzeichnet durch so unterschiedliche Elemente wie Stundenpläne, Gebäude, Personen, Rollen, Erwartungshaltungen, Kommunikationsstile, Lehrpläne, Gesetze, Infrastrukturen, Intake, Outcome, etc., respektive durch das Beziehungsmuster, mit dem diese Elemente verbunden sind.

> Als *Struktur* wollen wir bezeichnen: (a) die potentiellen Relationen zwischen den Elementen in einem gegebenen Bezugssystem zu einem gegebenen Zeitpunkt (Raumstruktur); und (b) die Abfolge der während einer gegebenen Periode tatsächlich aktualisierten Relationen (Prozeßstruktur).

(Ad b) Das Schulsystem ist – wenn man einen *Längsschnitt* zur Zeitachse macht – aber auch gekennzeichnet durch eine bestimmte Prozeßstruktur. Das durch die Elemente gebildete Netzwerk verändert sich in der Zeit, es lassen sich typische Prozesse beobachten, es kommt zu Entwicklungen, die von kürzerer oder längerer Dauer sind.

Von diesem Stand der Argumentation aus läßt sich nun idealtypisch beschreiben, worin der Unterschied zwischen der Schulqualitäts- und der Schulentwicklungsforschung begründet liegt. Der Aspekt der *Schulqualität* betont die Raumstruktur des Schulsystems zu einem bestimmten Zeitpunkt. Die Evaluation von Schulqualität arbeitet – von Ausnahmen abgesehen – vornehmlich mit einer querschnittlichen Erforschung, Beschreibung und Erklärung der am Schulsystem interessierenden Parameter. Typisch für diese Perspektive sind einmalige, meist eher geschlossene empirische Erhebungen (Befragung, Dokumentenanalyse, Beobachtung) und die Konstruktion von zeitlich und geografisch spezifizierten Modellen einer ‚guten Schule‘.

Im Gegensatz dazu fokussiert die Rede von *Schulentwicklung* den Prozeßcharakter des Schulsystems. Wie andere soziale Systeme, so sind auch Schulen darin verschieden, inwieweit sie sich dynamisch auf Innen- und Außenanforderungen neu einstellen, welche Ereignisse Entwicklungsprozesse auslösen, wie sie sich nach kritischen Phasen wieder stabilisieren, etc.. Die Schulentwicklungsforschung beschäftigt sich gezwungenermaßen mit (quasi-)längsschnittlichen Designs; ihr Interesse richtet sich weniger auf die Frage, welche Elemente und Relationen in einer Schule auffindbar sind, sondern darauf, wie ein Schulsystem zur Transformation seiner Relationen angestossen werden kann, wie es von innen oder außen zur Veränderung angeregt werden kann. Schulentwicklungsforschung arbeitet oft mit Aktions- und Handlungsforschung, mit prozeßbegleitenden Evaluationen und mit offenen Erhebungsverfahren (z.B. Fallstudien).

> *Schulqualitätsforschung* orientiert sich an Elementen und Strukturen, die zu einem ge-
> gebenen Zeitpunkt in einem Schulsystem beobachtbar sind, und die – nach normativ
> gesetzten Kriterien – für ‚qualitätsrelevant' gehalten werden. *Schulentwicklungsfor-*
> *schung* richtet sich auf die Bedingungen der Möglichkeit, ein Schulsystem zu Entwick-
> lungsprozessen anzuregen, wobei auch hier der Beobachter definiert, welchen Dimen-
> sionen der Veränderung er Relevanz zuschreibt.

Es würde natürlich nicht schwerfallen, eine Definition zu finden, die sich mit
der nebenstehenden nicht zur Deckung bringen läßt. Beispielsweise wird
oftmals eine Schule, die sich immer wieder Entwicklungen unterwirft, als
‚Gute Schule' bezeichnet. Auch die im englischen Sprachraum verwendete
Formel der ‚reflecting school' bezeichnet zweifellos eine Schule, die Schulqualität durch permanente Qualitätsevaluation und Schulentwicklung verbessern will. Daran ist soviel richtig, als sich Schulqualität und Schulentwicklung gegenseitig bedingen. Man könnte zudem sagen, daß sie in einem kom-
plementären, wenn auch nicht immer unproblematischen Verhältnis stehen
(vgl. Strittmatter 1999). Eine idealtypische Trennung dieser beiden Beob-
achtungsperspektiven dürfte aber aus heuristischen Gründen durchaus sinnvoll sein. Der nachfolgende Exkurs zur Entstehungsgeschichte von Qualitätsevaluation und Schulentwicklung arbeitet deshalb mit dem Begriffspaar
Schulqualitäts- und Schulentwicklungsforschung weiter. Der Begriff der
Qualitätsevaluation selber taucht im historischen Verlauf erst relativ spät auf
und wird deshalb gesondert behandelt.

2. Zur Entstehung der Qualitätsevaluation in Schulen

Die heutige Diskussion um Schulqualität und Schulentwicklung ist in höhe-
rem Maße von bestimmten historischen Konstellationen abhängig, als dies
gemeinhin angenommen wird. Insbesondere lassen sich zwischen der deutschen und der angelsächsischen Tradition, die in den letzten Jahren stark an
Einfluß gewonnen hat, einige bedeutsame Unterschiede feststellen. Dies läßt
sich schon daran ablesen, daß dort anstelle von „school quality" fast durchweg von „school effectiveness" gesprochen wird.

2.1 School Effectiveness Research

Während in deutsch- und französischsprachigen Ländern ein relativ breit ge-
faßter Qualitätsbegriff im Vordergrund steht, orientieren sich die angelsächsischen Länder eher an einem empirisch faßbaren und deshalb auf wenige
schulische Wirkungen enggeführten Effektivitätsbegriff (vgl. Szaday/Büeler/
Favre 1996: 19ff.). Dieser Unterschied hat seine Wurzeln in bestimmten hi-

storisch nachweisbaren Differenzen in der bildungspoltischen Ausgangslage zwischen diesen Sprachregionen. Ohne hier ins Detail zu gehen, sei auf das vielzitierte Initialereignis für die Schulwirkungsforschung in den USA higewiesen: unter dem Eindruck des Sputnik-Schocks wurde die Frage laut, wie es um die Qualität des amerikanischen Bildungssystems bestellt sei. Wie selbstverständlich stand dabei die Frage im Vordergrund, welche *Effekte* die Beschulung von Kindern auf deren Entwicklung habe. Darauf antworteten J. Coleman (1966) und C. Jencks (1973) singemäß folgendermaßen: „Schools don't make a difference". Ob gute Schule – ob schlechte Schule: viel entscheidender für die Laufbahn der Kinder seien Randbedingungen wie Rasse, soziale Schicht, Bildungsstand der Eltern oder väterliches Einkommen. Dieser Befund war für die Schulpädagogik und -politik alarmierend. Sollten die fünfzehntausend Stunden, die ein Kind durchschnittlich von der Einschulung bis zur Entlassung in der Schule verbringt, tatsächlich keinen Unterschied machen? Gibt es keine *effective schools*, die mehr aus den Voraussetzungen machen, die die Schüler bei der Einschulung mitbringen? Die bis dahin größte und sorgfältigste Studie zu diesen Fragen haben M. Rutter und seine Mitarbeiter Ende der 70er Jahre in England vorgelegt (Rutter/Maughan/Mortimore/Ouston 1980). Aufgrund von detaillierten und mehrjährigen Beobachtungen, Befragungen und empirischen Vergleichen konnten sie nachweisen: „Schools do make a difference!" Je nach Schulstruktur und -klima varieren Schülerleistungen, abweichendes Verhalten wie auch Schüler- und Lehrerzufriedenheit in hohem Maße. Ganz bestimmte schulinterne Faktoren bestimmen darüber, welche fachlichen und überfachlichen Kompetenzen dort erworben werden, und diese Faktoren sind veränderbar. Seither widmet sich die Schulforschung in Großbritanien, USA, Australien und den Niederlanden in bemerkenswerter Konsequenz der Suche nach einer Strategie „... for educational change that enhances student outcomes as well as strenghtening the school's capacity for managing change" (vgl. Hopkins 1989). In dieser Formulierung klingt bereits eine Neuorientierung der Schulqualitätsforschung an, die sich sowohl an Prozessen wie an Wirkungen orientiert.

2.2 Schulqualitätsforschung in deutschsprachigen Ländern

Aus dem Geist der „school effectiveness research" entstand im deutschsprachigen Raum mit starker Verzögerung und anderer Färbung die Schulqualitätsforschung. Etwa seit 1980 hat der Begriff der *Schulqualität* Eingang in die deutschsprachige wissenschaftliche Diskussion um die Erforschung, Gestaltung und Entwicklung des Schulsystems gefunden. Die Diskussion über Schulqualität begann in der Bundesrepublik mit der Rezeption anglo-amerikanischer Studien. Insbesondere die Übersetzung der oben erwähnten Studie von Rutter u.a., versehen mit einer provokativen Einführung Hartmut von Hentigs, scheint in Deutschland eine starke Resonanz ausgelöst zu haben.

Der Augenblick, in dem diese Studie kommt, ist in vielerlei Hinsicht günstig. Die Ergebnisse der wissenschaftlichen Begleitforschung zu den Gesamtschulen in Nordrhein-
Westfalen haben vor allem eins erbracht: daß der Leistungsvergleich zwischen Schulen, die
Verschiedenes wollen und Verschiedenes treiben (nicht das Gleiche auf andere Weise!),
nichts hergibt, gleich, ob es dabei um Leistungen in Mathematik, Deutsch und Englisch
oder um soziale Beziehungen oder um Disziplin oder um Schulangst oder um Abschlüsse
geht. ... Der aufschlußreichste Befund ... ist, daß die Unterschiede zwischen einzelnen Gesamtschulen sehr viel größer sind als zwischen den ... zu vergleichenden Schulsystemen.
(Hentig 1980: 9f.)

Dazu muß man vielleicht anfügen, daß die 60er und 70er-Jahre in Deutschland im Zeichen eines bildungsreformerischen Aufbruchs standen. Die Na-
men von Helmut Fend, Hans Haenisch, Ulrich Steffens, Kurt Aurin, Hans-
Günther Rolff, Klaus Tillmann (um nur einige zu nennen) stehen für eine
Forschungsgeneration, die auf diese Reformen reagiert hat.

Es ging um die strukturelle Umgestaltung des gesamten Schulsystems, also um die Einführung der Gesamtschule als aufhebende Regelschule und um Chancengleichheit, also um
Gesellschaftspolitik. Dementsprechend waren die genannten Bildungsforscher, die erstmals
in der deutschen Schulgeschichte großformatige empirische Untersuchungen finanziert be-
kamen, an ‚Makropolitik‘ orientiert. Ende der siebziger Jahre hatte diese Reformbewegung
ihren Rückenwind verloren und desto mehr Gegenwind erfahren. Die Einführung der Gesamtschule stagnierte, erlitt sogar Rückschläge. Forschungen zum Systemvergleich waren
nicht mehr gefragt. (Rolff 1993: 107)

Um zu sehen, welche Verschiebungen in der Forschung hier angetönt werden, sind wir zu einem Systematisierungsversuch gezwungen. Evaluation
schulischer Verhältnisse ist auf allen in Abbildung 1 bezeichneten Ebenen
möglich (vgl. Fend 1998: 200f.): auf der Ebene des gesamten Schulsystems,
auf der Ebene der Schule als lokale Einheit, auf der Ebene der Klasse und des
Unterrichts und auf der Ebene der Einzelpersonen.

Vor 1980 ging die Initiative für Reflexion und Reform des Bildungssystems in hohem Maße vom Politiksystem aus. Charakteristisch an der Diskussion dieser Periode war ebenfalls, daß sie vorwiegend auf makrosozialer
Ebene ausgetragen wurde und die Schule als lokale Einheit lediglich als an-
onyme Größe, als Mittel zum Zweck, als „black box" in den Blick geriet.
Bildungspolitiker verschiedener Couleur versuchten, ihre politischen Über-
zeugungen und Interessen innerhalb des Bildungssystems stärker zu veran-
kern, indem neue Schultypen (z.B. die Gesamtschulen) geschaffen wurden.
Begleitend dazu wurde die bis heute größte empirische Schulforschungswelle
(vgl. Fend 1990) in Deutschland und eine teils sehr engagiert ausgetragene
Ideologiedebatte in der Pädagogik ausgelöst.

In Anbetracht der weitreichenden Hoffnungen, die man mit der Reform-
politik verbunden hatte, mußte die Erkenntnis einigermaßen frustrieren, daß
Veränderungen auf der schulpolitischen Makroebene nur einen schwachen
Einfluß hatten auf pädagogisch relevante Dimensionen wie etwa Schülerleistungen und Sozialverhalten, um die es doch letztlich ging. Zudem deckte
sich diese Erkenntnis in hohem Maße mit Forschungsbefunden in den nicht-

deutschsprachigen Ländern (vgl. Wang/Haertel/Walberg 1993). So mußte es zwangsläufig zu einer Neuorientierung kommen, und in dieser Phase im Übergang zu den achtziger Jahren kam der Studie von Rutter programmatischer Charakter zu. In einer radikalen Kehrtwendung wurde hier statt nach makropolitischen Programmen nach Effekten auf der Ebene des Kindes gefragt: „Haben die schulischen Erfahrungen des Kindes Auswirkungen? Spielt es eine Rolle, *welche* Schule das Kind besucht? Welche Aspekte der Schule sind die entscheidenden?" (Rutter u.a. 1980: 25).

Schaubild 1: Systematisches Ebenenmodell des Bildungssystems und der relevanten Umweltsysteme (vgl. Büeler in Szaday u.a. 1996: 83f.)

Makroebene I:	Gesamtgesellschaftliche Kommunikation			
Makroebene II: Zentrale gesell-schaftliche Subsysteme	Wissenschafts-system	Erziehungs- und Bildungssystem	Politik- und Staatssystem (inkl. Rechts-system)	Wirtschafts-system
Mesoebene: Formale Organisa-tionen mit gesatzten Kommunikations-regeln	– Universitäten – Hochschulen – Publikations-wesen – Wissenschaft-liche Gesell-schaften –	Schule als organisatorische Einheit: – Schulleitung – Schulorgane – Infrastruktur –	– Regierung – Parlamente – Gerichte – Verwaltung –	– Betriebe – Märkte – Börsen – Kartelle – ....
Mikroebene:	– Schwach formalisierte, eher an diffus-intimer Kommunikation orientierte Systeme – Dominanz von „Face to face"-Interaktion. – Beispiele: Familien, Schulklassen, Lehrerkollegien, Gelehrtenzirkel, Wissenschaftliche Seminarien, Beratungs- oder Verkaufsgespräche, etc.			
Personale Ebene:	Ebene der intrapersonalen Verarbeitung von Kommunikation. Diese Ebene markiert den Übergang von Kommunikations- zu Bewußtseinssystemen, respektive den Übergang vom Gegenstandsbereich der Soziologie zu jenem der Psychologie. Beispiele: Motivation, Kognition, Verhaltensschemata, Bewältigungsstile, etc.			

Die Selbstverständlichkeit dieser Frage darf nicht darüber hinwegtäuschen, daß sie in Deutschland bis zu Helmut Fends Gesamtschuluntersuchungen nie empirisch aufgegriffen wurde. Im Gegensatz zum angelsächsischen Raum, wo sich Qualitätsevaluation in der Regel auf die systematische Überprüfung bestimmter fachlicher Leistungen konzentrierte, setzte sich im deutschsprachigen Raum ein Denken durch, das Schulqualität an einer breiten Palette von Merkmalen festmacht, die sich in der Praxis als qualitätsrelevant erwiesen haben. Die vielleicht am weitesten verbreitete Zusammenstellung stammt von Steffens & Bargel (1993) und umfaßt die folgenden 12 Merkmale *Guter Schulen:*

1. Orientierung der Schule an klaren fachlichen und überfachlichen Leistungszielen; Vermitteln wollen von Kenntnissen und Fähigkeiten
2. Forderndes Lernen, im Sinne eines ‚pädagogischen Optimismus‘, der davon ausgeht, daß die Schüler etwas lernen wollen und lernen können
3. Pädagogisches Engagement der Lehrer, ablesbar am erkennbaren Interesse am Wohlergehen jedes einzelnen Schülers
4. Kontrollierte Beobachtung und Begleitung der Lernfortschritte
5. Sicherung der Mindestbedingungen von Disziplin und Ordnung; klar erkennbare Regeln und Prinzipinen und konsistente Handhabung derselben
6. Führungsqualitäten von Leitungs- und Lehrpersonen im Sinne personaler und sozialer Kompetenzen (Optimismus, Konfliktfähigkeit, Kreativität, Begeisterungsfähigkeit, etc.)
7. Ein Klima des Vertrauens, resultierend aus persönlichen Kontakten (zwischen Lehrern, Schülern, Eltern), positiver Identifikation mit der eigenen Schule und einem Wir-Gefühl
8. Arbeitsorganisatorisches Funktionieren einer Schule im engeren Sinne
9. Lehrerkooperation (durch gemeinsame Projektarbeit, Hospitation, Supervision, etc.)
10. Innovationsbereitschaft und -fähigkeit der Lehrerschaft
11. Einbezug der Eltern
12. Schulaufsichtliche flankierende Stützmaßnahmen (personelle und finanzielle Ressourcen)

Allerdings existieren bis heute kaum gehaltvolle empirische Untersuchungen dazu, in welcher Weise solche Merkmaldimensionen mit Schulwirksamkeit gekoppelt sind (vgl. Hopkins 1999). Das hat zunächst damit zu tun, daß man sich Schulen nicht mehr als mechanische Input-Output-Systeme vorstellt, sondern als komplexe soziale Systeme, die sich an nachhaltigen Lernprozessen auf drei Ebenen orientieren (vgl. dazu ausführlich 3.1). Es wird denn auch häufig von einer selbstorganisierenden oder lernenden Schule (im Anschluß an Senge 1990) gesprochen. Wenn man aber als Funktion der lernenden Schule die Förderung einer ganzheitlichen Persönlichkeitsentwicklung bestimmt, wird jede Schulwirksamkeitsanalyse selbstredend zu einem schwierigen Unterfangen.

Eine selbstorganisierende Schule nach Dalin & Rolff (1994: 20ff.) begreift Lernen als Herausforderung in dreierlei Hinsicht:

– *Personales Lernen*: Jedes Individuum (Schüler/-in, Lehrer/-in, Leiter/-in) wird darin unterstützt, die der jeweiligen Aufgabe angemessenen Qualifikationen, Kompetenzen und Ressourcen zu erwerben.
– *Soziales Lernen*: Jede einzelne Gruppe in der Schule betrachtet sich als kollektive Lerngruppe und ist bereit, Zeit und Energie in die Zusammarbeit zu investieren.
– *Organisationslernen*: Die Schule begreift sich selber als lernendes System und institutionalisiert Strategien zur Förderung von Innovation, „vision-building“, Wirkungsdiagnose und Problemlösekompetenz.

Doch selbst dann, wenn man diese Perspektive engführt und Schulwirksamkeit alleine an fachlichen Lernprozessen ablesen möchte, sind große Vorbehalte angebracht. Noch lange nicht alle Lernerfolge oder Lernmißerfolge dürfen als „Produkt" der Schule gedeutet werden. Den Stand der Erkenntnis im Hinblick auf die damit angesprochene Anlage-Umwelt-Diskussion bringt F.E. Weinert folgendermassen auf den Punkt:

Weltweit ist zum gegenwärtigen Zeitpunkt niemand in der Lage, die Zusammenhänge zwischen individuellen Lernvoraussetzungen, typischen Lernprozessen und stabilen Leistungsunterschieden durch Erb-, Umwelt-, Entwicklungs- und Situationseinflüsse befriedigend zu erklären. Die wissenschaftlich zweifelsfrei nachgewiesenen Unterschiede in der Lernwirksamkeit und – damit zusammenhängend – im Leistungsniveau zwischen verschiedenen Kindern rechtfertigen aber die theoretische Annahme von stabilen interindividuellen Begabungsdifferenzen. (Weinert 1999: 45)

Ganz abgesehen davon ließen sich gute Argumente dafür vorbringen, als Qualitätsmerkmale von Schulen neben Schulleistungen auch die Reduzierung von Leistungsunterschieden oder die Entwicklung psycho-sozialer Kompetenzen zu evaluieren. Allerdings sind hier die Zusammenhänge mit schulischen Umwelten noch geringer als bei den Lernfortschritten (vgl. Baumert in GEB 2000a: 39ff.). So kommt denn Weinert (a.a.O.: 47) aufgrund seiner methodisch einzigartigen Längsschnittuntersuchungen zu folgendem Resümee: „Ist es nicht letztlich eine List der Vernunft, daß etwa 50% der geistigen Unterschiede zwischen Menschen genetisch determiniert sind, ungefähr ein Viertel durch die kollektive Umwelt und ein weiteres Viertel durch die individuelle, zum Teil selbstgeschaffene Umwelt erklärbar sind?"

Aus der Sicht der Qualitätsevaluation jedenfalls bedeutet der heutige Stand des Wissens im Bereich der Schulwirksamkeitsforschung, daß die Qualität von Bildungseinrichtungen keinesfalls alleine und noch nicht einmal zur Hauptsache aus Schulleistungen abgeleitet werden darf, wie dies in etlichen angelsächsischen Ländern der Fall ist. Alternativen dazu werden im Abschnitt 3 vorgestellt.

2.3 Von der Schulforschung zum Qualitätsmanagement in Schulen

Obwohl dieses Kapitel mit Qualitätsevaluation überschrieben ist, war bisher selten von Evaluation die Rede. Das hat damit zu tun, daß man im Schulbereich bis vor nicht allzu langer Zeit zwar vieles unternahm, was man heute auch mit Evaluation umschreiben würde, dafür aber andere Begriffe verwendet hat. Zwar hat Ralph W. Tyler (1971) den Begriff bereits 1949 im Zusammenhang mit der Evaluation von Unterricht eingeführt, und in diesem Kontext mit Unterricht verblieb der Terminus auch bis in die 70er-Jahre. Noch bis in die 80er-Jahre hinein wurde der Begriff in den einschlägigen pädagogischen Handbüchern und Fachlexika nicht oder kaum erwähnt.

Soweit ich sehe, waren drei Gründe dafür maßgebend, daß ab den 90er-Jahren der Begriff der Evaluation im Schulbereich so prominent wurde:

- Zunächst verschob sich ab 1980 das Interesse der Schulforschung zunehmend von der Makro- (oder Systemebene, wie sie oft genannt wurde) auf die Mesoebene. Die einzelne *Schule als gestalterische Einheit* (vgl. Fend 1987) rückte in den Vordergrund und verdrängte den Glauben an die Kraft der von oben verordneten Strukturreformen.
- Mit der Entdeckung der Schule als organisatorische Einheit machte man sich auf die Suche nach Möglichkeiten zu ihrer Verbesserung. Fündig wurde die Pädagogik bei der bereits etablierten Organisationsentwicklung, deren Leitideen und -programme man auf den Schulbereich übertrug. Die *Schulentwicklungsbewegung* war damit geboren und mit ihr der Gedanke, daß das *Qualitätsmanagement* zu den zentralen Gestaltungsdimensionen jeder Organisation zählt.
- Nicht zuletzt unter dem Eindruck der einsetzenden Reform der öffentlichen Verwaltung (New Public Management) wurden den Schulen höhere Autonomiegrade verliehen, allerdings um den Preis erhöhter *Rechenschaftspflichten*. Diese Pflicht wurde und wird zumeist über eine Kombination von internen und externen Evaluationen erfüllt.

Auf diesem Hintergrund wird verständlicher, weshalb neben der weiterlaufenden Schulqualitäts- und Schulentwicklungsforschung Qualitätsevaluation zunehmend auch als Aufgabe der einzelnen Schule verstanden wurde. Evaluation hat hier von der Schule her gesehen eine zentrale Funktion im Bereich des Qualitätsmanagements; von außen her gesehen dient sie der Rechenschaftslegung gegenüber dem Geldgeber.

Evaluation ist somit im Rahmen von Schulentwicklung in erster Linie ein Mittel zum Zweck der Verbesserung von Schulqualität. Zu den Führungsaufgaben von Schulleitung und Schulaufsicht gehört heute wie selbstverständlich die Installierung eines modernen Qualitätsmanagements (vgl. Dubs 1994: 270ff.). Dieses Qualitätsmanagement bedingt die regelmäßige Evaluation von zentralen Gestaltungsdimensionen (Lehrpläne, Schulklima, Unterricht usw.). Dazu werden neben selbstevaluierenden Verfahren zunehmend auch teil- oder vollstandardisierte Verfahren (ISO, 2Q, EFQM) angewendet.

Interessanterweise läßt sich seit einiger Zeit eine weitere Verlagerung des Interesses an Qualitätsevaluation beobachten. Nachdem über lange Zeit Indikatoren auf der Mesoebene (z.B. Schulklima, Einstellungen, Akzeptanz usw.) im Vordergrund standen, gerät nun zunehmend – wieder! – die Unterrichtsqualität in den Blickwinkel. Dieser Perspektivenwechsel läßt sich begründen mit der empirischen Einsicht, daß letzlich Unterrichtsvariablen einen wesentlich höheren statistischen Zusammenhang mit Schülerleistungen aufweisen als Variablen auf der Ebene der Schule allgemein.

3. Systematische Herleitung

Bevor allerdings auf konkrete Verfahren und Methoden der Evaluation im Schulbereich eingegangen werden kann, müssen einige systematische Überlegungen zum Ort und Stellenwert von Qualitätsevaluation im Schulbereich vorangestellt werden.

3.1 Die Lernende Schule

Es wurde andernorts ausführlich beschrieben, wie eine zeitgemäße Schule aussehen könnte (Rolff 1993). Es genügt für unseren Zusammenhang, auf einige zentrale Wirkungs- und Gestaltungsdimensionen einer Lernenden Schule einzugehen (Büeler 1997). Solche Schulen zeichnen sich dadurch aus, daß sie sowohl ihre realen Ziele wie auch ihre realen Möglichkeiten häufig reflektieren und systematisch nach Ansatzpunkten für innerschulische Initiativen und Verbesserungsmöglichkeiten suchen. Das Feld, das sich einer solchen Schule eröffnet, umfaßt die in Abbildung 2 skizzierten Gestaltungsdimensionen.

Lernende Schulen weisen eine starke *Outcome-Orientation* auf, d.h. ablaufende Lehr-/Lernprozesse werden kontinuierlich beobachtet, verglichen und es werden, wo angezeigt, Korrekturen angeregt. Im Zentrum der Aufmerksamkeit von effektiven Schulen stehen die Lern- und Entwicklungsprozesse aller Beteiligten, ja der Organisation insgesamt. Es geht also ausdrücklich nicht nur um Lernprozesse der Schüler/-innen, sondern genauso um diejenigen bei den Lehrpersonen usw.. Lernen wird auch nicht kognitivistisch verkürzt und reduziert auf Fachleistungen, sondern ganzheitlich gesehen. Begriffe wie emotionale Intelligenz oder Sozialkompetenz sind in einer solchen Schule genauso bedeutsam wie – beispielsweise – IQ oder mathematisches Wissen.

Gestaltungsmöglichkeiten eröffnen sich der Schule zunächst in ihrem traditionellen Gebiet, der Lehre und dem Unterricht. Die Rede von der Schule als organisatorischer Einheit darf nicht den Blick für die Tatsache verstellen, daß die entscheidensten innerschulischen Faktoren noch immer das Klassenklima und das Lehrerverhalten sind. Oberhalb dieser Mikroebene sollte eine Schule auch Zeit und Engagement in die Mesoebene investieren, zuvorderst in die Kreation gemeinsamer Visionen, in die Entwicklung eines Leitbildes und in ein individuelles Schulprofil. Die gemeinsame Arbeit an diesen Elementen verbessert nicht nur die Lehr-/Lernprozesse selber, sondern hat auch eine wichtige sozialintegrative Funktion für die Schule insgesamt (Corporate Identity).

Sodann zeichnen sich effektive Schulen dadurch aus, daß sie systematisch schulinterne und -externe Strukturen überprüfen und Anpassungen vornehmen. Dazu zählen wir auf der internen Seite beispielsweise Kommunikationsklima, Organisationsstrukturen, Informations- und Ressourcenmanagement, Weiterbildungswesen und Kooperationsverhalten; auf der externen Seite sollten etwa die sozio-ökonomischen Faktoren, aber auch die Kontakte zu Behörden, Politik und Wirtschaft berücksichtigt werden. Schlußendlich ist es unverzichtbar, daß Schulen vermehrt in Qualitätsevaluation investieren, wobei alle bisher umrissenen Gestaltungsdimensionen, vor allem aber die Lern- und Entwicklungsfortschritte selber einer kontinuierlichen Überprüfung und Sicherung unterworfen werden. Wenn eine Schule hier auf Professionalität setzt, wird sie interne und externe Kontrolle geschickt kombinieren müssen.

Schaubild 2: Ein Orientierungsrahmen für systemische Schulentwicklungs-
prozesse. Dunkel hinterlegt sind die primären Gestaltungs-,
resp. Wirkungsdimension(en).

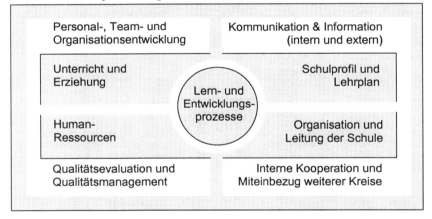

3.2 Qualität evaluieren und entwickeln

Damit ist ein entscheidender Punkt angesprochen. Die Dringlichkeit der laufenden Anpassungen der Schule an neue Rahmenbedingungen wird kaum bezweifelt, auch wenn das Ächzen über damit verbundene Belastungen unüberhörbar ist. Wesentlich weniger akzeptiert ist die Ansicht, daß Schulentwicklung sinnvollerweise immer mit Qualitätsevaluation verknüpft werden muß. Dabei stellt diese Verbindung eine Selbstverständlichkeit dar. Wenn immer wir in Lern- und Entwicklungsprozessen etwas grundlegend Neues ausprobieren, wollen wir am Schluß wissen, ob es – dieses Neue – einen Unterschied macht. Dieser Wille, aber auch diese Fähigkeit zur Selbstreflexion ist geradezu ein Kennzeichen erfolgreicher Personen und Organisationen. Schulentwicklung und Qualitätsevaluation können somit als zwei Seiten derselben Medaille betrachtet werden.

Dabei darf nicht vergessen werden, daß auch Qualitätsevaluation Zusatzbelastungen mit sich bringt. Statt diesen Umstand zu leugnen, müssen daraus die richtigen Schlüsse gezogen werden. Der wohl wichtigste ist: daß Qualitätsevaluation so organisiert werden muß, daß sie in bestmöglichem Umfang zur Schulentwicklung beiträgt. Evaluation ist also nicht Selbstzweck, sondern Mittel zum Zweck „besserer" Schulen. Doch dieses Kriterium alleine genügt nicht. Gefragt ist vielmehr eine Optimierung von mehreren Funktionen von Evaluation, wobei insbesondere die zwei folgenden bedeutsam sind:

– *formativ* wirksam ist eine Evaluation dann, wenn einerseits das Evaluationsdesign und andererseits die Ergebnisse (Berichte, Analysen, Daten) die Schule in ihrem Entwicklungsprozeß unterstützen;
– *summativ* gelungen ist eine Evaluation dann, wenn die verwendeten Methoden und Verfahren die Wirklichkeit der Schule zu einem gegebenen Zeitpunkt hinreichend genau (d.h. valide, reliabel und objektiv) abbilden.

Diese beiden Funktionen schließen sich nicht aus; sie schließen sich aber auch nicht zwanglos ein. Im Prinzip muß es darum gehen, ihr Verhältnis zu optimieren. Was als Optimum zu bezeichnen ist, kann wiederum nicht ein für allemal festgestellt werden, sondern muß von Fall zu Fall bestimmt werden. Zunächst müssen eine Reihe von Fragen beantwortet werden:

– Wer benötigt welche Informationen und weshalb?
– Wann werden die Resultate benötigt?
– Welchen Anforderungen müssen die Daten genügen?
– Welche methodischen Freiheitsgrade lassen die strukturellen und kulturellen Rahmenbedingungen zu?
– Wem werden die Resultate wann und zu welchem Zwecke rückgemeldet?

Eine sehr detaillierte und fundierte Diskussion solcher und anderer Grundprobleme der Evaluation findet sich in Sanders (1994), inklusive einer stark beachteten Zusammenstellung der wichtigsten Evaluationsstandards im Bildungssektor.

3.3 Vier Perspektiven der Qualitätsevaluation

Fragen dieser Art müssen geklärt werden, bevor man über einzelne Methoden, Instrumente oder Budgets zu diskutieren beginnt. In einer etwas systematischeren Sicht (vgl. Abb. 3) können vier grundlegende Perspektiven und Bezugsgruppen unterschieden werden. Diese Perspektiven sind nicht grund-

sätzlich unvereinbar. Vielmehr wird es in der Praxis oft auf eine Balancie-
rung und Kombination verschiedener Perspektiven und Erwartungen hinaus-
laufen (vgl. unten, Abschnitt 4).

Schaubild 3: Idealtypische Unterscheidung von vier Perspektiven im
Hinblick auf Ziele und Verfahren der Qualitätsevaluation in
Schulen.

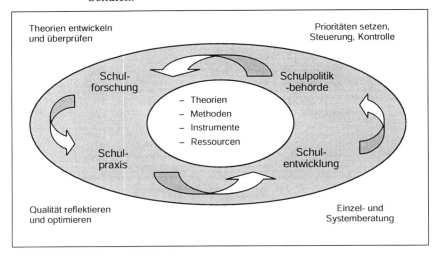

3.3.1 Schulbehörde und Schulpolitik

Qualitätsevaluation im Hinblick auf diese Bezugsgruppe dient in erster Linie
den zwei Zielen der *Legitimation* und der *Steuerung*. Schulen müssen sich
gegenüber den politischen Instanzen über die effektive und effiziente Verwendung der ihr zugewiesenen Ressourcen ausweisen. Gerade im Zeichen
der zunehmenden Autonomie lokaler Schulen gewinnt dieser Aspekt der Rechenschaftslegung an Bedeutung. Schulen mit ganz unterschiedlichen Profi-
len und Leitbildern werden sich zunehmend darüber ausweisen müssen, daß
sie die strategischen Ziele der Bildungspolitik einzulösen vermögen. Diese
Aufgabe geht natürlich weit über das hinaus, was die bisherige Schulaufsicht
leisten wollte und konnte, und zwar inhaltlich wie auch methodisch.

Damit ist der zweite Aspekt, jener der politisch-administrativen *Steuerung* von Schulen angesprochen. In vielen Schweizer Kantonen hat die politische Exekutive umgeschaltet von einer Steuerung des Inputs (gleiche Ressourcen und Strukturen) zu einer Steuerung des Outputs (wirkungsorientierte
Verwaltung, NPM, etc.). Im Hinblick auf beide Ziele benötigt Politik hinreichend präzise Informationen, und zwar hinsichtlich der Qualität einzelner

Schulen wie auch der Wirkungen anfälliger Reformen. Erst aufgrund solcher Daten können dann Prioritäten gesetzt und strategische Entscheide getroffen werden. Die Art der Daten richtet sich dabei nach den Fragen der Entscheidungsträger und diese wiederum stehen selbstredend in einem engen Zusammenhang mit der jeweiligen politischen Agenda.

3.3.2 Schulforschung

Das Wissenschaftssystem ist darauf ausgelegt, Theorien über die Wirklichkeit aufzustellen, sie empirisch auf ihren Wahrheitsgehalt hin zu überprüfen und weiter zu entwickeln. Die Wissenschaft knüpft mit ihren Theorien und Methoden gleichsam ein Netz und versucht, damit die Welt einzufangen. Was hängenbleibt, hängt allerdings vom Netz ab, nicht von der Welt. Wie fein auch immer dieses Netz geknüpft ist, immer fallen viele Sachverhalte durch die Maschen, die ebenfalls noch von Interesse sein könnten. Bezeichnend für die Wissenschaft ist, daß sie Forschung bestimmten methodischen Gütestandards unterwirft. Im Bereich der Empirie sind dies unter anderem die Prinzipien der Validität, der Objektivität und der Reliabilität.

Im Bereich der *Grundlagenforschung* geht es primär darum, grundlegende Aussagen über die Strukturen und Prozesse innerhalb des Systems Schule zu machen. Dieser Typ von Schulforschung geht etwa der Frage nach, wodurch sich gute oder effektive Schulen *im Allgemeinen* auszeichnen, welche Funktionen, Rollen und Dynamiken vorfindbar sind oder wie bestimmte schulische Merkmale mit den Leistungen der Schüler gekoppelt sind. Obwohl bei dieser Art von Forschung von konkreten Einzelfällen ausgegangen wird, sollen letztlich nach dem Prinzip der Induktionslogik verallgemeinernde Schlüsse ermöglicht werden. Solche Schlüsse nehmen im Bereich der Sozialwissenschaften meist den Charakter von Wahrscheinlichkeitsaussagen an und dürfen nicht als kausale Gesetze mißverstanden werden. Durch die logische Verknüpfung einer Vielzahl solcher Argumente entstehen dann eigentliche Theorien eines Gegenstandsgebietes, z.B. eine Theorie der Schule.

Das Interesse der *angewandten Forschung* liegt dagegen stärker beim Einzelfall, an den konkrete Fragestellungen herangetragen werden. Oft werden dabei bereits bestehende Theorien zum Ausgangspunkt für die Beobachtung einzelner Schulen oder einzelner Schulentwicklungsvorhaben verwendet (Prinzip der Deduktion). Gesucht wird dabei weniger das Allgemeine, sondern das Außergewöhnliche, das Überraschende, das Einmalige. Die Qualität der Forschungsbefunde liegt deshalb darin, daß sie ein begrenztes Feld möglichst präzise beschreiben und auf konkrete Fragen plausible Antworten liefern. Angewandte Forschung ist somit näher bei den Bedürfnissen der Schulpraxis anzusiedeln und nimmt in der Tat oft die Form von Auftragsforschung an.

3.3.3 Schulpraxis

Das Augenmerk des Systems Schule gilt, wie weiter oben postuliert wurde, zuallererst der Förderung von Lern- und Entwicklungsprozessen. Trotzdem gehörten qualitätsevaluierende Maßnahmen schon immer zum pädagogischen Geschäft, vor allem in Form der Überprüfung von Lernfortschritten bei den Schülerinnen und Schülern.

Ist man gewillt, dem Modell der lernenden Schule zu folgen, dann muß man allerdings Lernen in dreifacher Hinsicht berücksichtigen: als personales, als soziales und als organisationales Lernen. Und Qualitätsevaluation darf sich dann nicht mehr nur auf die Lernprozesse der Schüler/innen beschränken, sondern sie müßte in einer integralen Sicht die Lern- und Entwicklungsvorgänge aller Beteiligter miteinbeziehen. Dies stellt im Hinblick auf den in den 80er-Jahren eingeführten Begriff der Schulqualität ein erheblich erweitertes Konzept dar. Analog zum *Total Quality Management*-Konzept (Murgatroyd/Morgan 1993) werden nicht mehr nur einige organisationale Parameter erhoben, sondern man versucht, neben strukturellen und funktionalen Merkmalen auch die Qualität einzelner Prozesse zu evaluieren, beispielsweise eine Lehrplanimplementation.

Ein derart professionalisiertes Verständnis von Qualitätsevaluation ist allerdings in der Schulpraxis noch wenig verbreitet. Stattdessen dominieren vorderhand noch *ad-hoc-Evaluationen* zu den jeweils drängendsten Problemen: Gewalt auf dem Pausenhof, Elterneinstellungen oder Schülerzufriedenheit sind einige der Themen, die immer wieder auftauchen. Zum Einsatz gelangen möglichst einfache Erhebungsverfahren (z.B. Fragebogen), um die Daten mit kleinem Aufwand auswerten zu können. Die Prägnanz der so entstehenden Befunde darf allerdings nicht darüber hinweg täuschen, daß sie methodenkritischen Reflexionen oft nicht standhalten würden. Man kann dieses Problem natürlich auch positiv wenden: Der Prozeß der Reflexion ist wichtiger als die Ergebnisse. Dieser Schluß ist jedenfalls konsistent mit der These, wonach Qualitätsevaluation ein Mittel zum Zweck der Schulentwicklung darstellt, nicht mehr, aber auch nicht weniger. Man muß den unter Zeitdruck stehenden Lehrpersonen nachsehen, daß sie den diesbezüglichen Aufwand vorderhand so klein als möglich halten. Die Gefahr dabei ist, daß Selbstevaluation zu einem der christlichen Beichte verwandten Ritual verkommt, dessen Funktion in einer nach außen gekehrten Bereitschaft zu Einkehr und Reue liegt.

3.3.4 Schulentwicklung

Im Bereich der Schulentwicklung finden schon seit Jahren qualitätsevaluierende Verfahren aus der Organisationsentwicklung Verwendung. Diese Verfahren erfüllen dabei mehrere Funktionen. Sie müssen zunächst eine *Diagnose* ermöglichen, auf der dann die Einzel- oder Systemberatung aufbauen kann. Sodann sollen sie erlauben, laufende Entwicklungsprozesse zu reflektieren (*monitoring*), um allfällige Interventionen darauf abzustimmen. Und letztlich sollen diese Verfahren eine Form haben, die per se einen *formativen Effekt* hat, unabhängig von tatsächlichen Ergebnissen und den daraus resultierenden Interventionen.

Charakteristisch für die Perspektive der Schulentwicklung ist, daß sie Innovationen auslösen und steuern will. Qualitätsevaluierende Verfahren werden in der Regel nicht mit Blick nach außen (Legitimation) verwendet, sondern im Hinblick auf die Optimierung von internen Prozessen. Erhobene Daten und Befunde haben eine kurze Halbwertszeit und sie verbleiben denn auch meist im Besitz der Schule. Da Schulentwicklungsmoderatoren, Supervisoren, Coaches, usw. normalerweise spezielle Ausbildungsgänge absolviert haben, sind sie auch in der Lage, die Reichweite bestimmter Evaluationsverfahren abschätzen zu können und gegebenenfalls ein anderes Instrument „aus dem Methodenkoffer hervorzuzaubern". Im Gegensatz zur Schulforschung ist das Gütekriterium, an dem Resultate bemessen werden, nicht wissenschaftliche Präzision sondern *Passung* (Viabilität).

4. Evaluationsformen, -methoden und -modelle

Die soeben unterschiedenen vier Evaluationsperspektiven besitzen neben Unterschiedlichkeiten auch eine Reihe von Gemeinsamkeiten, namentlich im Bereich der herangezogenen Evaluationsmethoden und -modelle. Formallogisch betrachtet basieren alle Evaluationsansätze auf den in Abb. 4 skizzierten Grundformen der Qualitäts- und Wirkungsanalyse.

Diese Grundformen treten in der Regel in Mischformen auf. Dies ist auch sinnvoll, wie die Querverweise andeuten. Je mehr derartige Verknüpfungen aber in Analysen eingefügt werden, desto schwieriger wird die Handhabung der Evaluation und desto heikler die Interpretation der Befunde. Und nicht alle diese Formen sind gleich anspruchsvoll und aufwendig in ihrer *Handhabung*. Während einige problemlos auch als Selbstevaluation konzipiert werden können, bedingen andere fast zwingend den Beizug von externen Fachleuten.

Wie bereits ausgeführt wurde, gehen wir von einem Mehrebenenmodell (vgl. Abb. 1) aus, innerhalb dessen der Schule als lokaler organisatorischer Einheit eine Schlüsselrolle zukommt. Um der Klarheit in der Darstellung willen konzentrieren sich die folgenden Ausführungen auf den Ablauf von Evaluationsvorhaben auf dieser Mesoebene.

Schaubild 4: Fünf Grundformen der Qualitäts-/Wirkungsanalyse mit Erläuterungen und Beispielen aus dem Schulbereich. In eckigen Klammer [ ] sind die logischen Beziehungen mit anderen Grundformen vermerkt

Grundform: – Fokus:	Erläuterung und Beispiele aus dem Schulbereich:
1. *Analyse von* – System-Indikatoren – Struktur – Input – Output	In einem Querschnitt zur Zeitachse wird die gegenwärtige Systemstruktur erhoben. Bsp.: Elternzufriedenheit (Fragebogen), Schulleitungskompetenz (Assessment), Schülerleistungen (Test, TIMSS), Ressourcenallokation (Dokumentenanalyse; Recherche), Bildungsindikatoren im internationalen Vergleich (OECD), System-Monitoring (Schülerzahlen, Drop out)
2. *Vorher-Nachher Analyse* – Produkte – Outcome	In einem Quasi-Längsschnitt zur Zeitachse werden die Resultate von zeitlich verschobenen System-Analysen [1] verglichen, wobei die Differenz als „Produkt" des Systemverhaltens interpretiert wird. Bsp.: Schülerleistungen (added-value-Analysen), Wirkungen von Schulreformen (z.b. Erhebung Unterrichtsqualität V-N)
3. *Ist-Soll-Analyse* – Effektivität – Zielerreichung	[1, 2 und 5] können danach beurteilt werden, ob sie mit den Zielvorgaben übereinstimmen. Daraus kann auf die Wirksamkeit des Vermittlungsvorganges geschlossen werden. Bsp.: Lernzielkontrolle (Test, Anwendungsübung), SCHILF-Evaluation (z.B. durch Fallstudie), Programm-Pretest (Simulation, Evaluation).
4. *Aufwand-Ertrag-Analyse* – Effizienz – Kostenreduktion	[1, 2, 3 und 5] können nach dem Aufwand (Ressourcen) beurteilt werden, den sie zur Erreichung eines bestimmten Wirkungsgrades (Ertrag) benötigen. Als Ressourcen kommen personelle, zeitliche, finanzielle u.ä. Aufwendungen in Betracht. Bsp: Kalkulation einer Schulentwicklung oder Schulklassengrösse.
5. *Analyse von Prozeßindikatoren* – Prozeß – Systemdynamik	Im Anschluß an [2, 3 und 4] kann das Systemverhalten (d.h. die Interaktion zwischen Elementen) selber analysiert werden. Hier geht es darum, wirkungsvolle Prozeßmuster zu identifizieren. Bsp.: Beurteilung der Curriculum-Implementationsstrategie (Kausale Netzwerke) oder von Lehrverhalten (Beobachtung).

4.1 Ablauf eines Evaluationsvorhabens im Schulbereich

So verschieden die zur Anwendung gelangenden Evaluationsansätze in mancher Hinsicht auch sein mögen, so ähnlich sind sie sich doch im Hinblick auf ihren generellen Ablauf. Letztlich hat sich im Bildungssektor ein Denken durchgesetzt, das Evaluation als Kreislauf oder – im Sinne einer kontinuierlichen Qualitätsentwicklung – als Spirale vorstellt (vgl. Abb. 5).

Der Begriff des Qualitätsmanagements (Abk. QM) ist im Verhältnis zum Begriff Evaluation ein übergeordneter. Im QM-Konzept beschreibt eine Schule die Verfahren, mit denen die Qualität langfristig verbessert werden soll (vgl. Dubs in Tonhauser/Patry 1999: 154). Evaluation bezeichnet im Gegensatz dazu die Durchführung eines solchen Verfahrens, wobei in einem QM-Konzept durchaus auch sehr anders gelagerte Verfahren wie Supervision oder Q-Zirkel vorkommen können. Für eine ausführlichere Erläuterung der einzelnen Schritte in Abb. 5 vergleiche Kempfert & Rolff (1999: 96f.) oder Dalin, Rolff & Buchen (Dali/Rolff/Buchen 1995).

Schaubild 5: Der Kreislauf der Qualitätsevaluation, der zyklisch durchlaufen wird

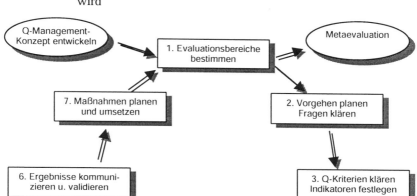

Die Auswahl von Evaluationsbereichen und -verfahren richtet sich also einerseits nach dem übergeordneten QM-Konzept, andererseits berücksichtigt sie die aktuellen Rahmenbedingungen und Notwendigkeiten in der betreffenden Schule. Hier wie bei jedem anderen Schritt ist darauf zu achten, die Beteiligten und Betroffenen an der Evaluation zu beteiligen, damit ein Bewußtsein von Selbstwirksamkeit, „ownership" und Verpflichtung und damit die erwünschte Verbindung von Q-Evaluation und Schulentwicklung entstehen kann. Auch die Einsetzung einer zuständigen Projekt- oder Steuergruppe kann sich als sinnvoll erweisen. Die Führungsverantwortung bezüglich Controlling und Qualitätsmangement verbleibt allerdings bei der Schulleitung (Dubs 1994: 266).

Aufgrund bisheriger Erfahrungen wird Schulen heute dazu geraten, mit einer Selbstevaluation zu beginnen. Die beteiligten Personen sollten die Gelegenheit erhalten, anhand eines überblickbaren und selbstgesteuerten Q-Projektes positive Erfahrungen zu sammeln, ganz in Übereinstimmung mit dem Leitsatz der Schulentwicklung Hartmut von Hentigs (1993: 25): „Wenn die Gedanken groß sind, dürfen die Schritte dahin klein sein". Selbst bei diesen ersten Schritten ist es ratsam, den Schulen Unterstützung anzubieten, sei es in Form leicht handhabbarer Instrumente, in Form von Fachberatung oder durch methodische Weiterbildung der Lehrpersonen.

Gleichzeitig ist heute aber auch weitgehend unbestritten, daß Selbstevaluation alleine nicht genügt, zumindest nicht aus der Perspektive der Schulforschung und der Schulpolitik (vgl. Abb. 3). Dies hat mehrere Gründe:

- Schulen verfügen intern oftmals nicht über die notwendigen methodischen Kompetenzen, um komplexere Evaluationsvorhaben selbständig durchführen zu können.
- Schulen verfügen selten über die für solche Vorhaben notwendigen zeitlichen, personellen und finanziellen Ressourcen.
- Aus Selbstevaluationen resultieren immer nur Binnensichten von Schule; der Vergleich mit anderen Schulen wie auch mit anderen Regionen kommt zu kurz.
- Schulen geht es nicht besser als allen anderen Organisationen: sie haben ihre blinden Flecken und sie haben zweifellos auch eigene Partikularinteressen, was nicht ohne Einfluß bleibt im Hinblick auf Evaluationsergebnisse.
- Form und Inhalt von Selbstevaluation sind oft nur begrenzt kompatibel mit den Bedürfnissen der Rechenschaftslegung und der Schulforschung.

Jedenfalls zeichnet sich zunehmend eine Kombination von vorgängig interner mit zeitlich nachgeordneter externer Evaluation ab, wobei teilweise auch voll synchronisierte Modelle zum Einsatz gelangen (vgl. etwa Büeler 2000). Im übrigen bin ich der Ansicht, daß extern konzipierte Evaluationsverfahren ebenfalls große Vorteile bieten: Sie sind für Schulen einfach zu kalkulieren und zu planen; die Lehrpersonen werden i.d.R. zeitlich weniger belastet; Aufgaben- und Rollenteilung ist klar geregelt; externer Support ist verfügbar. Im Zusammenhang mit dem mehrmaligen Einsatz des Verfahrens Peer Review Extended (ebd.) habe ich die Erfahrung gemacht, daß Schulen von solchen klar konzipierten und strukturierten Modellen profitieren, Überforderungen seltener und positive Erfahrungen häufiger werden. Inwieweit die Schule allerdings intern oder extern konzipierten Verfahren den Vorzug gibt, muß ihr überlassen bleiben. Der Entscheid für dieses oder jenes Verfahren bedarf jedenfalls seriöser Vorbereitung und sorgfältiger Güter- und Interessenabwägung. Alleine aufgrund von Hochglanzprospekten läßt sich die Spreu nicht vom Weizen trennen. Das Einholen von Referenzen und eine breit abgestützte interne Vernehmlassung scheinen in Anbetracht der investierten Mittel unerläßlich zu sein.

4.2 Verfahren zur Evaluation von Schulqualität im Überblick

Das Angebot an Evaluationsverfahren ist auch mit Blick auf den Bildungssektor in den letzten Jahren sehr unübersichtlich geworden. Dies widerspiegelt einerseits die Bedeutungszunahme von QM in Schulen und andererseits die zunehmende Professionalisierung des Angebots, wobei hier private Anbieter eine eigentliche Marktnische entdeckt haben. Zu unterscheiden sind zwei Typen von

Verfahren: auf der einen Seite existieren offene Verfahren, die im Hinblick auf Abb. 5 lediglich einzelne Schritte im Evaluationsablauf (z.b. die Datenerhebung) abdecken und normalerweise wenig standardisiert sind. Auf der anderen Seite gibt es standardisierte Q-Systeme, die meistens von privaten Institutionen entwickelt und angeboten werden. Die wichtigsten im Bildungssektor verwendeten Verfahren sollen in der Folge in aller Kürze skizziert werden.

4.2.1 Offene, systemunabhängige Evaluationsverfahren

Die nachfolgende Auflistung von Verfahren, resp. Verfahrenselementen ist selbstredend nicht vollständig. Sie deckt aber die im Schulbereich besonders häufig verwendeten Verfahren ab. Viele dieser Verfahren sind auch in Selbstevaluationen einsetzbar, andere sind typische Verfahren der Fremdevaluation (z.B. Audit oder Inspektion).

– *Test*: Bereits seit langem werden zur Kontrolle des Lernfortschrittes Schülertests eingesetzt. Diese „handgestrickten" Prüfungen und noch viel mehr die damit vergebenen Noten genügen höheren Anforderungen kaum; sie sind nur beschränkt valide, reliabel und objektiv. Problematisch ist dies deshalb, weil die Schule ihre Selektionsfunktion an diese Noten bindet. In angelsächsischen Ländern werden im Bereich kognitiver Leistungen zusätzlich standardisierte Tests eingesetzt, die diesbezüglich bessere Eckdaten aufweisen. Neuerdings werden solche Tests (IALS, TIMSS, etc.) in den OECD-Staaten auch zum Zwecke der Bildungsindikatorenforschung und des „system monitorings" verwendet. Auch zur Abklärung von Kindern mit über- oder unterdurchschnittlichen Begabungen werden testpsychologische Verfahren eingesetzt. Auch hier steht klar die summative Funktion im Vordergrund.

– *Survey*: Schriftliche Erhebungen haben eine lange Tradition, wobei sowohl offene Fragen wie auch multiple-choice-Fragen herangezogen werden. Fragebogenerhebungen werden sehr häufig herangezogen, um die Einstellungen, Erfahrungen, Wünsche usw. von Beteiligten und Betroffenen zu erfahren. Auch viele Leistungstests basieren auf diesem Datenerhebungsverfahren. Der Vorteil des Surveys ist seine Effizienz. Mit geringem Aufwand lassen sich große Populationen befragen, was eine Voraussetzung darstellt für statistische Auswertungen. Die scheinbare Einfachheit des Verfahrens darf nicht darüber hinwegtäuschen, daß die Validität der Instrumente wie auch die praktische Aussagekraft der Resultate oft recht bescheiden ist und wenig formatives Potential enthält.

– *Interview*: Mündliche Befragungen dürften die wohl häufigste Datenerhebungsmethode überhaupt darstellen. Sei es in formellen oder informellen Settings, sei es mit offenen oder halboffenen Fragen, seien es Einzel- oder Gruppeninterviews: Interviews stellen immer dann eine ernsthafte Alternative dar, wenn es um qualitative und explorative Da-

tenanalyse geht. Ein großer Vorteil dabei ist, daß auch Fragen zur Vergangenheit und Zukunft gestellt werden können und somit neben Ist-
Analysen auch prospektive und retrospektive Analysen vorgenommen
werden können. Eine gewisse Beschränkung stellt der Umstand dar, daß
die Arbeitsschritte sehr ressourcenintensiv sind (Befragung, Aufbereitung, Analyse) und daher zumeist keine repräsentativen Stichproben befragt werden können. Dieses Manko kann mit hilfe durchdachter Stich-
probenpläne minimiert werden.

- *Dokumentenanalyse*: Damit werden Verfahren bezeichnet, mit denen
  ausgewählte Belege sozialer Interaktion codiert und analysiert werden.
  Neben schriftlichten Belegen (Protokolle, Artikel, Aufsätze, usw.) wer-
  den heute zunehmend auch visuelle (Fotos, Videos) und auditive Daten
  (Tonbandaufzeichnungen) verwendet. Gerade letztere Datenquellen stellen sehr anschauungs- und aufschlußreiches Material (thick description)
  zur Verfügung. Inhaltsanalytische Verfahren eignen sich besonders im
  Verbund mit Portfolio- und Action Research-Ansätzen (vgl. unten).
- *Audit*: Es handelt sich dabei um die systematische Untersuchung oder
  Überprüfung einer Schule (resp. von Teilbereichen) durch offizielle In-
  spektoren oder durch unabhängige Fachexperten. Im Vergleich zur Inspektion werden Audits meistens durch Teams durchgeführt und haben einen größeren zeitlichen Umfang (z.B. zwei Wochen). Innerhalb eines Audits wird beispielsweise Unterricht hospitiert, es werden Gespräche mit
  Lehrpersonen geführt und schriftliche Unterlagen kontrolliert. Die Befunde
  werden protokolliert und der beauftragenden Behörde übergeben. Die
  summative Funktion steht beim Audit ganz klar im Vordergrund.
- *Action Research*: Innerhalb dieses Modells erforschen Lehrpersonen,
  Schüler (usw.) ihre Schule oder ihren Unterricht. Im Unterschied zu den
  anderen Verfahren handelt es sich um eine teilnehmende Beobachtung
  mit spezifischen Stärken (praxisnah, kontextualisiert, handlungsorientiert) und Schwächen (subjektiv, wenig analytisch). Ein Verfahren mit
  hohem formativem Potential.
- *Assessement* (AC): Es wird unterschieden in Entwicklungs- und Selekti-
  ons-AC sowie in Einzel- und Gruppen-AC. Eingesetzt werden AC's vorwiegend als Entwicklungsinstrument bei Personen in Kaderfunktionen,
  namentlich bei Schulleitungen. Eine weitere Verbreitung dieses Instruments wäre in Anbetracht seiner hohen summativen und formativen Funk-
  tionalität wünschenswert, scheiterte aber bisher an den hohen Kosten.
- *Hospitation*: Lehrpersonen besuchen sich wechselseitig im Unterricht
  und reflektieren ihre Erkenntnisse. Beobachtungskriterien und Rückmel-
  deprozedere sollten zuvor geklärt werden. Hospitation gewinnt zunehmend an Verbreitung und wird heute nachgerade als Grundmerkmal lernender Schulen betrachtet.
- *Inspektion/Pflichtvisitation*: Der periodische Besuch des Inspektors ist
  gleichermaßen unbeliebt wie verbreitet in der Schulwelt. Heute wird

vermehrt darüber nachgedacht, wie diese eher rituellen Besuche sinnvoll in den Gesamtzusammenhang des Q-Mangementes an Schulen gestellt werden könnten, ohne die Rechenschaftsfunktion preiszugeben (vgl. unter 4.2.2 die Systeme FQS oder PRE). Die bisherige Praxis leidet jedenfalls in erheblichem Maße an summativen wie formativen Schwächen.

– *Portfolio*: Im Zusammenhang mit Selbst- oder Fremdevaluationen werden Schulen gebeten, während einer bestimmten Periode alle verfügbaren Dokumente zum interessierenden Bereich zusammenzutragen. Die Schule selber kommentiert diese Dokumentation in knapper Form und zieht ein kurzes Fazit. Dieses Portfolio dient damit auch der Vorbereitung nachfolgender und weiterführender Evaluationsmaßnahmen.

– *Benchmarking*: Dieses bisher nur in Einzelfällen angewendete Verfahren dient der Suche nach der „best practice". Schule A sucht sich eine Schule B mit vergleichbaren Rahmenbedingungen von der sie glaubt, sie leiste Überdurchschnittliches (best in class). Schule B wird gebeten, in einen strukturierten Vergleichsprozeß einzutreten, anhand dessen Schule A seine Stärken und Schwächen eruieren kann. Das Verfahren hätte gerade im nicht-privatisierten Schulsektor durchaus Zukunftspotential, weil hier ein Kompetenztransfer nicht zum Ausscheiden eines „Konkurrenten" aus dem Markt führen kann. Gegen Benchmarking spricht wohl die bisher nicht gegebene Offenheit unter den Schulen und den zu erwartenden Arbeitsaufwand.

4.2.2 Standardisierte Qualitätssysteme

Bisher werden in Schulen noch vergleichsweise selten standardisierte Q-Systeme eingesetzt, insbesondere auf der Primar- und Sekundarstufe. Gründe dafür liegen im zu erwartenden Aufwand, aber auch darin, daß viele dieser Systeme wenig auf die effektiven Bedürfnisse und Rahmenbedingungen von Volksschulen eingehen. Volksschulen besitzen in der Regel die finanziellen und zeitlichen Ressourcen nicht, die von solchen Systemen – von FQS und PRE$^©$ einmal abgesehen – vorausgesetzt werden.

In Zukunft dürften standardisierte Systeme trotzdem an Bedeutung gewinnen. Bereits heute sind Schulen auf der Tertiärstufe häufig von Gesetzes wegen zu systematischer Evaluation verpflichtet und dieser Trend dürfte sich auch nach unten fortsetzen, gerade wenn die Bewegung hin zu Teilautonomie und New Public Management anhält. Ungelöst ist dann allerdings die Frage, wie den Schulen die dazu notwendigen Ressourcen und Kompetenzen zur Verfügung gestellt werden können. Ohne eine tiefgreifende Strukturreform wird dies kaum zu bewerkstelligen sein. Bei praktisch all diesen Systemen ist davon auszugehen, daß neben den direkten Kosten für das System zusätzliche Beratungsleistungen eingekauft werden müssen.

Die nachfolgende Auswahl beinhaltet Systeme, die nach Anspruch, Art und Umfang sehr unterschiedlich sind. Eine ausführliche Darstellung und entsprechende Literaturverweise zu einigen der nachfolgend erwähnten Q-Systeme finden sich bei Gonon, Hügli, Landwehr, Ricka & Steiner (1998).

– *ISO 9000ff*: Ein ursprünglich für Produktionsbetriebe entwickeltes System, das in einer an Dienstleistungsbetriebe angepaßten Version auch von Schulen angewendet werden kann. „Die Hauptarbeit … liegt darin, den Ist-Zustand der Aufbau und Ablauforganisation differenziert zu beschreiben" (a.a.O.: 21). Das hoch standardisierte System berücksichtigt das eigentliche schulische Kerngeschäft – d.h. Unterrichten – nur am Rande. Die formative Wirkung von ISO wird auch von Befürwortern als gering taxiert.

– *European Foundation for Quality Management (EFQM)*: Dieses auf der Philosophie des Total Quality Management aufbauende System wird in der Wirtschaft oft als zweiter, wesentlich aufwendigerer Schritt nach der ISO-Zertifizierung betrachtet. Das Ziel besteht in einer Verbesserung der Wettbewerbsfähigkeit mittels Selbstevaluation und einem Benchmarking, d.h. formative Effekte stehen im Vordergrund. Eine Anpassung des sehr differenzierten Modells an schulische Rahmenbedingungen scheint aufgrund bisheriger Erfahrungen machbar.

– *Peer Review Extended* (PRE©): Ein an der Universität Zürich entwickeltes Modell zur gemischt formativ-summativen Evaluation von Schulen, Schulnetzwerken und Schulreformprojekten. Nach der Bestimmung der Fragestellungen erstellt die Schule ein Portfolio und führt eine Selbstevaluation durch. Die an einer PRE© beteiligten 6-8 Schulen delegieren je zwei Vertreter in die Review-Teams, die nach einer zweitägigen Schulung wechselseitig durch Dokumentenanalyse, Beobachtung, Interviews und Schulbesuche eine externe Evaluation vornehmen. Die Beteiligung von externen Kreisen (Schulaufsicht, politische Behörden, Lehrmeister, Wissenschaftler) ist möglich und wünschbar. Neben den einzelnen Schulberichten entsteht durch fallvergleichende Methoden ein übergreifender Gesamtbericht.

– *Productivity Measurement and Enhancement System* (ProMES): ProMES wurde an der University of Texas entwickelt und stellt nicht ein fertiges Meßsystem dar, sondern definiert einen partizipativen Prozeß, mittels dem ein Selbstevaluationsinstrument vor Ort entwickelt und eingesetzt werden kann. ProMES versteht sich als vorwiegend formatives System, das beim Einsatz im Schulbereich stark angepaßt werden muß.

– *Formatives Qualitätsevaluations-System (FQS)*: Auch FQS gehört, wie schon der Name sagt, zu den formativen Systemen. Im Gegensatz zu ProMES, mit dem es sonst vieles gemein hat, wurde FQS vom Schweizerischen Lehrerverband spezifisch für Schulen entwickelt. Es soll Lehrpersonen zur Selbstevaluation anregen und der Schule zu einer transparenten Qualitätsentwicklung verhelfen. Das Verfahren ist vergleichsweise offen und bedarf erheblicher Anpassungsleistungen von Seiten der Schule. Wie ProMES definiert auch FQS weniger ein „was" als ein

„wie". Inwieweit auf das intern zu konzipierende FQS eine summative externe Evaluation folgen kann, ist umstritten.

- *2Q*: Die Abkürzung steht für Qualität und Qualifizierung. Das von Karl Frey entwickelte Verfahren hat weniger eine systematische Evaluation der Schule zum Ziel, als die berufsbezogene und persönliche Entwicklung der Mitarbeiter/-innen. Im Vordergrund steht dabei die zielorientierte Personalführung, die durch regelmäßige Beurteilungsgespäche gewährleistet wird. Bei 2Q steht die formative Funktion im Vordergrund; eine systematische Qualitätsevaluation ist nicht vorgesehen.

- *3-Säulen-Modell*: Das von Margrit Stamm entwickelte Verfahren stellt ein ganzheitliches Modell zur Evaluation von Schulen im sekundären und tertiären Bildungsbereich dar. Es enthält sowohl summative wie formative Elemente und berücksichtigt Variablen auf der Ebene Schule, Unterricht und Einzelperson (Lehrpersonen, Schüler). Zur Auswertung der Daten wird eine eigens entwickelte Software angeboten.

- *BfW*: Die Bewertungsstelle für Weiterbildungsangebote (BfW) bietet einen 20-Punkte Checkup an, mit dem Weiterbildungsgänge zertifiziert werden können. Das Verfahren ist rein summativ angelegt und beschränkt sich weitgehend auf die Prüfung eingereichter Dokumentationen.

5. Ausblick

Bereits einleitend wurde auf den Umstand verwiesen, daß das Bildungssystem als „größtes Unternehmen der öffentlichen Hand" zunehmend unter einen gewissen Entwicklungs- und Legitimationsdruck gerät. Schulentwicklung und Qualitätsevaluation werden künftig zum Normalprogramm von Schule gehören, genauso wie Unterricht oder Elternkontakte. Die diesbezüglichen Trends dürften irreversibel sein. Sie treffen aber im Schulbereich auf ein traditionelles Umfeld, in dem sich solche Richtungsänderungen nicht immer zwanglos realisieren lassen. Problem- und Spannungszonen werden denn auch bereits heute sichtbar.

Heiß diskutiert wird zur Zeit die Frage, ob die für Evaluation bereitstehenden Mittel eher der *Messung oder der Entwicklung* von Schulqualität zugeführt werden sollen. Insbesondere an den großen und teuren internationalen Leistungsstudien (TIMSS, PISA) scheiden sich die Geister. Ihnen wird vorgeworfen, sie würden Schulqualität auf Leistungserbringung reduzieren, wobei der Leistungsbegriff nochmals reduziert wird auf Fachleistungen in wenigen Hauptfächern. Die so entstehenden Befunde seien für die Schulpraxis weitgehend irrelevant, da in Lehrplänen und Schulprofilen ein sehr viel ganzheitlicheres Bild von Schule transportiert werde. Befürchtet werden auch „amerikanische Zustände", wo die Resultate von Schulen in solchen Leistungstests in Form von Rankings in den Massenmedien publiziert werden und zu einer Tri-

vialisierung der Schulforschung beitragen. Die teilweise berechtigten bildungs-
politischen wie auch forschungsmethodischen Bedenken können hier nicht
weiter ausgeführt werden (vgl. GEB 2000b; Zentrum für Schulentwicklung
1999).

Mit dem Einzug von Schulentwicklung und Qualitätsevaluation hat sich
auch das *Berufsbild und das Anforderungsprofil* des Lehrers verändert. Aus
dem Einzelkämpfer im Klassenzimmer soll nun der „Teamplayer" werden,
neben fachlichem und didaktischem Können sind neuerdings auch emotionale und soziale Intelligenz gefordert, und nun soll der Lehrer auch noch zum
Forscher werden? Nicht wenige Lehrpersonen fühlen sich durch diese Perspektiven verunsichert und reagieren mit Rückzug oder Widerstand. Es ist
einsichtig, daß solche Veränderungsprozesse ihre Zeit brauchen und nicht
ohne flankierende Ünterstützungssysteme (Weiterbildung, Coaching, Supervision, Beratung) zu realisieren sind. In der sich damit abzeichnenden Professionalisierung des Lehrerberufs liegt sicherlich auch eine große Chance.

Doch solche Perspektiven zeigen unvermittelt eine weitere Spannungs-
zone auf. Die für solche weiterführenden Maßnahmen *notwendigen Ressourcen* sind bisher schlicht nicht verfügbar. Wenn Organisationsentwicklung,
Qualitätsmanagement und Personalentwicklung tatsächlich im Schulbereich
Einzug halten sollen, müssen entweder neue Mittel bereitgestellt oder die
Allokation bisheriger Mittel verändert werden. Weil ersteres finanzpolitisch
quer in der Landschaft steht, wird man darüber nachdenken müssen, wo
schulintern Ressourcen eingespart oder schulextern beschafft werden können.
Im Zusammenhang mit neuen Formen selbsteuernden Lernens (z.B. per Internet) kann man sich durchaus vorstellen, das künftig Lernen nicht permanent in Gegenwart von Lehrpersonen stattfinden muß; andererseits dürften –
unbesehen der laufenden Kontroversen – Sponsoringverträge auch im Schulbereich häufiger werden und dadurch zu neuen Verbindungen zwischen dem
Bildungs- und dem Wirtschaftssektor führen.

Ein letzter, eher methodischer Knackpunkt der Evaluationsforschung betrifft die weitverbreitete Tendenz, das zu *messen, was einfach zu messen ist.* Sei
es in Schülerprüfungen, in Selbstevaluationen, in Leistungsvergleichsstudien
oder in Lehrerqualifikationssystemen: allzu oft wird kaum reflektiert, ob man
nun tatsächlich das mißt, was man messen wollte. Die damit angesprochene
Frage der Validität von Evaluationen darf aber nicht auf einzelne Konstrukte
reduziert betrachtet werden. Sie muß sich auf das insgesamt an qualitätsevalu-
ierenden Maßnahmen beziehen. Wenn also beispielsweise von Schulen ganz-
heitliche Erziehung und Bildung erwartet wird, darf man nicht zulassen, daß in
Schulleistungsvergleichen alleine eine kleine Bandbreite kognitiver Leistungen
berücksichtigt werden, auch wenn genau dafür besonders viele Meßinstrumente
vorliegen (vgl. Scheerens in Vedder 1992: 65ff.). Validität von Evaluation auf
dieser allgemeinen Ebene würde bedeuten, das zwischen schulischen Curricula
und getätigten Evaluationsmaßnahmen eine möglichst hohe Passung anzustre-
ben ist. Alles andere wäre auf lange Sicht fatal, wenn man die Negativerfah-

rungen des „teaching to the test" in angelsächsischen Ländern ernst nimmt (vgl. Broadfoot in a.a.O.: 109). Validität würde weiter bedeuten, daß die hohe Komplexität des Schulsystems sich widerspiegelt in vergleichsweise komplexen Evaluationsmodellen, die dem systemischen Charakter der Schule Rechnung tragen und nicht dazu neigen, singuläre und möglicherweise besonders spektakuläre Einzelbefunde herauszupartialisieren.

Daß sich damit ein erheblicher Entwicklungsbedarf in forschungsmethodischer Hinsicht abzeichnet, ist unübersehbar. Doch hier weiß sich die Schulforschung in bester Gesellschaft mit andern Disziplinen, die vor ähnlichen Problemlagen stehen. *Interdisziplinarität* ist deshalb das letzte Stichwort in dieser Aufzählung von Entwicklungsperspektiven der Schulevaluationsforschung. Die bereits seit einiger Zeit zu beobachtende Öffnung der Pädagogik gegenüber ihren Nachbardisziplinen wie auch gegenüber disziplinenübergreifenden Paradigmen (Systemtheorie, Kybernetik, Konstruktivismus usw.) wird sich wohl noch akzentuieren.

Die Schule findet ihren Ort und ihre Funktion in der Gesellschaft. Evaluation kann dazu beitragen, den Beitrag von Schule zum Wohlergehen der Gesellschaft insgesamt transparenter zu machen. Wenn man so seinen Blick auf das Ganze richtet, wird man Evauation im Schulbereich immer auch als Investition in die Schule der Zukunft verstehen.

Literatur

Bertalanffy, L. v. (1971): General System Theory: Foundations, Development, Applications. London: Allen Lane The Penguin Press.

Büeler, X. (1994): System Erziehung. Ein bio-psycho-soziales Modell. Bern: Haupt.

Büeler, X. (1997): Gute Schulen in systemischer Sicht. Grundschule, 29(4), S. 13-15.

Büeler, X. (2000): Peer Review Extended. Ein Verfahren zur Evaluation von Schulen und Schulentwicklungsprojekten (Manual). Zürich: FS&S.

Bundesamt für Statistik (Hg.) (1999): Bildungsindikatoren Schweiz 1999. Neuchâtel: BA.

Coleman, J. S. (1966): Equality of educational opportunity. Washington D.C.: U.S. Government Printing Office.

Dalin, P./Rolff, H.-G./Buchen, H. (1995):L Institutioneller Schulentwicklungs-Prozeß (ISP). Ein Handbuch. (2. Aufl.). Soest: LSW.

Dubs, R. (1994): Die Führung einer Schule. Leadership und Management. Stuttgart, Zürich: Steiner, Verlag d. Schweizerischen Kaufmännischen Verb.

Fend, H. (1981): Theorie der Schule. (2. Aufl.). München: Urban & Schwarzenberg.

Fend, H. (1987): ‚Gute Schulen' – ‚schlechte Schulen' – Die einzelne Schule als pädagogische Handlungseinheit, Qualität von Schule, H. 1: Erkundungen zur Wirksamkeit und Qualität von Schule . Wiesbaden: Hessisches Institut für Bildungsplanung und Schulentwicklung. S. 55-80.

Fend, H. (1990): Bilanz der empirischen Bildungsforschung. Zeitschrift für Pädagogik, 36, S. 687-709.

Fend, H. (1998):L Qualität im Bildungswesen. Schulforschung zu Systembedingungen, Schulprofilen und Lehrerleistung. Weinheim: Juventa.

GEB (Hg.) (2000a): Messung sozialer Motivation. (Bd. 14). Frankfurt: GEB.
GEB (Hg.) (2000b): Was leisten Leistungsvergleiche (nicht). Frankfurt: GEB.
Gonon, P./Hügli, E./Landwehr, N./Ricka, R./Steiner, P. (1998): Qualitätssysteme auf dem Prüfstand. Die neue Qualitätsdiskussion in Schule und Bildung. Aarau: Sauerländer.
Hentig, H. v. (1980): Einführung, Fünfzehntausend Stunden Schulen und ihre Wirkungen auf die Kinder. Weinheim: Beltz. S. 9-24.
Hentig, H. v. (1993): Die Schule neu denken. München: Carl Hanser.
Hopkins, D. (1989): Evaluation for school development. Milton Keynes: Open University Press.
Hopkins, D. (1999): Teaching and learning and the challenge of educational reform. School Effectiveness and School Improvement, 10, S. 257-267.
Jencks, C. (1973). Chancengleichheit. Reinbek: Rowohlt.
Kempfert, G./Rolff, H.-G.(1999): Pädagogische Qualitätsentwicklung. Ein Arbeitsbuch für Schule und Unterricht. Weinheim: Beltz.
Luhmann, N. (1987): Soziale Systeme. Grundriss einer allemeinen Theorie. (2. Aufl.). Frankfurt: Suhrkamp.
Murgatroyd, S./Morgan, C. (1993): Total quality management and the school. Buckingham: Open University Press.
OECD/CERI. (1997): Education at a Glance. OECD Indicators 1997. Paris.
Rolff, H.-G. (1993): Wandel durch Selbstorganisation. Theoretische Grundlagen und praktische Hinweise für eine bessere Schule. Weinheim: Juventa.
Roth, H. (1962): Die realistische Wendung in der Pädagogischen Forschung. Neue Sammlung, S. 481-490.
Rutter, M./Maughan, B./Mortimore, P./Ouston, J. (1980): Fünfzehntausend Stunden – Schulen und ihre Wirkungen auf die Kinder. Weinheim: Beltz.
Sanders, J. R. (1994): The program evaluation standards: how to assess evaluations of educational programs. (2. Aufl.). Thousand Oaks: Sage Publications.
Senge, P. (1990): The fifth discipline: the art and practice of the learning organization. New York: Doubleday.
Stamm, M. (1998): Qualitätsevaluation und Bildungsmanagement im sekundären und tertiären Bildungsbereich. Frankfurt: Sauerländer.
Steffens, U./Bargel, T. (1993): Erkundungen zur Qualität von Schule. Neuwied: Luchterhand.
Strittmatter, A. (1999): Qualitätsevaluation und Schulentwicklung. In: Thonhauser, J./ Patry, J.-L. (Hrsg.): Evaluation im Bildungsbereich. Wissenschaft und Praxis im Dialog. Innsbruck: Studienverlag. S. 173-188.
Szaday, C./Büeler, X./Favre, B. (1996): Schulqualitäts- und Schulentwicklungsforschung: Trends, Synthesen und Zukunftsperspektiven. Aarau: SKBF.
Tonhauser, J./Patry, J.-L. (Hg.) (1999): Evaluation im Bildungsbereich. Wissenschaft und Praxis im Dialog. Innsbruck: Studien Verlag.
Tyler, R. W. (1971): Basic principles of curriculum and instruction. Chicago: University of Chicago Press.
Vedder, P. (1992): Measuring the Quality of Education: Swets & Zeitlinger INC.
Wang, M. C./Haertel, G. D./Walberg, H. J. (1993): Toward a knowledge base for school learning. Review of Educational Research, 63, S. 249-294.
Weinert, F. E. (1999): Begabung und Lernen: Zur Entwicklung geistiger Leistungsunterschiede. In Max-Planck-Gesellschaft (Hrsg.), Jahrbuch 1999 . München: Max-Planck-Institut. S. 35-48.
Wottawa, H./Thierau, H. (1998): Lehrbuch Evaluation. (2. Aufl.). Bern: Hans Huber.
Zentrum für Schulentwicklung (Hrsg.) (1999): Evaluation und Qualität im Bildungswesen. Problemanalyse und Lösungsansätze am Schnittpunkt von Wissenschaft und Bildungspolitik. Graz: Zentrum für Schulentwicklung.

Stefan Kuhlmann

Evaluation in der Forschungs- und Innovationspolitik

1. Einführung

Die Institutionen der wissenschaftlichen Forschung und ihre Kommunikationen untereinander können als selbstreferentielles System beschrieben werden, dessen Leistungsorientierungen und Qualitätsmaßstäbe sich deutlich von denen anderer gesellschaftlicher Subsystem unterscheidet (Luhmann 1990). Ein Teil der heute verwendeten Evaluationsverfahren – vor allem die Praktiken der Bewertung wissenschaftlicher Leistungen, Projekte und Publikationen durch Fachkollegen (*peer review*) – wurzelt in dieser Selbstbezüglichkeit. Doch sie hat ihre Grenzen: Über ein Drittel aller (in Deutschland) betriebenen Wissenschaft und Forschung wird von der öffentlichen Hand alimentiert, knapp zwei Drittel von Unternehmen der Wirtschaft finanziert (European Commission 1999). Politik und Gesellschaft verlangen – seit den 1990er Jahren verstärkt – Rechenschaft über Leistungen, Qualität und Nutzen von staatlich geförderter Wissenschaft und Forschung, teils weil staatliche Mittel knapp sind und möglichst „effektiv" verwendet werden sollen, teils weil Politik und Öffentlichkeit einer gewissen Skepsis gegenüber dem selbstbezüglichen Wirken im Wissenschaftssystem hegen. Große Forschungsprojekte, übergreifende Forschungsförderungsprogramme und Forschungsinstitutionen wurden zusehends zum Gegenstand von Evaluationsverfahren.

Parallel zur Verbreitung und Ausdifferenzierung dieser Versuche der Erfolgsbewertung entfaltete sich auch eine Evaluationsforschung; sie analysiert die Anwendungsbedingungen sowie Erfolgsvoraussetzungen von Evaluation im Bereich der Forschungs- und Innovationsförderung und entwickelt die verwendeten Konzepte und Methoden weiter. Der vorliegende Beitrag skizziert diese Entwicklungen im Überblick.

Auch die Forschungs- und Entwicklungslaboratorien der Industrieforschung werden immer häufiger auf ihre Effizienz, Effektivität und auf ihre strategische Positionierung hin untersucht; diese industrielle Evaluationspraxis kann im vorliegenden Beitrag nur gestreift werden.

Im Folgenden findet der Leser zunächst (Abschnitt 2) eine knappe Darstellung der Entwicklungslinien der staatlichen Forschungs- und Technologieförderung, danach (Abschnitt 3) eine Übersicht der wichtigsten Konzepte, Anwendungsbereiche und Methoden evaluativer Verfahren in diesem Politikfeld, sodann (Abschnitt 4) eine Skizze des anhaltenden strukturellen Wandels in Forschung und Innovation sowie (Abschnitt 5) eine Diskussion seiner Konsequenzen für die Verwendung von Evaluationsverfahren im Prozeß politischer Entscheidungsfindung; ein Ausblick schließt den Beitrag (Abschnitt 6).

2. Entwicklungslinien der Forschungs- und Innovationsförderung

Staatliche Interventionen in Forschung, Technologie und Innovation haben eine lange Tradition und bilden heute unbestritten ein eigenständiges Feld staatlicher Politik (vgl. hierzu z.B. Grimmer u.a. 1992; Martinsen/Simonis 1995; Kuhlmann 1999). Wenn im folgenden von Forschungs- und Innovationspolitik die Rede ist, so sind damit zunächst alle Anstrengungen des politischen Systems gemeint, das „Forschungssystem" – verstanden als „Landschaft" forschender und Technologie entwickelnder Institutionen einschließlich der ihnen geltenden Regulationen – zu gestalten (hierzu auch Krull/ Meyer-Krahmer 1996; Ostry/Nelson 1995; Roobeek 1990); dies schließt, spätestens seit den 1970er Jahren, Bemühungen ein, das Innovationsverhalten industrieller Unternehmen positiv zu beeinflussen (vgl. Mowery 1994; Ergas 1987). Dabei ist zu betonen, daß Forschungs- und Innovationspolitik wichtige Schnittstellen zu anderen Politikfeldern aufweist, insbesondere zur Bildungspolitik (Aus-, Fort- und Weiterbildung), zur Wirtschaftspolitik (Strukturwandel, Handelspolitik), zur Rechts- und Innenpolitik, zur Umwelt- und Verkehrspolitik etc. Diese Politikbereiche beeinflussen entweder entscheidende Randbedingungen von Forschung und Innovation auf der Angebotsseite (Infrastruktur, qualifiziertes Personal etc.) oder wirken von der Nachfrageseite her (wie Verkehrsinfrastruktur, Arbeitsschutz, Umweltregulationen) (hierzu auch Kuhlmann u.a. 1998).

Das deutsche Forschungs- und Innovationssystem gilt im internationalen Vergleich als relativ gut entwickelt: 1995 waren knapp 460.000 Personen (Vollzeitäquivalente) mit Forschung und Entwicklung (FuE) beschäftigt; die Gesamtausgaben für FuE beliefen sich auf knapp 81 Mrd. DM, das entspricht 2,35% des Brutto-Inlandprodukts (Zahlen nach BMBF 1998)[1]. Die Forschungsinfrastruktur läßt sich als vergleichsweise differenziert charakterisieren:

– Die *Industrie* realisiert den größten Anteil von Forschung und Entwicklung (FuE) in Deutschland (283.000 FuE-Mitarbeiter): 1995 investierte die Industrie knapp 50 Mrd. DM überwiegend in angewandte Forschung

---

1 Der Spitzenwert lag 1987-89 bei 2,9%; zum Vergleich: 1997 erreichte Schweden 3,8%, Japan 2,9%, USA 2,7%.

und experimentelle Entwicklung. Nur einige wenige große multinationale Unternehmen, insbesondere in der Chemie und der elektrotechnischen Industrie, führen selber langfristig anwendungsorientierte Grundlagenforschung durch.

– Auf die *Hochschuleinrichtungen* (335 staatliche bzw. staatlich anerkannte Hochschulen, darunter 113 Universitäten und vergleichbare Einrichtungen; 101.000 FuE-Mitarbeiter) fällt der zweitgrößte Anteil der Forschungsausgaben (14,4 Mrd. DM). Sie konzentrieren sich auf Grundlagenforschung und auf langfristig anwendungsorientierte Forschung, zum größten Teil finanziert durch die Bundesländer sowie durch die Deutsche Forschungsgemeinschaft (DFG 1995: 1,8 Mrd. DM), eine staatlich finanzierte aber weitgehend unabhängige und selbstorganisierte Instanz der Forschungsförderung. Im Verlaufe den 1980er Jahren ist der Anteil industrieller Forschungsaufträge an den Forschungsbudgets einzelner Universitäten, insbesondere technische, signifikant gewachsen (auf 1,2 Mrd. DM).

– Die 16 „Großforschungseinrichtungen" der *Helmholtz-Gesellschaft* des Bundes (22.000 FuE-Mitarbeiter), leisten vor allem langfristig orientierte Forschung, die als risikoreich gilt, hohe Kosten verursacht (Anlagen) und große Forschungsteams benötigt. In den vergangenen Jahren haben die Großforschungseinrichtungen ihre Aktivitätsfelder deutlich verändert; ihr Aktivitätsspektrum reicht heute von der Hochenergiephysik über die Raumfahrttechnologie, die Medizin, die Biotechnologie, die angewandte Mathematik und die Software-Entwicklung bis hin zur Umwelttechnologie. Außerdem betreiben verschiedene Ministerien des Bundes sog. *Ressort-Forschungseinrichtungen* zur wissenschaftlich-technischen Unterstützung ihrer Aufgabenerledigung.

– Die Institute der *Max-Planck-Gesellschaft* (9.900 FuE-Mitarbeiter), eine Forschungsorganisation die auf die im Jahre 1911 gegründete „Kaiser-Wilhelm-Gesellschaft" zurückgeht, konzentrieren sich auf ausgewählte Felder der Grundlagenforschung in den Naturwissenschaften und Geisteswissenschaften. Sie beschäftigen sich vor allem mit solchen Forschungsschwerpunkten, bei denen ein großes Erkenntnis- und Entwicklungspotential vermutet wird, und die noch nicht in der Universitätsforschung verankert sind, oder die – wegen ihres interdisziplinären Charakters oder des erforderlichen Ressourcenaufwandes – dort keinen Platz finden werden.

– Die Institute der *Fraunhofer-Gesellschaft* (ca. 6.200 FuE-Mitarbeiter) sollen die praktische Verwendung wissenschaftlicher Erkenntnisse durch langfristig anwendungsorientierte und angewandte Forschung fördern. Die Fraunhofer-Gesellschaft führt in erster Linie Vorhaben der Auftragsforschung durch, die teils von der Industrie und teils von staatlichen Stellen finanziert wird. Die Gesellschaft betrachtet sich selbst als „Schnittstelle" zwischen Wissenschaft und Industrie in Deutschland. Sie wurde 1949 gegründet; keine andere Forschungsorganisation in Deutschland ist in den vergangenen 20 Jahren so schnell gewachsen.

- Die Forschungseinrichtungen der *Arbeitsgemeinschaft industrieller Forschungsvereinigungen* (AiF) führen vor allem angewandte Forschung und experimentelle Entwicklung für sektor-spezifische Bedürfnisse industrieller Unternehmen durch. Ihr Angebot, das teils aus öffentlichen Quellen und teils durch die Industrie finanziert wird, richtet sich insbesondere an kleine und mittlere Unternehmen, die in industrie-sektoralen Forschungsvereinigungen organisiert sind.
- Die Institute der *„Wissenschaftsgemeinschaft G.W. Leibniz (WGL)"* (früher „Blaue Liste") schließlich bilden eine Restkategorie, deren Gemeinsamkeit vor allem darin besteht, daß diese Einrichtungen von Bund und Ländern institutionell gefördert werden (rund 9.800 Mitarbeiter). Nach der Verschmelzung der beiden deutschen Forschungssysteme 1990 haben viele ostdeutsche Einrichtungen hier eine förderpolitische Heimat gefunden.

Abbildung 1: Instrumente staatlicher Forschungs- und Innovationspolitik (nach: Meyer-Krahmer/Kuntze 1992)

Instrumente im engeren Verständnis	Instrumente im weiteren Verständnis
1. Institutionelle Förderung	4. Aus- und Fortbildung

– Großforschungseinrichtungen
  – Max-Planck-Gesellschaft
  – Fraunhofer-Gesellschaft
  – Hochschulen
  – Andere Einrichtungen
	– Schulen, Hochschulen, Unternehmen
	
	5. „Diskursive" Maßnahmen

2. Finanzielle Forschungs- und Innovationsanreize	– Evaluation von Innovationspolitik
	  – Technikfolgenabschätzung
	  – Langfristvisionen
	  – *Awareness*-Maßnahmen

– Forschungsprogramme und Verbundprojekte
  – Innovationsprogramme (Indirekte Förderung)
  – Risikokapital
	6. Öffentliche Nachfrage

3. Sonstige Infrastruktur u. Technologietransfer	7. Benachbarte Politikfelder

– Information und Beratung für KMU
  – „Demonstrationszentren"
  – „Technologiezentren"
  – Kooperation, Netzwerke
	– Industrie- und Wettbewerbspolitik
	  – Regulative Politik, z.B. Beeinflussung der privaten Nachfrage
	  – Sozialpolitik

1996 gab der Bund insgesamt 16,7 Mrd. DM für Forschung und Entwicklung aus. Das Spektrum von Instrumenten der staatlichen Forschungs- und Innovationspolitik ist heute weit ausdifferenziert (siehe Abbildung 1) und reicht von der *institutionellen* Förderung von Forschungseinrichtungen (6,8 Mrd.

DM) über verschiedene Formen finanzieller Anreize (*Programme:* 7,5 Mrd.
DM) zur Durchführung von Forschung und experimenteller Entwicklung in
öffentlichen oder industriellen Forschungslaboratorien bis zur Gestaltung einer „*innovationsorientierten"* Infrastruktur einschließlich der Institutionen
und Mechanismen des Technologietransfers. Diese Instrumente kennzeichnen die Praxis der Forschungs- und Innovationspolitik in der Bundesrepublik
Deutschland seit den 1970er Jahren.

3. Evaluationsverfahren

3.1 Konzepte und Anwendungsgebiete

In historischer Perspektive kann man in Deutschland wie auch in anderen in-
dustrialisierten Ländern zwei heterogene Entwicklungslinien von Evaluationsverfahren im Bereich der Forschungs- und Innovationspolitik ausmachen
(vgl. zum Folgenden Kuhlmann 2000: 313/4; Kuhlmann/Bührer 1999: 239-
241). Sie lassen sich als ein *Drei-Schalenmodell* darstellen[2]:
Erste Schale – Individuelle Forschungsleistungen: Den „Kern" bilden
peer review-Verfahren und später zusätzlich Verfahren zur Messung der For-
schungsleistung einzelner Forscher und Gruppen (Bibliometrie etc.) als wis-
senschaftsinterne Instrumente für die Entscheidung über die Allokation von
Fördermitteln in Forschungseinrichtungen (vgl. hierzu Daniel 1993; Hornbostel 1997; van Raan 1988). Peer Review-Verfahren kommen im deutschen
Forschungs- und Innovationssystem weithin zur Anwendung, insbesondere
bei der ex-ante-Bewertung von Projekten der grundlagen- und der langfristig
anwendungsorientierten Forschung (Campbell/Felderer 1997). Dieses Verfahren ist das vorherrschende Evaluationsinstrument der Deutschen Forschungsgemeinschaft (DFG). Die DFG spielt eine zentrale Rolle bei der Förderung von Grundlagenforschung an Universitäten (1993: 835 Mio. DM),
vorwiegend indem sie einzelnen Forschern Zuwendungen auf Antrag gewährt
(sog. Normalverfahren). Förderanträge werden von *peers* bewertet, die im
Vier-Jahres-Rhythmus von der gesamten wissenschaftlichen Gemeinschaft
gewählt werden (vgl. Neidhardt 1988). Jeder Gutachter ist angehalten, den
Antrag allein auf der Grundlage seiner wissenschaftlichen Qualität zu beurteilen.

---

2   Die hier beschriebene deutsche Evaluationspraxis im Bereich von Forschungs- und
    Innovationspolitik steht in enger Beziehung zu ähnlichen „Evaluationskulturen" in
    anderen Industrieländern; Übersichten geben u.a. Bozeman & Melkers 1993; Geor-
    ghiou 1995 und 1998; OECD 1997.

Zweite Schale – Programme: Um diesen Kern der Peer Review-Verfahren herum legte sich eine Schale, die aus Evaluationsstudien im Sinne von *impact analyses* forschungs- und innovationspolitischer Programme besteht. Die in Deutschland bisher durchgeführten Studien schließen konzeptionell überwiegend an die Tradition der *Wirkungsforschung* an: Grundlage bilden die vielfältigen und traditionsreichen Arbeiten vor allem der amerikanischen Wirkungsforschung (*impact analysis*), in Verbindung mit Ansätzen der *policy analysis*, die sich zu einem in vielen Politikfeldern (insbesondere der Sozialpolitik) angewendeten Instrument der Politikberatung („policy-analytic movement"; vgl. Schön/Rein 1994: 11) entwickelt hat (Übersichten bei Widmer 1996; Patton 1997; Kuhlmann 1998a: 86-111; Wollmann 1998). Dieses Evaluationskonzept kann als wissenschaftsextern bezeichnet werden, denn es wird überwiegend von Akteuren des politisch-administrativen Systems in Gang gesetzt in der Absicht, die Erreichung politisch gesetzter wissenschaftlicher, technologischer, ökonomischer oder gesellschaftlicher Ziele zu prüfen. Wirkungsanalysen haben sich seit den 1970er Jahren in Deutschland mit der Verbreitung von Programm-Politik in vielen Politikfeldern durchgesetzt (vgl. Derlien 1976; Mayntz 1980 und 1983; Hellstern/Wollmann 1984). Seit dieser Zeit wurde etwa die Hälfte des Forschungshaushalts in die Projekt- bzw. Programmförderung gelenkt, die andere Hälfte in die institutionelle Förderung: Im Unterschied zur institutionellen Förderung verfolgen Programme gezielt politische Steuerungs- und Gestaltungsabsichten, etwa im Bereich der Förderung von „Schlüsseltechnologien" oder der Stimulierung von Innovationstätigkeit in der mittelständischen Wirtschaft. Weitreichende Steuerungsansprüche verlangten nach Erfolgskontrolle: Die Programmevaluation und Wirkungsforschung erlebten seither einen nachhaltigen Aufschwung (Meyer-Krahmer 1989). Die Ausbreitung von Evaluationsverfahren ist außerdem eng mit der wachsenden Zahl von strategischen Programmen (der EU-Kommission) zur Förderung von Wissenschaft und Technologie verbunden. In Deutschland zeigte sich insbesondere das Bundesforschungsministerium aktiv; zwischen 1985 und 1993 ließ man etwa 50 größere Evaluationsstudien anfertigen (Kuhlmann/Holland 1995a). Als Evaluatoren treten dabei üblicherweise unabhängige Forschungsinstitute im Auftrag forschungspolitisch-administrativer Akteure auf.

Die Erfahrung mit über zwei Jahrzehnten Programmevaluation führte zur Etablierung einer gewissen „Evaluations-Szene" im deutschsprachigen Raum, bestehend aus einer Gruppe von Experten und Instituten auf dem Gebiet der Wirtschaftswissenschaften und der Sozialwissenschaften, die ein relativ breites Spektrum von Evaluationskonzepten, -methoden und -instrumenten anwendet (vgl. Becher/Kuhlmann 1995) und seit den 1990er Jahren auch professionell in einer „Deutschen Gesellschaft für Evaluation (DeGEval)" organisiert ist.

Dritte Schale – Institutionen: Hier geht es um die Leistungsfähigkeit ganzer Forschungsinstitutionen. In Deutschland spielen seit langem die Begutachtungen durch den Wissenschaftsrat eine wichtige Rolle; bei der Neustrukturierung der „Forschungslandschaft" Ostdeutschlands nach der Vereinigung übernahmen sie sogar eine gestaltende Funktion (Block/Krull 1990). Seit den 1990er Jahren wurden institutionelle Evaluationen immer häufiger durchgeführt (Kuhlmann/Holland 1995b). Im Frühjahr 1999 schloß eine internationale Kommission eine „Systemevaluation" der Deutschen Forschungsgemeinschaft und der Max-Planck-Gesellschaft, ab (im Auftrag der Regierungschefs von Bund und Ländern; vgl. BLK 1999). Zeitlich parallel wurde auch eine Systemevaluation der Fraunhofer-Gesellschaft durchgeführt (vgl. FhG 1998). Eine Evaluation der Einrichtungen der „Wissenschaftsgemeinschaft G.W. Leibniz (WGL)" ist noch nicht abgeschlossen (Röbbecke/Simon 1999); Systemevaluationen der Großforschungseinrichtungen der „Helmholtz-Gesellschaft" sowie der Einrichtungen der „industriellen Gemeinschaftsforschung" befinden sich in Vorbereitung. Weitere Beispiele aus jüngerer Zeit ließen sich nennen.

Parallel zum gewachsenen Interesse an der Leistungsfähigkeit öffentlich geförderter Forschungsprogramme und -institutionen widmete auch die Privatwirtschaft der Effizienz, Effektivität und strategischen Ausrichtung ihrer Laboratorien erhöhte Aufmerksamkeit (z.B. Brockhoff 1999; Gerpott 1999; Bürgel u.a. 1996).

Zusammenfassend läßt sich die deutsche Evaluationspraxis im Bereich der Leistungen von Forschung und Forschungsinstitutionen als stark und zersplittert zugleich charakterisieren: stark wegen eines hohen Maßes an Selbstorganisation, das Konsens und Verpflichtung zwischen den Forschern fördert; unsystematisch und zersplittert, weil die institutionell orientierten Evaluationsbemühungen bisher nur wenig aufeinander abgestimmt werden konnten.

3.2 Methoden

Wir kennen heute vielfältige *Methoden* zur Feststellung erzielter oder erzielbarer Wirkungen. Die wichtigsten sind der Vorher-/Nachher-Vergleich, der Kontroll- oder Vergleichsgruppenansatz, sowie qualitative Analysen (u.a. Plausibilitätsüberprüfungen, Schätzurteile). Sie können mit unterschiedlichen Indikatoren (finanzieller Aufwand für Forschung und Entwicklung, Patente, ökonomische, soziale, technische Kenngrößen, Veröffentlichungen, Zitate etc.), Datensammlungsverfahren (Statistiken, Fragebögen, Interviews, Fallstudien, Panel etc.) und Datenanalyseverfahren (ökonometrische Modelle, Cost-/Benefit-Analysen, andere statistische Verfahren, Technometrie, Bibliometrie, Peer Review) einzeln oder kombiniert verwendet werden (ausführlich hierzu z.B. Meyer-Krahmer 1989: 60-71; Beiträge in Bozeman/Melkers 1993; Grupp/Kuntze/Schmoch 1995; Grupp 1997). Bei allen notwendigen Bemühungen um objektivierende Verfahren und geeignete Indikatoren muß jedoch davor gewarnt werden, quantitative Indikatoren allein als hinreichend für die Evaluation von Forschungs- und Innovationsförderung zu betrachten.

Der verständliche Wunsch nach einem standardisiert anwendbaren „Indikatoren-Werkzeugkasten" ist bei der Tendenz zur Verfolgung komplexer politischer Zielsetzungen nicht erfüllbar (Airaghi u.a. 1999).

Ein aus der Perspektive der Evaluationsforschung akzeptables, methodisch abgerundetes Konzept einer *ex-post*-Evaluation politischer *Programme* umfaßt grundsätzlich die folgenden Fragestellungen (hierzu ausführlich Kuhlmann 1998; Dreher 1997; Kuhlmann/Holland 1995a; Callon u.a. 1995; Meyer-Krahmer 1989: 50-60; Rip 1990; siehe auch *Abbildung 2*): Ermöglichte die evaluierte politische Maßnahme adäquate Lösungen für das zugrundeliegende technische, wissenschaftliche, wirtschaftliche oder gesellschaftliche Problem, das den Anlaß für die politische Intervention gab? Sind die dem Programmkonzept zugrundegelegten Annahmen hinsichtlich Problemwahrnehmung und -ursachen zutreffend, ist das Programm in diesem Sinne also „strategisch effizient"? Sind mögliche, im Förderfeld beobachtbare Strukturveränderungen Effekte der Maßnahme oder haben solche Strukturveränderungen ihrerseits die potentiellen Politikwirkungen beeinflußt? Der Versuch der Beantwortung wirft eine Reihe von methodischen, konzeptionellen und empirischen Problemen auf, die in jedem Fall neu bewältigt werden müssen. In den meisten Fällen erweist es sich, daß sie nur innerhalb wohl definierter konzeptioneller Grenzen überhaupt beherrschbar sind. Ein entscheidendes methodisches Problem hat seine Ursache unmittelbar in der Praxis der Politikgenerierung: Nur in seltenen Ausnahmefällen werden forschungs- und technologiepolitische Ziele explizit, klar und im Hinblick auf ihre Einlösung kontrollierbar formuliert (ausführlich untersuchten diesen Zusammenhang in verschiedenen Industrieländern Cunningham u.a. 1994; siehe auch Mowery 1994: 10).

Abbildung 2: Basiselemente eines Evaluationskonzeptes

1.	Ist das Programm geeignet? Sind die zugrundeliegenden Annahmen richtig?
2.	Wird/wurde die Zielgruppe erreicht?
3.	Welche direkten und indirekten Wirkungen gibt es/sind absehbar?
4.	Wurden die Ziele erreicht, bzw. sind sie erreichbar?
5.	Sind Implementation und Verwaltung effizient?

Die weiteren Fragestellungen eines Evaluationskonzepts betreffen die Wirkungen und die Durchführung des Programms: Wurde die Zielgruppe erreicht? Welche direkten und indirekten Wirkungen lassen sich dem Programm zuweisen? Wurden die Programmziele „erreicht"? Diese Frage ist keinesfalls trivial, nicht nur wegen der Unklarheit von Zielsetzungen, sondern zusätzlich wegen des Problems der Zuschreibung von feststellbaren Sachverhalten zu Anstoßwirkungen des Programms. Neben der Zielerreichung ist außerdem nach „Mitnehmereffekten" und nach der Angemessenheit der Implementation und der administrativen Abwicklung von Programmen zu fragen; diese Elemente betreffen die operative Effizienz der evaluierten Maßnahme und gehören zu den methodisch am weitesten Entwickelten der Evaluationspraxis.

Objektivität und Reichweite von Evaluationsverfahren

Auch wenn Evaluationsverfahren heute in weiten Bereichen staatlicher Forschungs- und Innovationspolitik Anwendung finden und Akzeptanz genießen, so läßt sich doch die „Richtigkeit" und Objektivität ihrer Ergebnisse und der daraus abgeleiteten Empfehlungen mit dem Hinweis auf unzureichende Evaluationsmethodik immer wieder in Zweifel ziehen. Bezweifelt wird die methodische Seriosität von Evaluationsstudien sowohl von Policy-Machern als auch von Sozialwissenschaftlern. Schön/Rein (1994: 12-13) identifizieren die folgenden Probleme:

–　Die verwendeten Evaluationskriterien vernachlässigen die Tatsache, daß die meisten Programme „multiple, conflicting, and evolving purposes" verfolgen.

–　Programmergebnisse werden häufig evaluiert, ohne daß ihr Entstehungskontext hinreichend verstanden worden ist („black box problem").

–　Evaluation erwarb vielfach den Ruf eines „Killers", wenn sie den (teilweisen) Mißerfolg eines Programmes nachwies, ohne sich mit den möglichen Ursachen zu beschäftigen.

–　Viele Kritiker von Programmevaluationen verweisen darauf, daß diese in der Regel die Perspektive der politisch-administrativen Programmverantwortlichen (oder staatlicher Aufsichtsorgane) einnehmen, aber die Interessen sonstiger „Betroffener" (z.B. Bürgergruppen) außer Acht ließen.

Zu diesen generellen Problemen von Programmevaluationen treten für das Politikfeld spezifische Effekte ein (Airaghi u.a. 1999): (1) Forschung und Innovation haben vielfältige Effekte. Zu den typischen kurzfristigen wünschbaren Wirkungen für die Teilnehmer geförderter Projekte gehören Umsatzsteigerungen und vergrößerte Marktanteile, Verbesserungen des Know-how sowie neuartige Kontakte. Die Effekte von Forschung gehen aber weit darüber hinaus: Ein Projekt übt auch vielfältige Wirkungen auf Akteure aus, die nicht unmittelbar daran teilgenommen haben – solche Einflüsse sind allerdings schwer zu messen. (2) Evaluationsergebnisse werden häufig frühzeitig für politische Entscheidungen benötigt, manchmal sogar bevor die Forschungsarbeiten abgeschlossen sind und normalerweise bevor sich die gesamte Breite möglicher sozio-ökonomischer Effekte entfaltet haben kann. (3) Viele Effekte lassen sich nicht eindeutig einem bestimmten Projekt oder Programm zuordnen. Sie können die Folge einer Kombination von Einflüssen sein, wozu auch die Verfahren der praktischen Umsetzung von Forschungsergebnissen zählen.

　Die offensichtlichen Begrenzungen der Leistungsfähigkeit von Evaluationsverfahren lassen sich nur kompensieren, wenn ihr Verwendungskontext

bewußt gehalten und ihre Ergebnisse mit Vorsicht bewertet werden (vgl.
Kuhlmann 1998a: 97-106):

– Evaluatoren und Evaluationsnutzer müssen sich klar darüber werden, was
  sie eigentlich wissen wollen, welche *Fragen* in welcher Breite, Tiefe und
  Radikalität zu stellen sind. Dabei bleibt die analytische Reichweite von
  Evaluationsstudien immer beschränkt: Wenn man einen prinzipiell unbe-
  grenzten Wirkungsraum politischer Maßnahmen annimmt, in den zugleich
  immer auch *andere Wirkkräfte* strahlen, dann bereitet die Rekonstruktion
  von Wirkungszusammenhängen umso mehr Probleme, desto umfassender
  und allgemeiner die Input- und Outputgrößen definiert werden.

– Die Evaluationsforschung im Bereich der Forschungs- und Innovationspolitik geht heute davon aus, dass „realistische" Informationen über ein
  Evaluationsobjekt nur durch die *kombinierte* Verwendung verschiedener
  sozialwissenschaftlicher *Methoden* und *Indikatoren* erarbeitet werden können.

– Dennoch sind der *„Objektivität"* von Evaluationsergebnissen *enge Grenzen* gesetzt, die durch eine gezielte Berücksichtigung verschiedenartiger
  Akteurperspektiven allerdings „überwunden" werden können.

Vorsicht und Sorgfalt sind also angebracht. Die Innovationsforschung weiß
heute, daß die Zusammenhänge zwischen „Investition" in Forschung und Innovation und möglichen wissenschaftlichen, wirtschaftlichen, sozialen oder
ökologischen „Erträgen" komplex sind und keinesfalls als schlichtes Input/
Output-Modell konstruiert werden können (z.B. Grupp 1998: 324-336).

4. Innovationssysteme im Wandel

Das „*Innovationssystem*" einer Gesellschaft umfaßt nach international akzep-
tiertem Verständnis die „Kulturlandschaft" all jener Institutionen, die wissenschaftlich forschen, Wissen akkumulieren und vermitteln, die Arbeitskräfte
ausbilden, die Technologie entwickeln, die innovative Produkte und Verfahren
hervorbringen sowie verbreiten; hierzu gehören auch einschlägige regulative
Regimes (Standards, Normen, Recht) sowie die staatlichen Investitionen in entsprechende Infrastrukturen (Freeman 1987; Lundvall 1992; Nelson 1993; Edquist 1997). Das Innovationssystem erstreckt sich also über Schulen, Universitäten, Forschungsinstitute (Bildungs- und Wissenschaftssystem), industrielle
Unternehmen (Wirtschaftssystem), die in diesem Felde tätigen politisch-administrativen und intermediären Instanzen (politischen System) sowie die formellen und informellen Netzwerke der Akteure dieser Institutionen. Als „hy-
brides System" repräsentiert es einen Ausschnitt der Gesellschaft, der weit in
andere Bereiche hineinstrahlt, etwa über das Bildungswesen, oder über unter-
nehmerische Innovationstätigkeit sowie deren sozio-ökonomischen Effekte

(Kuhlmann 1999: 13). Kein Innovationssystem gleicht dem anderen, ebenso wenig wie eine Gesellschaft der anderen (Amable u.a. 1997). Leistungsfähige Innovationssysteme entfalten ihre besonderen Profile und Stärken nur langsam, im Laufe von Jahrzehnten oder sogar Jahrhunderten. Sie beruhen auf stabilen Austauschbeziehungen zwischen den Institutionen der Wissenschaft und Technik, der Industrie sowie des politischen Systems.

Moderne Innovationssysteme standen immer und stehen gegenwärtig ganz besonders unter dem *Druck der Anpassung* an veränderte Umwelten (zum Folgenden Kuhlmann 1999: 19-25): Globalisierte Märkte, Umwälzungen der geopolitischen Situation sowie weltweit verflochtene, neuartige Kommunikationsinfrastrukturen und Technologien verändern das Innovationsgeschehen, das wiederum seinerseits durch eigendynamischen Wandel den internationalen Verflechtungsprozeß beeinflußt:

–   Die Entwicklung von Hochtechnologieprodukten hat in den vergangenen Jahren signifikante *Beschleunigung* erfahren; die Hervorbringung einer neuen Idee und ihre Kommerzialisierung am Markt folgen heute so schnell aufeinander wie nie. Veränderte Markterfordernisse und der Einsatz von Informations- und Kommunikationstechnik haben wesentlich dazu beigetragen.

–   In vielen Gebieten wächst die „*Wissenschaftsbindung*" des Innovationsgeschehens; die Funktionen und Verfahrensweisen der „zielgerichteten" Grundlagenforschung und ihre Schnittstellen zur Entwicklung von marktfähigen Produkten erfordern wachsende Aufmerksamkeit (Schmoch u.a. 1996a; Meyer-Krahmer/Schmoch 1998). Ein oft verwendetes Beispiel hierfür bildet die neue Bedeutung molekularbiologischer Forschungen für die pharmazeutische Industrie und die praktizierende Medizin.

–   Dabei erfordern komplexe Produkte und Prozesse eine dichtere Verflechtung und „Fusion" (Kodama 1995) heterogener Technikentwicklungen, wodurch traditionelle Grenzziehungen zwischen Wissens- und Technikgebieten verschwinden und *interdisziplinäre Kompetenzen* im Innovationsprozeß an Bedeutung gewinnen (Schmoch u.a. 1996b), neue disziplinäre Cluster entstehen und alte verschwinden.

–   Die genannten Trends steigern insgesamt das Erfordernis der *Kooperation* von Innovationsakteuren: Mit wachsender Komplexität des erforderlichen Wissens sind isolierte Akteure immer weniger in der Lage dieses ohne externe Unterstützung hinreichend zu beherrschen[3]. Innovationsorientierte

---

3   Hierzu auch Grupp/Schmoch (1992); van der Meulen/Rip (1994); Felt u.a. (1995: 211-218); Rammert (1997); Kuhlmann/Reger (1996: 74-78); Meyer-Krahmer (1997). Gibbons u.a. fassen diese Entwicklung als Übergang von „Mode 1" zu „Mode 2" zusammen: In „Mode 1 problems are set and solved in a context governed by the largely academic interests of a specific community. By contrast, Mode 2 knowledge is carried out in a context of application. Mode 1 is disciplinary while Mode 2 is transdisciplinary. Mode 1 is characterised by homogeneity, Mode 2 by heterogeneity. Organisatio-

Kooperation und die Pflege entsprechender Netzwerke (Callon 1992) gehören mittlerweile zum alltäglichen Innovationsgeschehen – zwischen Unternehmen sowie im Rahmen gemeinsamer Forschungs- und Entwick-
lungsvorhaben zwischen Unternehmen und öffentlichen Forschungseinrichtungen, zusehends auch in internationalen Verflechtungen (Jungmittag
u.a. 1999; Niosi 1999; Gerybadze u.a. 1997).

–   Nur scheinbar im Widerspruch hierzu steht ein Trend zur Herausbildung
    von besonders starken, an einen bestimmten Standort gebundenen, thema-
    tisch fokussierten Innovationskapazitäten, die weltweit im Wettbewerb mit
    nur ein oder zwei anderen Standorten stehen, wobei sich die Rangfolge
    durchaus ändern kann (z.B. Automobilbau in Deutschland und den USA;
    gentechnologische Pharmazeutik in den USA; Heimelektronik und Büro-
    technik in Japan; Segmente der Werkzeugmaschinenindustrie in Italien
    usf.). Man hat diese „locations" anschaulich auch als „Industrial Holly-
    woods" beschrieben (Meyer-Krahmer 1999): Wer erfolgreich innovieren
    will, muß sich an den Maßstäben dieser Zentren, die ein besonders lei-
    stungsfähiger Teil regionaler, nationaler oder sektoraler Innovationssyste-
    me sind, orientieren und gegebenenfalls mit ihnen kooperieren.

–   Einer neuen Dynamik ist schließlich auch das Verhältnis von kodifiziertem
    und nicht-kodifiziertem Wissen im Innovationsprozeß ausgesetzt; diese
    Unterscheidung bezieht sich auf das Ausmaß, in dem Wissensbestände fi-
    xiert und transferiert werden können. Computernetzwerke beschleunigen
    den Umlauf kodifizierten Wissens, das nur dann effektiv nutzbar ist, wenn
    es re-kontextualisiert werden kann, wenn also die Lernfähigkeit der Inno-
    vationsakteure wächst (Lundvall/Borrás 1998: 31).

Staatliche Politik reagiert auf diese Trends in Wissenschaft und Innovation,
indem sie mit ihrer Förderpolitik strukturellen Wandel in der „Forschungs-
und Innovationslandschaft" zu bewirken sucht und Modernisierungsdruck
auf Forschungsinstitutionen ausübt:

–   So werden seit Mitte der 1990er Jahre viele Programme der Forschungs-
    und Innovationspolitik als thematisch ausgerichtete Wettbewerbe ausge-
    schrieben, die auch einen strukturellen Wandel in Wissenschaft und
    Wirtschaft bewirken sollen: Konsortien von Bewerbern (i.d.R. Institutio-
    nen) sollen in einem selbstorganisierten Prozeß gemeinsame Projekte
    und deren Detailziele formulieren. Partnerschaften verschiedenster Ein-
    richtungen (Forschungseinrichtungen, Universitäten, private Firmen,
    Technologiezentren, Weiterbildungseinrichtungen etc.) zielen mit einem

---

nally, Mode 1 is hierarchical and tends to preserve its form, while Mode 2 is more
heterarchical and transient" (Gibbons u.a. 1994: 3). Ähnlich argumentiert auch Mit-
telstraß 1994. Etzkowitz/Leydesdorff (2000) entwickeln ein „Triple Helix" Modell,
nach dem Wissenschaft ko-evolutionär in die Dynamiken des Wirtschafts- und des
politischen Systems verflochten ist.

ganzen Bündel an aufeinander abgestimmten Maßnahmen auf eine Effektivierung ganzer Innovationssysteme. Solche *Multi-Akteur- und/oder Multi-Maßnahmen-Programme* können sich entweder auf Regionen und/oder bestimmte Missionen und/oder bestimmte Technologien und Branchen beziehen.

– Die *veränderten Anforderungen an Institutionen* wurden im Rahmen der „Systemevaluation" der Max-Planck-Gesellschaft und der Deutschen Forschungsgemeinschaft prägnant zusammengefaßt. Die Gutachter forderten unter anderem eine Lockerung der starken disziplinären Orientierung, die Entwicklung beweglicher und leistungsfähiger Organisationsformen für eine temporäre Zusammenarbeit verschiedener Disziplinen und Gruppen in problemorientierten Forschungsfeldern, wirksame Verfahren zur Qualitätssicherung unter externer Beteiligung, eine verbesserte Zusammenarbeit von Hochschulen und außeruniversitären Forschungseinrichtungen, die Förderung von Institutionen übergreifenden Forschungszentren sowie eine verstärkte internationale Orientierung und Vernetzung der Einrichtungen (BLK 1999).

5. Leistungsmessung *oder* Lernmedium: *Evaluation zwischen zwei funktionalen Polen*

Die skizzierten Veränderungen der Funktionsbedingungen von Forschung und Innovation haben seit den 1990er Jahren zu einem wachsenden Interesse an Evaluation geführt und der Anwendung entsprechender Verfahren Auftrieb gegeben (als Übersicht: OECD 1997). Die Erwartungen an Evaluationsverfahren bewegen sich dabei zwischen zwei funktionalen Polen: Evaluation kann in erster Linie der *Leistungsmessung* und damit der nachträglichen Rechtfertigung von Fördermaßnahmen dienen (*summative Funktion*), oder sie kann als „*Lernmedium"* verwendet werden, indem sie Erkenntnisse über Ursache-Wirkungszusammenhänge laufender oder abgeschlossener Maßnahmen als intelligente Information für laufende oder künftige Initiativen nutzt (*formative Funktion*).

Der summative Pol wird vor allem von der Evaluationspraxis angloamerikanischer Staaten genährt: Hier gewannen im Rahmen der Bemühungen zur Reform und Kostensenkung im öffentlichen Sektor („New Public Management") auch in der Forschungs- und Innovationspolitik Verfahren der Leistungsmessung („Performance Measurement") großen Einfluß (Osborne/Gaebler 1993; Shapira u.a. 1997). Die US-Regierung und eine Mehrheit der Bundesstaaten betreiben zusehends „performance-based management and budgeting systems" – nicht zuletzt in der Forschungs- und Innovationsförderung (Cozzens/Melkers 1997). Förderer und Geförderte stehen unter wachsendem Druck den Nutzen ihrer aus Steuergeldern finanzierten Aktivitäten unter Beweis zu stellen. Dies liegt nicht allein an entsprechenden neuen rechtlichen Erfordernissen – wie dem „Government Performance and Results Act (GPRA)" – oder knappen öffentlichen Haushalten sondern auch an einer intensiven öffentlichen Debatte über Berechtigung, Ausrichtung und Nutzen öffentlicher Investitionen in Forschung und Innovation. Ein Beispiel dafür ist das „Advanced Technology Program (ATP)" – ein heftig diskutiertes Programm des Bundes zur Förderung von kooperativen Forschungs- und Innovationsprojekten zwischen Wissenschaft und Industrie in risikoreichen Hochtechnologiebereichen, das langfristig auf weitreichende Diffusionseffekte zielt; dennoch wird das Programm immer wieder mit Erwartungen an kurzfristig meßbare Wirkungen konfrontiert. Ruegg (1998) stellt fest, daß das Programm „has met nearly continuous demand for measures of impact of the program since the day it was established".

Da aber die Komplexität forschungs- und innovationspolitischer Programme wie auch der Aufgaben von Institutionen eher gewachsen als zurück gegangen ist, stoßen summative Leistungsmessungen schnell an ihre Grenzen. Formative, lernorientierte Evaluationsansätze wurden deshalb – teils in Konkurrenz, teils als Ergänzung zu summativen – ebenfalls weiter entwickelt und eingesetzt. Von der nachhaltigen Erfahrung ausgehend, daß Evaluationsergebnisse häufig nur geringe Wirkung in politischen Entscheidungsprozessen zeigten und häufig nur wenige der in einer Policy-Arena vertretenen Erwartungshaltungen und Interessenpositionen unterstützten, versuchten Evaluationsexperten (und zunehmend auch Policy-Macher) die Grenzen zwischen Evaluation und Entscheidungsprozessen zu lockern, ja sogar beide Sphären teilweise zu integrieren. Prägnant haben Egon Guba und Yvonna Lincoln (1989) die Problematik skizziert. Sie sehen ein Grundproblem bisheriger Evaluationskonzepte in deren wissenschaftstheoretisch naiver Behauptung, daß Untersuchungsergebnisse darüber informieren, wie „die Dinge wirklich sind und funktionieren", so als ob sie nicht vom Evaluator, dessen Auftraggeber und von anderen hätten beeinflußt werden können.

Der Schlüsselbegriff des neuen, erweiterten Evaluationsverständnisses lautet „Verhandlung" in Akteursarenen. Das Ergebnis von Evaluationen, die entsprechend konzipiert wurden, ist, im Unterschied zur konventionellen Methodologie, nicht länger „a set of conclusions, recommendations, or value judgements, but rather an *agenda for negotiation* of those claims, concerns, and issues that have not been resolved in the hermeneutic dialectic exchanges" (Guba/Lincoln 1989: 13): Entscheidungen erfolgen eher als fortlaufender Prozeß, in welchem konkurrierende Akteure interaktiv Konsens erzielen, oder auch nicht. Evaluationsergebnisse sind dabei eine Information unter vielen. Hier treten also der Evaluations*prozeß*, genauer die Kommunikationen der beteiligten Akteure in seinem Verlauf in den Vordergrund; der Prozeß wird bewußt „partizipativ" gestaltet („Participatory Evaluation"; siehe Patton 1997: 100; Worthen u.a. 1997: 153-170). Der *mediale* Charakter des Evaluationsverfahrens tritt in den Vordergrund. Insbesondere folgende Eigenschaften des partizi-

pativen Ansatzes lassen sich für den Einsatz in forschungs- und innovationspo-
litischen Auseinandersetzungen weiterentwickeln:

– Evaluation wird als Verfahren der empirisch-analytisch aufbereiteten,
strukturierten Präsentation und Konfrontation von (teilweise widerstreiten-
den) *Akteurperspektiven* konzipiert; dabei kann das gesamte Spektrum von
Evaluationsmethoden (siehe Abschnitt 3) zum Einsatz gebracht werden.

– Der Evaluator agiert als *„facilitator"*, er unterstützt die *Moderation der
Auseinandersetzungen* im Verhandlungssystem durch Akteure des politisch-administrativen Systems.

– Das Evaluationsziel ist nicht allein die Bewertung von Sachverhalten aus
einer einzelnen Akteurperspektive (z.B. des politisch-administrativen Systems), oder die „objektive" Prüfung der Eignung einer Policy, sondern
die Stimulation von *Lernprozessen* durch Überwindung verfestigter Ak-
teursorientierungen.

Diese Evaluationskonzeptionen zielen vor allem darauf, ein „re-framing"
(Schön/Rein 1994) der Orientierungen korporatistischer und politisch-admi-
nistrativer Akteure zu erleichtern. Im Kontext des Forschungs- und Innovati-
onssystems können sie ein „intelligenter" Zulieferer zu den Verhandlungs-
und Bewältigungsstrategien der verantwortlichen politischen Akteure wie der
interessierten Öffentlichkeit sein. *„Intelligente" Politikentwicklungsverfah-
ren* in diesem Sinne[4] können darüber hinaus bereichert werden durch Kombination mit (vgl. Kuhlmann u.a. 1999)

– „Vorausschau-Verfahren" („Technology Foresight"; vgl. Cuhls 1998;
Cuhls /Kuwahara 1994), mit der Absicht, diskussionsfähige „Visionen"
von mehr oder weniger wünschbaren Zukunftsentwicklungen zu liefern,
und
– „Technology Assessment" (vgl. z.B. Rip u.a. 1995; Sundermann u.a.
1999) als dem Versuch, die möglichen positiven oder negativen Wirkungen technologischer Entwicklungen zu antizipieren und die in solchen
Studien gewonnenen Informationen in den Prozeß der Technikgenese
rückzukoppeln.

Dieses Potential methodisch angereicherter akteur- und prozeßorientierter
Evaluationsverfahren stößt in der Forschungs-, Technologie- und Innovationspolitik in Europa auf wachsendes Interesse. Aktuelle Beispiele für solche
Konzepte finden sich beispielsweise bei Maßnahmen des Bundesfor-
schungsministeriums zur strukturellen Modernisierung der interdisziplinären
Forschung an deutschen Universitätskliniken (Braun u.a. 1997; Bührer u.a.
1999), bei der Förderung von komplexen „Kompetenzzentren der Nanotechnologie" (Bührer 2000) oder bei der Maßnahme „Existenzgründer aus Hoch-

---

4 Ähnlich wie die für die Umwelt-, aber auch die Technikpolitik entwickelten „Diskurs-"
und „Mediationsverfahren"; z.B. van den Daele 1997.

schulen", die Initiativen einer engen regionalen Zusammenarbeit von Wissenschaft und Wirtschaft, von Hochschulen und deren Kooperationspartnern in der Region (wie z.b. Technologie- und Gründerzentren, Unternehmen, Kreditinstitute, Kammern, außeruniversitäre Forschungseinrichtungen) unterstützt, die zum Ziel haben, innovative Unternehmensgründungen von Studierenden sowie Hochschulabsolventen zu fördern und zu betreuen.

6. Ausblick

Jenseits des innerwissenschaftlichen Peer Review-Verfahrens zur Bewertung der wissenschaftlichen Leistungen von Fachkollegen erfolgt Evaluation im Bereich der Forschungs- und Innovationsförderung überwiegend als kritisch prüfender Eingriff von außen: Repräsentanten des politischen Systems veranlassen Bewertungen des Erfolges von Fördermaßnahmen gegenüber Wissenschaft und Innovationssystem. Solche Erfolgskontrolle kann als Frage nach dem „return on investment" von Steuergeldern konzipiert werden – dann droht die Gefahr kurzsichtig die Vielfalt möglicher langfristiger und indirekter, wünschbarer aber auch abzulehnender Wirkungen kreativer Wissenschaft und Innovationstätigkeit in Wirtschaft und Gesellschaft zu übersehen. Die Verwendung von Evaluationsverfahren als Medium der Moderation, das die divergierende Perspektiven beteiligter Akteure in Wissenschaft, Industrie und Politik nicht leugnet, sondern unterschiedliche Interessen bewußt als konkurrierende Erfolgskriterien thematisiert, kann hingegen eine „reflexive Wende" gegenüber älteren, häufig naiven rationalistischen Konzepten politischer Gestaltungsinitiativen einleiten. Umwälzende Richtungsänderungen in der Forschungs- und Innovationspolitik lassen sich auf diese Weise zwar nicht herbeiführen (dies kann letztlich nur in der Sphäre der Polity geschehen), doch die praktische Umsetzung solcher Richtungsänderungen wird durch Moderation erleichtert: Sie unterstützt die Lernfähigkeit der Akteure.

Literatur

Airaghi, Angelo/Busch, Niels E./Georghiou, Luke/Kuhlmann, Stefan/Ledoux, Marc J./van Raan, Anthony F. J./Viana Baptista, José (1999): Options and Limits for Assessing the Socio-Economic Impact of European RTD Programmes. Report to the European Commission, DG XII, Evaluation Unit. Brussels/Luxembourg (Office for Official Publications of the European Communities). – ISBN 92-828-3721-1.

Amable, Bruno/Barré, R./Boyer, R. (1997): Diversity, coherence and transformations of inovation systems. In: Barré, B./Gibbons, M./Maddox, Sir J./Marin, B./Papon, P. (Hg.): Science in tomorrow's Europe. Paris (Economica International), S. 33-49.

Becher, Gerhard/Kuhlmann, Stefan (Hg.) (1995): Evaluation of Technology Policy Programmes in Germany. Boston, Dordrecht, London :Kluwer Academic Publishers.

Block, Hans-J./Krull, Wilhelm (1990): What are the consequences? Reflections on the impact of evaluations conducted by a science policy advisory body. In: Scientometrics, Vol. 19, Nos. 5-6, S. 427-437.

Bozeman, Barry/Melkers, Julia (Hg.) (1993): Evaluating R&D Impacts: Methods and Practice. Boston, Dordrecht, London: Kluwer Academic Publishers.

Braun, Dietmar/Hinze, Sybille/Hüsing, Bärbel/Kuhlmann, Stefan/Menrad, Klaus/Peter, Viola (1997): Interdisziplinäre Zentren für Klinische Forschung in der Frühphase der Bundesförderung – Vergleichende Analyse. In: Zusammenarbeit mit Université de Lausanne. Stuttgart: Fraunhofer IRB Verlag.

Brockhoff, Klaus (1999): Forschung und Entwicklung. Planung und Kontrolle. München, Wien: R. Oldenbourg. 5. erg. u. erw. Aufl.

Bührer, Susanne/Peter, Viola/Braun, Dietmar/Kuhlmann, Stefan (1999): Interdisziplinäre Zentren für Klinische Forschung – Kommunikation & Kooperation: Prozeßevaluation der Fördermaßnahme „Interdisziplinäre Zentren für Klinische Forschung an den Hochschulkliniken". Stuttgart: Fraunhofer IRB Verlag.

Bührer, Susanne/Bierhals, Rainer/Erlinghagen, Robert/Hullmann, Angela/Lang, Christian/ Studer, Thomas (2000): Begleitende Evaluation der Kompetenzzentren der Nanotechnologie. Karlsruhe: Fraunhofer-Institut für Systemtechnik und Innovationsforschung; mimeo (im Erscheinen).

Bürgel, Hans D./Haller, Christine/Binder, Markus (1996): F & E-Management. München: Vahlen.

Bundesministerium für Bildung und Forschung, BMBF (1998): Bundesbericht Forschung. Faktenbericht 1998: Bonn.

Bund-Länder-Kommission für Bildungsplanung und Forschungsförderung, BLK (1999): Bericht der internationalen Kommission zur Systemevaluation der DFG und der MPG (Juni 1999) (56. Broschüre „Forschungsförderung in Deutschland"). Download http://www.blk-bonn.de/papers/forschungsfoerderung.pdf

Callon, Michel (1992): The Dynamics of Techno-Economic Networks. In: Coombs, R./ Saviotti, P./Walsh, V. (Hg.): Technological Change and Company Strategies: Economic and sociological perspectives. London u.a.: Academic Press Limited. S. 72-102.

Callon, Michel/Larédo, Philippe/Mustar, Philippe (1995): La gestion stratégique de la recherche et de la technologie. L'evaluation des programmes. Paris: Economica.

Campbell, David F. J./Felderer, B. (1997): Evaluating Academic Research in Germany. Patterns and Policies. Vienna: Institute for Advanced Studies. Political Science Series, No. 48.

Cozzens, Susan/Melkers, Julia (1997): Use and Usefulness of Performance Measurement in State Science and Technology Programs. In: Policy Studies Journal, No. 25(2).

Cuhls, Kerstin (1997): Retrospektive auf die Technikvorausschau und die technologiepolitische Anwendungen des Delphi-Verfahrens in Japan. Heidelberg: Physica, Springer: Reihe „Technik, Wirtschaft und Politik", Bd. 29.

Cuhls, Kerstin/Kuwahara, T. (1994): Outlook for Japanese and German Future Technology. Comparing Technology Forecast Surveys. Heidelberg: Physica, Springer Publishers, Series „Technology, Innovation and Policy", Vol. 1.

Cunningham, Paul N./Georghiou, Luke G./Barker, Kate E./Kuhlmann, Stefan/Reger, Guido/Marciano da Silva, C./Henriques, L. (1994): Analysis of Experience in the Use of Verifiable Objectives. Brussels, Luxembourg: Commission of the European Communities. (MONITOR/SPEAR – EUR 15634 EN).

Daniel, Hans-D. (1993): Guardians of Science. Fairness and Reliability of Peer Review. Weinheim u.a. (VCH).

Derlien, Hans-Ulrich (1976): Die Erfolgskontrolle staatlicher Planung. Eine empirische Untersuchung über Organisation, Methode und Politik der Programmevaluation, Baden-Baden: Nomos.

Dreher, Carsten (1997): Technologiepolitik und Technikdiffusion. Auswahl und Einsatz von Förderinstrumenten am Beispiel der Fertigungstechnik. Baden-Baden: Nomos.

Edquist, Charles (Hg.) (1997): Systems of Innovation. Technologies, Institutions and Organizations. London,Washington: Pinter.

Ergas, Henry (1987): Does Technology Policy Matter? In: Guile, B. R./Brooks, H. (Hg.): Technology and Global Industry. Companies and Nations in the World Economy. Washington D.C.: National Academy Press. S. 191-245.

Etzkowitz, Henry/Leydesdorff, Loet (2000): The dynamics of innovation: from National Systems and „Mode2" to a Triple Helix of university-industry-government relations. In: Research Policy, No. 29, S. 109-123.

European Commission (1999): Second European Report on S&T Indicators. Key Figures. Luxembourg: Office for Official Publications.

Felt, Ulrike/Nowotny, Helga/Taschwer, K. (1995): Wissenschaftsforschung. Eine Einführung. Frankfurt, New York: Campus.

Fraunhofer-Gesellschaft (1998): Systemevaluierung der Fraunhofer-Gesellschaft. Bericht der Evaluierungskommission. Download ftp://192.76.176.135/eval_fhg.pdf.

Freeman, Chris (1987): Technology Policy and Economic Performance: Lessons from Japan. London: Pinter.

Georghiou, Luke (1995): Research Evaluation in European National Science and Technology Systems. In: Research Evaluation, Vol. 5, No. 1, S. 3-10.

Georghiou, Luke (1998): Issues in the Evaluation of Innovation and Technology Policy. In: Evaluation, Vol. 4(1), S. 37-51

Gerpott, Torsten J. (1999): Strategisches Technologie- und Innovationsmanagement. Eine konzentrierte Einführung. Stuttgart: Schäffer-Poeschel.

Gibbons, Micheal/Limoges, C./Nowottny, H./Schwartzman, S./Scott, P./Trow, M. (1994): The new production of knowledge. The dynamics of science and research in contemporary societies. London u.a.: Sage.

Grimmer, K./Häusler, J./Kuhlmann, S./Simonis, G. (Hg.) (1992): Politische Techniksteuerung – Forschungsstand und Forschungsperspektiven. Opladen: Leske + Budrich.

Grupp, Hariolf (1998): Foundations of the Economics of Innovation: Theory, Measurement and Practice. Cheltenham: Edward Elgar Publishing.

Grupp, Hariolf/Schmoch, Ulrich (1992): Wissenschaftsbindung der Technik. Panorama der internationalen Entwicklung und sektorales Tableau für Deutschland. Heidelberg: Physica. Wirtschaftswissenschaftliche Beiträge 69.

Guba, Egon G./Lincoln, Yvonne S. (1989): Fourth Generation Evaluation. Newbury Park u.a.: Sage.

Hellstern, Gerd-Michael/Wollmann, Helmut (1984): Handbuch zur Evaluierungsforschung. Bd. 1. Opladen: Westdeutscher Verlag.

Hornbostel, Stefan (1997): Wissenschaftsindikatoren. Bewertungen in der Wissenschaft. Opladen: Westdeutscher Verlag.

Kodama, Fumio (1995): Emerging Patterns of Innovation. Sources of Japan´s Technological Edge. Boston: Harvard Business School Press.

Krull, W./Meyer-Krahmer, F. (Hg.) (1996): Science and technology in Germany. London: Cartermill

Kuhlmann, Stefan (2000): Moderation von Forschungs- und Technologiepolitik? Evaluationsverfahren als „reflexives" Medium. In: Martinsen, R./Simonis, G. (Hg.): Demokratie und Technik – (k)eine Wahlverwandtschaft? Leverkusen: Leske + Budrich, S. 303-332.

Kuhlmann, Stefan (1999): Politisches System und Innovationssystem in „postnationalen" Arenen. In: Grimmer, K./Kuhlmann, S./Meyer-Krahmer, F. (Hg.): Innovationspolitik in globalisierten Arenen. Leverkusen: Leske + Budrich, S. 9-37.

Kuhlmann, Stefan (1998a): Politikmoderation. Evaluationsverfahren in der Forschungs- und Technologiepolitik: Baden-Baden: Nomos.

Kuhlmann, Stefan (1998b): Moderation of Policy-making? Science and Technology Policy Evaluation beyond Impact Measurement: the Case of Germany. In: Evaluation, Vol. 4, No. 2, S. 130-148.

Kuhlmann, Stefan/Bührer, Susanne (1999): Evaluation von Forschungs- und Technologiepolitik. In: Sundermann, K./Bröchler, S./Simonis, G. (Hg.): Handbuch Technikfolgenabschätzung. Berlin: Sigma. S. 237-249.

Kuhlmann, Stefan/Holland, Doris (1995a): Evaluation von Technologiepolitik in Deutschland – Konzepte, Anwendung, Perspektiven. Heidelberg: Physica-Verlag.

Kuhlmann, Stefan/Holland, Doris (1995b): Erfolgsfaktoren der wirtschaftsnahen Forschung. Heidelberg: Physica-Verlag.

Kuhlmann, S./Reger, G. (1996): Technology-intensive SMEs: Policies Supporting the Management of Growing Technological Complexity. In: Cannell, W./Dankbaar, B. (Hg.): Technology Management and Public Policy in the European Union. Luxembourg, Oxford: Office for Official Publications of the European Communities, Oxford University Press. S. 73-102.

Kuhlmann, Stefan/Bättig, Christoph/Cuhls, Kerstin/Peter, Viola (1998): Regulation und künftige Technikentwicklung. Pilotstudien zu einer Regulationsvorausschau. Berlin: Physica-Verlag.

Kuhlmann, Stefan/Boekholt, P./Georghiou, L./Guy, K./Héraud, J.-A./Laredo. Ph./Lemola, T./Loveridge, D./Luukkonen, T./Polt, W./Rip, A./Sanz-Menendez, L./Smits, R. (1999): Improving Distributed Intelligence in Complex Innovation Systems. Brussels, Luxembourg: Office for Official Publications of the European Communities. (http://www.isi.fhg.de/abtlg/ti/pb_html/final.pdf).

Luhmann, Niklas (1990): Die Wissenschaft der Gesellschaft. Frankfurt/M.: Suhrkamp.

Lundvall, Bengt-Åke (Hg.) (1992): National Systems of Innovation: Towards a Theory of Innovation and Interactive Learning. London: Pinter.

Lundvall, Bengt-Åke/Borrás, S. (1998): The globalising learning economy: Implications for innovation policy. Luxembourg: Office for Official Publications of the European Communities, Targeted Socio-Economic Research.

Martinsen, Renate/Simonis, Georg (Hg.) (1995): Paradigmenwechsel in der Technologiepolitik? Opladen: Leske + Budrich.

Mayntz, Renate (1980): Implementation politischer Programme. Empirische Forschungsberichte. Königstein: Verlagsgruppe Athenäum, Hain, Scriptor; Neue Wissenschaftliche Bibliothek.

Mayntz, Renate (1983): Implementation politischer Programme II. Ansätze zur Theoriebildung. Opladen: Westdeutscher Verlag.

Meyer-Krahmer, Frieder (1989): Der Einfluß staatlicher Technologiepolitik auf industrielle Innovationen. Baden-Baden: Nomos.

Meyer-Krahmer, Frieder (1997): Science-based Technologies and Interdisciplinarity: Challenges for Firms and Policy. In: Edquist, Ch. (Hg.) (1997): Systems of Innovation. Technologies, Institutions and Organizations. London,Washington: Pinter. S. 298-317.

Meyer-Krahmer, Frieder (1999): Was bedeutet Globalisierung für Aufgaben und Handlungsspielräume nationaler Innovationspolitiken? In: Grimmer, K./Kuhlmann, S./ Meyer-Krahmer, F. (Hg.): Innovationspolitik in globalisierten Arenen. Neue Aufgaben für Forschung und Lehre: Forschungs- und Technologiepolitik im Wandel. Leverkusen: Leske + Budrich. S. 35-65.

Meyer-Krahmer, Frieder/Kuntze, Uwe (1992): Bestandsaufnahme der Forschungs- und Technologiepolitik. In: Grimmer, K./Häusler, J./Kuhlmann, S./Simonis, G. (Hg.): Politische Techniksteuerung – Forschungsstand und Forschungsperspektiven: Opladen: Leske + Budrich. S. 95-118.

Meyer-Krahmer, Frieder/Montigny, Philippe (1989): Evaluations of innovation programmes in selected European countries. In: Research Policy, 18, Vol. 6, S. 313-331.

Meyer-Krahmer, Frieder/Schmoch, Ulrich (1998): Science-based technologies: university-industry interactions in four fields. In: Research Policy 27, S. 835-851.

Mowery, David C. (1994): Science and Technology Policy in Interdependent Economies, Boston, Dordrecht, London: Kluwer Academic Publishers.

Neidhardt, Friedhelm (1988): Selbststeuerung in der Forschungsförderung. Das Gutachterwesen der DFG. Opladen: Westdeutscher Verlag.

Nelson, Richard R. (Hg.) (1993): National Innovation Systems: A Comparative Analysis. Oxford, New York: Oxford University Press.

OECD (1997) (Hg.): Policy Evaluation in Innovation and Technology. Towards Best Practices. Paris.

Osborne, D./Gaebler, T. (1993): Reinventing Government: How the Entrepreneurial Spirit is Transforming the Public Sector. New York: Plume.

Ostry, S./Nelson, Richard R. (1995): Techno-Nationalism and Techno-Globalism. Conflict and Cooperation. Washington: The Brookings Institution.

Patton, Michael Q. (1997): Utilization-Focused Evaluation. The New Century Text. Thousand Oaks u.a.: Sage.

Rammert, Werner (1997): Auf dem Weg in eine post-schumpeterianische Innovationsweise. Institutionelle Differenzierung, reflexive Modernisierung und interaktive Vernetzung im Bereich der Technikentwicklung. In: Bieber, D. (Hg.): Technikentwicklung und industrielle Arbeit. Frankfurt, New York: Campus. S. 45-71.

Rip, Arie (1990): Implementation and Evaluation of Science & Technology Priorities and Programs. In: Cozzens, S. (Hg.): The Research System in Transition, Boston, Dordrecht, London: Kluwer Academic Publishers. S. 263-280.

Rip, Arie/Misa, Th. J./Schot, J. (Hg.) (1995): Managing Technology in Society. The Approach of Constructive Technology Assessment. London, New York: Pinter.

Röbbecke, Martina/Simon, Dagmar (1999): Zwischen Reputation und Markt. Ziele, Verfahren und Instrumente von (Selbst)Evaluierungen außeruniversitärer, öffentlicher Forschungseinrichtungen. Berlin: Wissenschaftszentrum, WZB.

Roobeek, Annemieke J. M. (1990): Beyond the Technology Race. An Analysis of Technology Policy in Seven Industrial Countries. Amsterdam u.a.: Elsevier.

Ruegg, R. (1998): Symposium Overview. Symposium on Evaluating a Public Private Partnership: The Advanced Technology Program. In: The Journal of Technology Transfer, Vol. 23, No. 2, summer.

Schmoch, Ulrich/Hinze, S./Jäckel, G./Kirsch, N./Meyer-Krahmer, F/Münt, G. (1996a): The Role of the Scientific Community in the Generation of Technology. In: Reger, G./Schmoch, U. (Hg.): Organisation of Science and Technology at the Watershed. The Academic and Industrial Perspective. Heidelberg: Physica, Springer, Series: „Technology, Innovation, and Policy, Vol. 3, S. 1-138.

Schmoch, Ulrich/Breiner, S./Cuhls, K./Hinze, S./Münt, G. (1996b): The Organisation of Interdisciplinarity – Research Structures in the Areas of Medical Lasers and Neural Networks. In: Reger, G./Schmoch, U. (Hg.): Organisation of Science and Technology at the Watershed. The Academic and Industrial Perspective. Heidelberg: Physica, Springer, Series: „Technology, Innovation, and Policy, Vol. 3, S. 267-372.

Schön, D./Rein, M. (1994): Frame Reflection. Toward the Resolution of Intractable Policy Controversies. New York: BasicBooks.

Shapira, Philip/Kingsley, Gordon/Youtie, Jan (1997): Manufacturing Partnerships: Evaluation in the Context of Government Reform. In: Evaluation and Program Planning, 2(1), S. 103-112.

Shapira, Philip/Roessner, J. David (Hg.) (1996): Evaluation of Industrial Modernization. In: Research Policy, Vol. 25, No. 2, Special Issue.

Sundermann, Karsten/Bröchler, Stephan/Simonis, Georg (Hg.): Handbuch Technikfolgenabschätzung. Berlin: Sigma.

van den Daele, Wolfgang (1997): Risikodiskussionen am „Runden Tisch". Partizipative Technikfolgenabschätzung zu gentechnisch erzeugten herbizidresistenten Pflanzen. In: Martinsen, R. (Hg.): Politik und Biotechnologie. Die Zumutung der Zukunft. Baden-Baden: Nomos. S. 281-301.

van der Meulen, Barend/Rip, Arie (1994): Research Institutes in Transition. Delft: Eburon.

van Raan, Anthony F. J. (Hg.) (1988): Handbook of Quantitative Studies of Science and Technology. Amsterdam: Elsevier.

Widmer, Thomas (1996): Meta-Evaluation. Kriterien zur Bewertung von Evaluationen: Bern u.a.: Haupt.

Wollmann, Helmut (1998): Evaluation research and politics: Between a science-driven and a pluralist controversy-responsive policy-making model. Potential and limitations. Paper given to the Conference of the European Evaluation Society (EES). Roma: October 1998.

Worthen, Blaine R./Sanders, J. R./Fitzpatrick, J. L. (1997): Program Evaluation. Alternative Approaches and Practical Guidelines (2nd ed.). White Plains, NY: Longman.

Bettina Bangel, Christian Brinkmann & Axel Deeke

Arbeitsmarktpolitik

1. Konzeptioneller Rahmen[1]

1.1 Zum Stellenwert von Evaluation

Nachdem die Evaluierung von Politikfeldern in Deutschland im Vergleich zu anderen eurpäischen Ländern und den USA lange Zeit als Mauerblümchen eher ein Schattendasein führte, ist seit einiger Zeit eine Trendumkehr zu beobachten: Monitoring und Evaluation sind gleichsam Zauberwörter in Ansätzen des „new public management": Sie werden zum Ausdruck lernender Organisationen und einer effizienten und wirksamen Politikgestaltung.

Der zunehmende Stellenwert von Monitoring und Evaluation in der Arbeitsmarktpolitik spiegelt sich auf verschiedenen Politikebenen wider: Im Luxemburg-Prozeß der Europäischen Union, im Kontext des Benchmarking Europäischer Beschäftigungspolitik und in den Vorgaben der Europäischen Kommission zur Evaluierung ESF-kofinanzierter Arbeitsmarktprogramme. Auf Bundesebene in der im Dritten Buch des Sozialgesetzbuchs (§280 SGB III) nunmehr gesetzlich verankerten Verpflichtung der Bundesanstalt für Arbeit (BA), Wirksamkeitsanalysen zur aktiven Arbeitsmarktpolitik vorzunehmen oder der Verpflichtung der Arbeitsämter, im Rahmen von „Eingliederungsbilanzen" Rechenschaft über den Erfolg ihrer Aktivitäten nachzuweisen. Schließlich ist auch auf der Ebene der Bundesländer einiges in Bewegung geraten: Ein Beispiel ist hier das Land Brandenburg, in dem sich alle Ressorts der Landesregierung im Rahmen eines Kabinettbeschlusses zur Transparenz- und Wirksamkeitserhöhung durch Monitoring und Wirkungsforschung verpflichtet haben.

Die zunehmende Bedeutung von Evaluation hat die Diskussion um Möglichkeiten und Grenzen der Evaluierung von Arbeitsmarktprogrammen in Wissenschaft und Praxis neu belebt und seitens der politikberatenden Arbeitsmarktforschung eine Reflexion über die Rolle und Weiterentwicklung von Evaluationskonzepten angeregt.

Im folgenden werden zunächst die zentralen Diskussionslinien der Debatte anhand des Spannungsfeldes zwischen traditionellen Evaluationskonzepten einerseits und dem Ansatz der zielorientierten Evaluation andererseits nachgezeichnet (Kapitel 1.2).

---

1   Kapitel 1 basiert auf der leicht gekürzten Fassung des Beitrags von Bangel (1999).

Konzepte zur Evaluierung von Arbeitsmarktprogrammen, ihre konkreten Zielvorgaben, Fragestellungen und Verfahrensweisen lassen sich ferner nicht allgemeingültig bestimmen. Sie müssen vielmehr auf die Kontextbedingungen und die Erfordernisse der verschiedenen Nutzergruppen rückbezogen werden. Auch wenn es durchaus Fragestellungen von allgemeiner Relevanz gibt, werden Konzepte zur Erfolgsbewertung von Programmen je nach Adressatenkreis sei es etwa die Europäische Union, der Bund, ein einzelnes Bundesland oder aber ein Projektträger der Arbeitsförderung unterschiedlich akzentuiert sein. Dies wird bei der Entwicklung und Diskussion von Evaluationskonzepten und ihrer methodisch-empirischen Herangehensweise oftmals nur unzureichend berücksichtigt.

Der hier vorliegende Beitrag fragt daher aus verschiedenen Perspektiven der Bundesebene (Kapitel 2), der Landesebene (Kapitel 3) sowie aus europäischer Sicht (Kapitel 4) nach den Konzepten, Möglichkeiten, Grenzen und Entwicklungsperspektiven der Evaluation von Arbeitsmarktprogrammen.

1.2 Risiken traditioneller Evaluation oder: Zielorientierte Evaluation als Königsweg?

In der öffentlichen wie auch in der politischen Debatte steht das „ob" und „warum" der Evaluation von Programmen inzwischen außer Frage: Evaluation hat – darüber besteht Konsens – als eine auf nachvollziehbaren Kriterien beruhende Analyse und Bewertung der Wirkungen der Arbeitsförderung und dem Aufzeigen von Ansätzen zur Weiterentwicklung der Förderprogramme inzwischen auch in Deutschland ihren Platz. Kernpunkte sind dabei die Fragen nach der Effektivität der Maßnahme („wurden mit den eingesetzten Mitteln die Programmziele erreicht?") und der Effizienz der Maßnahme („wurden die gewünschten Effekte mit möglichst geringem Mitteleinsatz erreicht?").

Komplizierter – und strittiger – ist hingegen das „wie" von Evaluation. Das heißt konkret: Wie werden Ziele und Erfolge arbeitsmarktpolitischer Programme definiert, welche Evaluierungsmethoden werden verwandt, welche Untersuchungsebenen werden in die Evaluation einbezogen etc. Hier reichen die Ansätze – je nach Fachdisziplin und Blickwinkel – von einem stark standardisierenden, quantitativ orientierten Ansatz auf der einen Seite, bis hin zu einem ausschließlich qualitativ, projektbezogenen, der Aktionsforschung verpflichteten Ansatz auf der anderen Seite. Zwischen diesen Eckpunkten finden sich selbstverständlich eine Reihe von „Zwischentönen" im Umgang mit dem zuvor skizzierten Spannungsfeld.[2]

---

2   Aus der Fülle von Literatur sei hier insbesondere auf folgende Beiträge verwiesen: Schmid/O'Reilly/Schömann (1996a); Kromrey (1995); Brinkmann (1999).

1.2.1 Risiken traditioneller Evaluationskonzepte

Insbesondere hinsichtlich des „Wie" von Evaluation findet in der traditionellen Evaluationsforschung und auch in der öffentlichen Debatte auf verschiedenen Ebenen eine Verengung des Blickwinkels statt, die im folgenden anhand einiger Beispiele thesenhaft skizziert wird:[3]

Angebotsorientierte Schieflage bei der Frage nach dem Erfolg der Maßnahme
Bei der Frage nach dem Erfolg arbeitsmarktpolitischer Maßnahmen wird der Blick oftmals verengt auf den Verbleib der Teilnehmerinnen und Teilnehmer. Erfolgsindikatoren werden somit reduziert auf eindimensionale Leistungsindikatoren, wie z.B. die „Eingliederungsquote" und die „Eingliederungseffizienz". Nachfrageorientierte Kontextbedingungen, wie etwa die regionale Arbeitsmarktsituation oder sozioökonomische Determinanten der Beschäftigungsentwicklung bleiben ausgeblendet.

Vorrang der Vergleichbarkeit vor der Aussagekraft
In der Debatte zur Erfolgsmessung hat die Auswahl gleichlautender, quantifizierbarer Indikatoren zur Evaluation von Arbeitsmarktprogrammen oberste Priorität, um – vermeintlich eine Vergleichbarkeit der Wirksamkeit verschiedener Programme oder gar verschiedener Nationalstaaten sicherzustellen. Es findet somit eine Verengung auf einige wenige Indikatoren statt, die den Zielvorgaben einzelner Programme möglicherweise gar nicht oder nur unzureichend gerecht werden können. Das Spannungsfeld zwischen „Vergleichbarkeit" und „Aussagekraft" kann infolgedessen in eine Schieflage geraten und birgt die Gefahr eines Vergleiches von Äpfeln mit Birnen in sich.

Unzureichende Abgrenzung von Monitoring, Evaluation und Finanzkontrolle
Angesichts der noch wenig etablierten Monitoring-Systeme dient die Evaluation häufig überhaupt erst der Erhebung spezifischer Förderdaten. Die enge Anlehnung der Evaluation an die Monitoring-Systeme beschränkt die Aussagekraft und die Ziele von Evaluation insbesondere in ihrer Funktion der Wirkungs- und Ursachenanalyse über Erfolg und Mißerfolg von Programmen.

Gefahr unerwünschter Nebenwirkungen
Eine Vernachlässigung komplexer Wirkungszusammenhänge und Verengung des Blickwinkels auf einige wenige Leistungsindikatoren (z.B. Eingliederungsquote und Eingliederungseffizienz) birgt die Gefahr kontraproduktiver Wirkungen in sich, wie etwa Anreize zur reinen Mengenpolitik (möglichst viel zu geringen Kosten) oder eine Begünstigung der wettbewerbsfähigsten

---

3   Vgl. dazu auch: Schmid/O'Reilly/Schömann (1996b); Schmid (1996); Schmid/Schömann/Schütz (1997); Deeke/Hülser/Wolfinger (1997); Brinkmann (1999); Blaschke/Nagel (1999).

Arbeitslosen (creaming-Prozesse). Problematisch ist ferner die Fokussierung auf Bruttoeffekte der Wiedereingliederung: Mitnahmeeffekte, Substitutionseffekte oder Verdrängungseffekte können den Bruttoeffekt der Wiedereingliederung faktisch zunichte machen und bergen somit die Gefahr von Fehlallokationen bei der Mittelverteilung in sich.

Vernachlässigung von Prozessen der Politikformulierung und Implementation der Programme
Die traditionelle Programmevaluation fragt verkürzt nach Mitteleinsatz und Output und vernachlässigt somit die Ebenen der institutionellen Rahmenbedingungen und der Implementation von Programmen. Ein Beispiel ist hier die explizit arbeitsmarktorientierte Vorruhestandsregelung (West), die ihre Wirkung nur unzureichend entfalten konnte, da sie in Konkurrenz stand zu sogenannten 59er-Regelungen auf Basis der Rentenversicherung, die für die Unternehmen kostengünstiger waren (Bangel 1993).

Unzureichende Einbindung der Erfolgsbewertung in übergeordnete Ziele und Wirkungsgeflechte
Bei der Erfolgsbewertung sind oftmals übergeordnete Wirkungsziele und Wirkungsgeflechte nicht klar formuliert. Die Gesamtprogrammatik oder ihre Teilkomponenten sind jedoch nicht unabhängig von den à priori Zielsetzungen der Programmatik – wie etwa Bekämpfung der Jugendarbeitslosigkeit oder Verwirklichung des Postulats der Chancengleichheit – zu bewerten.

1.2.2 Die Konzeption der zielorientierten Evaluation

Demgegenüber rückt die zielorientierte Evaluation die Ziele von Programmen in das Zentrum der Analyse. Sie fragt nach den erwünschten Wirkungen und dem Politik-Mix sowie den institutionellen Rahmenbedingungen, mit denen die für einen bestimmten Adressatenkreis gewünschten Wirkungen am effizientesten erzielt werden können. Dabei werden auch Nebenziele, wie etwa der Ausgleich von Benachteiligungen am Arbeitsmarkt, einbezogen.

Die Konzeption der zielorientierten Evaluation bezieht Ergebnisse der traditionellen, programmorientierten Evaluation in ihre Analysen ein, erweitert jedoch den Blickwinkel um die Berücksichtung von Prozessen der Politikformulierung, den sozioökonomischen Kontext sowie die Umsetzungsbedingungen (Implementation) von Programmen. Die zielorientierte Evaluation vermeidet somit die negativen Effekte einer eindimensionalen, rigiden Erfolgskontrolle durch eine höhere Komplexität der Analyse, die von der Analyse des sozio-ökonomischen Kontextes über Monitoring und Wirkungsanalysen bis hin zu Kosten-Nutzen-Analysen oder Kosten-Wirksamkeitsanalysen reicht. Ferner präferiert sie prozeßhafte und dialogorientierte Verfahren der Erfolgskontrolle.[4]

---

4 Dieser Ansatz wurde im Rahmen eines „Handbuches zur Evaluierung der Arbeitsmarktpolitik" entwickelt, das mit der Unterstützung der Europäischen Kommission

Die Konzeption der zielorientierten Evaluation ist sicher ein Schritt in die richtige Richtung. Von ihrer Umsetzung sind wir allerdings – wie die nachfolgenden Kapitel deutlich machen – noch weit entfernt. Dennoch sind auf den unterschiedlichen Politikebenen (Bund, Land und EU) beachtliche Entwicklungen zu beobachten.

2. Aktive Arbeitsförderung auf Bundesebene

2.1 Organisatorische und gesetzliche Hintergründe

Es ist Bewegung gekommen in die Arbeitsförderung[5] der Bundesanstalt für Arbeit, und das nicht erst durch das SGB III, das Anfang 1998 das seit 1969 geltende Arbeitsförderungsgesetz (AFG) abgelöst hat (Deutscher Bundestag 1996). Im Rahmen des Organisationskonzepts „Arbeitsamt 2000" wurden die grundlegenden Organisationsziele neu bestimmt (Kundenorientierung, Wirksamkeit, Wirtschaftlichkeit und Mitarbeiterorientierung) und Handlungsfelder abgeleitet, zu denen ausdrücklich die Einführung von Controlling zählt (Bundesanstalt für Arbeit 1995, 1996; Kulozik 1998).

Die Leistungen der aktiven Arbeitsförderung[6] – neben Vermittlung und Beratung vor allem die „großen" Instrumente Förderung der beruflichen Weiterbildung (FbW) und Arbeitsbeschaffungsmaßnahmen (ABM) – wurden verändert und ergänzt. Ausgehend von einschlägigen Erfahrungen im Ausland wurde schon 1986 das Überbrückungsgeld als Starthilfe für den Sprung aus der Arbeitslosigkeit in die Selbständigkeit eingeführt und später in den Konditionen deutlich verbessert. Nach einer Erprobungsphase wurde Anfang 1994 eine Projektförderung für besonders schwer vermittelbare Arbeitslose eingeführt.[7] Vor allem die Erfahrungen in Ostdeutschland haben zu den jetzt „Strukturanpassungsmaßnahmen" genannten pauschalierten Lohnkostenzuschüssen geführt, mit denen Arbeitsbeschaffung mehr an die Beschäftigung im regulären Arbeitsmarkt gekoppelt werden soll.[8] Hinzugekommen ist weiterhin die gemeinnützige Arbeitnehmerüberlassung.

Mit dem SGB III wurde u.a. die schon vorhandene Palette betriebsbezogener Einstellungshilfen um neue Instrumente erweitert (Stichworte: Eingliederungsvertrag, Einstellungszuschuß bei Neugründungen). Besonders zu er-

---

von einem internationalen Netzwerk renommierter Arbeitsmarktforscher erarbeitet wurde, vgl. dazu: Schmid/O'Reilly/Schömann (1996a).

5   Dieser Begriff wird im SGB III zur Umschreibung der arbeitsmarktpolitischen Aktivitäten der BA verwendet.
6   Hierzu gehören nicht die (passiven) Lohnersatzleistungen.
7   Sie ist nunmehr im Rahmen der Freien Förderung nach §10 SGB III möglich.
8   Zur Zeit auf fünf Jahre im SGB III befristet verankert.

wähnen ist schließlich die nach holländischem Vorbild gerade auch im kommunalen Bereich nunmehr praktizierte Vermittlung nach der sog. „Maatwerk"-Methode, bei der private Vermittlungsagenturen für erfolgreiche Vermittlungen Prämien erhalten.

Zudem wird anders als früher in deutschen Landen nunmehr auch im Bereich der Arbeitsmarktpolitik viel experimentiert, zumindest im Sinne von Modellversuchen und der Erprobung neuer Ansätze. Zusätzlich zu einem schon mehrere Jahre existierenden BMA-Haushaltstitel[9] und zusätzlich zu den aus EU-Mitteln finanzierten (transnationalen) Modellprojekten der Gemeinschaftsinitiativen[10] kann nun auch die „Freie Förderung" nach §10 SGB III als „Innovationstopf" genutzt werden, und zwar mit einem beachtlichen Haushaltsvolumen.[11]

Das Sozialgesetzbuch III hat den laufenden Veränderungen in der Arbeitsverwaltung neue Impulse gegeben und einen Rahmen gezogen, der sich mit den Stichworten neue Förderphilosophie, neue Instrumente, Dezentralisierung und Regionalisierung umschreiben läßt. Es enthält neue Vorgaben für Controlling und Evaluation, wobei ein innerer Zusammenhang zwischen diesen Komponenten zu erkennen ist.

Die neue „Förderphilosphie" interessiert an dieser Stelle weniger, sie hat sich auch nur partiell im Instrumentarium niedergeschlagen (Brinkmann/ Kress 1997). In einem insgesamt sehr heterogenen Zielsystem (vgl. 2.4) wird mehr als früher der unmittelbare Arbeitsmarktausgleich in den Vordergrund gerückt, d.h. vorrangig individuelle Förderung von Problemgruppen des Arbeitsmarktes (§7 Abs. 3).

Auch auf die neuen *Förderinstrumente* ist an dieser Stelle nicht näher einzugehen. Gerade mit Neuansätzen zur beruflichen Eingliederung von Arbeitslosen oder den Zuschüssen zu Sozialplanmaßnahmen verbindet sich Evaluationsbedarf – dies aber nur am Rande.[12]

Mit dem neuen Instrument der Freien Förderung wurde bereits ein wesentlicher Baustein dessen angesprochen, was mit dem SGB III an erweiterten regionalen Kompetenzen der örtlichen Arbeitsämter angelegt ist. Ausgesprochene (und eingeschränkte) Zielsetzung war in diesem Zusammenhang

---

9   Förderung der Erprobung zusätzlicher Wege in der Arbeitsmarktpolitik (früher „neuer Wege"). Neben der SGB III-Förderung existieren noch weitere Bundesprogramme (u.a. Beschäftigungshilfen für Langzeitarbeitslose und das Jugendsofortprogramm).

10 Gemeinschaftsinitiativen Beschäftigung und ADAPT, in der neuen Förderperiode ab 2000 Gemeinschaftsinitiative EQUAL.

11 Maximal 10% des Eingliederungstitels (s.u.). In den Haushaltsplanungen für 2000 wurden deutlich mehr als 1 Mrd. DM für die Freie Förderung veranschlagt. Zur Evaluation der Freien Förderung vgl. Brinkmann 1998b und Luschei/Trube 1999.

12 Zum weiteren Spektrum betriebsbezogener Einstellungshilfen hat das IAB 1998 zwei längerfristig angelegte repräsentative Evaluationsprojekte begonnen (Jaenichen 1999). Zu den Sozialplanmaßnahmen führt das Institut Arbeit und Technik in Gelsenkirchen im Auftrag des IAB eine Begleitforschung durch (Kirsch u.a. 1999).

Effektivität und Effizienz der Arbeitsverwaltung zu erhöhen (Brinkmann 1998a). Nach §9 sollen die Leistungen der Arbeitsförderung vorrangig durch die örtlichen Arbeitsämter erbracht werden. Sie haben dabei mit den Beteiligten des örtlichen Arbeitsmarktes zusammenzuarbeiten. Diese im Vergleich zum AFG gar nicht so ganz neuen Formulierungen gewinnen dadurch Gewicht, daß weitere Änderungen im Sozialgesetzbuch (§71b SGB IV) festschreiben, daß die Ermessensleistungen der Arbeitsförderung in einem einzigen *Eingliederungstitel* zusammengefaßt werden und die darin veranschlagten Mittel (mit kleineren Ausnahmen) den Arbeitsämtern zur eigenverantwortlichen Bewirtschaftung zuzuweisen sind.[13]

Ganz allgemein: Dezentralisierung in den Verwaltungsabläufen, regionale Verantwortung und zunehmende Kooperationsnotwendigkeiten, um Arbeitsvermittlung und Förderung sinnvoll im Hinblick auf regionale Erfordernisse und effizient zu gestalten: All dies hat u.a. zur Voraussetzung, daß Transparenz hergestellt wird, auch um Fehlentwicklungen zu erkennen und Erträge feststellen zu können.

Deshalb legt §280 SGB III nunmehr erstmals gesetzlich fest, daß die Bundesanstalt für Arbeit nicht nur Lage und Entwicklung am Arbeitsmarkt, sondern auch „... die Wirkungen der aktiven Arbeitsförderung zu beobachten, zu untersuchen und auszuwerten (hat), indem sie 1. Statistiken erstellt, 2. Arbeitsmarkt- und Berufsforschung betreibt und 3. Bericht erstattet."

Die Gesetzesformulierung läßt deutlich erkennen, daß Erfolgsbeobachtung und Evaluation im SGB III-Zusammenhang nicht nur Aufgabe des zur BA gehörenden Instituts für Arbeitsmarkt- und Berufsforschung (IAB) bzw. der Wissenschaft ist, sondern *Aufgabe aller in der BA,* und zwar auf allen Ebenen.[14]

2.2 Das sich entwickelnde Monitoring-System

Genau aus diesem Grunde sind die Arbeitsämter in Deutschland nun verpflichtet, sog. Eingliederungsbilanzen über die Ermessensleistungen der aktiven Arbeitsförderung zu erstellen. Diese wurden Mitte 1999 erstmals (für das Geschäftsjahr 1998) veröffentlicht (Bundesanstalt für Arbeit 1999).

Nach den detaillierten Vorgaben von §11 SGB III enthält eine Eingliederungsbilanz *insbesondere* (nicht abschließend definiert) Angaben über den/die

---

13 Darauf hinzuweisen ist, daß noch weitere Entwicklungslinien im Umfeld der Arbeitsmarktpolitik zu einer Stärkung bzw. stärkeren Inanspruchnahme der regionalen Ebene führen: Zu erwähnen ist zum einen der komplementäre Ausbau des Sozialhilferechts in Richtung verstärkter Arbeitsförderung arbeitsloser Sozialhilfeempfänger durch Kommunen, zum anderen die Aufhebung des Vermittlungs- und Beratungsmonopols der Bundesanstalt für Arbeit zum Teil schon vor der Einführung des SGB III.

14 Zum notwendigen Zusammenspiel von Verwaltungscontrolling und Evaluationen vgl. Lenk (1993: 91).

- Umfang und Verteilung der Geldmittel,
- Durchschnittsausgaben je geförderten Arbeitnehmer,
- Umfang und Verteilung der einzelnen Ermessensleistungen sowie Beteiligung besonders förderungsbedürftiger Personengruppen,
- Frauenbeteiligung,
- Vermittlungsquote,
- Verbleibsquote,
- Rahmenbedingungen des regionalen Arbeitsmarktes,
- Entwicklung der Maßnahmen im Zeitverlauf.

Kernstück der Bilanzen sind Angaben zum Verbleib der Arbeitnehmer *„in angemessener Zeit im Anschluß an die Maßnahme"*. Nach groben Maßnahmebereichen weist demnach jedes Arbeitsamt aus, wie viele Geförderte ein halbes Jahr nach Abschluß der Maßnahme *arbeitslos gemeldet* sind (ein Verbleib in Beschäftigung bzw. in nicht geförderter Beschäftigung, wie ursprünglich angestrebt, ist in der vorgegebenen kurzen Zeit nicht flächendeckend ausweisbar). Differenziert wird soweit wie möglich auch nach *besonders förderungsbedürftigen Personengruppen.* Das werden im Hinblick auf die statistische Datenlage und die notwendige Übersichtlichkeit zunächst nur sein: Langzeitarbeitslose, Schwerbehinderte/Gleichgestellte, Ältere (50 Jahre und älter) sowie Berufsrückkehrer/-innen. Frauen werden gesondert berücksichtigt.

In der gesetzlich vorgegebenen Form werden Eingliederungsbilanzen im Controlling-System der BA einen unverzichtbaren Stellenwert haben, aber der Ergänzung bedürfen. *Übersicht 1* faßt die wesentlichen, in der Einleitung schon angedeuteten Kritikpunkte zusammen.[15]

Eingliederungsbilanzen enthalten sog. Input- und Outputindikatoren (Ausgaben, Verbleib) vorrangig zum Instrumenteneinsatz. Sie stellen allenfalls mittelbar und über ergänzende Informationen auf arbeitsmarktbezogene Wirkungen als „Outcome" ab. Hier setzt nun als zweiter Entwicklungsstrang das 1999 eingeführte Ziel-Controlling der BA an. Es handelt sich um die zunächst als Bundesziele entwickelten geschäftspolitischen Schwerpunkte, die im Vorfeld mit den regionalen Organisationseinheiten abgeklärt wurden und um regionale Zielsetzungen ergänzt werden können. Später sollen sie flächendeckend in förmliche Zielvereinbarungen einmünden, wie sie jetzt bereits in Modellarbeitsämtern praktiziert werden.

Grundsätzlich geht es um die Steuerung des Verwaltungshandelns (Vermittlung, Beratung, Einsatz arbeitsmarktpolitischer Instrumente) über verbindliche, quantitative, auf *den Arbeitsmarkt bezogene* Wirkungsziele.[16] Die-

---

15 Eingliederungsbilanzen machen das Zusammenführen unterschiedlicher Dateien innerhalb der BA erforderlich. Damit wird der Datenzugang für Forschung wesentlich erleichtert (s.u.).

16 Weitere Steuerungsebenen sind die gesetzlichen Rahmenbedingungen (Normen) und die Zuteilung von Ressourcen (verfügbares Budget).

se Ziele werden in einem komplexen Zielfindungsprozeß unter Beteiligung aller Ebenen der Gesamtorganisation entwickelt und vorgegeben, die Zielerreichung wird periodisch über das „Controlling-System" überprüft, Zielabweichungen werden im dialogischen Verfahren zum Anlaß genommen, Verhaltensänderungen vorzunehmen.

Geschäftspolitische Schwerpunkte für das Jahr 2000 mit den entsprechenden Handlungsfeldern sind (für alle Organisationseinheiten verbindliche Bundesziele, die regional ergänzt werden können):

- Langzeitarbeitslosigkeit senken (mehr Langzeitarbeitslose in Arbeit bringen, Übertritte in Langzeitarbeitslosigkeit verhindern)
- Jugendarbeitslosigkeit senken (Ausbildungsstellenakquisition verbessern, Jugendliche in Ausbildung oder Beschäftigung bringen)
- Vereinbarkeit von Beruf und Familie für Männer und Frauen verbessern (mehr „Mobilzeit"[17] als Beschäftigungsvariante anbieten, mehr Berufsrückkehrerinnen und Berufsrückkehrer in Arbeit bringen)
- Beschäftigungsmöglichkeiten marktgerecht erschließen (Einschaltung intensivieren, Ausschöpfung erhöhen)

Auch hier sind kritische Fragen zu stellen (*Übersicht 2*). Zum einen geht es um die Aussagekraft einiger der Indikatoren, ihre Validität und die Frage, inwieweit es möglich ist, realistische Erwartungswerte zu bilden, um Zielwerte sinnvoll definieren zu können, z.B. hinsichtlich des Zugangs in die Langzeitarbeitslosigkeit oder der Laufzeit der Offenen Stellen. Zum anderen geht es um ein Grundsatzproblem (Auer/Kruppe 1996): Solche Monitoring-Systeme sind zwangsläufig auf routinisierbare, quantifizierbare und i.d.R. kurzfristige Wirkungen (lediglich kurzfristiger Verbleib in Beschäftigung, nicht Qualität der Beschäftigungsverhältnisse wie Dauerhaftigkeit) beschränkt. Controlling und Evaluation muß über solches Monitoring hinausgehen, will es alle wichtigen Zieldimensionen von Arbeitsförderung im allgemeinen und von Vermittlung und Beratung im besonderen mit umfassen.

2.3 Wirkungsforschung

Wie verortet sich nun Wirkungsforschung im Evaluationssystem der BA (das noch gar nicht so systematisch ist, aber werden soll)? Wirkungsforschung ist primär kausalanalytisch orientiert[18] und dem Ziel-Controlling zuzuordnen[19]. Sie ersetzt nicht, sondern ergänzt notwendigerweise die sich entwickelnden Monitoring-Aktivitäten. Zur Evaluation der Arbeitsförderung müssen Moni-

---

17 Teilzeitarbeit und flexible Formen der Arbeitszeitgestaltung.
18 Vgl. Schmid/O'Reilly/Schömann (1996a). Erste und immer noch gültige konzeptionelle Vorstellungen sind enthalten in Mertens, Reyher & Kühl (1981).
19 Ziel-Controlling ist zu unterscheiden vom Haushalts-Controlling, Kosten-Controlling und Organisations-Controlling (Postlep 1994).

toring, Wirkungsforschung und qualitative Wirkungsanalysen von Wissenschaft und Praxis zusammenkommen – *dann erst ist Controlling in diesem Bereich vollständig.*

Mit der Einführung von Eingliederungsbilanzen wird auch ein neues „Datum" für Wirkungsanalysen zu den Instrumenten der Arbeitsförderung gesetzt. Durch die routinemäßige Verfügbarkeit von Brutto-Informationen zum kurzfristigen Verbleib von Geförderten und die dafür erforderliche Weiterentwicklung der Datenverarbeitung und -verknüpfung werden Informationslücken geschlossen. In der Vergangenheit konnten zu den „großen" Instrumenten der Arbeitsförderung nur sehr aufwendige, punktuelle Sonderuntersuchungen durchgeführt werden[20].

Die neuen prozeßproduzierten Dateien enthalten differenzierte Strukturinformationen von Maßnahmeteilnehmerinnen und -teilnehmern, sie werden längerfristige Datenabgleiche (z.B. mit der Datei über sozialversicherungspflichtig Beschäftigte) ermöglichen und es werden über die mit ihnen entstandenen DV-Systeme Stichproben gezogen werden können (zur Befragung von Geförderten usw.). Wirkungsforschung des IAB wird sich in Kooperation mit weiteren Instituten auf diese neuen Datenquellen stützen.[21]

In Wirkungsanalysen zum (individuellen) Eingliederungserfolg der Arbeitsförderung (als einer zentralen Zielsetzung des SGB III) setzt das IAB sehr stark auf das datenschutzrechtlich abgesicherte Zusammenführen von Dateien und den Aufbau von Historikdateien, soweit es nicht um Begleitforschung zu einzelnen Modellvorhaben geht. Eine grundsätzliche Schwierigkeit, auf diesem Wege Netto-Effekte der Förderung zu ermitteln, besteht darin, daß die Dateien für Evaluationszwecke nur unvollkommene Informationen enthalten, so daß die notwendigen „Kontrollgruppen" nicht ohne weiteres gebildet werden können. Für anspruchsvolle repräsentative Wirkungsforschung mangelt es gegenwärtig nicht an Konzepten und statistischen Verfahren, allerdings ist auch kein Königsweg erkennbar. Es sind vor allem die unzureichenden Datensätze, die Wirkungsforschung erschweren (abgesehen von den sich nunmehr lösenden Zugangsproblemen zu diesen Datensätzen).[22]

---

20 Z.B. Blaschke/Nagel (1995); vgl. auch Autorengemeinschaft (1997); Brinkmann (1999).

21 Zunächst einmal ging es darum, im Rahmen bzw. im Vorfeld des sich entwickelnden „Data-Warehouse" der BA die zentrale Verfügbarkeit der in den Arbeitsämtern entstehenden Individualdatensätze (einschließlich Verbleibinformationen im Sinne der Eingliederungsbilanzen) sicherzustellen. Im Hinblick auf begrenzte Kapazitäten werden auch Kooperations- und Auftragsprojekte durchgeführt bzw. angestrebt.

22 Entwicklungsarbeit an dieser Stelle betrifft zum einen das nachträgliche Rekonstruieren von Teilen der Erwerbsbiographie (Almus u.a. 1998 und Bender/Klose 2000) wie auch die Ergänzung der verfügbaren Prozeßdaten um valide Einschätzungen von Vermittlungshemmnissen durch Fachkräfte in den Arbeitsämtern (Jaenichen 1999).

2.4 Evaluation als „joint venture" von Wissenschaft und Praxis

Von einem umfassenden Evaluationssystem der aktiven Arbeitsförderung auf Bundesebene und darin fest verankerter Wirkungsforschung sind wir noch weit entfernt. Das Ziel umfassender Kosten-Nutzen-Analysen, auf der Mikro – wie auf der Makro-Ebene (teilnehmer- bzw. arbeitsmarktbezogen), mit Teilbeiträgen aus den sich entwickelnden Monitoring-Systemen und ergänzenden Aktivitäten von Wissenschaft und Praxis, bleibt zunächst noch Fernziel, obwohl die eingeschlagene Richtung stimmt.

Gründe hierfür sind auf verschiedenen Ebenen zu sehen, Verbesserungen setzen systematische Evaluationssysteme unter Einschluß von Wissenschaft und Praxis voraus, an denen gegenwärtig gearbeitet wird:

1. *Komplexität des Zielsystems*, das im Spannungsfeld steht von kurz- und langfristig zu erzielenden Wirkungen auf der individuellen Ebene, aber auch auf der Ebene des Arbeitsmarktes insgesamt, wobei es sich teils um (noch) nicht quantifizierbare „qualitative" Wirkungen handelt: Im Vordergrund der Rahmenzielsetzungen (§§1,5-8 SGB III) steht der (kurz- wie langfristige) Ausgleich am Arbeitsmarkt unter Betonung der individuellen Eingliederungszielsetzung namentlich für besonders förderungsbedürftige Personengruppen. Gefordert wird aber auch weiterhin die Einbettung der Arbeitsförderung in die beschäftigungspolitischen Zielsetzungen der Bundesregierung (Ammermüller 1997: 6), wobei es um „globale" und strukturelle Wirkungen am Arbeitsmarkt geht. Hinzu kommen instrumentenspezifische Zielsetzungen. So sollen mit ABM und SAM ausdrücklich auch Beiträge zum Entstehen neuer Arbeitsplätze geleistet werden, Zielsetzung ist weiterhin die Vorbereitung und Ergänzung strukturverbessernder Arbeiten, Verbesserung von sozialer Infrastruktur und Umwelt oder (nach jüngster Gesetzesnovellierung) der wirtschaftsnahen Infrastruktur (§§260, 273, 415 SGB III). Bei der beruflichen Weiterbildung sollen u.a. Kenntnisse an die technische Entwicklung angepaßt werden (§87 SGB III). Bei Beratung und Vermittlung gehört zu den Rahmenzielsetzungen, daß berufliche Entscheidungen sowie Auswahl- und Suchprozesse optimiert werden (§§30, 33, 34ff. SGB III).

2. *Heterogenität von Maßnahmen*, die sich nur scheinbar als „Arbeitsförderung" insgesamt oder als „Weiterbildungsmaßnahmen" usw. summarisch evaluieren lassen: Ohne daß bislang hinreichend Kenntnisse vorliegen über Wirkungsketten hinsichtlich einzelner Interventionsformen, werden Maßnahmen doch zumindest ansatzweise sehr unterschiedlich und „paßgenau" für unterschiedliche Zielgruppen und Teilzielsetzungen eingesetzt. Aussagen über den durchschnittlichen Erfolg von Maßnahmen, selbst wenn sie in Form von Netto-Ergebnissen der Förderung vorliegen (was z.B. bei Eingliederungsbilanzen noch gar nicht der Fall sein kann), ermöglichen keine abschließende Beurteilung, sondern können

(und müssen) Ausgangspunkt für Differenzierungen und weiterführende
Fragen, für den eingangs erwähnten unverzichtbaren Dialog aller Beteiligten, sein.

3. *Heterogenität von Zielgruppen,* die je nach Zielsetzung für bestimmte
Maßnahmen und nicht für andere in Frage kommen: So können ABM
und nunmehr insbesondere Strukturanpassungsmaßnahmen für ältere Arbeitslose eingesetzt werden, nicht um eine spätere reguläre Beschäftigung ohne Förderung vorzubereiten, sondern um einen für den Betroffenen erträglichen Übergang in den Ruhestand zu ermöglichen, mit dem
sich zugleich Wertschöpfung verbindet.

Abgesehen von der unzulänglichen Datenbasis, die in der Vergangenheit ein
differenziertes Monitoring und aussagefähige kausalanalytische Forschung
wesentlich erschwert hat, ist die Vernachlässigung der aufgeführten Gesichtspunkte Grund dafür, daß viele Studien bislang nur zu wenig praktisch
verwertbaren Ergebnissen kommen. Dies gilt namentlich für eine Reihe neuerer mikroökonometrischer Studien, die trotz ausgefeilter Evaluationsmethoden die angestrebte Kontrolle „nicht beobachteter Heterogenität" nicht zu
leisten vermögen (Brinkmann u.a. 1999; Schmid u.a. 1999; für die USA re-
sümierend Heckma/LaLonde/Smith 1999).

Verbesserungen lassen sich nur durch gemeinsame Anstrengungen als
„joint venture" erzielen: Es geht um differenziertere und validere Prozeßdaten für Monitoring und Forschung, um bessere Vergleichs- oder Kontroll-
gruppenbildung (z.B. durch Rekonstruktion von Teilen der Biographie als
Indikator für Eingliederungsschwierigkeiten, oder um entsprechende Einschätzungen durch Fachkräfte oder Betroffene), um die Einbeziehung weiterer, im Zielsystem enthaltener Wirkungsdimensionen und um ergänzende
Forschung über Einflußketten und günstige Rahmenbedingungen für einen
erfolgreichen Einsatz der Arbeitsförderung.

3. Arbeitsmarktpolitik auf Länderebene: Das Beispiel Brandenburg

Nachdem zuvor die Entwicklungslinien von Monitoring und Evaluation auf
Bundesebene beleuchtet wurden, werden in diesem Kapitel die Konzepte,
Möglichkeiten und Grenzen der Evaluierung der Arbeitsmarktpolitik aus
Ländersicht diskutiert. Dabei geht es zunächst um die Frage, welche Rolle
die Länder in der Arbeitsmarktpolitik im bundesdeutschen System spielen.
Im Anschluß daran wird am Beispiel des Landes Brandenburg, das bereits
1992/1993 mit der Evaluation seiner arbeitsmarktpolitischen Programme begonnen hatte, eine speziell auf die Ländersicht zugeschnittene Konzeption
zur Evaluierung der Arbeitsmarktpolitik vorgestellt.

3.1 Die Rolle der Länder in der Arbeitsmarktpolitik

Die Verantwortung für die aktive Arbeitsmarktpolitik liegt im bundesdeutschen System vordringlich beim Bund. Dies spiegelt sich in der Organisation der aktiven Arbeitsmarktpolitik deutlich wider: Die Umsetzung des SGB III erfolgt ausschließlich durch den Bund, und hier durch die Bundesanstalt für Arbeit (vgl. Kapitel 2). Dennoch spielen die Länder durchaus eine eigenständige Rolle in der Arbeitsmarktpolitik, indem sie die Arbeitsförderung des Bundes flankieren (z.b. durch die Kofinanzierung von Arbeitsbeschaffungsmaßnahmen) oder auch eigene Akzente setzen. Hierbei bietet insbesondere die Europäische Union über den Europäischen Sozialfonds den Ländern zusätzliche Möglichkeiten. Dies gilt vor allem für die neuen Länder, die auch in der neuen Förderperiode des ESF 2000-2006, als sogenanntes Ziel-1-Gebiet, zu den Gebieten mit höchster Förderpriorität zählen (vgl. Kapitel 4).

Geht es um die Einordnung der Förderpolitik auf Länderebene ist zunächst systematisch zu unterscheiden zwischen der aktiven Arbeitsmarktpolitik *im* Land und der aktiven Arbeitsmarktpolitik *des* Landes (Schmachtenberg 1999). Die Arbeitsmarktpolitik im Land ist geprägt durch unterschiedliche gesetzliche Rahmenbedingungen auf den verschiedenen Politikebenen: Die europäische Beschäftigungspolitik (über den ESF), die bundesdeutsche Arbeitsmarktpolitik (über das SGB III), die aktive Arbeitsmarktpolitik der Länder sowie diejenige der Kommunen (etwa durch aktive Maßnahmen im Rahmen des BSHG).

„Die Landesarbeitsmarktpolitik steht (in diesem Mehrebenensystem, d.A.) vor dem doppelten Koordinierungsproblem, erstens diese unterschiedlichen Anforderungen vertikal zwischen den Ebenen z.b. über geeignete Kofinanzierungen oder die Schließung von Förderlücken zu integrieren, zweitens aber auch auf der Landesebene zwischen den einzelnen Ressorts horizontal zu integrieren, um z.b. über die Verknüpfung von Infrastrukturmaßnahmen die Strukturwirksamkeit von Arbeitsförderung zu erhöhen." (Schmachtenberg 1999).

Die hohe Bedeutung der Bundesarbeitsmarktpolitik für die Arbeitsmarktpolitik im Land spiegelt sich auch im Finanzvolumen, das für aktive Arbeitsmarktpolitik bereitgestellt wird, deutlich wider: 1999 betrugen die Ausgaben des Bundes für aktive Arbeitsmarktpolitik[23] 44,5 Mrd. DM, ein Zehnfaches der entsprechenden Ausgaben der Bundesländer (4,5 Mrd. DM). Betrachtet man die Ausgaben der Länder für aktive Arbeitsmarktpolitik im Zeitverlauf, zeigt sich insbesondere seit 1990 ein erheblicher Anstieg, der bei näherer Betrachtung fast ausschließlich auf die neuen Länder zurückzuführen ist. Der Bedeutungszuwachs der Länder in der Arbeitsmarktpolitik basiert somit im Wesentlichen auf dem Engagement der neuen Länder, was angesichts des hohen Problemdrucks am Arbeitsmarkt auch nicht erstaunlich ist (Reissert 1999).

---

23 Eingliederungstitel, sonstige Leistungen der aktiven Arbeitsförderung nach SGB III sowie Ausgaben des Bundesarbeitsministeriums für aktive Arbeitsmarktpolitik (Beschäftigungshilfen für Langzeitarbeitslose, Eingliederungshilfen, Teil der Strukturanpassungsmaßnahmen u.a.).

Bei der arbeitsmarktpolitischen Ausrichtung der Länder handelt es sich keineswegs um einen monolithischen Block: Vielmehr nutzen die Länder – so eine Tübinger Studie (Blancke 1999) – ihre Spielräume auf ganz unterschiedliche Weise. Die Studie typisiert die Arbeitsmarktpolitiken der Länder anhand dreier idealtypischer Strategien, die mit „Push", „Pull" und „Stay" umschrieben werden. Eine Klassifizierung der Arbeitsmarktpolitiken der Länder zeigt, daß es durchaus eine Bandbreite für eine strategische Ausrichtung der Arbeitsmarktpolitik gibt, allerdings nicht in jedem Bundesland mit einem inhaltlich eigenständigen Politikansatz.[24]

3.1 Evaluierung der Arbeitsmarktpolitik aus Ländersicht – Die Brandenburger Konzeption der adressatenorientierten Evaluation

Angesichts der gravierenden und anhaltenden Ungleichgewichte am Arbeitsmarkt und damit verbunden dem hohen Stellenwert arbeitsmarktpolitischer Maßnahmen insbesondere in den neuen Bundesländern sind auch die Länder zunehmend mit Fragen nach dem Erfolg ihrer Politikkonzepte konfrontiert.

Wie kann eine Evaluation auf Länderebene aussehen? Wie sind Evaluationskonzepte hinsichtlich ihrer Untersuchungsebenen und Verfahrensweisen auszugestalten, damit die Erkenntnisse für die Entwicklung arbeitsmarktpolitischer Programme sowie ihrer Bewertung und Weiterentwicklung unmittelbar in die Verwaltungspraxis einfließen können? Wo liegen die Möglichkeiten und Grenzen einer Evaluierung der Arbeitsmarktpolitik aus Ländersicht?

Im folgenden wird am Beispiel der speziell für das Land Brandenburg entwickelten „Konzeption der adressatenorientierten Evaluation" ein Ansatz zur Evaluierung der Arbeitsmarktpolitik aus der Perspektive eines Bundeslandes vorgestellt. Es handelt sich dabei um eine systematische Ausrichtung der Konzeption auf die Verwaltungspraxis aus Ländersicht, die die drei zentralen Elemente verwaltungsinternes Monitoring, Vergabe von vertiefenden Evaluationsstudien an Dritte sowie gezielte Nutzung von Erkenntnissen aus der politikberatenden Arbeitsmarktforschung umfaßt und systematisch aufeinander bezieht (Bangel 1999).

Wo ist die Brandenburger Konzeption im Spannungsfeld zwischen traditionellen Evaluationskonzepten einerseits und dem Ansatz der zielorientierten Evaluation anderseits zu verorten? Zunächst einmal ist die Konzeption

---

24 So werden beispielsweise Nordrhein-Westfalen, Thüringen und Brandenburg als Länder mit einer vergleichsweise eigenständigen, mit relativ vielen Mitteln ausgestatteten Arbeitsmarktpolitik klassifiziert („Push") während etwa für Baden-Württemberg eine relativ geringe Bedeutung der Arbeitsmarktpolitik konstatiert wird, was möglicherweise auch auf den geringeren Problemdruck zurückzuführen ist („Pull"). Schließlich zählen etwa das Saarland und Schleswig-Holstein zu den Ländern mit einem zwar hohen Mittelvolumen für aktive Arbeitsförderung, allerdings einer hohen inhaltlichen Ausrichtung an der aktiven Arbeitsförderung des Bundes („Stay"). Vgl. dazu Blancke (1999).

der zielorientierten Evaluation ein sehr umfassender und ambitionierter Ansatz, dem gegenüber traditionellen Evaluationskonzepten der Vorzug zu geben ist (vgl. Kap. 1). Dieser Ansatz wird jedoch – und dies muß ganz klar herausgestellt werden – auf Länderebene in der Praxis nur in Teilbereichen umsetzbar sein: So erfordern etwa Kosten-Nutzen-Analysen oder Kosten-Wirksamkeits-Analysen ein äußerst komplexes Untersuchungsdesign mit ausgefeilten Methoden, wie z.B. einen Kontrollgruppenansatz, multivariate Analysemethoden, die Berücksichtigung institutioneller Rahmenbedingungen – hier Bundes- und Landesregelungen – sowie die Einbettung in einen gesamtwirtschaftlichen, wenn nicht gar gesamtgesellschaftlichen Kontext. Dies geht weit über das hinaus, was ein einzelnes Bundesland mit seinen bescheidenen Ressortforschungsmitteln leisten kann und soll.

Hier muß ein Bundesland aus Effizienz- und Machbarkeitsgründen – sofern vorhanden – auf Wirkungsuntersuchungen aus der politikberatenden Arbeitsmarktforschung zurückgreifen. Das IAB ist in diesem Kontext ein wichtiger Partner. Dort wurden bereits Ansätze für die Verknüpfung von Massendaten der Bundesanstalt für Arbeit (Daten aus der Leistungsstatistik, Betriebsdatei, Beschäftigtenstatistik etc.) entwickelt, die wiederum für aggregierte Wirkungsanalysen nutzbar gemacht werden können.

Aus Landessicht gilt es, die Erkenntnisse hieraus systematisch zu nutzen und sich – soweit möglich – für eine Weiterentwicklung der Ansätze und ihrer Methoden einzusetzen. Dabei ist die Verwendung rein quantitativer Leistungsindikatoren zu den unmittelbaren Programmwirkungen, wie sie in den traditionellen Evaluationskonzepten meist erfolgt, eine notwendige, aber keineswegs hinreichende Bedingung für ein Evaluationskonzept, das für sich den Anspruch erhebt, politikberatend wirksam zu werden.

Die Brandenburger Konzeption der *adressatenorientierten Evaluation* versucht – aus Ländersicht – das Spannungsfeld zwischen konzeptioneller Überfrachtung einerseits und rigider Erfolgskontrolle andererseits mit einem pragmatischen Ansatz auszugleichen, indem sie Elemente der zielorientierten Evaluation aufgreift und die Risiken traditioneller Evaluation zu vermeiden sucht. Im folgenden wird zunächst die spezifische Akzentuierung des Brandenburger Ansatzes im Hinblick auf die Untersuchungsebenen und Verfahrensweisen bei der Programmevaluation im Rahmen der Vergabe von Forschungsaufträgen an Dritte dargelegt. Im Anschluß erfolgt eine zusammenfassende Darstellung des Brandenburger Ansatzes anhand einer Typologie seiner zentralen Funktionsbereiche und Analysefelder.

3.1.1 Untersuchungsebenen und Evaluationsverfahren

Kernstück der Brandenburger Konzeption der adressatenorientierten Evaluation ist die Programmevaluation im Rahmen der Vergabe von Forschungsaufträgen an Dritte. Konzeption und Projektdesign folgen dabei einem integrierten Analyseansatz: In die Programmbewertung werden die Prozesse der

Politikformulierung, die Verortung des Untersuchungsgegenstandes im Kontext der Brandenburger Arbeitsmarktsituation und Programmatik, Fragen der Implementierung und des unmittelbaren Programmvollzuges, der Programmwirkungen und Fragen der Akzeptanz von Programmen einbezogen. Ziel ist dabei eine umfassende Programmbewertung sowohl aus der Binnenperspektive der Programmentwickler, Umsetzer und Nutzer als auch einer Außensicht auf die Programme, etwa durch die regionalen Arbeitsmarktakteure. Dabei geht es auch darum, Handlungsoptionen für die Verbesserung von Programmen anzuregen.

Damit die Evaluierung von Arbeitsmarktprogrammen politikgestaltend wirksam werden kann, präferiert die adressatenorientierte Evaluation prozeßhafte, dialogorientierte und somit reflexive Verfahren der Erfolgskontrolle, indem sie die unmittelbaren und mittelbaren Adressaten staatlicher Förderung systematisch in die Untersuchung einbezieht und den Evaluationsprozeß als Lernprozeß begreift. Das heißt konkret:

–   Sozialwissenschaftlicher Ansatz, der die Analyse prozeßproduzierter Daten mit der Analyse von gezielt erhobenen, repräsentativen Befragungsdaten sowie Expertengesprächen verknüpft (quantitativ-qualitativer Methodenmix).

–   Es hat sich insbesondere bewährt, die unmittelbaren Nutzerinnen und Nutzer der Programme im Rahmen von Befragungen selbst zu Wort kommen zu lassen und die klassischen quantitativen Indikatoren zur Erfolgsmessung um qualitative Zieldimensionen, wie etwa Einschätzungen zum „subjektiv empfundenen Nutzen" zu ergänzen.

–   Einbindung der Akteure, die die Maßnahme unmittelbar umsetzen (z.B. Betriebe, Weiterbildungsträger etc.) und somit Aktivierung von Expertenwissen bereits im Evaluationsprozeß. Anstoßen von Prozessen der Selbstreflexion und Selbstevaluation beim Maßnahmeträger.

–   Einbindung weiterer Arbeitsmarktakteure als Experten für eine „Fremdeinschätzung" (z.B. regionale Arbeitsmarktakteure, Arbeitgeber- und Arbeitnehmerverbände etc.).

–   Einbindung der Akteure, die die Programme entwickeln und umsetzen (Ministerium, Umsetzungsagenturen). Ergebnistransfer durch Rückkoppelung von (Teil-)Ergebnissen bereits im Evaluierungsprozeß. Ausloten von Handlungsempfehlungen zur Verbesserung von Förderprogrammen anhand eines diskursiven Verfahrens anstelle eines kontrollorientierten Verfahrens.

–   Transparenz, u.a. auch durch Veröffentlichung der Ergebnisse.

3.1.2 Die drei zentralen Elemente der adressatenorientierten Evaluation –
      Typologie der Funktionsbereiche und Analysefelder

Die Brandenburger Konzeption der adressatenorientierten Evaluation folgt einem mehrstufigen Ansatz mit den drei zentralen Elementen: Verwaltungsinternes Monitoring, Vergabe von Forschungsaufträgen zur Evaluierung der Arbeitsmarktpolitik an Dritte sowie gezielte Nutzung der Erkenntnisse der politikberatenden Arbeitsmarktforschung (vgl. *Übersicht 3*).

Verwaltungsinternes Monitoring
Das verwaltungsinterne Monitoring hat die prozeßbegleitende Dokumentation, Programmanalyse und Programmsteuerung zum Ziel. Sie dient der laufenden Beobachtung der unmittelbaren Ergebnisse der Förderung anhand der Erhebung und Auswertung ausgewählter materieller und finanzieller Indikatoren, wie z.b. die Ausschöpfung des Programms, Teilnehmerzahlen und Abbrecherquoten, Zielgruppenberücksichtigung, regionale Verteilung der Fördermittel.

Das verwaltungsinterne Monitoring hat vorwiegend die Funktion des unmittelbaren Programmcontrollings. Darüber hinaus liefert das verwaltungsinterne Monitoring die zentralen quantitativen Daten für einfache Struktur- und Wirksamkeitsanalysen zur Arbeitsmarktpolitik, bezogen auf einzelne Programme sowie für Querschnittanalysen. Ferner sind die im Rahmen der unmittelbaren Programmbegleitung gewonnenen Daten die Basis für die vertiefende Evaluation anhand sozialwissenschaftlicher Evaluationsstudien.

Insbesondere hier setzt bisher auch die Europäische Kommission mit ihren Anforderungen an die Bewertung ESF-kofinanzierter Programme an. Inwiefern hier künftig eine Spezifizierung nach Programminhalten und eine qualitative Fundierung stattfinden wird, ist gegenwärtig noch offen. Ansätze hierfür lassen sich in der gegenwärtigen Diskussion um die Anforderungen der Europäischen Kommission an das neue ESF-Begleitsystem finden (vgl. Kapitel 4).

Vergabe von Evaluierungsstudien an Dritte
Die Vergabe von Evaluierungsstudien an Dritte dient der vertiefenden Analyse zur Paßfähigkeit, Akzeptanz, Wirkung und Wirksamkeit bestehender Förderprogramme sowie deren Weiterentwicklung und der Entwicklung neuer Programme.

Hier gilt es, im Rahmen von sozialwissenschaftlichen Untersuchungen zur Beschäftigungs- und Arbeitsmarktentwicklung zum einen die Paßfähigkeit von Programmen zu untersuchen und Handlungsfelder für die Entwicklung von neuen Programmen zu lokalisieren. Die Flankierung von Erkenntnissen aus dem verwaltungsinternen Monitoring sowie der Praxiserfahrung mit sozialwissenschaftlichen Befragungs- und Analysemethoden zielt auf eine fundierte Untersuchung und Weiterentwicklung bestehender Programme hinsichtlich ihrer Programmkonzeption und -administration, der Implementation und Akzeptanz sowie ihrer Wirkung und Wirksamkeit. Dabei sind neben den unmittelbaren Programmzielen auch mittelbare Ziele wie etwa der Ausgleich von Benachteiligungen am Arbeitsmarkt einzubeziehen.

Im Kontext der „vertiefenden Evaluation durch Vergabe von Evaluationsstudien an Dritte" ist dementsprechend nicht allein an Programmevalua-

tionen im Sinne traditioneller Evaluationskonzepte gedacht. Vielmehr sind
hierunter Studien zur Beschäftigungs- und Arbeitsmarktentwicklung, wie etwa die amtliche Statistik ergänzende Betriebsbefragungen zur Beschäfti-
gungsdynamik und Personalrekrutierung oder etwa die Analyse spezifischer
Problemfelder für die Entwicklung präventiver Arbeitsmarktprogramme
ebenso zu fassen, wie Programmevaluationen zur Untersuchung der Akzeptanz, Wirkung und Wirksamkeit von Förderprogrammen, Begleitforschung
etwa zur innovativen Modellförderung oder Querschnittstudien, in denen verschiedene Programme hinsichtlich ihrer Zielerreichung für bestimmte Adres-
satengruppen vergleichend untersucht werden.

Ein Beispiel ist hier der Aufbau eines Betriebspanels zur Entwicklung
von Betrieben und Beschäftigung, das das Land Brandenburg gemeinsam mit
anderen neuen Bundesländern und in Kooperation mit dem IAB aufbaut (vgl.
z.B. für die Brandenburger Ergebnisse aus der dritten Befragungswelle: Ministerium für Arbeit, Soziales, Gesundheit und Frauen 1999a). Weitere Beispiele aus dem Land Brandenburg sind ferner die Studien zur Evaluierung
von Beratungsstrukturen, wie der „Weiterbildungsberatungsstellen" oder der
„Regionalstellen Frauen und Arbeitsmarkt" (Ministerium für Arbeit, Soziales, Gesundheit und Frauen 1998, 1999b), programmbezogene Evaluationen
etwa zum Förderprogramm „Arbeit statt Sozialhilfe" (Ministerium für Arbeit, Soziales, Gesundheit und Frauen 1996a) oder zur wirtschaftsnahen Weiterbildung (Ministerium für Arbeit, Soziales, Gesundheit und Frauen 1993),
sowie programmvergleichende Evaluationen wie die Studie zur Brandenburger Existenzgründungsförderung, in der die Programme des Arbeits- sowie
des Wirtschaftsministeriums vergleichend untersucht wurden (Ministerium
für Arbeit, Soziales, Gesundheit und Frauen 1996b).

In *Übersicht 3* sind die verschiedenen Untersuchungsfelder idealtypisch
aufgeführt.

Erkenntnisse der politikberatenden Arbeitsmarktforschung nutzen
Das dritte Element zielt ferner darauf, die vorliegenden Ansätze und Erkenntnisse der politikberatenden Arbeitsmarktforschung systematisch zu nutzen.
Hierzu zählen programmbezogene Wirkungsstudien ebenso wie etwa international vergleichende Untersuchungen zur Ausgestaltung der Arbeitsmarktpolitik. Nicht zuletzt sind hierunter auch Kosten-Nutzen oder Kosten-Wirksamkeitsanalysen zu fassen, die sowohl aus Gründen der Effizienz als auch
aus konzeptionell-methodischen Gründen einen gesamtgesellschaftlichen
Analyseansatz erfordern. Hier wären etwa Ansätze zur aggregierten Wirkungsforschung oder aber auch volkswirtschaftliche Modellrechnungen zur
Ausgestaltung einer erfolgversprechenden Beschäftigungs- und Arbeitsmarktpolitik zu nennen, wie sie etwa das IAB in seiner Agenda 98 vorgelegt
hat (Autorengemeinschaft 1998).

4. Arbeitsmarktpolitik im Rahmen des Europäischen Sozialfonds (ESF)

4.1 Der Europäische Sozialfonds – Kofinanzierung der Arbeitsmarktpolitik von Bund und Ländern im Rahmen der Europäischen Beschäftigungsstrategie

Im Rahmen der Europäischen Strukturfonds ist der Europäische Sozialfonds das entscheidende Instrument zur Förderung der „Humanressourcen" (Strukturfonds-Ziel 3). Die Gelder aus dem ESF sollen insbesondere als qualitative Ergänzung zur nationalen aktiven Arbeitsmarktpolitik, in Deutschland also des Bundes und der Länder, eingesetzt werden. Angesetzt wird bei Problemlagen auf dem Arbeitsmarkt und im Beschäftigungssystem, für die das nationale Fördersystem aus europäischer Sicht nicht ausreichend erscheint, und deshalb durch Kofinanzierung ergänzt wird. Auf diese Weise soll ein „europäischer Mehrwert" („added value") im Vergleich zur nationalen Arbeitsmarkt- und Beschäftigungspolitik erreicht werden.

Die Mittel des ESF können zum einen zur Kofinanzierung von Programmen eingesetzt werden, die auf eine integrierte Förderung im Zusammenspiel mit den anderen EU-Strukturfonds angelegt sind.[25] So haben die ostdeutschen Bundesländer sogenannte Multifondsprogramme aufgelegt, weil Ostdeutschland als Ziel-1-Gebiet auch Fördergebiet z.B. des Europäischen Regionalfonds (EFRE) ist, und hier die verschiedenen Strukturfonds zusammenwirken sollen, also aktive Arbeitsmarktpolitik und regionale Strukturpolitik aufeinander abzustimmen sind. Zum anderen können auch sog. Monofondsprogramme formuliert werden. Dies war in der Vergangenheit und ist auch aktuell von Bund und Ländern für die Förderung arbeitsmarktpolitischer Zielgruppen im Rahmen des Ziel 3 in Westdeutschland vorgesehen, in Ostdeutschland allein für den Bundesteil des ESF.

Im Wechsel von der alten Strukturfondsphase 1994 bis 1999 zur neuen Phase von 2000 bis 2006 hat es einige Änderungen in der Zielausrichtung der Strukturfonds insgesamt wie auch des ESF im Besonderen gegeben, auf die hier nicht näher eingegangen werden soll.[26] Wichtiger ist an dieser Stelle, daß alle ESF-Programme in den politischen Bezugsrahmen der Europäischen Beschäftigungsstrategie gestellt sind. Im Rahmen des sog. Luxemburg-Prozesses werden seit 1998 jährlich Beschäftigungspolitische Leitlinien der EU beschlossen, zu denen die nationalen Staaten dann jeweils einen Nationalen

---

25 An dieser Stelle geht es zunächst nur um die offiziellen, von der EU zu genehmigenden Operationellen Programme und Einheitlichen Programmplanungsdokumente. Die konkreten Einzelprogramme von Bund und Ländern können wiederum auch anders zugeschnitten sein.

26 Vgl. dazu die vergleichende Darstellung in: Europäische Kommission 1999a.

Aktionsplan vorlegen, in dem sie aufzeigen, wie sie die Leitlinien umsetzen wollen.[27] Inhaltlich geht es um konkrete Maßnahmen in den Politikfeldern der folgenden vier Säulen (pillars) der Leitlinien (Rat der EU 1999a):

1. „Verbesserung der Beschäftigungsfähigkeit",
2. „Entwicklung des Unternehmergeistes",
3. „Förderung der Anpassungsfähigkeit der Unternehmen und ihrer Beschäftigten",
4. „Verstärkung der Maßnahmen zur Förderung der Chancengleichheit von Frauen und Männern".

Zu den einzelnen Maßnahmen im Nationalen Aktionsplan werden quantitative Zielwerte vorgegeben (z.B. zum Abbau der Langzeitarbeitslosigkeit), die den Grad der Zielerreichung meßbar und im internationalen Benchmarking bewertbar machen sollen.[28] Zu den Ergebnissen der Umsetzung wird dann ein Bericht vorgelegt, auf dessen Basis die Kommission und der Rat wiederum beschäftigungspolitische Empfehlungen an die einzelne Mitgliedstaaten aussprechen.

Für die hier interessierende Frage nach den EU-seitigen Vorgaben für das Monitoring und die Evaluation des ESF-Einsatzes ist nun wichtig, daß aus Sicht der EU der ESF ein zentraler Hebel zur Umsetzung der Beschäftigungspolitischen Leitlinien bzw. der Vorhaben der Nationalen Aktionspläne sein soll (Rat der EU 1999a: 3). Damit geht es beim ESF nicht allein um den added value hinsichtlich der nationalen Arbeitsmarktpolitik, sondern um diese selber. Von Seiten der EU wird der ESF als Instrument zur Beeinflussung der Zielsetzungen und der Umsetzung der nationalen Arbeitsmarkt- und Beschäftigungspolitik angesehen.

Dieser beschäftigungspolitische Kontext des ESF und seiner Ergänzung nationaler Arbeitsmarktpolitik ist neu und hat sich auf die jetzt abgelaufene Strukturfondsphase noch nicht auswirken können. In Verbindung mit dem aktuellen Bemühen um einen Wechsel von der bisher bürokratischen Regulierung der Umsetzung der Strukturfonds hin zu einer strategischen Zielsteuerung (vgl. unten) hat die beschäftigungspolitische Einbindung erhebliche Konsequenzen für die zukünftige Umsetzung des ESF und damit auch für die Ausgestaltung des darauf bezogenen Feedbacksystems von Monitoring, Evaluation und Finanzkontrolle.

4.2 Programmierung und Steuerung des ESF in der neuen Phase von 2000 bis 2006

Das System der EU-Strukturfonds-Politik wird in der einschlägigen Policy-Forschung als ein verflochtenes Mehrebenensystem charakterisiert, in das in

---

27 Zum Konzept der Europäischen Beschäftigungsstrategie vgl. Rhein (1999a und 1999b).
28 Zum Benchmarking der Nationalen Aktionspläne vgl. Tronti 1999.

vertikaler Hinsicht (EU, Mitgliedstaat, Region) und in horizontaler Hinsicht (staatliche Akteure auf den einzelnen Ebenen, die Sozialpartner und weitere Nichtregierungsorganisationen) eine Vielzahl von Akteuren eingebunden sind. Dies impliziert in hohem Maße Transparenzprobleme und das Risiko einer „Politikverflechtungsfalle" (Scharpf 1994), bei der jeder Beteiligte nur „sein eigenes Süppchen kochen" will, und die übergeordneten, als gemeinsam erklärten politischen Ziele zugunsten des „kleinsten gemeinsamen Nenners" oder gar durch Selbstblockaden aus den Blick geraten können.

In Reaktion auf diese Probleme wurde ein neues System der Programmierung und Steuerung der Strukturfonds entwickelt. Das bisherige bürokratische, an der Einhaltung von Regeln und deren Überwachung orientierte Regulierungsmodell soll zugunsten eines strategischen Management überwunden werden, bei dem die Zielsteuerung im Vordergrund steht, Entscheidungen über die konkreten Programme und deren Umsetzung auf die Ebenen der Mitgliedstaaten und Regionen dezentralisiert werden, dafür aber im Sinne von Zielcontrolling das Monitoring und die Evaluation einschließlich der Finanzkontrolle als Feedbacksystem systematisiert und verbindlicher werden (Lang/Naschold/Reissert 1998).

Für die Programmierung und Steuerung des ESF ab 2000 (nicht nur) in Deutschland bedeutet dies u.a., daß ein detailliertes Konzept von Monitoring und Evaluation verbindlich wird – in organisatorischer Hinsicht (Zuständigkeiten und Ablauf) und in Gestalt eines Katalogs von Indikatoren, die den Verlauf und die Ergebnisse der Implementation auf der konkreten Ebene einzelner Maßnahmen und aggregiert meßbar machen. Unter dem Aspekt eines Soll-Ist-Vergleichs mit Kontextindikatoren zur Entwicklung von Arbeitsmarkt und Beschäftigung und mit Kontingentindikatoren zur Zielgruppenerreichung soll die Umsetzung bewertet werden. Und mit Hilfe von Wirkungsindikatoren soll Auskunft gegeben werden über den individuellen Nutzen der Förderung wie auch z.B. über die Auswirkungen auf die Strukturen und das Niveau der Arbeitslosigkeit (vgl. dazu unten 4.4).

Die einzelnen Schritte der mehrstufigen Programmierung des ESF ab 2000 (und entsprechend bei den anderen Strukturfonds) sind in „Arbeitspapieren" der Kommission im Einzelnen dargelegt und leiten den Prozeß der Ausarbeitung und Verhandlung (Europäische Kommission 1999b).[29] Zusätzlich gibt es für den ESF einen „Leitfaden zur Begleitung und Bewertung", in dem die Anforderungen genauer beschrieben sind (Europäische Kommission GDV Beschäftigung und soziale Angelegenheiten 1999). Das Monitoring („Begleitung") ist Aufgabe der für die Programmumsetzung zuständigen Verwaltungsbehörde, die Evaluation („Bewertung") obliegt den ESF-Begleitausschüssen, die ihrerseits hierzu unabhängige wissenschaftliche Eva-

---

29 Dabei handelt es sich u.a. um ein Vademecum zur Programmerstellung (Arbeitspapier 1), Vorschläge für die ex-ante-Evaluation (Arbeitspapier 2) und für Indikatoren für die Begleitung und Bewertung aller Strukturfonds (Arbeitspapier 3).

luatoren einsetzen. Vorgesehen sind nach der ex-ante Evaluation im Zuge der Programmplanung eine „Halbzeitbewertung" im Jahr 2003, eine „ergänzende Zwischenevaluation" im Jahr 2005 und eine ex-post-Evaluation am Ende der Strukturfondsphase.[30]

In formaler Hinsicht entspricht diese organisatorische Struktur von „Begleitung" und „Bewertung" auf den ersten Blick den Regelungen der vorherigen Programmphase bis 1999. Gleichwohl gibt es wichtige Neuerungen. An den für die Begleitung und Bewertung zuständigen ESF-Begleitausschüssen will die Kommission im Sinne der Dezentralisierung von Verantwortung nur noch beratend teilnehmen. Die Programmverantwortlichen sollen nun anders als zuvor eine wissenschaftliche Evaluation von Beginn an und durchgehend einsetzen. Dies gilt nicht nur für die oberste Programmebene, sondern auch für die jeweiligen Einzelprogramme von Bund und Ländern. Vor allem ist nun mit der Vorgabe von Indikatoren einschließlich Wirkungsindikatoren, die auf Nettoeffekte zielen, ein neues Datum gesetzt.

Die Neuregelungen von Monitoring und Evaluation sind zum einen als Reaktion auf entsprechende Defizite in der Vergangenheit anzusehen. Diese werden zum besseren Verständnis im folgenden kurz dargestellt (4.3.). Dabei geht es vor allem um bessere Informationen über die Implementation im Interesse einer Optimierung der Implementationsprozesse, und um mehr Kenntnisse über die Wirkungen der ESF-Förderung. Weiterhin zielen die Neuregelungen auf bessere Vergleichsmöglichkeiten des ESF-Einsatzes innerhalb eines Mitgliedstaates und auch international in Hinblick auf die Europäische Beschäftigungsstrategie sowie nicht zuletzt darauf, Monitoring und Evaluation als Instrumente von Zielcontrolling und Finanzcontrolling zu nutzen. Dies ist eine neue Herausforderung für die wissenschaftliche ESF-Evaluation, die hier abschließend charakterisiert werden soll (4.4.).

4.3 Monitoring und Evaluation des ESF bis 1999

Für die jetzt abgelaufene Phase der Strukturfonds gab es zunächst kein verbindliches System von Monitoring und Evaluation.[31] Zwar waren von den Fondsverwaltern des ESF jährliche Durchführungsberichte zur finanziellen

---

30 Europarechtlich sind diese Vorgaben in der Verordnung des Rates der EU (1999b) mit den allgemeinen Bestimmungen über die Strukturfonds fixiert. Für die Zwecke eines internationalen Vergleichs sind diese Vorgaben von Indikatoren und allgemeinen Regeln der Begleitung und Bewertung wichtig. Dabei besteht aber die Gefahr, daß jeweilige nationale Besonderheiten (z.B. Erfassung von Arbeitslosigkeit durch Register oder Befragungen, Unterschiede in den rechtlichen Systemen sozialer Sicherung usw.) zugunsten formaler Einheitlichkeit aus dem Blick geraten.

31 So wurden z.B. die „Gemeinsamen Leitlinien für die Begleitung und Zwischenbewertung" erst 1996, also im dritten Jahr nach dem Start der Strukturfonds (1994) veröffentlicht (Europäische Kommission 1996).

Abwicklung und zur Zahl der geförderten Personen und Projekte an die Begleitausschüsse und die Kommission zu richten, aber es gab kein differenziertes Indikatorensystem zu Input, Verlauf und Ergebnissen der Förderung. Eine Halbzeitbewertung und eine spätere „ergänzende Zwischenevaluation" wurden europaweit durchgeführt – dies aber auf äußerst unzureichender Datenbasis und mit erheblichen inhaltlichen und methodischen Anlaufschwierigkeiten.[32]

In Deutschland hat es nur für den von der Bundesanstalt für Arbeit umgesetzten Teil des ESF-Bundesprogramms, das ESF-BA-Programm, eine durchgehende Begleitforschung gegeben. Die Länder hatten sich – mit wenigen Ausnahmen (vgl. hier Kap. 3) – auf die Einrichtung und den Ausbau von Umsetzungsorganisationen konzentriert, denen auch das Monitoring mit primärer Ausrichtung auf die Zahlungsströme der ESF-Mittel übertragen war. Nur punktuell wurden von den Ländern Evaluationsstudien zur Programmimplementation und zur Ermittlung von Förderergebnissen in Auftrag gegeben.

Deshalb war nicht überraschend, daß die vom Bundesarbeitsministerium zur Mitte der Laufzeit in Auftrag gegebenen Arbeiten zur übergreifenden ersten Zwischenevaluation des ESF – getrennt für West- und Ostdeutschland – mit erheblichen Schwierigkeiten verbunden waren. Probleme bereitete schon die Antwort auf die Frage, wie viele Personen vom ESF gefördert wurden, zu welchen Zielgruppen sie gehörten und an welchen Maßnahmearten sie mit welchem Erfolg teilgenommen hatten. Fragen zum Verbleib nach der Förderung konnten schon aus zeitlichen Gründen (erforderliche Beobachtungszeiträume waren noch nicht abgelaufen), aber auch mangels valider Daten noch nicht beantwortet werden. Es blieben erhebliche Datenlücken. Wirkungsanalysen im Sinne der Ermittlung von Nettoerträgen lagen nicht vor. Die Evaluationsberichte fielen entsprechend unbefriedigend aus, mußten viele Fragen offen lassen.[33]

Im Zuge dieser Erfahrungen wurde von einer Arbeitsgruppe der Länder- und Bundesevaluatoren in Zuarbeit für die ESF-Begleitausschüsse und mit Zustimmung der Kommission dann ein sogenannter „ESF-Minimalkatalog" erarbeitet, der die Rahmendaten für die „ergänzende Zwischenevaluation" im Jahr 1999 abdecken sollte. Die Arbeiten daran sind noch nicht abgeschlossen. Sie sind nach wie vor davon geprägt, daß das Monitoring und die Evaluation zu den Einzelprogrammen unterschiedlich weit entwickelt ist, die Daten und

---

32 Die zusammengefaßten nationalen Berichte zur Halbzeitbewertung sind im Internet zugänglich: http://europa.eu.int/comm/dg5/esf/en/public/mid_term/tocde.htm.

33 Vgl. dazu ausführlicher die Schwächen des Berichts zur Ziel-3-Förderung in Westdeutschland von Prognos Köln (1997) und demgegenüber kritisch und weiterführender den Bericht zur Bundes- und Landesförderung von Zielgruppen in Ostdeutschland von IfS und FBAE Berlin (1997). Die Zwischenergebnisse zum bundesweiten ESF-BA-Programm wurden gesondert veröffentlicht (Deeke/Hülser/Wolfinger 1997; Deeke 1999).

Befunde nur schwerlich vergleichbar und für die übergeordnete Bewertung des ESF-Einsatzes in West- und Ostdeutschland nur mit erheblichen Vorbehalten aggregierbar sind. Selbst Ansprüche einer konventionellen Evaluation, wie sie hier eingangs angesprochen und als unzureichend charakterisiert worden sind (Kapitel 1), sind damit nicht hinreichend erfüllbar. Wirkungsuntersuchungen auf der Basis von Vergleichsgruppenanalysen usw. fehlen nach wie vor. Erfolgseinschätzungen müssen weitgehend auf den Vergleich von kurzfristigen Bruttoeffekten der Förderung beschränkt bleiben und beinhalten damit die gleichen Probleme, wie im Falle der Verbleibsquoten der Eingliederungsbilanz des SGB III (vgl. Kapitel 2). Die Balance zwischen dem übergreifenden vergleichenden Bewertungsanspruch und der erforderlichen Berücksichtigung länderspezifischer bis hin zu maßnahmespezifischer Kontexte gelingt nur zum Teil. Und schließlich: gemessen am Anspruch einer adressenorientierten, auf den untersuchten politischen Prozeß bzw. Programmablauf gezielten Evaluation kommen die Ergebnisse zu spät.

4.4 Neue Ansätze von Monitoring und Evaluation als Instrumente der Zielsteuerung und strategischen Reflexion des ESF in Deutschland

Der gewachsene Stellenwert von Monitoring und Evaluation in der neuen Strukturfondsphase und die Erfahrungen der Vergangenheit haben die ESF-Begleitausschüsse in Abstimmung mit der Kommission zu einer grundlegenden Verbesserung des Systems von Begleitung und Bewertung veranlaßt (Indikatoren-Arbeitsgruppe 1999). Nach derzeitigem Stand soll das vorgelegte Konzept umgesetzt werden für alle einzelnen ESF-kofinanzierten Programme wie insbesondere für die übergeordnete Begleitung und Bewertung durch die Begleitausschüsse bzw. die zuständigen Verwaltungsbehörden und beauftragten wissenschaftlichen Evaluationsprojekte. Einzelheiten des neuen Konzepts und seiner Umsetzung können zwar nur in einem mittelfristigen Abstimmungsprozeß zwischen allen Beteiligten auf Bundes- und Länderebene ausgearbeitet und realisiert werden. Gleichwohl drängt von Beginn an die Zeit, wenn die Defizite der Vergangenheit behoben werden sollen.

Als ein Grundgerüst für das Monitoring und die Evaluation ist im Anschluß an den sog. ESF-Minimalkatalog, in Anlehnung an die SGB-III-Eingliederungsbilanz und in Konkretion der Indikatorenvorgaben aus den einschlägigen Arbeitspapieren der Kommission folgende Systematik entwickelt worden:

- Inputindikatoren (quantifizierte Ziele zum finanziellen und materiellen Verlauf),
- Verlaufsindikatoren (finanziell und materiell)
- Ergebnisindikatoren (u.a. Verbleib im ersten und sechsten Monat nach Austritt)

- Wirkungsindikatoren (u.a. Nettoeffekte individueller Förderung)
- Effizienzindikatoren (Verhältnis Nettoefekte zu eingesetzten Mitteln).

Im Zentrum der Überlegungen zu diesem Indikatorenschema steht eine funktionale Arbeitsteilung zwischen Monitoringsystem und Evaluationsarbeiten. Die Evaluation soll ihren Schwerpunkt bei Implementations- und vor allem bei Wirkungsanalysen haben, also als analytischer Beitrag zur übergreifende Begleitung und Bewertung konzipiert sein.

Im Rahmen des Monitoring sollen vor allem die Indikatoren zum Input, zum Verlauf und zu den Ergebnissen einschließlich dem Verbleib nach der Förderung abgedeckt werden. Voraussetzung ist für jedes Einzelprogramm eine Individualdatenbank, in die alle Eintritte in die Förderung aufgenommen werden, und die als Historik ereignisbezogen fortgeschrieben wird. Darauf sollen die analytischen Evaluationsarbeiten, die in der Vergangenheit aufgrund gravierender Datenlücken nicht möglich waren, aufsetzen, differenzierte Zielgruppenanalysen und Soll-Ist-Vergleiche durchführen, im Schwerpunkt den Bereich der Wirkungsindikatoren mit Hilfe von Vergleichsgruppenanalysen abdecken und nach Möglichkeit auch die Effizienz der Förderung ermitteln.

Insgesamt handelt es sich bei diesem Konzept in mehrfacher Hinsicht um ein ehrgeiziges Vorhaben – angefangen von der Lösung der in der Vergangenheit dominanten Probleme der Zugänglichkeit und Validität von Mikrodaten bis hin zur Verpflichtung auf Wirkungsanalysen, die über Nettoerträge der Förderung für die Einzelnen wie hinsichtlich der ESF-Programme insgesamt und ihrer Beiträge zu den Nationalen Aktionsplänen im Zusammenspiel mit der sonstigen Arbeitsmarktpolitik Auskunft geben.[34]

Die Aufgabe kausalanalytisch ausgerichteter Wirkungsuntersuchungen wird noch erhebliche Anstrengungen verlangen. Bedenkt man die hier in Kapitel 2 dargelegten methodischen und inhaltlichen Probleme sowie Perspektiven einer wirkungsanalytischen Untersuchung zu den zentralen Förderinstrumenten des SGB III, so wird deutlich, daß auch entsprechende Analysen der ESF-Ergänzung des Einsatzes dieser und weiterer Instrumente mit den beschriebenen Schwierigkeiten zu kämpfen haben werden, und daß der mögliche empirisch-analytische Ertrag nicht zuletzt von der Arbeit an der Wirkungsforschung zu den Regelinstrumenten abhängen wird.

---

34 Dabei bedeutet die funktionale Zuweisung von Monitoring- und Evaluationsaufgaben nicht, daß im Rahmen der begleitenden Evaluationsprojekte nicht zum Teil auch Monitoringaufgaben übernommen werden müssen. So wird es z.B. für die Länder, die ihre ESF-Förderung über Projektträger abwickeln, erfahrungsgemäß schwer sein, von diesen Trägern valide Verbleibsdaten zu den geförderten Personen zu erhalten, muß dies also ggf. erst noch durch Befragungen geförderter Personen erhoben werden. Beim ESF-BA-Programm werden diese Daten voraussichtlich über Datenabgleich aus Prozeßdatenbanken gewonnen, müssen aber ebenfalls durch Befragungen noch ergänzt werden.

Dabei müssen auch Risiken des hier nur kurz vorgestellten Konzepts bedacht werden. Die bisherige Evaluationspraxis (nicht nur beim ESF) zeigt, daß Wirkungsforschung nur dann mit Aussicht auf inhaltlichen Gewinn möglich ist, wenn sie in ein kooperatives Verhältnis von Monitoring, Controlling und gemeinsamer Bewertung von Wissenschaft und Praxis eingebettet ist und dabei hinreichend Zeit und Ressourcen hat. Dies gilt insbesondere, wenn es wie im Falle des ESF um eine begleitende Evaluation geht. So kann z.b. aufgrund des Zusammenhangs mit dem ESF-Finanzcontrolling nicht vorab ausgeschlossen werden, daß es bei der jährlichen Berichterstattung an die Kommission auf der Basis finanzieller und materieller Verlaufs- und Ergebnisindikatoren sowie Kontextindiaktoren zu einem neuen bürokratischen System – jetzt der Regulierung von Monitoring und Evaluation – kommt, welches an die Stelle der vormaligen Regulierung der bürokratisch verflochtenen Umsetzungsstrukturen tritt. Dies wäre aber weder im Interesse des neuen Anspruchs der EU auf zielorientierte Steuerung bei dezentraler Umsetzung, noch im Interesse eines Evaluationsanspruchs, der sich – ganz im Einklang mit den bisher entwickelten Vorgaben und Vorhaben – in die Richtung der hier eingangs beschriebenen Konzeption ziel- und prozeßorientierter Evaluation bewegt.

5. Ausblick

Die gravierenden und anhaltenden Ungleichgewichte am Arbeitsmarkt und damit verbunden der hohe Stellenwert arbeitsmarktpolitischer Maßnahmen haben auf den verschiedenen Politikebenen (Bund, Land und EU) die Fragen nach der Wirkung und Wirksamkeit von Programmen der Arbeitsförderung neu belebt.

Angesichts des hohen Problemdrucks bei knappem Mittelvolumen wird zu Recht die Frage aufgeworfen, welche Maßnahmen oder Maßnahmebündel einer Strukturalisierung der Arbeitslosigkeit am wirkungsvollsten entgegenwirken und den Abbau der Arbeitslosigkeit befördern können. Dies hat auch in Deutschland die Bedeutung der Programmevaluation gestärkt. Dazu hat die Europäische Union mit ihrer Verpflichtung zur Begleitung und Erfolgskontrolle ESF-kofinanzierter Maßnahmen nicht unwesentlich beigetragen. Daher gilt es um so mehr, die Möglichkeiten, aber auch die Grenzen der Evaluierung von Arbeitsmarktprogrammen auszuloten und machbare Konzepte zu entwickeln.

Zunächst ist die Rolle von Monitoring und Wirkungsforschung in ihrer jeweils spezifischen Arbeitsteilung klarer zu bestimmen. Auch wenn hier bereits Ansätze erkennbar sind, ist die Diskussion bisher noch stark verhaftet im reinen Monitoring: Konkret, welche Daten im einzelnen – durchaus mit dem Vorteil eines quantifizierbaren Querschnittvergleiches über Programme oder

Ländergrenzen hinweg – zu erfassen seien. Demgegenüber wird die hypothesengeleitete Bestimmung von Erfolgsindikatoren sowie der erwarteten Wirkungszusammenhänge im Rahmen der Datenauswahl für das Monitoring nur unzureichend diskutiert.

Ferner können Daten aus dem Monitoring einerseits und bislang für mikro-analytische Studien verfügbare Datensätze über Teilnehmerinnen und Teilnehmer sowie Vergleichsgruppen andererseits angesichts der hohen Anzahl von Kontextvariablen verbunden mit der Spezifik einzelner Programme nur eine schmale Basis für die notwendigen Evaluationen bieten. Deshalb möchte dieser Beitrag eine Lanze brechen für das hier dargelegte differenzierte und mehrstufige Vorgehen.

Damit die Ergebnisse schon im Programmvollzug unmittelbar in die Programmentwicklung einfließen können, sollte gerade bei neuen Förderansätzen die Rolle von On-ging-Evaluationen (im Sinne von Begleitforschung während der Programmlaufzeit) zu Lasten von ex-post-Evaluationen (im Sinne einer Bewertung nach Ablauf einer Förderperiode) gestärkt werden. Letztere haben gleichwohl einen unverzichtbaren Stellenwert namentlich für die Evaluation der großen Standardinstrumente.

Ferner hat sich das in der Konzeption der adressatenorientierten Evaluation verankerte reflexive und diskursive Vorgehen, das quantitative mit qualitativen Indikatoren, Methoden und Verfahrensweisen verbindet, bewährt. Hier geht es um eine Stärkung der Rolle von Evaluation als Instrument der Qualitätsbewertung, -sicherung und -verbesserung durch Einbindung der an der Programmgestaltung und Programmumsetzung beteiligten Akteure gegenüber einer auf wenige Maßzahlen reduzierten Erfolgskontrolle von außen.

Schließlich bedarf die Evaluationsforschung einer kritischen Selbstreflexion. Wirkungsforschung im Sinne eines Benchmarking erfolgreicher Politikkonzepte ist angesichts komplexer Wirkungszusammenhänge und aufwendiger Methoden zur Bestimmung der Effekte verschiedener Förderprogramme (z.B. Vergleichs- oder Kontrollgruppenansatz) kein leichtes Unterfangen. Hier sollten die Möglichkeiten und Grenzen stärker in das Blickfeld gerückt werden. Neben einer Weiterentwicklung von Konzepten und Methoden im Bereich der problemorientierten Grundlagenforschung gilt es u.E. insbesondere, ihre Machbarkeit an den Möglichkeiten und Anforderungen der Praxis zu spiegeln.

Die befruchtende Wirkung des Blickes über die Grenzen – etwa im Rahmen international vergleichender Evaluationsstudien – soll hier keineswegs in Abrede gestellt werden. Gleichwohl werden bei international vergleichenden Studien die Grenzen der Übertragbarkeit von Politikkonzepten schon aufgrund unterschiedlicher institutioneller Arrangements schnell deutlich. Dies gilt für international vergleichende Studien, angesichts der föderalen Struktur der Bundesrepublik Deutschland in abgeschwächter Form auch für einen Vergleich der Arbeitsmarktförderung der Bundesländer. Hier bieten vertiefende Evaluationsstudien von Arbeitsmarktprogrammen gleicher Ziel-

richtung über einzelne Bundesländer hinweg gegenüber dem flächendeckenden Monitoring weit mehr Möglichkeiten, Anhaltspunkte zu finden, unter
welchen Bedingungen spezifische Programme ein hohes Maß an Wirksamkeit entfalten können

Literatur

Almus, Matthias u.a. (1998): Die gemeinnützige Arbeitnehmerüberlassung in Rheinland-
Pfalz – eine ökonometrische Analyse des Wiedereingliederungserfolgs. In: Mitteilun-
gen aus der Arbeitsmarkt- und Berufsforschung (MittAB) 3.

Ammermüller, Martin (1997): Reform der Arbeitsförderung – Grundlinien. In: Bundesar-
beitsblatt 7-8.

Auer, Peter/Kruppe, Thomas (1996): Monitoring of Labour Market Policy in EU Member
States. In: Schmid, Günther/O'Reilly, Jacqueline/Schömann, Klaus (Hg.): International Handbook of Labour Market Policy and Evaluation. Chaltenham und Brookfield.

Autorengemeinschaft (1997): Arbeitsmarktentwicklung und aktive Arbeitsmarktpolitik im
ostdeutschen Transformationsprozeß 1990-1996. IAB-Werkstattbericht Nr. 5 vom
21.02.1997.

Autorengemeinschaft (1998): IAB-AGENDA'98, IAB-Werkstattbericht Nr. 10 vom
28.09.1998.

Bangel, Bettina (1993): Geografie der Altersgrenzen. Frühverrentung im regionalen Strukturwandel. Berlin.

Bangel, Bettina (1999): Evaluierung der Arbeitsmarktpolitik aus Ländersicht. Die Brandenburger Konzeption der adressatenorientierten Evaluation: In: ibv Nr. 45/99, Nürnberg. S. 3745-3754.

Bender, Stefan/Klose, Christoph (2000): Ein Ansatz zur Evaluation eines arbeitsmarktpolitischen Programms mit prozeßproduzierten Längsschnittdaten. In: MittAB (i. Erscheinen).

Blancke, Susanne (1999): Push, Pull und Stay – Strategien gegen Arbeitslosigkeit in
Deutschland. Bericht aus dem Forschungsprojekt „Aktive Arbeitsmarktpolitik der
Bundesländer". In: Blancke, Susanne/Schmid, Josef (Hg.): Die aktive Arbeitsmarktpolitik der Bundesländer. Dokumentation des Workshops „Push, Pull und Stay –
Strategien gegen Arbeitslosigkeit in Deutschland". Occasional Paper Nr. 6 des Arbeitsbereichs „Politische Wirtschaftslehre und Vergleichende Politikfeldanalyse". Institut für Politikwissenschaft der Universität Tübingen: S. 28-36. In: http://www.uni-
tuebingen.de/uni/spi/polwihp.htm.

Blasche, Dieter/Nagel, Elisabeth (1999): Statistische Explorationen im Vorfeld der Ein-
gliederungsbilanz-Monitoring der Verbleibsquoten. In: MittAB 2/1999: 185-202.

Blaschke, Dieter/Nagel, Elisabeth (1995): Beschäftigungssituation von Teilnehmern an
AFG-finanzierter beruflicher Weiterbildung. In: MittAB 2.

Brinkmann, Christian (1998a): Regionalisierung der Arbeitsmarktpolitik. In: ibv-Zeit-
schrift für berufskundliche Information und Dokumentation, Nr. 17 vom 29. April
1998. Nürnberg.

Brinkmann, Christian (1998b): Wissenschaftliche Begleitung innovativer Ansätze der Arbeitsmarktpolitik, die mit Mitteln der „Freien Förderung" nach §10 des Sozialgesetz-
buches III gefördert werden. IAB-Werkstattbericht Nr. 3 vom 08.05.1998.

Brinkmann, Christian (1999): Zielcontrolling und Evaluation im Rahmen von Arbeitsförderung. IAB-Werkstattberichte, Nr. 2/1999.

Brinkmann, Christian/Kress, Ulrike (1997): Reformierung der Arbeitsförderung – Sozialabbau oder Finanzierung des Strukturwandels. In: ibv Nr. 30 vom 23. Juli 1997. Nürnberg.

Brinkmann, Christian u.a. (1999): Instrumente aktiver Arbeitsmarktpolitik in Ostdeutschland. In: Wiedemann, Eberhard u.a. (Hg.): Die arbeitsmarkt- und beschäftigungspolitische Herausforderung, BeitrAB 223. Nürnberg.

Bundesanstalt für Arbeit (1995 und 1996): Leistungsorientierte Führung in der Bundesanstalt für Arbeit, Zwischenberichte der Fachprojektgruppe, unveröffentlichte Manuskripte. Nürnberg.

Bundesanstalt für Arbeit (1999): Daten zu den Eingliederungsbilanzen 1998. Sondernummer der Amtlichen Nachrichten der Bundesanstalt für Arbeit. Nürnberg, 31. Juli 1999.

Deeke, Axel (1999): Vier Jahre ESF-BA-Programm. Die Umsetzung der ergänzenden Förderung zum AFG und SGB III aus dem Europäischen Sozialfonds (ESF) von 1995 bis 1998. IAB-Werkstattbericht Nr. 17 vom 30.09.1999.

Deeke, Axel/Hülser, Oliver/Wolfinger, Claudia (1997): Zwei Jahre „AFG-Plus". Zwischenbilanz zur ergänzenden Förderung zum AFG aus dem Europäischen Sozialfonds. BeitrAB 208. Nürnberg.

Deutscher Bundestag (1996): Entwurf eines Gesetzes zur Reform der Arbeitsförderung (Arbeitsförderungs-Reformgesetz – AFRG). BT-Drucksache 13/4941. Bonn.

Europäische Kommission (1996): Strukturfonds der EU 1994-1999: Gemeinsame Leitlinien für die Begleitung und die Zwischenbewertung. Luxemburg: Amt für amtliche Veröffentlichungen der Europäischen Gemeinschaften.

Europäische Kommission (1999a): Reform der Strukturfonds 2000-2006. Eine vergleichende Analyse (Juni 1999). In: www.inforegio.cec.eu.int/wbdoc/docoffic/ sf20002006/pdf/irfo_de.pdf.

Europäische Kommission (1999b): Arbeitsdokumente Strukturfonds 2000-2006. In: www.inforegio.ce.eu.int/wbdoc/docoffic/working.

Europäische Kommission GDV Beschäftigung und soziale Angelegenheiten (1999): Leitlinien für die Begleit- und Bewertungssysteme der Interventionen des ESF für den Zeitraum 2000-2006. Brüssel. Juli 1999.

Heckman, James J./LaLonde, R. J. /Smith, Jeffrey A. (1999): The Economics And Econometrics of Active Labor Market Programs. In: Handbook of Labor Economics, Vol. III A, chapter 31, pp. 1865-2097.

IfS/FBAE (1997): Institut für Stadtforschung und Strukturpolitik, Forschungsstelle für Berufsbildung, Arbeitsmarkt und Evaluation: Zusammenfassende Zwischenbewertung (1994-1996) der vom Europäischen Sozialfonds kofinanzierten Bundes- und Länderprogramme zur Erreichung des Zieles 1 in der Bundesrepublik Deutschland. Abschlußbericht. Berlin.

Indikatoren-Arbeitsgruppe (1999): FHVR Berlin, IfS Berlin, ISG Köln, ism Mainz, HLT Wiesbaden, Laewitz-Stiftung Hamburg: Vorschlag zur Begleitung und Bewertung der ESF-Förderung im Förderzeitraum 2000-2006. Stand: 09.11.1999.

Jaenichen, Ursula (1999): Betriebliche Einstellungshilfen. Erste Ergebnisse zu Förderstrukturen, IAB-Werkstattbericht Nr. 6 vom 28.04.1999.

Kirsch, Johannes/Knuth, Matthias/Krone, Sirikit/Mühge, Gernot (1999): Vorerst geringe Inanspruchnahme, Konzentration auf Kleinbetriebe, Nothilfe in Konkursfällen. IAB-Werkstattbericht Nr. 5 vom 19.04.1999.

Kromrey, H. (1995): Evaluation. Empirische Konzepte zur Bewertung von Handlungsprogrammen und Schwierigkeiten ihrer Realisierung. In: ZSE, H. 4 (1995): S. 312-336.

Kulozik, Ehrenfried (1998): Modell ‚Arbeitsamt 2000' im Arbeitsamt Dortmund – eine Zwischenbilanz. In: Arbeit und Beruf 9.

Lang, Jochen/Naschold, Frieder /Reissert, Bernd (1998): Management der EU-Strukturpolitik. Steuerungsprobleme und Reformperspektiven. Berlin.

Lenk, Klaus (1993): Evaluationsbedarf? Evaluationsprobleme beim GAO. In: Derlien, Hans-Ulrich (Hrsg.): Programm „Gemeinschaftswerk Aufschwung-Ost" – Planung, Vollzug, Evaluation. Werkstattbericht Nr. 15. München.

Luschei, Frank/Trube, Achim (1999): Qualitätsmanagement in der Arbeitsmarktpolitik und lokalen Beschäftigungsförderung. Grundsätzliche Überlegungen und exemplarische Darstellungen anhand eines Praxisprojektes. IAB Werkstattbericht Nr. 7 vom 21.05.1999.

Mertens, Dieter/Reyher, Lutz/Kühl, Jürgen (1981): Ziele und Möglichkeiten von Wirkungs-Analysen. In: MittAB 3.

Ministerium für Arbeit, Soziales, Gesundheit und Frauen (Hg.) (1993): Förderung der wirtschaftsnahen Weiterbildung. Pilotstudie zum brandenburgischen Programm „Förderung der Qualifizierung von Beschäftigten in kleinen und mittleren Unternehmen". Reihe Forschungsberichte des MASGF, Potsdam.

Ministerium für Arbeit, Soziales, Gesundheit und Frauen (Hg.) (1996a): Arbeit statt Sozialhilfe. Studie zur Implementation und Wirksamkeit des Brandenburger Förderprogramms. Reihe Forschungsberichte des MASGF. Potsdam.

Ministerium für Arbeit, Soziales, Gesundheit und Frauen (Hg.) (1996b): Wirkungsstudie zu den Brandenburger Existenzgründungsprogrammen. Reihe Forschungsberichte des MASGF. Potsdam.

Ministerium für Arbeit, Soziales, Gesundheit und Frauen (Hg.) (1998): Weiterbildungsberatungsstellen im Land Brandenburg. Akzeptanz, Inanspruchnahme, Tätigkeitsspektrum und Handlungspotentiale. Reihe Forschungsberichte des MASGF. Potsdam.

Ministerium für Arbeit, Soziales, Gesundheit und Frauen (Hg.) (1999a): Entwicklung von Betrieben und Beschäftigung in Brandenburg. Ergebnisse der dritten Welle des Betriebspanels Brandenburg. Reihe Forschungsberichte des MASGF. Potsdam.

Ministerium für Arbeit, Soziales, Gesundheit und Frauen (Hg.) (1999b): Tätigkeitsspektrum, Wirksamkeit, Akzeptanz und Handlungspotentiale der Regionalstellen Frauen und Arbeitsmarkt im Land Brandenburg. Reihe Forschungsberichte des MASGF. Potsdam.

Postlep, Rolf-Dieter (1994): Controlling zur Rationalisierung in der Kommunalpolitik. In: Bunde, Jürgen/Postlep, Rolf-Dieter (Hg): Controlling in Kommunalverwaltungen. Marburg.

Prognos Köln (1997): Zwischenbewertung der Effizienz von Durchführung und Mitteleinsatz der Bundes- und Länderprogramme im Rahmen der Interventionen des ESF zur Erreichung des Zieles 3. Endbericht. Köln.

Rat der Europäischen Union (1999a): Entschließung des Rates vom 22. Februar 1999 zu den beschäftigungspolitischen Leitlinien für 1999 In: Amtsblatt der Europäischen Gemeinschaften C 69/2-8 vom 12.03.1999.

Rat der Europäischen Union (1999b): Verordnung (EG) Nr. 1260/1999 des Rates vom 21. Juni 1999 mit allgemeinen Bestimmungen über die Strukturfonds. In: Amtsblatt der Europäischen Gemeinschaften L 161/1-142 vom 26.06.1999.

Reissert Bernd (1999): Die Rolle der Länder in der Arbeitsmarktpolitik. In: Ministerium für Arbeit, Soziales, Gesundheit und Frauen (Hg.): Dokumentationsreihe zum partnerschaftlichen Abstimmungsprozeß Nr. 10: Neue Akzente mit dem ESF in Brandenburg. Potsdam. S. 33-52. In: http://www.bbj.de/potsdam.

Rhein, Thomas (1999a): Rolle der Europäischen Union in der Beschäftigungspolitik. IAB-Kurzbericht Nr. 13 vom 23.09.1999.

Rhein, Thomas (1999b): Europäische Beschäftigungspolitik. Dokumentation 1994-1999, Dokumentationsdienste zur Arbeitsmarkt- und Berufsforschung, Informationsmappe. Nürnberg.

Scharpf, Fritz W. (1994): Optionen des Föderalismus in Deutschland und Europa. Frankfurt/M, New York.

Schmachtenberg Rolf (1999): Schlußfolgerungen des MASGF aus dem bisherigen Programmplanungsprozeß-Konturen des zukünftigen Landesprogramms „Arbeit und Qualifizierung für Brandenburg". In: Ministerium für Arbeit, Soziales, Gesundheit und Frauen (Hrsg.): Dokumentationsreihe zum partnerschaftlichen Abstimmungsprozeß Nr. 10: Neue Akzente mit dem ESF in Brandenburg: Potsdam. S. 5-32. In: http://www.bbj.de/potsdam.

Schmid Günther (1996): Process Evaluation: Policy Formation and Implementation. In: Schmid/O'Reilly/Schömann (Hg.) (1996a): S. 198-231.

Schmid, Günther/O'Reilly, Jacqueline/Schömann, Klaus (Hg.) (1996a): International Handbook of Labour Market Policy and Evaluation. Cheltenham und Brookfield.

Schmid, Günther/O'Reilly, Jacqueline/Schömann, Klaus (1996b): Theory and Methodology of Labour Market Policy and Evaluation: An Introduction. In: Schmid/O'Reilly/Schömann (Hg.) (1996a): S. 131.

Schmid Günther/Schömann, Klaus/Schütz, Holger (1997): Evaluierung der Arbeitsmarktpolitik. Ein analytischer Bezugsrahmen am Beispiel des Arbeitsmarktpolitischen Rahmenprogramms. Discussion Paper FS I S. 97-204. Wissenschaftszentrum Berlin für Sozialforschung.

Schmid, Günther u.a. (1999): Zur Effektivität aktiver Arbeitsmarktpolitik. Erfahrungen aus einer integrierten Wirkungs- und Implementationsstudie. In: MittAB 4.

Tronti, Lionello (1999): Benchmarking employment performance and labour market policies: the results of the Research project. In: TRANSFER. European Review of Labour and Research, Vol. 5, No. 4, S. 542-562.

Übersicht 1: Eingliederungsbilanz (§11 SGB III)

I. Vorzüge
- Transparenz als Voraussetzung für wirksameren Einsatz
- Vergleichbarkeit, „managed competition"
- neue Datenzugänge

II. Kritikpunkte
- nur kurzfristiger Verbleib
  (arbeitslos ½ Jahr)
- keine qualitativen Zieldimensionen
  („employability", qualifikationsadäquate Beschäftigung, Vermittlung gewichtet nach Schwierigkeitsgrad, z.b. Dauer der vorausgegangen Arbeitssuche)
- nur am Rande Arbeitsmarktwirkungen
  (Entlastungswirkung wurde einbezogen, „Strukturverbesserung" fehlt)
- Brutto- statt Nettoeffekte
- Gefährdung von Zielgruppenerreichung
  („creaming"-Effekte)
- mögliche Verzerrungen beim Querschnittsvergleich
  (Einfluß von regionalen Arbeitsmarktstrukturen)

III. Fazit:
ein schwieriger Schritt in die richtige Richtung, darf nicht isoliert gesehen werden, bedarf der Ergänzung und Weiterentwicklung

Übersicht 2: Geschäftspolitische Schwerpunkte der Bundesanstalt für Arbeit

I. Vorzüge
- Arbeitsmarktbezogene Wirkungsziele
- an mittelfristigen Problemlagen des Arbeitsmarktes orientiert
- orientiert an beschäftigungspolitischen Leitlinien der EU sowie der Bundesregierung
- hohes Ausmaß an Objektivierbarkeit

II. Kritikpunkte
- weitgehendes Fehlen realistischer „Erwartungswerte" für die Bildung von Zielen („Soll-Werten")
- Fixierung auf kurzfristig erreichbare Zielsetzungen
- Fehlen von qualitativen Wirkungsdimensionen wie
  Erhöhung der Berufswahlkompetenz
  dauerhafte Eingliederung in das Erwerbsleben
  qualifikationsadäquate Beschäftigung (u.a. nach FbW)
  Verbesserung der regionalen Angebotsbedingungen
- Ausblenden weiter Bereiche des BA-Handelns aus dem „obersten" Zielsystem (Beratungsdienstleistungen)

III. Fazit:
Entwicklungarbeit zur Behebung der Defizite (Ableitung von „Erwartungswerten", „Objektivierung" von Zielerreichung im Bereich qualitativer Wirkungsdimensionen, Ergänzung um längerfristige Erfolgsaspekte), Verknüpfung weiterer Controllinginstrumente zu einem (umfassenderen) System arbeitsmarktbezogener Wirkungsziele

Übersicht 3: Adressatenorientierte Evaluation der Arbeitsmarktpolitik
Typologie der Funktionsbereiche und Analysefelder

Zielvorgabe:
* Informationsbasis für die Entwicklung arbeitsmarktpolitischer Programme erhöhen
* Paßfähigkeit und Wirkungen der Arbeitsförderung untersuchen
* Ansätze zur Weiterentwicklung der Arbeitsmarktpolitik aufzeigen

Umsetzung: 3-stufiger Ansatz mit den Elementen:

I. Verwaltungsinternes Monitoring	II. Vergabe von Evaluations-studien an Dritte	III. Politikberatende Arbeits-marktforschung nutzen
Zielvorgabe: Prozeßbegleitende Dokumentation, Programmanalyse und Programmsteuerung	*Zielvorgabe:* vertiefende Analyse zur Paßfähigkeit, Akzeptanz, Wirkung und Wirksamkeit bestehender Förderprogramme sowie deren Weiterentwicklung, Entwicklung neuer Programme	*Zielvorgabe:* Konzeptentwicklung und Synergieeffekte für I. und II., Weiterentwicklung bestehender Förderprogramme, Entwicklung neuer Programme
durch: laufende Beobachtung der unmittelbaren Ergebnisse der Förderung anhand der Erhebung und Auswertung ausgewählter Indikatoren, z.B. – Ausschöpfung des Programms – Anzahlen und Abbrecherquoten – Zielgruppenberücksichtigung – Regionale Verteilung – Verbleib Struktur- und Wirksamkeitsanalysen zur Arbeitsmarktpolitik Gewinnung von Basisdaten für II.	*durch:* sozialwissenschaftliche Untersuchungen zur Arbeitsmarktentwicklung sowie zur Wirksamkeit der Arbeitsförderprogramme (Programmkonzeption und -administration, Implementation und Akzeptanz, Wirkung und Wirksamkeit) *ex-ante:* – Studien zur Beschäftigungs- und Arbeitsmarktsituation – programmvorbereitende Studien *on-going:* – Wirkungsuntersuchungen zur Arbeitsförderung – förderpunktbezogene Eval. – Evaluation von Beratungsstrukturen – Begleitforschung zu Modellförderung – Querschnittstudien *ex-post:* – Querschnittstudie ex post-Bewertung	*durch:* Aufbereitung der vorliegenden Ansätze und Erkenntnisse der politikberatenden Arbeitsmarktforschung als Impulsangebote für die Programmwickler, z.B. – Grundsatzarbeit zur Konzeptentwicklung für internes Monitoring und externe Evaluation – Programmbezogene Wirkungsstudien – Gesamtwirtschaftlich orientierte Wirkungsanalysen zur Arbeitsmarktpolitik – Erfahrungen aus anderen Ländern

Methode:
Konzeption der adressatenorientierten Evaluation als handlungsleitender Ansatz: Sozialwissenschaftlicher, interdisziplinärer Ansatz; dialogorientiertes, reflexives Vorgehen; Rückkoppelung von (Teil-)Ergebnissen; Anstoßen von Prozessen der Selbstevaluation, methodisch-empirischer Methodenmix.
Zitiert nach: Bangel (1999).

Joseph Huber und Axel Müller

Zur Evaluation von Umweltschutz-Maßnahmen in Staat und Unternehmen

1. Zum Gegenstandsbereich von Evaluationen im Umweltschutz

Staatliche Umweltpolitik entwickelt sich seit rund drei Jahrzehnten, industrielles Umweltmanagement seit rund 15 Jahren. Dennoch hat man erst in jüngerer Zeit zu fragen begonnen, ob und wie weit der viele Aufwand, der ersichtlich betrieben wird, den Umweltnutzen, den man sich davon verspricht, auch effektiv erbringt, und wie weit der Aufwand in Anbetracht der ermittelten Ergebnisse, ggfls. auch nicht-intendierter Effekte, als vertretbar gelten kann. Bartlett (1994: 169) stellt fest: „The challenge of identifiying environmental policy success and failure has been insufficiently recognized. The problems are partly political, partly theoretical, and partly methodological. Some difficulties are inherent in the business of policy, others in the task of evaluation".

1.1 Vergesellschaftung der Politik und des Politikzyklus

Bezüglich des Gegenstandsbereiches von Evaluationen im Umweltschutz erscheint es erforderlich, zumindest zwei Spezifizierungen vorzunehmen. Die eine betrifft den etatistischen Bias des Evaluationsbegriffes, die andere den Unterschied zwischen Maßnahmen-Evaluation und Politikevaluation. Bei Bussmann, Klöti & Knoepfel (1997: 39ff.) wird Evaluation rigoros auf staatliche Maßnahmen eingeschränkt. Auch für Jänicke (1999: 62f.) ist Umweltpolitikevaluation „die Prüfung der Effektivität und Effizienz sowie der Wirkungsbedingungen politischer Maßnahmen und Programme", wobei „politische Maßnahmen" synonym mit öffentlich-rechtlichen Maßnahmen gebraucht wird.

Trotz der ansonsten vorhandenen Zustimmung zu den in beiden Referenzen angestellten Betrachtungen, sehen wir in der Einschränkung auf staatliche Aktivitäten eine nicht sachgerechte Verkürzung der Aufgabenstellung, um so mehr, als hiermit oft genug eine weitere Verkürzung auf Verwaltungsmaßnahmen verbunden ist, neben denen Gesetzgebung und Rechtsprechung sowie der Politikprozeß auf Parlaments-, Kabinetts- und Ministerialebene in den Hintergrund treten. Vor allem aber ist gerade im Umweltschutz festzustellen, daß ein zusätzlicher Schwerpunktbereich besteht in Gestalt von privatrechtlichen Umweltmaßnahmen im Rahmen der Unternehmensführung und Betriebsleitung. Im Zeichen der Schwerpunktverlagerung vom ordnungsrechtlichen zum marktlich-zivilrechtlichen Umweltschutz besitzen nicht-staatliche Akteure wie Industrie und Gewerbe, Handel, Forschung und Entwicklung, private Haushalte, Aktionsgruppen und Bürgerbewegungen eine erhebliche Bedeutung. Deshalb müssen auch Umweltmaßnahmen von para-staatlichen, intermediären und privaten Akteuren Gegenstand von Evaluationen sein.

Im Rahmen der Policy-Analysis bildet Evaluation einen der Schritte in der Abfolge des Policy-Zyklus. Die Darstellung eines Politikzyklus pflegt je nach Autor und Anlaß in Einzelaspekten zu variieren. Im Wesentlichen werden zu einem vollständigen Politikzyklus folgende Schritte gezählt (Windhoff-Héritier 1987; Jänicke 1999: 52):

- Problemwahrnehmung (Problem perception)
- Thematisierung (Agenda setting)
- Politikformulierung (Policy formulation)
- Entscheidung (Decision making)
- Politik- und Verwaltungsvollzug (Implementation)
- Ergebnisbewertung (Evaluation)
- Politikneuformulierung oder -beendigung (Termination)

Abgesehen von der Frage, wie realitätsgerecht dieses Ablaufmodell sei, bleibt zu sagen, daß, sofern man dem Modell folgt, es auch auf Politikprozesse jenseits des Staates anzuwenden ist. An die Stelle des institutionellen, etatistischen Politikbegriffes tritt – nicht nur theoretisch, sondern in Praxis – ein funktionaler Politikbegriff (Huber 1998: 320ff.). Demzufolge ist Politik, psychologisch gesprochen, der kognitive und affektive Prozeß der Meinungs- und Willensbildung zusammen mit dem konativen Prozeß der Verhaltensdisponierung, soziologisch gesprochen ein formativer Prozeß der intentionalen und sinnvermittelten Norm- und Zielbildung sowie der Programmierung und Konditionierung des Handelns. Formative Politikprozesse in einem solchen zivilgesellschaftlich verallgemeinerten Sinne finden überall statt – im Management von Unternehmen und Finanzinstitutionen, der Leitung von Kirchen und Medienanstalten, Forschungs- und Bildungseinrichtungen, im Rahmen privatrechtlicher Vereinigungen und gemeinschaftlicher Sozialbeziehungen ebenso wie nach herkömmlichem Verständnis in Gesetzgebung, Rechtsprechung und hoheitlichen Exekutivfunktionen auf überstaatlicher bis kommunaler Ebene.

1.2 Maßnahmen-Evaluation und Politik-Evaluation

Eine Umweltmaßnahme bezeichnet jegliche Art von Gesetz, Verordnung, operativem Programm, Vorhaben, Anleitung, Richtlinie, Anordnung, Anweisung o.ä., im Unterschied zum allgemeineren Begriff des Umwelt*handelns*. Dieses beinhaltet intentionale Handlungsstrategien, eventuell beruhend auf Grundsatzprogrammen, Positionsbeschlüssen o.ä., ebenso wie faktische Handlungsmuster oder stabilisierte Verhaltenskomplexe. In diesem Sinne ist zu unterscheiden zwischen der Evaluation von Umweltmaßnahmen und der Evaluation von Umweltpolitikprozessen, die teils zu Maßnahmen führen, teils auch unabhängig und jenseits davon umweltrelevante Folgen nach sich ziehen. Bartlett (1994: 170-176) unterscheidet in diesem Sinne die „Outcome evaluation" von exekutiven oder operativen Maßnahmen einerseits von der „Policy process evaluation" andererseits. Letztere fokussiert auf die Qualität und Problemadäquanz von strategischen Weichenstellungen und Maßnahmedefinitionen.

Wenn zum Beispiel eine mäßig weit reichende Ökobilanzierung des Abgaskatalysators zu dem Ergebnis gelangt, die Vorrichtung erfülle ihren Zweck der Abgasminderung zu vertretbaren Kosten, so heißt dies noch nicht, es handle sich um eine richtige Maßnahme, die einen nachhaltigen Beitrag zur Luftreinhaltung leistet. Selbst wenn eine Evaluation der Einführung von KFZ-Abgaskatalysatoren denkbar weit ginge, und sie auch den gesamten Ressourceninput sowie zudem langfristige Trends im Verkehrsaufkommen u.ä. berücksichtigen würde, so kann die Evaluation der Katalysatortechnik dennoch kein Ersatz sein für die vergleichende Begutachtung von strategischen Alternativen.

In einem analogen Sinne bedarf auch die politische Setzung von Umweltzielen und Meßindikatoren einer kritischen Prüfung. Es ist zunächst einmal anerkennenswert, wenn zum Beispiel das deutsche Umweltministerium sich in fast allen Umweltbereichen überprüfbare operationalisierte Ziele setzt. So soll, immer zur Basis 1990, im Hinblick auf das Klima-Problem der jährliche CO_2-Ausstoß bis 2005 um 25% gesenkt werden; die Luftschadstoffe Schwefeldioxid SO_2, Stickoxide NO_x, Ammoniak NH_3 und flüchtige organische Verbindungen VOC sollen bis 2010 insgesamt um 70% reduziert werden; für alle Fließgewässer soll bis 2010 die chemische Güteklasse II erreicht werden; die spezifische Energieproduktivität (gemessen als BIP im Verhältnis zum Energieverbrauch) soll bis 2020 verdoppelt werden; usw. (Bundesumweltministerium 1998). Die staatliche Umweltpolitik leistet damit ihrer eigenen Evaluation löblichen Vorschub. Gleichwohl bleibt kritisch zu hinterfragen, ob derartige Ziele und ihre Meßindikatoren überhaupt richtig gewählt sind, inwiefern es sich eventuell um kühne Ziele handelt oder vielleicht um Pseudo-Ziele, die aufgrund laufender Entwicklungen sozusagen „von alleine" erreicht werden.

Es gibt Fälle, bei denen strategisch-formative Aspekte und exekutive Vollzugs- und Ergebnis-Aspekte sich berühren. Viele Gesetze, die Handlungsbereiche im Grundlegenden kodifizieren, etwa das Bundesimmissionsschutzgesetz oder das Kreislaufwirtschafts- und Abfallgesetz, besitzen in den vorderen Paragraphen noch strategisch-formativen Charakter, während später mehr exekutive Schritte festgelegt oder vorbereitet werden, die dann folgen in Form einer Verordnung (hier Bundesimmissionsschutz-Verordnung oder Abfallanlagenbetriebsverordnung) und daran wiederum geknüpfter Technischer Anleitungen (hier TA Luft und TA Lärm sowie TA Abfall).

Gleichwohl handelt es sich bei der Maßnahmen-Evaluation und der Politik-Evaluation um zwei verschiedene Arten von Aufgaben, die *nicht* mit den gleichen Fragestellungen und Methoden bearbeitet werden können. Maßnahmen-Evaluation ist, wenn man so will, Evaluation sensu strictu, und zwar desto ausgeprägter, je mehr sie von empirisch erfaßten *Wirkungen* ausgeht *und* diese ursächlich bezogen werden können auf konkrete, eindeutig abgrenzbare und absichtsvoll zielgerichtete *Maßnahmen* von deutlich operativem Charakter. Sie hat einen doppelten Gegenstand – zum einen die Evaluation des Vollzuges (Implementation), also der praktischen Umsetzung eines Programms oder einer Maßnahme, zum anderen die Evaluation der Wirkungen bzw. Ergebnisse (Outcomes), seien diese intendiert, nicht-intendiert, oder ausbleibend. Die Leitfragen der *Vollzugsevaluation* lauten nach Rossi u.a. (1988) „Erreicht das Programm die Zielpopulation? Wird die Maßnahme so implementiert wie geplant?" Hier geht es also um die Richtigkeit, Vollständigkeit und Planentsprechung der Maßnahmendurchführung. Die Teilfragen der *Ergebnisevaluation* lauten „Ist die Intervention effektiv? Was kostet sie, wie steht es um das Verhältnis von Kosten, Effektivität und Nutzen?". Hier geht es also um die Beurteilung des effektiven Erfolges oder Mißerfolges von Maßnahmen.

Bei einer Politik-Evaluation dagegen kann die Zuschreibung feststellbarer Wirkungen oft nur vermittelt erfolgen, was es schwierig machen kann, klarsichtige Analytik von spekulativen Mutmaßungen zu unterscheiden. Es liegt selten offen zutage, inwiefern meßbare Veränderungen der nationalen Öko-Performance mit Maßnahmen der Regierung in einem erkennbaren Zusammenhang stehen. Zum Beispiel ist es seit den 70/80er Jahren in allen fortgeschritteneren Industrieländern zu einem Rückgang der groben Luftverschmutzung unter anderem durch Schwefel gekommen (vgl. für Voss, D. 1996: 54). Umweltpolitiker verbuchen dieses Ergebnis gerne als Erfolg der von ihnen verabschiedeten Luftreinhalte-Verordnungen. Allerdings wurde in Japan festgestellt, daß allenfalls ein Drittel der erzielten Verringerung der Schwefel-Emissionen auf die per Ordnungsrecht oktroierten End-of-Pipe-Maßnahmen zurückzuführen waren. Der größere Teil der Emissionsminderung, unabhängig von der Gesetzeslage, entstand durch verbesserte Verbrennungstechnik und andere Energiesparmaßnahmen der Betriebe und privaten Haushalte, sowie durch veränderte Brennstoff-Zusammensetzung (EAJ 1989 Fig. 1-2-23). Ein solcher Befund begründet Zweifel an Sinn und Nutzen der erheblichen Kosten und Bürokratielasten einer ordnungsrechtlichen Umweltpolitikstrategie.

Eindeutige empirische Befunde sind in der Politik-Evaluation eher die Ausnahme. Öfter bleibt es bei der eher summarischen Zusammenfassung von

Expertenurteilen. Dabei kommen wissensparadigmatische und eventuell auch politische Präferenzen zum Tragen. Zum Beispiel bewerten Umweltverbände und ihnen nahe stehende Institute die offizielle Umweltpolitik habituell etwas ungnädig, während eine Studie der OECD von 1993 die Umweltpolitik der konservativ-liberalen Regierung in Deutschland als besonders gut bewertete. Der Sachverständigenrat für Umweltfragen, sozusagen als umweltwissenschaftlicher Aufsichtsrat der Regierung, stellte im gleichen Zeitraum der deutschen Umweltpolitik wiederum ein eher kritisches Zeugnis aus, mit dem Tenor, anfänglich sei besonders bei der Abluft- und Abwasserreinigung sowie der herkömmlichen Abfallbehandlung Anerkennenswertes geleistet worden, während jedoch Aufgaben der innovativen Energie-, Verkehrs- und Landwirtschaftspolitik vernachlässigt worden seien (RSU 1987, 1994: 177ff.).

Dennoch besteht heute eine bemerkenswerte Übereinstimmung dahingehend, die bisherige Umweltpolitik sei generell zu bürokratisch, zu staatsfixiert, zu sehr am administrativen und technischen Verfahren und zu wenig am ökologischen Ergebnis orientiert. Aufwand und Kosten gemessen am Nutzwert werden durchgehend als zu hoch eingeschätzt (Weidner 1995, 1997; Huber 1993). Auch Evaluationen einzelner Gesetzespakete kommen meist zu ähnlichen Schlußaussagen, darunter relativ bekannt geworden eine Evaluation des amerikanischen „Superfund" als „superfailure", weil ein großer Teil der Kosten dieses Programms zur Deponien- und Altlastensanierung für Rechtsstreitigkeiten de facto zweckentfremdet wurde, während die eigentliche Standortsanierung nur ungenügend erfolgte (Mazmanian/Morell 1992).

1.3 Expertokratische und partizipative Evaluation

Auch Evaluation unterliegt einem Prozeß der Professionalisierung. Berater und Spezialisten der angewandten Forschung werden zu Evaluations-Experten und betrachten Evaluation als ihre berufliche Domäne. Es reproduziert sich hierbei eine demokratiebedeutsame Problematik, die bereits bei den Planungstheorien der 60er und 70er Jahre eine Rolle spielte, nämlich die Spannung zwischen Eliten und Experten einerseits und Publikum, Beteiligten und Betroffenen andererseits. Unter Demokratie-Aspekten sollte es vermieden werden, Evaluation zu einer bloßen expertokratischen Outsider-Diagnose im Rahmen bürokratisierter Verfahren werden zu lassen. Evaluationen *mit Hilfe* von Experten bzw. unter Federführung von Experten sind gewiß der bessere Weg. Aber es macht einen großen Unterschied, ob eine Evaluation unter Ausschluß *über* jemanden, oder *im Feld unter Einbeziehung* der Beteiligten und Betroffenen erfolgt.

Im Bereich des Umwelthandelns haben in den zurückliegenden Jahren, als Reaktion auf die erreichten Grenzen der bürokratischen Umweltpolitik, Diskursverfahren deutlich an Gewicht gewonnen. Diese Verfahren sind in hohem Maße evaluierend, insofern zu einem betreffenden Umweltproblem und darauf bezogenen Maßnahmen Fachwissen systematisch herangezogen und in einem öffentlichen Diskurs, unter Einbeziehung verschiedenster Interessenstandpunkte, bewertet wird. Abschließend kann eine Handlungsempfehlung beschlossen werden. Die definitive Entscheidung über bestimmte Maßnahmen pflegt freilich nicht im Rahmen eines öffentlichen Diskursverfahrens zu fallen, sondern bleibt den betreffenden kommunalen oder korporativen Gremien vorbehalten.

Im parlamentarischen Rahmen bilden Enquete-Kommissionen oder andere Kommissionen mit Anhörungen das diesbezügliche Verfahren. Es geht hierbei meist um die (Neu)Thematisierung eines Interventions- und Regelungsfeldes, zum Beispiel Klimapolitik oder Stoffstrompolitik. Auf kommunaler oder korporativer Ebene dagegen geht es meist um Anrainerprobleme an einem Standort, zum Beispiel wegen Gefährdungen, die von einem Chemiewerk ausgehen, oder die Neuansiedlung zum Beispiel einer Müllverbrennungsanlage, oder Trassenführungen von Verkehrswegen. In diesem Zusammenhang sind in den 90er Jahren verschiedenste Mediationsverfahren entwickelt worden (Renn 1999; Fietkau/Weidner 1998; Feindt 1997). Statt Mediation finden sich auch Begriffe wie „Kooperativer Diskurs" (Carius/Renn 1998: 336ff.) oder „Umweltforum" (Glaser 1997). Die betreffenden Kommunikationsverfahren können auch Bestandteil einer amtlichen Umweltverträglichkeitsprüfung sein.

2. Ansätze zur Erfassung und Bewertung von Umweltmaßnahmen

Im Folgenden werden Ansätze zur Erfassung und Bewertung von Umweltmaßnahmen erläutert und unter dem Aspekt ihrer Eignung als Evaluationsmethoden charakterisiert. Die Reihenfolge beginnt bei Methoden, deren Schwerpunkt mehr auf der Erfassung liegt, und geht schrittweise über zu Ansätzen, bei welchen die evaluierenden Aspekte überwiegen.

2.1 Amtliche und betriebliche Umweltberichterstattung

Umweltberichterstattung UBE bedeutet die regelmäßige Erhebung von Umweltmeßdaten, ihre statistische Verarbeitung sowie ihre Bekanntmachung gegenüber einem begrenzten oder öffentlich uneingeschränkten Adressatenkreis. Der statistische Teil wird auch Umwelt-Monitoring genannt (Weidner/Zieschank/Knoepfel 1992). Als gebietsbezoge Statistik ist die UBE zu einem bedeutenden Bestandteil der öffentlichen amtlichen Statistik geworden. Als anlagen-, werks-, und unternehmensbezogene Statistik erfolgt UBE mit zunehmender Verbreitung in Form von regelmäßig erstellten Umweltberichten sowie in Umwelterklärungen und den Geschäftsberichten von Unternehmen (Corporate environmental reporting – vgl. Coming Clean 1993). Jenseits ihrer Gegenstandsspezifik liegt den amtlichen UBE und den privaten Betriebs- und Unternehmens-UBE im Prinzip die gleiche Herangehensweise und Indikatorenbildung zugrunde. Deren Aussagekraft nimmt zu mit der Zeitreihen-Länge der Meßwerte, wodurch Trendanalysen möglich werden.

Sofern Indikatoren anthropogene Umweltwirkungen widerspiegeln, können sie auch als industrielle Leistungsparameter verstanden werden. Die Veränderung solcher Parameter, etwa im jährlichen Bilanzzeitraum, heißt in der Finanzsprache Performance. Zum Beispiel dienen der Cash-Flow oder die Aktienkursbewegung als Leistungsparameter für den Finanzerfolg. Im Umweltbereich dienen heute in analoger Weise die Veränderung des spezifischen oder absoluten Energie- und Materialverbrauchs einer Industrieanlage, oder die Veränderung der Abluftqualität, u.v.m. als Leistungsparameter. Man spricht in diesem Sinne von der Öko-Performance. Am deutlichsten zeigt sich die Öko-Performance wiederum, wenn die Meßwerte relevanter Umweltindikatoren in Zeitreihen dargestellt werden (James 1994; Azzone/Manzini 1994).

Inzwischen hat sich eine spezielle naturwissenschaftlich-ökologische Forschungsrichtung unter dem Stichwort der „Umweltbewertung" herausgebildet (u.a. Theobald 1998; Poschmann u.a. 1998; Umweltbewertung 1999). Es geht hierbei nicht direkt um eine Evaluation von Umweltmaßnahmen und Umwelthandeln im hier diskutierten Sinne, sondern um die Beurteilung von geo- und biosphärischen Gegebenheiten, ökosystemischen Zuständen i.S. stabil – labil, intakt – gestört, aber auch um die Einschätzung der ökologischen Folgen bestimmter menschlicher Natureingriffe sowie damit zusammenhängend auch um die Frage ihrer Zulässigkeit, Erwünschtheit, Vermeidbarkeit o.ä. Insofern bilden naturwissenschaftlich-ökologische Umweltzustandsbewertungen doch eine notwendige Grundlage oder selbst einen Bestandteil von mehr sozialwissenschaftlich geprägten Maßnahmen- und Politikevaluationen.

Ähnlich, wie die Kenngrößen der amtlichen Wirtschafts- und Sozialstatistiken vom Stand der Wissenschaft und dem Bedarf der Regierungsstellen geprägt werden, so ist auch die Entwicklung der Umweltberichterstattung geprägt vom Gang der Umweltforschung, der Umweltpolitik und des Umweltmanagements. Das ökosystemische Grundproblem liegt hierbei darin, relevante Aspekte der Umweltqualität zu bestimmen und in statistischen Indikatoren zu operationalisieren. Tausende von Indikatoren regelmäßig zu erfassen, wäre zwar möglich, aber weder sinnvoll noch bezahlbar. Inzwischen zeichnet sich ein gewisser Bestand von Indikatoren ab, der in einer Größenordnung von um die 200, im Kern um die 50 liegen dürfte.

Die Systematisierungsversuche der Statistiker folgen zunächst den Umwelt-Ressorts oder auch Umweltproblembereichen wie zum Beispiel Luft, Klima, Ozonschicht, Ozeane, Wasser und Grundwasser, Abfall, Boden, Flächen, Wälder, Biodiversität, Verbrauch erschöpflicher und regenerativer Ressourcen, Konsum, u.a. Für jeden Problembereich wird eine Auswahl von Stoffen oder Stoffaggregaten gemessen, bei welchen es sich um die betreffenden Indikatoren handelt, zum Beispiel bezüglich der Luft Ruß und Staub, Schwefel, Stickoxyde, Kohlendioxyd u.a. Auch Lebewesen, ihr Vorhandensein und Wachstum, werden als Bioindikatoren erfaßt. Ähnliche aber andere Systematisierungen folgen Umweltproblemgruppen wie Klima, Ozon, Versauerung, Toxika in Luft und Wasser, Biodiversität o.ä.

Das Statistische Bundesamt verfolgt aktuell einen anspruchsvollen Ansatz (Radermacher u.a. 1998). Es unterscheidet Akzeptoren wie Athmosphäre, Boden, Grundwasser, Mensch, Tier und Pflanze, die ihrerseits in verschiedene Ökosysteme eingebunden sind, etwa die Vegetation in Agrarökosystemen. Die Stoffindikatoren bezüglich Akzeptoren und Ökosystemen sind ihrerseits gegenwartsrelevanten Umweltproblematiken zugeordnet. Beispielsweise ist der Cadmium- und Zinngehalt in Milligramm je Kilogramm Nutzpflanzen-Trockensubstanz einer der Indikatoren für Kontamination. Die Indikatoren werden außerdem unterschieden nach direkten und medialen Belastungsindikatoren, Akkumulations-, Wirkungs- und Risikoindikatoren.

Verbreitung gefunden hat bereits die Unterscheidung von Bestands- und Flußgrößen sowie die Kategorisierung nach dem Pressure-State-Response-Modell (RSU 1994: 86ff.; 1996: 251-316; Pfister 1998: 242ff.). Pressure-Größen messen Umwelteinwirkungen, zum Beispiel Ressourcenverschleiß und Flächendenaturierung, Agrarchemikalieneinsatz, Emissionen von Stickoxyden oder Abwässern; State-Größen bilden den Umweltzustand ab, zum Beispiel als Güteklasse von Gewässern, als Asbestfasern oder bodennahes Ozon in der Luft, oder den Wald- und Artenbestand; Response-Größen spiegeln Umweltmaßnahmen wider, zum Beispiel die Ausweisung von Natur- oder Wasserschutzgebieten, oder Wiederaufforstung. Hinzu kommen außerdem sozio-ökonomische Indikatoren über das Ausmaß jener Produktions- und Konsumtätigkeiten, die in besonders ausgeprägter Weise umweltwirksam sind, zum Beispiel Verbrauch und Preise von Rohstoffen und Energie, Endkonsum, Transport, Landwirtschaft u.a., sowie auch Ausgaben für Umweltschutz (OECD 1998b).

Im Unterschied zur flächendeckenden amtlichen Umweltberichterstattung kann die betriebliche Umweltberichterstattung selektiver angelegt sein, zugeschnitten auf die Produktions-Spezifika eines Standortes, aber auch auf spezifische Anspruchsgruppen eines Unternehmens wie Eigenkapitalhalter, Kreditgeber, Versicherungen, Lieferanten, Kunden, Wettbewerber, Behörden, Anrainer, Umweltgruppen, die medienbestimmte Öffentlichkeit, nicht zuletzt die Mitarbeiterschaft (Steven u.a. 1997). Als Muster können die Publikationen der Henkel KGaA gelten. Bei der Beurteilung ihrer Informationspolitik und Umweltberichterstattung, vorgenommen vom Hamburger Umweltinstitut im Rahmen einer inzwischen wiederholt durchgeführten vergleichenden Umweltmanagement-Evaluation (weiter unten als Ranking diskutiert), schnitt die Firma Henkel unter den 50 weltweit führenden Chemiekonzernen am besten ab (manager magazin 9/99: 128ff.). An allen Standorten des Konzerns gelten in gleicher Weise insgesamt 15 Standards of Safety, Health, Environment. Diese bilden die Grundlage von 55 Richtlinien des Umweltmanagements, speziell auch der Umwelt-Kommunikation nach innen und außen (Henkel KGaA 1998). Erfassungsmethoden von Umweltwirkungen werden dargelegt, es wird auf vorhandene Lücken oder offene Fragen hingewiesen, und es werden Wege der Beseitigung von Mängeln aufgezeigt (Henkel KGaA 1998: 20).

Es gibt inzwischen einen Kanon von Mindestanforderungen an eine ordnungsgemäße Umweltberichterstattung von Firmen (Steven u.a. 1997: 165). Zunächst bedarf es einer möglichst vollständigen Abdeckung bestimmter Umweltthemen. Relevante Themen dürfen nicht fehlen. Die einzelnen Positionen des Umweltberichts müssen übersichtlich dargestellt und kommentiert sein. Die Nachvollziehbarkeit der Angaben muß gewährleistet sein (Steven u.a. 1997: 167ff.). Weiterhin sollen Umweltberichte periodisch regelmäßig erstellt werden bei thematischer und formaler Kontinuität, so daß Zeitreihen und andere Vergleiche ersichtlich werden. Erwartete Umweltwirkungen sind so früh wie möglich anzuzeigen und bei deren Quantifizierung ist grundsätzlich von der maximal möglichen Auswirkung auszugehen. Prinzip sollte es sein, „daß grundsätzlich *eher eine Über- als eine Unterbewertung* von Schadwirkungen erfolgt" (Steven u.a. 1997: 170). Entsprechend sollten Umweltentlastungen erst bei erfolgter Realisierung Eingang in die Darstellung finden, nicht als bloße Ankündigung.

2.2 Umweltgesamtrechnung

Mit der Entwicklung der Umweltberichterstattung sind Versuche einhergegangen, die Umweltwirkungen nicht nur stofflich, sondern auch monetär zu erfassen, also die ökologischen Kosten und den Nutzen bzw. Schaden des industriellen Metabolismus in Geldgrößen oder anderen aggregierten Buchungsgrößen auszudrücken. Am Beginn stand eine Kritik der Volkswirtschaftlichen Gesamtrechnung VGR, die alle Umsätze positiv kumuliert, gleich, ob es sich in sozialer und ökologischer Hinsicht um positive oder negative Vorgänge handelt. Unfall- und Rehabilitationskosten steigern ebenso das BIP wie nachträgliche Umweltschutz- und Umweltschadenskosten (Binswanger u.a. 1978). Es wurde ermittelt, daß solche „defensiven Kosten" des Wirtschaftswachstums sich heute auf circa 10-15 Prozent des BIP belaufen (Wicke 1987; Leipert 1989).

In Fortführung dieses Gedankens wurde versucht, ausgehend von einem Ansatz von Nordhaus und Tobin, dem Bruttoinlandsprodukt ein Ökoinlandsprodukt entgegen zu setzen. Es soll entstehen, indem man vom BIP erst die Wertminderung des Anlagevermögens (= Nettoinlandsprodukt), dann die Wertminderung des Naturvermögens abzieht (van Dieren 1995: 251ff.). Das

Problem liegt hierbei ersichtlich darin, wie das Naturvermögen überhaupt zu erfassen und dann auch noch monetär zu bewerten sein soll – abgesehen von der grundsätzlichen Frage, ob eine solche Totalökonomisierung der Natur überhaupt sinnvoll sein kann. Hier sind die Kritiker sich selbst gegenüber ziemlich unkritisch.

Ähnlich anspruchsvoll sind Ansätze, die auch noch sozio-ökonomische Wertberichtigungen einbringen wollen, zum Beispiel, nach einem Ansatz von Daly und Cobb, der Index of Sustainable Welfare (Diefenbacher 1995; van Dieren 1995: 171ff.). Dieser korrigiert das BIP unter anderem mit einem Koeffizienten der Einkommensverteilung, weil ungleichere Einkommen die Gesamtwohlfahrt weniger steigern, sodann werden unbezahlte Arbeitsleistungen des informellen Sektors wie Hausarbeit, Eigenarbeit, Ehrenamt u.ä. hinzuaddiert, und es werden wiederum defensive Umweltschutzaufwendungen oder andere „regrettable costs" wie etwa für Wachschutzdienste und Militär abgezogen.

Ohne Zweifel thematisieren solche Ansätze relevante Probleme der Definition, Geltung und Bewertung von Umwelt- und Sozialindikatoren. Das Problem mit den Ansätzen selbst ist nur, daß erstens eine Vielzahl pauschaler ungefährer Schätzungen an Stelle zuverlässiger Messungen vorgenommen werden müssen, und zweitens in die Postenabgrenzungen eine Reihe unvermeidlich wertender Beurteilungen ex-ante eingehen. Wenn Hausarbeit als informelle Leistung der Wohlfahrtssteigerung berücksichtigt wird, warum nicht die Schwarzarbeit? Und warum werden die wohlfahrtsmindernden Effekte einer überhöhten Staatsquote nicht abgezogen? Welche Gesundheitskosten soll man als wohlfahrtssteigernde Invesition in die Gesunderhaltung, welche als „bedauerliche" defensive Kompensationskosten verbuchen? Sicherheits- und Militärdienste mögen in gewisser Weise „bedauerliche" Notwendigkeiten sein, aber sind sie deshalb nicht doch Notwendigkeiten, die eine grundsätzliche Aktivposten-Einschätzung verdienen? Und ist ein Deich eine positive Vorsorgeinvestition wie eine vor Erosion schützende Hecke am Feldrand, oder eine defensive Ausgabe zur Kompensation des anthropogenen Treibhauseffektes? Man kann skeptisch bleiben bezüglich der Frage, ob es in Zukunft gelingen wird, etwas robustere und allgemein akzeptablere Ansätze zu einer die VGR ergänzenden UGR (Umweltgesamtrechnung) zu entwickeln.

2.3 Ökologische Buchhaltung

Parallel zu den Versuchen einer Umweltgesamtrechnung wurden auch entsprechende betriebliche Ansätze verfolgt. Sie orientierten sich an Buchhaltungs- und Bilanzierungsmethoden. Ein von Müller-Wenk (1978) entwickelter Ansatz sah vor, sämtliche Materialinputs und -outputs sowie Energieumsätze in einer betrieblichen Ökobilanz zu erfassen. Die Materialien und Emissionen sollten zunächst in physischen Größen erfaßt und dann mittels eines Äquivalenzkoeffizienten umgerechnet werden in eine einheitliche Recheneinheit als Buchungsgröße. Der Äquivalenzkoeffizient sollte die ökologische Knappheit ausdrücken – eher eine theoretische als eine praktikable Idee. Welchem „Zentralkommittee" möchte man die Wissensanmaßung überlassen, die betreffenden ökologischen Knappheiten von lokaler bis nationaler und globaler Ebene festzulegen? Ein dagegen eher unbedeutender Einwand galt dem Sachverhalt, daß eine solche Buchhaltung nicht alle Umweltaspekte erfassen kann. Aus ökosystemischer Sicht genügt es, die wirklich wichtigen zu erfassen. Unbeachtet jedoch blieb in der Diskussion, daß in dieser „Bilanz" fast alles debitorisch auf der Passivseite verbucht wurde, Ressourceninputs ebenso wie Emissionen, während lediglich die Material-Weiterlieferungen kreditorisch behandelt wurden. Das konnte immer nur zu einer negativen Bilanz führen und dem Defätismus der thermodynamischen Schule der Umweltökonomie Vorschub leisten, jegliche ökonomische Wertschöpfung sei eine ökologische Schadschöpfung.

Auch eine Reihe von Anwendungsexperimenten, etwa im Rahmen der kommunalen Ökonomie (Braunschweig u.a. 1984), machten deutlich, daß die Festlegung der Äquivalenzkoeffizienten der eigentliche Schwachpunkt dieser Art Öko-Buchhaltung war. Als Verdienst erwies sich jedoch, daß man begonnen hatte, Materialströme und Energieflüsse zu erfassen. Weitere Versuche, eine ökologische Buchhaltung zu entwickeln, die in Deutschland vor allem vom Berliner Institut für ökologische Wirtschaftsforschung vorangetrieben wurden, gingen in eben diese Richtung weiter und nahmen dann bezüglich der Buchung eine realistische Wendung: Im Rahmen einer ökologischen Unternehmensführung gebucht wird heute praktisch nur, was wirklich Geld kostet oder einbringt (Schaltegger 1992; Wicke u.a. 1992: 213-284). Dazu müssen diverse Konten der kaufmännischen Buchführung nach Kostenarten, Kostenstellen und Kostenträgern umweltkostenorientiert abgeändert und regruppiert werden. Viele der effektiven Umweltkosten verschwanden früher in Umlagen oder Pauschalen, anstatt sie gesondert und transparent auszuweisen.

2.4 Stoffstromanalyse

Die betrieblichen Untersuchungen zum Umsatz und Verbleib von Materialien mündeten in den Ansatz der Stoff- und Energiebilanzen (Immler 1975; Hofmeister 1989). Ingenieuren war die Erstellung von Energiefluß-Diagrammen im Zusammenhang mit der Konstruktion und dem Betrieb von Industrieanlagen oder Großbauten eine durchaus vertraute Aufgabe. Mit der Thematisierung der ökologischen Frage jedoch entstand ein neuer Kontext, der eine Systematisierung und Verallgemeinerung der Aufgabe erforderte. Sie wird heute unter dem Überbegriff der Stoffstromanalyse behandelt. Zunächst ging es dabei um die möglichst vollständige Erfassung von Ressourcenverbräuchen und Emissionen jeglicher Art, in diesem Sinne um eine Umweltbilanzierung als physische Erfassung der Nutzung von Umweltfaktoren auf Mate-

rial-, Energie- und Emissionskonten (Bechmann u.a. 1987). Eine Erfassung
von Umwelt*wirkungen* im eigentlichen Sinne ist damit noch nicht, jedenfalls
nicht systematisch verbunden, aber zweifellos handelt es sich um eine Voraussetzung dafür oder schon um den ersten Schritt einer Wirkungsanalyse.
Auf dem Weg vom ursprünglichen, eher noch eng verstandenen Abfallmana-
gement und Recycling, über Vorstellungen eines umfassenderen Stoffstrom-
managements, bis hin zur Konzeption einer möglichst geschlossenen Kreis-
laufwirtschaft seit den 90er Jahren, spielte die Stoffstromanalyse natürgemäß
eine zentrale Rolle. Die Fortentwicklung der Stoffstromanalyse widerspiegelt
ihrerseits die Entwicklung von der Abfall- und End-of-Pipe-Politik zur integrierten Prozeß-, Produkt- und Stoffpolitik (Friege u.a. 1998; Enquete-Kommission 1993: 106-290; 1994). Will man die industrietraditionale „Durch-
satz"-Wirtschaft mit geringen Stoffausbeuten und schlechten energetischen
Wirkungsgraden überführen in eine nachhaltig binnenoptimierte und natu-
rintegrierte „Ökonomie der Reproduktion" (Hofmeister 1998), dann gehört
die genaue Kenntnis der Stoffströme und Energieflüsse zum zentralen Fundus der dafür erforderlichen Wissensbasis.

2.5 Umweltintensität, MIPS (Material-Intensität pro Nutzeneinheit)

Unter Material- und Energieinensität versteht man einen Ressourceninput bezogen auf eine Vergleichsbasis, in der Regel den Input pro Einheit technischem
Produkt, oder pro Einheit Wirtschaftsergebnis oder Kostenaufwand. In diesem
Fall handelt es sich um die *spezifische* Umweltintensität, zum Beispiel in Form
des PKW-Benzinverbrauchs pro 100 km Fahrleistung, oder des Gesamteinsat-
zes von Primärenergie pro Einheit BIP. Bezieht man den Input auf die Bevölkerung, spricht man von der *relativen* Intensität oder *Pro-Kopf*-Intensität, zum
Beispiel in Form des durchschnittlichen täglichen Wasserverbrauchs privater
Haushalte (in D derzeit etwa 140 l) oder des jährlichen Abfallaufkommens (in
D derzeit etwa 345 kg) pro Kopf der Bevölkerung. Das Abfallbeispiel zeigt,
daß Umweltintensität auch als Output-Intensität, als Intensität der Emission
bzw. der Senkenbelastung gemessen werden muß. So spielt in der heutigen
Klimapolitik der Ausstoß von CO_2 absolut, spezifisch und pro Kopf eine wichtige Rolle. Unter Umweltintensität kann also im Prinzip auch das *absolute*
Ausmaß eines Inputs oder Outputs verstanden werden. Aber im Allgemeinen
verbindet man damit eine spezifische oder pro-Kopf-Intensität.
    Als Quotient von Input zu Output, oder Input und/oder Output zu einer
sonstigen sinnvollen Vergleichsbasis, sind Umweltintensitäten typische Pro-
duktivitäts-Koeffizienten. Das Interesse daran wuchs seit Beginn der 80er
Jahre mit der Einsicht in den Sachverhalt, daß im Falle von Produktivitäts-
gewinnen durch Steigerung der Stoffeinsatz-Effizienz und Emissionsminde-
rungs-Effizienz der bis dahin berüchtigte „Konflikt von Ökonomie und
Ökologie" sich zumindest in dieser Hinsicht in Wohlgefallen auflöst. Die

Rationalisierung des ökologischen Material- und Energieeinsatzes bedeutet eine relative ökonomische Kostenersparnis und trägt insoweit auch zu einer Ertragsverbesserung bei.

Ein Ansatz, der in diesem Zusammenhang Beachtung gefunden hat, ist das Konzept der Maßeinheit MIPS nach Schmidt-Bleek (1994). MIPS bedeutet Material-Intensität pro Serviceeinheit oder Endnutzeneinheit. Das Besondere an dem Ansatz ist die Einbeziehung der so genannten „ökologischen Rucksäcke". Wenn man zum Beispiel ein Telephongespräch führt oder mit einem Computer arbeitet, so repräsentieren der direkte Stromverbrauch oder das Material der benutzten Geräte noch längst nicht den ganzen involvierten Aufwand an Material und Energie. Vielmehr stehen dahinter große materialintensive Infrastrukturen sowie eine vertikale Produktionskette bis zurück zur Rohstoffgewinnung. Nicht zuletzt dort werden Stoff-„Rucksäcke" gesehen, die normalerweise unkenntlich bleiben, zum Beispiel Abraum und Grundwasservernichtung durch Bergbau.

Ein MIPS-Maß der Art „X Tonnen Stoffumsatz pro 1000 Flugkilometer" kann sicherlich manche Produktion oder Dienstleistung ökologisch in einem anderen Licht erscheinen lassen. Jedoch fehlt dem Maß die ökosystemische Eichung. Man weiß nicht, wieviel MIPS wofür genug oder zu viel sind (Huber 1995: 134ff.). Daß einem „alles irgendwie viel zu viel" vorkommt, ist keine wissenschaftliche Bewertung. Der Ansatz sah sich deshalb u.a. auch der Kritik ausgesetzt, eine unqualifizierte „Tonnenideologie" darzustellen – eine Kritik, die berechtigt ist sowohl im Hinblick auf die fehlende ökosystemische *Qualifizierung* der umgesetzten Stoff*quantitäten* als auch im Hinblick auf das mitgelieferte Umwelt-„Qualitäts"-Ziel der so genannten „Dematerialisierung" der industriellen Produktion (was seinerseits wiederum mit dem o.g. „thermodynamischen" Schrumpfungsdenken zu tun hat).

2.6 Ecological Footprint (angeeignete Tragekapazität)

Der „ökologische Fußabdruck" ist ein anderer Versuch, die anthropogenen Stoffumsätze in einer griffigen statistischen Kenngröße auszudrücken (Rees/ Wackernagel 1994, 1997). Es handelt sich um einen aggregierten Indikator, der Stoffumsätze in ein Flächenmaß umrechnet, sinngemäß analog der Umrechnung von Energieverbräuchen in Steinkohleeinheiten. Der Anspruch besteht darin, den Naturfaktorenverbrauch der Industriebevölkerung und damit die von ihr angeeignete ökologische Tragekapazität zu objektivieren. Wie schon die anderen Versuche einer ökologischen Buchhaltung, erfordert der Footprint-Indikator eine längere Reihe von mehr oder weniger plausiblen Setzungen bezüglich Verfügbarkeit von Ressourcen und Senken, Reproduktionsraten von Ressourcen sowie Regenerationsfähigkeit und Resilienz von Ökosystemen, technischen und natürlichen Produktivitätsraten, u.ä., mithin also eine Ex-ante-Setzung der Tragekapazität.

Eine solche Ex-ante-Einschätzung ist nicht grundsätzlich abzulehnen, im Gegenteil, denn es geht um geosphärische Aufrechterhaltung und biosphärische Gesunderhaltung, nicht um die ebenso „sichere" wie sinnlose Feststellung von irreversiblen Systemzusammenbrüchen ex-post. Das Problem ist nur, daß das dafür erforderliche Wissen aus der Ökosystem- und Umweltbewertungs-Forschung im nötigen Umfang und Detail noch lange nicht vorhanden ist. So muß auch der Footprint-Ansatz, etwa bei der Umrechnung von Verbräuchen in Flächenbedarf, ähnlich den Äquivalenz-Koeffizienten der ökologischen Buchhaltung, mit einer Vielzahl von ungefähren und eben auch nicht immer plausiblen Annahmen operieren. Das macht die Sache anfechtbar, unter normativem Aspekt tatsächlich unhaltbar, und gibt ihr den Status einer bloßen Modellrechnung. Immerhin konnte auf diese Weise neuerlich vorgerechnet werden, was schon um 1970 die Computersimulation der „Grenzen des Wachstums" besagte, nämlich, daß eine Übertragung von Art und Volumen der industrietraditionalen Produktion der bisherigen reichen Länder auf die ganze Erdbevölkerung nicht möglich ist, weil die Menschheit dafür mehrere Erden benötigen würde.

2.7 Kontingentierter Umweltraum

Vollends normativ werden Ansätze einer aggregierten Erfassung der Ressourcen- und Senkennutzung, die beanspruchen, den vorhandenen Umweltraum objektiv zu messen, und außerdem eine gerechte Aufteilung des verfügbaren Umweltraumes zu definieren (Milieudefensie 1992; BUND/Misereor 1996). Umweltraum ist ein anderes Wort für Lebensraum. Er bedeutet die Gesamtheit der Ressourcen und Senken, die eine Population in Raum und Zeit nutzen kann, ohne den nachhaltigen Bestand der betreffenden Ökosysteme zu beeinträchtigen. Die Grenze des Umweltraumes wird bestimmt durch die Tragekapazität. Insofern gilt hier alles in gleicher Weise, was zuvor bereits zum MIPS- und Footprint-Ansatz gesagt wurde. Hinzu kommt nun allerdings noch ein politisches Verteilungsdiktum in Form einer zentralplanerisch gedachten Kontingentierung des angeblich verfügbaren Umweltraumes. Unter Rückgriff auf die bevölkerungsökologische IPAT-Formel[1] kann man sagen, „Population" und „Technologie" werden als gegeben vorausgesetzt, und es wird der „Umweltraum" durch die „Population" dividiert. Es ergeben sich „Affluence"-Quoten, also Konsumanspruchs-Quoten pro Kopf.

Eine solche Modellrechnung mag veranschaulichen, wie ungleich der Umweltnutzen und die Umweltschäden auf der Welt verteilt sind, wo das wohlhabende eine Fünftel der Erdbevölkerung vier Fünftel bis drei Viertel

---

1   Die IPAT-Formel geht zurück auf die Bevölkerungswissenschaftler Paul und Anne Ehrlich in den 60er Jahren und bedeutet: Ecological Impact = Population × Affluence × Technology.

der Ressourcen an fossiler Energie, Agrarland, Wasser, Holz u.ä. zu beanspruchen pflegte. Wollte man, und könnte man überhaupt, eine diesbezügliche Verteilungsgleichheit herstellen, würden den Holländern zum Beispiel 80% weniger Aluminium, 45% weniger Agrarfläche, 40% weniger Wasser oder 60% weniger CO_2-Emission zustehen. Würde dies allerdings nicht nur eine bewußtseinsbildende Modellbetrachtung, sondern eine praktische Handlungsanleitung sein sollen, würde sie unversehens einen Ressourcenkommunismus begründen, dessen Realität voraussichtlich nicht weniger bestürzend wäre wie die des realhistorisch schon erlebten.

2.8 Ökobilanz und Produktlinienanalyse (Life Cycle Assessment)

Ökobilanzierung und Produktlinienanalyse sind zwei Varianten des Life Cycle Assessment, das heißt, der Erfassung und Bewertung der Umweltwirkungen von Produkten, mit dem Anspruch, alle wesentlichen Umweltwirkungen eines Produktes bzw. seiner Produktion und Nutzung zu erfassen und sie in ihrer gesamten ökologischen und auch ökonomischen Reichweite zu bewerten (Berkhout 1996). Es handelt sich um Evaluationsmethoden, auf deren Grundlage Entscheidungen bezüglich Maßnahmen der Produktpolitik sowie überhaupt der Stoffstrom- und Kreislaufwirtschaftspolitik vorbereitet oder ihr Erfolg kontrolliert werden soll (Übersicht in Enquete-Kommission 1993: 72-105). In der Idealvorstellung sollten die betreffenden Umwelt- und Kostenwirkungen eines Produktes „von der Wiege bis zur Bare" erfaßt werden, das heißt, von den ursprünglichen Rohstoff-Inputs bis zur endgültigen Reststoffausschleusung und damit der Wiedereinbringung der Stoffe in weitere industrielle oder natürliche Kreisläufe. Daher „Life Cycle" Assessment, auf Deutsch auch Lebenswegbilanz. Gemäß den inzwischen etablierten Standards besteht eine Ökobilanzierung aus vier bis fünf Abschnitten.

1. Im ersten Schritt erfolgt die *definitorische Abgrenzung* und die *Aufgabenstellung* der möglichst komparativ zu untersuchenden Umweltwirkungen bestimmter Produkte, Verfahren oder Maßnahmen. Das Maximalprogramm einer vollumfänglichen Lebenswegbilanz kann aufgrund des Aufwandes meist nur in exemplarischen Projekten der Grundlagenforschung ins Auge gefaßt werden. Meist bleibt es bei der selektiven Untersuchung einzelner Problem- und Stoffsegmente.

2. Zweitens folgt die *Sachbilanz*. Diese erfaßt sämtliche Inputs und Durchflüsse von Materialien und Energie, sodann outputseitig Produkte, Kuppelprodukte, Emissionen und sonstige ökologische Impakte jeglicher Art (Abwasser, Abluft, Abfall, Flächen, Lärm, Strahlungen, sonstige Natureingriffe). Dies soll im Idealfall über alle Stufen der vertikalen und horizontalen Erzeuger-Überbringer-Verbraucher-Ketten hinweg in der Form von Input-Output-Diagrammen nachvollziehbar gemacht werden. In der

Sachbilanz sind die vorgenannten Ansätze der „ökologischen Buchhaltung" und der Stoffstromanalyse enthalten bzw. aufgehoben.

3. Auf der Grundlage der so erfaßten industriellen Stoffwechselvorgänge sollen sodann drittens in der *Wirkungsbilanz* die unmittelbar absehbaren Umweltwirkungen dargelegt werden, insbesondere die Umweltproblemfolgen, darunter etwa allergene, toxische oder karzinogene Wirkungen auf die Gesundheit von Menschen, Tieren und Pflanzen, oder Wirkungen bezüglich wichtiger Umweltproblem-Komplexe wie Verschleiß erschöpflicher Ressourcen, Übernutzung regenerativer Ressourcen, Dispersion persistenter Schadstoffe, Niederschlags- und Bodenversauerung, Gewässereutrophierung, Boden- und Grundwasserdegradation, Erosion, Klimawandel, bodennahe Ozonbildung, stratosphärische Ozonschutzschicht-Zerstörung, o.a.

4. Im vierten Abschnitt folgt die *Bewertung* der Sach- und Wirkungsbilanz. Hier werden u.a. ökologische Problemschwerpunkte erörtert, Vor- und Nachteile verschiedener Produkt- oder Maßnahmevarianten gegeneinander abgewogen, Kosten-Nutzwert-Erwägungen angestellt und sonstige vergleichende Güterabwägungen vorgenommen, wobei ggfls. auch ethische, wirtschafts- und sozialpolitische Aspekte zum Tragen kommen können. Schließlich kann außer der ökosystemischen Tolerabilität auch die gesellschaftliche Akzeptabilität eingeschätzt werden.

5. In einem fünften Schritt sollen schlußfolgernd *Handlungsalternativen* aufgezeigt werden, und es können eventuell außerdem, noch ein Schritt weiter, auch Handlungs*empfehlungen* abgegeben werden. Dieser Schritt ist jener, der über die Erfassung und Bewertung von Umweltwirkungen hinausgeht und sich bereits auf dem politischen Terrain der Maßnahmen-Re-Konzeption bewegt. In offiziellen Dokumenten zum Beispiel des VDI*, des UBA*, des DIN/NAGUS* oder ISO* wird das Aufzeigen von Handlungsalternativen ausdrücklich erwartet, teils wird es per Gesetz verlangt, während die Formulierung von Entscheidungs-Empfehlungen fakultativ bleibt.

Ökobilanzen im engeren Sinne beschränken sich auf naturwissenschaftlich-technisch objektivierbare Umweltwirkungen. Aus Gründen der Praktikabilität und Wirtschaftlichkeit sind sie meist eingegrenzt auf spezifische Aspekte wie zum Beispiel Energiebilanz, Verbrauch und Verschmutzung von Wasser, o.ä. (UBA 1992, 1997 a+b; Kytzia 1995). So lassen sich zum Beispiel die ökologischen und ökonomischen Vor- und Nachteile von Alu, Plastik und Papier als Verpackungsalternativen für Lebensmittel untersuchen, oder diverse Varianten von Waschmitteln, oder es lassen sich Energieeinsparung und Wasserschonung durch Papier-Recycling objektivieren. Ökobilanzen in diesem

---

*   VDI = Verein deutscher Ingenieure. UBA = Umweltbundesamt. DIN = früher Deutsche Industrie Norm, danach Deutscher Normenausschuß, jetzt Deutsches Institut für Normung. NAGUS = Normenausschuß Grundlagen des Umweltschutzes, ISO = International Organization for Standardization.

Sinne werden eher von der Industrie und kooperierenden Forschungsinstituten befürwortet.

Im Unterschied dazu sind Produktlinienanalysen sozusagen „Ökobilanzen plus", indem bereits in ihre Sachbilanz weitest möglich auch allgemeinwirtschaftliche sowie politische, gesellschaftliche und kulturelle Wirkungen einbezogen werden sollen, zum Beispiel Wirkungen auf die lokale Ökonomie und Beschäftigungslage (Projektgruppe Ökologische Wirtschaft 1987; Baumgartner 1986). In der politisch-gesellschaftlichen Ausweitung des Evaluationsgegenstandes liegt der strittige Unterschied zwischen beiden Ansätzen. Im Hinblick auf die Erfassung und Bewertung ökologischer Wirkungen und deren ökonomische Bedeutung bestehen in der Sache keine wesentlichen Unterschiede. Produktlinienanalysen werden von Nichtregierungsorganisationen und unabhängigen Forschungsinstituten befürwortet. Das Freiburger Öko-Institut spricht im Hinblick auf seine Produktlinienanalysen inzwischen auch von Product Sustainability Assessment.

Auch die Formen des Life Cycle Assessment sehen sich mit dem Grundproblem jeder „ökologischen Buchhaltung" konfrontiert, das darin liegt, Ungleiches vergleichbar machen zu sollen. Ist Luftreinhaltung wichtiger als Minderung des Wasserverbrauchs oder Abfallaufkommens? Sind flüchtige organische Kohlenstoffe weniger bedeutend als Schwermetalle? Versuche der Aggregierung solcher Aspekte sind problematisch und werden es vermutlich auch bei fortgeschrittenerem Ökosystemwissen bleiben. Von daher versteht es sich auch, daß Öko- oder Produktlinienbilanzen zwar relevantes Material für diskursive Bewertungen liefern können, sie jedoch keinesfalls einen Bewertungsautomatismus im Sinne der unzutreffenden Vorstellung einer „objektiv richtigen Lösung" begründen.

2.9 Umweltcontrolling

Manche Autoren behandeln die weiter oben erläuterte Erfassung von Stoffströmen und die umweltorientierte Buchführung, zusammen mit ihrer regelmäßigen Überprüfung und Auswertung, unter dem Oberbegriff des Umweltcontrolling oder Öko-Controlling in Analogie zum Finanzcontrolling (Hallay 1992, 1996: 219-298). In noch weiter gehender Sichtweise wird daraus ein gänzlicher Überbegriff, der auch Ökobilanzen und die nachfolgend besprochenen Öko-Audits mit einschließt, somit im Prinzip fast alle der hier besprochenen Erfassungs- und Bewertungsansätze, sofern sie betriebs-, unternehmens- oder verwaltungsbezogen angelegt sind oder sie eine solche Anwendung finden (Hopfenbeck 1991: 480-519; BMU/UBA 1995; Orwat 1996).

Umwelt-Controlling in einem solchen umfassenden Sinne steht dann für sämtliche umweltdatenrelevanten Erfassungs- und Bewertungsmethoden, die dem Betriebsmanagement und der Unternehmensführung oder Verwaltungsleitungen als Steuerungs- und Kontrollinformation dienen (Haasis u.a. 1995)

– von der sachgerechten Abbildung von umweltrelevanten Vorgängen in Buchhaltung, Statistik oder sonstigen formalisierten Berichterstattungen, über die laufende oder stichprobenartige Prüfung solcher Informationen auf Stimmigkeit, auf (un)erwünschte Veränderungen, und die Ermittlung ihrer Ursachen, bis zur auswertenden Zusammenführung solcher Daten in manageriellen (Umwelt-)Informationssystemen und der Korrektur oder Neuformulierung von Maßnahmen aufgrund kritischer Befunde. Controlling-Methoden sind bei öffentlichen Verwaltungen in prinzipiell gleicher Weise anwendbar wie in Privatunternehmen. Tatsächlich ist Controlling ein fester Bestandteil der Ansätze des New Public Management.

Was speziell die stichprobenartige Prüfung von finanziellen Vorgängen in Büchern angeht, sind diese dem Publikum eher durch eine bestimmte Art des öffentlichen Controllings bekannt, das sich immer wieder in skandalartig aufgemachten Presseberichten niederschlägt, nämlich den Prüfungen des Finanzgebarens öffentlich-rechtlicher Einrichtungen durch die Rechnungshöfe der Länder und des Bundes. Sie prüfen auch kommunale Einrichtungen. Auf Umweltmaßnahmen beziehen sich solche Prüfungen zwar nicht generell, aber doch im Einzelfall, zum Beispiel bei der Prüfung des Neubaus von Kläranlagen in den neuen Bundesländern zu Beginn der 90er Jahre. Nicht wenige solcher Anlagen erwiesen sich bald als überdimensioniert. Sie weisen von daher ein schlechtes Kosten-Nutzen-Verhältnis auf. Aufwand-Nutzwert-Analysen, als Prüfung der „Effizienz" von Maßnahmen, sind grundsätzlich Bestandteil einer jeden Evaluation. Das Beispiel verdeutlicht, daß öffentliches ebenso wie privates Controlling einen unmittelbaren und wichtigen Beitrag zu Evaluationen leisten kann, und zwar nicht nur, insoweit es um die Wirtschaftlichkeit von Maßnahmen geht, sondern auch um ihre Effektivität, denn eine Feststellung des materialen Nutzens oder Nutzwertes einer Maßnahme bedeutet nichts anderes als etwas über die Effektivität der Maßnahme auszusagen.

2.10 Öko-Audit nach EG-Verordnung (EMAS-Verordnung)

Öko-Audit ist eine Bezeichnung, die abermals dem Finanzwesen entlehnt worden ist. Audit (engl.) heißt betriebliche Finanzprüfung. Öko-Audit bedeutet die interne und/oder externe Überprüfung von Betriebsstätten im Hinblick auf ihre Umweltwirkungen und ihre Übereinstimmung mit gesetzlichen und behördlichen Umweltschutz-Vorschriften sowie auch unternehmens- und betriebseigenen Leitlinien und Aktionszielen des Umwelthandelns, darunter insbesondere auch die Einhaltung von Grenzwerten und anderen Soll-Vorgaben (Leicht-Eckart u.a. 1996; Janke 1995; Lindlar 1995). Aufgrund ihres Soll-Ist-vergleichenden Ansatzes dienen Audits auch der Ermittlung von Ursachen für eventuelle Abweichungen, und sie können in diesem Zusammenhang auch zur Stärken-Schwächen-Analyse der Öko-Performance genutzt werden. Werden aufgrund von Auditierungen Maßnahmen beschlossen, deren Erfolg im nächsten Durchgang evaluiert werden soll, werden damit Kontinuierliche Verbesserungsprozesse etabliert.

Für Öko-Audits gibt es inzwischen gesetzliche Regelungen oder offizielle Richtlinien der nationalen und internationalen Normeninstitutionen (wie DIN**, BSI**, ISO**). In der EU gilt seit 1995 die EG-Öko-Audit-Verordnung 1836/93. Aufgrund unterschiedlicher nationaler Vorgeschichten heißt die Verordnung außerhalb Deutschlands EMAS-Verordnung (EMAS = Environmental Management and Audit System). Der Management-Teil davon ist nach dem British Standard 7750 modelliert. Die Beteiligung an dem Verfahren ist freiwillig. Teilnehmende Firmen müssen die nicht unerheblichen Kosten und den Verwaltungsmehraufwand tragen, sich der Richtlinie gemäß mindestens alle drei Jahre evaluieren lassen, und erhalten dafür ein Zertifikat mit Logo, mit dem sie öffentlich werben können. Solche Unternehmen bezeichnet man auch als validierte Unternehmen. Die Vorteile für sie liegen vor allem in einer auch kostenökonomisch interessanten Verbesserung des betrieblichen Umweltschutzes, Herstellung von Rechtssicherheit, Vorbeugung gegen Schadens- und Haftungsrisiken, sowie Imageverbesserung bei relevanten Bezugsgruppen.

Ein Umweltaudit umfaßt im Wesentlichen vier Komponenten – erstens eine Produktionsprüfung im Sinne einer spezifisch anlagen- und betriebsstättenbezogenen, mithin selektiven Stoffstromanalyse bzw. Sach- und Wirkungsbilanz, zweitens das so genannte Compliance-Prüfung, das heißt, die Überprüfung der Einhaltung von öffentlich-rechtlichen Vorschriften und manageriellen Vorgaben (Wagner 1996). Beide Komponenten zusammen dienen auch als eine Risiko-Analyse, die dem vorbeugenden Ausschluß von Haftungs- und Strafrechtsrisiken dienen soll. Drittens ist mit der Zulassung zum Verfahren die Einführung eines Umweltmanagement-Systems verbunden. Es kann natürlich auch ohne Audit eingeführt werden, aber zum Audit muß es eingeführt werden. Ein solches Managementsystem hat einer Reihe von Organisations-, Personal- und Kommunikationskriterien zu genügen, darunter, viertens, die Erstellung eines internen Umwelthandbuches und eine regelmäßige, auch öffentlich zugängliche Umweltberichterstattung, insbesondere auch die Bekanntmachung zumindest des öffentlichen Teils der Audit-Ergebnisse. Die Audits werden, meist unter der Leitung des Umweltbeauftragten der Firma, von Expertengruppen durchgeführt. Darin können Betriebsangehörige ebenso wie externe Berater vertreten sein. Die Abnahme des Audits muß durch einen externen, amtlich zugelassenen Gutachter erfolgen (Freimann 1995, 1996: 400ff.). Bis November 1999 haben sich 2290 deutsche Unternehmen nach EMAS validieren lassen (UBA 1999). Außerhalb Deutschlands findet EMAS jedoch eine erheblich geringere Akzeptanz.

** DIN = früher Deutsche Industrie Norm, danach Deutscher Normenausschuss, jetzt Deutsches Institut für Normung. BSI = British Standards Institution, ISO = International Organization for Standardization.

2.11 Umweltqualitätsmanagement nach ISO 14001

Öko-Audits sind um 1980 herum zwar von amerikanischen Pionierunternehmen begonnen, dann aber von europäischen Konzernen übernommen und weiterentwickelt worden. So gelten Öko-Audits, zumal mit Blick auf die Gesetzgebung, heute vor allem als ein europäischer Ansatz. Bezüglich Art und Umfang der Evaluationsmaßnahmen besteht ein Verfahrenswettbewerb mit den ähnlich, teilweise gleich angelegten Methoden des ISO-Standard 14001 sowie 14040. Diese werden vor allem von amerikanischer, auch von japanischer Seite verfolgt.

Der mit Öko-Audits implizierte Prozeß des Umweltmanagements ist als ein Rückkopplungsprozeß angelegt – zwischen Konzeption, Durchführung, Erfolgskontrolle und Korrektur von Umweltmaßnahmen, zwischen Führungspersonal und Belegschaft. Dem wohnt eine beabsichtigte Tendenz zur rollierenden Planung und zu Kontinuierlichen Verbesserungs-Prozessen KVP inne, zum Beispiel im Hinblick auf die fortlaufende, explizit und systematisch betriebene Rationalisierung des Energieeinsatzes oder des Abfallaufkommens auf allen Ebenen eines Unternehmens. Öko-Audits sind daher nichts anderes als eine umweltpolitikspezifische Ausprägung des Total Quality Managements TQM (Löwe 1996; Stauss 1994; Malorny 1994). Dieses orientiert sich ursprünglich vor allem an Kundenbedürfnissen, der Marktnachfrage, flexiblen Produktions- und Preisanpassungen und der Produktqualität. Es lag nahe, die Logik von TQM/KVP auf das Umweltmanagement zu übertragen. Dieser konzeptionelle Ansatz beeinflußte das EMAS-Verfahren und begründete vor allem die ISO-Standards 9000ff. sowie inzwischen 14001 und 14040 seit 1997.

Ein Vergleich des europäischen EMAS- und des amerikanischen ISO-Ansatzes läuft meist auf ein Statement der Art hinaus, EMAS sei strenger und ziele auf Verbesserung der Öko-Performance, ISO sei flexibler und offener, damit auch beliebiger, und diene nur der laufenden Verbesserung des Managementsystems (Dyllick 1995; Schimmelpfeng/Machmer 1996). ISO definiert vor allem einen Verfahrensstandard, aber weder Umweltstandards (Grenzwerte, Umweltqualitätsziele) noch technische Ausführungsstandards. Im Übrigen stellt der ISO-Verfahrensstandard kein Gesetz dar, lediglich eine Leitlinie des internationalen Dachverbandes der nationalen Normen-Institute. Das ISO-Design beruht auf der erklärten Absicht, ein weltweit verbreitungsfähiges Evaluationsverfahren zu formulieren, das von allen Betrieben in allen Ländern der Erde angewandt werden kann, das indirekte Handelsbarrieren in Form von präskriptiven Umweltschutz- und Produktvorschriften vermeidet, und das darauf gerichtet ist, sowohl das Umweltmanagement-System als auch die Öko-Performance kontinuierlich zu verbessern. Eine Compliance-Prüfung ist angelegt, aber nicht zwingend. ISO legt es zwar nahe, stellt es aber frei, die an einem Standort geltenden gesetzlichen und anderen Standards in einer Compliance-Prüfung einzubeziehen. Die ISO-Befürworter erwarten, daß eine laufende Evaluation des Umweltmanagement-Systems automatisch eine Verbesserung der Compliance und der Öko-Performance induziert (Bell 1995).

Auch das EG-Öko-Audit beinhaltet den KVP-Auftrag, jedoch richtet dieser sich ausdrücklich lediglich darauf, den wirtschaftlich vertretbaren Stand der Technik zu implementieren (EVABAT = economically viable best available technology). Aus der Kritik des bürokratischen ordnungsrechtlichen Umweltschutzes ist bekannt, daß sich die EVABAT-Orientierung Status-quo-konservierend auswirkt und sie innovative Schritte eher behindert. Dies muß als ernstlicher Einwand gegen EMAS gelten.

Die Teilnahme an EMAS oder ISO ist freiwillig. Es sieht gegenwärtig so aus, als ob ISO auch in Europa EMAS den Rang abläuft. Dahinter steckt ein Kosten- und ein Qualitätsaspekt. Audits sind relativ aufwendig. Das ISO-Verfahren scheint meist weniger teuer auszufallen, wohl vor allem, weil die Beteiligungs- und Ausführungsstruktur weniger detailliert vorgegeben ist. Die größere Offenheit erweist sich außerdem nicht als Beliebigkeit, sondern als Vorteil der ortsspezifischen Auslegbarkeit. Der Schwerpunktverlagerung des Umwelthandelns vom Staat zur Industrie liegt unter anderem ja auch die Einsicht zugrunde, daß der Staat sein Wissen ohnedies von der Industrie und der kooperierenden Forschung beziehen muß. Entscheidend ist, wie weit die Unternehmen sich Umweltschutz offensiv und positiv zur Aufgabe gemacht haben. Aufgrund der weltweiten Bevorzugung von ISO wird EMAS gegenwärtig überarbeitet. EMAS II wird ISO voraussichtlich sehr ähnlich werden, wobei der hauptsächliche Streitpunkt in der Aufrechterhaltung oder Öffnung der EVABAT-Orientierung liegt.

Die Freiwilligkeit hat sich bei beiden Konkurrenzverfahren nicht als der befürchtete Schwachpunkt erwiesen. Denn eine Zertifizierung nach EMAS oder nach ISO 14001 ist unter verschiedensten Stakeholder-Aspekten zunehmend zu einem Muß für viele Betriebsstätten geworden. Auch haben die Unternehmen erkannt, daß durch Umweltaudits in der Tat Einsparpotentiale realisiert und Risikoquellen offengelegt werden (UBA 1999). Der Nutzen für organisatorische und technische Innovationen, die über Statusmodifikationen hinausgehen, ist dagegen weniger ersichtlich.

2.12 Ökologische Produktions- und Produkt-Zertifizierung

Im Unterschied zu den vorgenannten Audit-Zertifizierungen gibt es auch Produktions*qualitäts*spezifische Zertifikate für Betriebe sowie Öko-Labels für Produkte, zum Beispiel das Markenzeichen „demeter" für biologisch-dynamisch erzeugte und verarbeitete Nahrungsmittel, oder der amtliche „Blaue Engel" für allerlei Gebrauchsgüter. Gegenstand der Evaluationen zur Zuerkennung solcher Gütesiegel sind komparative Ökobilanz-Vorteile oder die Einhaltung materialer Umweltschutz-Standards. Die Prüfzertifikate werden je nach Konstitution der Gütegemeinschaft von staatlichen, verbandlichen oder privaten Instanzen vergeben. Aus staatlicher Sicht handelt es sich um die Möglichkeit, relativ unbürokratisch umwelt-produktpolitische Anreize zu setzen, deren Realisierung sich für die betreffenden Unternehmen bezahlt macht durch ein verbessertes Image und eine größere Kundennachfrage. Von Seite der Unternehmen werden Umwelt-Qualitätszertifikate für Betriebe und Produkte als wichtiges Marketing-Instrument behandelt, teilweise aber auch, aus einer Überzeugungsmission heraus, als politisches Mittel der Verbreitung neuer Umweltqualitätsstandards und ethisch-sozialer Ziele (Meffert/Kirchgeorg 1992; Altmann 1997: 200ff.; Haberer 1996: 353-386; Wendorf 1994).

Der „Blaue Engel" mit dem Umweltemblem der Vereinten Nationen wird in Deutschland seit den 70er Jahren vergeben, und zwar vom Umweltbundesamt in Zusammenarbeit mit dem Deutschen Institut für Gütesicherung und Kennzeichnung (vormals Reichsausschuß für Lieferbedingungen, daher „RAL-Gütezeichen", mit denen heute eine Vielzahl von Lebensmitteln und anderen Produkten vertrieben werden, von der amtlichen Qualitätsbutter bis zum Deutschen Weinsiegel). Der „Blaue Engel" findet sich heute auf etwa 4.000 Waren und Geräten. Sie erfahren dadurch meist gewisse Umsatzsteigerungen, in Einzelfällen bis zu 40%. Die EU hat inzwischen ein ähnliches Öko-Label eingeführt.

Der häufig kritisierte Schwachpunkt am „Blauen Engel" besteht darin, daß die als „umweltfreundlich" validierten Produkte nicht unbedingt umweltfreundlich sind, sondern sie sich lediglich als vergleichsweise weniger umweltbelastend darstellen. So konnte zum Beispiel ein PVC-Bodenbelag, per se ein Umweltproblem, mit dem „Blauen Engel" ausgezeichnet werden, weil er im Vergleich zu anderen asbestfrei war (Stellpflug 1997: 78). Freilich war diese Problematik von vornherein bewußt, und es kommt darauf an, den Erfolgsnutzen verschiedener Verfahren für die Fortentwicklung von Umweltmaßnahmen pragmatisch abzuwägen (Janiszewski 1992).

Neben der offiziellen ökologischen Produktvalidierung haben sich mit der neueren Ökologiebewegung wettbewerbliche Qualitätsalternativen etablieren können. So haben sich zum Beispiel eine Reihe von ökologisch orientierten Agrarerzeugern in der Arbeitsgemeinschaft Ökologischer Landbau AGÖL zusammengeschlossen, darunter Marken wie demeter, Bioland, Naturland oder Ökosiegel. Um diese Umweltqualitätssiegel zu erlangen, müssen sowohl die Produktion als auch die Produkte bestimmten ökologischen Erzeugungs- und Verarbeitungskriterien genügen, die regelmäßig überprüft werden, zum Beispiel Befolgung eines ganzheitlichen Konzeptes der Landbewirtschaftung, Verzicht auf synthetische Agrarchemikalien und Mineraldünger, Erhalt der Bodenfruchtbarkeit, sowie artgerechte Tierhaltung. Ähnliche Labels sind zum Beispiel auch „Transfair" für Kaffee und „Flower-Label" für Blumen aus Dritte-Welt-Ländern, die zu „fairen" Arbeits- und Lohnbedingungen sowie Handelspreisen erzeugt und importiert werden. Um die Validierung „fair" zu erlangen, müssen in Handel und Herstellung eine Reihe von ökologischen *und* sozio-ökonomischen Kriterien erfüllt werden, deren Einhaltung regelmäßig überprüft werden soll.

2.13 Benchmarking, Öko-Ranking, Öko-Rating

Benchmarking bedeutet ursprünglich den Vergleich von Leistungsparametern zwischen Unternehmen. Die Übertragung des Prinzips auf den Umweltschutz bedeutet eine vergleichende Bewertung der Umweltschutzleistungen eines Unternehmens, oder auch einer öffentlichen Verwaltung, einer Kommune o.ä. In der Regel gelten die jeweils Höchstplazierten als Maßstab (Leistungsziel) für die Nächstplazierten (Dyllick/Schneidewind 1995). Die komparative Umweltpolitikforschung hat das Prinzip auch übertragen auf den Vergleich der Maßnahmen und Ergebnis-Performances von nationalen Umweltpolitiken, wobei das „best achievement" in einem jeweiligen Segment zum allgemeinen Maßstab erhoben wird (Jänicke/Weidner 1995).

Beim Vergleich der Öko-Performance verschiedener Akteure durch Benchmarking ergibt sich ein Öko-*Ranking*. Die verallgemeinernde Klassifizierung von Öko-Performance-Kriterien, unabhängig von situativen Vergleichen, führt zu einem Öko-*Rating*. In sinngemäßer Anlehnung an das finanzielle Bonitätsrating werden Ratings von A+, A, A- (beste) bis D, D- (schlechteste) vergeben. Kriterien sind dabei Art und Ausmaß des betrieblichen Umweltmanagements, der Umweltberichterstattung und -kommunikation, der umweltorientierten Forschungs-, Entwicklungs- und Investitionspolitik u.a. Von Benchmarking spricht man eher, wenn ein Akteur seine eigene Öko-Performance mit anderen vergleicht; von Öko-Ranking und Öko-Rating, wenn externe Analysten die Öko-Performances einer Gruppe von Akteuren vergleichend bewerten.

Es gibt inzwischen eine Reihe von Instituten und Agenturen, die sich auf Öko-Rankings und Öko-Ratings spezialisiert haben. Sie veröffentlichen entsprechende Evaluationslisten, ähnlich den gerne publizierten Evaluations-Hitlisten von Universitäten. Die Ergebnisse der Rankings und Ratings dienen Banken, Fonds und anderen institutionellen Investoren als Anhaltspunkt für „grüne" oder „ethische" Investment- oder Kreditentscheidungen, und faktisch auch Behörden, Aktionsgruppen, Medien und anderen Akteuren als Anhaltspunkt dafür, ob ein Unternehmen aus ihrer Sicht Vertrauen und Kooperation verdient.

Die vom Hamburger Umweltinstitut durchgeführten Rankings von Chemiekonzernen sowie vergleichbare Untersuchungen der Münchner oekom research AG oder der Sustainable Performance Group AG Zürich haben gezeigt, daß Unternehmen, die bei Umwelt-Evaluationen gut abschneiden, auch beim Geschäftserfolg hoch skalieren. Im Zeitraum 1994-1999 lag die Jahresrendite der "Ökoleaders" um durchschnittlich 9,2% höher als die der "Ökolaggards" (Sustainable Performance Group 1997; manager magazin 9/99: 143). Die Interpretation des Zusammenhangs ist freilich strittig. Haben die betreffenden Unternehmen Finanzerfolg, weil sie umweltorientiert sind? Oder können sie sich Umweltorientierung leisten, weil sie geschäftlich erfolgreich sind? Oder sind erfolgreiche Unternehmen so beschaffen, daß sie für neue Themen und Trends generell offen sind, für Umfeldanpassungen, für technische und institutionelle Innovationen, für Geschäftschancen, für Ökologie, soziale Fragen u.a., so daß sie bezüglich allen solchen Angelegenheiten stets unter den Gruppenführern zu finden sind? Jedenfalls, die Chancen, Innovationspotentiale zu nutzen, neue Produkte und Prozesse auch und gerade im Rahmen einer ökologischen Unternehmensführung entwickeln und anwenden zu können, erlangen bei Entscheidungen über langfristige Investitionen zunehmende Bedeutung. Die Sustainable Performance Group hat inzwischen in Zusammenarbeit mit Dow Jones einen nach Weltregionen gegliederten Aktien-Performanceindex von „grünen" Unternehmen erstellt.

Häufig wird das ökologische mit einem so genannten ethischen Ranking oder Rating verbunden, oder als Teil davon behandelt (Hoffmann 1997). An der Börse gehandelte Anteile von Öko-Fonds oder „Green baskets" laufen auch unter der Bezeichnung „Ethical investment". In solche Fonds aufgenommen werden nur die Aktien solcher Unternehmen, die außer einer bestimmten Öko-Performance auch ansonsten ein sozial verantwortliches Verhalten an den Tag legen, sei es im Hinblick auf ihre Mitarbeiter, Kunden und ihre Nachbarschaft, sei es im Hinblick auf Operationen in Entwicklungsländern, ihr Kooperationsverhalten gegenüber diktatorischen und korrupten Regimes u.ä. Bestimmte Institute und Verbraucherzentralen haben inzwischen ähnliche, nicht gar so weit gehende Rankings mit einer Vielzahl von Unternehmen des Konsumgüter-Sektors durchgeführt. Die Rankings erfolgen vergleichend aber getrennt nach den Bereichen Informationsoffenheit, Verbraucherinteressen, Arbeitnehmerinteressen, Frauenförderung, Behindertenengagement, und Umweltengagement (imug 1997; Der Unternehmenstester... 1998, 1999).

2.14 Umweltverträglichkeitsprüfung

Bei einer Umweltverträglichkeitsprüfung UVP handelt es sich um eine gesetzlich vorgeschriebene und unter Behördenkontrolle durchgeführte Prüfung von genehmigungspflichtigen Vorhaben wie zum Beispiel dem Bau und Betrieb von Infrastrukturen und Fabrikanlagen, Straßen, Bahntrassen, Entsorgungseinrichtungen, Sportstätten, verschiedensten Neuansiedlungen auf der grünen Wiese u.a.m. (Hübler 1989 a+b; RSU 1996: 81-85; UBA 1997: 282-284). Die UVP wurde teilweise unter Orientierung an dem amerikanischen Environmental Impact Assessment EIS entwickelt.

UVPs sind Bestandteil eines amtlichen Verfahrens zur Planung und Genehmigung von Vorhaben. Sie können von der betreffenden Behörde selbst durchgeführt oder bei unabhängigen externen Gutachtern in Auftrag gegeben werden. Es handelt sich um eine Ex-ante-Abschätzung der Umweltbeeinträchtungen, die eine geplante Maßnahme voraussichtlich mit sich bringen wird, insbesondere Emissionen, Flächenumwandlung/Denaturierung und Flächenverbrauch, Wirkungen auf Flora und Fauna, Lärm, Abfälle, u.ä. Es sollen möglichst mehrere Maßnahmen-Alternativen zur vergleichenden Prüfung vorgelegt werden. Die Prüfung hat die Umweltbeeinträchtigungen sowohl während des Baues als auch während des Betriebes als auch eventuell bei Abbruch/Stillegung zu untersuchen. Die prüfende und die genehmigende Behörde ist in der Regel die selbe (was Anlaß zu Kritik gibt).

Bei der Gesetzgebung zur UVP in den 80er Jahren hat es Diskussionen darüber gegeben, ob außer den Umweltwirkungen nicht auch soziale Auswirkungen einbezogen werden sollten, zumal sich der Auftrag der UVP ausdrücklich auch auf den Schutz von Denkmälern, Kulturlandschaften und anderen Sachgütern bezieht, die als kulturelles Erbe gelten. Wie so oft, hat sich die Praxis der UVP als ernüchternder herausgestellt als die hohen Ansprüche, die man zuvor damit verbunden hat. Das Grundproblem liegt hier weniger darin, Ex-ante-Feststellungen zu treffen (welche Fläche eine Maßnahme beanspruchen wird, selbst, wieviel Verkehr induziert werden wird und anderes, ist einigermaßen zutreffend kalkulierbar), als vielmehr, Güterabwägungen vorzunehmen, die auf rein wissenschaftlicher Grundlage nicht vorgenommen werden können. Sind Frösche, Kraniche und Restsümpfe wirklich Grund genug, eine Eisenbahntrasse unter Inkaufnahme erheblicher Verkehrsnachteile umzulegen? Eine UVP soll eine wissenschaftliche Entscheidungshilfe liefern. Oftmals jedoch wird sie unversehens zum Vehikel politischer Interessens- und Konfliktaustragung. Und so wird sie oft genug auch bürokratisch und juristisch mißbraucht, um Planungs- und Genehmigungsverfahren zu behindern oder gar zu verhindern.

2.15 Technikfolgen- und Risiko-Assessment

Die Ansätze zum Technikfolgen- und Risiko-Assessment TA sind typische Hervorbringungen der 70er und 80er Jahre, in denen die Umweltdebatte vor allem auch als Technikrisiko-Debatte geführt wurde. TA hat ihren Schwerpunkt bei der vergleichenden Beurteilung sehr langfristiger strategischer Weichenstellungen im Hinblick auf Wissenschafts- und Technologiepfade sowie sonstige Innovationspfade (Rip u.a. 1995; von Westphalen 1997; Renn/Zwick 1997) In einem solchen Kontext ist es in der Tat fast selbstverständlich, daß es nicht nur um die Abschätzung von Umweltwirkungen geht, sondern ebenso um verschiedenste gesellschaftliche Auswirkungen. Aber der ökologische Aspekt ist sehr bedeutend gewesen, insbesondere unter dem Aspekt der Abschätzung des Sicherheitsrisikos für Mensch und Umwelt, zunächst vor allem der Atomtechnik sowie allgemein der „Großtechnik" (um 1975-1980), anschließend der Informations- und Kommunikationstechnik (80er Jahre), und schließlich auch der Bio- und Gentechnik (80er und 90er Jahre).

Mit der TA eng verbunden war die Technik-Akzeptanzforschung seit den 70er Jahren und die daraus hervorgegangenen Ansätze der Risikokommunikation (Renn/Zwick 1997). Dabei geht es im Wesentlichen um die Bewertung von Risiken und das Herausarbeiten von Handhabungsstrategien im offenen und auch öffentlichen, zumindest teilöffentlichen Dialog (Jungermann u.a. 1988). Die Akzeptanzforschung fand in Wirklichkeit vor allem in Form demoskopischer Umfragen statt. Der Ansatz der Risikokommunikation dagegen wurde zu einem festen Bestandteil im Konzept der Umweltkommunikation und Umweltberichterstattung von Großunternehmen, Ministerien und Verbänden (Röglin/Grebmer 1988; Röglin 1994).

In den USA wurde das Office of Technology Assessment Anfang der 90er Jahre wieder geschlossen – was symptomatisch ist für die Fluktuationen des Zeitgeistes, und was durchaus zu Bedauern ist im Hinblick auf die Sache, denn die qualifizierte Einschätzung strategischer Perspektiven ist zu jeder Zeit so wichtig wie sie es in den 70er und 80er Jahren gewesen ist. TA besteht jedoch auch ohne Regierungsauftrag durchaus weiter, in verschiedensten privaten und öffentlichen Think Tanks, strategischen Planungsstäben, Forschungseinrichtungen, insbesondere solchen, die Zukunftsforschung weiterbetreiben. Auch kann man sagen, daß ein Teil der TA-Impulse in der Konzeption von Öko- und Lebenswegbilanzen, Product Sustainability Assessments, Umweltverträglichkeitsprüfungen u.a. ihren Niederschlag gefunden hat.

3. Zusammenfassung und Ausblick

Während die Umweltpolitik der letzten Jahrzehnte dazu tendierte, über ordnungsrechtliche Verwaltungsmaßnahmen Einfluß zu nehmen, tendiert sie in ihrer neueren Ausrichtung verstärkt zu koordinativen und indirekten Lenkungskonzepten. Dies gilt um so mehr im Hinblick auf die Umsetzung komplexer Programme wie zum Beispiel CO_2-Reduktionen im Zuge des Rio-Prozesses und daraus sich ableitender nationaler Umweltpläne. Evaluationen des Instrumentenmix, des Politikprozesses und der Ergebnisse werden zu einem integralen Bestandteil derartiger komplexer Programme, auch im Sinne einer laufenden prozeßbegleitenden Evaluation. Mittels einer begleitenden Evaluation können eventuell auftretende nicht-intendierte Effekte erkannt sowie nicht-wirksame Maßnahmen rechtzeitig abgebrochen werden.

Auf unternehmerischer Seite erlangen Audits im Rahmen von ISO oder EMAS wie beschrieben zunehmende Bedeutung. Die fortlaufende Bewertung und Neujustierung betrieblicher Umweltschutzmaßnahmen wird sich auf Dauer positiv auf die Ökoperformances der Unternehmen und, kumuliert, auch auf die Umweltgesamtrechnung der Volkswirtschaften auswirken. Im Sinne einer umweltökonomischen Rechnung werden die Umweltfolgekosten eines Unternehmens tendenziell sinken. Da betrieblicher Umweltschutz in bestimmten Branchen ein erheblicher Kostenfaktor ist, müssen dessen Elemente permanent auf ihre Wirksamkeit überprüfbar gestaltet sein. Um diese Ziele zu erreichen, bedarf es einer breiten und stets aktuellen Datenbasis sowie der kooperativen Mitwirkung aller relevanter Akteure. An diesen Stellen werden in Zukunft Evaluationen von Umweltschutzmaßnahmen in Staat und Unternehmen noch an Bedeutung gewinnen.

Literatur

Altmann, Jörn (1997): Umweltpolitik. Daten, Fakten, Konzepte für die Praxis. Stuttgart: Lucius & Lucius. UTB.

Azzone, Giovanni/Manzini, Raffaella (1994): Measuring Environmental Performance. Business Strategy and the Environment, Vol. 3, Part 1, Spring 1994, S. 1-14.

Bartlett, Robert V. (1994): Evaluating Environmental Policy Success and Failure. In: Vig, Norman J./Kraft, Michael E. (Hg.): Environmental Policy in the 1990s. Washington: Congressional Quarterly Press. S. 167-187.

Baumgartner, Thomas (1986): Die Produktlinienanalyse als neue Form der Informationserhebung und -darstellung. In: Beckenbach, Frank/Schreyer, Michaele (Hg.) (1986): Gesellschaftliche Folgekosten, Frankfurt: Campus. S. 150-169.

Bechmann, Arnim/Hofmeister, Sabine/Schultz, Stefanie (1987): Umweltbilanzierung. Darstellung und Analyse zum Stand des Wissens. Forschungsbericht des Umweltbundesamtes Berlin. UBA-Texte 5/1987.

Bell, Christopher L. (1995): Environmental Management Systems and ISO 14001. Business and the Environment, Special Insert, December 1995.

Berkhout, Frans (1996): Life Cycle Assessment and Innovation in Large Firms. In: Angel, David/Huber, Joseph (Hg.): Business Strategy and the Environment. Special Issue, Vol. 5, No. 3, September 1996, S. 145-155.

Binswanger, Hans-Christoph u.a. (1978): Der NAWU-Report. Wege aus der Wohlstandsfalle. Frankfurt: S.Fischer.

BMU/UBA (Hg.) (1995): Handbuch Umweltcontrolling. München: Vahlen (BMU = Bundesministerium für Umwelt, UBA = Umweltbundesamt)

Braunschweig, Arthur u.a. (1984): Ökologische Buchhaltung für eine Stadt. Hg.v.d. Arbeitsgemeinschaft Umweltökonomie an der Hochschule St.Gallen.

BUND/Misereor (1996): Zukunftsfähiges Deutschland. Ein Beitrag zu einer global nachhaltigen Entwicklung. Im Auftrag durchgeführt vom Wuppertal Institut für Klima, Umwelt, Energie. Basel: Birkhäuser.

Bundesumweltministerium (1998): Nachhaltige Entwicklung in Deutschland. Entwurf eines umweltpolitischen Schwerpunktprogramms. Bonn: Bundesministerium für Umwelt, Naturschutz und Reaktorsicherheit.

Bussmann, Werner/Klöti, Ulrich/Knoepfel, Peter (Hg.) (1997): Einführung in die Politikevaluation. Basel/Frankfurt: Helbing & Lichtenhahn.

Carius, Rainer/Renn, Ortwin (1998): Partizipation als Instrument einer Nachhaltigkeitspolitik am Beispiel Abfallplanung. In: Knaus/Renn (Hg.), S. 336-354.

Coming Clean (1993): Coming Clean. Corporate Environmental Reporting – Opening Up for Sustainable Development. Co-ed. and co-publ. by Deloitte Touche Tohmatsu International. International Institute for Sustainable Development, SustainAbility. London.

Conrad, Jobst (Hg.) (1998): Environmental Management in European Companies. Success Stories and Evaluation. Amsterdam: Overseas Publ. Assoc./Gordon & Breach.

Der Unternehmenstester Lebensmittel 1999, Ein Ratgeber für den verantwortlichen Einkauf. Hg.v. imug (Institut für Markt, Umwelt, Gesellschaft) und Verbraucherverbänden. Reinbek: rororo.

Der Unternehmenstester Kosmetik, Körperpflege und Waschmittel 1998, Ein Ratgeber für den verantwortlichen Einkauf. Hg.v. imug (Institut für Markt, Umwelt, Gesellschaft) und Verbraucherverbänden. Reinbek: rororo.

Diefenbacher, Hans (1995): Der Index of Sustainable Welfare. Heidelberg: Forschungsstätte der Evangelischen Studiengemeinschaften. Texte Reihe B, Nr. 24, Juli 1995.

Dyllick, Thomas (1995): Die EU-Verordnung zum Umweltmanagement und zur Umweltbetriebsprüfung (EMAS-Verordnung) im Vergleich mit der ISO-Norm 14001. Zeitschrift für Umweltpolitik und Umweltrecht, Heft 3/95, S. 299-339.

Dyllick, Thomas/Schneidewind, Uwe (1995): Ökologische Benchmarks. Erfolgsindikatoren für das Umweltmanagement von Unternehmen, Diskussionsbeitrag Nr. 26 des Instituts für Wirtschaft und Ökologie der Hochschule St.Gallen.

EAJ (Environment Agency, Government of Japan) (1989): Report Quality of the Environment in Japan. Tokyo: Government of Japan.

Enquete-Kommission „Schutz des Menschen und der Umwelt" des Deutschen Bundestages (1993): Verantwortung für die Zukunft. Wege zum nachhaltigen Umgang mit Stoff- und Materialströmenl. Bonn: Economica.

Enquete-Kommission... (1994): Die Industriegesellschaft gestalten. Perspektiven für einen nachhaltigen Umgang mit Stoff- und Materialströmen. Bonn: Economica.

Feindt, Peter Henning (1997): Kommunale Demokratie in der Umweltpolitik. Neue Beteiligungsmodelle. In: Aus Politik und Zeitgeschichte, B 27/97, 27. Juni 1997.

Fietkau, Joachim/Weidner, Helmut (1998): Umweltverhandeln. Konzepte, Praxis und Analysen alternativer Konfliktregelungsverfahren. Berlin: Edition Sigma.

Friege, Henning/Engelhardt, Claudia/Henseling, Karl Otto (1998): Das Management von Stoffströmen. Heidelberg: Springer.

Freimann, Jürgen (1996): Betriebliche Umweltpolitik. Bern: Haupt/UTB.

Freimann, Jürgen (1995): Pilot-Öko-Audits. Hg. v. Hessischen Ministerium für Wirtschaft. Wiesbaden, September 1995.

Glasze, Georg (1997): Das Umweltforum. Schriftenreihe zur ökologischen Kommunikation Bd.5. München: ökom-Verlag

Haasis, Hans Dietrich u.a. (Hg.) (1995): Umweltinformationssysteme in der Produktion. Marburg: Metropolis.

Haberer, Axel (1996): Umweltbezogene Informationsasymetrien und transparenzschaffende Institutionen. Marburg: Metropolis.

Hallay, Hendric (1996): Ökologische Entwicklungsfähigkeit von Unternehmen. Marburg: Metropolis.

Hallay, Hendric (1992): Öko-Controlling.Umweltschutz in mittelständischen Unternehmen. Frankfurt: Campus.

Henkel KGaA (1998): Daten und Fakten für 1998. Umwelt, Sicherheit, Gesundheit. Düsseldorf .

Hoffmann, Johannes (Hg.) (1997): Ethische Kriterien für die Bewertung von Unternehmen. Frankfurt: Verlag für interkulturelle Kommunikation.

Hofmeister, Sabine (1998): Von der Abfallwirtschaft zur ökologischen Stoffwirtschaft. Wege zu einer Ökonomie der Reproduktion. Opladen: Westdeutscher Verlag.

Hofmeister, Sabine (1989): Stoff- und Energiebilanzen. Zur Eignung des physischen Bilanzprinzips als Konzeption der Umweltplanung, Landschaftsentwicklung und Umweltforschung, Bd. Nr. 58 der Schriftenreihe des Fachbereichs Landschaftsentwicklung der TU Berlin.

Hopfenbeck, Waldemar (1991): Umweltorientiertes Management und Marketing. Landsberg: Moderne Industrie.

Huber, Joseph (1998): Vollgeld. Beschäftigung, Grundeinkommen und weniger Staatsquote durch eine modernisierte Geldordnung. Berlin: Duncker & Humblot.

Huber, Joseph (1995): Nachhaltige Entwicklung. Berlin: Edition Sigma.

Huber, Joseph (1993): Ökologische Modernisierung. Bedingungen des Umwelthandelns in den neuen und alten Bundesländern. In: Kölner Zeitschrift für Soziologie und Sozialpsychologie, Jg. 45, Heft 2/93, S. 288-304.

Huber, Joseph/Protzmann, Elle/Siegert, Ulrike C. (1998): Environmental Management at the Ciba Corporation in: Conrad (Hg.), S. 223-242.

Hübler, Karl-Hermann/Otto-Zimmermann, Konrad (Hg.) (19890a): Umweltverträglichkeitsprüfung. Taunusstein: E. Blottner.

Hübler, Karl-Hermann/Otto-Zimmermann, Konrad (Hg.) (1989b): Bewertung der Umweltverträglichkeit. Taunusstein: E. Blottner.

Immler, Hans (1975): Die Notwendigkeit von Stoff- und Energiebilanzen im Betrieb. In: Das Argument, Jg. 17, 1975, Nr. 93, S. 822-834.

Imug (Institut für Markt, Umwelt, Gesellschaft) (1997): Unternehmenstest. Neue Herausforderungen für das Management der sozialen und ökologischen Verantwortung. München: Vahlen.

Janiszewski, Jörg (1992): Umweltzeichen. Rechtliche Analyse und Neuorientierung. Berlin: E.Schmidt.

Jänicke, Martin/Kung, Philip/Stitzel, Michael (1999): Umweltpolitik. Politik, Recht, und Management des Umweltschutzes in Staat und Unternehmen. Bonn: Verlag J.H.W. Dietz Nachf.

Jänicke, Martin/Weidner, Helmut (1995): Successful Environmental Policy. An Introduction. In: Jänicke/Weidner (Hg.): Successful Environmental Policy. A critical evaluation of 24 cases. Berlin: Edition Sigma, S. 10-26.

James, Peter (1994): Business Environmental Performance Measurement. Business Strategy and the Environment, Vol. 3, Part 2, Summer 1994, S. 59-67.

Janke, Günter (1995): Öko-Auditing Handbuch. Berlin: Erich Schmidt.

Jungermann, Helmut/Kasperson, Roger E./Wiedemann, Peter M. (1988): Themes and Tasks of Risk Communication. Hg.v.d. Zentralbibliothek der Kernforschungsanlage Jülich.

Knaus, Anja/Renn, Ortwin (1998): Den Gipfel vor Augen. Unterwegs in eine nachhaltige Zukunft. Marburg: Metropolis.

Kytzia, Susanne (1995): Die Ökobilanz als Bestandteil des betrieblichen Informationsmanagements. Chur: Rüegger.

Leicht-Eckart, Elisabeth u.a. (Hg.) (1996): Öko-Audit.Grundlagen und Erfahrungen. Frankfurt: VAS.

Leipert, Christian (1989): Die heimlichen Kosten des Fortschritts. Frankfurt: S. Fischer.

Lindlar, Angela (1995): Umwelt-Audits. Ein Leitfaden. Bonn: Economica Verlag.

Löwe, Carsten (1996): Qualitätsmanagement in der Weiterbildung. Köln: Dt. Wirtschaftsdienst.

Malorny, Christian (1994): Brennpunkt Total Quality Management. Stuttgart: Schäffer-Poeschel.

managermagazin 9/99. Hamburg: manager magazin Verlagsgesellschaft mbH.

Mazmanian, Daniel/Morell, David (1992): Beyond Superfailure: America's Toxics Policy for the 1990s. Boulder: Westview.

Meffert, Heribert/Kirchgeorg, Manfred (1992): Marktorientiertes Umweltmanagement. Stuttgart: Poeschel.

Milieudefensie 1992: Action Plan Sustainable Netherlands – A perspective for changing nothern lifestyles. Publ. by Milieudefensie (Friends of the Earth Netherlands). Amsterdam.

Müller-Wenk, Ruedi (1978): Die ökologische Buchhaltung. Frankfurt: Campus.

OECD 1998: Eco-Efficiency, Paris: OECD Publishing.

OECD 1998b: Towards Sustainable Development. Environmental Indicators. Paris: OECD Publishing.

OECD 1993: Environmental Performance Reviews: Germany. Paris: OECD Publishing.

Orwat, Carsten (1996): Informationsinstrumente des Umweltmanagements. Ökologische Bilanzierung und Controlling. Berlin: Analytica.

Pfister, Gerhard (1998): Ein Konzept zur Messung einer nachhaltigen Entwicklung. In: Knaus/Renn (Hg.) (1998), S. 235-255.

Poschmann, Christian/Riebenstahl, Christoph/Schmidt-Kallert, Einhard (1998): Umweltplanung und -bewertung. Gotha: Justus Perthes Verlag.

Projektgruppe Ökologische Wirtschaft 1987: Produktlinienanalyse. Köln: Kölner Volksblatt Verlag.

Radermacher, Walter/Zieschank, Roland/Hoffmann-Kroll, Regina/van Nouhuys, Jo/Schäfer, Dieter/Seibel, Steffen (1998): Entwicklung eines Indikatorensystems für den Zustand der Umwelt in Deutschland. Stuttgart: Metzler-Poeschel.

Rees, William E./Wackernagel, Mathis (1994): Ecological Footprints and Appropriated Carrying Capacity. Measuring the Natural Capital Requirements of the Human Economy. In: Jansson, Annmari/Hammer, Monica/Folke, Carl/Costanza, Robert (Hg.) (1994): Investing in Natural Capital. The Ecological Economics Approach to Sustainability. Washington/Covelo: Island Press. S. 362-391. Dt. als Monographie 1997: Unser ökologischer Fußabdruck. Basel: Birkhäuser.

Renn, Ortwin (1999): Abfallwirtschaft 2005. Bürger planen ein regionales Abfallkonzept. Baden-Baden: Nomos.

Renn, Ortwin/Zwick, Michael M. (1997): Risiko- und Technikakzeptanz. Berlin/Heidelberg: Springer.

Rip, Arie/Misa, Thomas/Schot, Johan (Hg.) (1995): Managing Technology in Society. The approach of Constructive Technology Assessment. London/New York: Pinter Publishing.

Röglin, Hans-Christian/von Grebmer, Klaus (1988): Pharma-Industrie und Öffentlichkeit. Basel: Buchverlag Basler Zeitung.

Röglin, Hans-Christian (1994): Technikängste und wie man damit umgeht. Düsseldorf: VDI-Verlag.

Rossi, Peter H./Freeman, Howard E./Hofmann, Gerhard (1988): Programm-Evaluation. Einführung in die Methoden angewandter Sozialforschung. Stuttgart: Enke.

RSU (Rat von Sachverständigen für Umweltfragen) (1996): Umweltgutachten 1996. Stuttgart: Metzler-Poeschel.

RSU (Rat von Sachverständigen für Umweltfragen) 1994: Umweltgutachten 1994. Für eine dauerhaft-umweltgerechte Entwicklung. Stuttgart: Metzler-Poeschel.

RSU (Rat von Sachverständigen für Umweltfragen) (1987): Umweltgutachten 1987. Stuttgart/Mainz: Kohlhammer.

Schaltegger, Stefan (1992): Ökologieorientierte Entscheidungen im Unternehmen. Ökologisches Rechnungswesen statt ökologischer Bilanzierung. Bern: Haupt.

Schimmelpfeng, Lutz/Machmer, Dietrich (Hg.) (1996): Öko-Audit und Öko-Controlling gemäß ISO 14000ff. und EG-Verordnung 1836/93. Taunusstein: Blottner.

Schmid-Bleek, Friedrich (1994): Wieviel Umwelt braucht der Mensch? MIPS – das Maß für ökologisches Wirtschaften. Berlin: Birkhäuser.

Stauss, Bernd (Hg.) (1994): Qualitätsmanagement und Zertifizierung. Wiesbaden: Gabler.

Stellpflug, Jürgen (1997): Der schöne Schein der Gütesiegel. In: Trendsetter – Schritte zum nachhaltigen Konsumverhalten der privaten Haushalte. Hg. v. Umweltbundesamt Berlin, Texte 64/1997, S. 77-79.

Steven, Marion/Schwarz, Erich J./Lethmate, Peter (1997): Umweltberichterstattung und Umwelterklärung nach der EG-Öko-Audit-Verordnung. Grundlagen, Methoden, Anwendung. Berlin: Springer.

Sustainable Performance Group AG (1997): Sustainability und Aktienperformance. Chancen für Investoren am Beispiel der Chemie- und Pharmaindustrie, erarbeitet von Sustainable Asset Management und Hamburger Umweltinstitut. Zürich.

Theobald, Werner (Hg.) (1998): Integrative Umweltbewertung. Theorie und Beispiele aus der Praxis. Berlin: Springer.

UBA (Umweltbundesamt) (1997): Nachhaltiges Deutschland. Wege zu einer dauerhaft umweltgerechten Entwicklung. Berlin: Erich Schmidt Verlag.

UBA (Umweltbundesamt) (Hg.) (1992): Ökobilanzen für Produkte. Texte 38/92. Berlin.

UBA (Umweltbundesamt) (Hg.) (1997a): Produktlinienanalyse Waschen und Waschmittel. Texte 1/97. Berlin.

UBA (Umweltbundesamt) (Hg.) (1997b): Materialien zu Ökobilanzen und Lebensweganalysen. Texte 26/97. Berlin.

UBA (Umweltbundesamt) (1999): EG-Umweltaudit in Deutschland. Erfahrungsbericht 1995-1998. Berlin .

Umweltbewertung (1999): Umweltbewertung aus ethischer und ökonomischer Sicht. Grundfragen und ihre Anwendung auf Nutzung und Schutz der Biosphäre, Sondergutachten des Wissenschaftlichen Beirats der Bundesregierung „Globale Umweltveränderungen". Marburg: Metropolis.

Umweltdaten 1998, hrsg. v. Umweltbundesamt und Statistisches Bundesamt. Stuttgart: Metzler-Poeschel.

Van Dieren, Wouter (Hg.) (1995): Mit der Natur rechnen. Vom Bruttosozialprodukt zum Ökosozialprodukt. Basel: Birkhäuser.

Von Westphalen, Graf Raban (1997): Technikfolgenabschätzung als politische Aufgabe. München: Oldenbourg.

Voss, Gerhard (1996): Sustainable Development. Erfolge beim Materialverbrauch. IW-Trends zur empirischen Wirtschaftsforschung, 23. Jg., 3/96, S. 4759.

Wagner, Bernd (1996): Konkurrenten oder Partner? Ökobilanz und Öko-Audit im Vergleich. München: Gesellschaft für ökologische Kommunikation.

Weidner, Helmut (1995): 25 Years of Modern Environmental Policy in Germany. Wissenschaftszentrum Berlin, Papers FS II, S 95-301.

Weidner, Helmut (Hg.) 1997: Performance and Characteristics of German Environmental Policy. Overview and Expert Commentaries from 14 Countries, Wissenschaftszentrum Berlin, Papers FS II, S. 97-301.

Weidner, Helmut/Zieschank, Roland/Knoepfel, Peter (Hg.) (1992): Umwelt-Information. Berichterstattung und Informationssysteme in zwölf Ländern. Berlin: Edition Sigma.

Wendorf, Gabriele (1994): Umweltzeichen im Spannungsfeld zwischen Konsumenten und Unternehmen. Frankfurt: P. Lang.

Wicke, Lutz (1987): Die ökologischen Milliarden. Was die zerstörte Umwelt kostet. München: Koesel.

Wicke, Lutz/Haasis, Hans-Dietrich/Schafhausen, Franzjosef/Schulz, Werner (1992): Betriebliche Umweltökonomie. München: Vahlen.

Windhoff-Héritier, Adrienne (1987): Policy-Analyse. Eine Einführung. Frankfurt: Campus.

Reinhard Stockmann

Evaluation staatlicher Entwicklungspolitik

1. Problemstellung

Die Entwicklungszusammenarbeit (EZ) zählt zu den wenigen Politikfeldern in Deutschland, in denen Projekte und Programme kontinuierlich evaluiert werden.[1] Hierzu wurde ein ausgefeiltes Evaluationssystem aufgebaut und in den staatlichen Steuerungs- und Durchführungsorganisationen institutionalisiert. Das in der Entwicklungszusammenarbeit federführende Bundesministerium für Wirtschaftliche Zusammenarbeit und Entwicklung (BMZ) richtete bereits Anfang der 70er Jahre ein „Inspektionsreferat" ein, das später in „Zentrale Erfolgskontrolle" umbenannt wurde. Auch die beiden wichtigsten Durchführungsorganisationen, die Kreditanstalt für Wiederaufbau (KfW), die vor allem mit der Vergabe entwicklungspolitischer Kredite beauftragt wird (Finanzielle Zusammenarbeit) und die Deutsche Gesellschaft für Technische Zusammenarbeit (GTZ), die Partnerländer bei der Planung und Durchführung von Entwicklungsprojekten berät und unterstützt (Technische Zusammenarbeit), institutionalisierten umfangreiche Evaluationssysteme. Deshalb ist es um so erstaunlicher, daß Evaluationen im EZ-Bereich ein hohes Theorie- und Methodendefizit aufweisen. Die Evaluationsverfahren der einzelnen Organisationen waren bisher wenig aufeinander abgestimmt; es fehlen gemeinsame Standards und Bewertungsmaßstäbe; Wirkungsanalysen, vor allem ex-post durchgeführte Evaluationen werden stark vernachlässigt; methodisch anspruchsvolle Designs (Längsschnittstudien, Verwendung von Multimethodenansätzen) sind selten und vor allem fehlt Transparenz. Bis 1999 wurden Evaluationsstudien der staatlichen Geber nicht veröffentlicht und waren somit der wissenschaftlichen und gesellschaftlichen Diskussion weitgehend entzogen.

Bei den Nicht-Regierungsorganisationen (NRO) sieht es keineswegs besser aus. Im Gegenteil, die meisten NRO setzen nur einfache Evaluationsinstrumente ein, evaluieren nicht systematisch, sondern vertrauen mehr auf persönliche Kontakte und Netzwerke und behandeln Evaluationsergebnisse oft wie eine Geheimsache.[2]

---

1 Die Begriffe „Evaluation" und „Evaluierung" werden hier synonym verwendet.
2 Allerdings sind einige NRO derzeit sehr aktiv dabei, ihre methodischen Evaluationsdefizite abzubauen. Vgl. z.B. VENRO (2000). Vgl. auch Misereor (1992); Mayer

Seit einigen Jahren findet nun jedoch eine umfassende Diskussion[3] über die Evaluation in der EZ statt, die zu einem durchgreifenden Wandel der vorhandenen Evaluationssysteme zu führen scheint. Es ist deshalb besonders reizvoll, sich mit der Evaluation in diesem Politikfeld auseinanderzusetzen. Dabei konzentriert sich der vorliegende Beitrag auf die staatliche Entwicklungszusammenarbeit. Ziel ist es, die bisherige Evaluationspraxis zu skizzieren, Defizite aufzuzeigen, die derzeitigen Reformbemühungen zu bewerten sowie den weiteren Reformbedarf zu benennen.

2. Evaluationssystem der staatlichen EZ

2.1 Das Bundesministerium für wirtschaftliche Zusammenarbeit und Entwicklung

Seit fast 50 Jahren leistet die Bundesrepublik Deutschland Entwicklungshilfe. Zehn Jahre dauerte es, bis für dieses Politikfeld ein eigenes Ministerium gegründet wurde und weitere zehn Jahre, bis es wesentliche, in anderen Ministerien angesiedelte Kompetenzen bei sich vereinen konnte[4]. Seitdem ist es maßgeblich für die „Planung, Grundsätze, Programme und Koordinierung der gesamten bi- und multilateralen Entwicklungspolitik" zuständig (BMZ 1998: 40)[5]. Und seitdem verfügt es auch über ein eigenes Referat zur Erfolgskontrolle, dessen Ziel es ist, die Wirksamkeit der deutschen Entwicklungszusammenarbeit zu überprüfen, indem die durchgeführten Projekte und Programme und die dafür eingesetzten Instrumente unter Berücksichtigung der sektoralen, regionalen und kulturellen Rahmenbedingungen evaluiert werden. Aus den Ergebnissen werden allgemeine Empfehlungen und Kritierien abgeleitet, die in die Grundsatz- und Sektorpapiere des BMZ Eingang finden und als Entschei-

---

(1993); Weiter/Huber (1994); Barth/Kasch (1996), Barth (1996, 1998); Tepel (1997); Bohnsack (1998); Dolzer u.a. (1998); Dütting (1998); Polak (1998); Wiener (1998).

3   Zur Diskussion vgl. u.a. Derlien (1976); Bodemer (1976), Bodemer (1979); Glagow (1983); Lotz (1984); Bohnet (1985); Schwefel (1987); Grashoff (1987); Deutscher Bundestag (1989a, 1989b, 1990, 1996, 1998); Brüne (1998); Hoebink (1998); Kenneweg (1998); Barthelt (1998); Breier (1998); Mutter (1998); Erlbeck (1998); Stockmann (1990, 1996, 1998).

4   Zur Geschichte des BMZ vgl. Martinek (1981); Schimank (1983a & b); Bodemer (1985); Stockhausen (1986); Stockmann (1990); Nuscheler (1995).

5   Nach wie vor muß sich das BMZ die Zuständigkeit auf dem Gebiet der Entwicklungspolitik vor allem mit drei mächtigen Partnern teilen, dem Außen-, dem Wirtschafts- und dem Finanzministerium. Seit einiger Zeit ist zudem eine deutliche Kompetenzerosion des BMZ zu beobachten, so daß die seit seiner Gründung nicht verstummende Diskussion, das BMZ institutionell als eigenständiges Ministerium aufzulösen, wieder verstärkt geführt wird (vgl. Stockmann 1990: 39ff.).

dungshilfen für die Auswahl, Planung und Durchführung ähnlicher Projekte in der Zukunft dienen: „Hierdurch sollen eine ständige Verbesserung der Qualität deutscher Entwicklungsprojekte erreicht und entwicklungspolitische Fehlschläge auf ein Minimum reduziert werden" (BMZ 1998: 44).

Seit Gründung des Evaluationsreferats wurden zwar etwa 1.000 Evaluierungen durchgeführt, doch dies entspricht nur einem Anteil von rund einem Prozent aller Projekte. Bei den BMZ-Evaluationen[6], früher Inspektionen genannt, handelte es sich in der Regel um Verlaufskontrollen, die aus den unterschiedlichsten Gründen durchgeführt wurden. Auslöser konnten akute Probleme bei der Durchführung sein, Fragen der Projektfortführung, lange Laufzeiten, hohes Mittelvolumen, Komplexität des Vorhabens, Besonderheiten des Projektansatzes oder sein Modell- oder Pilotcharakter. Projektabschlußkontrollen waren und sind hingegen selten und Ex-post-Evaluationen werden fast gar nicht durchgeführt[7]. Gemessen an den seit 1989 erfolgten Evaluationen bezogen sich 85% auf die Technische Zusammenarbeit und nur 15% auf die Finanzielle Zusammenarbeit. Begründet wird dieses Mißverhältnis durch das bei der KfW weiterentwickelte Evaluationssystem (vgl. Borrmann 1998: 68). 70% der Evaluationen beziehen sich auf einzelne Projekte, 16% auf Programme. Daneben werden auch sogenannte Querschnittsevaluationen durchgeführt, die sich auf Sektoren, Länder, Institutionen, Themen sowie Instrumente und Verfahren der EZ beziehen. Die jährlich rund 50 Einzelevaluationen des BMZ werden in einer Jahresquerschnittsanalyse metaevaluiert. Die dadurch gewonnenen Ergebnisse sind jedoch keineswegs repräsentativ, da die Auswahl weder dem Zufallsprinzip noch anderen klaren Kriterien folgt.

Insgesamt betrachtet, nimmt die Evaluation im BMZ trotz wechselnder Regierungen und Minister einen untergeordneten Stellenwert ein. Dies läßt sich unter anderem daran erkennen, daß das zuständige Referat nie seine anfangs vorgesehene Sollstärke von neun Mitarbeitern erreichte. Mit durchschnittlich vier Mitarbeitern weist das Referat gerade mal die Personalstärke seines Schweizer Pendants auf, obwohl die staatlichen Entwicklungshilfeleistungen der Schweiz mit ca. einer Milliarde US $ rund acht Mal niedriger liegen als die der BRD (vgl. Hoebink 1998: 80-82). Zudem konnte das BMZ-Referat seinen Status als Stabsstelle nicht aufrecht erhalten, was seine Unabhängigkeit stark einschränkt. Auch die Finanzmittel, die für „Zentrale Erfolgskontrolle" zur Verfügung stehen, sind äußerst gering. Der Budgettitel beträgt nur 1,8 Millionen DM. Hinzu kommen noch rund fünf Millionen DM aus anderen Titeln. Damit wendet das BMZ, bezogen auf die bilaterale EZ gerade mal ein Promille für Evaluation auf.

---

6   Der Zeitaufwand für eine BMZ-Evaluation beträgt ca. 30 Tage (davon rund 2 Wochen Feldaufenthalt) pro Gutachter. Der Berichtskoordinator erhält einige zusätzliche Tage (vgl. BMZ 2000: 3).

7   Eine seltene Ausnahme war die Ex-post-Evaluation von zwei Berufsbildungsprojekten. Vgl. Stockmann und Resch (1990 a & b).

Zwar wird zu recht darauf verwiesen, daß das BMZ den größten Teil der Erfolgskontrolle auf die Durchführungsorganisationen verlagert hat, doch damit gibt das BMZ ein zentrales Instrument an die Organisationen ab, deren Arbeit sie eigentlich steuern, koordinieren und kontrollieren soll.

2.2 Die Deutsche Gesellschaft für Technische Zusammenarbeit (GTZ)

Für die GTZ sind Evaluationen Teil ihres Qualitäts-Managementsystems[8] und werden vor allem durch die operativen Einheiten selbst – oft mit externer Unterstützung – durchgeführt.[9] Hierfür hat die GTZ ein umfassendes Evaluationssystem aufgebaut, das bisher stark mit der Methode der Zielorientierten Projektplanung (ZOPP) verknüpft war.[10] Dabei werden Oberziel, Projektziele, Ergebnisse, Aktivitäten und Indikatoren säuberlich voneinander getrennt, Indikatoren definiert sowie Annahmen und Risiken spezifiziert und zuletzt schließlich in eine Projektplanungsübersicht (PPÜ)[11] gegossen. Diese bildet die wesentlichen Elemente des Plans und ihre Beziehungen zueinander ab (vgl. GTZ 1997).

In den Planungsprozeß sind Feasibility-Studien eingebunden, die als exante Evaluationen gelten können. Die Projektplanungsübersicht bildet nicht nur den Orientierungsrahmen für die Projektsteuerung, sondern sie ist auch handlungsleitend für das M+E-System der GTZ. Das projektinterne Monitoring ist daran ausgerichtet und bildet die Grundlage für die in der Regel jährlich zu erstellenden Projektfortschrittsberichte (vgl. GTZ 1997b: 12). Diese wurden in ihrer Struktur mehrfach verändert. Doch allen Mustern ist gemeinsam, daß sie stark auf einen Soll-Ist-Vergleich ausgerichtet sind und kaum Projektwirkungen thematisieren. Dies rührt vor allem daher, daß die GTZ stark Input-Output-orientiert war und bisher in ihren Projekten kaum wirkungs- oder gar nachhaltigkeitsbezogene Monitoring-Systeme etabliert hat. (Vgl. Übersicht 1).

Dies galt bis 1999 auch für die wichtigste Evaluationsform der GTZ, die Projektsfortschrittskontrolle (PFK)[12], die eine systematische Überprüfung der Planung und Durchführung leisten soll, um dem verantwortlichen Projektmanagement handlungsorientierte Empfehlungen für die Zielerreichung bereitzustellen. D.h., auch PFK waren stark am Soll-Ist orientiert. Planungsvorgaben wurden mit der Projektrealität verglichen. Differenzen mußten erklärt werden. Der Erfolg eines Projekts wurde vor allem danach bemessen, inwie-

---

8   Zum Qualitätsmanagementsystem der GTZ vgl. Preuss/Steigerwald (1996), Donner (1998), Donner/Steigerwald (1998), Steigerwald/Rapp (1998).
9   Auf die Etablierung einer hausinternen, „unabhängigen" Evaluationseinheit wird in Kap. 4 eingegangen.
10   Zur Bewertung von ZOPP vgl. u.a. Kohnert (1998).
11   Orientiert sich am Logical Frame Work Ansatz aus den USA.
12   Für eine PFK werden in der Regel insgesamt 30-50 Fachtage vorgesehen. Der Kostenumfang bewegt sich je nach Fragestellung zwischen 40 und 100 Tausend DM. (Quelle: GTZ).

weit die Planungsvorgaben eingehalten wurden. Die entwicklungspolitischen Wirkungen stellten bisher in den GTZ-Leitfäden zur PFK kein Prüfungsthema dar. Diese Aufgabe war – gemäß dem Leitfaden – dem BMZ vorbehalten[13]. Im Zuge der Dezentralisierung der GTZ wurde das Verfahren grundlegend überarbeitet. Neuerdings soll der sogenannte „Soll-Ist-Vergleich" zwar immer noch durchgeführt werden, doch das Hauptaugenmerk richtet sich jetzt auf die „Leistungen und Entwicklungswirkungen des Vorhabens" (GTZ 1999: 5). Dabei soll sowohl der deutsche Beitrag als auch der Veränderungsprozeß beim Partner und den Zielgruppen betrachtet werden.

Projekte werden in der Regel mit einem Schlußbericht abgeschlossen, für den es allerdings keine bestimmte Form gibt. Ex-post Evaluationen hat die GTZ bisher kaum durchgeführt[14].

Übersicht 1: Monitoring- und Evaluationsinstrumente der Deutschen Gesellschaft für Technische Zusammenarbeit (GTZ)

Eingesetzte Instrumente	Zweck	Zeitpunkt	intern/ extern	Turnus	Erstellungs- ort
Projektfort- schrittsbericht (PFB)	stellt fest, ob: – die Aktivitäten auftragsge- mäß durchgeführt werden u. zu den vorgesehenen Ergebnissen führen, – die Zwischenergebnisse in der aktuellen Förderphase voraussichtlich erreicht werden, – Anpassungen der Planung erforderlich sind, – Ergänzungen bzw. Ände- rungen erforderlich sind.	während der Durchfüh- rung	intern (durch Ansprech- partner)	jährlich	vor Ort erstellt
Projektfort- schrittskontrolle (PFK)	Soll die Wirksamkeit der Pro- jektarbeit erfassen, unter ent- wicklungspolitischen und fach- lichen Aspekten beurteilen u. ggf. Maßnahmen zu ihrer Ver- besserung empfehlen.	während der Durchfüh- rung	intern/ extern	unregelmä- ßig, mit mehrjähri- gem Ab- stand	mit Vor-Ort- Besuch ver- bunden
Schlußbericht	nicht genau definiert	Ende Förde- rung (Ausreise des letzten Langzeitex- perten)	intern	1 x	teilweise mit Vor-Ort-Be- such verbun- den, teilweise nur Akten- studium

---

13 Daneben führt die GTZ noch sogenannte Projekt-Verlaufskontrollen durch (PVK), die jedoch keine formalisierte Form der Evaluierung darstellen und in der Regel im Zusammenhang mit Dienstreisen durchgeführt werden.

14 Die erste und bisher einzige umfassende Ex-post Analyse wurde im Bereich der Berufsbildung durchgeführt. Vgl. Stockmann/Resch (1991 a, b, c, d; 1992 a, b, c, d); Stockmann (1993, 1996, 1997, 1998).

2.3 Die Kreditanstalt für Wiederaufbau (KfW)

Im Unterschied zur GTZ fördert die Kreditanstalt für Wiederaufbau (KfW) vorrangig Investitionen und unterstützt Projekte und Programme nicht mit eigenem Personal vor Ort. Die von der KfW finanzierten Lieferungen und Leistungen werden in der Regel von Privatfirmen im Auftrag einheimischer Träger erbracht.

Die KfW verfügt über ein weitreichendes Qualitätssicherungssystem, das vor allem auf interne Evaluationen aufbaut. Die Hauptverantwortung dafür liegt bei den operativen Länderabteilungen. Diese werden vom sogenannten „Auslandssekretariat" (AS), dem „ASa", das u.a. für Grundsatzfragen und dem „ASb", das u.a. für Evaluierungsmethoden in der FZ zuständig ist, unterstützt. Ein von den operativen Abteilungen unabhängiges Referat (wie im BMZ oder der GTZ) existierte bisher in der KfW nicht. [15] Da keine strikte Trennung von Kontrolle und Durchführung möglich ist, kann die KfW weder genaue Aufgaben zu den personellen Ressourcen machen, noch weiß sie, wie hoch sich die finanziellen Mittel belaufen, die für Evaluation eingesetzt werden.

Das Evaluationssystem der KfW umfaßt den gesamten Projektzyklus[16]. Am Anfang werden Feasibility-Studien (ex-ante Evaluationen) durchgeführt, um die Projektkonzeption zu entwickeln. Während der Durchführung kontrolliert die KfW die Mittelverwendung sowohl anhand der mit den Mittelabrufen eingereichten Belege als auch anhand detaillierter Fortschrittsberichte des Projektträgers. Dieser soll die KfW auch außerhalb des üblichen Berichterstattungsrhythmus' unverzüglich über alle Probleme unterrichten, die die Durchführung, den Betrieb und die nachhaltige entwicklungspolitische Wirksamkeit eines Vorhabens wesentlich beeinträchtigen oder gefährden. Zudem führt die KfW in regelmäßigen Zeitabständen selbst örtliche Fortschrittskontrollen durch. Damit wird das Ziel verfolgt, den Durchführungsstand des Vorhabens festzustellen und Veränderungen im Projektumfeld (insbesondere innerhalb des Fördersektors und beim Projektträger) und Abweichungen von der Projektkonzeption daraufhin zu prüfen, welchen Einfluß sie auf den Projekterfolg haben. Über die Fortschrittskontrollen fertigt die KfW Berichte mit Handlungsempfehlungen an, die an das BMZ weitergeleitet werden. (Vgl. Übersicht 2)

Nach dem Ende der Investitionsphase (Abschluß der Auszahlungen) unterzieht die KfW die Projekte einer „Abschlußkontrolle" und erstellt einen Abschlußkontrollbericht. Dabei wird in erster Linie untersucht, ob es Kostenabweichungen und Zeitverzögerungen bei der Projektabwicklung gab und welche Ursachen dazu führten. Die Abschlußkontrollberichte werden entweder allein auf der Grundlage vorhandener Berichte gemäß Aktenlage erarbeitet oder sind

---

15 Auf die Gründung einer hausinternen, „unabhängigen" Evaluierungseinheit wird in Kap. 4 eingegangen.

16 Zum Evaluationssystem der KfW vgl. auch Kary (1992), Polte (1992), Kroh (1993), Raschen (1998).

mit Vor-Ort-Besuchen verbunden. Vor-Ort-Besuche sind hierfür nicht zwingend vorgeschrieben, aber nach Aussage der KfW die Regel. Für Abschlußkontrollen können KfW-Mitarbeiter, Mitarbeiter der Treuarbeit[17] und gegebenenfalls auch externe Gutachter jeweils allein oder im Team eingesetzt werden. Der weitere Projektverlauf (nach Ablauf der Auszahlungen) wird von der KfW weiterhin mit einem Monitoring-System überprüft. Zeichnen sich Probleme ab, werden diese gemeinsam mit dem Projektträger analysiert und zu lösen versucht (vgl. KfW 1996a: 98; Stockmann/Caspari 1998: 116).

Übersicht 2: Monitoring- und Evaluationsinstrumente der Kreditanstalt für Wiederaufbau (KFW)

Eingesetzte Instrumente:	Zweck:	Zeitpunkt:	intern/ extern:	Turnus	Erstellungs- ort
Fortschrittsberichte des Projektträgers	Informiert über alle Probleme, die die Durchführung, den Betrieb und die nachhaltige entwicklungspolitische Wirksamkeit eines Vorhabens wesentlich beeinträchtigen oder gefährden.	während der Durchführung	intern	viertel- bis halbjährlich	vor Ort erstellt
Fortschrittskontrollen (FK)	Durchführungsstand des Vorhabens feststellen und Veränderungen im Projektfeld (insb. innerhalb des Fördersektors u. beim Träger) u. Abweichungen von der Projektkonzeption daraufhin prüfen, welchen Einfluß sie auf den Projekterfolg haben. Handlungsempfehlungen formulieren.	während der Durchführung	intern	jährlich (letzte FK ein Jahr vor Ende Projektdurchführung)	in der Regel mit Vor-Ort-Besuch verbunden
Abschlußkontrolle*	Untersucht Kostenabweichungen und Zeitverzögerungen bei der Projektabwicklung und die Ursachen dafür, Mittelverwendungsprüfung.	Ende der Investitionsphase (Abschluß der Auszahlungen)	intern/extern (KfW, Treuarbeit, ggf. externe Gutachter)	1 x	in der Regel mit Vor-Ort-Besuch verbunden
Schlußprüfung* (Ex-post-Kontrolle)	Abschließende Bewertung Zielerreichung, entwicklungspolitische Wirksamkeit, Nachhaltigkeit.	drei bis fünf (bis zu zehn) Jahre nach Inbetriebnahme einer Investition	intern/extern (zu zwei Drittel ohne externe Beteiligung)	1 x	mit Vor-Ort-Besuch verbunden

* gelegentlich zusammen durchgeführt

Das Instrument der Ex-post Evaluation setzt die KfW ein, um eine abschließende Bewertung der Wirkungen und der Nachhaltigkeit vornehmen zu können. Der Evaluationszeitpunkt kann drei bis fünf, manchmal sogar acht bis zehn Jahre nach Inbetriebnahme einer Investition liegen, d.h. die Evaluation erfolgt zu einem Zeitpunkt, zu dem Anlaufschwierigkeiten überwunden oder

---

17 Die Treuarbeit heißt mittlerweile „Price Waterhouse Coopers Dt. Revision" (PWC)

weitere Unterstützungsmaßnahmen zur Beseitigung aufgetretener Probleme nicht mehr aussichtsreich sind. Diese „Schlußprüfungen" werden von der KfW durchgeführt, „um die Zielerreichung sowie generell die entwicklungspolitischen Wirkungen des Vorhabens und damit den Projekterfolg festzustellen. Außerdem sollen die Voraussetzungen für die Nachhaltigkeit des Vorhabens beurteilt werden" (KfW 1996a: 98). Die Ergebnisse der Schlußprüfungen werden mit den Partnern vor Ort diskutiert und systematisch ausgewertet, „um sie für die laufende Projektarbeit nutzen zu können" (ebenda). Auf die methodische Vorgehensweise wird später eingegangen[18].

3. Evaluationsdefizite in der EZ

3.1 Unzureichende Wirkungs- und Nachhaltigkeitsorientierung

Ein wesentliches Defizit im Evaluationsbereich der deutschen EZ ist darin zu sehen, daß der Wirksamkeit oder gar Nachhaltigkeit von Projekten oder Programmen zu wenig Beachtung geschenkt wird. Dies scheint auch bei anderen Gebern ein Problem darzustellen. „(...) there is often very extensive monitoring of foreign aided projects during the period of implementation, but there is much less evaluation of how well projects operate, how effectively they are sustained, and to what extend they produce the intended impacts" (Bamberger 1991: 3). Hierfür können eine Reihe von Gründen verantwortlich gemacht werden:

Über Jahrzehnte hinweg konzentrierten sich die Evaluationen der Geber in der EZ auf die Planung und Steuerung laufender Projekte. Besonders ausgeprägt war diese Entwicklung in der GTZ, die die Methode des Logical Framework Anfang der 80er Jahre zur sogenannten Zielorientierten Projekt Planung (ZOPP) weiterentwickelte und darauf vertraute, daß eine „gute" Planung zu wirkungsvollen Projekten führen würde. Mit dieser planungsfixierten Perspektive war lange Zeit auch eine stark Input-Output orientierte Betrachtungsweise verbunden. Ausgerichtet an einer Projekt-Planungsübersicht (PPÜ) wurden vor allem Soll-Ist-Vergleiche vorgenommen, um den Erfolg der EZ zu belegen. Dieser wurde vor allem an der Zielerreichung und der Verwirklichung der vorher festgelegten Ergebnisse gemessen. Dies führte dazu, daß die Wirkungen vernachlässigt wurden – sowohl die intendierten, als auch die nicht-intendierten.

Eine solche Betrachtungsweise, die im wesentlichen das geplante „Soll" mit dem erreichten „Ist" vergleicht und dem eingesetzten Input den erzielten Output gegenüberstellt, greift zu kurz, weil die entstandenen Wirkungen unberücksichtigt bleiben. Doch diese sind letztendlich entscheidend für eine

---

18 Der Zeitaufwand für eine „normale" Schlußprüfung liegt bei ca. 5 Wochen (inklusive 10 Tage Feldaufenthalt) für einen Gutachter. Hinzu kommen noch Arbeitstage interner Stellen. Insgesamt werden rund 7 Wochen Arbeitszeit veranschlagt. (Quelle: KfW).

entwicklungspolitische Erfolgsbeurteilung. Dies wird schnell an einem Beispiel deutlich: Wenn der Erfolg einer Maßnahme nur am Input festgemacht wird, also z. B. an den finanziellen Aufwendungen für den Bau einer Straße oder den Aufbau eines Krankenhauses, oder wenn der Erfolg nur mit Hilfe von Outputindikatoren gemessen wird, wie z.b. in Metern fertiggestellter Straße oder der Anzahl neu geschaffener Krankenhausbetten, dann bleibt offen, welche *Wirkungen* entstanden sind. Also, wer auf der Straße fährt, welche Folgen für die Umwelt eingetreten sind, wer die Betten des Krankenhauses nutzt, wer die Kosten dafür zahlen kann etc. Doch dies sind die entscheidenden Fragen, die Auskunft über die Wirksamkeit und damit den entwicklungspolitischen Erfolg einer Maßnahme geben.

In den letzten Jahren ist zwar eine verstärkte Thematisierung von Wirkungs- und Nachhaltigkeitsfragen im BMZ und seinen Durchführungsorganisationen festzustellen. Das BMZ hat in sein neues Evaluationsraster (vgl. BMZ 1998) eine Reihe von Wirkungsfragen aufgenommen und will künftig auch Ex-post-Evaluationen einen erhöhten Stellenwert einräumen, hat aber bis 1998, mit einer Ausnahme[19], keine Nachhaltigkeitsuntersuchungen durchgeführt. Nur bei der KfW waren bisher ex-post durchgeführte Wirkungsanalysen in das Evaluationssystem integriert. Dies ist insoweit erstaunlich, als die Entwicklungspolitik vorgibt, an nachhaltigen Lösungen interessiert zu sein. So hat eine um die Jahreswende 1997/98 durchgeführte Führungskräftebefragung bei BMZ und GTZ mit großer Einmütigkeit ergeben, daß Evaluation prozeßhaft betrachtet wird und eine kontinuierliche Wirkungsbeobachtung beinhalten muß. Deshalb wurde nicht nur dafür plädiert, die Wirkungsevaluation während der Projekt- bzw. Programmdurchführung zu intensivieren, sondern auch auf die Zeit nach dem Förderende auszudehnen, um festzustellen, ob nachhaltige Strukturwirkungen erzielt werden konnten und um für die Zukunft zu lernen (vgl. Stockmann/Caspari 1998: 18).

Immer wieder wurde in den Interviews darauf verwiesen, daß der Gebereinfluß während der Förderzeit sehr stark ist und den Partner dazu verleiten kann, eigene Interessen zurückzustellen und Ziele zu akzeptieren, die er eigentlich gar nicht verfolgen möchte, „damit der Geldstrom nicht abreißt" (BMZ-Interview). Auch der personelle Input der deutschen Experten dürfe nicht unterschätzt werden. Erst wenn der Partner nach dem Förderende auf sich allein gestellt ist, – „wenn der Kleister des deutschen Geldes und die persönliche Präsenz des Projektleiters nicht mehr vorhanden sind" (BMZ-Interview) – dann zeigt sich, ob dauerhafte Strukturen geschaffen wurden, die Trägerstrukturen zusammenwirken und die Ziele akzeptiert sind: „Nur langfristig kann festgestellt werden, inwieweit sich der deutsche Beitrag mit dem des Partners mischt" (BMZ-Interview).

Alle Befragten waren der Auffassung, daß die Erfahrungen aus abgeschlossenen Projekten „nicht Schnee von gestern sind", sondern wertvolle

---

19 Vgl. Stockmann/Resch (1990a & b).

Informationen für die Neugestaltung von Konzepten, Programmen und Projekten darstellen. Dabei wurde auch betont, daß viele Projekte genügend Ähnlichkeiten aufweisen, um Erfahrungen generalisieren zu können.

3.2.1 Mangelhaftes Methodeninstrumentarium

3.2.1.1 Regelinstrumente
Die vom BMZ in Auftrag gegebenen Evaluationen werden mit einem Evaluierungsraster durchgeführt, das mehrfach modernisiert und 1998 erneut überarbeitet wurde. Im Gegensatz zu früher ist dieses Raster nunmehr weitaus detaillierter gegliedert. Zwar wird noch immer schwerpunktmäßig die Projektzielerreichung geprüft (Ist-Abweichungen vom Soll sind zu erklären, aber den entwicklungspolitischen Wirkungen und der Signifikanz eines Vorhabens wird erhöhte Aufmerksamkeit geschenkt (vgl. BMZ 1996, 1998). Das Evaluationsraster ist als Berichtsgliederung verbindlich vorgegeben. Da es allerdings auch auf die jeweilige Themenstellung einer Evaluierung hin ausgerichtet werden soll, sind begründete Modifikationen erlaubt.

Neu ist auch der „Leitfaden zur Durchführung von BMZ-Evaluierungen" (BMZ 2000), der allerdings keine Erläuterung des Evaluationsinstruments darstellt, sondern lediglich allgemeine Ausführungen zum Ziel und Zweck von BMZ-Evaluierungen enthält sowie die organisatorische Vorgehensweise aufzeigt (Gutachterauswahl, vertragliche Vereinbarungen, Vorbereitung der Gutachter, Partnerbeteiligung etc.). Ein Fortschritt gegenüber früher ist immerhin, daß die Gutachter sich im Rahmen eines sogenannten „Inception Reports" vor ihrer Ausreise zur beabsichtigten Vorgehensweise und Methodik äußern sollen. Zur Verbesserung der häufig unzureichenden Datenlage können die Gutachter sogar vorab Fragenkataloge in ein Partnerland verschicken, die dort verteilt und ausgefüllt werden sollen. In Einzelfällen sind zukünftig sogar Reisen zur Vorbereitung von Datenerhebungen möglich. Vergleichbare Anforderungen oder Möglichkeiten sind bei KfW und GTZ nicht zu finden. (Vgl. BMZ 2000: 4)

Bewertend ist festzuhalten, daß das Raster weiterhin als „Check-Liste" verstanden wird, von der abgewichen werden kann. Einheitliche und bindende Begriffsdefinitionen oder gar Meßindikatoren, Bewertungsmaßstäbe und Qualitätsstandards oder methodische Orientierungshilfen werden nicht mitgeliefert. Auch spezielle Analyseraster für einzelne Förderbereiche und Projekttypen gibt es nicht. Die zur Datenerhebung bemessene Zeit ist kurz. In der Regel wird eine Evaluation von zwei Personen in zwei Wochen vor Ort durchgeführt.

Inwieweit die gewählten methodischen Möglichkeiten von den Gutachtern genutzt werden, wird in hohem Maße davon abhängen, ob das BMZ künftig erhöhte Ansprüche an Evaluationsdesign, Instrumenteneinsatz und Datenerhebungsverfahren auch durchsetzt, oder ob die bisherige Evaluationspraxis weitgehend beibehalten wird, die sich zumeist in Aktenanalysen und im Führen von Gesprächen mit Programmverantwortlichen auf verschiedenen Steuerungsebenen erschöpfte. Dabei wurden in der Regel keine strukturierten Auswertungs- bzw. Interviewleitfäden genutzt oder gar standardisierte Interviews durchgeführt. Zielgruppenbefragungen wurden in der Regel nicht vorgenommen, so daß die Perspektive der Betroffenen oder potentiellen Nutznießer nur sehr vermittelt erfaßt wurde. Ein breites Spektrum der Methoden der empirischen Sozialforschung kam bisher nicht zur Anwendung. In einer vom BMZ selbst in Auftrag gegebenen Studie zur Analyse und Bewertung des Systems der Erfolgskontrolle in der deutschen EZ werden den Gutachtern „unzureichende oder gänzlich fehlende methodische Anstrengungen" attestiert (Borrmann 1998: 71). Oft spiegeln die Evaluationen nicht belegte und deshalb intersubjektiv auch nicht nachvollziehbare persönliche Urteile der Gutachter wider, die mehr intuitiven Eingaben als empirisch überprüften Fakten folgen. Dabei dürften die stark subjektiv geprägten Urteile in hohem Maße von der Erfahrung, Professionszugehörigkeit und den Wertvorstellungen der Gutachter abhängen und schon deshalb von Fall zu Fall stark variieren.

Die von der GTZ durchgeführten PFK orientieren sich – auch in der 1999 überarbeiteten Form des Instruments – an einer sehr allgemein gehaltenen Gliederung. Der neue Wegweiser für die PFK (GTZ 1999) enthält lediglich einige einführende Erläuterungen über den künftigen Zweck von PFK sowie eine Checkliste für die Vorbereitung und Durchführung der Kontrolle. Das methodische Vorgehen ist vollkommen freigestellt und die Gliederung des Berichts gibt nur wenige Stichworte vor, unter denen die Qualität der Planung und des Planungsprozesses, der Durchführungsstand sowie die erbrachten Leistungen und erzeugten Wirkungen erfaßt werden sollen.

Deshalb gilt die hier an der BMZ-Vorgehensweise geäußerte Kritik für die PFK der GTZ sogar noch in verstärktem Umfang. Es fehlen konkrete Handlungsanweisungen, einheitliche und bindende Begriffsdefinitionen, Qualitätsstandards und spezielle Analyseraster für einzelne Förderbereiche und Projekttypen.

Die hohe Bedeutung der PFK, die die GTZ selbst als „das wichtigste interne Evaluierungsinstrument" [20] bezeichnet, steht in krassem Gegensatz zur Gestaltung dieses Instruments. Während die GTZ ihren Projektmitarbeitern und Gutachtern für den Planungsbereich umgangreiche Hilfen an die Hand gibt und ein Monitoring-Leitfaden zumindest für einen ersten orientierenden Überblick sorgt (GTZ 1998), gibt es zu dem Bereich Evaluation keine Handreichungen oder praktische Leitfäden. Auch im hausinternen Weiterbildungsprogramm der GTZ ist dieses Mißverhältnis deutlich zu erkennen. Während es für den Planungsbereich reichhaltige Angebote gibt, wird der M+E-Bereich vernachlässigt.

Von diesem Problem sind nicht nur die deutschen Mitarbeiter betroffen, sondern in noch viel stärkerem Umfang die Partnerfachkräfte, die in Deutsch-

---

20 Kuby (GTZ-Team Interne Evaluierung): Vortrag im AK „Evaluation von Entwicklungspolitik" am 12. Mai 2000

land und vor Ort in Kurz- und Langzeitausbildungen aus- und weitergebildet werden. Technikbezogene und in den letzten Jahren zunehmend auch managementorientierte Angebote überwiegen. Selbst im Planungsbereich – vor allem in ZOPP-Methoden und Moderationstechniken – wurden Partnerkräfte fortgebildet, doch für den Aufbau und Betrieb von (insbesondere Wirkungs-) Monitoring-Systemen oder die Durchführung von Evaluationen gibt es nahezu keine Angebote. Vor dem Hintergrund der so häufig betonten Partnerschaftlichkeit fällt dieses Mißverhältnis besonders auf. Da Partnerkräfte in vielen Ländern für Evaluationen nicht ausreichend qualifiziert sind, übernehmen sie oft nur Hilfsarbeiten oder „ihre Funktion erschöpft sich in Reisebegleitung" (GTZ 1999: 14). In dem neu erstellten „Wegweiser für die Projektfortschrittskontrolle" (GTZ 1999) findet sich kein Hinweis wie in Zukunft die Partnerbeteiligung verbessert werden kann. Es bleibt deshalb zu befürchten, daß die GTZ zwar immer wieder betont, daß es sich um Projekte des Partners handelt zu denen sie einen Beitrag leistet, daß aber der Partner bei der Evaluation seiner Projekte nicht ausreichend aktiv mitwirken kann.

Da die GTZ bisher keine systematischen Wirkungskontrollen durchgeführt hat, versucht sie über schriftliche Befragungen die Wirksamkeit der von ihr unterstützten Projekte zu eruieren. Anhand eines standardisierten Fragebogens sollen die Projektverantwortlichen selbst gegen Förderende ihre Bewertungen abgeben.

Diese Form der Selbsteinschätzung stellt ohne Zweifel eine wichtige Informationsquelle dar, denn sie nutzt die Detailkenntnisse der verantwortlichen Mitarbeiter und bietet die Möglichkeit, die Erfahrungen aus den Projekten weiterzugeben. Dennoch reicht ein solches Verfahren schon wegen seiner Subjektivität allein nicht aus, um die Erfolge und die Wirksamkeit der GTZ-Arbeit beurteilen zu können. Daran ändern auch nachträglich durch externe Gutachter vorgenommene Plausibilitätsprüfungen nichts, die ebenfalls nur auf das Material zurückgreifen, das in der GTZ vorliegt.

Wie sehr die Selbsteinschätzung schwankt, wird schon daran deutlich (um nur ein Beispiel zu geben), daß in einem Jahr 50% der abgeschlossenen Vorhaben als „sehr erfolgreich" und 23% als „erfolgreich" eingestuft wurden, im darauffolgenden Jahr hingegen nur noch 37% der abgeschlossenen Vorhaben (Rückgang um 13%) als „sehr erfolgreich" und 35% als erfolgreich bewertet wurden. Kaum jemand wird glauben, daß diese Zahlensprünge auf Veränderungen in der empirischen Realität zurückzuführen sind. Sie sind vielmehr eine Folge der Subjektivität des Verfahrens. Angesichts der Tatsache, daß es sich um Projekte des Partners handelt, muß darüber hinaus erstaunen, daß dieser nicht in die Befragungsaktion mit einbezogen wurde. Um eine einseitige Sichtweise zu vermeiden, hätte dies allein schon ein wertvolles Korrektiv dargestellt.

Kern des methodischen Ansatzes der KfW bildet seit 1990 die sogenannte „Log Frame-Matrix", die eine ähnliche Logik aufweist wie die Projekt-Planungs-Übersicht (PPÜ) der GTZ. Für die Durchführung von Feasibility-Studien und Projektprüfungen wird ein allgemeiner Prüfungsleitfaden verwendet (vgl. KfW 1996b), der durch sektorspezifische Prüfungsleitfäden ergänzt wird (vgl. KfW 1994c, 1994e, 1996c, 1997f). Darüber hinaus gibt es für einige wenige Sektoren auch sogenannte „Kenndatenblätter", die als wichtige Hilfen zur Erhebung von Indikatoren für die in den Prüfleitfäden angesprochenen Fragestellungen dienen können.

Die eingesetzten Methoden umfassen vor allem ökonomische Verfahren wie Cost-Benefit-Analyse, interner Zinsfuß, Kapitalwertmethode, dynamische Gestaltungskostenrechung sowie die Berechnung der langfristigen Grenzkosten und der gesamtwirtschaftlichen Durchschnittskosten (vgl. Borrmann u.a. 1998: 235)[21]. Anders als die GTZ führt die KfW regelmäßig Ex-post Evaluationen (Schlußprüfungen) durch, für die in der Regel ein Aufenthalt im Partnerland von einer Woche vorgesehen ist. Methodisch wird so vorgegangen, daß im Rahmen eines Soll-Ist-Vergleichs ermittelt wird, inwieweit die Zielvorstellungen verwirklicht werden konnten und wo die Ursachen für Erfolge und Mißerfolge lagen. Am Ende eines Schlußprüfungsberichts nimmt die KfW eine Gesamtbewertung vor, indem sie das Projekt in eine von sechs Erfolgsstufen einordnet.

Als wichtigste „Kriterien" zur Erfolgseinstufung von EZ-Projekten nennt die KfW: Sektorale Rahmenbedingungen, Erreichung der Projektziele, betriebswirtschaftliche Wirkungen, gesamtwirtschaftliche Effekte, sozioökonomische und soziokulturelle Folgen, Umweltwirkungen und Nachhaltigkeit. Diese Bereiche sind jedoch z.T. so umfassend, daß sie nicht alle als „Erfolgskriterien" geeignet sind. Zudem liegen keine weiteren operationalisierten Indikatoren vor, so daß die Subjektivität der Einschätzung nur schwer zu begrenzen ist. Darüber hinaus ist nicht klar, wie die einzelnen Faktoren innerhalb einer Gesamtbeurteilung gewichtet werden. Da die Schlußprüfungen in der Regel durch einen Ökonomen und einen Ingenieur vorgenommen werden, kann der Verdacht nicht ausgeräumt werden, daß die ökonomischen und technischen Implikationen überbewertet und andere (soziale, politische, kulturelle und ökologische) Projektwirkungen nicht ausreichend erfaßt und gewürdigt werden. Auch die einer Wirtschaftsprüfungsgesellschaft überlassene Kontrolltätigkeit, gibt kaum Anlaß zu der Vermutung, daß diese auf nichtökonomische Faktoren besonders spezialisiert sei.

Hinzu kommt, daß es sich bei der KfW weitgehend um Eigenevaluationen handelt. Während die GTZ z.B. bei fast allen Projektfortschrittskontrollen mit dem Einsatz von Gutachtern für ein Korrektiv sorgt, werden die Schlußprüfungen der KfW zu über zwei Dritteln von den KfW-Experten selbst vorgenommen.

Als Fazit bleibt festzuhalten, daß die KfW im Unterschied zur GTZ im Rahmen ihrer Wirkungsbeobachtung zwar auf Ex-Post-Erhebungen zurück-

---

21 Die KfW nutzt mitunter die Möglichkeit im Vorfeld von Erfolgskontrollen über vor Ort durchgeführte Datenerhebungen (z.B. mit Befragungen) Informationen zu beschaffen.

greift; allerdings ist die dabei angewendete Methodik stark an ökonomischen Kriterien ausgerichtet.

3.2.2 Spezielle Wirkungsstudien

Um sich einen Überblick über das methodische Niveau speziell von Ex-post Evaluationen zu verschaffen, wurden für sämtliche von BMZ, GTZ und KfW (außer Schlußberichten) zur Verfügung gestellten Fallstudien eine Metaevaluation durchgeführt (vgl. Stockmann/Caspari 1998). Als „Kontrollgruppe" wurden einige Studien anderer Geber ausgewertet.

Übersicht 3: Bewertung der analysierten Studien im Überblick[*]

	Theoretische Konzeption	Untersu- chungs- design	Erhebungs- methoden	Breit angelegte Wirkungs- analyse	Wirkungs- indikatoren	Kausalitäts- problem
BMZ 1984	–	–	0	–	–	–
BMZ 1984[a]	–	–	–	–	–	–
BMZ 1994	–	–	–	–	–	–
BMZ 1995a	–	–	0	–	–	0
BMZ 1995b	–	–	0	–	–	–
BMZ 1997	–	–	0	0	–	–
GTZ 1988[b]	0	–	+	0	0	0
GTZ 1995[c]	–	–	–	–	–	–
KfW 1994	–	–	0	–	0	–
KfW 1995	0	–	0	–	0	–
IOV 1994a	–	–	–	–	–	–
IOV 1994b	–	–	–	–	–	–
DEZA 1991/95[d]	+	+	+	+	+	+
OED 1989	+	+	+	+	+	+
OED 1994a	0	+	0	+	+	+
OED 1994b	0	+	0	0	+	0

Ergänzende Quellenangaben:
a Schubert/Agrarwal 1984; b Carls/Große-Rüschkamp 1988; c Lindauer/Raabe u.a. 1995; d INFRAS 1991 und INFRAS 1995.

---

[*]   Zu den einzelnen Kriterien:

	+	0	-
Theoretische Konzeption für Wirkungsanalyse geeignet:	Ja	Ansatzweise	Nein
Untersuchungsdesign für Wirkungsanalyse geeignet:	Ja	Ansatzweise	Nein
Erhebungsmethoden, d.h. Multimethodenansatz und nicht nur 1 bis 2 Erhebungsmethoden:	Mulitmetho- denansatz	Wenige, aber mehr als 2	Nur 1 bis 2
Breit angelegte Wirkungsanalyse, d.h. nicht nur Soll-Ist-Vergleich, sondern auch intendierte und nicht-intendierte Wirkungen erfaßt:	Ja	Ansatzweise	Nein
Wirkungsindikatoren, z.B. ökonomische, soziale, kulturelle, ökologische, geschlechtsspezifische etc.:	Mehrere	Wenige	Nur ökono- mische
Kausalitäsproblem angemessen behandelt	Ja	Ansatzweise	Nein

(*Quelle*: Stockmann & Caspari 1998: 71)

Übersicht 3 zeigt die Evaluationsergebnisse der analysierten Studien im Überblick. Die Beurteilungskriterien sind:

– Das zugrundeliegende Konzept: Liegt eine (theoretische) Analysekonzeption vor und ist diese für eine Wirkungsanalyse angemessen?
– Das Untersuchungsdesign: Wurde statistisch angemessen verfahren? Wurde eine Längs- oder eine Querschnittuntersuchung durchgeführt?
– Die Erhebungsmethoden: Wurde ein Multimethodenansatz gewählt, d.h. ein Mix aus verschiedenen Erhebungstechniken zur Absicherung der Daten, oder wurden lediglich Aktenanalysen und „Gespräche" durchgeführt?
– Die Wirkungsanalyse: Wurde die Wirkungsanalyse breit angelegt, d.h. auch nicht-intendierte Effekte erfaßt, oder wurde nur ein Soll-Ist-Vergleich durchgeführt?
– Die Wirkungsindikatoren: Wurden mehrere Indikatoren genutzt, wie z.B. soziale, kulturelle, ökologische und geschlechtsspezifische oder nur rein ökonomische?
– Das Kausalitätsproblem: Wurde die Kausalitätsfrage angemessen behandelt oder nicht?

Die Zuordnung der einzelnen Berichte wurde nur grob über drei „Beurteilungen" vorgenommen: ja, angemessen berücksichtigt (+); ansatzweise berücksichtigt (0); nein, nicht angemessen berücksichtigt (-). Die Tabelle stellt lediglich eine allgemeine Klassifikation der Berichte dar. Ziel ist, ein „Strukturbild" der analysierten Studien zu zeichnen. Insgesamt zeigt sich ein deutlicher Qualitätsunterschied zwischen den von der Weltbank und den von deutschen Geberorganisationen durchgeführten Evaluationsstudien. Im einzelnen ist zu beobachten, daß den wenigsten ein ausgearbeitetes Evaluationskonzept oder Untersuchungsdesign zugrunde liegt. Eine Ausnahme stellen die schweizerische DEZA und die Studien des Operations Evaluation Departments (OED) der Weltbank dar. Diese sind die einzigen Studien, in denen zumindest ein konzeptioneller Rahmen erarbeitet wird, der Hypothesen zuläßt, die eine Untersuchung leiten.

Aussagen zu einem Untersuchungsdesign, das zumindest die Wirkungsproblematik diskutiert und Anstrengungen unternimmt sie zu lösen, finden sich ebenfalls nur in diesen DEZA- und OED-Berichten. Längsschnittuntersuchungen sind eine Ausnahme.

Bezüglich der Evaluationsmethode ergibt die Analyse der vorliegenden Studien ein ähnliches Bild: Bei der überwiegenden Zahl von Berichten wird auf eine Darstellung der genutzten Methoden verzichtet. Nur wenige Berichte gehen wenigstens ansatzweise auf die Untersuchungsform und die Datenerhebungstechnik ein. Zumeist werden nur Schlagwörter wie „Aktenanalyse", „Gespräche", „Befragung" oder „Interviews" erwähnt. Unklar bleibt oft, ob es sich um „Gespräche im üblichen Verständnis" oder um Gespräche im Sinne von Intensivinterviews gehandelt hat. Auch wird nicht ersichtlich, ob die als „Befragungen" und als „Interviews" titulierten Verfahren anhand standardisierter Fragen durchgeführt wurden. Ausnahmen sind die Berichte des OED, die eine genauere Darstellung der Erhebungsmethoden beinhalten. Auch das hierbei zugrundeliegende Auswahlverfahren wird in kaum einem der Berichte angesprochen.

Ein weiteres Problem zeigt sich dahingehend, daß selten differenziert wird, ob es sich bei einer Untersuchung um eine „echte" Ex-post Evaluation handelt oder um eine Evaluation laufender Projekte/Programme. Trotzdem werden Aussagen über die Nachhaltigkeit der Interventionen gemacht, ohne allerdings zuvor eine Definition des Begriffes „Nachhaltigkeit" zu geben.

Ansonsten werden in den Berichten selten Indikatoren für die Messung der Effekte der Projektintervention aufgeführt – wenn überhaupt, wird lediglich auf ökonomische Daten zurückgegriffen. Auf nicht intendierte Effekte, die die untersuchten Projekte/Programme hervorgebracht haben könnten, wird überhaupt nicht eingegangen. Folglich werden in den analysierten Berichten weder die intendierten noch die nicht intendierten Effekte angemessen methodisch erhoben. Lediglich die bereits erwähnte OED-Studie (1989) führt detailliert alle relevanten – sowohl intendierten als auch nicht intendierten Effekte – auf.

Die Kausalitätsproblematik wird ebenfalls in den meisten Berichten nicht thematisiert. Problem hierbei ist die Tatsache, daß die intendierten Effekte oft nicht angemessen erhoben wurden bzw. die nicht-intendierten Effekte nicht berücksichtigt wurden. Werden solche Effekte nicht erfaßt, kann auch keine aussagekräftige Wirkungsanalyse durchgeführt werden. Trotzdem werden Kausalitätsaussagen getroffen, die dann notwendigerweise im Konjunktiv gehalten werden müssen. Lediglich bei der bereits erwähnten OED-Studie (1989) wurden Hauptkomponentenanalysen und Faktoranalysen durchgeführt, so daß angemessene Aussagen möglich waren. Die INFRAS-Berichte (1990, 1995) lassen ebenso anspruchsvolle Interdependenzanalysen vermuten. In nur wenigen Berichten wird erwähnt, daß eine Ursache-Wirkungs-Analyse schwierig möglich ist, sofern das untersuchte Projekt noch nicht abgeschlossen ist. Auch die Ursachenzuschreibung wird meist vorschnell vorgenommen. Zwar werden in den meisten Berichten die gesellschaftspolitischen Rahmenbedingungen beschrieben, Veränderungen werden jedoch meist auf die Projektintervention zurückgeführt, wobei aus den oben beschriebenen methodischen Gründen die Aussagen hierzu nur vage formuliert werden. Dies ist auch darauf zurückzuführen, daß in den wenigsten Berichten Begriffsbestimmungen erfolgen.

In den Fällen, in denen der Kausalitätsproblematik eine größere Bedeutung beigemessen wird, reduzieren die Autoren in den untersuchten Berichten ihre Ursache-Wirkungsanalyse auf einen einfachen Soll-Ist-Vergleich, dem dann lediglich ökonomische Wirkungsindikatoren zugrunde liegen.

Erwähnt werden muß an dieser Stelle, daß die Berichte selten Aussagen über die Finanzierung, die finanziellen Aufwendungen, die Dauer der Durchführung sowie die Anzahl der daran beteiligten Mitarbeiter enthalten. Somit fehlen Informationen, die eine Erklärung für die unterschiedliche Qualität der Studien liefern könnten. Im Grunde kann eine Untersuchung, für die nur ein sehr schmales Finanzvolumen bereitgestellt wurde, nicht mit einer Studie verglichen werden, für die hohe personelle und materielle Ressourcen zur Verfügung standen. Eine vom Finanz- und Zeitvolumen breiter ausgelegte Studie kann prinzipiell natürlich auch mehr Möglichkeiten nutzen. Ob dies dann auch geschieht, ist allerdings zu prüfen, denn eine kostenaufwendige Studie wird natürlich nicht automatisch zu einer „guten" Studie.

3.2 Fehlende Transparenz, Unabhängigkeit und Legitimität

Evaluationen in der EZ sind vor allem interne Evaluationen oder werden im Auftrag von Geberinstitutionen durchgeführt. Was Bamberger (1991: 237) für die U.S.-amerikanische Evaluationsliteratur feststellt, gilt deshalb auch für Deutschland: „Most of the literature relating to evaluation in developing countries is produced by, or for, donor agencies and is mainly concerned with the donor's perspective".

Hinzu kommt, daß die Geberorganisationen sehr restriktiv mit Evaluationsberichten umgehen. Aufgrund ihrer Monopolstellung kontrollieren sie die Datenzugänge, die für empirische Studien notwendig sind. Zwar werden viele Studien und Gutachten unter der Mitarbeit von Wissenschaftlern erstellt, doch da die Entwicklungshilfegeber die meisten Studien nicht freigeben, sind sie der wissenschaftlichen Diskussion weitgehend entzogen (vgl. auch Bamberger 1991: 325). Bis 1999 wurden die Evaluationsberichte des BMZ wie eine Geheimsache behandelt. Selbst die Mitglieder des für EZ zuständigen Parlamentsausschusses, des AWZ, durften die Berichte nicht einsehen. Bei GTZ und KfW sind nach wie vor die meisten Studien nicht öffentlich zugänglich.

Dies hat zum einen zur Folge, daß Ergebnisse nicht transparent gemacht werden, zum anderen führt die fehlende fachliche Kritik an den Evaluationen zu mangelnder Qualität. Während wissenschaftliche Studien einer professionellen Beurteilung standhalten müssen und Kritik zu einer Weiterentwicklung von Theorien und Methoden führt, kann sich ein solcher Prozeß im Evaluationsbereich der EZ nicht entfalten. Insoweit sind die konstatierten Evaluationsdefizite nicht zuletzt auch auf das Informationsverhalten der Geberorganisationen zurückzuführen.

Wie schlecht es um die Transparenz bei der Evaluation der EZ bis vor kurzem bestellt war, wird auch daran deutlich, daß selbst der Leiter des BMZ-Evaluierungsreferats erklärte: „Von anekdotischem und verstreutem Wissen abgesehen, ist leider viel zu wenig darüber bekannt, was die einzelnen Akteure[22] der deutschen EZ unter dem Stichwort Erfolgskontrolle treiben,

---

22 Mit Akteuren sind die Durchführungsorganisationen, Stiftungen, NGO etc. gemeint.

z.B. welche Ziele sie prioritär verfolgen, welche Inhalte und Verfahren sie entwickelt haben, welche Methoden sie anwenden, welche Mittel sie einsetzen u.s.w." (Breier 1998: 75). Deshalb gab das BMZ eine Studie in Auftrag, um die Erfolgskontrolle in der deutschen EZ zu durchleuchten (vgl. Borrmann u.a. 1999).

Neben einer eingeschränkten Transparenz ist auch eine weithin fehlende Unabhängigkeit der Evaluationen festzustellen. Das BMZ verfügt zwar über ein eigenes Evaluationsreferat, das jedoch noch nicht einmal als Stabsabteilung verankert ist und deshalb allenfalls eine eingeschränkte Unabhängigkeit besitzt. Das BMZ greift in großem Umfang auf externe Gutachter zurück, deren Unabhängigkeit auf dem relativ kleinen Evaluationsmarkt der EZ mit nur wenigen Auftraggebern zumindest gefährdet ist.

Das Evaluationssystem der GTZ beruht vor allem auf internen Evaluationen, die im wesentlichen von den operativen Abteilungen selbst durchgeführt werden. Die GTZ setzt für ihre Evaluationen jedoch in erheblichem Umfang auch externe Gutachter ein. So waren z.B. im Jahr 1996 an 239 durchgeführten Projektprüfungen 136 und im Rahmen von 299 PFK 212 externe Gutachter beteiligt. Für den Einsatz externer Gutachter wendet die GTZ seit 1993 jährlich zwischen sechs und neun Millionen DM auf (vgl. Borrmann u.a. 1998: 206). Gemessen an der jährlichen Auftragssumme der GTZ von rund 2 Milliarden DM stellt dies jedoch nur einen Anteil von durchschnittlich 0,37% dar.

Der Auftragsverantwortliche entscheidet, ob, wann und durch wen eine PFK durchgeführt wird (vgl. GTZ 1997h: 13). Dadurch werden die durch die Dezentralisierung der Auftragsverantwortung gestärkten Teamleiter vor Ort zunehmend „unabhängig" von der GTZ-Zentrale, dem BMZ und der Öffentlichkeit. Dieser Prozeß wird noch durch die zu beobachtende Praxis verstärkt, daß zunehmend GTZ-Mitarbeiter aus fachlichen „Nachbarprojekten" PFK durchführen, sich die GTZ-Mitarbeiter vor Ort also selbst evaluieren.

Eine von den operativen Einheiten getrennte Evaluierungseinheit wurde in der GTZ 1988 etabliert. Sie ist der Abteilung „Grundsatzfragen der Unternehmensentwicklung" untergeordnet, die der Geschäftsführung untersteht. Bisher war ihre personelle und materielle Ausstattung jedoch so gering, daß sie im gesamten M+E System der GTZ nur eine sehr begrenzte Wirkung entfalten konnte. Auf die Frage, inwieweit sich dies im Rahmen der Neuordnung des Evaluationssystems der staatlichen EZ zukünftig ändern soll, wird im folgenden Kapitel eingegangen.

Wie auch die GTZ veröffentlicht die KfW ihre Evaluationsberichte in der Regel nicht, da sie als interne Steuerungsinstrumente betrachtet werden. Da es sich bei den Schlußprüfungen der KfW jedoch um summative Evaluationen zur abschließenden Erfolgsbeurteilung handelt – und nach eigenem Bekunden nicht um ein Projektsteuerungsinstrument – ist erklärungsbedürftig, warum nicht wenigstens diese Berichte der Öffentlichkeit zugänglich gemacht werden. Dies gilt in noch stärkerem Maße für die ex-post durchgeführten Sektor- und Querschnittsanalysen. Dadurch könnte die Arbeit der KfW deutlich an Legitimität gewinnen.

Auch im Hinblick auf das Kriterium der Unabhängigkeit schneidet die KfW schlecht ab. Die KfW läßt nur wenige externe Evaluationen durchführen und beteiligt kaum externe Gutachter an ihren Evaluationen. Im Unterschied zu den PFK der GTZ werden die Fortschrittskontrollen der KfW ohne externe Gutachter durchgeführt. Zwar kann man anführen, daß vor Ort nicht die Leistung von KfW-eigenem Personal bewertet wird, sondern die Arbeit Dritter (Generalunternehmer oder Consultings), doch insgesamt wird selbstverständlich auch die Steuerungsleistung der KfW selbst beurteilt. Lediglich in den Schlußprüfungen sind unabhängige Gutachter involviert, allerding auch nur bei einem Drittel aller Schlußprüfungen.

Die Kritik an der „unzureichenden Unabhängigkeit" wurde in der KfW ernst genommen und soll noch in diesem Jahr (2000) zur Einrichtung einer vom „operativen Geschäft" unabhängigen Evaluierungseinheit führen, auf deren Funktion im folgenden Kapitel eingegangen wird.

4. Reformanstrengungen und Reformbedarf

Die umfangreiche Kritik an der Evaluationspraxis der staatlichen EZ, die vom DAC aufgestellten „Principles for Effective Aid" (OECD 1992), die jährlich erstellten DAC-Reports und auch die Forderungen des Deutschen Bundestages haben zu einer Reihe von Aktivitäten in den Förderorganisationen selbst und im wissenschaftlichen Umfeld geführt, um die genannten Evaluationsdefizite abzubauen:

1. Neue Evaluationskonzeption des BMZ
Die neue Evaluationskonzeption des BMZ geht von der Überlegung aus, daß der Charakter von Evaluationen als Managementinstrument sowie als Mittel zur Legitimierung der EZ zu stärken ist. Daraus folgt, daß der bisher vorherrschende, kleinteilige Ansatz, der sich durch die Evaluation einzelner Projekte auszeichnete, zugunsten eines strategischen Ansatzes überwunden werden soll. In Zukunft soll eine Evaluationskultur in der EZ entstehen. Evaluationen sollen zwar wie bisher an vielen verschiedenen Stellen stattfinden, jedoch in einer systematisch besser aufeinander angestimmten Form (vgl. Schaubild 1).

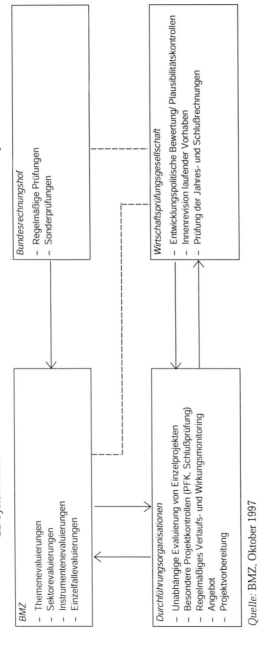

Schaubild 1: Neugliederung des Systems der Erfolgskontrolle der deutschen EZ

EZ-System intern

EZ-System extern

BMZ
– Themenevaluierungen
– Sektorevaluierungen
– Instrumentenevaluierungen
– Einzelfallevaluierungen

Bundesrechnungshof
– Regelmäßige Prüfungen
– Sonderprüfungen

Durchführungsorganisationen
– Unabhängige Evaluierung von Einzelprojekten
– Besondere Projektkontrollen (PFK, Schlußprüfung)
– Regelmäßiges Verlaufs- und Wirkungsmonitoring
– Angebot
– Projektvorbereitung

Wirtschaftsprüfungsgesellschaft
– Entwicklungspolitische Bewertung/ Plausibilitätskontrollen
– Innenrevision laufender Vorhaben
– Prüfung der Jahres- und Schlußrechnungen

Quelle: BMZ, Oktober 1997

Im Rahmen des internen EZ-Systems soll der Steuerungs- und Entscheidungsbedarf der projektführenden Referate durch Evaluationen gedeckt werden, die die Durchführungsorganisationen selbst durchführen. Das BMZ kann sich dann – derart entlastet – auf drei Hauptschwerpunkte konzentrieren:

a) *Thematische Evaluationen* sollen in enger Kooperation mit der Leitung konzipiert werden. Sie sollen Themen gewidmet sein, die aus der Sicht der BMZ-Führung von besonderer entwicklungspolitischer Bedeutung sind, z.B.
   – Wirkungskontrolle/ Nachhaltigkeit,
   – Umsetzung des Konzepts der Armutsorientierung,
   – Genderfragen,
   – Krisen- und Konfliktprävention.
b) *Sektor-Evaluationen* sind am Entscheidungs- und Entwicklungsbedarf orientiert. Die Evaluationsergebnisse sollen der Erarbeitung von sektorbezogenen Policy-Papieren dienen, die als Steuerungsinstrumente politische und sektorale Vorgaben formulieren, z.B. zur Energie, Grundbildung, Umwelt oder auch zur Bedeutung bilateraler Tropenwaldmaßnahmen.
c) *Instrumenten-Evaluationen* umfassen die Überprüfung und Bewertung von entwicklungspolitischen Instrumenten im weitesten Sinne, z.B.
   – Zusammenarbeit mit den Kirchen und politischen Stiftungen,
   – Regionaltitel für osteuropäische Länder und GUS-Staaten,
   – Sozial- und Investitionsfonds in Lateinamerika,
   – KfW-Begleitmaßnahmen,
   – Langzeitstipendienprogramm der DSE,
   – Handelsbezogene TZ-Aktivitäten.

Einzelfall-Evaluationen sollen nur noch in Ausnahmefällen durchgeführt werden, z.B.

– wenn ein Projekt von besonderer entwicklungspolitischer Bedeutung ist,
– wenn ein Projekt Modellcharakter für einen entwicklungspolitischen Ansatz oder Sektor hat,
– wenn es sich um eine „Feuerwehraktion" handelt.

Die Durchführungsorganisationen sollen *wie* bisher Evaluationen zur Planung und Durchführung von Projekten durchführen (z.B. Feasibility Studien, Monitoring, PFK, Schlußprüfung*), dabei aber die Wirkungsbeobachtung verstärken.* Die unabhängige Evaluation von Einzelprojekten, die bisher dem BMZ vorbehalten war, soll nun von den Durchführungsorganisationen selbst organisiert werden. Dabei sind die inhaltlichen Vorgaben des BMZ (Evaluierungs-Raster) und die DAC-Principles für Evaluation zu beachten.
   Damit eine gemeinsame Evaluationskultur wachsen kann, soll der Dialog zwischen allen Partnern der EZ intensiviert werden.
   Die strategische Ausrichtung des neuen Evaluationssystems soll einerseits dazu führen, die Legitimität der EZ zu erhöhen. Die traditionellen Jah-

resberichte, die über die EZ informieren, sollen auf eine solidere Grundlage
gestellt werden und sich stärker an thematischen Fragestellungen orientieren.
Andererseits soll dadurch das institutionelle Lernen im BMZ erleichtert werden, indem z.b. zweiseitige, besser beschriebene Kurzfassungen über die Ergebnisse einer Evaluation verbreitet werden, Fortbildungen und thematisch
ausgerichtete Workshops stattfinden.

Das externe EZ-Kontrollsystem (vgl. Schaubild 1) besteht vor allem (wie
bisher) aus den Aktivitäten des Bundesrechnungshofs. Zudem sollen zunehmend Wirtschaftsprüfungsgesellschaften eingebunden werden. Diese sollen
nicht nur die Prüfung von Jahres- und Schlußrechnungen und die Innenrevision laufender Vorhaben übernehmen, sondern auch (wie schon bei der KfW)
entwicklungspolitische Bewertungen und Plausibilitätskontrollen vornehmen.
Dieses Modell, das sich bei der KfW bewährt habe, soll nun auch die GTZ
übernehmen. Dabei soll allerdings noch getestet werden, inwieweit sich das
„KfW-Modell" auf andere Durchführungsorganisationen übertragen läßt.

Ex-post Analysen zur Untersuchung der Wirksamkeit der EZ sollen in
diesem veränderten Evaluationssystem der EZ eine deutliche Rolle spielen.
Im Kontext der vom BMZ durchgeführten Evaluationen soll das Instrument
insbesondere im Rahmen von Sektor- und Instrumenten-Untersuchungen
eingesetzt werden.

2. Gründung hausinterner Evaluationsstäbe bei GTZ und KfW

Die Kritik an der mangelnden Unabhängigkeit der Evaluation hat in der GTZ
zu der Etablierung einer internen, vom operativen Bereich getrennten Evaluationseinheit geführt, die mit sechs Fachkräften ausgestattet ist. Nach eigenem Selbstverständnis will die Einheit in der GTZ ein „center of competence
for evaluation" sein (GTZ-handout 2000). Zu den Hauptaufgaben der Stab-
stelle gehören,

- die Durchführung von Einzelprojekt-Evaluationen im Auftrag des BMZ,
  der Geschäftsführung oder anderer,
- das Controlling strategischer Projekte (wie z.B. der Dezentralisierungs-
  prozeß der GTZ, die Optimierung von Dienstleistungen, Personalentwicklung, Know-how-Management, Entwicklung eines Management-
  Informations-Systems, Private Public Partnership),
- die Durchführung der jährlich durchgeführten Querschnittsanalysen laufender und abgeschlossener TZ-Vorhaben,
- die Beratung von TZ-Vorhaben und GTZ-Organisationseinheiten,
- die Optimierung des GTZ-Evaluierungssystems durch die Weiterentwicklung von Verfahren, Methoden und Instrumenten,
- die Verbreitung von Evaluationsergebnissen und
- die Zusammenarbeit mit den Evaluationseinheiten anderer Geber und
  Durchführungsorganisationen (GTZ-internes Papier vom Juni 1999).

Ob sich diese Einheit tatsächlich zu einem Nukleus für die Evaluation in der GTZ entwickeln kann bleibt abzuwarten. Angesichts der Vielfalt der selbst gestellten Aufgaben, den genannten Problemen die sich im Rahmen der Dezentralisierung für die Qualitätssicherung der GTZ ergeben und dem massiven Übergewicht der weiterhin von den operativen Abteilungen durchgeführten Evaluationen scheint ein operatives Budget von 1,2 Mill. DM nur sehr begrenzte Aktivitäten zuzulassen.

Die KfW will eine Evaluierungseinheit einrichten, die direkt dem Vorstand unterstellt ist, so daß weitgehend interne Unabhängigkeit gegeben ist. Der neue Stab soll „sowohl dem Ziel der Rechenschaftslegung als auch dem des institutionellen Lernens Rechnung" tragen (KfW-internes Papier von Mai 2000). Das Problem, daß Rechenschaftslegung eine möglichst weitgehende Unabhängigkeit, das institutionelle Lernen demgegenüber eine möglichst enge Einbindung des verantwortlichen Personals impliziert, soll durch ein besonderes Modell gelöst werden. Vorgesehen ist, daß der feste Personalstamm von fünf Mitarbeitern (inkl. Abteilungsleiter) durch rotierende Abordnungen von Mitarbeitern aus dem Länderbereich für einzelne Prüfungsaufgaben und durch externe Experten ergänzt wird. Vorgegeben ist, daß die Evaluierungseinheit u.a.

– die Einzelevaluationen im Auftrag des BMZ koordiniert,
– nach und nach die ex-post durchgeführten Schlußprüfungen von den bisher zuständigen Länderabteilungen übernimmt,
– sektor- und themenübergreifende Querschnittsauswertungen vornimmt,
– Evaluationsverfahren und Instrumente weiterentwickelt und
– „alle anderen mit der Evaluierung verbundenen Aufgaben" übernimmt (ebenda).

3. Studie zur Erfolgskontrolle

Das BMZ hat eine Studie zur Bewertung der Erfolgskontrolle in der deutschen EZ durchführen lassen (Borrmann u.a. 1999), um Ansatzpunkte für eine Fortentwicklung einzuleiten. Hierzu wurden die vom BMZ, den staatlichen und nicht-staatlichen Institutionen der deutschen EZ praktizierten Erfolgskontrollen im Hinblick auf ihre Organisation, Konzeption, Methoden und Verfahren sowie Umfang und Struktur untersucht (ebenda: S. 13).

Die hier aufgezählten Defizite in der Wirkungsevaluation werden in der Studie nachdrücklich bestätigt:

„Wirkungs- und nachhaltigkeitsorientierte Erfolgskontrollen sind jedoch bei vielen EZ-Institutionen nicht oder nur in Ansätzen anzutreffen. Wirkungsmonitoring in der Verlaufsphase der Vorhaben ist oft nicht existent oder steckt in den Anfängen. Die größten Defizite bestehen bei den Ex-post-Kontrollen" (ebenda: 327).

4. BMZ – Wirkungsanalyse abgeschlossener Projekte

Das BMZ hat zum ersten Mal (!) in seiner Geschichte eine breit angelegte Wirkungsanalyse ex-post durchgeführt. Ziel der Studie ist es „empirisch abgesicherte Aussagen zur Nachhaltigkeit der bundesdeutschen Entwicklungszusammenarbeit zu gewinnen" (BMZ, Entwurf der QA vom Okt. 1999: 12). Hierzu wurden 32 Projekte in 19 Ländern aus vier Fördersektoren, nämlich Landwirtschaft (16), Wasser/Abwasser (10), Basisgesundheit (4) und Grundbildung (2) evaluiert.

Um der häufig geäußerten Kritik zu begegnen, daß das BMZ bei seinen Erfolgskontrollen bisher nur einen geringen methodischen Aufwand betreibt und seinen Gutachtern und Gutachterinnen zu viel methodische Freiräume läßt (vgl. Stockmann 1995: 255ff., 1996b, 1998a: 104ff., 1999:268ff.; Borrmann u.a. 1999: 69ff.), wurde für diese Ex-post-Evaluation ein wissenschaftlich unterstütztes Vorgehen gewählt. Es kam eine theoretisch und methodisch fundierte und bei zahlreichen Ex-post-Evaluationen bereits getestete Analysekonzeption zum Einsatz (vgl. Stockmann 1996a), die in einem Methodenworkshop an der Universität des Saarlandes im August 1998 an die Evaluationserfordernisse der vier Fördersektoren angepaßt wurde. Erst nach der Durchführung von vier Pretests, einem Auswertungsworkshop und einer methodischen Gutachterschulung wurde 1999 die eigentliche Feldphase durchgeführt. An der Erstellung des Ergebnisberichts wird derzeit gearbeitet.

5.   Arbeitskreis zur „Evaluation von Entwicklungspolitik" in der DeGEval

Der Arbeitskreis „Evaluation von Entwicklungspolitik"[23] wurde auf der ersten Jahrestagung der Deutschen Gesellschaft für Evaluation (DeGEval) im September 1998 konstituiert, um einen Beitrag zur Verbesserung der Evaluation in der Entwicklungszusammenarbeit zu leisten. Er stellt ein Forum dar, das allen mit der Evaluation von Entwicklungspolitik befaßten Personen und Institutionen (BMZ, Durchführungsorganisationen, NROs, Politische Stiftungen, Kirchen, Universitäten, Freie Gutachter) offensteht und einen regelmäßigen Erfahrungsaustausch über aktuelle Entwicklungen und Probleme ermöglicht. Dabei soll eine Brücke zwischen Politik, Theorie und Praxis geschlagen werden.

Aus der Diskussion unterschiedlicher Perspektiven soll ein dauerhafter Dialog entstehen, um miteinander und voneinander zu lernen, neue Denkanstöße zu vermitteln und um letztlich in der EZ eine neue Evaluationskultur entstehen zu lassen.

Die Evaluationsdiskussion soll sich deshalb keineswegs nur auf Methodenfragen konzentrieren, sondern sich selbstverständlich auch mit dem Evaluationskontext beschäftigen. D.h., dem Feld der Entwicklungspolitik und seinen spezifischen Bedingungen und Erfordernissen im Spannungsfeld von Zielgruppen, Partnerinstitutionen, Geberorganisationen, Evaluatoren, Förderprogrammen und internen und externen Strukturbedingungen, etc. Während der letzten Jahrestagung der DeGEval (September 1999) hat der AK über

---

23   Informationen zum AK erhalten Sie vom Arbeitskreissprecher Prof. Dr. Reinhard Stockmann, Lehrstuhl für Soziologie, Im Stadtwald, Postfach 15 11 50, 66041 Saarbrücken, email: r.stockmann@rz.uni-sb.de

seine Ziele und Aufgaben diskutiert, die zu einem Arbeitsprogramm verdichtet werden. Im einzelnen werden folgende Ziele angestrebt:

- Förderung des interinstitutionellen Lernens durch dauerhaften Dialog über die Erfahrungen in unterschiedlichen Handlungsfeldern.
- Beiträge zur Methodenentwicklung durch offene Diskussion über in Planung oder in Anwendung befindliche Konzeptionen und Austausch der jeweiligen Erfahrungen und Ergebnisse.
- Auf Grundlage der im gegenseitigen Austausch gewonnenen Erkenntnisse: Entwicklung praxisbezogener methodischer Handreichungen für Gutachter.
- Beiträge zur Fortbildung und Qualifizierung von Gutachtern, zunächst durch eine recherchierbare Zusammenfassung vorhandener Angebote, langfristig möglicherweise sogar durch eigenständige Organisation von Fortbildungsveranstaltungen.
- Entwicklung von Standards und Qualitätskriterien als professionelle Orientierungshilfe für entwicklungspolitische Gutachter.[24]

6. Vorschlag zur Gründung eines Zentrums für Evaluation
Die bisherigen Aktivitäten sind bei weitem noch nicht ausreichend, um die vielfältigen Aufgaben für eine Verbesserung der Qualitätskontrolle in der EZ, zu der vornehmlich auch die Evaluation entwicklungspolitischer Wirkungen zählt, zu bewältigen. Das BMZ kann die Koordinations- und Entwicklungsleistungen schon allein aus personellen Gründen nicht leisten. Die Durchführungsorganisationen sind zu sehr mit ihrer eigenen Arbeit beschäftigt und ihr Blickwinkel ist durch die jeweilige Besonderheit ihrer Aufgabenstellung eingeengt. Zudem fehlt den Durchführungsorganisationen, die in den DAC-Principles ausdrücklich geforderte Unabhängigkeit. Zur Methoden- und Instrumentenentwicklung und um das Problem einer unabhängigen Begutachtung zu lösen, wurde deshalb die Gründung eines Zentrums für Evaluation der EZ vorgeschlagen (vgl. Stockmann 1996b).

Dieses Institut sollte politisch und administrativ unabhängig sein (d.h. auch keiner Durchführungsorganisation organisatorisch angehören), um seine Aufgaben möglichst frei von politischem und administrativem Druck, objektiv und mit höchster Glaubwürdigkeit professionell ausführen zu können. Die Erarbeitung anwendungsbezogener Lösungen steht im Vordergrund. Deshalb

---

24 Um die inhaltliche Arbeit auch über die Plenarsitzungen hinaus zu vertiefen, hat der AK Arbeitsgruppen eingerichtet, die auch zwischen den Tagungsterminen aktiv sind und deren Ergebnisse in die inhaltliche Vorbereitung der Plenarsitzungen einfließen. Derzeit sind folgende Gruppen tätig: „Vergleich der Methodik von Wirkungsanalysen (auf der Grundlage von Leitfäden)" (Sprecher: Prof. Dr. Franz Thedieck, DSE), „Politische Bildung und ihre Evaluierung" (Sprecherin: Rita Krommen, Kolping-Institut), „Transparenz, Information und Follow-up von Evaluierungen" (Sprecherin: Dr. Petra Feil, Misereor).

soll das Zentrum eng mit allen deutschen Durchführungsorganisationen zusammenarbeiten. Dadurch würden nicht nur unnötige Doppel- und Mehr-
facharbeiten vermieden, sondern es könnten auch leichter einheitliche Standards (Definitionen, gemeinsame Beurteilungskriterien, Evaluationsverfahren
etc.) entwickelt werden. Das Institut soll keineswegs ein Monopol für Evaluationsfragen darstellen, sondern ein Nukleus, eine Art Informations- und
Entwicklungszentrum, in dem u.a.

- sektor-, programm- und fördertypspezifische Methoden und Instrumente
  unter Beachtung soziokultureller Aspekte anwendungsbezogen gemeinsam mit den Beteiligten erarbeitet werden,
- „best practices" der Organisationen gesammelt, ausgewertet und verar-
  beitet werden, um das „institutional learning" zu verbessern,
- Partnerinstitutionen in der Dritten Welt bei der Durchführung von Evaluationen sowie beim Aufbau von eigenen Evaluationsstellen und -abtei-
  lungen unterstützt werden,
- in und -ausländische Gutachter und Projektmitarbeiter in Monitoring-
  und Evaluationstechiken fortgebildet werden.

5. Bewertung des Reformprozesses und Zukunftsaufgaben

Das Evaluationssystem der staatlichen EZ steht zu Beginn des 21. Jahrhunderts vor einem durchgreifenden Wandel. BMZ, KfW und GTZ haben Reformen eingeleitet, die bisherige Schwächen überwinden sollen. Positiv zu
vermerken ist:

- die strategische Neuausrichtung des staatlichen Evaluationssystems
  durch das BMZ,
- die stärkere Orientierung der Erfolgsbeurteilung der EZ an Wirkungen,
  an langfristiger Wirksamkeit und Nachhaltigkeit,
- an dem Bemühen, die methodischen Standards zu verbessern und die
  Methodenvielfalt zu vergrößern,
- der Versuch, mehr Transparenz zu schaffen, mit allen Beteiligten in einen verstärkten Dialog zu treten und vorhandene Defizite offen zu diskutieren,
- die Umgestaltung der jeweiligen hausinternen Evaluationssysteme hin zu
  einer größeren Unabhängigkeit.

Diese Entwicklungen sind im Hinblick auf eine Steigerung der Effizienz und
Glaubwürdigkeit der Evaluation in der EZ uneingeschränkt positiv zu beurteilen. Inwieweit diese Anstrengungen jedoch zum Ziel führen werden, kann
erst in den kommenden Jahren beurteilt werden. Dabei wird es wichtig sein,

- das Wirkungsmonitoring für Projekte und Programme deutlich zu intensivieren,
- die Zahl von Wirkungs- und ex-post durchgeführten Nachhaltigkeitsuntersuchungen deutlich zu erhöhen,
- gemeinsame Definitionen, Standards und Bewertungsmaßstäbe zu entwickeln und
- die Evaluationsverfahren der einzelnen Durchführungsorganisationen (auch der nicht-staatlichen) stärker aufeinander abzustimmen, um die Möglichkeiten gemeinsamer Evaluationen (joint evaluations) zu verbessern,
- methodisch anspruchsvolle Evaluationsdesigns anzuwenden, die nicht nur ein theoretisches Konzept oder zumindest einen konzeptionellen Rahmen erkennen lassen, die untersuchungsleitende Hypothesen zulassen, um kausale Ursachenzuschreibungen zu erleichtern,
- die Vielfalt empirischer Datenerhebungsverfahren auszuschöpfen,
- die Evaluationsinstrumente und Methoden sektor- und programmspezifisch unter Berücksichtigung der gängigen Standards der empirischen Sozialforschung und den Standards of Evaluation sowie kultureller Adaptionen weiter zu entwickeln,
- die Evaluatoren methodisch fortzubilden,
- in den Partnerländern Evaluationskapazitäten aufzubauen, um eine echte Partizipation erreichen und die bisherige Geberfixierung überwinden zu können,
- den Transfer von bei Evaluationen gewonnenen Erkenntnissen (methodisch: best practices, inhaltlich: lessons learned) in die administrativen und politischen Entscheidungsgremien zu verbessern, um das „institutional learning" zu erleichtern,
- die Transparenz der Evaluationen (insbesondere bei GTZ und KfW und vielen NGO) weiter zu erhöhen, um sie einer öffentlichen und wissenschaftlichen Kritik zugänglich zu machen,
- die Unabhängigkeit von Evaluationen zu stärken; intern durch die organisatorische Umgestaltung der Evaluationseinheiten und extern durch die Erweiterung und die Nutzung professioneller Evaluationskapazitäten (in Deutschland und in den Partnerländern)
- die Außendarstellung der EZ (jährliche Berichterstattung, PR) mit Hilfe von empirisch anspruchsvoll durchgeführten summativen Evaluationen auf eine solide, empirische Grundlage zu stellen.

Wenn es gelingt, die bisherigen Defizite in der Evaluation der EZ zu überwinden, kann die EZ nicht nur dem Rechtfertigungsdruck der Finanzverwalter angesichts knapper Haushaltsmittel besser standhalten, sondern vor allem auch die Glaubwürdigkeit der Ergebnisse der Zusammenarbeit in der Öffentlichkeit und damit ihre Legitimität insgesamt erhöhen. Des weiteren könnten auch andere Politikfelder mit bisher erst relativ gering ausgeprägten Evalua-

402   *Reinhard Stockmann*

tionssystemen von der Weiterentwicklung im EZ-Bereich profitieren. Hierzu
ist nicht nur ein fachspezifischer, sondern auch ein politikfeldübergreifender
Dialog notwendig, um gegenseitige Lernprozesse auslösen zu können.

Literatur

Bamberger, Michael (1991): The Politics of Evaluation in Developing Countries. In: Evaluation and Program Planning. Jg. 14, S. 325-339.
Barth, Jutta (1998): Planung, Monitoring und Evaluierung (PME) in der kirchlichen Entwicklungszusammenarbeit – Erfahrungen der EZE mit Wirkungsbeobachtungen. In: Brüne, Stefan (Hg.), (1998): Erfolgskontrolle in der entwicklungspolitischen Zusammenarbeit. Hamburg: Deutsches Übersee-Institut. S. 222-239.
Barth, Jutta/Kasch, Volker (1996): Haben NRO eigene Bewertungskriterien? In: Entwicklung und Zusammenarbeit, Jg. 37, H. 8, S. 203-205.
Barth, Jutta/Kasch, Volker/Rusteberg, Elke (1996): Welche Wirkungen hat die kirchliche Entwicklungszusammenarbeit? EZE (Hg.). Bonn.
Barthelt, Rainer (1998): Erfolgsbebachtung und Wirkungsoptimierung. Die Aufgabe der Evaluierung im BMZ. In: E+Z, 39. Jg., Nr. 1, S. 4-5.
BMZ (Hg.) (2000): Leitfaden zur Durchführung von BMZ-Evaluierungen. Bonn: BMZ.
BMZ (Hg.) (2000): Journalistenhandbuch. Bonn: BMZ.
BMZ (Hg.) (1999): Querschnittsauswertung: „Wirkungsuntersuchung abgeschlossener Vorhaben der deutschen EZ". Entwurf. Bonn: Gutachten im Auftrag des Bundesministeriums für Wirtschaftliche Zusammenarbeit und Entwicklung.
BMZ (Hg.) (1999): Journalistenhandbuch. Bonn: BMZ.
BMZ (Hg.) (1998): Evaluierungsraster. Bonn: BMZ.
BMZ (Hg.) (1998): Journalistenhandbuch. Bonn: BMZ.
BMZ (Hg.) (1997): Leitfaden, Zielsetzung und Durchführung von Evaluierungen. Bonn: BMZ.
BMZ (Hg.) (1986): Raster für Evaluierungen. Bonn: BMZ.
Bodemer, Klaus (1997): Erfolgskontrolle der deutschen Entwicklungshilfe – improvisiert oder systematisch? Meisenheim.
Bodemer, Klaus (1985): Programmentwicklung in der Entwicklungspolitik der Bundesrepublik Deutschland. In: Politische Vierteljahresschrift Jg. 26, H. 16 (Sonderheft); S. 279ff.
Bodemer, Klaus (1979): Erfolgskontrolle der deutschen Entwicklungshilfe – improvisiert oder systematisch? Meisenheim: Anton Hain.
Bohnet, Michael (1985): Methodik und Praxis der Evaluierung. Bonn.
Bohnsack, Friedrich-Karl (1998): Für transparente und flexible Projektstrukturen. Anfragen an die Entwicklungszusammenarbeit kirchlicher Organisationen. In: Entwicklung und Zusammenarbeit, Jg. 39, Nr. 1, S. 14-16.
Borrmann, Axel (1999): Erfolgskontrolle in der Deutschen Entwicklungszusammenarbeit. Baden-Baden: Nomos.
Borrmann, Axel u.a. (1998): Analyse und Bewertung der Erfolgskontrolle in der deutschen Entwicklungszusammenarbeit. Vorläufige Fassung Hamburg: HWWA.
Breier, Horst (1998): Neukonzeption des Systems der EZ-Erfolgskontrolle. In: GTZ (Hg.): Nachhaltige Wirkungen durch Qualitätsmanagement – eine Herausforderung für die Technische Zusammenarbeit. Eschborn: GTZ.

Breier, Horst (1998): Erfolgskontrolle in der Entwicklungszusammenarbeit. In: E+Z, 39. Jg., S. 128-130.

Brüne, Stefan (1998): Evaluierung als öffentliche Kommunikation – Zu den politischen und institutionellen Rahmenbedingungen entwicklungsbezogener Wirkungsbeobachtung. In: Brüne, Stefan (Hg.): Erfolgskontrolle in der entwicklungspolitischen Zusammenarbeit. Hamburg: Deutsches Übersee-Institut.

Carls, J./Große-Rüschkamp A. (1988): Wirkungen und Wirtschaftlichkeit der Counterpartfortbildung in TZ-Projekten dargestellt am Beispiel aus Pflanzenbau, Pflanzenschutz und Forst. Eschborn: GTZ.

DEH (Hg.) (1992): Zusammenarbeit Planen. Eine Arbeitshilfe für erfahrene Planer und solche, die es werden wollen. Bern: DEH.

DEH (Hg.) (1990): Externe Evaluation von Entwicklungsprojekten. Bern: DEH.

Derlien, Hans-Ulrich (1976): Die Erfolgskontrolle staatlicher Planung. Eine empirische Untersuchung über Organisation, Methode und Politik der Programmevaluation. Schriften zur öffentlichen Verwaltung und öffentlichen Wirtschaft, hrsg. von Peter Eichhorn und Peter Friedrich, Band 17. Baden-Baden: Nomos Verlag.

Deutscher Bundestag (1998): Beschlußempfehlung des Ausschusses für Wirtschaftliche Zusammenarbeit zu dem Antrag der Abgeordneten Dr. R. Werner Schuster, Brigitte Adler, Klaus Marthel, weitere Abgeordneter und der SPD-Fraktion – Drucksache 13/4120, Systematische Erfolgskontrolle von Projekten und Programmen der bilateralen Entwicklungszusammenarbeit, Drucksache 13/10857. Bonn.

Deutscher Bundestag (1996): Evaluation über Projekte und Maßnahmen in den Bundesministerien und nachgeordneten Behörden und Organisationen, Ausarbeitung des Wissenschaftlichen Dienstes, Fachbereich III, Verfassung und Verwaltung. Bonn (unveröffentlicht).

Deutscher Bundestag (1990): Beschlußempfehlung und Bericht des Ausschusses für Wirtschaftliche Zusammenarbeit (20. Ausschuß) zu dem Antrag der Abgeordneten Bindig, Brück, Dr. Hauchler, Dr. Holtz, Luuk, Dr. Niehus, Dr. Osswald, Schanz, Schluckebier, Toetemeyer, Dr. Vogel und der Fraktion der SPD, Drucksache 11/5666, Erfolgskontrolle in der Entwicklungspolitik, Drucksache 11/8059. Bonn.

Deutscher Bundestag (1989a): Beschlußempfehlung und Bericht des Ausschusses für Wirtschaftliche Zusammenarbeit (20. Ausschuß) zu der Unterrichtung durch die Bundesregierung – Drucksache 11/2020 – Siebenter Bericht der Entwicklungspolitik der Bundesregierung, Drucksache 11/4381. Bonn.

Deutscher Bundestag (1989b): Kleine Anfrage der Abgeordneten Dr. Niehus, Schluckebier, Bindig, Brück, Dr. Hauchler, Dr. Holtz, Luuk, Schanz, Toetemeyer, Dr. Osswald, Dr. Vogel und der Fraktion der SPD, Erfolgskontrolle in der Entwicklungspolitik, Drucksache 11/4863. Bonn.

DEZA (Hg.), (1996): PEMU – Ein Einstieg. Bern: DEZA.

Donner, Franziska/Steigerwald, Volker (1998): Qualitätsmanagement in der GTZ: Grundverständnis, zentrale Aspekte und deren Umsetzung. In: GTZ (Hg.): Nachhaltige Wirkungen durch Qualitätsmanagement – eine Herausforderung für die Technische Zusammenarbeit. Eschborn: GTZ.

Donner, Franziska (1998): Das Qualitätsmanagement der GTZ – zum Grundverständnis. In: Entwicklung und Zusammenarbeit, Jg. 39, Nr. 516, S. 131-133.

Dolzer, Hermann u.a. (1998): Wirkungen und Nebenwirkungen. Wirkungsverständnis und Wirkungserfassung in der Entwicklungszusammenarbeit. Hg. Misereor. Aachen.

Dütting, Martin (1998): Projekt-, Wirksamkeits- und Strategieorientierung. Anmerkungen zur Evolution der Evaluierungsarbeit von Misereor. In: Brüne, Stefan (Hg.): Erfolgskontrolle in der entwicklungspolitischen Zusammenarbeit. Hamburg: Deutsches Übersee-Institut.

Eggerstedt, Harald (1988): Bewertungsprobleme nicht-projektgebundener Entwicklungshilfe. Berlin: Deutsches Institut für Entwicklungspolitik (DIE).

Erlbeck, Ruth (1998): Wirkungsbeobachtung in der Personellen Zusammenarbeit (PZ). In: Brüne, Stefan (Hg.): Erfolgskontrolle in der entwicklungspolitischen Zusammenarbeit. Hamburg: Deutsches Übersee-Institut.

Glagow, Manfred (1990): Deutsche und internationale Entwicklungspolitik: zur Rolle staatlicher, supranationaler und nicht-regierungsabhängiger Organisationen im Entwicklungsprozeß der dritten Welt. Opladen: Westdeutscher Verlag.

Glagow, Manfred (Hg.) (1983): Deutsche Entwicklungspolitik: Aspekte und Probleme ihrer Entscheidungsstruktur, Bielefelder Studien zur Entwicklungssoziologie Band 19, Saarbrücken.

Grashoff, Sabine (1987): Methodik und Ergebnisse von Projektevaluierungen, ein Vergleich der Erfahrungen der Bundesrepublik Deutschland mit denen anderer westlicher Industrieländer und der Weltbank. Bonn.

GTZ (1999): Wegweiser für die PFK. Eschborn.

GTZ (Hg.) (1998): Jahresbericht 1998 Eschborn: GTZ.

GTZ (Hg.) (1998): Monitoring im Projekt – Eine Orientierung für Vorhaben in der Technischen Zusammenarbeit. Eschborn: GTZ.

GTZ (Hg.) (1997b): Die Verantwortung der Ansprechpartnerinnen und Ansprechpartner. Ein praktischer Leitfaden durch die „Regelungswelt" der GTZ. Eschborn: GTZ.

GTZ (Hg.) (1997): Ziel Orientierte Projekt Planung – ZOPP. Eschborn: GTZ.

GTZ (Hg.) (1997): Das Leitbild nachhaltiger Entwicklung – handlungsleitende Orientierung der GTZ? Eschborn: GTZ.

GTZ (Hg.) (1995): Project Cycle Management (PCM) und Zielorientierte Projektplanung (ZOPP). Eschborn: GTZ.

GTZ (Hg.) (1995): Orientierungsrahmen für die Durchführung von Vorhaben der deutschen Technischen Zusammenarbeit durch die GTZ. Eschborn: GTZ.

GTZ (Hg.) (1991): Leitfaden für die Projektfortschrittskontrolle (PFK). Eschborn: GTZ (Hg.) (1989): ZOPP-Leitfaden. 2. Überarbeitete Fassung. Eschborn.

GTZ (Hg.) (1987b): ZOPP. Zielorientiertes Planen von Projekten und Programmen der Technischen Zusammenarbeit. Eschborn.

GTZ (Hg.): Die GTZ stellt sich vor. Eschborn: GTZ.

GTZ (Hg.): Wege zur Zusammenarbeit. Wie funktioniert das „F-Verfahren"? Eschborn: GTZ.

Hoebink, Paul (1998): Bewertungsanstrengungen der EU-Geberländer im Vergleich. In: Brüne, Stefan (Hg.): Erfolgskontrolle in der entwicklungspolitischen Zusammenarbeit. Hamburg: Deutsches Übersee-Institut. S. 80-82.

INFRAS (1995): Development Trends in Dolakha and Sindhupalchik, Nepal (1975-1995). Zürich, Kathmandu: INFRAS.

INFRAS (1991): Impact Status Report No. 2: 1990, Summary. Zürich, Kathmandu: INFRAS.

Kary, Matthias (1992): Evaluierung von Entwicklungsprojekten, Analyse und konzeptionelle Vorschläge am Beispiel der bundesdeutschen Finanziellen Zusammenarbeit, Studien zur Entwicklungsökonomie Bd. 7. Münster, Hamburg.

Kenneweg, Jochen (1998): Evaluierungen – Fragestellungen eines Praktikers aus der Entwicklungsverwaltung. In: Brüne, Stefan (Hg.): Erfolgskontrolle in der entwicklungspolitischen Zusammenarbeit. Hamburg: Deutsches Übersee-Institut. S. 124-131.

KfW (Hg.) (1999): Jahresbericht über die Zusammenarbeit mit Entwicklungsländern 1999. Frankfurt a. Main: KfW.

KfW (Hg.) (1998): Geschäftsbericht 1998 – Kurzfassung. Frankfurt am Main: KfW.

KfW (Hg.) (1997f): Prüfungsleitfaden für Vorhaben der Finanziellen Zusammenarbeit – Finanzsektor. Frankfurt a. Main: KfW.

KfW (Hg.) (1996b): Allgemeiner Prüfungsleitfaden für Vorhaben der Finanziellen Zusammenarbeit. Frankfurt a. Main: KfW.

KfW (Hg.) (1996c): Prüfungsleitfaden für Vorhaben der Finanziellen Zusammenarbeit – Grundbildung. Frankfurt a. Main: KfW.

KfW (Hg.) (1994): Prüfungsleitfaden für Vorhaben der Finanziellen Zusammenarbeit – Trinkwasser. Frankfurt a. Main: KfW.

KfW (Hg.) (1994): Wirtschaftliche Prüfkriterien für Stromversorgungsprojekte. Frankfurt a. Main: KfW.

Kohnert, Dirk (1998): Lehren aus 15 Jahren ZOPP. In: Entwicklung und Zusammenarbeit, Jg. 39, Nr. 516, S. 137-140.

Kroh, Wolfgang (1993): Nachhaltigkeit von Vorhaben der Finanziellen Zusammenarbeit. In: Stockmann, Reinhard/Gaebe, Wolf (Hg.): Hilft die Entwicklungshilfe langfristig? Bestandsaufnahme zur Nachhaltigkeit von Entwicklungsprojekten. Opladen. S. 149-157.

Kuby, Thomas (1999): Analyse des PFK-Wegweisers der GTZ. Unveröffentlichtes Manuskript 1999.

Lindauer, Gerd/Raabe, Christa u.a. (1995): Längsschnittanalyse zu den indonesisch-deutschen EZ-Projekten in Ost-Kalimanatan, West-Pasaman und Sumatra. Gutachten (5 Bde.). Eschborn: GTZ.

Lotz, Rainer (1984): Das Inspektionsreferat des Bundesministeriums für wirtschaftliche Zusammenarbeit und Entwicklung. In: Hellstern, Gerd-Michael/Wollmann, Hellmut (Hg.): Handbuch zur Evaluierungsforschung. Opladen. S. 289-301.

Martinek, Michael (1981): Die Verwaltung der deutschen Entwicklungshilfe und ihr Integrationsdefizit. Bad Honnef: Bock und Herchen.

Mayer, Peter (1993): Die Nachhaltigkeit von Entwicklungsprojekten der Friedrich-Ebert-Stiftung. In: Stockmann/Gaebe: Hilft die Entwicklungshilfe langfristig? Bestandsaufnahme zur Nachhaltigkeit von Entwicklungshilfeprojekten. Opladen. S. 167-181.

Misereor (1992): Evaluierung in der Kirchlichen Zusammenarbeit. Ein Handbuch für Partnerorganisationen und Hilfswerke. Stuttgart, Aachen.

Mutter, Theo (1998): Aussagefähigere Erfolgskontrolle durch verbesserte Methoden? In: Brüne, Stefan (Hg.): Erfolgskontrolle in der entwicklungspolitischen Zusammenarbeit. Hamburg: Deutsches Übersee-Institut.

Neubert, Susanne (1999): Die soziale Wirkungsanalyse in armutsorientierten Projekten: ein Beitrag zur Methodendiskussion in der Evaluationspraxis der Entwicklungszusammenarbeit. Köln: Weltforum Verlag.

Nuscheler, Franz (1995): Lern- und Arbeitsbuch Entwicklungspolitik 4., völlig neubearb. Aufl.. Bonn: Dietz.

Polak, Hanns P. (1998): Plädoyer für gemeinsame Wirkungskontrolle. Perspektiven einer besseren Zusammenarbeit der NRO. In: Entwicklung und Zusammenarbeit, Jg. 39, H. 1, S. 17-19.

Polte, Winfried (1992): Erfolgskontrolle bei KfW-Projekten. In: Entwicklung und Zusammenarbeit, Jg. 33, Nr. 8, S. 16-18.

Preuss, Hans-Joachim/Steigerwald, Volker (1998): Von Projektfortschrittskontrolle zu Qualitätsmanagement – Wirkungsbeobachtung der Deutschen Gesellschaft für Technische Zusammenarbeit (GZT) GmbH. In: Brüne, Stefan (Hg.): Erfolgskontrolle in der entwicklungspolitischen Zusammenarbeit. Hamburg: Deutsches Übersee-Institut.

Preuss, Hans-Joachim/Steigerwald, Volker (1996): Wirkungsbeobachtung in der GTZ – Von der Projektfortschrittskontrolle zu Qualitätsmanagement. Eschborn: GTZ.

Raschen, Martin (1998): Die Erfolgsmessung in der Finanziellen Zusammenarbeit durch die Kreditanstalt für Wiederaufbau. In: Brüne, Stefan (Hg.): Erfolgskontrolle in der entwicklungspolitischen Zusammenarbeit. Hamburg: Deutsches Übersee-Institut. S. 168-188.

Schimank, Uwe (1983a): Das außenpolitische Interorganisationsnetz als Hemmnis einer eigenständigen Entwicklungspolitik In: Glagow, Manfred: Deutsche Entwicklungspolitik: Aspekte und Probleme ihrer Entscheidungsstruktur (Bielefelder Studien zur Entwicklungssoziologie Bd. 19). Saarbrücken: Breitenbach.

Schimank, Uwe (1983b): Illusionen der Organisationsreform politischer Verwaltungen: Das Beispiel des Bundesministeriums für wirtschaftliche Zusammenarbeit In: Glagow, Manfred: Deutsche Entwicklungspolitik: Aspekte und Probleme ihrer Entscheidungsstruktur (Bielefelder Studien zur Entwicklungssoziologie Bd. 19). Saarbrücken: Breitenbach.

Schubert, Bernd/Agarwal R. C. (1984): Die Nachhaltigkeit der Wirkungen von Agrarprojekten. Fachberichte des BMZ (Bd. 64). Köln u.a.: Weltforum.

Schwefel, Detlef (Hg.) (1987a): Soziale Wirkungen von Projekten in der Dritten Welt Baden-Baden: Nomos.

Steigerwald, Volker/Rapp, Kerstin (1998): Das Qualitätsmanagement der GTZ – Aufbau- und Ablaufstrukturen, Instrumente und Verfahren. In: Entwicklung und Zusammenarbeit, Jg. 39, Nr. 516, S. 133-136.

Stockhausen, Joachim v. (1986): Theorie und Politik der Entwicklungshilfe. Eine Einführung in die deutsche bilaterale Entwicklungszusammenarbeit Köln u.a.: Weltforum.

Stockmann, Reinhard (1999): Wirkungsevaluation in der Entwicklungszusammenarbeit: Notwendige Grenzüberschreitungen. In: Pfaffenweiler, Centaurus: Kongreßband 2 des 29. Kongresses der Deutschen Gesellschaft für Soziologie.

Stockmann, Reinhard (1998a): Viel Kritik – aber wenig profundes Wissen: Der Mangel an Erkenntnissen über die Wirksamkeit der Entwicklungszusammenarbeit und wie er behoben werden könnte. In: Brüne, Stefan (Hg.): Erfolgskontrolle in der entwicklungspolitischen Zusammenarbeit. Hamburg: Deutsches Übersee-Institut.

Stockmann, Reinhard (1998b): La eficacia de la ayuda al desarollo. Baden-Baden: Nomos Verlag.

Stockmann, Reinhard (1997a): The Evaluation of the Sustainability of Development Projects Baden-Baden: Nomos Verlag.

Stockmann, Reinhard (1996a): Die Wirksamkeit der Entwicklungshilfe. Opladen: Westdeutscher Verlag.

Stockmann, Reinhard (1996): Defizite in der Wirkungsbeobachtung. Ein unabhängiges Evaluationsinstitut könnte Abhilfe schaffen. In: Entwicklung und Zusammenarbeit. H. 8.

Stockmann, Reinhard (1995): Die Krise der Entwicklungszusammenarbeit: Viel Kritik – aber wenig empirisches Wissen über Nachhaltigkeit. In: Trappe, Paul: Krisenkontinent Afrika – Ansätze zum Krisenmanagement. Basel.

Stockmann, Reinhard (1993): Die Nachhaltigkeit von Entwicklungsprojekten. Eine Methode zur Evaluierung am Beispiel von Berufsbildungsprojekten. Opladen: Westdeutscher Verlag (2. Auflage).

Stockmann, Reinhard (1990): Administrative Probleme der staatlichen Entwicklungszusammenarbeit – Entwicklungsengpässe im Bundesministerium für wirtschaftliche Zusammenarbeit. In: Glagow, Manfred: Deutsche und internationale Entwicklungspolitik: zur Rolle staatlicher, supranationaler und nicht-regierungsabhängiger Organisationen im Entwicklungsprozeß der dritten Welt. Opladen: Westdeutscher Verlag.

Stockmann, Reinhard/Caspari, Alexandra (1998): Ex-Post Evaluation als Instrument des Qualitätsmanagements in der Entwicklungszusammenarbeit. Eschborn: Gutachten im Auftrag der Deutschen Gesellschaft für Technische Zusammenarbeit (GTZ).

Stockmann, Reinhard/Gaebe, Wolf (Hg.) (1993): Hilft die Entwicklungshilfe langfristig? Bestandsaufnahme zur Nachhaltigkeit von Entwicklungsprojekten. Opladen: Westdeutscher Verlag.

Stockmann, Reinhard/Resch, Annegret (1992a): Die Nachhaltigkeit von Entwicklungsprojekten der beruflichen Bildung in Ecuador (SECAP). Eine Fallstudie durchgeführt im Auftrag der GTZ Mannheim.

Stockmann, Reinhard/Resch, Annegret (1992b): Die Nachhaltigkeit von Entwicklungsprojekten der beruflichen Bildung in Mexiko: Deutsch-Mexikanische Technikerschule CETMA Mannheim: Fallstudie.

Stockmann, Reinhard/Resch, Annegret (1992c): Die Nachhaltigkeit von Entwicklungsprojekten der beruflichen Bildung in Kolumbien: Centro Colombo-Alemán Barranquilla. Mannheim: Fallstudie.

Stockmann, Reinhard/Resch, Annegret (1992d): Die Nachhaltigkeit von Entwicklungsprojekten. Eine Methode zur Evaluierung und eine Untersuchung von Berufsbildungsprojekten in Lateinamerika (Abschlußbericht). Mannheim.

Stockmann, Reinhard/Resch, Annegret (1991a): Die Nachhaltigkeit von Entwicklungsprojekten der beruflichen Bildung in Honduras: Deutsch-Hondurenisches Ausbildungszentrum in San Pedro Sula (CTHA). Eine Fallstudie durchgeführt im Auftrag der GTZ Mannheim.

Stockmann, Reinhard/Resch, Annegret (1991b): Die Nachhaltigkeit von Entwicklungsprojekten der beruflichen Bildung in Honduras (INFOP). Eine Fallstudie durchgeführt im Auftrag der GTZ Mannheim.

Stockmann, Reinhard/Resch, Annegret (1991c): Die Nachhaltigkeit von Entwicklungsprojekten der beruflichen Bildung in Guatemala: Facharbeiterschule Mazatenango. Eine Fallstudie durchgeführt im Auftrag der GTZ Mannheim.

Stockmann, Reinhard/Resch, Annegret (1991d): Die Nachhaltigkeit von Entwicklungsprojekten der beruflichen Bildung in Guatemala (INTECAP). Eine Fallstudie durchgeführt im Auftrag der GTZ Mannheim.

Stockmann, Reinhard/Resch, Annegret (1990a): Die Nachhaltigkeit des Berufsbildungsprojekts: Thai-German Technical Teacher College in Bangkok, Thailand. Mannheim: Fallstudie.

Stockmann, Reinhard/Resch, Annegret (1990b): Die Nachhaltigkeit des Berufsbildungsprojekts: Korean-German Busan Vocational Training Institute in Busan, Südkorea. Mannheim: Fallstudie.

Sülzer, Rolf (1995): Nachhaltigkeit und Instrumente der Wirksamkeitskontrolle in der deutschen Entwicklungszusammenarbeit. Berlin: DED.

Tepel, Ralf (1997): Projektevaluation – Kontrollinstrument oder Ansatz zur Steigerung von Erfolgschancen. In: EPD-Entwicklungspolitik, 20. November, S. d13-d16.

VENRO (Hg.) (2000): Prüfen und lernen. Praxisorientierte Handreichung zur Wirkungsbeobachtung und Evaluation. Bonn: VENRO.

Weiter, Matthias/Huber, Rudolf (1994): Wirkungskontrolle bei Nichtregierungsorganisationen. In: Entwicklung und Zusammenarbeit, Jg. 35, S. 291-292.

Wiener, Manuel (1998): Das Evaluierungsinstrumentarium der Deutschen Welthungerhilfe. In: Brüne, Stefan (Hg.): Erfolgskontrolle in der entwicklungspolitischen Zusammenarbeit. Hamburg: Deutsches Übersee-Institut. S. 264-269.

Autorenverzeichnis

Bangel, Bettina; Dr.
Referentin im Referat Grundsatzfragen der Arbeitsmarktpolitik im Ministerium für Arbeit, Soziales, Gesundheit und Frauen des Landes Brandenburg.
Referentin für Evaluierung der Arbeitsmarktpolitik, Mitglied der Deutschen Vereinigung für Sozialwissenschaftliche Arbeitsmarktforschung e.V (SAMF).
Arbeitsschwerpunkte: Arbeitsmarkt- und Beschäftigungspolitik, Struktur und Entwick-lung von Beschäftigung und Arbeitslosigkeit, Evaluierung der Arbeitsmarktpolitik aus Ländersicht - Konzeption und Umsetzung im Rahmen der Vergabe von Wirkungsuntersuchungen.
Adresse:
MASGF, Abt. 3, Ref. 31
Postfach 601 163
14411 Potsdam
Tel.:   0331/866 5341
Fax: 0331/866 5499
e-Mail: bettina.bangel@masgf.brandenburg.de
Web-Seite: http://www.brandenburg.de/land/masgf

Brinkmann, Christian; Dipl.-Soz.
Leiter des Arbeitsbereichs wissenschaftliche Praxisbegleitung im Institut für Arbeitsmarkt- und Berufsforschung (IAB) der Bundesanstalt für Arbeit (BA).
Mitglied der Gesellschaft für Programmforschung e.V. (GfP) und der Deutschen Vereinigung für Sozialwissenschaftliche Arbeitsmarktforschung e.V. (SAMF).
Arbeitsschwerpunkte: Wirkungsforschung zur aktiven Arbeitsförderung, Mitwirkung am Aufbau eines Evaluationssystems in der BA.
Adresse:
Institut für Arbeitsmarkt- und Berufsforschung der Bundesanstalt für Arbeit
Regensburger Str. 104
90327 Nürnberg
Tel: 0911/179 3121
Fax: 0911/179 3297
e-Mail: Christian.Brinkmann@iab.de
Web-Seite: http://www.iab.de

Büeler, Xaver; Dr.
Universitätsdozent. Leiter des Forschungsbereichs Schulqualität und Schulentwicklung der Universität Zürich. Internationale Forschungs- und Beratungstätigkeit in diesem Bereich, u.a. in Entwicklungsländern.
Vorstandsmitglied der Schweizerischen Gesellschaft für Bildungsforschung (SGBF), Mitglied der European Educational Research Association (EERA) und Mitglied des International Congress for School Effectiveness and Improvement (ICSEI).
Arbeitsschwerpunkte: Forschungs- und Lehrtätigkeit zu Schulqualität, Schulentwicklung, Qualitätsmanagement und Schulreform; Entwicklung von Forschungs- und Evaluationsinstrumenten, beispielsweise zur Erhebung überfachlicher Kompetenzen (Schlüsselqualifikationen); theoretische Arbeiten im Bereich von Systemtheorie und Konstruktivismus.
Adresse:
Universitaet Zürich
Forschungsbereich Schulqualität und
Schulentwicklung (FS&S)
Scheuchzerstrasse 21
CH-8006 Zurich
Tel.:   (0041) 01 634456 3
Fax: (0041) 01 634436 5
e-Mail: bueler@paed.unizh.ch
Web-Seite: www.unizh.ch/~fss/

Caracelli, Valerie; Dr.
Senior Social Science Analyst at the U.S. General Accounting Office in the Advanced Studies and Evaluation Methodology Group.
Editorial Advisory Board (1996-present). American Journal of Evaluation Associate Editor. Evaluation Review (1993-1996) Chair (1995-present). Evaluation Use a topical interest group, American Evaluation Association. President, 1997-1998 and current Board Member of the Washington Evaluators (WE)
Address:
U.S. General Accounting Office
GGD/ASEM room 2440
441 G Street NW
Washington, D.C. 20548
USA
Tel.:   (001) 202 5129792
Fax: (001) 202 5123774
e-Mail: caracelli.ggd@gao.gov
Web-Seite: http://www.gao.gov

Deeke, Axel; Dr.
Wissenschaftlicher Mitarbeiter im Institut für Arbeitsmarkt- und Berufsforschung (IAB) der Bundesanstalt für Arbeit.
Mitglied der Deutschen Vereinigung für Sozialwissenschaftliche Arbeitsmarktforschung e.V. (SAMF).
Arbeitsschwerpunkte: sozialwissenschaftliche Arbeitsmarktforschung, Wirkungsforschung zu Arbeitsmarktpolitik.
Adresse:
Institut für Arbeitsmarkt- und Berufsforschung
Bundesanstalt für Arbeit
Regensburger Str. 104

90478 Nürnberg
Tel.:   0911/179 3132
Fax: 0911/179 3297
e-Mail: Axel.Deeke@iab.de
Web-Seite: http://www.iab.de

Huber, Joseph; Prof. Dr.
Lehrstuhl für Wirtschafts- und Umweltsoziologie an der Martin-Luther-Universität Halle-Wittenberg. Daneben auch politikberatend und als Forschungsgutachter tätig.
Arbeitsschwerpunkt: Ökologische Modernisierung und industriegesellschaftliche Entwicklungstheorie.

Adresse:
Martin-Luther-Universität
Institut für Soziologie
Emil-Abderhalden-Str. 7
06099 Halle an der Saale
Tel: 0345/552 4242
Fax: 0345/552 7149
e-Mail: huber@soziologie.uni-halle.de
Web-Seite: www.soziologie.uni-halle.de/huber/index.html

Kromrey, Helmut; Prof. Dr. rer.pol.
Lehrstuhl für Soziologie und Empirische Sozialforschung am Institut für Soziologie der Freien Universität Berlin; stellvertretender Vorsitzender des Berufsverbandes Deutscher Soziologinnen und Soziologen.
Arbeitsschwerpunkte: Lehre und Forschung zur Methodik der Evaluation (insb. Implementations- und Wirkungsforschung), Evaluationsprojekte in den Bereichen Neue Medien einschl. Lernmedien, Hochschule und betriebliche Weiterbildung, Lehre zur Methodik empirischer Sozialforschung (insbesondere standardisierte Verfahren und anwendungsorientierte Forschung), Forschungen zu Bildung und Weiterbildung, neue Medien und Stadtentwicklung.

Adresse:
Institut für Soziologie
FU Berlin
Babelsberger Str. 14-16
10715 Berlin
Tel: 030/850 02230
Fax: 030/850 02138
e-Mail: kromrey@zedat.fu-berlin.de

Kuhlmann, Stefan; Privatdozent Dr. rer.pol.
Leiter der Abteilung "Technikbewertung und Innovationsstrategien"
Mitglied des Editorial Advisory Board der Zeitschrift "Evaluation", Mitglied der "International Evaluation Research Group (INTEVAL)", seit 1999.
Mitglied des Vorstandes der Deutschen Gesellschaft für Evaluation (DeGEval), seit 1997 (Details: www.degeval.de/degeval.htm), Deutscher Vertreter im "European RTD Evaluation Network" der Europäischen Kommission, Generaldirektion Forschung, seit 1997.
Arbeitsschwerpunkte: Analysen des politisches Systems in Deutschland und Europa, schwerpunktmäßig Policy-Forschung sowie Planung, Steuerung und Evaluation politischer Prozesse in den Bereichen Forschung, Technologie und Innovation; Analyse industrieller Innovationsstrategien, -netzwerke und Innovationssysteme; Technikfolgenabschätzung.

Adresse:
Fraunhofer-Institut für Systemtechnik und Innovationsforschung (ISI)
Breslauer Straße 48
76139 Karlsruhe
Tel: 0721/680 91704
Fax: 0721/680 91260
e-Mail: stefan.kuhlmann@isi.fhg.de;
Web-Seite: www.isi.fhg.de/ti/index.htm

Lee, Barbara; Ph.D., Research Psychologist
Assistant in Research
Member of the American Evaluation Association, the Evaluation Theory Topical Interest Group (TIG), the Empowerment Evaluation TIG, the Mulitcultural TIG.
Working emphasis: Evaluation of public mental health programs.
Address:
Louis de la Parte Florida Mental Health Institute
University of South Florida
Tampa, FL 33612
USA
Phone: (001) 813 9747011
e-Mail: lee@fmhi.usf.edu

Leeuw, Frans L.; Prof. Dr.
Chief Review Officer of Higher Education in the Netherlands and Professor, Policy and Program Evaluation, Department of Sociology, Utrecht University.
President of the European Evaluation Society, consultant for the World Bank and member of several national/international evaluation groups.
Working emphasis: Work within the department of Sociology focusing on program theory analysis, evaluation theory and evaluating public management. Involvement in an evaluation of results-based management in the Netherlands public sector. Supervision of World Bank/University of Utrecht project evaluating anticorruption initiatives of the World Bank Institute.
Address:
Inspectie van het Onderwijs
Park Voorn 4, P.O. Box 2730
3500 GS Utrecht
Netherlands
Tel.: (0031) 30 669075 3
e-Mail: f.leeuw@owinsp.nl; flleeuw@cuci.nl.

Mertens, Donna M.; Prof. Dr.
Professor of Educational Research, Gallaudet University, Washington, DC.
Past-President of American Evaluation, currently serve on AEA's Board; Chief evaluator for many projects, national and international, including Improving Access to the Courts for Deaf and Hard of Hearing People in the United States.
Working emphasis: Conducting of evaluations with marginalized populations, especially deaf people, and write about evaluation from the transformative persepctive in terms of theory and practice.
Address:
Donna M. Mertens
4600 Marie St.

Beltsville, MD 20705
USA
Tel.:   (001) 202 651520 2
e-Mail: Donna.Mertens@gallaudet.edu
Web-Seite: www.gallaudet.edu

Müller, Axel; Dipl.-Soz.
Wissenschaftlicher Mitarbeiter am Lehrstuhl für Wirtschafts- und Umweltsoziologie an der
Martin-Luther-Universität Halle-Wittenberg.
Arbeitsschwerpunkt: Innovationsforschung.
Adresse:
Martin-Luther-Universität
Institut für Soziologie
Emil-Abderhalden-Str. 7
06099 Halle an der Saale
Tel: 0345/552 4234
Fax: 0345/552 7149
e-Mail: mueller@soziologie.uni-halle.de

Stockmann, Reinhard; Prof. Dr.
Lehrstuhl für Soziologie an der Universität des Saarlandes.
Gründungsmitglied der Deutschen Gesellschaft für Evaluation, Leiter des Arbeitskreises
„Evaluation von Entwicklungspolitik", Leiter der AG „Evaluation" in der Deutschen Ge-
sellschaft für Soziologie, Herausgeber der Reihe „Evaluationsforschung" im Leske + Bu-
drich Verlag.
Arbeitsschwerpunkte: Methoden der empirischen Sozialforschung, insb. Evaluations-
forschung, Entwicklungs-, Bildungs- Umweltsoziologie, Politikberatung und Evaluation in
der Entwicklungszusammenarbeit und im Umweltbereich.
Adresse:
Universität des Saarlandes
Lehrstuhl für Soziologie FR 5.2
Postfach 15 11 50
66041 Saarbrücken
Tel.:   0681/302 3372
Fax: 0681/302 3899
e-Mail: r.stockmann@rz.uni-sb.de
Web-Seite: www.uni-saarland.de/fak5/stockmann

Vedung, Evert; Prof. Dr.
Professor of political science esp. housing policy, Uppsala University, Institute of Housing
and Urban Research (Gävle) and Department of Government (Uppsala).
Jan 1985-Dec 1991 Special research position, evaluation research, at the National Swedish
Council for the Humanities and the Social Sciences (Humanistisk-Samhällsvetenskapliga
Forskningsrådet, HSFR), Stockholm.
Working emphasis: Evaluation methods, utilization of research and evaluation, policy in-
struments theory, public information campaigns, public policy studies, global environ-
mental regimes, urban land use, sustainable ecology, energy conservation, nuclear energy
policy.
Address:
Uppsala University, Institute for Housing Research
P O Box 785,

SE-801 29 Gävle
Sweden
Tel: (0046) 264/206 515
Fax: (0046) 264/206 501
Mobile phone: (0046) 7070 4401315
e-Mail: Evert.Vedung@ibf.uu.se
Homepage: http://www.ibf.uu.se/person/evert-v.html
Visiting address, Gävle: Rådhuset (City Hall), Rådhustorget (City Hall Square)

Wollmann, Hellmut; Prof. Dr. jur.,
Professor für Verwaltungslehre an der Humboldt-Universität zu Berlin seit 1993 (davor: Freie Universität Berlin).
Deutsches Gründungsmitglied der European Evaluation Society, 1997-1999, deren Präsident; Mitglied des Gründungsbeirats der Deutschen Gesellschaft für Evaluierung.
Forschungsschwerpunkte: Policy-Forschung, Verwaltungsmodernisierung, Implementations-/Evaluierungsforschung, institutionelle Transformation in post-sozialistischen Ländern.

Adresse:
Humboldt-Universitaet zu Berlin
Institut für Sozialwissenschaften (Institute of Social Science)
Politikwissenschaft/Political Science
Unter den Linden 6
10099 Berlin
Tel.:   030/209 31532 (Sekr.), 1533 (direkt)
Fax: 030/209 31500
e-mail: hellmut.wollmann@rz.hu-berlin.de
Web-Seite: http:// www2.rz.hu-berlin.de/verwaltung